Culture and Counseling

New Approaches

Frederick D. Harper
Howard University

John McFadden
University of South Carolina

Boston   New York   San Francisco
Mexico City   Montreal   Toronto   London   Madrid   Munich   Paris
Hong Kong   Singapore   Tokyo   Cape Town   Sydney

Executive Editor: *Virginia Lanigan*
Editorial Assistant: *Robert Champagne*
Marketing Manager: *Taryn Wahlquist*
Composition and Prepress Buyer: *Linda Cox*
Manufacturing Buyer: *Andrew Turso*
Cover Administrator: *Kristina Mose-Libon*
Editorial-Production Service: *Omegatype Typography, Inc.*
Electronic Composition: *Omegatype Typography, Inc.*

For related titles and support materials, visit our online catalog at www.ablongman.com.

Between the time Website information is gathered and then published, it is not unusual for some sites to have closed. Also, the transcription of URLs can result in unintended typographical errors. The publisher would appreciate notification where these errors occur so that they may be corrected in subsequent editions.

Library of Congress Cataloging-in-Publication Data

Culture and counseling : new approaches / [edited by] Frederick D. Harper, John McFadden.— 1st ed.
p.   cm.
Includes bibliographical references and indexes.
ISBN 0-205-35901-9
1. Cross-cultural counseling.   I. Harper, Frederick D.   II. McFadden, John.

BF637.C6 C778 2003
158'.3—dc21

2002074774

Printed in the United States of America
10 9 8 7 6 5 4 3 2 1   07 06 05 04 03 02

CONTENTS

About the Contributors   vii

Introduction   xv

PART ONE   Cultural Viewpoints of Counseling   1

1 Background: Concepts and History   1

   Frederick D. Harper

2 On Becoming an Existential Cross-Cultural
   Counselor   20

   Clemmont E. Vontress

3 Increasing the Cultural Awareness, Knowledge,
   and Skills of Culture-Centered Counselors   31

   Paul B. Pedersen

4 Transcultural Counseling Theory Development
   Through the Liberal Arts   47

   John McFadden

PART TWO   Ethnicity and Counseling   66

5 Native American Mental Health: An Examination of
   Resiliency in the Face of Overwhelming Odds   66

   Susan Chavez Cameron and imani turtle-song

6 Therapeutic Approaches With African American
   Populations   81

   Thomas A. Parham and Sherlon Brown

iii

7   Counseling Approaches With Asian Americans
     and Pacific Islander Americans   99

         Daya Singh Sandhu, S. Alvin Leung, and Mei Tang

8   Counseling Paradigms and Latina/o Americans:
     Contemporary Considerations   115

         Patricia Arredondo and Patricia Perez

9   Counseling European Americans   133

         Lee J. Richmond

PART THREE   International and Intercultural Dimensions   147

  10   The International Counseling Movement   147

         Frederick D. Harper and Nathan Deen

  11   Understanding Immigrants: Acculturation
         Theory and Research   164

         Gargi Roysircar

  12   Integrating Spirituality in Multicultural
         Counseling: "A Worldview"   186

         Mary A. Fukuyama

PART FOUR   Innovative Cross-Cultural
Models and Theories   196

  13   Existential Worldview Counseling Theory:
         Inception to Applications   196

         Farah A. Ibrahim

14 Stylistic Model for Counseling Across Cultures   209

John McFadden

15 Transcendent Counseling: An Existential, Cognitive-Behavioral Theory   233

Frederick D. Harper and Winifred O. Stone

PART FIVE   Intervention and Prevention   252

16 Culture-Specific Counseling Cases   252

17 Using Bibliotherapy in Transcultural Counseling   285

John McFadden and MaryAnne Banich

18 Preventive Counseling in a Multicultural Society   296

Charles E. Durant and John McFadden

19 Breaking Barriers for Multiracial Individuals and Families   313

Bea Wehrly

PART SIX   Special Topics, Issues, and Trends in Culture and Counseling   324

20 Cultural Considerations in Counselor Training and Supervision   324

Don C. Locke and Marie Faubert

21   Traditional Counseling Theories and
        Cross-Cultural Implications   339

         Marty Jencius and John West

22   Applications of Technological Advances for
        Multicultural Counseling Professionals   350

         Marty Jencius

23   Ethical Issues and Multicultural
        Competence in Counseling   363

         Barbara Herlihy and Zarus E. Watson

24   Conclusions, Trends, Issues,
        and Recommendations   379

         Frederick D. Harper and John McFadden

        Glossary   394

        Appendix A: Annotated Bibliography
        on Culture and Counseling   403

        Appendix B: Past Presidents of the Association
        for Multicultural Counseling and Development (AMCD)   410

        Appendix C: Thirty-One Multicultural Counseling
        Competencies of the Association for Multicultural
        Counseling and Development (AMCD)   411

        Author Index   415

        Subject Index   421

ABOUT THE CONTRIBUTORS

Editors

Frederick D. Harper is professor of counseling at Howard University, former editor of the *Journal of Multicultural Counseling and Development,* and immediate past managing editor of the *International Journal for the Advancement of Counselling.* Dr. Harper has presented 110 conference papers and authored or edited more than 100 publications, including twelve books and monographs. He is a past president of the D.C. Counseling Association, cofounder of the theory of transcendent counseling (with W. O. Stone), and recipient of numerous awards in counseling and education. Dr. Harper has served as adjunct or visiting professor of counseling at a number of universities, including Florida A and M University, George Washington University, Johns Hopkins University, the University of the Virgin Islands, and Virginia Polytechnic Institute and State University. He has presented counseling or psychology papers at international conferences in a number of countries, including Argentina, France, Greece, India, Ireland, and Sweden. Dr. Harper received his Ph.D. in counselor education from Florida State University and has done postdoctoral study in experimental psychology at George Mason University and alcohol studies with the National Institute on Alcohol Abuse and Alcoholism.

John McFadden, Ph.D., is the Benjamin Elijah Mays Professor, Department of Educational Psychology, University of South Carolina. He is the first African American scholar in the history of USC to be named to an endowed chair, which was in 1988. Dr. McFadden has authored in excess of 150 professional publications and has made more than 225 research conference presentations. He is an editorial adviser for the *International Journal for the Advancement of Counselling* and a former member of editorial boards for the *Journal of Counseling and Development,* the *Journal of Multicultural Counseling and Development,* the *Educational and Social Analysis Journal,* and *Counselor Education and Supervision.*

Dr. McFadden has held various administrative positions at the University of South Carolina, including senior vice president for intercultural affairs and professional development. His international experiences span forty countries in North America, South America, Africa, Asia, Europe, and the Caribbean.

Among his books and monographs is the lettered text *Transcultural Counseling,* Second Edition. An international authority on stylistic and transcultural counseling, Dr. McFadden has lectured and conducted seminars at select universities throughout the world.

His notable contributions to the profession have resulted in his having been identified as one of the twenty-three distinguished counselor educators biographically included in the book, *Leaders and Legacies: Contributions to the Profession of Counseling.*

Contributing Authors

Patricia Arredondo, associate professor at Arizona State University, is known for her contributions in the development of multicultural counseling competencies, her dedication to Latina/o issues, and her leadership in promoting organizational change through a focus on diversity. Dr. Arredondo is a past president of the Association for Multicultural Counseling and Development and the American Psychological Association's (APA) Division 45, Society for the Psychological Study of Ethnic Minority Issues. Her major publications include *Successful Diversity Management Initiatives, Key Words in Multicultural Interventions—A Dictionary,* and *Counseling Latinas/os and La Familia: A Practioners Guide.* She is co-author or lead author of several major multicultural competency documents, including *Multicultural Counseling Competencies and Standards: A Call to the Profession.* In her organizational diversity work, she has consulted to universities, corporate clients, and nonprofit organizations. Dr. Arredondo is the recipient of many awards and is a Fellow of the APA Division 45. She is a former professor of the University of New Hampshire, Boston University, and Columbia University, and she has served as president of Empowerment Workshops, Inc., since 1985. Dr. Arredondo earned her doctorate in counseling psychology at Boston University and is a licensed psychologist.

MaryAnne Banich, Ed.S., marriage and family therapy, University of South Carolina, holds the M.P.H. with a concentration in health education and promotion as well as a B.A. degree in journalism. Ms. Banich is also the adolescent services coordinator for Sexual Trauma Services and has worked as a counselor in the USC Counseling Center in Columbia. She has made presentations at the annual conferences of the South Carolina Counseling Association and the South Carolina Association for Marriage and Family Therapy. She recently co-authored a journal article, entitled "A Model of Brief Narrative Strength-Focused (B.E.S.T) Therapy in Family Counseling With Abused Women and Their Children," and continues to be active in a variety of training activities in play therapy.

Sherlon Brown received her doctorate from the University of Toledo. She is associate professor and graduate coordinator for the counseling program in the Division of Intervention Services, College of Education and Human Development, at Bowling Green State University. In addition, Dr. Brown works as a multicultural consultant with ASASA Consulting, Inc. She has presented nationally and internationally and has authored or co-authored extensively in the field of multicultural counseling, including numerous articles, books, book chapters, and a training video. Dr. Brown has served as president of the Association for Multicultural Counseling and Development (AMCD) and as chair of the American Counseling Association's (ACA) Ethics Committee. In recognition of her many contributions, she is the recipient of the Ohio Counseling Association's (OCA) Dave Brooks Award for meritorious service promoting the counseling profession and the Association for Multicultural Counseling and Development's (AMCD) Distinguished Samuel H. Johnson Award for Exemplary Service and/or Scholarship. Her greatest source of life satisfaction comes from her relationships with her three adult children (Allison Sherlon Brown-Smith, Scott Allen Brown, and Tony Brown) and three grandchildren (Taylor Sheral, Courtney Breanna, and Camryn Charles Smith).

Susan Chavez Cameron, Ph.D., LPCC, is the quality and risk manager at Santa Fe Indian Hospital in Santa Fe, New Mexico. Her academic career involves teaching as adjunct faculty at Humboldt State University in the Indian Teacher Education and Personnel Program, the American Indian Teaching Institute, Webster University, and Johns Hopkins University. She has also taught at the University of New Mexico and Purdue University. Dr. Cameron has a Ph.D. in counselor education; an M.S. in marriage, family, and child counseling; and a B.S. in nursing. She worked for thirteen years as an intensive-care RN and has directed a Native American mental health clinic in California and Su Vida in Santa Fe. Dr. Cameron has served on numerous Native American advisory boards throughout the country and is an advisory board member for the California Wellness Foundation's Violence Prevention Initiative. She regularly conducts workshops on multicultural issues, ethics, and Native American mental health issues.

Nathan Deen is professor emeritus of guidance and counseling with the University of Utrecht, the Netherlands. In 1972, the first initiative was taken to develop a Department of Guidance and Counseling in the Netherlands at the University of Utrecht, and Dr. Deen became head of the new department. He served as associate professor in this department until 1987 and as Special Professor of Guidance and Counselling at the University of Utrecht until his retirement in 1995. Dr. Deen was a key figure in the development of counseling in the Netherlands and in the international arena. In 1977, he founded the *International Journal for the Advancement of Counselling* and served for fifteen years as its managing editor. Dr. Deen has written several books and numerous chapters on education and counseling (most of them in the Dutch language) and published numerous articles in both Dutch and English. On several occasions, Dr. Deen served as visiting professor in various universities in the United States. The American Counseling Association granted him the Arthur A. Hitchcock Distinguished Professional Service Award in 1997. Dr. Deen is a leading authority on international and cross-cultural counseling.

Charles E. Durant; Ed.D., is senior research associate with the Center for Literacy Studies at the University of Tennessee. He has extensive experience in higher education.

Marie Faubert, Ed.D., is director of the Counselor Education Program at the University of Saint Thomas, Houston, Texas. She received her doctorate from North Carolina State University.

Mary A. Fukuyama received her doctorate in counseling psychology from Washington State University in 1981. She has worked primarily at the University of Florida Counseling Center in Gainesville, where she has engaged in clinical practice; training; and teaching courses in career development, multicultural counseling, and spiritual issues in counseling. She recently co-authored a book with Todd Sevig titled *Integrating Spirituality Into Multicultural Counseling* and is interested in exploring multidimensional ways of articulating spirituality in counseling, healing, and health. She is an active member of an interdisciplinary group at the University of Florida, which has established a Center for Spirituality and Health.

Barbara Herlihy is a professor in the Counselor Education Program at the University of New Orleans. She received her Ph.D. from Northwestern University. She is a National Certified Counselor, Licensed Professional Counselor (Texas), and a former counselor in schools, agencies, and private practice. She has a long-standing interest in counselor ethics, which has resulted in the publication of five books, several book chapters, and numerous journal articles. Her books include *Ethical, Legal, and Professional Issues in Counseling*, with Theodore P. Remley, and *Boundary Issues in Counseling* and the *ACA Ethical Standards Casebook* (5th ed.), with Gerald Corey. She is a former chair of the American Counseling Association's (ACA) Ethics Committee and has served on the ethics committees of three ACA divisions. Dr. Herlihy has presented workshops and seminars on ethics across the United States and internationally. She combines her work in ethics with her other research interests in feminist therapy, multicultural counseling, and counselor supervision.

Farah A. Ibrahim is an immigrant scholar and a licensed psychologist. She is program director and professor of counseling psychology at Howard University in Washington, D.C., and former program director and professor of counseling psychology at the University of Connecticut, Storrs. She has written a number of articles and chapters on Asian American women, identity development of South Asians, multicultural counseling issues, and existential wordview theory. Dr. Ibrahim is co-author (with Harris Kahn) of the *Scale to Assess World View* and *Cultural Identity Check List*. She is currently on the editorial boards of the *International Journal for the Advancement of Counselling* (also, its book review editor) and the *Journal of Multicultural Counseling and Development*. In addition, she has served on the editorial boards of *The Counseling Psychologist*, the *Journal of Counseling and Development*, and *Psychotherapy*. Dr. Ibrahim was recently elected president of Counselors for Social Justice, a division of the American Counseling Association.

Marty Jencius is an assistant professor in counselor education in the Department of Adult, Counseling, Health, and Vocational Education at Kent State University. His teaching includes multicultural counseling and counseling theory courses. He serves on the American Counseling Association Cyber/Technology Committee and as the technology advisor to the president of the Association for Counselor Education and Supervision. He is cofounding editor of the *Journal of Technology in Counseling* at http://jtc.colstate.edu, and his research interests include transcultural counseling models, acculturation models, and use of technology in the development of intercultural collaboration.

S. Alvin Leung is a professor in the Department of Educational Psychology, The Chinese University of Hong Kong, China. He received his Ph.D. in counseling psychology from the University of Illinois at Urbana-Champaign in 1988 and served as a faculty member in the Counseling Psychology Programs at the University of Nebraska–Lincoln and the University of Houston. He is currently associate editor of *The Counseling Psychologist* and editor of the *Asian Journal of Counselling* (published in Hong Kong). His research interests include career development and assessment, multicultural and cross-cultural issues in counseling, and counselor training and development.

Don C. Locke is director of the ACCE Doctoral Program at the Asheville Graduate Center of North Carolina State University and professor of counselor education at the same university. He is former president of the Association for Counselor Education and Supervision and former president of the North Carolina Counseling Association. Dr. Locke has served on editorial boards of journals, has received numerous awards and honors in counseling and education, and has authored a number of publications. He is author of *Increasing Multicultural Understanding: A Comprehensive Model* and lead editor of the recently published book, *The Handbook of Counseling* (with co-editors Jane E. Myers and Edwin L. Herr). Dr. Locke received his doctorate from Ball State University.

Thomas A. Parham, Ph.D., is assistant vice chancellor for counseling and health services and director of the Counseling Center, as well as adjunct professor at the University of California, Irvine. Dr. Parham received his bachelor's degree in social ecology from the University of California, Irvine. He received his Ph.D. in counseling psychology from Southern Illinois University at Carbondale. A licensed psychologist, Dr. Parham is a past president of the Association of Black Psychologists and past president of the Association for Multicultural Counseling and Development. He has served on several editorial boards including the *Journal of Multicultural Counseling and Development.* Dr. Parham has focused his research efforts on psychological nigrescence, racial identity development, and multicultural counseling. He is co-author of *The Psychology of Blacks: An African American Perspective* (2nd ed.) and *The Psychology of Blacks: An African Centered Perspective,* and author of *Counseling African Descent People: Raising the Bar of Practitioner Competence* and *Psychological Storms: The African American Struggle for Identity.* Dr. Parham has received a number of honors and awards and has lectured and consulted in numerous settings.

Paul B. Pedersen is a visiting professor in the Department of Psychology at the University of Hawaii. He has taught at the University of Minnesota, Syracuse University, the University of Alabama at Birmingham, and, for six years, at universities in Taiwan, Malaysia, and Indonesia. He has authored, co-authored, or edited forty books, ninety-nine articles, and seventy-two chapters on aspects of multicultural counseling. He is a Fellow in Divisions 9, 17, 45, and 52 of the American Psychological Association.

Patricia Perez is a doctoral student in the Counseling Psychology Program at Arizona State University. She earned her bachelor's and master's degrees in psychology at California State University, Los Angeles (CSULA). For nearly four years,

Ms. Perez was a research assistant at CSULA's Center for Cross-Cultural Research, where she conducted research in the area of racial identity. This work resulted in a publication in the *Journal of Counseling and Development,* as well as several conference presentations. Ms. Perez is a Fellow of the American Psychological Association Minority Fellowship Program.

Lee J. Richmond is professor of education at Loyola College in Maryland, where she coordinates the graduate program in school counseling. A National Certified Counselor and career counselor, Dr. Richmond is also a licensed psychologist who is involved in corporate training in Japan and China as well as in the United States. A former president of the National Career Development Association and the American Counseling Association, her major emphasis has been the development and dignity of diverse populations. She has co-authored three books and has authored several book chapters that focus on spirituality, work, and cross-culturalism. Dr. Richmond is the mother of four adult children and the grandmother of eleven children. Her profoundest hope is for a just world with the kind of peace and understanding that will enable her children and the children of others to live together in harmony and in joy.

Gargi Roysircar is the founding director of the Antioch New England Multicultural Center for Research and Practice (www.multiculturalcenter.org) and professor in the Department of Clinical Psychology (APA-accredited), Antioch New England Graduate School, Antioch University. She does research on the interface of acculturation and ethnic identity with the mental health of immigrants and ethnic minorities, worldview differences between and within cultural groups, multicultural competencies and training in professional psychology, and multicultural assessment and instrumentation. Gargi Roysircar has written approximately 125 journal articles, book chapters, books, and national papers/presentations. She is a Fellow of the American Psychological Association (APA), immediate past president of the Association for Multicultural Counseling and Development, and the editor of APA's *Division 17 Counseling Psychology Newsletter.* Dr. Roysircar is on the editorial board of several professional journals. At the Antioch New England Multicultural Center for Research and Practice, she integrates research with clinical services, consultation, and education. Prior to joining Antioch New England in 2000, Dr. Roysircar was a tenured associate professor in the Counseling Psychology Program (APA-accredited) of the Department of Educational Psychology, University of Nebraska–Lincoln, where she began her academic career in 1988.

Daya Singh Sandhu, Ed.D., NCC, is chairperson and professor in the Department of Educational and Counseling Psychology at the University of Louisville. He received his doctor of counselor education degree from Mississippi State University and has taught graduate courses in counseling and counseling psychology for the past fifteen years. Dr. Sandhu has an interest in school counseling, multicultural counseling, neurolinguistic programming, and the role of spirituality in counseling and psychotherapy. In addition to more than 50 refereed journal articles, Dr. Sandhu has authored or edited seven books, including *Counseling for Prejudice Prevention and Reduction* (1997), *Empowering Women for Equity: A Counseling Approach* (1999), *Asian and Pacific Islander Americans: Issues and Concerns for Counseling and Psychotherapy* (1999), *Violence in American Schools: A Practical Guide for Counselors* (2000), *Faces of Violence: Psychological Correlates, Concepts, and Intervention Strategies* (2001), *Elementary School Counseling in the New Millennium* (2001), and *Counseling Employees: A Multifaceted Approach* (2002). Dr. Sandhu has received several distinguished awards, including a Fulbright Research Scholar Award (2002), the AMCD Research Award (2001), and the Multicultural Teaching Award (2000). Recently, he was cited in the *Handbook of Multicultural Counseling* as one of the twelve pioneers in multicultural counseling.

Winifred O. Stone, Ph.D., is associate professor emeritus of the Department of Ethnic Studies, Bowling Green State University. He is former associate dean of the graduate school and director of graduate admission, Bowling Green State University. Dr. Stone has received and managed numerous grant programs for the development of ethnic minority students. Currently, he is a member of the Governor's Council, Ohio Department of Aging. Dr. Stone is cofounder of Transcendent Counseling with Frederick D. Harper, and he has authored a number of publications on ethnicity and career counseling.

Mei Tang, Ph.D., is assistant professor in the Counseling Program, University of Cincinnati. Dr. Tang coordinates the School Counseling Program and teaches in the areas of school counseling, counseling children, career development, and testing and research methods in counseling. She serves on the editorial boards of the *Journal of Career Development* and the *Journal of College Counseling*, as well as on various committees of the American Counseling Association and the American Psychological Association. She has published and presented in the areas of career development and assessment, counseling ethnic minorities, counseling school-age populations, and cross-cultural issues in counselor education. Dr. Tang obtained her Ph.D. from the University of Wisconsin–Milwaukee in 1996, her M.Ed. from the University of Central Oklahoma, and her B.A. from Shanghai International Studies University in China.

imani turtle-song, M.A., LPC (Navajo/African American), is a practicing counselor and intake coordinator at PB&J Family Services, Inc., in Albuquerque, New Mexico—an agency that provides services to developmentally delayed parents and their children. Speaking both Navajo and Spanish, Ms. turtle-song often provides special services to these populations. She received her M.A. in counselor education in 1999 from the University of New Mexico. Her research and applied interests include ethnic identity development, multicultural counseling competencies, philosophy, and therapeutic interventions to families with developmental delays who are experiencing and living with domestic violence.

Clemmont E. Vontress, Ph.D., is a frequent contributor to the counseling literature, especially cross-cultural psychotherapeutic intervention. His book, *Counseling*

Negroes (1971), was one of the first to call attention to the impact of culture on counseling. A university professor for more than thirty-five years, he has taught at Howard University and George Washington University, among several other universities. Active in professional, local, state, and national associations during his career, Dr. Vontress has served twice as president of the D.C. Counseling Association and has been on editorial boards of several professional journals. Currently, he is on the editorial boards of the *Journal of Mental Health Counseling* and *Ethical Human Sciences and Services: An International Journal of Critical Inquiry.* Dr. Vontress has made several trips to Africa to study traditional healing, and he has traveled, taught, and/or researched in the Middle East, the Caribbean Islands, Europe, and Africa. His most recent book is *Cross-Cultural Counseling: A Casebook* (1999) with Jake A. Johnson and Lawrence R. Epp. Dr. Vontress is a licensed psychologist who is in private practice in Washington, D.C.

Zarus E. Watson is a tenured associate professor in the Counselor Education Program with the Department of Educational Leadership, Counseling, and Foundations at the University of New Orleans (UNO). He holds a B.A. degree from Tulane University and M.A. and Ph.D. degrees in counseling and research methods from the University of New Orleans. He is the cofounder, research director, and principal investigator of the UNO Research Center for Multiculturalism and Counseling, which includes the funded operation of the Child Crisis Unit (a dedicated site for sexually abused children under the age of six years) and the Families for Learning Literacy Project (a counseling-supported family/community-oriented workforce literacy program). His teaching and research interests include macrosystemic conditioning; cultural competence issues in counseling and consultation; sociorace, class, and gender identity development within and between groups; and adaptive employee assistance program and evaluation designs.

Bea Wehrly, Ph.D., NCC, has forty years of experience in teaching and counseling, the past twenty-five of which were in the Counselor Education/College Student Personnel Department at Western Illinois University, Macomb, Illinois. She is the senior author of *Counseling Multiracial Families* (1999) and the author of *Counseling Interracial Individuals and Families* (1996) and *Pathways to Multicultural Counseling Competence: A Developmental Journey* (1995). Dr. Wehrly developed and taught the multicultural counseling course at Western Illinois University for the eight years before she retired. She has been active in local, state, national, and international professional counseling endeavors since 1970. Most recently, Dr. Wehrly has been conducting seminars on multiracial counseling in the United States, Canada, and Europe. She is the recipient of the 1999 American Counseling Association Professional Development Award; the 1986 Illinois Counseling Association Michelman Award; the 1982 Distinguished Alumni Award from the University of Wisconsin, Whitewater; and the 1998 and 2001 Western Illinois University Diversity Award.

John D. West is a professor and coordinator of the Counseling and Human Development Services Program at Kent State University. His current scholarly interests include the study of social construction theory and the use of Q methodology in the study of human subjectivity.

INTRODUCTION

The late 1970s ushered in the era of culture and counseling as an attempt to be more inclusive of special populations and diverse groups. Therefore, today we have a plethora of culture-related terms that have flooded the literature and, to a degree, confused counseling professionals as to which are interchangeable, which overlap, and which are inclusive of others. Some of these culture-specific terms include *counseling across cultures* (Pedersen, Draguns, Lonner, & Trimble, 2002), *cross-cultural counseling* (Vontress, 2001), *multicultural counseling* (Pedersen, 1991; Lee, 1999; Ponterotto, Casas, Suzuki, & Alexander, 2001; Lee, 2002), *transcultural counseling* (d'Ardenne & Mahtani, 1999; McFadden, 1999), *intercultural counseling* (Pedersen, 1976), and *counseling the culturally different* (Smith 1973; Sue & Sue, 1999).

Weinrach and Thomas (1998) observe that the whole cultural movement grew out of a need to address "differentness" between the counselor and client. During the ethnic and minorities counseling movement of the 1960s and the 1970s, a cross-racial counseling dyad often referred to or focused on the White counselor and the non-White client. In the past couple of decades, the popularity of the culture-centered counseling movement has been demonstrated by the increased number of textbooks and required counselor training courses on the subject of culture and diversity. This increased prevalence has been driven mainly by the requirements of (1) counselor training accreditation groups, (2) counselor certification boards, and (3) a multicultural counseling competence movement as presently reflected in standards of professional associations (e.g., Sue, Arredondo, & McDavis, 1992).

Because of professional requirements and the increasing diversity of groups and cultures in the United States and the global community, it seems that the need for multiculturally competent and diversity-sensitive counselors is here to stay. In the counseling profession, cultural awareness, understanding, and tolerance are increasingly becoming more and more important in the United States and throughout the world. Cross-cultural migration is on the rise as people of the world seek opportunity and occasionally refuge in distant or nearby countries. In the United States, demographic statistics are shifting from what was once considered a society of mainstream European Americans to a nation of diverse cultural and ethnic groups. According to the U.S. Bureau of the Census (2001, 2002), the 2000 census count indicated a total U.S. population of 281,421,906, which included 69.1 percent White (not of Hispanic/Latino origin), 12.5 percent Latino or Hispanic "origin" (the actual Latino population, versus "origin," was 12.0 percent), 12.3 percent African Americans, 3.6 percent Asian Americans, 0.9 percent Native Americans and Alaskan Natives, and 0.1 percent Native Hawaiian and other Pacific Islanders. The remaining several percentage points represent those who reported other races. By 2050, it is estimated that U.S. demographics and inherent political, economic, and social structures will reflect an even more ethnoculturally diverse society.

Because of an increasing diversity of immigrant populations, U.S. citizens have been forced into greater awareness of and tolerance for the global world and its diverse cultures, ethnic groups, and religions. This increased awareness and tolerance, compared to the past, has developed, in part, because of the diversity of immigrants who have settled in the United States from various regions of the world. In a number of major U.S. cities, one can find communities of persons with physical features and ethnic surnames that reflect this increasing diversity, for example, communities where there are concentrated populations of U.S. citizens or residents of Caribbean, Central American, Chinese, Asian Indian, Ethiopian, Korean, Mexican, Middle Eastern, Japanese, Puerto Rican, or Vietnamese origin. Considering an increasing diversity of ethnic groups in the United States, counselors and counseling textbooks can no longer limit their focus to the historically traditional U.S. ethnic groups of color. Moreover, counselors and counseling authors have become more sensitive to or aware of diverse ethnic, gender, religious, identity, status, and affiliation groups.

As regards international cross-cultural exchange, rapidly developing technological advances have had a profound influence on the United States's sense of being a part of a global community, especially technological advances in computer sciences, the Internet, and telecommunications. Electronic mail (e-mail) can be transmitted from any location in North America to a country on the other side of the globe in a matter of seconds. The World Wide Web not only facilitates e-mail but it also enables individuals to access or exchange cultural and professional information on Web sites with relative ease and minimal to no cost.

Individuals connected with schools, colleges, and universities are keenly aware of the momentous changes that are taking place demographically and technologically. Institutions of higher education have called for increased initiatives to meet the cultural mix of campus populations and the related challenges that include language and communication, cross-cultural adjustment, and intergroup conflict. Grants from educational, governmental, and private sectors have funded numerous projects to bring technological advances into institutions of higher education and local school systems. As with educational institutions and U.S. society at large, the profession of counseling is responding to changes and challenges that are evident at home and abroad, changes and challenges that give credence to the importance of and need for a comprehensive book on "culture and counseling" as a resource for practice, research, counselor preparation, supervision, and consultation.

Culture and Counseling: New Approaches reflects the writings of a group of leading scholars on the topic and includes up-to-date discussions of their theories, research, counseling approaches, and cultural viewpoints. The numerous chapters cover national and international cultural perspectives and encompass a variety of counseling concerns and clientele groups. Our position is that the United States is not an insulated, multicultural capsule that is isolated from and unaffected by the rest of the world. Therefore, it is necessary to present a book, such as this one, that addresses the cultural dynamics within the United States as well as ways in which U.S. culture interfaces with world cultures in this exciting and challenging era of one interdependent and interactive global community. We have done this by including a section in the book (Part Three) that presents chapters on international and intercultural dimensions of counseling.

As editors, we invited authors to contribute chapters based on our personal and professional knowledge of their writings and scholarly leadership in the field of culture and counseling. This does not imply that there are other authors who are not worthy of being included as chapter contributors. There were several invited authors whose commitments did not allow them to participate, and there are others whom we may have invited if space or the nature of our selected topics would have allowed. Nevertheless, within the book, we have attempted to document and include the contributions of leading pioneers, researchers, theorists, and other professional leaders in the field of culture and counseling.

Regarding the title of the book, we labored over an appropriate name before settling on *Culture and Counseling: New Approaches*. Our thinking was to agree on a phrase that would be inclusive of the wide range of language in the counseling literature as related to culture and diversity—that is, language that includes terms such as *multicultural counseling* (Ponterotto et al., 2001), *cross-cultural counseling* (Vontress, Johnson, & Epp, 1999; Vontress, 2001), *transcultural counseling* (d'Ardenne & Mahtani, 1999; McFadden, 1999), *counseling across cultures* (Pedersen et al., 2002), and *counseling the culturally different* (Smith, 1973; Sue & Sue, 1999). The idea for the book's subtitle, "new approaches," was to address approaches and themes that are often overlooked or underemphasized in culture and counseling books. Overlooked and underemphasized themes and approaches that are addressed in the book include healing and other nontraditional therapeutic approaches (Chapters 2 and 16), counseling White or European American ethnicities (Chapter 9), the international counseling movement (Chapter 10), spiritual approaches to therapy (Chapter 12), culture-specific and diversity-sensitive intervention and prevention strategies (Chapters 16 to 18), and the possible uses of the Internet and technology by counseling professionals (Chapter 22).

We encouraged authors to share with readers, if they chose, how they developed as a person and a professional to the point of their current thinking and theoretical position. Therefore, you will see this refreshing orientation in some chapters, including those by Vontress, Ibrahim, Arredondo, and Fukuyama. We believe that such an approach helps the reader to understand the cultural pathways and developing worldviews of authors. In addition, we made conscious attempts to ensure contributions from a diverse group of authors in terms of ethnic background and gender. We also made a conscious effort to select counseling cases (Chapter 16) that reflect a diversity of clientele in terms of gender, sexual identity, ethnicity, cultural origin, national origin, age, and spiritual or religious affiliation. The counseling cases were also selected to represent a variety of clientele problems that are influenced by or interact with culture.

Culture and Counseling: New Approaches is divided into six parts with a total of twenty-four chapters. Part One, Cultural Viewpoints of Counseling, has four chapters. Chapter 1, by Harper, presents explanations of basic concepts and a discussion of historical events during the overall ethnocultural movement in counseling (i.e., both the ethnic and cultural movements). In Chapter 2, Vontress traces the pathway of his work on culture and human existence, existential psychotherapy as a cross-cultural theory, and recent research on traditional healing as an alternative or supplement to Western therapies. In Chapter 3, Pedersen presents his latest thinking on a model of "culture-centered counseling competence" and presents a "cultural grid" for training culturally competent counselors. McFadden, in Chapter 4, discusses "transcultural counseling" from an intercultural perspective and interfaces this viewpoint with interdisciplinary insights.

Part Two, Ethnicity and Counseling, includes five chapters on the major ethnic groups in the United States. In Chapter 5, Cameron and turtle-song delineate specific phases of the history of Native Americans, current health and social issues of Native Americans, and a holistic model of treatment and counseling from a Native American perspective. Parham and Brown, in Chapter 6, focus on treatment dynamics in working with African Americans, that is, in terms of the mental health system, role of the healer, specific counseling techniques, concepts of competence (awareness, knowledge, and skill), conditions of an effective counseling relationship, and social engineering. In Chapter 7, Sandhu, Leung, and Tang address counseling Asian and Pacific Islander Americans from the viewpoints of immigration patterns, ethnic identities, acculturative stress, values conflict, Asian women's issues, and relevant counseling models and strategies. Arredondo and Perez, in Chapter 8, discuss Latina/o Americans within the framework of historical factors, sociopolitical contexts, explanations of Spanish terms, Latino worldviews, gender socialization (machismo versus marianismo), la familia (the family), religion and spirituality, ethnic identity, and Latino-centered counseling. Chapter 9, the final chapter in Part Two, discusses European Americans. Richmond helps the reader to understand the migration patterns of White immigrants to the United States, including (1) Spanish, Dutch, Portuguese, French, and English explorers, starting in the fifteenth century; (2) Jewish, Irish, Italian, and Swedish immigrants, primarily during the late 1800s and early 1900s; and (3) recent White immigrants from Russia, Eastern Europe, and South America. By using counseling cases and counseling strategies, Richmond demonstrates how White U.S. immigrants (including European Americans) are not one monolithic ethnic group but a diversity of ethnic groups with unique cultural styles, worldviews, and values, that is, between groups and within groups.

Part Three, International and Intercultural Dimensions, includes three chapters related to international counseling or global implications for counseling. Chapter 10, by Harper and Deen, discusses the international movement of counseling in terms of international associations and journals, pioneers and contributors, international counseling Web sites, and the development of organized counseling efforts in various parts of the world, such as North America, Western and Eastern Europe, Africa, South America, Asia, and the South Pacific. In Chapter 11, Roysircar provides a comprehensive discussion of immigrants, demography, theories of acculturation, and psychometric measures of cultural phenomena. Fukuyama's Chapter 12 concludes Part Three with a discussion of multicultural spirituality from a global perspective.

Part Four, Innovative Cross-Cultural Models and Theories, contains three chapters of theoretical models of cross-cultural or multicultural counseling. In

Chapter 13, Ibrahim presents an up-to-date account of her existential worldview theory. In doing so, she traces her life development, starting in Pakistan, and explains how her life experiences influenced her thinking and theoretical development. In Chapter 14, McFadden presents his most recent conceptualization of stylistic counseling, a model that is based on three dimensions (the cultural-historical, the psychosocial, and the scientific-ideological) and twenty-seven cubes (or descriptors)—nine cubes for each dimension. In Chapter 15, Harper and Stone present an update of their existential, cognitive-behavioral theory of transcendent counseling, a metacultural theory that focuses on lifestyle change and holistic health for clients of all cultures, identities, statuses, and age groups.

Part Five focuses on intervention and prevention strategies and commences with nine culture-centered counseling cases (Chapter 16) that overlap cultural dynamics with counseling themes or concerns, such as racial identity, sexual identity, drug abuse, AIDS and holistic healing, family conflict, biracial youth problems, and a posttraumatic experience. Chapter 17, by McFadden and Banich, presents a model of bibliotherapy as a culture-specific paradigm for counseling, while Chapter 18, by Durant and McFadden, discusses cultural implications and strategies for preventive counseling. Wehrly's Chapter 19 concludes Part Five with a discourse on working with multiracial individuals and interracial families. Wehrly defines and clarifies a number of related concepts (e.g., biracial, multiracial, interracial, LatiNegra, and transracial adoption) and provides a variety of counseling strategies for the counselor's use with interracial families and multiracial individuals.

Part Six, Special Topics, Issues, and Trends in Culture and Counseling, has five chapters, including our wrap-up or concluding chapter (Chapter 24). In Chapter 20, Locke and Faubert examine cultural considerations in both counselor preparation and counselor supervision. The authors include criteria of a "sound" training program and strategies for "infusing" multiculturalism into counselor training and supervision. In Chapter 21, Jencius and West analyze traditional theoretical groups in counseling (psychoanalytic and ego psychology, cognitive-behavioral, and humanistic approaches) in terms of relevance to multicultural counseling and examine the social constructionist approach as a possible multicultural fit. Chapter 22, by Jencius, addresses technological advances and their applications for multicultural counseling, especially in the area of computer science and the Internet. As editor of the *Journal of Technology in Counseling,* Jencius shares the latest technological and Internet resources that are available to counseling professionals. In Chapter 23, Herlihy and Watson discuss ethical issues; legal concerns; and competence with regard to multicultural or cross-cultural counseling, supervision, diagnosis, and assessment, among other professional roles and areas of focus.

Within the various chapters of *Culture and Counseling* there are discussion questions, counseling cases, vignettes, and examples to stimulate creative thoughts in the classroom and in the counseling work setting. Moreover, as a limited reference or resource, we have included a glossary of culture-related terms. In addition, there is an annotated bibliography of recent multicultural and cross-cultural counseling books in Appendix A, a list of names of past presidents of the

Association for Multicultural Counseling and Development (AMCD) in Appendix B, and AMCD's thirty-one multicultural counseling competencies in Appendix C.

As co-editors, we anticipate that readers of this volume will assess themselves, confront others, and reevaluate their personal lives and professional involvement with the intent of growing and developing into stronger and more effective human beings. Our hope and spirit are transmitted to each of you as you gain insight and learn from the varied and knowledgeable contributors of this work.

Acknowledgments

We express appreciation to our wives, Jacqueline A. Harper and Grace Jordan McFadden, for their untiring support and patience with us during the very demanding period of preparing the manuscript of this book for publication with Allyn and Bacon. In addition, we acknowledge the cooperation of graduate assistants and other students who did library research and helped review parts of the manuscript at various stages of its development. These persons include Stephanie McVea and Alicia Murray, doctoral students in the Counseling Psychology Program at Howard University, and Robert A. Horak, Jr., doctoral student in the Counselor Education Program at the University of South Carolina. Also, research assistance and consultation were rendered by Charles E. Durant, Marty Jencius, Amanda B. Thompson, MaryAnne Banich, and Terry Carter.

We also acknowledge persons who provided interview information for the development of specific chapters of the book. These counseling authorities include Jean Guichard, who provided information on the history of counseling in France; Lothar R. Martin, who provided information on the history of counseling in Germany; Paul Collins, Gloria S. Smith, Aaron B. Stills, and Clemmont E. Vontress, who provided information on the history of the ethnocultural counseling movement in the United States; and Morris Jackson, who shared information on his development of the multicultural listserv and the American Counseling Association Multicultural Counseling Summit.

We wish to thank the following manuscript reviewers: Mark S. Kiselica, The College of New Jersey; Donna M. Talbot, Western Michigan University; and Clemmont E. Vontress, George Washington University. We thank Anne Rogers and others at Omegatype Typography, Inc., for their production coordination and copyediting contributions. Lastly, we express our appreciation to Virginia Lanigan, Executive Editor at Allyn and Bacon, who supported our idea and efforts for this book from the very beginning to its publication.

Frederick D. Harper and **John McFadden**

REFERENCES

d'Ardenne, P., & Mahtani, A. (1999). *Transcultural counseling in action* (2nd ed.). Newbury Park, CA: Sage.

Lee, C. C. (Ed.). (2002). *Multicultural issues in counseling: New approaches to diversity* (3rd ed.). Alexandria, VA: American Counseling Association.

Lee, W. M. L. (1999). *An introduction to multicultural counseling.* Philadelphia, PA: Accelerated Development.

McFadden, J. (Ed.). (1999). *Transcultural counseling* (2nd ed.). Alexandria, VA: American Counseling Association.

Pedersen, P. B. (1976). The field of intercultural counseling. In P. Pedersen, W. J. Lonner, & J. G. Draguns (Eds.), *Counseling across cultures* (pp. 17–44). Honolulu: East-West Center Press.

Pedersen, P. B. (Ed.). (1991). Multiculturalism as a fourth force in counseling [Special issue]. *Journal of Counseling & Development, 70*(1).

Pedersen, P. B., Draguns, J. G., Lonner, W. J., & Trimble, J. E. (2002). *Counseling across cultures* (5th ed.). Thousand Oaks, CA: Sage.

Ponterotto, J. G., Casas, J. M., Suzuki, L. A., & Alexander, C. M. (2001). *Handbook of multicultural counseling* (2nd ed.). Thousand Oaks, CA: Sage.

Smith, E. J. (1973). *Counseling the culturally different black youth.* Columbus, OH: Merrill.

Sue, D. W., Arredondo, P., & McDavis, R. J. (1992). Multicultural counseling competencies and standards: A call to the profession. *Journal of Multicultural Counseling and Development, 20,* 64–88.

Sue, D. W., & Sue, D. (1999). *Counseling the culturally different: Theory and practice* (3rd ed.). New York: Wiley.

U.S. Bureau of the Census. (2001). The Hispanic population in the United States. Retrieved March 25, 2002, from http://www.census.gov/population/socdemo/hispanic/p20-535/p20-535.pdf

U.S. Bureau of the Census. (2002). U.S. Census Bureau QuickFacts. Retrieved March 25, 2002, from http://quickfacts.census.gov/qfd/states/00000.html

Vontress, C. E., Johnson, J. A., & Epp, L. R. (1999). *Cross-cultural counseling: A casebook.* Alexandria, VA: American Counseling Association.

Vontress, C. E. (2001). Cross-cultural counseling in the twenty-first century. *International Journal for the Advancement of Counselling, 23,* 83–97.

Weinrach, S. G., & Thomas, K. R. (1998). Diversity-sensitive counseling today: A postmodern clash of values. *Journal of counseling and development, 76,* 115–122.

1 Background: Concepts and History

FREDERICK D. HARPER

This chapter addresses concepts and historical events related to the cultural movement in counseling. Culture, diversity, ethnicity, and race are intertwined and elusive concepts that commonly appear in the literature on "culture and counseling." Nevertheless, these concepts have not found a consensus among authors in terms of their definitions and their relationships to each other (Copeland, 1983; Das, 1995; Smart & Smart, 1997). Persons who have a specific culture of origin tend to have an ethnic identity and, in a broader, more sociopolitical sense, a racial identity (Helms, 1990), whether persons define ethnic or racial identity for themselves or whether others define it by law or by perception of their image.

A concept that is inclusive of culture is diversity, which tends to include multiculturalism plus concerns related to special clientele groups such as (1) American ethnicities; (2) lesbian, gay, bisexual, and transgender (LGBT) clients; (3) persons with disabilities; (4) age groups; and (5) gender or clients with gender-related concerns. Weinrach and Thomas (1998) use the term *diversity-sensitive counseling* and, in doing so, define diversity in an even more comprehensive manner to include "age, culture, disability, education level, ethnicity, gender, language, physique, race, religion, residential location (i.e., urban, suburban, rural), sexual orientation . . . socioeconomic situation, trauma, and multiple and overlapping characteristics of the preceding" (p. 115). In parsimonious language, diversity refers to ethnic heritage, cultural background, group affiliation, identity, and status. Within this context, "identity" refers to sexual identity and other nonethnic identities and "status" refers to any biosocial or socioeconomic status, including state of disability and social-class status.

Culture can be defined broadly as the sum of intergenerationally transmitted and cross-culturally acquired lifestyle ways, behavior patterns, and products of a people that include their language, music, arts and artifacts, beliefs, interpersonal styles, values, habits, history, eating preferences, customs, and social rules. Furthermore, culture can be characterized by people who share a common geographic place, common experiences, and a specific time in history. Nowadays, most cultures are fluid or in flux and not static, impermeable, or rigidly isolated from other cultural influences. In a world of telecommunication, rapid jet air travel, and global migration, many cultures of the world are changing rapidly and many are becoming blended cultures composed of multiple ethnic groups and cultural mixes.

Vontress (Chapter 2) posits that one's culture can be national (e.g., U.S. culture), regional (e.g., Southeast U.S. culture), and racio-ethnic (e.g., Korean American culture). There are commonalities within a culture and variations between cultures. Although often overlooked in the literature, there are also variations within culture. For example, as regards regional, geographic cultural differences within the United States, there is much variance between the cultural ways of people who reside in Texas and those who reside in Massachusetts. In Texas, persons are more likely than those in Massachusetts to greet each other with "howdy," to favor Mexican food, and to engage in square dancing. Furthermore, there are within-ethnic group differences between African Americans who grow up in Texas and those who grow up in Massachusetts, although African Americans are members of the same ethnic group and have other cultural ways in common. By the same token, there are within-ethnicity cultural differences among Hispanic or Latino/a immigrants who originate from different geographic regions of the Americas, for example, Cuba, Puerto Rico, Mexico, Central America, and various countries in South America (Herring, 1997; see also Chapter 8).

Culture is important in counseling because it plays a significant role in influencing the worldviews of both the counselor and the client, and the worldviews of both participants in the counseling process can affect the quality and outcome of the counseling relationship (Ibrahim, 1999). Das (1995) states that "Culture is an inevitable silent participant in all counseling because counseling is a culture-specific human invention. Each form of counseling is a reflection of the culture that produces it" (p. 50). Although culture is an important factor in counseling, it must be kept in mind that there are other factors that influence the outcomes and effectiveness of counseling such as the nature of the client's problem, client resistance, counselor empathy, and counselor acceptance and respect for the client (Rogers, 1961; Lambert & Cattani-Thompson, 1996).

Culture and counseling, as used to title this book, includes the expanding potpourri of culturally characterized concepts that are used in the counseling literature to describe a counseling relationship between counselors and clients who have different cultural backgrounds. Such terms include *cross-cultural counseling, multicultural counseling, counseling the culturally different, counseling across cultures, intercultural counseling,* and *transcultural counseling.* The following discussion is an attempt to make some sense of these culture-and-counseling concepts and how they relate to each other; nevertheless, it is not necessarily an attempt to bring about a consensus regarding their meaning and usage.

- Cross-cultural counseling, counseling across cultures, and intercultural counseling appear to be used in the counseling literature interchangeably. Cross-cultural counseling appears to be the most popular among these concepts in terms of frequency of use in the counseling literature (Pedersen, 1976; Pedersen et al., 1981; Copeland, 1983; Vontress, 2001).

- Multicultural counseling was adapted primarily as an alternative to cross-cultural counseling and counseling the culturally different. It is viewed as a broader and more inclusive term that suggests counseling clients from a variety of ethnic groups, cultural backgrounds, "affiliations," and status situations (Pedersen, 1991b, p. 7).
- Counseling minorities or counseling U.S. ethnic minorities basically refers to counseling clients from specific U.S., non-White ethnic groups. Atkinson, Morten, and Sue (1998), over the past couple of decades, have used the concept of "American minorities" in book titles. In addition, Henderson (1979) and Herring (1997) have used the terms *ethnic minorities* and *ethnic youth* respectively in their book titles.
- Transcultural counseling, associated with d'Ardenne and Mahtani (1999) and McFadden (1999), purports to be a broad term that transcends culture and nations and is a reciprocal process between the counselor and the client.
- Counseling the culturally different was more prevalent in the counseling literature during the late 1960s and the decade of the 1970s (Vontress, 1969a; Smith 1973; S. Sue, 1977a). The rare exception is that the phrase "counseling the culturally different" continues to be used by Sue and Sue (1999) in titles of subsequent editions of their book by the same name (the first edition was published in 1981). The term fell out of favor with a number of counseling writers because it raised the question of different from what cultural norm. Moreover, "culturally different" seems to imply a difference from the dominant cultural norm, that is, in a deviant manner, or it implies a difference from so-called socially acceptable cultural ways of mainstream U.S. society.
- Culture-centered counseling is associated with Pedersen's (1999) multicultural counseling Triad Training Model as well as Pedersen and Ivey's (1993) training in interviewing skills for multicultural counselors.
- Other cultural or ethnocultural concepts that can be found in the counseling literature include cultural diversity (Herr, 1987), counseling special populations (Larson, 1982; Gelso & Fretz, 2001), culture-specific counseling (Nwachuku & Ivey, 1991), diversity-sensitive counseling (Weinrach & Thomas, 1998), and ethnopsychiatry (Vontress & Epp, 2000).

To confuse the issue even more, although Pedersen (1991b) views multicultural counseling as broader and more inclusive in focus as compared to cross-cultural counseling, there are other authors who see no essential differences between multicultural counseling, cross-cultural counseling, and transcultural counseling, but see them basically as terms that can be used interchangeably (Das, 1995; Smart & Smart, 1997). The literature suggests that multicultural counseling and cross-cultural counseling are probably the most frequently used language among the currently and recently used culture-and-counseling concepts (Heath, Neimeyer, & Pedersen, 1988; Speight, Myers, Cox, & Highlen, 1991; Holcomb-McCoy & Myers, 1999; Lee, 1999; Ponterotto, Casas, Suzuki, & Alexander, 2001; Lee, 2002).

As a summary schema, Table 1.1 presents concepts related to race and ethnicity (Rubric 1) and concepts related to diversity and ethnocultural counseling

TABLE 1.1   **The Relationship of Cultural and Ethnocultural Concepts**

Race, Ethnicity, and Culture (Rubric 1)

Human race: The global race of human beings

Racial groups: Three primary divisions of the human race

Culture: Human-made environment and ways of a people of a particular time and place

Ethnic groups: A group with common features, ways, and heritage residing within a culture or across cultures

Diversity/Ethnocultural Counseling Concepts (Rubric 2)

Diversity counseling: Diversity-sensitive counseling of cultural, ethnic, identity, and status groups

Multicultural counseling: Counseling focus on a variety of cultural or ethnocultural groups

Cross-cultural counseling: Counseling a client or clients from a different culture

Ethnic/minority counseling: Counseling clients from a particular ethnic or U.S. minority group

Note: The concepts under both rubrics are ranked from the most to least comprehensive in scope. Cultural diversity suggests diversity within culture. Diversity includes diversity within culture and across cultures.

(Rubric II) as an attempt to define these concepts in a capsule and to explain their relationships to each other. Under each rubric, the various concepts are briefly defined and ordered or ranked from the most comprehensive or inclusive to the least comprehensive or inclusive. "Ethnocultural" is used throughout this chapter to refer to the counseling process or the counseling historical movement as they relate to both ethnic and cultural themes.

The Historical Movement

Several authors have written about historical perspectives and events of the ethnocultural movement in counseling (Copeland, 1983; McFadden & Lipscomb, 1985; Jackson, 1995; Wehrly, 1995; Ponterotto, et al., 2001). Among these works, (1) Copeland presents a history of cross-cultural counseling, (2) Jackson discusses themes and events of the ethnocultural counseling movement based on publications from the counseling literature and personal interviews with historical participants, (3) McFadden and Lipscomb present a brief history (1972–1985) of the Association for Non-White Concerns in Personnel and Guidance (ANWC), now the Association for Multicultural Counseling and Development (AMCD), (4) Ponterotto et al. provide culture-oriented life stories by prominent multicultural counseling authorities, and (5) Wehrly examines multicultural counseling themes, theoretical viewpoints, and training foci from a historical perspective.

To a significant degree, one could refer to the cultural movement in counseling as an ethnocultural movement because the cross-cultural and multicultural movements grew out of and are intertwined with earlier writings and research on counseling U.S. minorities or counseling non-White ethnic groups. Recent textbooks on culture and counseling, including this volume, continue, as appropriate, to include a sequence of chapters on counseling U.S. ethnicities (Axelson, 1998; McFadden, 1999; Sue & Sue, 1999; Ponterotto et al., 2001; Lee, 2002; Pedersen, Draguns, Lonner, Trimble, 2002). Moreover, there are books that continue to focus primarily on counseling U.S. ethnic groups and secondarily on culture, books such as Atkinson et al.'s (1998) *Counseling American Minorities* (5th ed.) and Herring's (1997) *Counseling Diverse Ethnic Youth.*

The discussion that follows presents themes and developments of the ethnocultural or cultural movement in counseling over the past 40-plus years.

The 1960s: The Pioneering Years

The etiology of the ethnocultural movement in counseling is rooted in the U.S. civil rights movement of the 1950s and 1960s—organized protests that forced the United States to change its laws and sociocultural structure (Parker & Myers, 1991; Jackson, 1995; Wehrly, 1995). During this time, the United States began to change from a country of White "encapsulated" institutions, to use Wrenn's (1962) term, to a country of racially mixed social and educational institutions. Westbrook and Sedlacek (1991) note that the social transformation of the 1960s forced White educators and counselors to try and understand, educate, and counsel the growing numbers of "nontraditional" or non-White students who were entering what were previously all-White schools, colleges, and universities. Patterson (1996) and Pedersen, Lonner, and Draguns (1976) indicate that White counselors of the 1960s were not trained to work with persons of color; therefore, they were not prepared to counsel African American and other non-White youth. In response to this need for ethnocultural awareness and knowledge, Vontress (1966, 1967a, 1967b, 1969a, 1969b) was the only counselor educator who wrote consistently about White–Black, cross-cultural counseling during the 1960s. Wehrly (1995) states that, "He [Clemmont Vontress] was also a pioneer in helping White counselors understand the special challenges of working with Black clients" (p. 27). In two separate published interviews with Clemmont Vontress, Jackson (1987) and Lee (1994) reveal his pioneering contributions to and consistent involvement in the history of the cultural movement in counseling. Lee posits that "His [Vontress's] early thoughts and writings about human diversity helped to shape the development of multicultural counseling as a major discipline" (p. 66).

Copeland (1983) and Westbrook and Sedlacek (1991) report that during the decade of the 1960s, African Americans and other ethnic minorities of color, especially low-income students, were often labeled in the education and counseling literature with terms such as *culturally deprived* and *disadvantaged.* These terms were soon perceived to be deficit-oriented or negative labels, thus leading to alternative language such as *culturally different* (Vontress, 1967b, 1969a; Smith, 1973) and *non-White* (McFadden & Lipscomb, 1985). More than 30 years ago, Vontress (1967b, 1969a) was among the first to use the expression "counseling the culturally different" in the counseling literature, that is, as an alternative to "culturally deprived" and "disadvantaged."

Prior to the 1960s, the American Personnel and Guidance Association (APGA), now the American Counseling Association (ACA), was primarily a White professional association in leadership and membership, just as most other traditionally White U.S. organizations and institutions were during that time. As African Americans increased their membership in the APGA, there became a developing sense of frustration among them that APGA was neither addressing their professional needs nor the needs of African American counseling clients. In addition, the assassination of civil rights leader Dr. Martin Luther King exacerbated tensions among African American APGA members, as evidenced at the 1968 Annual Convention of the APGA in Detroit (C. E. Vontress, personal communication, February 21, 2002). At the next APGA convention, of 1969 in Las Vegas, a small group of African Americans held a "Black Caucus," and, during the convention, William (Bill) Banks represented the group in presenting a resolution to the APGA Senate calling for a national office within the APGA that would address the concerns of African Americans and other non-White persons. In the article "History of the Association for Non-White Concerns in Personnel and Guidance," McFadden and Lipscomb (1985) note that during the 1969 APGA convention, the APGA Senate adopted a resolution to establish a salaried National Office of Non-White Concerns within the executive structure of APGA. The 1969 APGA Black Caucus and the Office of Non-White Concerns became the forerunners to the founding of the Association for Non-White Concerns in Personnel and Guidance.

Although there were numerous college and university courses on the subject of teaching students who were disadvantaged or culturally deprived during the 1960s (Riessman, 1962), there were few to no training courses for counselors on how to counsel ethnic minorities. Therefore, there was not a perceived market for or need to publish textbooks on this topic. One of the very few, if not the only significant book, on the topic at the time was Amos and Grambs's (1968) *Counseling the Disadvantaged Youth.*

The 1970s: Non-Whites and Ethnic Minorities

The 1970s brought with it a number of new courses on counseling ethnic minorities as well as an increase in the number of published articles and books on counseling non-White ethnic groups (Ponterotto, 1986; Ponterotto & Casas, 1991). This decade also marked the beginning of a focus on ethnic-racial identity development, originating with Cross's (1971) model of Black Identity Development. In addition, the Association for Non-White Concerns in Personnel and Guidance was chartered as an APGA division in 1972, stimulating use of the term *non-Whites* as an interchangeable term with *ethnic minorities*. Furthermore, in 1972, Samuel H. Johnson became the first president of the new ANWC and Gloria Smith became the first editor of the *Journal of Non-White Concerns in Personnel and Guidance*, the affiliate journal of the ANWC. The journal became a popular conduit for readings on counseling non-Whites or ethnic minorities, mainly due to the paucity of available information on the topic. Moreover, the journal became a vehicle for non-White authors to share their ideas and research during a time when traditionally White journals were not fully open to publishing articles on race and ethnicity. Nevertheless, the APGA flagship journal, *Personnel and Guidance Journal*, was compelled to address the needs of its readership and, therefore, to publish ethnic- and gender-sensitive articles and special issues during the decade of the 1970s (Smith, 1970; Lewis, 1972; S. Sue, 1977a).

Through the early and middle 1970s, a series of books were published that addressed counseling clients from specific ethnic and racial groups. Among publications in its Guidance Monograph Series, Houghton Mifflin published *Counseling Negroes* (Vontress, 1971), *Indian Students and Guidance* (Bryde, 1971), *Spanish-Speaking Students and Guidance* (Pollack & Menacker, 1971), and *The Counselor and Black/White Relations* (Beck, 1973). Books by other publishers on ethnic-racial counseling for this historical period included Smith's (1973) *Counseling the Culturally Different Black Youth*, Harper's (1975) *Black Students/White Campus: Implications for Counseling*, and DeBlassie's (1976) *Counseling with Mexican American Youth*. In the latter half of the decade, the first edition of Atkinson, Morten, and Sue's (1979) *Counseling American Minorities: A Cross-Cultural Perspective* appeared along with Henderson's (1979) *Understanding and Counseling Ethnic Minorities*.

As regards journal articles on specific ethnicities, S. Sue (1977b) along with Sue and Sue (1973) took leadership in writing about counseling Chinese and other Asian clients. Sue and Sue referred to Asian Americans as the "neglected minority," and Seligman (1977) followed Sue and Sue's cue by writing on Haitians as another neglected minority group. Ruiz and Padilla (1977) wrote on counseling Latino Americans. Publications that addressed theories of counseling African Americans included Gunnings and Simpkins's (1972) systemic counseling, Harper and Stone's (1974) transcendent counseling, and Vontress's (1971) aggressive counseling. In addition, a number of articles were authored or co-authored on topics of counseling and student-personnel concerns regarding non-White ethnic students in higher education by Sedlacek and colleagues (Brooks, Sedlacek, & Mindus, 1973; Sedlacek & Webster, 1978; Westbrook & Sedlacek, 1991).

The latter half of the decade witnessed a developing prevalence of cultural language in publication titles, for example, "counseling the culturally different" (S. Sue, 1977a), "counseling across cultures," and "cross-cultural counseling" (Pedersen, Lonner, & Draguns, 1976; Pedersen, 1978). The emphasis on cultural themes was more evident in titles of books (e.g., Pedersen, et al., 1976) and special issues of the *Personnel and Guidance Journal* (S. Sue, 1977a; Pedersen, 1978) and less prevalent in articles published in the *Journal of Non-White Concerns in Personnel and Guidance*, which continued to focus primarily on African Americans, other non-White ethnic minorities, and ethnocultural issues and strategies in counseling (Ponterotto, 1986).

1980s: The Cultural Movement

The developing trend in the counseling literature during the late 1970s of favoring cross-cultural counseling and counseling across cultures continued into the decade of the 1980s. The early 1980s marked an increasing use of culture-characterizing terms as an attempt to be more inclusive of special populations, gender, and various identity groups in addition to non-White ethnic minorities. The interest in cross-cultural counseling got a push from Pedersen and colleagues' revised edition of *Counseling Across Cultures* (Pedersen, Draguns, Lonner, & Trimble, 1981) and a special issue of the *Counseling Psychologist* on "Cross-cultural Counseling" (Smith & Vasquez, 1985). While books were beginning to focus on cultural inclusiveness, Ponterotto's (1986) content analysis on the themes of articles published in the *Journal of Non-White Concerns in Personnel and Guidance* from November 1979 to April 1984 indicated a different trend or focus. Ponterotto found that a majority (77 percent) of the articles in the journal for this 5-year period focused on ethnicity and race, including 51 percent that addressed African American concerns.

Regardless of the focus of its affiliate journal on ethnic-minority themes, the Association for Non-White Concerns in Personnel and Guidance conceded to the growing trend of inclusiveness, and therefore changed its name to the Association for Multicultural Counseling and Development in 1985. Aaron B. Stills, the first president of the newly named association, indicated that, as president-elect, he and other officers of the association encouraged the name change for the simple reason of inclusion or welcoming all ethnic groups, including Whites. Stills further stated that the ANWC's membership had declined, and that some previous members and potential members perceived the division as an association for non-Whites only— if not for Blacks only (A. B. Stills, personal communication, February 28, 2002). Along with the notion of inclusiveness of human beings of all cultures, ethnicities, and affiliations was a reemphasis on human rights and peace during the mid-1980s, as led by Farah Ibrahim, chairperson of the Human Rights Committee of the American Association for Multicultural Counseling and Development (AACD) (Ibrahim, 1985).

Upon the eve of a new decade, Courtland Lee (1989), then editor of the *Journal of Multicultural Counseling and Development*, challenged the leadership and membership of AMCD to (1) ensure greater inclusiveness of diverse groups, (2) provide more leadership for the field of multiculturalism, and (3) get more involved in international leadership, collaboration, and outreach with regard to cross-cultural issues and concerns. Lee stated, "AMCD must be an integral part of the international outreach efforts now being initiated within AACD [now ACA]. For it must be understood that the term international implies multicultural" (p. 169).

1990s: Multicultural Competence and Professional Expansionism

As fulfillment of Lee's (1989) challenges of the late 1980s, the 1990s found AMCD leaders and members taking greater leadership for changes in a number of ways. The AMCD board of directors approved 31 multicultural competencies in 1991 (see Appendix C). Moreover, at the annual ACA conference of 1992, the AMCD board of directors, upon a resolution from the editor of the *Journal of Multicultural Counseling and Development,* approved to increase the volume of each issue of the journal (Harper, 1992a). Therefore, in October 1992, the *JMCD* increased in size from 48 to 64 pages per issue, and it was changed to perfect binding (with a spine) instead of the previous stapled or saddle-stitched binding. These changes allowed for additional material or articles per issue and made for a more attractive looking journal.

There was a focus on the development and testing of cultural assessment inventories and multicultural competence instruments (Ibrahim & Owen, 1994; Ponterotto, Rieger, Barrett, & Sparks, 1994; Sodowsky, Taffe, Gutkin, & Wise, 1994) as well as a significant increase in the publication of printed materials on culture and counseling. As regards printed materials, there was a significant increase in the publication of multicultural and cross-cultural textbooks, including revised editions of previously published textbooks (e.g., Lee, 1995; Ponterotto, Casas, Suzuki, & Alexander, 1995; Wehrly, 1995; Pedersen, Draguns, Lonner, & Trimble, 1996; Herring, 1997; Atkinson et al., 1998; McFadden, 1999; Sue & Sue, 1999; Vontress, Johnson, & Epp, 1999).

This increasing interest in and prevalence of books on the topic of "culture and diversity" was apparently influenced by (1) the increasing number of required "culture and diversity" courses in counselor preparation programs throughout the country, (2) multicultural counseling requirements of credentialing groups for counseling program accreditation and counselor certification, and (3) the developing professional demands for multicultural competence, including AMCD's 31 competencies for multicultural counselors that were approved in 1991 (Sue, Arredondo, & McDavis, 1992). (See Appendix C for the AMCD statement of the 31 competencies for multicultural counselors.)

In addition, there was a significant increase in the number of publications on the topics of racial identity and ethnic identity (Helms, 1990; Helms & Carter, 1991; Smith, 1991). During the 1990s, Janet E. Helms was the most influential in leading and shaping the literature in the area of racial identity and race as related to counseling and psychotherapy (Helms, 1990; Helms & Carter, 1991; Helms, 1994; Helms & Talleyrand, 1997). Moreover, Carter (1990), Helms (1994), Locke and Kiselica (1999), Parham and McDavis (1987), and Ridley (1995) discussed the importance of race and racism in counseling and psychotherapy and argued how these sociopolitical concepts had been obscured and overshadowed by an excessive focus on multiculturalism and cultural inclusiveness.

In 1992, the first "Multicultural Summit," organized by Morris Jackson, was presented at the ACA conference in Baltimore, Maryland (American Counseling

Association [ACA], 1992). Since the first Multicultural Summit, additional summits have become a reoccurring feature at ACA conferences. At these summits, leading authorities of multicultural counseling present their viewpoints on various issues in the field, and their presentations are videotaped by the ACA for distribution.

During the late 1990s, there was increased leadership and involvement of AMCD and ACA members in the international counseling movement, starting with the attendance at the 1998 Annual Conference of the International Association for Counselling (IAC) in Paris. The significance of this year was that a former AMCD president became secretary of the IAC, a former *JMCD* editor became editor of the *International Journal for the Advancement of Counselling*, outgoing ACA and AMCD presidents attended and participated, and, for the first time, a non-White AMCD/ACA member from the United States was the lead keynote speaker. The decade of the 1990s was not only a decade of focus on multicultural competence and assessment but it was also a period of significant professional expansion in terms of the development of standards, development and publication of multicultural materials, and AMCD's international leadership and involvement in cross-cultural counseling.

Chronology of Historical Events

As a sequential profile of significant events in the ethnocultural movement in counseling, the following chronology is presented as a delineation of developments over the past 40-plus years:

1954 ▪ The National Association of Personnel Workers (now the National Association of Student Affairs Professionals [NASAP], 2002) is founded at Howard University as a professional association for African American counselors and student personnel workers, primarily in higher education. The association is founded mainly because African Americans are not allowed to join all-White counseling and student personnel associations during the time. (See the association's webpage: http://www.angelfire.com/ga/nasap.)

1962 ▪ Gilbert Wrenn (1962) calls for culturally sensitive counseling in his publication on the "culturally encapsulated counselor."

1967 ▪ Clemmont E. Vontress (1967b) is among the first to author an article that uses the phrase "culturally different."

1969 ▪ African Americans hold a Black Caucus at the Annual Convention of the APGA in Las Vegas and petition the APGA Senate to approve a resolution for the establishment of a National Office for Non-White Concerns within APGA. The APGA Senate approves the resolution, and Richard Kelsey becomes the first director of the Office of Non-White Concerns and serves in the position for a brief period, 1969–1970 (McFadden & Lipscomb, 1985).

1970 ▪ Paul Collins becomes executive assistant for Human Rights Opportunity and assumes the responsibility for the Office of Non-White Concerns as part of his responsibilities (P. Collins, personal communication, March 2, 2002).

- In May, Paul M. Smith (1970) is guest editor of a special issue of the *Personnel and Guidance Journal* by the title, "What Guidance for Blacks?"

1971 ■ William E. Cross (1971) develops one of the first theories of "Black Identity Development," which becomes the seminal work for the development of additional models of racial and ethnic identity development. Cross identifies his five stages of "Black Identity Development" as (1) Pre-Encounter, (2) Encounter, (3) Immersion-Emersion, (4) Internalization, and (5) Internalization-Commitment.

- In October, Uvaldo H. Palomares (1971) is guest editor of a special issue of the *Personnel and Guidance Journal* by the title of "Culture as a Reason for Being."

1972 ■ The Association for Non-White Concerns in Personnel and Guidance is chartered as a division of APGA. Black Caucus members Samuel H. Johnson, Gloria Smith, Joyce Clark, Charles E. Gordon, Loretta Price, and Phil Layne play a significant role in the founding of ANWC (McFadden & Lipscomb, 1985). Samuel H. Johnson becomes the first president of ANWC, serving in the position for 2 years (1972–1974).

- In October, the first issue (Volume 1, Number 1) of the *Journal of Non-White Concerns in Personnel and Guidance* is published; Gloria Smith is the journal's first editor.

- In October, Judith A. Lewis (1972) is guest editor of a special issue of the *Personnel and Guidance Journal* titled "Women and Counselors."

1973 ■ In February, Derald Wing Sue (1973) is guest editor of a special issue of the *Personnel and Guidance Journal* by the title of "Asian-Americans: The Neglected Minority."

1975 ■ Thelma T. Daley is the first African American to become president of the American Personnel and Guidance Association, 1975–1976 (ACA, 2001).

1976 ■ Pedersen, Lonner, & Draguns (1976) edit the first edition of their *Counseling Across Cultures*.

1978 ■ In April, Paul B. Pedersen (1978) is guest editor of a special issue of the *Personnel and Guidance Journal* by the title of "Counseling Across Cultures."

- During this year, the first issue of the *International Journal for the Advancement of Counselling (IJAC)* is published. *IJAC*'s aim is to address cross-cultural counseling issues and concerns from an international perspective and to create an opportunity for persons of different cultures throughout the world to exchange ideas about counseling.

1985 ■ The Association for Non-White Concerns in Personnel and Guidance changes its name to the Association for Multicultural Counseling and Development (AMCD).

- Elsie J. Smith and Melba J. T. Vasquez (1985) guest edit a special issue of *The Counseling Psychologist* by the title of "Cross-Cultural Counseling."

1990 - Janet E. Helms (1990) is editor of *Black and White Racial Identity: Theory, Research and Practice,* the first comprehensive and significant work on racial identity and counseling.

1991 - AMCD's Professional Standards Committee develops 31 competencies for multicultural counselors. The competencies are approved by the AMCD Board of Directors (Appendix C).

- Paul Pedersen (1991a) is guest editor of a special issue of the *Journal of Counseling and Development* by the title of "Multiculturalism as a Fourth Force in Counseling." In this issue, Pedersen describes multiculturalism as a "fourth force" in counseling.

- Ponterotto and Casas's (1991) *Handbook of Racial/Ethnic Minority Counseling Research* is published. It is the first significant, comprehensive guide for counseling research related to racial and ethnic U.S. minority groups.

1992 - Sue, Arredondo, and McDavis (1992) author "Multicultural Counseling Competencies and Standards: A Call to the Profession" in the *Journal of Multicultural Counseling and Development* (*JMCD*) based on the 1991, AMCD-approved 31 multicultural competencies for counselors. The same article is also published during the same year in the *Journal of Counseling and Development* as a means of reaching a broader audience.

- In October, Frederick D. Harper (1992b) is editor of a special issue of the *JMCD* by the title of "Gender and Relationships."

- The first "Multicultural Counseling Summit" is held at the Annual Conference of the American Counseling Association in Baltimore, Maryland.

1994 - In October, Phoebe Dufrene and Roger Herring (1994) are guest editors of a special issue of the *JMCD* by the title of "Native American Indians."

1997 - In January, Daya S. Sandhu (1997) is guest editor of a special issue of the *JMCD* by the title of "Asian and Pacific Islander Americans."

- In April, Roberto J. Velasquez (1997) is guest editor of a special issue of the *JMCD* by the title of "Counseling Mexican Americans/Chicanos."

- Courtland C. Lee is the first African American male to become president of the American Counseling Association, 1997–1998 (ACA, 2001).

1998 - This year marks significant international involvement and leadership of ACA and AMCD leaders and members in the International Association for Counselling. Courtland C. Lee is elected secretary of the Association and Frederick D. Harper becomes managing editor of the IAC-affiliated *International Journal for the Advancement of Counselling.*

- On November 16, 1998, the multicultural and diversity listserv is established, Diversegrad-L@listserv.american.edu, as a forum for counseling professionals and counseling students to exchange ideas and information about diversity and multiculturalism in counseling (M. Jackson, personal communication, March 8, 2002).

2000 ▪ During the Multicultural Summit at the Annual Conference of the ACA in Washington, D.C., the feasibility, viability, and future of multicultural counseling are fervently debated by invited speakers.

2002 ▪ With support of the IAC (2002), the African Conference on Guidance and Counselling is held in Nairobi, Kenya, April 22 to 26, resulting in the formation of the African Association for Guidance and Counselling.

Gender and Ethnocultural History

Both females and males have been actively involved in the ethnic and cultural movement in counseling since its visible beginning in the late 1960s. The history of ethnocultural counseling in the United States cannot be written without mentioning the pioneering contributions and leadership of Katherine "Kitty" Cole, for whom the Kitty Cole Human Rights Award is named. In a published interview with Jackson (1987), Vontress recalls that Kitty Cole, as she was affectionately called, was the first African American to serve on the APGA board of directors and was an instrumental leader in organizing the APGA Black Caucus of 1969. Furthermore, as executive assistant for branch relations, Kitty Cole was the first African American executive staffer at APGA headquarters and among the few non-Whites involved at the executive and policymaking level of APGA during the early 1970s (P. Collins, personal communication, March 2, 2002). Without question, Cole was a significant force in pushing the APGA toward a sensitivity to human rights and the inclusion of both non-White ethnic minorities and women.

Kitty Cole seemingly paved the way for greater representation of female leadership in both AMCD and ACA. For example, as compared to men, women have taken equal or greater instances of presidential leadership in AMCD and ACA over the past couple of decades. Among 30 AMCD presidents from 1972 to 2002 (Appendix B), there has been an even split of leadership by gender, 50 percent female and 50 percent male (Association for Multicultural Counseling and Development [AMCD], 2002). Moreover, females have dominated the presidential leadership of ACA over the past 12 years (1990 to 2002), except for one male ACA president, Courtland C. Lee, during the 1997–1998 ACA year (ACA, 2001). Moreover, over the years, women have provided significant leadership of and membership on AMCD committees and ACA's human rights and diversity-related committees.

As regards publications related to ethnic minorities and culture and counseling, males have had greater representation in the authorship and editorship of textbooks. Nevertheless, over the past three decades, women have consistently authored and co-authored published articles, chapters, and books, and they have served as editors and co-editors of some books in the area of ethnocultural and multicultural counseling. Instead of a tendency to focus on generic cross-cultural or multicultural publications, women have been more likely to author works on special topics and theories of culture and counseling (e.g., children, families, women's issues, racial/ethnic identity, worldview, biracial identity/children, spirituality, spousal abuse, gender and relationships, cultural assessment, acculturation, and multicultural competence). Table 1.2 presents a list of female authors who have written over a sustained period of time on a specific topic or topics of ethnocultural counseling or who have authored or edited a single, significant work (e.g., a book) in the field. This list is not all-inclusive; however, it provides some representation of leading female writers in the areas of culture and counseling and ethnocultural counseling.

Conclusion

The cultural movement in counseling is really a phase of the overall ethnocultural counseling movement, which grew out of the reverberations from the civil rights movement of the 1960s and later the Black Caucus meeting at the 1969 APGA convention. A resolution by the Black Caucus at the convention led to the APGA Senate approval of an Office of Non-White Concerns of APGA, established in 1969, and the Association for Non-White Concerns in Personnel and Guidance, an APGA division chartered in 1972. White counselors' need for knowledge and techniques for counseling non-White students generated conference dialogues and

TABLE 1.2   Leading Female Authors in Ethnocultural Counseling by Areas of Contributions

Name	Areas of contributions to ethnocultural counseling or culture and counseling
Patricia Arredondo	Latinas/os, cultural competence
Lillian Comas-Diaz	Multicultural counseling and gender issues, Puerto Ricans
Madonna G. Constantine	Ethnic career counseling, racism
Mary A. Fukuyama	Multicultural counseling and spirituality
Janet E. Helms	Racial identity and counseling, womanist identity
Farah A. Ibrahim	Worldview, existential multicultural counseling, cultural assessment instruments
Teresa D. LaFromboise	Native Americans, cross-cultural counseling assessment
Elsie J. Smith	Ethnic minorities, ethnic identity development
Gargi Roysircar (Sodowsky)	Multicultural assessment, acculturation, immigrants
Bea Wehrly	International/cross-cultural, biracial-multiracial individuals

journal articles on counseling African American and other non-White clientele; clients who were labeled as "culturally deprived," "disadvantaged," and "culturally different" in the 1960s; and American minorities or non-Whites in the 1970s. A focus on counseling ethnic and racial minorities during the early and mid-1970s yielded somewhat to a growing interest in cross-cultural counseling and other counseling-and-culture themes during the latter half of the decade and into the early 1980s. Although an interest in the concept of cross-cultural counseling has persisted over the years, the multicultural counseling movement, originating in the mid-1980s, began as a new thrust that pushed for greater cultural diversity and cultural inclusiveness. This new clarion call for inclusiveness perceived culture broadly to involve gender, all ethnic groups, special populations, various group affiliations and identities (e.g., sexual identity), and status groups (e.g., persons with disabilities).

In order to accommodate the changing mood of inclusiveness and diversity-sensitive counseling, the Association for Non-White Concerns in Personnel and Guidance changed its name to the Association for Multicultural Counseling and Development in 1985. Moreover, ANWC's affiliate journal, the *Journal of Non-White Concerns in Personnel and Guidance* changed its name to the *Journal of Multicultural Counseling and Development* during the same year.

The decade of the 1990s plus the past couple of years witnessed a proliferation of books on culture and diversity, a focus on training strategies and standards for multicultural competence, the development of cultural assessment instruments, and increased international leadership and involvement of cross-cultural counseling professionals from the United States.

DISCUSSION QUESTIONS

1. Do you support the idea that there are differences among the concepts of cross-cultural, multicultural, and transcultural counseling? If so, explain the differences. Do you agree with Pedersen, that multicultural counseling should be comprehensively inclusive as to encompass practically all groups that can be defined in terms of ethnicity, identity, affiliation, and status?

2. Do you believe that the counseling needs of ethnic minorities of color have been masked or sidetracked by a generic and theoretical focus on multicultural counseling, or do you believe that the multicultural counseling division of ACA has been too focused on the needs of African Americans and other non-White ethnicities? State your position and explain or justify.

3. In reference to Vontress's viewpoint of a national culture, would you go so far as to posit that there are continental cultures (e.g., Asia or Europe) or even a global culture of human beings? If so, explain and justify.

4. As argued at the Multicultural Summit of the 2000 ACA annual conference in Washington, D.C., do you believe that the counseling profession has put too much focus on "culture and counseling" and, thus, has neglected other areas of interest in the counseling relationship and the counseling profession? Discuss.

REFERENCES

American Counseling Association (Producer). (1992). Multicultural counseling summit: A town meeting [Videotape]. (Available from the American Counseling Association, 5999 Stevenson Avenue, Alexandria, VA 22304.)

American Counseling Association. (2001). *American Counseling Association annual conference program guide.* Alexandria, VA: Author.

Amos, W. E., & Grambs, J. D. (Eds.). (1968). *Counseling the disadvantaged youth.* Englewood Cliffs, NJ: Prentice-Hall.

Association for Multicultural Counseling and Developments. (2002). *Past presidents of the Association for Multicultural Counseling and Development.* Retrieved February 24, 2002, from http://www.amcd-aca.org/pastpres.html.

Atkinson, D. R., Morten, G., & Sue, D. W. (Eds.). (1979). *Counseling American minorities: A cross-cultural perspective.* Dubuque, IA: William C. Brown.

Atkinson, D. R., Morten, G., & Sue, D. W. (Eds.). (1998). *Counseling American minorities* (5th ed.). Boston: McGraw-Hill.

Axelson, J. A. (1998). *Counseling and development in a multicultural society* (3rd ed.). Pacific Grove, CA: Brooks/Cole.

Beck, J. D. (1973). The counselor and Black/White relations. *Guidance Monograph Series* [Series 7: Special Topics in Counseling]. Boston: Houghton Mifflin.

Brooks, G. C., Jr., Sedlacek, W. E., & Mindus, L. A. (1973). Interracial contact and attitudes among university students. *Journal of Non-White Concerns in Personnel and Guidance, 1,* 102–110.

Bryde, J. F. (1971). Indian students and guidance. *Guidance Monograph Series* [Series 6: Minority Groups and Guidance]. Boston: Houghton Mifflin.

Carter, R. T. (1990). The relationship between racism and racial identity among White Americans: An exploratory investigation. *Journal of Counseling and Development, 69,* 46–50.

Copeland, E. J. (1983). Cross-cultural counseling and psychotherapy: A historical perspective, implications for research and training. *The Personnel and Guidance Journal, 62,* 10–15.

Cross, W. E., Jr. (1971). The Negro-to-Black conversion experience: Toward a psychology of Black liberation. *Black World, 20,* 13–27.

d'Ardenne, P., & Mahtani, A. (1999). *Transcultural counseling in action* (2nd ed.). Newbury Park, CA: Sage.

Das, A. K. (1995). Rethinking multicultural counseling: Implications for counselor education. *Journal of Counseling and Development, 74,* 45–52.

DeBlassie, R. R. (1976). *Counseling with Mexican American youth: Preconceptions and processes.* Austin, TX: Learning Concepts.

Dufrene, P., & Herring, R. (Eds.). (1994). Native American Indians [Special issue]. *Journal of Multicultural Counseling and Development, 22*(3).

Gelso, C. J., & Fretz, B. R. (2001). *Counseling psychology* (2nd ed.). Fort Worth, TX: Harcourt Brace Jovanovich.

Gunnings, T. S., & Simpkins, G. (1972). A systemic approach to counseling disadvantaged youth. *Journal of Non-White Concerns in Personnel and Guidance, 1,* 4–8.

Harper, F. D. (1975). *Black students/White campus: Implications for counseling.* Washington, DC: American Personnel and Guidance Association Press.

Harper, F. D. (1992a). Celebrating 20 years of *JMCD* publishing [Editorial]. *Journal of Multicultural Counseling and Development, 20,* 147–148.

Harper, F. D. (Ed.). (1992b). Gender and relationships [Special issue]. *Journal of Multicultural Counseling and Development, 20*(4).

Harper, F. D., & Stone, W. O. (1974). Toward a theory of transcendent counseling with Blacks. *Journal of Non-White Concerns in Personnel and Guidance, 2,* 191–196.

Heath, A. E., Neimeyer, G. J., Pedersen, P. B. (1988). The future of cross-cultural counseling: A delphi poll. *Journal of Counseling and Development, 67,* 27–30.

Helms, J. E. (Ed.). (1990). *Black and White racial identity: Theory, research and practice.* Westport, CT: Greenwood Press.

Helms, J. E. (1994). How multiculturalism obscures racial factors in the therapy process. *Journal of Counseling Psychology, 41*, 162–165.

Helms, J. E., & Carter, R. T. (1991). Relationships of White and Black racial identity attitudes and demographic similarity to counselor preferences. *Journal of Counseling Psychology, 38*, 446–457.

Helms, J. E., & Talleyrand, R. (1997). Race is not ethnicity. *American Psychologist, 52*, 1246–1247.

Henderson, G. (Ed.). (1979). *Understanding and counseling ethnic minorities.* Springfield, IL: Charles C. Thomas.

Herr, E. L. (1987). Cultural diversity from an international perspective. *Journal of Multicultural Counseling and Development, 15*, 99–109.

Herring, R. D. (1997). *Counseling diverse ethnic youth: Synergetic strategies and interventions for school counselors.* Fort Worth: Harcourt Brace.

Holcomb-McCoy, C. C., & Myers, J. E. (1999). Multicultural competence and counselor training: A national survey. *Journal of Counseling and Development, 77*, 294–302.

Ibrahim, F. A. (1985). Human rights and ethical issues in the use of advanced technology. *Journal of Counseling and Development, 64*, 134–135.

Ibrahim, F. A. (1999). Transcultural counseling: Existential worldview theory and cultural identity. In J. McFadden (Ed.), *Transcultural counseling* (2nd ed., pp. 23–57). Alexandria, VA: American Counseling Association.

Ibrahim, F. A., & Owen, S. V. (1994). Factor analytic structure of the Scale to Assess Worldview. *Current Psychology, 13*, 201–209.

International Association for Counselling (2002). *African conference on Guidance and Counselling, April 22–26, Nairobi, Kenya.* Retrieved July 7, 2002, from http://www.iac-irtac.org/ nairobi/nairobi.html

Jackson, M. L. (1987). Cross-cultural counseling at the crossroads: A dialogue with Clemmont E. Vontress. *Journal of Counseling and Development, 66*, 20–22.

Jackson, M. L. (1995). Multicultural counseling: Historical perspectives. In J. G. Ponterotto, J. M. Casas, L. A. Suzuki, & C. M. Alexander (Eds.), *Handbook of multicultural counseling.* (pp. 3–16). Thousand Oaks, CA: Sage.

Lambert, M. J., & Cattani-Thompson, K. (1996). Current findings regarding the effectiveness of counseling: Implications for practice. *Journal of Counseling and Development, 74*, 601–608.

Larson, P. C. (1982). Counseling special populations. *Professional Psychology, 13*, 843–858.

Lee, C. C. (1989). AMCD: The next generation. *Journal of Multicultural Counseling and Development, 17*, 165–170.

Lee, C. C. (1994). Pioneers of multicultural counseling: A conversation with Clemmont E. Vontress. *Journal of Multicultural Counseling and Development, 22*, 66–78.

Lee, C. C. (Ed.). (1995). *Counseling for diversity: A guide for school counselors and related professionals.* Boston: Allyn & Bacon.

Lee, C. C. (Ed.). (2002). *Multicultural issues in counseling: New approaches to diversity* (3rd ed.). Alexandria, VA: American Counseling Association.

Lee, W. M. L. (1999). *An introduction to multicultural counseling.* Philadelphia, PA: Accelerated Development.

Lewis, J. A. (Ed.). (1972). Women and counselors [Special issue]. *Personnel and Guidance Journal, 51*(2).

Locke, D. C., & Kiselica, M. S. (1999). Pedagogy of possibilities: Teaching about racism in multicultural counseling courses. *Journal of Counseling and Development, 78*, 80–86.

McFadden, J. (Ed.). (1999). *Transcultural counseling* (2nd ed.). Alexandria, VA: American Counseling Association.

McFadden, J., & Lipscomb, W. D. (1985). History of the Association for Non-White Concerns in Personnel and Guidance. *Journal of Counseling and Development, 63*, 444–447.

National Association of Student Affairs Professionals. (2002). National Association of Student Affairs Professionals. Retrieved February 27, 2002, from http://www.angelfire.com/ ga/nasap/

Nwachuku, U. T., & Ivey, A. E. (1991). Culture-specific counseling: An alternative training model. *Journal of Counseling and Development, 66*, 106–111.

Palomares, U. H. (Ed.). (1971). Culture as a reason for being [Special issue]. *Personnel and Guidance Journal, 50*(2).

Parham, T. A., & McDavis, R. J. (1987). Black men, an endangered species: Who's really pulling the trigger? *Journal of Counseling and Development, 70,* 24–27.

Parker, W. M., & Myers, J. E. (1991). From ANWC to AMCD: Goals, services, and impact. *Journal of Multicultural Counseling and Development, 19,* 52–64.

Patterson, C. H. (1996). Multicultural counseling: From diversity to universality. *Journal of Counseling and Development, 74,* 227–231.

Pedersen, P. B. (1976). The field of intercultural counseling. In P. Pedersen, W. J. Lonner, & J. G. Draguns (Eds.), *Counseling across cultures* (pp. 17–44). Honolulu: East-West Center Press.

Pedersen, P. B. (Ed.). (1978). Counseling across cultures [Special issue]. *Personnel and Guidance Journal, 56*(8).

Pedersen, P. B. (Ed.). (1991a). Multiculturalism as a fourth force in counseling [Special issue]. *Journal of Counseling and Development, 70*(1).

Pedersen, P. B. (1991b). Multiculturalism as a generic approach to counseling *Journal of Counseling and Development, 70,* 6–12.

Pedersen, P. B. (1999). *Hidden messages in culture-centered counseling: A Triad Training Model,* Thousand Oaks, CA: Sage.

Pedersen, P., Draguns, J. G., Lonner, W. J., & Trimble, J. E. (Eds.). (1981). *Counseling across cultures* (Rev. ed.). Honolulu: University of Hawaii Press.

Pedersen, P., Draguns, J. G., Lonner, W. J., & Trimble, J. E. (Eds.). (1996). *Counseling across cultures* (4th ed.). Thousand Oaks, CA: Sage.

Pedersen, P. B., Draguns, J. G., Lonner, W. J., & Trimble, J. E. (Eds.). (2002). *Counseling across cultures* (5th ed.). Thousand Oaks, CA: Sage.

Pedersen, P. B., & Ivey, A. (1993). *Culture-centered counseling and interviewing skills: A practical guide.* Westport, CT: Praeger Publishers.

Pedersen, P. B., Lonner, W. J., & Draguns, J. G. (Eds.). (1976). *Counseling across cultures.* Honolulu: East West Center Press.

Pollack, E., & Menacker, J. (1971). Spanish-speaking students and guidance. *Guidance Monograph Series* [Series 6: Minority Groups and Guidance]. Boston: Houghton Mifflin.

Ponterotto, J. G. (1986). A content analysis of the *Journal of Multicultural Counseling and Development. Journal of Multicultural Counseling and Development, 14,* 98–107.

Ponterotto, J. G., & Casas, J. M. (1991). *Handbook of racial/ethnic minority counseling research.* Springfield, IL: Charles C. Thomas.

Ponterotto, J. G., Casas, J. M., Suzuki, L. A., & Alexander, C. M. (Eds.). (1995). *Handbook of multicultural counseling.* Thousand Oaks, CA: Sage.

Ponterotto, J. G., Casas, J. M., Suzuki, L. A., & Alexander, C. M. (Eds.). (2001). *Handbook of multicultural counseling* (2nd ed.). Thousand Oaks, CA: Sage.

Ponterotto, J. G., Rieger, B. P., Barrett, A., & Sparks, R. (1994). Assessing multicultural counseling competence: A review of instrumentation. *Journal of Counseling and Development, 72,* 316–322.

Ridley, C. R. (1995). *Overcoming unintentional racism in counseling and therapy: A practitioner's guide to intentional intervention.* Thousand Oaks, CA: Sage.

Riessman, F. (1962). *The culturally deprived child.* New York: Harper & Row.

Rogers, C. R. (1961). *On becoming a person.* Boston: Houghton Mifflin.

Ruiz, R., & Padilla, A. (1977). Counseling Latinos. *Personnel and Guidance Journal, 55,* 401–408.

Sandhu, D. S. (Ed.). (1997). Asian and Pacific Islander Americans [Special issue]. *Journal of Multicultural Counseling and Development, 25*(1).

Sedlacek, W. E., & Webster, D. W. (1978). Admission and retention of minority students in large universities. *Journal of College Student Personnel, 29,* 242–248.

Seligman, L. (1977). Haitians: A neglected minority. *Personnel and Guidance Journal, 55,* 409–411.

Smart, D. W., & Smart, J. F. (1997). DSM-IV and culturally sensitive diagnosis: Some observations for counselors. *Journal of Counseling and Development, 75,* 392–398.

Smith, E. J. (1973). *Counseling the culturally different Black youth.* Columbus, OH: Charles E. Merrill.

Smith, E. J. (1991). Ethnic identity development: Toward the development of a theory within the majority/minority context status. *Journal of Counseling and Development, 70,* 181–188.

Smith, E. J., & Vasquez, M. J. T. (Eds.). (1985). Cross-cultural counseling [Special issue]. *The Counseling Psychologist, 13*(4).

Smith, P. M. (Ed.). (1970). What guidance for Blacks [Special issue]. *Personnel and Guidance Journal, 48*(9).

Sodowsky, G. R., Taffe, R. C., Gutkin, T. B., & Wise, S. (1994). Development of the Multicultural Counseling Inventory (MCI): A self-report measure of multicultural competencies. *Journal of Counseling Psychology, 41,* 137–148.

Speight, S. L., Myers, L. J., Cox, C. I., & Highlen, P. S. (1991). A redefinition of multicultural counseling. *Journal of Counseling and Development, 70,* 29–36.

Sue, D. W. (1973). Asian-American: The neglected minority [Special issue]. *Personnel and Guidance Journal, 51*(3).

Sue, D. W., Arredondo, P., & McDavis, R. J. (1992). Multicultural counseling competencies and standards: A call to the profession. *Journal of Multicultural Counseling and Development, 20,* 64–88.

Sue, D. W., & Sue, D. (1973). Understanding Asian Americans: The neglected minority. *Personnel and Guidance Journal, 51,* 386–389.

Sue, D. W., & Sue, D. (1999). *Counseling the culturally different: Theory and practice* (3rd ed.). New York: Wiley.

Sue, S. (Ed.). (1977a). Counseling the culturally different [Special issue]. *Personnel and Guidance Journal, 55*(7).

Sue, S. (1977b). Psychological theory and implications for Asian Americans. *Personnel and Guidance Journal, 55,* 381–389.

Velasquez, R. J. (Ed.). (1997). Counseling Mexican Americans/Chicanos [Special issue]. *Journal of Multicultural Counseling and Development, 25*(2).

Vontress, C. E. (1966). The Negro personality reconsidered. *The Journal of Negro Education, 35,* 210–217.

Vontress, C. E. (1967a). Counseling Negro adolescents. *The School Counselor, 15,* 86–91.

Vontress, C. E. (1967b). The culturally different. *Employment Service Review, 4,* 35–36.

Vontress, C. E. (1969a). Counseling the culturally different in our society. *Journal of Employment Counseling, 6,* 9–16.

Vontress, C. E. (1969b). Cultural barriers in the counseling relationship. *Personnel and Guidance Journal, 48,* 11–17.

Vontress, C. E. (1971). Counseling Negroes. *Guidance Monograph Series* [Series 6: Minority Groups and Guidance]. Boston: Houghton Mifflin.

Vontress, C. E. (2001). Cross-cultural counseling in the 21st century. *International Journal for the Advancement of Counselling, 23,* 83–97.

Vontress, C. E., & Epp, L. R. (2000). Ethnopsychiatry: Counselling immigrants in France. *International Journal for the Advancement of Counselling, 22,* 273–288.

Vontress, C. E., Johnson, J. A., & Epp, L. R. (1999). *Cross-cultural counseling: A casebook.* Alexandria, VA: American Counseling Association.

Wehrly, B. (1995). *Pathways to multicultural counseling competence: A developmental journey.* Pacific Grove, CA: Brooks/Cole.

Weinrach, S. G., & Thomas, K. R. (1998). Diversity-sensitive counseling today: A postmodern clash of values. *Journal of Counseling and Development, 76,* 115–122.

Westbrook, F. D., & Sedlacek, W. E. (1991). Forty years of using labels to communicate about nontraditional students: Does it help or hurt? *Journal of Counseling and Development, 70,* 20–28.

Wrenn, C. G. (1962). The culturally encapsulated counselor. *Harvard Educational Review, 32,* 444–449.

2 On Becoming an Existential Cross-Cultural Counselor

CLEMMONT E. VONTRESS

Retrospectively, my formative years were filled with disparate thoughts about my existence. The ruminations darted through my mind such that I was unable to make sense of the babble that at times threatened my psyche. When I matured, I was able to organize the musings into meaningful wholes. In writing them down in notebooks, I realized the source of my troubled soul. During my sojourn in Europe in the early 1950s, I understood the psychological implications of humankind's inhumanity to its own kind. I comprehended quickly from afar what I was unable to grasp mentally up close—my lifelong racial oppression in the United States (Vontress, 1996).

After spending nearly two years in France and Germany, I returned to the United States and enrolled in graduate school at Indiana University, in Bloomington, Indiana, where I received M.S. and Ph.D. degrees in counseling. In the 1950s there were few African American students at the university. Usually, I was the only one in my classes. Even so, my studies were uneventful, except for what I experienced in my sociology classes. The professors lectured a great deal about culture and how many people were deprived of it. I was startled and felt personally attacked by their views. Although I suppressed my hostility at the time, I swore to get to the bottom of the matter once I graduated. I did just that. I have devoted my entire professional career to studying culture and how it impacts counseling. I turned a negative experience into a positive pursuit.

The purpose of this chapter is to describe the course of my journey in search of truth. Specifically, the intent is to define culture, to indicate how it relates to counseling, to explicate existential intervention, to provide a snapshot of my research on traditional healing in Africa, to highlight my research on counseling immigrants in France, and to decry biopsychiatry, the antithesis of existential counseling.

Culture

In trying to understand throughout my career the nature of culture, I have concluded that it is a way of life passed from one generation to another to ensure the survival of the human species (Vontress, 1988a; Vontress, Johnson, & Epp, 1999). It shapes, directs, and maintains our existence. There are at play five forces that make us who and what we are. They are biological, ecological, national, regional, and racio-ethnic cultures.

The design, requirements, and finiteness of the human organism dictate in large measure our way of life. The sexual impulse and the propagation of humankind suggest two dependent life stages—youth and old age, which implies the need for humans to live in groups or herds as do most animals. Existence in collectivities in which there are many differences among the members gives rise to role allocations. For example, in most of the cultures of the world, women look after children; men provide food for the family. Children must be prepared to assume adult roles as their elders grow old and die. This behavioral repertoire cuts across geographical boundaries of the world (van den Berghe, 1975). It is reasonable to call it the biologically motivated or *universal culture.*

Humans, not unlike other animals, forage the environment to survive (Vontress, 1988a). The world's terrain is variform. It is hot and cold, peaked and flat, wet and dry, and much more. Regardless of the nature of the habitat, humans are apt to be present. In pooling their creativity and resources, members of each generation adapt to their natural surroundings and improve on the way of life appropriate to a particular location (Reader, 1988). Such was the case of the Europeans who settled in the "New World." In order to survive, they had to learn how to relate to their new surroundings. Over the course of several centuries, the indigenous people, now called Native Americans, had already adapted to the environment. Behaviors reflective of an adaptation to a natural location may be called the *ecological culture.*

People live in groups, both large and small. The nation is the largest. It is characterized by a set of rules, regulations, laws, and bureaucratic procedures to which all who reside in its confines are expected to abide. In due course, the expectations become ingrained in the psyche of the inhabitants of the territory (van den Berghe, 1975). Sojourners may perceive a general conformity in behavior, values, and attitudes. However, their perceptions are usually superficial, because culture is simultaneously visible and invisible, cognitive and affective, and conscious and unconscious. Individuals residing in a foreign country are usually aware of the host country's *national culture,* even though they are generally unable to describe their own way of life back home. Like most people, they are hard pressed to specify their native culture.

In many countries, a *regional culture* is also evident. Specific areas of a country may be unique because of geography, ethnicity of inhabitants, "ghettoization" of immigrants, and for other reasons. For example, the Hausas, an Islamic people

straddling the border separating Northern Nigeria and Southern Niger are culturally different from the majority of the citizens in either of the two countries in
which they reside. Also illustrative are American-born citizens who live in Texas in
communities along the Mexican border. Many of them are culturally more Mexican
than they are American.

Finally, the *racio-ethnic culture* is a product of exclusion. When groups exist
separately for whatever reason, in time they develop a way of life that meets their
peculiar needs (Vontress, 1967, 1971b, 1975). I offered *culturally different* as a
replacement for terms such as "culturally deprived," "educationally deprived,"
"underprivileged," and "disadvantaged." Even though a group may be rejected by
the larger society, its members are still influenced by that society. If the national
society is shot through with pernicious racism, the anti–African American attitudes
also implant themselves in the psyche of African Americans, the oppressed. That is
why I conceptualized *self-hatred* as the basic component of the African American
personality (Vontress, 1966, 1971b, 1971d).

The cultural model discussed here suggests that all people are multicultural
in that their genetic endowment and life experiences are sifted through a five-
tiered cultural filter. Although racial and ethnic minorities may suffer injustices in
the national society, the fact remains that they are still human beings who are
shaped and constrained by the universal, ecological, national, regional, and racio-
ethnic cultures (Vontress, Johnson, & Epp, 1999). It is inappropriate to consider
them members of a single culture. In spite of the brutality to which their forebears
were subjected in the United States, today's African Americans are Americans who
happen to reside in a black skin. It only takes a trip to Africa for them to realize
that they are Americans, not Africans. They are several hundred years removed
from the land of their ancestors. Any cultural similarity to them has now been
erased by the sands of time.

Cross-Cultural Counseling

Cross-cultural counseling is a psychotherapeutic interaction in which at least one
of the participants is perceived to be culturally different from the other (Jackson,
1987). Perceived differences are usually as important to the outcome of the relationship as are real differences (Vontress, 1971c, 1979, 1988b). It is for this reason
and others that counseling across cultures is so challenging to most counselors. In
order to diagnose the presenting problems of clients, develop treatment plans, and
intervene effectively on their behalf, they need to attend to several matters simultaneously. Importantly, they need to develop a cultural profile of each client (Vontress, Johnson, & Epp, 1999). The profile should help them to determine the extent
to which the client is influenced by each culture discussed previously. In this connection, it is important to avoid confusing culture with race. That is, the counselor
should not assume that clients with black skins are culturally African American
(Vontress, 1971c). They may be adoptees who were raised in white families,
African immigrants, or other individuals who identify exclusively with the
national culture for any number of reasons. Counselors do not want to get off to a

bad start with clients by making mistakes that can impede the establishment of rapport and effective intervention.

Today, most psychotherapeutic professionals are expected to diagnose clients according to the requirements of the *Diagnostic and Statistical Manual of Mental Disorders* (APA, 1994). This means that they must define the presenting problems of clients on Axis I; make an assessment of their personality on Axis II; indicate their physical condition on Axis III; ascertain any psychosocial and environmental problems on Axis IV; and decide a global assessment of their functioning on Axis V. This is a tall order for cross-cultural counselors. In addition to developing a cultural profile of each client, counselors must be able to determine the extent to which the personality of their clients is reflective of a particular culture influencing them. In general, personality is the internalization of culture. For example, White children adopted by African American families may, in due time, think, feel, and respond as if they were biological children in the families.

Existential Counseling

In graduate school, I was fascinated with Carl Rogers's theory of counseling. However, when I became a counselor in an urban high school in Indianapolis, Indiana, I soon learned that the theory was not very useful in my efforts to help adolescents who yearned for meaning and direction in life. It was in the 1960s that I started searching for a theory that would enable me to help the hopeless. I began to read the works of the European existential writers (Vontress, 1988a). Still impressed with Rogers, whom I met at Indiana University, I did not abandon his theory. Instead, I integrated my understanding of existentialism with his views of helping (see Ivey, Ivey, & Simek-Morgan, 1997).

Whereas multicultural counseling during the civil rights movement tended to focus on differences, I was committed to getting Black clients to recognize that they were human beings just like everybody else (Ivey, Ivey, & Simek-Morgan, 1997). I needed to develop a philosophical vantage point that would enable me and other counselors to bridge cultural differences, not to perpetuate or increase them (Vontress, 1979). I took well-known concepts from existential philosophy and applied them to counseling all people, regardless of their cultural background (Jackson, 1987). This was not easy to do in the sixties, a period in our history when some African American militants were against theory because they were suspicious of anything developed by Whites (Vontress, 1972). I was under frequent attack at national conventions where I presented my views on cross-cultural counseling. One African American scholar lambasted me for "defecting from the ranks of revolutionary African scholars" (Vontress, 1971a, p. 45).

Initially, I believed that existentialism was a philosophy rooted in Europe (Vontress, 1988a). Later I learned that ideas European philosophers called existential were evident in writings by scholars and thinkers throughout the world (Vontress, Johnson, & Epp, 1999). The focus on life, death, self-knowledge, authenticity, courage, becoming, existential anxiety, meaning in life, spirituality, and responsibility highlight concerns of all human beings (Vontress, 1988a).

I analyzed five psychotherapeutic theory groups—rationalism, behaviorism, psychoanalysis, phenomenology, and existentialism—to determine which approach is most useful to cross-cultural counselors (Vontress, 1985). I concluded that all of them, with the exception of behaviorism, could be classified as insight theories. Counselors use a variety of techniques designed to get clients to think, feel, and act differently. Behavioral therapists are most interested in getting them to act differently because they maintain that thinking, feeling, and acting are inseparable. Responding to their clients as fellow human beings, existential counselors generally disavow interest in techniques. Methods follow commitment to clients. An existential orientation would seem to hold the most promise for effective cross-cultural counseling. However, this assertion does not mean that counselors should abandon all psychological theory. Psychology is an offshoot of philosophy (Voelke, 1993). Counselors can and should draw on psychological understandings and tools as long as existentialism is their umbrella approach to helping (Vontress, Johnson, & Epp, 1999).

Traditional Healing

I became interested in traditional African healing after learning how much it parallels existential counseling. To Africans, healing is more than curing the body or the administration of medicine (Katz, 1982). Healers are renowned for treating the whole person, as Torrey (1986) explained. Usually, individuals are out of sorts because of disharmony in their existence. There is a disconnection of the client's psychological, physiological, social, and spiritual worlds (Hewson, 1998; Vontress, 1991). This way of understanding human problems is closely related to the existential cross-cultural counseling that I have described over the years. I use the German concepts *Umwelt* (physical world), *Mitwelt* (social environment), *Eigenwelt* (self-system), and *Uberwelt* (spiritual world) to explain human existence (Vontress, Johnson, & Epp, 1999).

In diagnosing the problems of their clients, traditional African healers look at all dimensions of human existence. They devote considerable attention to the spiritual component of their clients' lives (Diallo & Hall, 1989). However, the word "spiritual" should not be understood as a synonym for "religious," which generally suggests an institutionalized body of believers who accept a common set of beliefs, practices, and rituals regarding spiritual concerns and issues, as Krippner and Welch (1992) explain. The concept of spirituality as used in Africa has a broader meaning. It may refer to the spirit that is embodied in all of nature, often described as animism, or it may connote the spirit of departed ancestors. In any case, being able to connect with the spirits is an essential aspect of traditional African healing (Halifax, 1982). The spiritual is also an important component of existential counseling as I have conceptualized it. Although we in the West generally define spirituality differently from the way Africans define it, it is nevertheless an often unacknowledged but significant element of our existence. We especially appeal to this "higher power" during times of loss, trials, and tribulations.

There are other aspects of traditional healing in Africa that are interesting. The role that music plays in the therapeutic process is noteworthy. Barrois (1991), Diallo and Hall (1989), and Storr (1992) have discussed the power of music in promoting the curative process. It profoundly affects muscle tone, body rhythms, and emotions; and respiration, heartbeat, digestive peristalses, and brain waves tend to become synchronized to music. In Africa, music draws people together and creates a joyful and therapeutic sense of unity. Diallo and Hall (1989) consider the drum to be a healing instrument. Instead of just considering music and other methods used in traditional African healing as quaint, Western counselors can learn much from the practices of healers, some of which they may want to include in their psychotherapeutic repertoire as French psychotherapist Tobie Nathan (1988, 1993, 1994) has done.

Ethnopsychiatry

During the past 25 years, I have made six field trips to Africa—one to North Africa and five to West Africa—to interview traditional healers and their patients and former patients (Vontress, 1991, 1999). I learned that everybody, regardless of socioeconomic class or position in life, consults healers for all kinds of problems. Their clients' presenting complaints include headaches, backaches, suspicion of being victims of a hex, concern about a poor crop yield, lack of rain, trouble with a love affair gone sour, a wandering spouse, conflict with a neighbor, or the fear of the wrath of a departed ancestor. These respected psychologists, physicians, social workers, and religious ministers, all rolled up into one person, the healer, are generalists. They do it all.

During the same period, I interviewed African immigrants in Europe and the United States to ascertain their experience and level of satisfaction with Western therapeutic professionals whom they had consulted. Only about 10 percent of the nearly 100 persons whom I contacted reported that they had ever sought help from a Western counselor or psychologist. If they could not find a traditional healer working in the host country, they would call home to get counseling or treatment suggestions from a family member or friend. About 5 percent of those interviewed said that they had consulted a Western physician only as a last resort. In general, they did not believe that American or European health care providers could really help them. The main reason for not consulting them was their belief that they did not reflect the dominant values of their culture, which, according to Frank (1963), is an absolute essential for effective cross-cultural therapy. That is, the client must believe that the helper understands where he or she "is coming from." The ability of therapists to speak the client's ethnic or national language is the first indication of their ability to empathize with them and to intervene on their behalf.

I heard about a French psychotherapist who was effective counseling African immigrants. One of my graduate students, a French immigrant, went to

Paris to interview Dr. Tobie Nathan, who makes frequent field trips to Third World countries, especially those in Africa, to study techniques used by traditional healers to cure their patients. Nathan and his colleagues at a counseling center at the University of Paris VIII have fanned out across Africa, the Caribbean, and other parts of the world to learn directly from traditional healers their therapeutic methods (Laplantine, 1988; Nathan, 1988).

Intrigued by the reports about the effectiveness of *ethnopsychiatry*—what Nathan calls the intervention methods he uses for counseling African immigrants and their families—I spent five years (1994–1999) researching his work. I wanted to find out how he was able to combine, with considerable success, Western psychotherapeutic methods with traditional healing practices used by African and other non-Western healers. He and his associates regularly publish their findings in the *Nouvelle Revue d'Ethnopsychiatrie* (*The New Journal of Ethnopsychiatry*), a professional refereed journal launched and edited by Nathan. They publish numerous articles and books in which they argue that Western therapists should be open to learning from traditional healers in non-Western societies.

I share Nathan's view that Western therapists can learn a great deal from traditional healers in other parts of the world. There is an obligation to do so because the majority of the people in the world consult them (Dickinson, 1999; Tchetche, 1998). Without them, many people would have no medical or psychological services at all. The recognition of this fact led the World Health Organization nearly a quarter of a century ago to recommend that Western health care professionals reach out to their traditional counterparts and to collaborate with them in the healing enterprise (Torrey, 1986). The world needs this collaboration, a point that I emphasized in a keynote address that I presented at the conference of the International Association for Counseling, held in Thessaloniki, Greece, May 4–7, 2000 (Vontress, 2001).

Biopsychiatry

U.S. society has changed significantly since I entered the counseling profession almost a half century ago. As things changed in the social order at large, so did they change in the counseling profession. Counseling used to be restricted almost exclusively to school settings. Today, many counselors work alongside social workers, psychologists, and psychiatrists in a variety of settings. In general, they understand and use the same theories, tools, and procedures employed by their colleagues. Working under the constraints of managed health care and the *Diagnostic and Statistical Manual of Mental Disorders* (APA, 1994), counselors necessarily perceive themselves and their work unlike they did two decades ago. The last part of the twentieth century has seen the medicalization of Western culture (Cornett, 1998). We are told that problems heretofore considered to be the concern of counselors and psychologists are really not caused by psychosocial factors (Frattaroli, 2001). Instead, they are caused by subtle neurochemical malfunctions in the brain (Breggin, 1991). Increasingly, people, when called to task for irresponsible behavior, attempt to make the case that their brain made them do it.

In many schools throughout the Western world, pills are replacing counselors and other professionally trained people who formerly helped children adjust to the expected decorum of the classroom (Cadier, 2001). However, nowadays there is a new attitude toward children who squirm, jump, or otherwise move about without permission. Parents and teachers, eager to correct these distracting behaviors, accept with alacrity the advice of drug company representatives and physicians, most of whom declare that hyperactive children suffer from brain disorders that can be corrected easily by medication.

The drug-based approach to classroom discipline has contributed significantly to an increase in the sale of prescription drugs. According to Cadier (2001), the sale of tranquilizers increased 38 percent in the last five years. In some U.S. schools, one out of every five children is on drugs, especially boys. The more the use of prescribed drugs increase among our school population, the more the need for school counselors is apt to decrease (Frattaroli, 2001). Increasingly, the referral route is from the teacher to the school nurse or from the teacher to the parent and then to the school nurse. In some cases, the counselor is left out of the referral loop altogether.

Two years before I retired from George Washington University where I was professor of counseling and director of the counseling program, I invited Peter Breggin to speak to a seminar at the university. An internationally known psychiatrist and founder and director of the International Center for the Study of Psychiatry and Psychology, he posits that sedative medicine is dangerous to adults and children (Breggin, 2000). It is especially dangerous for young children to take tranquilizers and other medicines to reduce their energy and activity, because their brains are still developing. Research has yet to show the possible long-range effects of medicine on their bodies. Breggin (1991) and Breggin and Breggin (1994) declare that as long as we respond to the signals of conflict and distress in our children by subduing them with drugs, we will not address their genuine needs. As parents, teachers, therapists, and physicians, we need to retake responsibility for children, he points out. They need love and attention, not medicine.

I found a philosophical soul mate in Peter Breggin. Human life is unimaginable without pain, suffering, and sorrow. When I was a boy, "feeling down and out" was an expression I often heard around my neighborhood. Usually, it meant that people feeling depressed were about to burst out with a rendition of a blues song or a stamping and arousing spiritual, either of which would soon make things all right. Back then, nobody had heard of Prozac, Ritalin, and other medicines designed to "take your troubles away." Today, I think that the haste to medicate away all human problems robs individuals of the opportunity for growth and development that come from overcoming them. Psychological distress is more than a chemical imbalance in the brain (Frattaroli, 2001). Rather, it is a disharmony of the psychological, physical, social, and spiritual dimensions of the whole person, as I have pointed out already. People suffering from philosophically based or spiritual problems are not apt to find anything on the pharmacist's shelves that will provide permanent relief.

Conclusion

This segmented retrospective on my life, career, and professional contributions is unified by a common thread—the human condition held up to different angles of the same light, in order to get a holistic understanding of the condition. First, I explain that human culture is a product of many influences, some biological and some social. Second, I maintain that counselors must have a clear understanding of it before they can know who is a cross-cultural client. In large measure, cultural differences are based on perception. Are clients in need of cultural considerations if they do not perceive themselves to be culturally different? Are counselors who insist on treating such clients as if they were culturally different out of line? Third, in considering various counseling theory groups available to counselors, I conclude that the philosophically based existential theory discussed in this chapter is most useful because it is supported by ideas about human existence from all parts of the world. It is not rooted only in Europe as some writers have suggested. Fourth, traditional healers and modern healers serve the same purpose—to improve human existence. Therefore, they should learn to work together toward that goal. Fifth, ethnopsychiatry, as practiced in France, offers direction to Western psychotherapeutic professionals who want to learn healing methods used by Third World traditional healers. Finally, biopsychiatry, so much in vogue in Europe and the United States, may be doing humankind more harm than good. Psychotropic drugs often produce the psychological conditions they are supposed to alleviate. Agony and ecstasy are twin conditions of human existence.

DISCUSSION QUESTIONS

1. What is the relationship of the universal culture to the ecological culture? How would an understanding of the relationship aid you in helping a newly arrived West African student adjust to New Hampshire?

2. Is there a difference between cross-cultural counseling and multicultural counseling? Discuss.

3. What is existential counseling as discussed in this chapter? Do you believe that it is the most effective approach to use in cross-cultural counseling?

4. How do you feel about including some of the methods used by traditional African healers in your repertoire of counseling techniques? Discuss.

5. How does biopsychiatry differ from ethnopsychiatry? Do you think that biopsychiatry is a viable substitute for psychotherapy? Discuss.

REFERENCES

American Psychiatric Association. (1994). *Diagnostic and statistical manual of mental disorders* (4th ed.). Washington, DC: American Psychiatric Association.

Barrois, C. (1991). *La musique, la violence et la mort: Métphores du temps?* [Music, violence and death: Contemporary metaphors?]. In P. Fédida & J. Schotte (Eds.). *Psychiatrie et existence* [Psychiatry and existence] (pp. 339–362). Genoble: Éditions Jérôme Millon.

Breggin, P. R. (1991). *Toxic psychiatry.* New York: St. Martin's.

Breggin, P. R. (2000). Confirming the hazards of stimulant drug treatment. *Ethical Human Sciences and Services, 2*(3), 203–204.

Breggin, P. R., & Breggin, G. R (1994). *Talking back to prozac.* New York: St. Martin's.

Cadier, J.-B. (2001, September 14). Trop de petits américains sous calmants [Too many American children on sedatives]. *Le point, 1513,* 95.

Cornett, C. (1998). *The soul of psychotherapy: Recapturing the spiritual dimension in the therapeutic encounter.* New York: Free Press.

Diallo, Y., & Hall, M. (1989). *The healing drum: African wisdom teachings.* Rochester, VT: Destiny Books.

Dickinson, G. (1999). Traditional healers face off with science. *CMAJ: Canadian Medical Association Journal, 160*(5), 629.

Frank, J. D. (1963). *Persuasion and healing.* New York: Schocken.

Frattaroli, E. (2001). *Healing the soul in the age of the brain: Becoming conscious in an unconscious world.* New York: Viking.

Halifax, J. (1982). *Shaman: The wounded healer.* London: Thames and Hudson.

Hewson, M. G. (1998). Traditional healers in Southern Africa. *Annals of Internal Medicine, 128*(12), 1029–1034.

Ivey, A. E., Ivey, M. B., & Simek-Morgan, L. (1997). *Counseling and psychotherapy: A Multicultural perspective* (4th ed.). Boston: Allyn & Bacon.

Jackson, M. L. (1987). Cross-cultural counseling at the crossroads: A dialogue with Clemmont E. Vontress. *Journal of Counseling and Development, 66*(1), 20–23.

Katz, R. (1982). *Boiling energy.* Cambridge, MA: Harvard University Press.

Krippner, S., & Welch, P. (1992). *Spiritual dimensions of healing.* New York: Irvington.

Laplantine, F. (1988). *L'ethnopsychiatrie* [Ethnopsychiatry]. Paris: Presses Universitaires de France.

Nathan, T. (1988). *Le sperme du diable: Éléments d'ethnopsychothérapie* [The devil's sperm: Elements of Ethnopsychiatry]. Paris: Presses Universitaires de France.

Nathan, T. (1993). Ethnopsy 93 [Ethnopsychiatry 93]. *Nouvelle Revue d'Ethnopsychiatrie, 20, 7–14.*

Nathan, T. (1994). *L'influence qui guérit* [Healing influence]. Paris: Éditions Odile Jocob.

Reader, J. (1988). *Man on earth.* Austin: University of Texas Press.

Storr, A. (1992). *Music and the mind.* New York: Free Press.

Tchetche, G. D. (1998). *Psychiatrie en afrique noire et contexte socio-culturel* [Psychiatry in black Africa in socio-cultural context]. Paris: L'Harmattan.

Torrey, E. F. (1986). *Witchdoctors and psychiatrists: The common roots of psychotherapy and its future.* New York: Harper & Row

van den Berghe, P. L. (1975). *Man in society: A biosocial view.* New York: Elsevier Scientific.

Voelke, A-J. (1993). *La philosophie comme thérapie de l'âme: Études de philosophie hellénistique* [Philosophy as psychotherapy: Studies in hellenic philosophy]. Fribourg, Switzerland: Éditions Universitaires.

Vontress, C. E. (1966). The Negro personality reconsidered. *The Journal of Negro Education. 35*(3), 210–217.

Vontress, C. E. (1967). The culturally different. *Employment Service Review, 4*(10), 35–36.

Vontress, C. E. (1971a). A black scholar debate: A response to Robert Staples. *The Black Scholar, 3*(3), 46–49.

Vontress, C. E. (1971b). *Counseling Negroes.* Boston: Houghton Mifflin.

Vontress, C. E. (1971c). Racial differences: Impediments to rapport. *Journal of Counseling Psychology, 18*(1), 7–13.

Vontress, C. E. (1971d). The black male personality. *The Black Scholar, 2*(10), 1–16.

Vontress, C. E. (1972). The black militant as a counselor. *Personnel and Guidance Journal, 50*(7), 574–580.

Vontress, C. E. (1975). Counseling: Racial and ethnic factors. In H. J. Peters & R. F. Aubrey (Eds.). *Guidance: Strategies and Techniques* (pp. 456–472). Denver, CO: Love.

Vontress, C. E. (1979). Cross-cultural counseling: An existential approach. *The Personnel and Guidance Journal, 58*(2), 117–122.

Vontress, C. E. (1985). Theories of counseling: A comparative analysis. In R. J. Samuda & A. Wolfgang (Eds.), *Intercultural counseling and assessment: Global perspectives* (pp. 19–31). Toronto: C. J. Hogrefe.

Vontress, C. E. (1988a). An existential approach to cross-cultural counseling. *Journal of Multicultural Counseling. 16*(2), 73–83.

Vontress, C. E. (1988b). Social class influences on counseling. In R. Hayes & R. Aubrey (Eds.), *New directions in counseling and human development* (pp. 346–364). Denver, CO: Love.

Vontress, C. E. (1991). Traditional healing in Africa: Implications for cross-cultural counseling. *Journal of Counseling and Development, 70*(1), 242–249.

Vontress, C. E. (1996). A personal retrospective on cross-cultural counseling. *Journal of Multicultural Counseling and Development, 24*(3), 156–166.

Vontress, C. E. (1999). Interview with a traditional African healer. *Journal of Mental Health Counseling, 21*(4), 326–336.

Vontress, C. E. (2001). Cross-cultural counseling in the 21st century. *International Journal for the Advancement of Counseling, 23*(2), 83–97.

Vontress, C. E., Johnson, J. S., & Epp, L. R. (1999). *Cross-cultural counseling: A casebook.* Alexandria, VA: American Counseling Association.

3 Increasing the Cultural Awareness, Knowledge, and Skills of Culture-Centered Counselors

PAUL B. PEDERSEN

Culture as a construct has in recent years moved from the exotic edge of the counseling profession to a central position. Making wrong culturally learned assumptions will result in wrong decisions, regardless of how skilled and/or intelligent the provider might be. An appreciation for the generic importance of a culture-centered perspective has evolved. An understanding of the many culturally different ways that counseling services are provided has been documented. An awareness of how a culture-centered approach adds value to the literature about how theory and practice are being applied is essential to good counseling practice (Pedersen, 2002).

All behaviors are learned and displayed in a cultural context. Consequently, accurate assessment, meaningful understanding, and appropriate intervention must attend to each consumer's cultural context. Culture, in this case, is defined broadly to include ethnographic, demographic, status, and affiliation identities. Culturally encapsulated providers make the serious mistake of interpreting behaviors without regard for the consumer's cultural context. Providers can escape cultural encapsulation by *first* increasing their awareness of culturally learned assumptions, *second* increasing their access to culturally relevant knowledge, and *third* increasing their appropriate use of culturally sensitive skills. Kiselica, Maben, and Locke (1999) published a critical review of the research indicating that the awareness, knowledge, and skill three-stage developmental model does reduce prejudice and increase racial identity development among trainees who completed multicultural education and diversity appreciation training.

Culture is complex and dynamic in each context. By accepting the complexity of culture, it becomes possible to manage more variables efficiently, generate more potential answers to each question, identify contrasting perspectives, tolerate ambiguity more comfortably, and recognize the diversity within each cultural context. By accepting the dynamic nature of culture, it is possible to identify the changing cultural salience in each situation, avoid simple solutions to complicated problems, escape rigid stereotypes, interpret cultural stories, and understand behaviors in their changing cultural context.

The serious mistake of seeking a simplistic solution leads to three errors: (1) to overemphasize diversity, which leads to chaotic disconnected groups and typically hostile engagement, (2) to overemphasize similarities, in which the stronger group imposes their will and deprives minorities of their identity, or (3) to assume that there are only two choices. The only acceptable option is to emphasize both similarities and differences simultaneously, minimizing neither in the process. The alternative to accepting cultural complexity is cultural encapsulation. Cultural encapsulation occurs when we (1) define reality according to one set of assumptions, (2) become insensitive to cultural variations, (3) protect unreasoned assumptions against scrutiny, (4) prefer quick and easy solutions to complex problems, and (5) ignore other people's cultural viewpoints (Wrenn, 1962, 1985).

Increasing Multicultural Awareness

Developing multicultural awareness is the first stage of a culture-centered approach. Increased cultural awareness is indicated in a variety of ways. First, each of us becomes aware of the culture teachers we have accumulated over our lifetime. Individual differences such as skin color or gender were determined at birth but since birth have taken on cultural meanings through contact with culture teachers. Second, we discover our own identity or identities, recognizing that cultural identity is orthogonal (Oetting & Beauvais, 1991), therefore allowing each individual to claim membership in many different cultures at the same time. Third, we come to understand how culture controls each of us, with or without our permission, through culturally learned rules of perception. Fourth, we learn to be comfortable with differences between self and others without having to assume self-reference criteria of right and wrong. Fifth, we learn that all situations are multicultural and attempts to eliminate cultural considerations are misleading illusions. Sixth, we learn to identify those culturally learned assumptions—by ourselves and others—that are the basis for meaningful comprehension.

Culture is emerging as one of the most important and perhaps most misunderstood constructs in contemporary social theories. Culture may be defined narrowly as limited to ethnicity and nationality or it may be defined broadly to include any and all potentially salient ethnographic, demographic statuses or affiliations. Applying the broad definition of culture helps us identify many positive consequences of a culture-centered perspective (Pedersen, 1997a, 1997b, 2000a, 2000b).

First, the common ground of shared values or expectations can be expressed by contrasting culturally learned behaviors so that reframing conflict in a culture-centered perspective will allow two people or groups to display different behaviors without either one necessarily being wrong according to shared values and expectations. Discovering common ground across cultures enables win/win outcomes from conflicts between people who are expressing the same shared value for fairness, respect, success, and survival but where each is expressing that value through contrasting behaviors.

Second, an articulate awareness of the thousands of "culture teachers" (friends, family, enemies, fantasies, etc.) accumulated by each of us will help us comprehend the complexity of our multicultural identity. When you and your client enter the same room it would be a mistake to disregard the influence of these internalized culture teachers that each person depends on for advice, support, and guidance.

Third, just as a healthy ecosystem requires biodiversity, so does a healthy socioecosystem require a diversity of cultural perspectives. A diversity of perspectives increases the choices available for each problem or decision and enriches the range of cultural perspectives about that problem or decision.

Fourth, a culture-centered perspective protects us from inappropriately imposing our own culturally encapsulated self-reference criteria in the evaluation of others. We have learned to "do unto others as you would have them do unto you." However, what if they do not want those particular things done unto them? Should you do it unto them regardless? The self-reference criterion, however well intentioned, becomes the basis of racist exclusion.

Fifth, contact with culturally different groups provides an opportunity to rehearse adaptive-functioning skills for our own multicultural future in the global village. We are quickly moving toward a future that is probably different beyond our imagination, and those who are unable to adapt will not survive.

Sixth, understanding social justice and moral development in a multicultural context helps us differentiate necessary absolutes from culturally relative expediencies. Historically, those societies that have defined justice and morality in monocultural terms have tended to be oppressive and exploitative.

Seventh, a culture-centered cognitive style reflects the complementarity of the quantum metaphor in the nonlinear thinking processes, where the same event or phenomenon can be perceived to be both good and bad, right and wrong, and desirable and undesirable at the same time, that is, in the complementarity of opposites. It is not merely the content of what we are thinking that must be modified; the thinking process itself requires examination.

Eighth, all learning and change involve some degree of "culture shock," that is, to the degree that it influences our basic perspectives. Reframing the various events of change as journeys through different cultural contexts helps us to comprehend the meaning of social change.

Ninth, a culture-centered perspective enhances our spiritual completeness by linking culturally different spiritual perspectives of the same cosmic reality. Our spiritual understanding is enhanced by knowing the answers other cultures have discovered for our spiritual questions.

Tenth, a culture-centered perspective builds toward a pluralistic, political alternative to the other two possible futures of authoritarianism or anarchy in our sociopolitical organization. Pluralism remains an unrealized ideal in modern society but, nonetheless, provides the only acceptable future choice as a political alternative.

These elements of multicultural awareness enhance the competence of a provider in at least ten ways. Having audited one's culturally learned assumptions prepares the provider to move to the next stage of competence by identifying culturally relevant knowledge.

Developing Multicultural Knowledge

Developing multicultural knowledge, comprehension, or understanding is the second stage of culture-centered competence. Having multicultural knowledge and comprehension is indicated in a variety of ways. First, every action or inaction has political meaning for the consumer if not the provider of services. What one does and what one chooses not to do has political consequences that change the environment. Second, a competent provider will know the salient features of the consumer's cultural context and how that context supports or fails to support the provider's strategy. Third, it is important to know how the consumer perceives the provider as well. How does the consumer describe the provider when the provider is not present? Fourth, it is important to understand the symbolic meaning of ideas, concepts, and words from the perspective of the client's cultural context. Fifth, it is important to have a thorough understanding of the meaning each of us gives to ideas, concepts, and words we use in treatment. Otherwise, the same words may have different meanings and different words may have the same meaning.

The Basic Behavioral Science Task Force of the National Advisory Mental Health Council (1996) in its U.S. national plan for behavioral science research identified areas in which social and cultural factors were evident in the research literature. Although this report is focused on mental health and mental illness, the implications for the other fields of health services are clear. First, anthropological and cross-cultural research has demonstrated that cultural beliefs influence the diagnosis and treatment of mental illness. Second, the diagnosis of mental illness differs across cultures. Third, research has revealed differences in how individuals express symptoms in different cultural contexts. Fourth, culturally biased variations in diagnosis vary according to the diagnostic categories relevant to the majority population. Fifth, most providers come from a majority culture, whereas most clients are members of minority cultures. If each behavior occurs in a cultural context, then all theories of human behavior are fundamentally—but usually implicitly—cultural theories. Attempts to assess, understand, or change behaviors without regard for their cultural contexts are misguided, naive, and dangerous.

There are many examples of culturally learned principles that guide our knowledge systems and by which we organize our thinking about problems or solutions. Ten of these principles are provided as examples of cultural bias (Pedersen, 2000a, 2000b).

First, the term *normal* is not universally meaningful because what is normal is defined differently in each cultural context. However, the artificially established criteria for "normal behavior" is frequently used to guide our knowledge about clients and their possible pathologies.

Second, individualistic perspectives are not always appropriate nor are individuals the basic building blocks of a collectivistic society. While most industrialized societies have protected the individualistic perspective, that will change as more collectivistic societies gain economic and political power.

Third, a preference for specialized boundaries in diagnosis or in providing treatment for a "disease" tends to ignore the systemic context of an "illness" perspective. Each aspect of the individual influences every other aspect in profoundly important ways. Otherwise, the diagnosis becomes an artifact of the measure.

Fourth, abstract, specialized language or jargon has been presumed to be more sophisticated because it can be applied across cultural contexts. High-context cultures, where all meaning is necessarily contextual, are unlikely to understand abstract jargon in the way a provider intends.

Fifth, contrary to the individualistic perspective of more industrialized societies, dependency is not always undesirable. In many cultural contexts, dependency becomes a desirable or even essential element of a meaningful relationship between the consumer and the provider.

Sixth, individuals are not separated from their support systems of actual people or internalized identities from past experience. Whatever advice a provider may offer will be filtered by the support systems, separating what is acceptable from what is not acceptable. The competent provider will acknowledge the importance of these support systems.

Seventh, nonlinear thinking is becoming more widely used as developing non-Western cultures gain visible power. Until recently, linear thinking was considered inviolate as an essential element of modern science and scientific scrutiny.

Eighth, individuals should not adapt or adjust to the system when the individual is right and the system is wrong. Providers need to become more advocatory and less objectively detached from the good and bad consequences of their treatment.

Ninth, although historical background has been devalued in the search for quick and easy solutions to complicated and urgent problems, many if not most cultures consider historical ignorance to be barbaric or uncivilized.

Tenth, to assume that one has already discovered all of one's cultural biases is the most dangerous assumption of all. We need to do the best job we can, knowing deliberately that we are biased in undiscovered ways, and then discard dysfunctional cultural biases as we become aware of them.

During the past twenty years, multicultural theory has become a powerful "fourth force" (Pedersen, 1999), complementing the other three psychological forces of psychodynamics, behaviorism, and humanism. This fourth-force perspective does not compete with the other alternatives but rather complements them much as the fourth dimension of time complements three-dimensional space. A multicultural theory for counseling (Sue, Ivey & Pedersen, 1996) seeks to provide a conceptual framework that includes both the complex cultural diversity of a plural society and the shared concerns of common ground. Sue et al. (1996) have attempted to describe a multicultural counseling theory (MCT) based on six propositions to demonstrate this culture-centered perspective.

1. Each Western or non-Western theory represents a different worldview.
2. The totality and interrelationships of client–counselor experiences and contexts must be the focus of treatment.
3. A counselor or client's racial/cultural identity will influence how problems are defined and dictate or define appropriate counseling goals or processes.
4. The ultimate goal of a culture-centered approach is to expand the repertoire of helping responses available to counselors.
5. Conventional roles of counseling are only some of the many alternative helping roles available from other cultural contexts.
6. MCT emphasizes the importance of expanding personal, family, group, and organizational consciousness in a contextual orientation.

As these MCT propositions become more accepted, the provider will be led to ask new questions leading to a more comprehensive culture-centered understanding basic to the discussion of outcomes resulting from appropriate or inappropriate treatment. Under what circumstances and in which culturally circumscribed situations does a given psychological theory or methodology provide valid explanations for the origins and maintenance of behavior? What are the cultural boundary conditions potentially limiting the generalizability of psychological theories and methodologies? Which psychological phenomena are culturally robust in character and which phenomena appear only under specified cultural conditions (Gielen, 1994)?

There is a pervasive awareness of cultural similarities and differences in the social sciences today that require the rethinking of psychological theories of human behavior. Smith, Harre, and van Langenhove (1995) contrast the new with the old paradigms. The new paradigms emphasize understanding and description more than mere measuring; counting or predicting meanings more than just causation; interpretation of data more than just statistical analysis; language, discourse, and symbols more than just numerical reductionism; holistic perspectives more than atomistic; particularities more than universals; cultural context more than context-free perspectives; and subjectivity more than objectivity. The old and new rules are seamlessly connected in the cultural context of psychology as alternative perspectives of the same phenomena.

Levine (1985) suggests that the social sciences have favored a less complicated perspective because of the problems presented by ambiguity as an empirical phenomenon that is difficult to measure in objective terms. "The tolerance of ambiguity can be productive if it is taken not as a warrant for sloppy thinking but as an invitation to deal responsibly with ideas of great complexity" (p. 17). Complexity theory in the hard and more recently in the soft sciences has grown out of chaos theory, seeking to redefine conventional categories of analysis. Those working to apply nonlinear dynamics to the social sciences see themselves as pioneers of a dramatic new perspective. As Waldrop (1992) states, "They believe that they are forging the first rigorous alternative to the kind of linear, reductionistic thinking that has dominated science since the time of Newton—and that has now gone about as far as it can go in addressing the problems of our modern world" (p. 13). This is not "skeptical postmodernism," which rejects any quest for certainty or unitary truth, but rather an "affirmative post-modernist" position. This position reacts against modernism, but rejects a world without meaning while recognizing the importance of plural identities and ambiguous truth to ask questions even without having all the answers beforehand.

Developing Multicultural Skill

Developing multicultural skill is the third stage in developing multicultural competency. Having multicultural skill is indicated in a variety of ways. First, the skilled provider will generate a diversified response repertoire to each and every situation, problem, or decision, based on increased awareness and knowledge of various cultural contexts. Second, verbal and nonverbal messages will be sent and received more accurately, with attention to the culturally defined language, or nuances of meaning, that contributes to the message. Third, the skilled provider will know when to change the consumer to fit the system and when to change the system to fit the consumer, advocating for the consumer as appropriate and necessary. Fourth, the skilled provider will be able to recover after having said or done the wrong thing, getting out of trouble and furthering treatment goals in the process (Pedersen, 2000b).

Two different approaches to skill training are offered to increase provider competence in working with culturally different clients. The first model is The Cultural Grid, for teaching providers to separate culturally learned behaviors from the basic values or expectations that shape those behaviors. The second model is The Triad Training Model, for teaching providers to hear the hidden messages that the culturally different client might be thinking but not saying out loud.

The Cultural Grid

The Cultural Grid helps providers to increase their awareness of the client and their knowledge of the client's cultural context. Cultural contact can be either negative or positive. Negative cultural contact occurs when different behaviors presume negative expectations or values, when victims seek to "get even" with oppressors, when the more powerful force others to behave, and when potential friends become enemies. Positive cultural contact occurs when one or both persons positively interpret behaviors in their cultural context, when they identify positive shared expectations to find common ground, when that common ground becomes strong enough to allow each person or group to behave differently, when the common ground is protected and preserved by both parties, and when the behaviors of all parties are adapted and revised to enhance the common ground values or expectations.

The Cultural Grid is a visual attempt to demonstrate how a personal-cultural orientation can be derived by separating behaviors from expectations (Pedersen, 1997a). The Cultural Grid was developed to describe the complexity of each dynamic cultural context in a way that suggests research hypotheses and guides the training of people for multicultural contact. The Cultural Grid matches the social system (cultural) factors with the personal (behavior-expectation-value) variables in a personal-cultural orientation to each cultural context. The Cultural Grid provides a means to describe and understand each person's behavior as constructed by "culture teachers" from the client's social systems and cultural context, who teach the correct values, generate the correct expectations, and finally identify the correct behavior for that particular context.

The Intrapersonal Cultural Grid is useful to demonstrate the complexity of "cultural context." If you were asked, "What is your culture?" you would have a difficult time answering because you belong to more than one cultural affiliation, broadly defined. If, however, you use Figure 3.1 to describe the ways that your "cultural context" has shaped a particular behavior of yours, such as reading this book or making a particular decision, you will see how "culture teachers" from each of the many broadly defined affiliations has influenced your behavior. The Intrapersonal Cultural Grid demonstrates how to articulate the complex cultural context of each decision we make without being overwhelmed.

As shown in Figure 3.1, the categories of the Intrapersonal Cultural Grid provide a conceptual framework for how cultural and personal factors interact in a

FIGURE 3.1   Intrapersonal Cultural Grid

Cultural Teachers	Personal Variables		
	Where you learned to do it	Why you did it	What you did
1. Family relations relatives fellow countrypersons ancestors shared beliefs			
2. Power relationships social friends sponsors and mentors subordinates supervisors and superiors			
3. Memberships co-workers organizations gender and age groups workplace colleagues			

combined context, linking each behavior to expectations, each expectation to values, and each value to those social systems in which that value was learned. Each cultural context is complicated and dynamic, influenced by many culture teachers from social system contexts as each perspective takes its turn at being salient. An awareness of one's cultural identity requires being able to identify how a specific behavior is the expression of specific expectations, how each expectation developed from specific values, and how each value was learned from the culture teachers. On the cultural dimension, the social system contexts of ethnographic factors (ethnicity, nationality, language, religion, etc.), demographic factors (age, gender, place of residence, etc.), status (social, educational, economic, etc.), and affiliations (formal and informal) are combined and overlap in reinforcing the client's values, expectations, and ultimately his or her behavior. The Intrapersonal Cultural Grid is intended to show the complex relationship among behaviors, the many expectations behind a behavior, the many values behind each expectation, and the many social system variables through which each value was taught.

The Interpersonal Cultural Grid (see Figure 3.2), however, is an attempt to describe the relationship between people or groups by separating expectations from behaviors. The Interpersonal Cultural Grid includes four quadrants. Each quadrant explains one large or small part of any relationship between two individuals or groups. There will be some data in all four cells for any relationship, but the salience may change from one cell to another over time as the relationship changes.

The Interpersonal Cultural Grid can be useful in the classroom by asking for two volunteers, a male and a female for example, to role play a couple getting a divorce. Each partner speaks to the class for a couple of minutes explaining why they want to separate from the other. The class members then take on the role of "marriage counselors" to make comments or suggestions, or counsel one or the other partner. You will notice the importance of finding shared positive common ground between the two partners ("Tell me about when you first fell in love and decided to get married.") before attempting to change either partner's behaviors. The class will tend to focus on changing behaviors prematurely and the result will be to escalate the conflict. Only after the common ground of shared positive expectations has been clearly established can the discussion of "best behaviors" consistent with those expectations proceed. The task of the counselor is to focus on the second quadrant, where the two persons in conflict have similar positive expectations but express those expectations in different behaviors. Any attempt to

FIGURE 3.2 Interpersonal Cultural Grid

Why It Was Done	What Was Done	
	Perceived positive action	Perceived negative action
Perceived positive reasons		
Perceived negative reasons		

prematurely force behavior change will move the conflict to the third and ultimately the fourth quadrant.

In the first quadrant, two individuals have similar behaviors and similar positive expectations. The relationship is congruent and harmonious. There is a high level of accuracy in both individuals' interpretation of one another's behavior and the positive shared expectations behind that behavior. Both persons are smiling (behavior) and both persons expect friendship (expectation). There is little conflict in this quadrant and few surprises.

In the second quadrant, two individuals have different behaviors but share the same positive expectations. There is a high level of agreement in that both persons expect trust and friendliness, but there is a potentially low level of accuracy because each person perceives and incorrectly interprets the other's behavior as different and probably hostile. This quadrant is characteristic of cultural conflict in which each person is applying a self-reference criterion to interpret the other person's behavior. The conditions described in the second quadrant are very unstable and, unless the shared positive expectations are quickly found and made explicit, the salience is likely to change toward the third quadrant. It is important for at least one of the two persons or groups to discover and identify the presence of shared positive expectations of trust, respect, fairness, and so on in their shared cultural context despite the differences in their behavior as they express those expectations.

In the third quadrant, the two persons have the same behaviors but now they have different or negative expectations. The similar behaviors give the appearance of harmony and agreement through displaying the congruent or same behaviors, but the hidden different or negative expectations may ultimately destroy the relationship. Although both persons are now in disagreement, this might not be obvious or apparent. One person may continue to expect trust and friendliness, whereas the other person is now distrustful and unfriendly, even though they are both presenting the same smiling and glad-handing behaviors. If these two people discover that at an earlier time they shared positive expectations, they might be able to return to the second quadrant and reverse the escalating conflict between them. If the difference in expectations is ignored or undiscovered, the conflict will ultimately move to the fourth quadrant.

The fourth quadrant is where two people have different and/or negative expectations and they stop pretending to be congruent. The two persons are "at war" with one another and may not want to increase harmony in their relationship any longer. They may just want to hurt one another. Both persons are in disagreement and that disagreement is now obvious and apparent. This relationship is likely to result in hostile disengagement. It is very difficult to retrieve conflict from the fourth quadrant because one or both parties have stopped trying to find shared positive expectations. Unfortunately, most conflicts between people and groups remain undiscovered until they reach the fourth quadrant. An appropriate prevention strategy would be to identify the conflict in behaviors—as indicated in quadrant two—early in the process, when those differences in behaviors might be in the context of shared positive expectations, allowing both parties to build on the common ground they share without forcing either party to lose integrity.

Therefore, two people may both share the positive expectation of trust but one may be loud and the other quiet; they may share respect but one may be open and the other closed; they can both believe in fairness but one may be direct and the other indirect; they may value efficiency but one may be formal and the other informal; they can seek effectiveness but one may be close and the other distant; or they may want safety but one may be task oriented and the other relationship oriented. Only when each behavior is assessed and understood in its own cultural context does that behavior become meaningful. Only when positive shared expectations can be identified will two individuals or groups be able to find and build on common ground.

The Triad Training Model

The Triad Training Model is designed to increase the provider's skill in accurately interpreting the client's statements by better understanding the hidden messages. Every health care interview will include three simultaneous conversations. The client and the provider will have a verbal conversation they can both hear; the provider will have her or his own internal dialogue exploring related or unrelated factors, which the provider can monitor but the client cannot hear; the client will have her or his own internal dialogue exploring related or unrelated factors, which he or she can monitor but the provider cannot hear. The provider does not know what the client is thinking, but the provider does know that some of the client's internal dialogue will be positive and some will be negative. The more cultural differences there are between the provider and the client, the less likely that the provider will accurately understand what the client is thinking but not saying.

The Triad Training Model assumes that these three dialogues are going on at the same time for the client and provider (Pedersen, 2000b). Although the provider will not know what the culturally different client is thinking, he or she may well assume that part of the client's internal dialogue is negative and part is positive. The Triad Training Model assigns a culturally similar procounselor and an anticounselor to the coached client in a role-played training interview to make explicit the positive and negative internal dialogue of the client through the four-way interaction where there are often two or more people talking at the same time.

The anticounselor exaggerates the negative thoughts of the client toward the interview, emphasizing differences in behavior that drive the provider farther apart from the client. The anticounselor does this using a variety of techniques that include building on positive aspects of a problem, keeping the interaction superficial, obstructing communication, distracting or annoying the provider and/or client, building a barrier of cultural differences, demanding immediate results from the counselor, using a foreign language or whispering private messages to the client, finding a scapegoat to blame for the problem, or requesting a more appropriate provider. By involving the anticounselor in a simulated interview, the provider is likely to gain insight in cultural self-awareness, explicit negative unspoken thoughts of the client, opportunities for developing recovery skills, and a better understanding of the client's cultural context.

The procounselor is a deliberately positive force that helps articulate the client's positive unspoken messages about the interview, emphasizing similarities of common ground and positive expectations between the provider and the client and bringing the provider and client closer together. The procounselor accomplishes this by restating messages in a positive framework, relating statements to regular cultural patterns, offering approval and encouragement, reinforcing progress of the client, providing verbal and nonverbal encouragement, and helping the provider to focus accurately. The learning that results from the procounselor demonstrates the importance of making cultural information explicit to the provider, providing a teammate or friend to support the provider, reframing messages in a positive direction, and helping the provider track the changing cultural salience in the interview.

Research on the Triad Training Model in multicultural groups doing simulated interviews has been supportive and a variety of variations in the Triad Training Model have emerged (Pedersen, 2000b). The research literature clearly demonstrates the importance of a client's internal dialogue and the provider's accurate understanding of the client's internal dialogue for successful service delivery.

Intentional Group Microskills

Intentional group counseling is based on interpreting all behaviors in the multicultural context so that counselors are aware of their own values, attitudes, beliefs, and behaviors as these are similar and different across cultures (Ivey, Pedersen, & Ivey, 2001). Group workers learn microskills, beginning with (1) culturally appropriate attending and observation skills, (2) focusing, (3) basic listening sequence, (4) open and closed questions, (5) identifying themes of group interaction, (6) influencing skills, (7) conflict management, and (8) integration and application of microskills. The same behavior across cultures can have different meanings and different behaviors can have the same meaning.

Effective leadership demands the ability to observe what is occurring in a group. This can be learned through practice of the "3Vs plus B" (visuals, vocals, verbals, and body language). Intentional group leadership is a complicated process, especially when the leader considers the different national, ethnic, demographic, status, and affiliations of group members. The microskills approach provides the tools to quickly adapt to the changing cultural salience in a group and generate culturally appropriate responses.

Given a general topic, such as how to deal with "resistance" in a group, the group leader is taught a repertoire of microskills so the leader can "observe, focus, and listen" to identify salience, and then proceed to use questions and focusing skills, then confront, manage, and influence the discussion in a meaningful way. When the cultural salience changes, the leader can return to the basic listening skills again to reframe the group interaction. Microskills provide a fluid and flexible framework to train group leaders across cultures as an alternative to the more rigid "one-right-way" approaches, which are too easily biased toward a particular cultural perspective.

Intentional group counseling provides a model for how counselor education needs to be changed to meet the globalized needs of the future. It is not just the content of our teaching that is culturally biased but the process as well. We need to invent new ways that are less dependent on the assumptions of the dominant culture and more sensitive to cultural diversity in every context.

Multicultural Counselor Education

The literature on counseling has vigorously promoted the necessity for and advantages of a curriculum for training counselors to work with clients from a variety of different cultures, but very little has actually changed in the way counselors are educated. There are a few more single courses on cultural issues in each counselor education curriculum and a couple of dozen more books each year on the importance of culture in counseling, and the "word count" of culture-related terms has increased in professional mission statements or ethical guidelines, but very little has really changed about how counselors are being educated. It is important to infuse a culture-centered perspective throughout the counselor education curriculum, rather than marginalizing the topic in a single required course.

We know that behaviors are *learned* in a cultural context and are *displayed* in a cultural context; therefore, it makes sense that *accurate* assessment, *meaningful* understanding, and *appropriate* intervention require that counselors be educated to deal with their client's behavior in the cultural context where that behavior was learned and is being displayed. Every test and theory in counseling was developed to fit the precise needs of a particular cultural context, so it should not surprise us when a particular test or theory is less of an exact fit with radically different cultural contexts. Our search for culture-free and culture-fair tests has failed. We are left with the mandate to train counselors to translate data from culturally biased tests and theories *accurately, meaningfully,* and *appropriately.* Even those of our colleagues who react negatively to the infusion of multiculturalism into the curriculum are probably in favor of accurate assessment, meaningful understanding, and appropriate interventions. The message going unheard is that we are all on the same side. We differ in how to achieve accuracy but we strive for accuracy nonetheless. We need to get beyond the rhetoric and begin the process of real change in the curriculum of counselor education.

I would like to suggest an approach that failed when I tried it years ago at the University of Minnesota. I assembled a group of graduate students for a "topical seminar" on "infusing culture into the counseling curriculum." Each student was instructed to bring the syllabus for the other classes they were taking into the seminar. The class discussion would focus on preparing the students to generate questions about the relevance of culture into their other classes for discussion in those other classes and in that way infuse a culture-centered perspective throughout the other courses in counselor education. At the last minute, the students, who were originally very enthusiastic, approached me to apologize for withdrawing from the seminar because they were concerned that the other faculty would resent their bringing up culture-related questions and thereby "disrupting" the classes. Perhaps now we are at a point in time where these questions can be safely discussed.

Conclusion

A three-stage developmental structure was presented and described, beginning with increased awareness of culturally learned assumptions, moving next to increased knowledge about cultural information in the client's cultural context, and finally introducing the importance of competent skill based on cultural awareness and knowledge.

Three models were introduced to demonstrate how providers can be trained to increase their culture-centered competence. The first model was a cognitive framework, the Cultural Grid, designed to separate culturally learned behaviors from underlying values or expectations as a means of finding win/win outcomes in conflict. The second model was the Triad Training Model, to demonstrate how providers can be trained to hear what their culturally different clients are thinking but not saying. The third model was Intentional Group Microskills, describing a fluid and flexible model for preparing group leaders to track cultural salience in a dynamic group.

The final section described the implications of multicultural thinking for counselor education. We need to modify both the content and the process of counselor education to reflect the client's multicultural context. This greater task will be difficult but necessary for our survival in the global context.

As examples of discussion questions, I refer the reader to an article by Pedersen, Carter, and Ponterotto (1996) where several hundred "unanswered questions" on the "cultural context of psychology" were generated by thirty multicultural specialists and were listed for discussion. Some examples of these questions follow.

DISCUSSION QUESTIONS

1. Do the political aspects of culture further increase the controversy in culture-related language and terms? Moreover, is culture a conversation about sharing power?

2. Is race a pseudobiological term that has sociopolitical meaning? Does race influence human development and personality through perception?

3. Is most psychological research really about race—the "White" race? Moreover, is the Native American identity more than a race?

4. From various cultural perspectives, do we need more attention on a spiritual emphasis regarding healing processes?

5. How can we identify the changing "salience" of broadly defined cultural variables in a counseling interview?

6. How do/can we train counselors to assess the extent to which their own cultural backgrounds affect their working relationships?

7. Do we need new norms that are sensitive to different cultural contexts and groups?

8. Can clinicians provide quality care if they cannot communicate accurately and meaningfully with their clients?

9. Does DSM-IV's attention to cultural issues define clinical skills in a cultural context rather than putting culture in a clinical context?

10. What would be the incentives for counseling professionals to participate in diversity training for cultural competency, even when they are themselves minority group members?

11. Are groups that are more culturally diverse easier to teach than homogenous and particularly dominant culture groups?

12. What are the steps that need to be taken to measure the cultural competency of the service providers?

13. Do we need to identify indigenous helping frameworks as alternatives to traditional counseling approaches?

REFERENCES

Basic Behavioral Science Task Force of the National Advisory Mental Health Council. (1996). Basic behavioral science research for mental health: Sociocultural and environmental processes. *American Psychologist, 51,* 722–731.

Geilen, U. P. (1994). American mainstream psychology and its relationship to international and cross-cultural psychology. In A. L. Comunian & U. P. Gielen (Eds.), *Advancing psychology and its applications: International perspectives.* Milan, Italy: Franco Angeli Press.

Ivey, A. E., Pedersen, P. B., & Ivey M. B., (2001) *Intentional group counseling: A microskills approach.* Belmont CA: Brooks/Cole

Kiselica, M. S., Maben, P., & Locke, D. C. (1999). Do multicultural education and diversity appreciation training reduce prejudice among counseling trainees? *Journal of Mental Health Counseling, 21*(3), 240–254.

Levine, D. N. (1985). *The flight from ambiguity.* Chicago: The University of Chicago Press.

Oetting, E. R., & Beauvais, F. (1991). Orthogonal cultural identification theory: The cultural identification of minority adolescents. *International Journal of the Addictions, 25,* 655–685.

Pedersen, P. (1997a). *Culture-centered counseling interventions: Striving for accuracy.* Thousand Oaks, CA: Sage.

Pedersen, P. (1997b). Recent trends in cultural theories. *Applied and Preventive Psychology, 6,* 621–631.

Pedersen, P. (1999). *Multiculturalism as a fourth force.* Philadelphia: Taylor & Francis.

Pedersen, P. (2000a). *Handbook for developing multicultural awareness* (3rd ed.). Alexandria, VA: American Counseling Association.

Pedersen, P. (2000b). *Hidden messages in culture-centered counseling: A Triad Training Model.* Thousand Oaks, CA: Sage.

Pedersen, P. (2002). Ethics, competence and other professional issues of culture-centered counseling. In P. Pedersen, J. Draguns, W. Lonner, & J. Trimble (Eds.), *Counseling across cultures* (5th ed., pp. 3–27). Thousand Oaks, CA: Sage

Pedersen, P., Carter, R., & Ponterotto, J. (1996). The cultural context of psychology: Questions for accurate research and appropriate practice. *Cultural Diversity and Mental Health, 2*(3), 205–216.

Smith, J. A., Harre, R., & van Langenhove, L. (1995). *Rethinking psychology.* London: Sage.

Sue, D. W., Ivey A. E., & Pedersen, P. (1996). *A multicultural theory of counseling and psychotherapy.* Pacific Grove, CA: Brooks/Cole.

Waldrop, M. M. (1992). *Complexity: The emerging science at the edge of order and chaos.* New York: Touchstone.

Wrenn, C. G. (1962). The culturally encapsulated counselor. *Harvard Educational Review, 32,* 444–449.

Wrenn, C. G. (1985). Afterward: The culturally encapsulated counselor revisited. In P. Pedersen (Ed.), *Handbook of cross-cultural counseling and therapy* (pp. 323–329). Westport, CT: Greenwood.

4 Transcultural Counseling Theory Development Through the Liberal Arts

JOHN McFADDEN

Cultures attribute meaning to events for individuals and groups, which increases the predictability of people's psychological and physical worlds. Trends toward transculturalism are continuous in the counseling profession. This emerges out of a modern tendency toward the processing of models that are deterministic, mechanistic, and reductionistic and which serve to promote fragmentation and alienation of human life and relations endemic to this period of history. "Culturally mediated interpretations and predispositions ultimately end up in an individual's cognition as assumptions and representations of a world that is, in the last analysis, unique to each individual, but is, in a less specific sense, unique to different cultures" (Herr, 1999, p. 128). Transcultural models for counseling approach a stage of adequacy when they embrace synthetic views of whole persons in relationship to others while acknowledging the fact that no such view can ever completely capture the complexity and mystery of human beings or their respective communities. Even the culture of the only nonimmigrant population in the United States, Native Americans, was not monolithic. Religious beliefs and practices of Hopis and Navajos are quite different, despite the fact that they frequently share some of the same geographic area (Capuzzi & Gross, 1997). Cultural beliefs define acceptable behavior while providing criteria against which people judge themselves and others when applying a social norm. These beliefs affect how individuals and groups of people express themselves; respond to illness; rear children; and interact with family, friends, and strangers.

Counseling theories have tended to take a universalistic view of human behavior rather than acknowledge the cultural uniqueness of people (McFadden, 1999). This view of human behavior does not acknowledge cultural differences among people, which explains variations in verbal behavior, interpersonal interactions, work ethic, individualism, and group identity, making it easy for the counselor to resort to one theoretical model of behavior. Therefore, individuals who may be acting appropriately within their cultural traditions are characterized as behaviorally abnormal. Herr (1999) believes that cultural differences vary through human experience and also represent differences in general conceptions of our place in the universe and of factors that cause human beings to function the way in which one observes.

Vontress, Johnson, and Epp (1999) state that "as a helping profession, counseling, unlike psychology and psychiatry, was less 'scientific.' Its practitioners came from undergraduate programs in education, sociology, philosophy, religion, social sciences, and many other disciplines new to helping. These individuals were more willing to apply the insights gleaned from these other disciplines, along with psychological insights, to construct a more holistic vision of the client" (p. 4).

Emergent psychological models with a cultural base are projected in the future to be a multimodel synthesis of several models, theories, and methodologies. Beyond eclecticism, these models will be constructively interdisciplinary, endeavoring to address the complexity of human persons and their relations with self, others, and the environment. It becomes important, therefore, to build on sources in the liberal arts, such as philosophy, religion, sociology, international studies, art/music, and theater/dance, in addition to counseling and psychology as we move from nondisciplinary to transdisciplinary models of human life and relationships in an effort to frame historical and cultural foundations for a holistic transcultural theory.

Before engaging readers in a pertinent discussion for building a transcultural theory through the liberal arts, this chapter presents a discussion of cultural counseling terminology; this information should provide a foundation from which to conceptualize and digest the theoretical content that follows.

Cultural Counseling Terminology

Terminology pertaining to cultural descriptions for different points of view for counseling is as varied as each person's wish to label it. A sampling of these terms includes *monocultural, bicultural, bilateral, tricultural, cross-cultural, intercultural, international, multicultural, multiethnic, multilateral, pluralistic, transnational, transcultural,* and *transpiritual.* In an effort to move counselor education students from monolithic thinking to a more global perspective, it is useful to be familiar with some of the aforementioned terms. For example, the term *multicultural* accurately reflects the converging pluralism of cultures in a global community, but it also represents the study of a conglomeration of people from east to west and from north to south. Within any cultural grouping, it is not unusual for the individual to sit in the camp of more than one cultural belief system.

The term *multiculturalism* is becoming increasingly nebulous because its meanings continue to expand in relationship to an individual's political orientation, core values, early recollections, and social agenda. At one end, multicultural refers to reappraising the role of Western or European culture in world history as dedicated largely to oppression, injustice, gender bias, and rape of the natural world. Moderate views advocate for time and space for all cultures in a world strongly influenced by European cultural forces and norms. Pedersen (1988) states, "developing multicultural awareness is not an end in itself, but rather a means toward increasing a person's power, energy, and freedom of choice in a multicultural world. Multicultural awareness increases a person's intentional and purposive decision-making ability by accounting for the many ways that culture influences different perceptions of the same situation" (p. 3)

Multicultural counseling and transcultural counseling need to be differentiated. Although both terms contain elements of cultural inclusiveness, there are degrees by which they can be distinguished from each other. Multicultural counseling facilitates "client insight, growth and change through understanding and perpetuating multiple cultures within a psychological and scientific-ideological context" (McFadden, 1993, p. 6). Along these lines, counselors, within their own cultural contexts, attempt to understand cultural differences of those clients whom they might counsel.

Transcultural counseling, however, parallels a stage of internalization from which counselors function. It is broad based to the extent that a multiplicity of cultures can be included simultaneously and effectively as helping professionals fulfill their charge. Transcultural counseling extends itself as it embraces a transnational perspective and attains cultural transcendency. Moreover, transcultural counseling includes the counselor's and the client's ethnicity, locale, region, nation, ecology, and universality. Through this mode, counselors smoothly transcend cultural differences by engaging and understanding external cultures from intellectual and experiential analysis. Counselors actively accept opportunities for challenges presented through real-life situational vignettes. In light of recent world events and as technology makes it possible for our world to be even smaller, counseling may be seen by world governments as important in helping achieve national and international goals of work, spirituality, health, holistic healing, and happiness.

Liberal Arts

The field of liberal arts may include an extended number of academic disciplines, such as anthropology, government, history, international studies, literature, psychology, linguistics, art, music, religion, philosophy, sociology, theater, and others. This chapter focuses on the areas of philosophy, religion, sociology, international studies, art/music, and theater/dance in providing academic diversity toward the formation of transcultural counseling theory development. Each of these subjects is discussed relative to its base of thinking for putting in perspective the developing of a transcultural counseling theory through the liberal arts.

Philosophy

Philosophy is one of the academic disciplines in the liberal arts that represents "a set of ideas or beliefs relating to a particular field or activity." (*American Heritage Dictionary of the English Language,* p. 1,319). Historically, philosophy, in the midst of critical analysis, has been associated with counseling for many years. In fact, there exist individuals who have an identity as philosophical counselors, most of whom are based in countries such as Austria, Belgium, Denmark, France, Japan, Spain, and Switzerland (Shuster, 1989).

The German philosopher Gerd B. Achenback conceived the idea of the philosopher as a private "institution," as a person working independently outside the ivory tower of the university. During his nonclinical practice, Achenback began in 1981 receiving individuals for private consultation about their life problems and questions. His approach to philosophical counseling is that of creating a "free place" where persons use philosophy to develop their own thoughts on reluctant topics (Schuster, 1989).

Philosophy, critically analyzing basic assumptions or beliefs, is an idea that can be used to alleviate stress and, in doing so, assists individuals to come to acquire more insight into themselves and their environment. Epicurus described philosophy more than 2,000 years ago as "therapy of the soul." He believed that a number of theses advocated by philosophers are null and void if they do not provide a basis for relief of human suffering. So, as counselors seek to develop a theory for transcultural counseling, they should recall the need to ascertain a place in their profession where their theory and practice focus on relieving human suffering and learning the "art of living well," according to the Stoics (Raabe, 1999). Philosophical counseling requires a movement for philosophy from the ivory academic tower of academe to the world of reality.

Philosopher Martin Buber's teaching for counseling and other helping professions is embedded in the principle that dialogue is at the core of meeting life's challenges. Philosophical counselors Maurice Friedman and Maria da Venza Tillmanns of Solana Beach, San Diego County, California, concur with this idea (Knox, 1999). Even though philosophical counseling is not a new concept within mental health, it is continuing to expand within the field, for this form of counseling was born out of positive elements of the New Age movement whereby individuals began to exercise more control over their own lives (Knox, 1999).

Both Britain and the United States in recent years have increased the number of counselors within their respective countries who subscribe to having a philosophical emphasis in their work. University professors are beginning to include philosophy and counseling as compatible disciplines in their course syllabi, and this is particularly evident in advanced transcultural counseling courses (McFadden, 1999).

One of the varying definitions of philosophy is the critique and analysis of fundamental beliefs as they come to be conceptualized and formulated. As we seek a thorough understanding of the pedagogy aimed at enhancing the theory of transcultural counseling, there must be critical examination and reflection of reality and relationships accomplished by everyone involved in the counseling process. Such philosophical understanding is exemplified in Paulo Freire's writings, particularly noted in the *Pedagogy of the Oppressed* (2000) where the counselor can be seen as the oppressor and the counselee of color as the oppressed one.

Locke and Faubert (1999) state that culturally competent counselors have the responsibility to recognize and challenge the neutrality of traditional psychology and counseling theories and models and to gain substantive insights that are critical in developing a transcultural counseling theory. To initiate "awareness" (conscientization), Freire states that education is the path to permanent liberation involving a two-pronged process: the coming aware (conscientization) and the praxis, consisting of a lifelong process of liberation, cultural action, and reflection. This lifelong process is used for raising awareness, encouragement to action, and vigorous reflection. All of these are known to be essential elements in the preparation of culturally competent counselors.

Philosophically, counselor education programs that use the Freirian model as a basis for an instructional methodology in the formation of a transcultural counseling theory continually challenge students to think critically, to act dialogically, and to reflect openly on thoughts, feelings, and behaviors. Critical consciousness becomes the essence of effective transcultural counselor education curricula. Implementation of the Freirian model places the onus of reflecting on cultural realities, looking behind immediate cultural situations to determine their root sources, and examining the implications and consequences of the issues squarely on counselor education students. Ultimately, one might conclude that philosophy can certainly become a foundation upon which to build an instructional methodology in order to enhance a developing transcultural counseling theory.

Religion

Relatively speaking, the academic disciplines of counseling and psychology, compared with religious rituals, are in their early stages of development when we examine a bicultural, cross-cultural, multicultural, or transcultural theory. The field of religious studies has provided a substantial body of academic research and scholarship on culture across nationalities for many decades. A transcultural perspective within the study of religions around the globe continues to prevail in academic settings.

As counselor educators and psychologists promote a cultural paradigm within their teaching, learnings from the transcultural perspective in religious studies can be adapted from scholars such as J. Krishnamurti (1975) who conveyed, "The beginning of meditation is self-knowledge, which means being aware of every movement of thought and feeling, knowing all the layers of my consciousness, not only the superficial layers, but the hidden, the deeply concealed activities" (p. 219). However, religion and meditation are only one portion of what counselors consider in transcultural counseling theory development. "Although the connection between spirituality and counseling have not been central topics in these fields in the past, the historic barriers to such integration seem to be slowly dissolving as the practice of scientific inquiry and the practice of faith are beginning to build bridges and acknowledge that each may be complementary to the other and, indeed, that each has a significant contribution to make in facilitating human development, human healing, and human purpose" (Herr, 1999, p. 355).

Even before recent events of terrorism linked to religious fundamentalism, there seemed to be renewed attention to personal spirituality, faith, and religion as issues not only for clients but also psychotherapists. Covey (1989) has contended that among the four dimensions of adult renewal—physical, spiritual, mental, and social/emotional—an individual needs to be focused on the spiritual and meditate in order to enjoy a healthy and balanced life (Herr, 1999).

As the profession considers future challenges for psychotherapists, including the importance of achieving the goals of Maslow's hierarchy, it seems clear that issues related to reaching meaning in life and security in a fluctuating environment are pervasive to say the least. According to Herr, many people may feel that the possibility of a better quality of life through science and technology is unsatisfying and it is inner peace that they seek. An aspect of therapy that many psychotherapists using insight theories will face is that as clients strive for meaning in their lives they will come face to face with their own destiny and whether there is eternal life of the soul or spirit. In this process, clients will look for something or someone bigger than themselves, which may lead them to an organized religion, nature, or cults. Therefore, psychotherapists will need to take notice of such meaning making, which sometimes come in the form of anxiety, depression, and general discontent. Also, transcultural counseling theorists could adhere to a belief system grounded in their own spirituality.

In research, Myers and Diener (1997) found that actively religious people are much less likely to abuse drugs, divorce, and commit adultery, and that they also report greater happiness than those not religiously active. What's more, they found that those with strong faith are less vulnerable to depression and more likely to recover after divorce, serious illness, and unemployment. Hansen (1996) found that concepts of spirituality were important in the work of many prominent theorists in psychology and counseling, including Viktor Frankl, Carl Rogers, Carl Jung, and Rollo May. Although these greats differed in whether they believed in organized religion, they did agree that humans are characterized by the search for meaning, purpose, and wholeness. Herr (1999) states that even though connections between spirituality and psychotherapy have not been central topics in the past, the historic barriers seem to be eroding as the practice of scientific inquiry and the practice of faith are beginning to build bridges by acknowledging that each may be complementary and that each has a significant contribution to human development and human healing. Transcultural counseling theory development may represent another avenue for the interconnectedness between spirituality and psychotherapy.

Sociology

Sociology is "the scientific study of human social behavior." Sociologists investigate all group activities dealing with economic, social, political, and religious events. Sociologists may study broad areas such as bureaucracy, community, deviant behavior, family, public opinion, social change, social mobility, social stratification, as well as, specific areas such as crime, divorce, child abuse, poverty, and substance addiction (*Columbia Electronic Encyclopedia,* 2001). Sociologists seek to find relationships between events, describe these relationships by forming hypotheses and theories, and engage in research to find evidence to support or refute their hypotheses and theories.

Sociologists have four major research methods. These include surveys, observations and ethnography, experiments, and analysis of existing data. The historical development of sociology involves the pure science model from the 1930s to the 1960s and the unmasking inequality model since the 1970s. The reducing inequality model, which was developed in the 1970s and 1980s, takes into account the existence of race, gender, ethnic, sex, and class differences in society (Cancian, 1995).

Since the 1970s, there has been an increase in the literature and graduate training programs that address the need to develop and incorporate multicultural awareness in our society (Sue, Arredondo, & McDavis, 1992). As towns, cities, states, countries, and nations change, so do the opportunities for more cross-cultural and cross-national research. When examining and comparing different societies, certain ethnic values and cultural differences need to be considered as well as the diversity within societies. Not only do researchers need to understand different cultures and societies but they also need to be able to generalize and explain their findings to and across societies (May, 1997).

Collaboration between counselors and sociologists could result in positive gains in sociology and counseling tracks. In the field of sociology, there are three theoretical perspectives: functionalist, conflict, and symbolic interactionist. The functionalist and conflict perspectives offer a macro, or large, picture of society. The symbolic interactionist perspective concentrates on a micro view that deals with immediate social interactive situations (Thio, 2000). Sociologists, as well as counselors, work with children, adolescents, and adults that represent the diverse population of our society.

One's culture acts as a means to define an individual's identity and ensure social order and stability. Some practices, such as meeting the same human needs, are found in all cultures (Thio, 2000). However, counselors and sociologists should also recognize that there are many values, beliefs, and characteristics that are only represented in certain cultures. In realizing this important aspect, Mobley and Cheatham (1999) introduce and explain a self-awareness model for multiculturally oriented counselor educators. This model, which could benefit sociologists and other educators as well, is used to help counselor educators learn about their own culture and that of others and how they are related. Attention is focused on counselor training and cultural learning and is reflected in how counselors can be taught based on their level of racial and cultural development. Communities will continue to become more diverse and more controversial leading to many more studies and theories about society. It is baffling, however, that society still tends to incorporate and generalize negative stereotypes toward those who are not like "us." Counselors, educators, sociologists, psychologists, and other professionals are to be reminded that oppression and biases continue to prevail, whether intentionally or unintentionally. It is important throughout one's work to take time to monitor, assess, and adjust in order to decrease biases and increase the level of social awareness. These learnings are substantiating points to guide the development of a relevant transcultural counseling theory.

Wehrly, Kenney, and Kenney (1999) present a transcultural counseling theory that helps counselors explain, understand, recognize, and deal with diversity within and among different ethnic groups. This theory could help further explain existing data and findings of sociologists' research. When working with a multicultural population, counselors as well as sociologists are often faced with the negative aspects of stereotypes that stimulate emotional responses and reactions toward others (Wehrly, Kenney, & Kenney, 1999). Certain life experiences, along with values and beliefs, can certainly impact our entire socialization process. The White, middle-class value system is often considered the norm and reflected in counseling research involving race and ethnic issues (Sue, Arredondo, & McDavis, 1992). Models used to research and generalize socialization among those other than White, middle-class groups may have been harmful because of certain biases, generalizations, and limitations that exist from the chosen subject group being studied. Society's acknowledgment of cultural differences will hopefully lead to understanding the differences, which in time will lead to respecting the differences. Transcultural counseling theorists could also find this useful.

International Studies

Transcultural counseling theory and international studies are complementary disciplines that can be integrated for the enhancement of both fields of study. In combination, these disciplines have a reciprocal relationship and share some valuable issues such as effective intercultural communication and ethical dilemmas.

International research provides extremely valuable information that can be useful in transcultural counseling theory development. International studies utilizes a global worldview in research, observations, and interactions. A significant portion of this discipline involves immersion in other cultures through visiting, research, or exchange programs. This extensive interaction with other cultures can provide some valuable information about relating to different cultures through intercultural communication as well as knowledge of cultural norms.

Both international studies and counseling are significantly dependent upon effective communication. For counselors, communication has a critical role in the therapeutic process. It is central to developing a beneficial therapeutic relationship as well as applying successful therapeutic interventions. Communication also has a key role with international studies. This discipline works directly with many cultures, which makes communication and relating key components of global studies. In order to research, observe, or interact on a global basis effectively, it is imperative to develop a good understanding of intercultural communication as one seeks to formulate a transcultural counseling theory.

When communicating interculturally, it is vital to consider cultural differences as well as similarities (Zaharna, 2001). Often professionals may work to find common ground and may neglect important cultural differences. Although it is advantageous to find common ground to connect with people from different cultures, neglecting differences may inhibit effective communication. With international studies, failure to take differences into consideration may inhibit relational attempts and counselors could experience similar clinical difficulty. Neglecting differences may limit the therapeutic relationship or lead to misunderstanding between the counselor and client and, at the same time, restrict momentum toward transcultural counseling theory.

International studies also has explored the importance of being knowledgeable about the culture's influence on communication (Zaharna, 2001). Even with recent trends toward globalization, it has become evident that a common language is merely a beginning point for intercultural and transnational communication. Although a common language can be useful with intercultural communication, this form of communication may be limited if the cultural context is ignored. In some instances verbal expressions are insufficient. Without an appropriate cultural context, it is likely that misinterpretations will occur and the intercultural relationship could become ineffective.

Both counselors and international researchers are confronted with ethical dilemmas across cultural lines. A recent article by Mazrui (1999) explores the fine line between cultural norms and humane principles. This area of international studies can also be helpful for transcultural counselors. In therapy, it is a counselor's responsibility to take into consideration the best interests of the client. This may be complicated when the client has culturally different and opposing values. The counselor would have to take these cultural values into consideration during therapy. This situation could be further complicated if the client appears to be in a harmful situation, even if the circumstances are culturally normative. It leads to the difficult debate over working ethically as a counselor and protecting the client while at the same time respecting the client's culture.

International studies has produced some tremendous resources for transcultural counseling theory. Because international studies takes a global perception, it contributes a great deal of knowledge about other cultures. This knowledge can be a beginning point for counselors to work transculturally with clients. Counselors can build on this basic knowledge to develop an understanding of cultural similarities and differences and understand transcultural counseling theory. With this insight and comprehension, a counselor may be effective in communicating interculturally and hopefully in constructing a beneficial therapeutic relationship based on a relevant transcultural counseling theory.

Art and Music

Our aesthetic experience is based on our familiarity with art and music. We may gain interest or appreciation of diversity in art and musical forms, but it is essential to discover the historical, anthropological, and sociological foundations focusing on works of art and music. Looking at and exploring art through an educated eye offers insight into the intentions, motivation, and purpose found within the artist/musician and the expressive artist's culture can be identified (Blocker, 1993). Similar to spirituality, language, and tradition, art and music are important components in one's culture. Peter S. Li (1994) explains that "An essential feature of culture is that through symbolic manifestations in art, but also in religion and rituals, the philosophical and artistic meaning of existence that transcends the present day life of a people, its past and its mythologies, is infused into their experiences" (p. 2).

One's interpretation of art as well as music relies on an individual's past exposure to these disciplines, one's interest, and one's appreciation for art in a broad sense and in all forms. However, appreciation for these creative forms does not translate into a universal aesthetic. A universal language of art and music is not spoken and does not exist without the value of cultural designation. One must know the cultural foundations in order to understand the cultural designation and classification (Chanda, 1992).

Artifacts presented or discovered and classified as works of art must be considered simultaneously with the intentions, motivation, and purpose of their maker. When considering art and music from a Chinese, Native American, or African American perspective, knowledge about the individual's worldview is essential. Determining an artist's background, interests, significance of culture, and importance in the world allows an audience to experience the complexity, the richness, and the pain surrounding a particular piece (Blocker, 1993).

By the year 2050, it is presumed that the world will be more diverse than ever imagined. Communication between individuals, societies, and cultures is essential in maintaining a continual hermeneutical process of dialogue (Blocker, 1993). From a counseling perspective, dialogue allows for an opportunity of understanding. Exploring artifacts, tracing history, and establishing dialogue allow one to move closer to an artist's point of view. This reflects an impression that is made, a perspective that is offered, and potential change that may enhance one's being. This is visual and performing art that can be a basis on which transcultural counseling theory development begins.

The value of transcending art and music lies primarily in enriching our aesthetic appreciation of a diverse range of artistic genres but also in enhancing our understanding and motivation to dialogue with those in other cultures and finally to comprehend and appreciate our place in a multicultural and diverse world (Zaretti, 1998). Discovering, exploring, and offering opportunities for dialogue are important in gaining an appreciation for the arts. Works of art and musical forms exist everywhere from museums to the parks and from subways to the classrooms. A successful teaching methodology incorporates a multitude of opportunities for all people, young and old, to gain insight into the world of visual and performing art, both in theory and practice. Furthermore, studying the structure and dynamics of waves and vibrations represents fundamentals of art, music, and life.

"To understand anything, we must assimilate that thing within the orbit of our many concerns, and to that extent there will always be distortion" (Blocker, 1993, p. 7). To transcend cultures, perspectives must be expanded to incorporate beliefs, traditions, and rituals that comprise art and drive music. Expanding and changing one's consciousness is important, but influencing and potentially enhancing perspectives of those is of equal importance and value. Imposing systems of appreciation is not acceptable; however, the key is working to discover and enhance art and music appreciation opportunities that are offered through experiences of diverse people who share their artistic expressions, considering their culture, their environment, and their beliefs about themselves (Chanda, 1992). Both art and music represent a primary mode for intercultural communication and understanding. They likewise present themselves as vehicles through which transcultural counseling theories might be operationalized.

The environment plays an important role in the life of an individual. It can be documented that the environment (low socioeconomic status, abusive living environment, few role models, substance abuse, and other factors) determines the perceptions and behavior of an individual and the behavior can be related to the system (environment). This is nowhere more apparent than through art and opportunities to communicate through music. Just as transcendent and systemic counselors must familiarize themselves with the family structure, basic organization patterns of communication styles, modes of showing affection, decision making, and the power infrastructure, so too must the educator who utilizes a multicultural methodology surrounding art and music.

The stylistic model (McFadden, 1999) is built using cubicle descriptors that are hierarchical in nature and are described using three dimensions. From a stylistic perspective, it is very important for the educator to consider the cubicle descriptors in the model with regard to art and music. These dimensions are cultural/historical, psychosocial, and scientific-ideological. This model allows the counselor to have an intuitive and accurate perspective into the cultural identity of the individual. Then the counselor may view the psychosocial level, which is described as the interaction between people inside or outside the culture. The top level of the stylistic cube is the scientific-ideological dimension, which is the action-oriented aspect of stylistic counseling. Counselors will be able to do a great deal if they have a clear understanding of the history, structure, and culture of students while providing successful cultural and artistic experiences in an effort to build on students' self-image. These are inculcated in the artistic thinking of the transcultural counseling theorist.

Theater and Dance

There is growing interest for cognitive restructuring with creative arts. Both theater and dance can be used as a vehicle of self-discovery and as a mode for increasing awareness and appreciation of others. Dance therapy and drama therapy are well established fields but are not capitalized optimally across disciplines.

To refer to the rudiments of theater and dance in developing a transcultural counseling theory is useful. "The creative arts have the power to arouse and inform emotionally and physically" (Henderson & Gladdings 1998, p. 183). There are numerous components to formulating a transcultural counseling theory and developing curriculum because students begin to recognize and explore their ability and uniqueness, their sociohistorical context of being, and their ability to learn and express themselves in order to create and maintain a climate of understanding. Students have the opportunity to be brought out of self-consciousness to self-awareness (Henderson & Gladdings, 1998). Building on the transcultural counseling theory foundation, this curriculum could be a source for transcending cultures through communication and understanding as follows:

- Calling attention to the power of expression
- Providing experiences to help individuals interact and relate to others
- Bringing people together to discover new interests and gain new experiences
- Building positive feelings and affect within people that can help them cope with uncomfortable situations
- Helping people gain confidence and insight (Henderson & Gladdings, 1998)

An important philosophical aspect of transcultural theater is giving voice to and creating connections between different cultures, not simply using different cultures as tokenism (Uno, 1995). As students explore themselves and reach out to others, they will help bring together the professionals who are working with them. This transcultural theory and curriculum could build a new professional culture for the educational institution (Wengrower, 2001).

The human body may express itself in a number of ways. All of the senses are used to some degree as a means for signifying one person's emotions to another person. These expressions are frequently universal in nature while also unique in their meaning. Many individuals use movement in order to express their emotions and character of being. This mode of self-expression extends itself among cultures throughout the world. Dance is one of the numerous ways that people of various cultures assert their individuality and uniqueness. Through the use of dance, individuals use their body to communicate or express their way of life. The body can be used to dance through a variety of modalities, such as moving, turning, jumping, rotating, and bending (Jonas, 1998). Individuals in any culture may utilize any or all of the primary elements of dance: body weight, time, energy, and space.

The art of dance has been celebrated universally by cultures for centuries. Dancing represents one form for individuals to express physically their innermost soul and convictions without verbalizing them in prose form. Among cultures, dance may be for a celebration; mourning; a rite of passage; storytelling; expressing a wide range of emotions; religious narratives; educating others; and passing traditions, rituals, and heritage. Without regard to culture, people around the world use dance as a method of free expression (Gere, Segal, Koelsch, & Zimmer, 1995). Within each culture, particular styles and movements may be emphasized in order to signify the uniqueness of the culture. Historical preservation of dances has prevailed for generations. Many cultures use a number of universal movements to symbolize ideas and themes. In addition, these cultures may create particular forms of self-expression through dance that are distinctively unique in order to symbolize themes or ideas.

Dance therapy is a versatile form of therapy that may be used with a wide range of clients. Counselor educators can use dance therapy as a basis from which to develop a transcultural counseling theory. Dance is universal—it is not mandated to any particular culture. As a means of self-expression, dance therapy may help clients from any culture. Dance itself provides a medium for expression that may be safer for some clients than being verbal (Dreamer, 2001). It extends itself beyond words of culture. It is possible to use dance therapy with virtually any population or culture.

Within a transcultural context, counselors may choose to work with the dance of a client's culture with which they may or may not previously be familiar. Clients—from children to the elderly—may benefit from the use of dance therapy. The universality of dance transcends culture and may help clients deal with an issue from a specific cultural perspective. The physical and psychological effects of dance serve many functions (Bernstein, 1975). Dance may help clients in ways that counselors may never be able to accomplish alone, for dance and movement can be extremely therapeutic to clients. Dance therapy is transcultural in the sense that it transcends beyond cultures. Not only can dance therapy assist clients in appreciating the uniqueness of expression through their culture but it also allows clients to become aware of the totality of dance in all cultures and human beings. These insights for dance and theater serve a very valuable purpose in developing a transcultural counseling theory.

Transcultural Theory: A Counselor Development Model

Toward understanding the concept supporting the development of a transcultural counseling theory, inclusive of liberal arts components, a counselor development model has been designed by John McFadden (University of South Carolina) and Marty Jencius (Kent State University) (see Figure 4.1). The circular layers range from self-inquiry (A) to skills and techniques (H), representing progressive development from introspective reflections by the theorist to an ultimate level of theoretical application. The six pie-shaped sections of the cylinder with an aerial view are select disciplines in the area of liberal arts and permeate circular layers of the model. The social forces axis through the center of the cylinder depicts the core that holds together all components of this transcultural design. It actually constitutes the centrifugal force around which each academic discipline resides and upon which each circular layer (A–H) depends. In developing a transcultural counseling theory that is meaningful and relevant, the counselor acknowledges the prevalence of social forces and their impact on counseling functions and on society in general. The following discussion explains the eight circular layers of the cylinder and their interrelatedness.

This model is designed geometrically in the form of a cylinder that ranges from self-inquiry to skills and techniques. The foundation layer is self-inquiry (A),

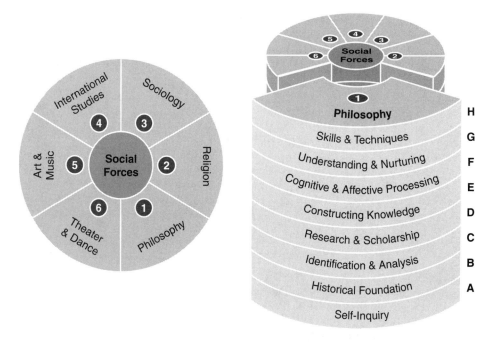

FIGURE 4.1   Transcultural Theory: A Counselor Development Model
Source: J. McFadden and M. Jencius, *Transcultural Theory: A Counselor Development Model*. 2002.

which lies at the base of the cylinder. If a counselor educator or other helping professional is to develop a transcultural counseling theory, it is mandatory to master an intuitive sense of self. This represents the initial step toward an individual's development of a model upon which to build a transcultural theory.

The second layer, historical foundation (B), follows self-inquiry. At this level the researcher is interested in discovering a foundation in terms of a narrative past of humanity. Identification and analysis (C) represents a layer for the realization of one's ability to conceptualize terminology and a visionary framework that can be analyzed, reviewed, and discussed.

Circular layer (D) is identified by research and scholarship and offers a challenge for the counselor educator to research quantitatively and qualitatively the previously identified concepts. Scholarly review is done in order to build toward a theory. A fifth layer or disk is called constructing knowledge (E), which follows thorough research and analysis. The researcher at this stage constructs a framework around what has been learned in previous stages. Assimilation of knowledge through a mode of constructivism leads to theory foundation.

The sixth layer, cognitive and affective processing (F), represents dimensions of knowing (knowledge) and feeling (emotion). As previously acquired insights blend through an element of processing, the researcher seizes an opportunity to assimilate them. Understanding and nurturing (G) is a natural outgrowth and depicts a window through which the counselor educator realizes advantages of cultivating and promoting that which has been learned.

The epitome of this cylindrical model is the layer of skills and techniques (H). At this point, it becomes obvious that the construction of systematic procedures for transcultural counseling theory development is inevitable for application across cultures.

Synthesizing Principles for and Beyond Liberal Arts

The area of liberal arts, for the purpose of this book, addresses philosophy, religion, sociology, international studies, art/music, and theater/dance even though the author acknowledges that liberal arts spans other disciplines. Transcultural counseling theory development manifests itself through interdisciplinary foundation building. In assessing the effectiveness of this type of theory, it is incumbent on the theorist to ensure intellectual stimuli representing age, gender, race, ethnicity, religion, sexual orientation, disability, and class. Principles to follow are guidelines to use in determining the sustaining foundation for transcultural counseling theory development and steering the enhancement of counselor education programs not only through the liberal arts but also through disciplines in scientific fields.

Principles for Transcultural Counseling Theory Development

Toward conceptualization, developing, and testing concepts for transcultural counseling theory development, the following principles should be considered:

- Build on traditional concepts and theoretical constructs historically known to have value.
- Permit intellectual dialogue to permeate developing notions for theory development.
- Incorporate a holistic view for healthy living and a productive lifestyle.
- Interface the thinking of trends for application of liberal arts in counseling.
- Embed a framework for globalization and mutual respect and appreciation for all cultures.
- Ensure that ideas incorporated are congruent with optimal human growth and development of human beings across ages, genders, races, ethnicities, religions, sexual orientation, and socioeconomic groups.
- Periodically test mini- and maxi-components of theory development to ensure validity and reliability.
- Permit the counseling theory to incorporate interdisciplinary thought and subjects. Include constructivistic discussion and debate on a continuous basis, remaining client oriented.
- Allow for futuristic development and application of transculturalism in theory formation as individuals transgress universally toward future generations.

Futuristic View

"The contents of counseling and its importance have become a function of political, social and economic events in the larger society. Counselors cannot function effectively in a world of comprehensive change with a limited understanding of the contexts, images, events, or cultural traditions within which people negotiate their identity and security" (Herr, 1999, p. 342). In our contemporary world, travel, trade, commerce, and communications have made it possible for people of different cultures to experience the food, music, art, clothing, folkways, and science of other cultures. The media has dubbed it an international lifestyle. For some people this is the antithesis of what should be evolving. The phenomenon that is readily observable today throughout many societies reflects a blending of cultures. We find ourselves being confronted with recognition of "the prickly and potentially combustible issues surrounding the growing acknowledgement of ethnically mixed Americans and the practical, intellectual and political impact of this new category of citizens upon each of us" (Johnson, 2001, p. 53). Furthermore, we can expand and redefine what society believes people of color—Blacks, Whites, Latinos, Indians, Asians, or any combination—can achieve and the arenas in which they can succeed (Johnson, 2001).

There are those who are angry about the homogenization of cultures and have launched an effort to preserve their cultural identity through racial and religious cleansing. This is one theory of the actions of the Islamic peoples on September 11, 2001. However, even in 1999 Naisbitt and Aburdene stated, "The trend toward a global lifestyle and countertrend toward cultural assertion represents the classic dilemma: how to preserve individuality within the unity of the family or community."

Conclusion

Counseling is being transfigured from a profession that mostly provides treatment for phobias, anxiety, or depression to one that puts more emphasis on such terms as *optimization of behavior, personal resilience, self-renewal,* and *personal flexibility.* As Herr (1999) stated, "whether at the global level or in a local town or family, changes tend to stimulate needs for new behavioral patterns and skills. Often this requires that former definitions of counseling be revisited and expanded and that these terms be invested with new metaphors, processes and practices, and used across wider audiences" (p. 343). As boundaries between ethnicity groups become indistinct, uncertainties arise. Counselors will need to be able to use transcultural theories to help clients learn conflict resolution and systems to live in culturally diverse environments. During the twenty-first century, the rapidity of familiar changes is challenging counselors to help their clients put meaning to various psychological, physical, and spiritual events. Therefore, the counselor's role is expanding in addition to the traditional role of behavior change to that of the client's need for reaching self-actualization as individuals and within cultural settings.

We live in a society inundated daily by media analyses and accounts of natural and political chaos, including terrorism around the globe. Counselors have a renewed role in helping people identify resources to deal with uncertainty and ambiguity with tangible steps to be able to manage their psychological, spiritual, and physical world as well as navigate those of people around them.

In addition to introducing the foundation and principles for developing a transcultural counseling theory, this chapter offers a perspective on several cultural and curricular aspects of counseling as a profession. Transcultural counseling by definition is truly interdisciplinary and allows for a blend of the liberal arts in addition to science in the academy. The collective approaches herein include visions on organizing one's transcultural counseling theory with thought, meaning, and perspectives on the world.

DISCUSSION QUESTIONS

1. What considerations would you make in defining and forming a transcultural theory for counseling?

2. What challenges do counselors face in the twenty-first century that they were not confronted with in the twentieth century?

3. What curriculum design would you develop in order to ensure that a counseling program incorporates cultural components for student competency as they enter counseling profession?

4. Discuss strategies for excellence of instruction as professors examine inculcating liberal arts in counselor training throughout our multicultural society.

5. Why is professional identity significant among counselors and counselor educators in view of public and political expectations for competency and performance?

REFERENCES

American heritage dictionary of the English language (4th ed.). Boston: Houghton Mifflin.

Bernstein, P. (1975). *Theory and methods in dance-movement therapy: A manual for therapists, students, and educators.* Dubuque, IA: Kendall/Hunt.

Blocker, H. G. (1993). Aesthetic value in cross-cultural, multicultural art study. *Arts Education Policy Review, 95*(2), 26–30.

Cancian, F. (1995, Fall). Truth and goodness: Does the sociology of inequality promote social betterment? *Sociological Perspectives, 38*(3), 339.

Capuzzi, D., & Gross, D. R. (1997). *Introduction to the counseling profession.* Boston: Allyn & Bacon.

Chanda, J. (1992). Multicultural education and the visual arts. *Arts Education Policy Review, 94*(1), 12–17.

Covey, S. R., (1989). *The seven habits of highly effective people: Restoring the character ethic.* New York: Simon & Schuster.

Dreamer, O. (2001). *The dance: Moving to the rhythms of your true self.* San Francisco: HarperCollins.

Einstein, A. (1954). *Ideas and opinions.* New York: Crown.

Freire, P. (2000). *Pedagogy of the oppressed* (30th anniversary ed.). New York: The Continuum International Publishing Group, Inc. [Original work published 1970]

Gere, D., Segal, L., Koelsch, P., & Zimmer, E. (Eds.). (1995). *Looking out: Perspectives on dance and criticism in a multicultural world.* Portland, OR: MacMillan Library.

Hansen, L.S. (1996). *Integrative life planning: Critical tasks for career development and changing life patterns.* San Francisco: Jossey-Bass.

Henderson, D., & Gladdings, S. (1998). The creative arts in counseling: A multicultural prospective. *The Arts in Psychotherapy, 25*(3), 183–187.

Herr, E. L. (1999). *Counseling in a dynamic society: Contexts and practices for the 21st century.* Alexandria, VA: American Counseling Association.

Johnson, R. S. (2001). Stand and deliver. *Savory, 1*(1), 49–55.

Jonas, G. (1998). *Dancing: The pleasure, power, and art of movement.* Chicago, IL: Abrams.

Knox, J. (1999, May 10). Scholars blend counseling, philosophy. *North County Times.* [Electronic version] Retrieved April 3, 2002, from http://psy.ucd.edu/~hdp/Philcounseling.html, Houghton Mifflin.

Krishnamurti, J. (1975). *The first and last freedom.* New York: Harper & Row.

Li, P. S. (1994). A world apart: The multicultural world of visible minorities and the art world of Canada. *The Canadian Review of Sociology and Anthropology, 31*(4), 365–392.

Locke, D. C., & Faubert, M. (1999). Innovative pedagogy for critical consciousness in counselor education. In M. S. Kiselica (Ed.), *Confronting prejudice and racism during multicultural training* (pp. 43–58). Alexandria, VA: American Counseling Association

May, T. (1997). *Social research: Issues, methods, and process.* London: Open University Press.

Mazrui, A. A. (1999, Summer). Globalization and cross-cultural values: The politics of identity and judgment. *Arab Studies Quarterly, 21*(3), 97–108.

McFadden, J. (ed.) (1993). *Transcultural counseling.* Alexandria, VA: American Counseling Association.

McFadden, J. (ed.) (1999). *Transcultural counseling.* (2nd ed.) Alexandria, VA: American Counseling Association.

McFadden, J. (2002). EDCE 820: Advanced transcultural counseling, University of South Carolina, Columbia.

McFadden, J. & Jencius, M. (2002). Transcultural theory: A counselor development model. Columbia, SC: University of South Carolina.

Mobley, M., & Cheatham, H. (1999). R.A.C.E.—Racial Affirmation and Counselor Educators. In M. S. Kiselica, (Ed.), *Confronting Prejudice and Racism during Multicultural Training* (pp. 89–105). Alexandria, VA: *American Counseling Association.*

Montaldo, J. (Ed.) (2000). *Entering the silence: The journals of thomas merton.* Volume II 1941–1952. San Francisco: Harper.

Myers, D. G., & Diener, E. (1997). The science of happiness. *The Futurist, 31*(5), 1–7.

Naisbitt, J., & Aburdene, P. (1999). *Megatrends 2000.* New York: Simon & Schuster.

Pedersen, P. (1988). *Multicultural handbook for developing awareness.* Alexandria, VA: American Association for Counseling and Development.

Raabe, P. B. (1999, May 2). What is philosophical counseling. A philosophical counseling website. Retrieved March 4, 2002, from http://www.interchange.ubc.ca/raabe/Raabe-articlel.html

Schuster, S. C. (1989). The philosophical counseling website. Retrieved April 3, 2002, from http://www.geocities.com/Athens/Foram/5914

Sociology. (2001). *The Columbia Electronic Encyclopedia* (6th ed.). New York: Columbia University Press.

Sue, D. W., Arredondo, P., & McDavis, R. (1992, April). Multicultural counseling competencies and standards: A call to the profession. *Journal of Multicultural Counseling and Development, 20,* 64–88.

Thio, A. (2000). *Sociology: A brief introduction.* Boston: Allyn & Bacon.

Uno, R. (1995). The way of inclusiveness. *The Arts in Psychotherapy, 2*(3), 183–187.

Vontress, C. E., Johnson, J. A., & Epp, L. R. (1999). *Cross-cultural counseling: A casebook.* Alexandria, VA: American Counseling Association.

Wehrly, B., Kenney, K., & Kenny, M. (1999). *Counseling multiracial families: Multicultural aspects of counseling series 12.* Thousand Oaks, CA: Sage.

Wengrower, H. (2001). Arts therapies in educational settings: An intercultural encounter. *The Arts in Psychotherapy, 28*(2), 109–155.

Zaharna, R. S. (2001, Summer). In-awareness approach to international public relations. Public *Relations Review, 27*(2), 135–150.

Zaretti, J. L. (1998). *Multicultural music education: An ethnography of process in teaching and learning.* Unpublished doctoral dissertation, Indiana University, Bloomington.

5 Native American Mental Health: An Examination of Resiliency in the Face of Overwhelming Odds

SUSAN CHAVEZ CAMERON (NAVAJO) AND
IMANI TURTLE-SONG (NAVAJO/AFRICAN
AMERICAN)

With more than 550 federally recognized tribes (U.S. Census Bureau, 1999) speaking more than 200 languages (Fleming, 1992), Native Americans represent the most ethnically diverse cultural group in the United States. Although many tribes share similar values and beliefs, their cultural practices, traditions, and social organization vary and are influenced not only by geographic location but also by the historical traumas experienced by individual tribal groups. The purpose of this chapter is to put Native Americans into a historical context so that the social, political, physical, and mental problems confronting contemporary Native Americans can be better understood.

Precontact

When Europeans arrived in the Americas, they encountered a thriving, self-governing people living in harmony with nature. At that time, most indigenous peoples believed humans to be connected to one another and to all creation—one part of a greater interdependent piece of the universe; one part no greater than another. These beliefs were manifested in Native Americans' deep respect for the land and their reverence for their kinship with wildlife. Contrary to the stereotype that they simply lived off the land, Native Americans managed their environments. They used fire not only to cook but also to modify the landscape, prevent forest fires, and create prairies, which encouraged larger game animals to congregate and, thus, made hunting easier. Plants were domesticated not only for food, but also as a source of fiber to create fishing and hunting equipment, clothing, medicines, and for making baskets and food utilities. And even though they lived in harmony with their environments, adapting to available resources, Native Americans also developed very complex trading routes, which traversed the Americas (Waldman & Braun, 1985).

Native American religions presented a wondrous variety of beliefs, sacraments, and systems, and spirituality was an important and intricate part of early Native American daily life. An especially holistic and reverent people, natural phenomena were inseparable from the supernatural, and most Native Americans believed in a special kinship between themselves and the plants, animals, and inanimate objects that inhabited their world. Prayers were used for food quests, hunting, healing rituals, and for giving thanks for all with which they had been blessed (Adams, 1997).

Although there are enormous discrepancies among scholars, it is estimated that in 1492, when the first Europeans landed in the Americas, there were between 10 and 15 million indigenous peoples living in what is now the United States (Waldman & Braun, 1985). Nevertheless, the actual population will remain forever elusive because early estimates were made after Native Americans had been exposed and ravaged by European diseases and warfare. What is known is at their lowest point, between 1890 and 1910, approximately 250,000 to 300,000 Native American people had survived European contact. Using the conservative number of 10 million at the time of first contact, this represents a loss of 97 to 97.5 percent of the entire indigenous population in the United States in about 400 years (Thornton, 1987).

Postcontact

It is not the intent of this chapter to cast blame or to moralize about the past. Simply, it is our goal to put things into historical perspective so that contemporary Native American issues are more understandable. Having said this, it is important to note that the authors understand and appreciate that not all the Whites in early U.S. history were racist, cruel, or sought to exploit the Native Americans. We also recognize and appreciate that many Whites, be they traders, settlers, missionaries, or members from other religious groups, defended Native American rights. This said, it is impossible for readers to understand current problems in Native American country without first understanding the devastating effects Europeans have had on Native Americans and their culture.

The history of the Native Americans after the arrival of the Europeans is a history of warfare and dispossession. The 400 year war between Native Americans and White settlers spanned from colonial times through the nineteenth century (Waldman & Braun, 1985; Pevar, 1992). As a result of these conflicts, the lives of many great individuals were lost, millions of acres of land were confiscated, tribes were disbanded or removed from their ancestral homelands, and Native American children were forcibly removed from their families.

For the early Europeans, the Native Americans became the villains. To many, they were viewed as violent, a menace to peaceful settlers, and an obstruction to manifest destiny, therefore, to be removed by whatever means necessary. Although there were times in which governmental policies sought to protect their interests from scofflaws, according to Pevar (1992), "there has never been a consistent federal Indian policy" (p. 2). In fact, there have been six distinct policies, five of which have exacted a devastating toll on Native Americans, contributing to the social, political, physical, and mental health problems that indigenous peoples confront today.

The first policy was annihilation. As devastating as war and forced relocation was to Native American peoples, even more debilitating and deadly were the spread of European diseases. Beginning early in the seventeenth century, Whites purposely exposed indigenous peoples to infectious diseases for which they had no natural immunity. For instance, by passing out smallpox-infected blankets, the Mandan of upper Mississippi were reduced from a population of 1,600 to 131 (Waldman & Braun, 1985). Besides smallpox, Native Americans lacked resistance to chicken pox, measles, scarlet fever, typhoid, typhus, influenza, tuberculosis, cholera, diphtheria, and venereal infections. It is estimated that infectious diseases alone accounted for a 25 to 50 percent loss of tribal life. In addition, the wholesale slaughter of Native American peoples by White raiding parties was an acceptable practice. Many times, "respectable" community members would gather after church to kill neighboring tribes (Kirby, 1991). Between infectious diseases and the unbridled slaughter of Native American peoples, European contact had a shattering effect not only on indigenous populations but also on their faith and religion.

The second policy was the forced removal of tribes from their ancestral homelands. Well known as an "Indian fighter" ("Sharp Knife" to the Native Americans), Andrew Jackson had been elected as president of the United States in 1830. Believing tensions between the Native Americans and land-hungry White Europeans could be settled by relocating eastern tribes to a designated Indian Territory west of the Mississippi River, Jackson signed the Indian Removal Act (Pevar, 1992). Outraged, the Cherokees resisted attempts to be removed from their ancestral lands by fighting and winning their case before the Supreme Court, unfortunately without avail. Overriding the court's decision, Jackson ordered the army to evict the Cherokees, Choctaws, Creeks, Chickasaws, and Seminoles, with particular attention to the Cherokees who were to be rounded up in the winter of 1832. At a cruel pace, the soldiers marched Cherokee men, women, and children during the rain and then freezing snow and ice. Starvation was rampant because of inadequate food rations, and disease and bandits were uncontrolled. During the 800-mile march, 4,000 died. The Cherokees were neither given the opportunity to grieve for their dead nor to bury them (Thornton, 1987).

The Treaty of Payne's Landing was also passed in 1832. This treaty targeted the Seminoles who had given refuge to escaped slaves. The Treaty of Payne's Landing required all Seminoles with African American ancestry to be treated as runaway slaves and returned to their masters. This meant the disintegration of many Seminole families (Waldman & Braun, 1985; Canby, 1998).

Between 1887 and 1934, the third policy of assimilation was initiated. This process required Native Americans to integrate into White society by breaking up tribal governments and abolishing reservations (Canby, 1998). To accomplish this, Congress passed the Dawes Act in 1887, also known as the General Allotment Act. This divided communally held tribal lands into separate 160-acre land parcels for farming, while selling off the "surplus" lands to White farmers at bargain prices. It was believed that by placing Whites on Native American lands, it would break up tribal relationships and they would learn to live using White ways (Waldman & Braun, 1985). Unfortunately, many of the parcels were unfit for farming and thousands of desperately poor Native Americans sold their lands to White farmers or lost them to foreclosures when they were unable to pay state real estate taxes. By the time the allotment system was abolished, almost two thirds of Native American lands had been lost (Canby, 1998). During these times of assimilation, although Congress conferred citizenship on American-born Native Americans (1924), it was the Fourteenth Amendment of the Constitution that made them citizens of the state in which they resided. Whereas Native Americans are now entitled to vote in every state in the Union, in New Mexico, it was not until 1962 when this issue was finally settled in the courts (Canby, 1998).

Although other legislation during this time encouraged Native Americans to cut their traditionally long hair and outlawed the Sun Dances of the Plains Indians, it was the boarding schools that had the most devastating effect. This, according to Adams (1997), was where the last Native American war was fought—in the schools and dormitories of the government schools. In 1875, Lieutenant Richard Pratt, a former fighter of Native Americans, founded the original Indian School in Carlisle, Pennsylvania. Eventually, twenty-six off-reservation schools spanning fifteen states would be established. Lieutenant Pratt relocated Native American children, ages 5 to 14, from the plains reservations to the Carlisle Indian School. Cutting their hair, exchanging their traditional clothes for military uniforms, assigning them Christian names, relentlessly attacking Native American religious beliefs and indoctrinating them in Christianity, Pratt began a program designed to reconstruct the psychological and cultural identities of these children (Adams, 1997). "In fear they would return to the blanket" (McCullough, 1992), rather than allow the children to return home during the summer months, many were farmed out to middle-class White families to work as domestics and hired hands. Some of the children would not return home for periods of five to eight years, whereas others would die from depression, feelings of abandonment, and disease (Cooper, 1999). During the 1930s to 1940s, almost half the Native American children attending school would do so in the Bureau of Indian Affairs (BIA) or mission school systems. And sadly, throughout these times, many of the children endured humiliating punishments, along with physical, sexual, and emotional abuse (Brookings Institute, 1971; Horejsi, Craig, & Pablo, 1992). According to McGoldrick, Giordiano, and Pearce (1996), the "boarding school system was one of the most ruthless and inhumane methods of assimilation available to the U.S. government" (p. 50).

As they entered the twentieth century, Native Americans continued to be exposed to federal policies that sought to eliminate tribal landholding and political organizations, suppress community customs, and terminate trust status. From 1953 to 1968, the fourth and fifth policies came into effect: termination and relocation. With regard to termination, Congress decided to abdicate its trust responsibilities to Native Americans by abolishing "their status as wards of the United States" (Canby, 1998, p. 25), in essence, abandoning all the treaties signed by the federal government and legislating them out of existence. Federal services promised by treaty agreement were withdrawn and federal protection of Native American lands was removed.

At the same time, in response to the high unemployment rate on reservations, the BIA established the Voluntary Relocation Program, offering reservation-based Native Americans relocation, as well as assistance in finding employment in large metropolitan cities such as Los Angeles, San Francisco, New York City. Although some were successful in securing lasting employment, many indigenous peoples were unprepared for the sweeping differences they encountered. Many had relocated without marketable job skills and without the family and tribal support to which they were accustomed. Consequently, many of the families experienced the usual problems of the urban poor with the added trauma of dislocation (Canby, 1998).

The sixth and current policy is self-determination. By the late 1960s it became evident that the termination and relocation policies had been largely unsuccessful, as were the assimilation efforts. In 1968, Congress passed the Indian Civil Rights Act, which granted Native Americans the "privileges" of the Bill of Rights, which until this time had been denied them. Along with other acts passed by Congress, there were moves to restore tribal sovereignty, encourage cultural renewal, and develop reservation resources and self-sufficiency, while maintaining the ongoing special trust relationship between the U.S. government and tribes (Canby, 1998). This act also prohibited states from acquiring any authority over Native American reservations without the consent of the tribe and extended to the tribes many of the taxation rights enjoyed by the states (Pevar, 1992).

As part of this movement, the Freedom of Religion Act (1978) was passed, stating that Native American religion was now protected by the First Amendment of the Constitution, while in that same year the Indian Child Welfare Act was passed in order to remedy the shameful "wholesale removal of reservation Indian children by state welfare and state courts" (Pevar, 1992, p. 296). According to the Honorable William Thorne, Jr., at the time this act was passed, "25 to 35% of all Indian children were raised at some time by non-Indians in homes and institutions" (as cited in Southern California Indian Center, 1991, p. 1).

Another piece of legislation passed during this time was the Self-Determination and Education Act (1975). Until 1975, the BIA, directed by non–Native Americans, was the only agency in the world that administered a conquered people (Richardson, 1981). With the advent of the Self-Determination and Education Act, for the first time in history, American indigenous peoples were given the right to oversee and direct their own health care agencies and school systems.

Contemporary Historical Issues

There are three things that make Native Americans different from other ethnic minority peoples. First, tribes are sovereign nations within the boundaries of the United States (Canby, 1998). This means that, like Canada, Japan, India, and so on, each tribe has power and authority over the people who reside within its tribal lands. Consequently, like any other country, tribes can determine citizenship requirements, create their own laws, establish their own courts and legal system, and so on. Second, federally recognized tribes enjoy a government-to-government relationship with the federal government. Just after the Revolutionary War, in 1787, the U.S. Congress ratified the Northwest Ordinance, recognizing Native American tribes as having the same status as a foreign country and declaring, "The utmost good faith shall never be taken from them without their consent" (as cited in Pevar, 1992, p. 3). And third, via treaty agreements, tribes surrendered lands and were relocated onto reservations with the understanding that they would be provided housing, health care, educational opportunities for their children, and food subsidies.

Who Is a Native American?

In general, "Indianness" is a confusing concept to understand, and an even more divisive issue in Native American country. For the purpose of the U.S. Census Bureau, every person who claims to be Native American is listed as one, whereas in other situations an individual is required to prove Indianness by blood quantum via a Certificate of Indian Blood (CIB). A person may qualify as Native American for educational benefits but be ineligible for health care services.

For federal purposes, an individual must be a member of a federally recognized tribe to be regarded as a Native American person. Generally this means that the individual must be at least one-quarter blood quantum to be considered Native American, although a full-blooded Native American with grandparents from eight different tribes may be considered a non–Native American (U.S. Department of the Interior, Bureau of Indian Affairs, 1991) because she or he fails to meet the one-quarter minimum requirements by federal law. This is further complicated because Cherokees need only show that they are a descendant of an Allotment Act awardee or be 1/2004 Cherokee in order to be considered a "card carrying Indian"; whereas in other tribes an individual must be at least 50 percent of that tribal group to be considered a member.

Although the Census Bureau and federal regulations define "Indianness," there are three other criteria used to identify who is a Native American. The first, and most important, is political status. In short, the question is, "Are you an enrolled member of a particular tribal group?" It is citizenship within the tribe that gives an individual voting powers within the tribe, the right to directly petition the U.S. government on behalf of the tribe, and the right to secure tribal resources, if any are available. The second criterion is culture. The question here is, "Have you been raised in and/or do you understand the cultural norms and mores of the tribe?" And third, biology: "Are you a biological decedent of a given tribe?" Because of the high rate of intermarriage of Native Americans to non–Native Americans (Eschbach, 1995), the second and third criteria have taken on somewhat less importance.

Contemporary Health Issues in Native American Country

Most Native Americans believe that "what happens to the body reflects what is happening in the mind and spirit" (Mehl-Madrona, 1997, p. 16). This means that the mind, body, and spirit are interwoven—no one part is greater than another. It also means that an individual happens in a context and is transformed and impacted by both her or his environment and the events of his or her daily life. The history discussed thus far is an attempt to place contemporary health problems in a context, in short, to demonstrate how everything is intertwined. Although separated into individual subsections to facilitate a clearer understanding, remember everything discussed is intertwined with the historical experiences of tribal peoples—no one is greater than another.

Spirituality.   It is difficult to discuss the health issues confronting Native American communities without first understanding the time-honored importance of spirituality in the daily lives of indigenous peoples. According to Adams (1997), "traditional Indian cultures were so thoroughly infused with the spiritual that Native languages generally had no single word to denote the concept of religion" (p. 165). In the daily lives of indigenous peoples, they were in constant contact with the Creator, with dreams and special ceremonies providing them a way to communicate directly with the spirits. Although tribal groups differed in how ceremonies were conducted, the use of these rituals allowed them to gain power, knowledge, and to master the lifespan transitions fluidly with the help of family, community, and spiritual guidance.

But this changed when the children were rounded up and placed in mission and boarding schools. Through the use of daily lessons and moral instructions, the children were under systematic attack to be Christianized; they were taught the "evils" of being Native American and the virtues of being European/American. Because these children were so young, many were not yet privy to the nuances of tribal customs and traditions, which made them much easier to indoctrinate. Consequently, some students became confused by this constant proselytizing, whereas others became rapt Christians, denying their cultural traditions and losing their "Indianness."

Another major assault to indigenous people's spirituality was the misrepresentation and theft of sacred ceremonies. Traditionally, most religious ceremonies were open to nontribal members, including non–Native Americans. Abusing the spiritual gifts given them, some non–Native Americans took photos, audiotaped, or wrote about the sacred rituals or traditions in which they had been invited to partake. To protect themselves from further theft, traditional Native American peoples began excluding nonmembers from certain ceremonies; however, later, even Native Americans were not privy to some of their own ceremonies. Consequently, this loss of openness diminished the fluidity that had once been an integral part of their daily lives.

Today, for many, Native American traditional practices remain relatively intact, whereas for others, spirituality and Christianity are intricately interwoven. For many more, Native American practices have been completely surrendered. For those retaining traditional spiritual practices, it has lost much of the fluidity it once knew. Native Americans have been able to find the uniqueness in all religions, which makes it easier to incorporate Christian spiritual beliefs into their own. Even though many may separate the trinity of body, mind, and spirit, they find that this leads not only to a new way of viewing religion but also to a new way of life. Within recent years, there has been a renaissance in Native American spirituality as many attempt to reclaim and recapture the wisdom of past generations.

Physical Health.   With the inception of Indian Health Services (IHS) in 1955, significant gains have been made in the health status of Native Americans, although they still lag behind the general U.S. population. In part, this is because many Native Americans live in isolated communities and reservation areas where the roads are poor and the distances from services are great. It is also because of unsafe water conditions, poor nutrition, and poor waste disposal and sanitation, which create a high incidence of disease and illness. Exacerbating these situations is the lack of medical professionals available to provide basic medical, dental, or mental health services to Native communities.

During 1994 to 1996, the life expectancy for Native Americans was 71.1 years, whereas that of all U.S. races was 75.8 years, a difference of 4.7 years. The infant mortality rate was 9.3 per 100,000, which is 22 percent higher than that of the U.S. general population, whereas the birthrate among Native Americans was 1.6 times that of all U.S. races (U.S. Department of Health and Human Services (DHHS), 2000).

According to the U.S. Department of Health and Human Services (2000), the major causes of illness and death among Native Americans are heart disease, alcoholism, tuberculosis, diabetes, accidents, suicides, and homicide. When compared to the death rate among all U.S. races it was found that Native Americans die from heart disease at a rate 13 percent higher; from tuberculosis 533 percent more often, and from alcoholism 627 percent more often. Respectively, the rates for diabetes, accidents, suicide, and homicide were 249 percent, 204 percent, 72 percent, and 63 percent higher than the U.S. general population (U.S. DHHS, 2000).

The high rate of alcohol use and abuse among Native Americans contributes strongly to the high rate of suicides, homicides, injuries (intentional and unintentional), deaths, and domestic violence (U.S. DHHS, 2000). The high rate of alcohol use among Native American women contributes to a higher rate of fetal alcohol syndrome (FAS). The rate of FAS is 2.97 percent per 1000 compared to 0.6 percent for African Americans, 0.09 percent for whites, 0.08 percent for Hispanics, and 0.03 percent for Asian Americans (Chavez, Cordero, & Becarra, 1988).

Poverty. "American Indians and Alaskan Natives are the most impoverished ethnic minority group in the United States" (U.S. DHHS, 2001, p. 88). Although the conditions vary, most live in poverty relative to all other U.S. races. Approximately 40 percent of Native Americans reside on reservations with the majority living in urban areas. Although Native Americans comprise less than 1 percent of the U.S. population, they constitute 8 percent of the homeless people, and an estimated 4 percent are incarcerated (U.S. DHHS, 2001). Whether in reservation or urban settings, most Native Americans are poor, live in substandard housing, are underemployed and undereducated, and many receive government subsidies. According to the U.S. Bureau of the Census (1995), in 1989 Native Americans had a median household income of $19,897 as compared to $30,056 for all U.S. races. Although the Native American poverty rate may have decreased slightly by the year 2000, the median household income would have had to increase by almost 400 percent for Native Americans to be living at a rate near that of all other ethnic groups in the United States.

Educational Achievement. The rate of academic achievement is below the national average. Though Native American children enter school on par with or beyond their non-Native peers, there is a marked decline in academic performance between the fourth and seventh grades (Barlow & Walkup, 1998), which is attributed to differences in cognitive and teaching styles.

For Native Americans 25 years or older, 65.3 percent, as compared to 75.2 percent for all races, have graduated from high school, but in areas such as Tucson, Navajo, and Phoenix, the rate is less than 60 percent (U.S. DHHS, 2000). Native Americans securing postsecondary education are significantly less than the national averages for all races. According to the 1990 Census, only 8.9 percent of the Native American population had a bachelor's degree or higher, compared to 20.3 percent for all races.

Mental Health and Disorders. Children and adolescents have fairly similar rates of disorders for general psychiatric problems as non-Native youth (17 percent); the five most common disorders are attention deficit/hyperactivity, major depression, alcohol dependence/abuse, marijuana dependence, and other substance dependence/abuse (U.S. DHHS, 2000). According to Manson, Shore, and Bloom (1985), for the adult population, almost 70 percent of those sampled in a 20-year study had experienced a mental health problem in their lifetime, whereas 30 percent were experiencing problems at the time of the follow-up. Among the elderly, more than 30 percent seeking outpatient services at IHS do so for complaints of depression, compared to 9 percent to 31 percent of non-Natives (Berkman et al., 1986).

The most prevalent mental health issues are alcohol abuse and suicide. The rate of death because of alcohol in 1995 for the IHS service area was 48.7 percent, which is seven times greater than that for all U.S. races. With regard to suicide, the rate in the same year was 19.3 percent as compared to 11.2 percent for other U.S. races. This is 72 percent greater than the overall U.S. population (U.S. DHHS, 2000). According to the Bureau of Statistics the rate of suicide among Alaskan Native males is the highest in the world.

Service-Related Issues. The previous statistics clearly speak to the overwhelming need for mental health services in the Native American community. IHS, which provides at least 50 percent of the medical and mental health services that Native Americans receive, reported that as of fiscal year 2000, in the continental United States, there were only 21 psychiatrists and 63 psychologists to serve American Indians (U.S. DHHS, 2000). As IHS had a reported user population of approximately 1,300,000 Native Americans, this amounts to a combined psychologist and psychiatrist clinician-to-patient ratio of 1 to 15,000 (U.S. DHHS, 1990).

Treatment Approaches

Although it may seem that specific counseling approaches should be given to guide non-Natives working with Native American clients, this would not be advisable because the within-group difference needs to be taken into account when working with such a diverse clientele. Because of the aforementioned issues of differing levels of trauma, acculturation, and assimilation, strategies and approaches that may be viable for one Native American individual might not be appropriate for another (Choney, Berryhill-Paapke, & Robbins, 1995). Thus, presenting a list of concrete values, strategies, techniques, and practical suggestions may lead clinicians to gain a set of stereotypical notions about how to counsel all Native Americans.

It would be unrealistic for Native Americans to relinquish the positive aspects of Western culture, just as it would be ridiculous to expect a total return to traditional/indigenous healing. Long before it was either appreciated or fashionable, medicine people/healers recognized that certain diseases or illnesses were better treated with the "White man's medicine," whereas others responded best to Native approaches. In 1996, the importance of integrating these different styles of medicine was recognized in a Native American health care meeting in Santa Fe, New Mexico, when a conference committee concluded that traditional practices can compliment present Western medicine and recommended that the two should be integrated "to better serve Native community health needs" (Native American Educational Services, 1996, p. 5). Therefore, the recommendations presented here attempt to integrate Western and indigenous healing techniques in order to address the multidimensional mental health needs of Native American peoples.

In 1997 and 1998, at the Post-Colonial Conference in Albuquerque, New Mexico, four Native American treatment models were presented: the Red Road, Corn Jar, First Nations, and Postcolonial Models. Although these constructs vary on minor points, they share the same basic principles, which can be divided into three overlapping groups. The first premise is related to the therapist as a cultural being.

In short, the assertion here is that therapists cannot give away what they do not have. As with all ethnic groups, in order for therapists to successfully work with Native Americans, they need to have an authentic understanding of themselves. This first premise involves knowing themselves historically, culturally, and emotionally, and requires examining their own biases, prejudices, and stereotypes, as well as their predecessors' role, if any, in the trauma suffered by Native Americans. Second, the therapist should have an emic knowledge of the community in which he or she has chosen to work, which requires living genuinely within the Native American community. This might include being able to talk with the tribal chair, attending religious ceremonies, and being able to collaboratively work with respected community members, such as a community health representative, medicine people, and community-based school boards. Third, therapists must have acquired a thorough knowledge and skill base within a broad arena of philosophical perspectives so that they can draw from culturally relevant theoretical orientations that will best meet the unique needs of this clientele. Thus, Native American clients must be approached using a biopsychosocial method in order to treat their multifaceted issues within a context. Finally, it is important that therapists understand that it is not the client's job to teach them about the cultural or historical issues affecting tribal members.

With regard to the therapeutic relationship, it is important for therapists to understand that in many, if not most, traditional Native American communities, healing is a spiritual journey, with each person in the relationship having well-defined roles and responsibilities. Most medicine people are cognizant that they play a minor role in the client's healing because the responsibility rests with the client. The healer's job is to listen carefully and to come to understand the client's concerns in a context. These qualities are what many, if not most, Native Americans are seeking in a therapist. This also means that the therapist is able to interact with cultural intentionality, a clear understanding of multiple therapeutic actions (Ivey, D'Andrea, Ivey, & Simek-Morgan, 2002).

Cultural intentionality also implies that the therapist is comfortable with the cultural use of silence; aware of and capable of accurately interpreting nonverbal communication, including cultural taboos; and is able to mirror that understanding in the therapeutic relationship. Intrinsically interwoven in this understanding are the issues of acculturation and assimilation that were discussed earlier in the chapter. It should be further noted that therapeutic goals are mutually driven or determined and not ultimately set by the therapist.

Regarding treatment approaches, the therapist needs to be able to offer holistic approaches that integrate indigenous and Western healing techniques (see Table 5.1). Because the body, mind, and spirit of the client have to be healed in order to effect wellness, it is necessary that the core component in therapy involve a medicine person at each juncture. This is best accomplished by maintaining a medicine person on staff who collaborates with and has an equal say in the treatment direction. This also means that, on occasion, treatment or therapeutic interventions are conducted outside the fifty-minute hour, as well as outside the facility.

TABLE 5.1   A Summary of Holistic Treatment

Therapist	Therapeutic Relationship	Treatment Approaches
Know thyself	Consensus treatment agreements	Holistic approaches
Historical/cultural self-understanding	Well-defined roles	Integrative
Understanding of how ancestors impacted NA history	Cultural intentionality	Core approaches based on NA traditional practices
Emic understanding of the history and culture of the tribal groups	Biopsychosocial context	A medicine person maintained on staff
Broad skills and knowledge base	Ability to interpret nonverbal communication	
	Client-centered goals	
	Ability to understand cultural use of silence	
	Awareness of assimilation and acculturation issues	

Note: NA = Native American

Discussion

Though there has been an increase in multiculturally based psychology and counseling education (Axelson, 1998; D'Andrea, Daniels & Heck, 1991; Sue, Arredondo, & McDavis, 1992; Ponterotto, Casas, Suzuki, & Alexander, 1995), it is the contention of the authors that counseling and psychology theory and practice have failed to meet the needs of Native Americans. This likely relates to mental health services being based primarily in Western ideology and theory, which are grounded in an individualistic worldview that contrasts sharply with that of Native Americans. Additionally, this theoretical base has historically been insensitive to the culture and experiences of indigenous peoples and has viewed them from a place of pathology.

Nevertheless, we believe that Western medicine is beginning to appreciate and understand the interconnectiveness between the mind, body, and spirit. According to Mehl-Madrona (1997), "everything in our lives, including disease, is simultaneously a physical, emotional, social, and spiritual phenomenon" (p. 18). This perspective is clearly evident in the Native American community.

Conclusion

We end with a story that we believe best demonstrates how traditional and Western healing practices can be fully integrated:

A 5-year-old Native American child who was sexually abused by her uncle was brought into the clinic by her parents. They reported that even though the uncle was in jail and awaiting trial, the child was becoming increasingly more depressed and less responsive to her environment. Initially, the child was seen twice a week for three weeks but continued to deteriorate despite our best treatment efforts. During the case review, it was determined that a healing ceremony was needed if we were to keep the child from being hospitalized.

The family, which included extended family members, gathered around the child for the ceremony, as did the clinical staff. Because the child was fairly unresponsive to the questions of the medicine man, her parents spoke on her behalf. As the medicine man listened carefully to the words and observed the tears of the parents and other family members, and as he asked the therapists to express their concerns, the medicine man mixed various herbs and made different prayers on behalf of the child. After everyone had spoken, he turned to the child and told her a story of how a coyote had violated the trust of his relatives in the animal world. Then, because he is a man, and, therefore, represents all men (brothers, sons, fathers, uncles, and grandfathers) the medicine man apologized for what a man, her uncle, had done to her. As he apologized, he cried and told her how sorry he (representing the uncle) was for having violated her trust, and then asked her for her forgiveness. As the ceremony drew to a close, he blessed her and told her, "Leave the pain here with the fire, you are well." With this, the child was taken home and returned the next day to the therapeutic playroom where she began to actively work out the pain of her abuse.

DISCUSSION QUESTIONS

1. In what ways might historical events continue to impact Native American communities today?

2. What unique challenges confront non-Native counselors who work with Native American clients?

3. Compare and contrast the primary differences in working with contemporary urban Native Americans as opposed to working with reservation-based Native Americans.

4. Why might a strong client-centered approach not work with some Native Americans?

5. Why would it be important for the non-Native clinician to gain an emic knowledge of the community in which he or she is working, even if he or she has worked with Native Americans elsewhere?

REFERENCES

Adams, D. W. (1997). *Education for extinction: American Indians and the boarding school experience, 1875–1928.* Lawrence: University Press of Kansas.

Axelson, J. (1998). *Counseling and development in a multicultural society* (3rd ed.). Pacific Grove, CA: Brooks/Cole.

Barlow, A., & Walkup, J. T. (1998). Developing mental health service for Native American children. *Child and Adolescent Psychiatry Clinic of North American, 7,* 555–577.

Berkman, L. F., Berkman, C. S., Kasl, S., Freeman, D. H., Jr., Leo, L., Ostfeld, A. M., Cornoni-Huntley, J., & Brody, J. A. (1986). Depressive symptoms in relation to physical health and functioning in the elderly. *American Journal of Epidemiology, 124,* 372–388.

Brookings Institute. (1971). *The problem of Indian administration.* Institute for Government Research. New York: Johnson Reprint.

Canby, W. C., Jr. (1998). *American Indian law in a nutshell* (3rd ed.). St. Paul, MN: West Group.

Chavez, G. F., Cordero, J. F., & Becarra, J. E. (1988). Leading major congenital malformations among minority groups in the United States, 1981–1986. *Morbidity and Mortality Weekly Reports,* Centers of Disease Control and Prevention Surveillance Summary, 37, 17–24.

Choney, S. K., Berryhill-Paapke, E., & Robbins, R. R. (1995). The acculturation of American Indians: Developing frameworks for research and practice. In J. G. Ponterotto, J. M Casas, L. A. Sukuki, & C. M. Alexander (Eds.), *Handbook of multicultural counseling.* (pp. 73–92). Thousand Oaks, CA: Sage.

Cooper, M. L. (1999). *Indian school: Teaching the White man's way.* New York: Houghton Mifflin.

D'Andrea, M., Daniels, J., & Heck, R. (1991). Evaluating the impact of multicultural counseling training. *Journal of Counseling and Development, 70,* 143–150.

Eschbach, K. (1995). The enduring and vanishing American Indian: American Indian population growth and intermarriage in 1990. *Ethnic and Racial Studies, 18,* 89–108.

Fleming, C. M. (1992). American Indians and Alaskan Natives: Changing Societies Past and Present. In M. A. Orlandi, R. Weston, & L. G. Epstein (Eds.), *Cultural competence for evaluators: A guide for alcohol and other drug abuse prevention practitioners working with ethnic/racial communities. (OSAP cultural competence series 1* (pp. 147–171). Rockville, MD: U.S. Department of Health and Human Services.

Horejsi, C., Craig, B. H. R., & Pablo, J. (1992). Reactions by Native American parents to child protections agencies: Cultural and community factors. *Child Welfare, 71,* 329–342.

Ivey, A. E., D'Andrea, M., Ivey, M. B., & Simek-Morgan, L. (2002). *Counseling and psychotherapy: A multicultural perspective* (5th ed.). Boston: Allyn & Bacon.

Kirby, K. (Producer). (1991). *Time machine: Savagery and the American Indian: "Wilderness."* London, England: BBC-TV Productions.

Manson, S. M., Shore, J. H., & Bloom, J. D. (1985). The depressive experience in American Indian communities: A challenge for psychiatric theory and diagnosis. In A. Kleinman & B. Good (Eds.), *Culture and depression* (pp. 331–368). Berkeley: University of California Press.

McCullough, D. (Producer). (1992). *The American experience: In the White man's image.* New York: WNET.

McGoldrick, M., Giordiano, J., & Pearce, J. (1996). *Ethnicity and family therapy.* New York: Guilford Press.

Mehl-Madrona, L. (1997). *Coyote medicine: Lessons from Native American healing.* New York: Simon & Schuster.

Native American Educational Services. (1996). Native American issues related to health: Paths to healing—Information gathering. Conference of the Native American Educational Services, Santa Fe, NM.

Pevar, S. L. (1992). *The rights of Indians and tribes* (2nd ed.). Carbondale: Southern Illinois University Press.

Ponterotto, J. G., Casas, J. M., Suzuki, L. A., & Alexander, C. M. (Eds.). (1995). *Handbook of multicultural counseling.* Thousand Oaks, CA: Sage.

Richardson, E. H. (1981). Cultural and historical perspectives in counseling American Indians. In D. W. Sue (Ed.), *Counseling the culturally different: Theory and practice* (pp. 216–255). New York: Wiley.

Southern California Indian Center, Indian Child and Family Services. (1991). *The Indian Child Welfare Act of 1978.* Garden Grove, CA: Author.

Sue, D. W., Arredondo, P., & McDavis, R. J. (1992). Multicultural counseling competencies and standards: A call to the profession. *Journal of Counseling and Development, 70,* 477–486.

Thornton, R. (1987). *American Indian holocaust and survival: A population history since 1492.* Norman: University of Oklahoma.

U.S. Bureau of the Census. (1995). Population profile of the United States. In D. W. Sue & D. Sue, *Counseling the culturally different: Theory and practice* (3rd ed.). New York: Wiley.

U.S. Bureau of the Census. (1999). *Statistical abstract of the United States: The national data book.* Washington, DC: Author.

U.S. Department of Health and Human Services. (1990). *Healthy people 2000.* Rockville, MD: Author.

U.S. Department of Health and Human Services. (2001). *Mental Health: Culture, Race, and ethnicity: A supplement to the mental health report of the Surgeon General.* Rockville, MD: Author.

U.S. Department of Health and Human Services, Indian Health Services. (2000). *Regional difference in Indian health 1998–1999.* Rockville, MD: Author.

U.S. Department of the Interior, Bureau of Indian Affairs. (1991). *American Indians today* (3rd. ed.). Washington, DC: U.S. Department of the Interior.

Waldman, C., & Braun, M. (1985). *Atlas of the North American Indian.* New York: Facts on File.

6

Therapeutic Approaches with African American Populations

THOMAS A. PARHAM AND SHERLON BROWN

The African American population nationally represents a community of approximately 33.9 million people and 9 million families (U.S. Bureau of the Census, 2001). Most populate the southern region of the United States (53 percent), with 37 percent in the Northeast and Midwest, and 10 percent in the West. Nearly 80 percent of African Americans earn a high school diploma, and 17 percent attain a bachelor's or graduate degree. Despite these advances in educational achievement when compared to previous census data, African Americans continue to suffer as a people under a veil of poverty, with 22 percent of families being at or below the poverty line of approximately $17,000 per year (U.S. Bureau of the Census, 2001). Poverty rates vary across the lifespan but impact children and older adults more significantly. And despite a growing number (25 percent) of middle-class African Americans with incomes of $50,000 and above, their median income levels continue to represent only 87 percent of what their white counterparts earn.

As a group, African Americans bear a disproportionate burden of health problems according to the U.S. Department of Health and Human Services (DHHS), with diabetes, heart disease, cancer, HIV/AIDS, and infant mortality being high on the affliction list (DHHS, 2000). For a people who represent approximately 12 percent of the U.S. population, they are overrepresented in inner cities and in their health concerns and poverty rates but underrepresented in degree of higher education attainment, middle- and upper-class social status, and employment viability. This is the demographic profile of many U.S. African American citizens who either seek or are exposed to mental health services across the United States.

Within the backdrop of these data, providing mental health and counseling services to African American populations has been a subject of interest in the psychological and counseling literature over the past several decades (White, 1972; Adebimpe, 1981; Jackson, 1983; Atkinson, Morton, & Sue, 1989). Within that body of research and writing have come concerns over therapist/client match (Vontress, 1971), counselor preference (Jackson & Kirshner, 1973; Parham & Helms, 1981), influences of identity development on the therapeutic process (Helms, 1986), and the most effective approaches to take in working with African American populations (Jones, 1980), as well as the need for more social advocacy in addressing perceived dysfunctionality in clients (White & Parham, 1990; Parham, White, & Ajamu, 1999). More recent writings have raised concerns over therapist comfort with issues of race (Carter, 1995), questions of whether proposed interventions are empirically supported (Atkinson, Bui, & Mori, 2001), and how issues of competence need to be considered at a multidimensional level (Sue, 2001). Also discussed are issues of cultural mistrust (Whaley, 2001), the potential for misdiagnosis and mistreatment (Lindsey & Paul, 1989; Neighbors, Jackson, Campbell, & Williams, 1989), and the need to develop more cultural competencies across individual, institutional, and societal domains (Sue, 2001).

Although this body of research and literature has sought to clarify issues in counseling and psychotherapy, less conspicuous in the literature has been much discussion of how to deliver services once clients are in the therapeutic dyad with the service provider. This perspective is particularly important given the professional and ethical mandates to provide competent care. Who are the African American clients being treated? What life experiences color and shape their worldview? What counselor attributes are necessary to facilitate a healthy therapeutic alliance? These and other questions are addressed in this chapter. Therefore, its purpose is to provide some additional insight into exploring therapeutic interventions with African American populations in particular.

The Practice of Therapy

The practice of counseling and psychotherapy does not begin or occur in a vacuum. Rather, counseling and therapy occur in a specific cultural context. By cultural context, we mean to suggest that individual behavior should not be assessed and cannot be understood outside of an analysis of the personal and collective realities each person confronts on a daily basis. In fact, Neville and Mobley (2001) argue that ecological models are a good way of better understanding how life experiences are confounded by systems that influence human behavior. For African-descent people, the social cultural context is framed by a set of issues that challenge the intellectual, emotional, behavioral, and spiritual adaptations they make. These contexts include the struggle against oppression, the development of identity where decisions about cultural retention are balanced against perceptions of opportunity and privileges, and a context where one tries desperately to retain a sense of cultural integrity in a world that fundamentally does not support or affirm one's humanity as an African-descent person (Parham, 1993). Working effectively with African American people requires a sensitivity to and a recognition of these realities, not simply an acknowledgment of the demographic variables described earlier in this text.

The need to modify one's perspective is underscored by Franklin's (1999) analysis of the *Invisibility Syndrome.* Franklin, like others before him (Ellison, 1947;

Ani, 1994) points out that within the life space of African Americans are chronic confrontations with racist, dehumanizing experiences he characterizes as micro-agressions. Consequently, the willingness to seek counseling services must be understood in the context that the psychic abrasions African-descent people seek to heal are not simply issues of depression, stress, careers, relationships, and so on. Rather, these and other issues are compounded by the devastating effects of social oppression and the need to navigate the pathways to productivity and success without losing their sanity in the process (Parham, White, & Ajamu, 1999).

The necessity for counselors to help clients wade through the seas of micro-agressions is further reinforced by Utsey, Bolden, and Brown (2001) in their model of liberation psychology. Using the work of Algerian psychiatrist Frantz Fanon, Utsey et al. remind us that theories (and by extension therapists) that ignore the role of an oppressive social structure tend to blame the victim for their own oppression as well as underestimate the client's power to transform the forces responsible for their personal and collective misery. Clearly then, the practice of therapy with African American people must both acknowledge and address this reality.

Future Directions in Counseling African Americans

The disciplines of psychology and counseling continue to expand their level of sensitivity in working with culturally different populations in general and African Americans in particular. However, it is important that practitioners of this newfound sensitivity not get stuck in a time warp by assuming that personal compassion or heightened sensitivity combined with outdated or inappropriate methods and constructs are a recipe for therapeutic success. As such, we would contend that any efforts that hope to be successful in working with African American people must address five critical criteria. These include the need to delineate worldview assumptions, the need to clarify definitions of mental health for African-descent people, the mandate to extend culture beyond skin color and demographics, the need to define and describe the role of the healer, and the need to delineate any specific techniques that can be used in working in the counseling and therapy context.

Delineation of Worldview Assumptions

Among the assumptions that are important for working with African American people is a recognition of the construct of *spiritness*. In the African tradition, there is a belief that whatever is in the first place is spirit. This statement suggests that there is a spiritual essence that permeates everything that lives and exists in the universe. Spiritness is the energy, life force, or power that is both the inner essence and the outer envelope of human beingness (Nobles, 1998). As energy, divine spirit becomes human spirit as we recognize the connectiveness between individuals and the creative force in the universe. Thus, the worldview of African-descent people incorporates a spiritual reality, where the manifestations of spiritness are the essence of one's humanity and the basis of existence, and the source of that spirit energy is divine (Grills, 2002).

A second assumption relates to the notion of *inner connectedness* by suggesting that there is an interrelationship between all things that exist on the planet. In the African tradition, this is represented by the notion of *consubstantiation*, meaning that elements of the universe are of the same substance. Nobles (1998) helps to crystallize this notion of cultural unity by teaching us that African American retentions of African culture do exist and thrive in our communities. The anthropocentric ontology (as he describes it) was a complete unity that nothing could destroy or dissipate. Everything was functionally connected and interconnected to everything else in the universe. The Creator is seen as the originator and sustainer of humankind. The spirits explained man's destiny. Human beings are the center of the ontology (an orientation to reality with a belief about what the essential nature of reality is), with animals, plants, and natural phenomena constituting the environment in which man and woman live (p. 50).

The third worldview assumption relates to the notion of *collectivity* and the idea that the collective rather than the individual is the most salient element of existence. In life, individuals do not exist alone but rather exist as part of a larger social network. Recognition is also given to the belief that each person owes his or her existence to other members of the "tribe," or kinship unit (Mbiti, 1970). Unlike Western-oriented systems, African-centered philosophical beliefs do not place a heavy emphasis on individuals. Rather, only in terms of others does one come to know and understand one's own beingness. Thus, the Ashanti proverb, "I am because we are; and because we are, therefore I am," holds a particular salience for African-descent people because it reinforces the notion of collective survival.

A fourth assumption relates to the notion of *self-knowledge*. For African-descent people, self-knowledge is the key to mental health. This realization is not simply a focus on how one thinks, feels, or behaves but rather how one comes to know *who* one is. Humanity can only be understood in the context of an inner relationship between each individual and the divine force in the universe. Fundamentally then, it is believed that people possess a "spiritual anatomy" that seeks out opportunities for growth and transformation through the exercise of morally grounded relations with others. "Who one is" is also a question of identity, where people come to recognize that the answer is always a consolidation of individual valuations and the sociocultural context in which that self is nurtured and supported (Parham, 2002). Thus, clinicians need to recognize the fact that everything an individual needs to be successful and to confront life's challenges is already within the individual him- or herself. Consequently, the task of counselors and therapists is to assist each individual in understanding that he or she is a seed of divinely inspired possibility, which when nurtured in its proper context, can and will grow into the fullest expression of all one is supposed to become. Therapists and counselors must help clients analyze those factors in their lives that both contaminate their growth and contribute to stagnation.

Clarifying Definitions of Mental Health for African-Descent People

The effectiveness with which African-descent people have been treated in the mental health system historically has left a lot to be desired. Ironically, African Americans represent a population that has been traumatized by the mental health system as much as it has been helped by it (Gary & Weaver, 1991). However, despite the negative history that exists, the mental health system generally and the professions of counseling and psychology specifically are struggling to be more sensitive with regard to treatment approaches for African American populations. However, it is our belief that this task will be much more daunting to the degree that clinicians who treat African American people have difficulty understanding the dynamics of mental health and mental illness as they relate to this population. Further, it is our belief that as therapists, counselors, and clinicians seek to assist clients who are in distress, and help them to heal and otherwise return to a normal state of mental health, they are at a decided disadvantage. You can not help an individual to achieve a level of mental health if you have no idea about what constitutes mental health for that people or that person (Parham, 2002).

Historically, epidemiologic community surveys were used as a barometer of the prevalence of mental illness in the general population and among African Americans as well. These surveys were administered to community residents and sought to screen for psychiatric symptoms and other dysfunctional behaviors (Gary & Weaver, 1991). When combined with the incidence and prevalence data from hospital and mental institution admission rates, these methods were thought to provide useful data on understanding mental health and mental illness. Unfortunately, inferring "mental health" from an absence of mental illness seems like a questionable leap or faith.

Despite this drawback, Gary and Weaver (1991) remind us that these mental health data were informative in documenting the types of institutions used by African American people, the types of diagnoses African Americans received, a comparison between African Americans and other groups, and the demographic profile of those African Americans who received psychiatric care. This point is born out in analyzing the most recent psychiatric trends with African Americans. Zhang and Snowden (1999) have found that African Americans are less likely to be diagnosed with major depression, dysthymia, obsessive compulsive disorders, antisocial personalities, and eating disorders. However, they also found that African Americans had a higher incidence of phobias and somatization complaints when compared to other ethnic groups.

Beyond the consideration of traditional markers of mental illness, attention must also be given to the idea that diagnostic labels developed by and for White people may not capture the psychological experiences and reactions of their African American counterparts. Akbar (1991) makes this point very clear in proposing a cultural-specific classification system for African Americans involving the Alien-Self, Anti-Self, Self-Destructive, and Organic Disorders. Akbar further suggests that any classification system must be functional and not simply descriptive. Functionally, his system of mental disorders isolates dangerous conditions, suggests the origins of the condition, and provides suggestions for correcting the condition. Disorders articulated by Akbar and others have also been consolidated into a diagnostic nosology used to classify mental disorders and disease among African Americans (Atwell & Azibo, 1992). Use of these systems are considered to be equally beneficial in understanding the psychological debilitations of African-descent people.

In conceptualizing the notion of mental health for African Americans, it is important to remember that operationalizing the construct cannot simply be reflected in the absence of mental illness or freedom from disease notions. Fundamentally, mental health is a state of personal well-being where each person is able to successfully confront life's challenges using cognitive, emotional, and behavioral attributes in appropriate ways. Although this definition is an important marker in extending the polarity between mental health and mental illness, relegating mental health to the domains of cognition, affect, and behavior may be insufficient when attempting to understand what mental health is for African people.

Grills (2002) again invites us to understand that in the African cultural worldview, the essential ingredient and essence of everything, including humans, is spirit. To have spirit is to be in harmony with life, mind and soul, energy, force, and passion. Thus, human beings not only have spirit; each person is spirit. Nobles (1998) continues by asserting that spirit is the essence of all things human. Thus, one can not conceive of the concept of mental health for African people without a fundamental recognition of the spiritness that permeates everything that is.

Central to the notion of mental health for African people is also the idea that everyone must know and understand their nature. This notion relates to the idea that self-knowledge is the key to mental health. For African-descent people, that profile of a mentally healthy individual, in our view, is characterized as a relationship with and connectedness to the Divine; a sense of self that holistically integrates cognitive, affective, behavioral, and spiritual aspects; a positive sense of identity in one's self and one's people; the value of connectedness to one's community sustained by a healthy sense of interdependence; a reservoir of emotional vitality; the ability to persevere through adversity; and an ability to sustain the attributes of intellectual, emotional, and spiritual growth, self preservation, and regeneration.

Understanding the notion of mental health also requires a recognition that in the African tradition, each of us is endowed with an energy or life force that is a self-healing power (Fu-Kiau, 1991). This self-healing power represents a reservoir of energy that can be drawn upon to assist in managing the challenges and obstacles of daily living. In some respect, this self-healing power is a manifestation of the spiritual energy each individual possesses at a given moment and time. That energy allows us to laugh when we feel good, to cry when we hurt, and to seek the security of one's inner essence when we are in pain. Mental health in this regard represents the mastery over oneself. It is the process of becoming consciously accountable for one's actions, on intellectual, emotional, and behavioral levels (Vanzant, 1996). Effective therapists must be able to assist African American clients with this process.

A final thought on mental health relates to the notion of destiny, and the need to align one's daily activities with that inner passion. In speaking of destiny, we do not mean to suggest that everyone has a predetermined course or direction their lives should take. Rather, we contend that, like the African concept of "Ore-Ire," one's consciousness must be in harmony with one's destiny in order to achieve a level of personal congruence and, ultimately, mental health. Indeed, therapists must be able to assist clients in exploring their passions and helping them explore ways to focus their personal and professional activities that incorporate greater degrees of fulfillment.

Extending the Notion of Culture
Beyond Skin Color and Demographics

Fundamentally, a discipline concerned with being more sensitive to African American clients cannot continue to confuse variables of culture, race, and demographics. First of all, race is a socially derived construction used to classify people into supposed discrete categories of humanness, based upon a phenotypic feature or other ideological assumption. To know that an African American client is of African descent is interesting but tells you nothing about the individual him- or herself. Second, the use of demographic profiles (including race, gender, age, class, etc.) as indicators of diversity, and by extension culture, distorts one's image of culture and reduces its essence to a frequency distribution. Although each of those variables plays a role in the construction of a person's personal identity and reference group orientation, the variables themselves are not the substance of culture.

It is fascinating to see how many mental health practitioners strive to be culturally competent, yet have difficulty defining and operationalizing the notion of culture in and of itself. Culture is typically thought of in ways that are relegated to demographic variables or fashion statements. As clinicians and the agencies they work in seek to be culturally diverse, diversity in many respects is defined by demographic frequency distributions that indicate that a particular agency or center has the staff that represents various percentages of ethnic, racial, gender, or some other variable. Beyond this distorted logic, many clinicians operate as if skin color and phenotype are tantamount to culture as well. In this regard, clinicians believe that the racial differences between a therapist and client create a potential cross-cultural dyad. If one assumes that skin color is synonymous with culture, then this reasoning makes sense. If, however, one recognizes that culture is not related to skin color at all, then this logic needs to be challenged and reframed.

We believe that culture is more than a demographic frequency distribution. Culture is more than food, music, or artwork on the wall. Culture is more than ethnic dress, or holidays celebrated during various times of the year. Culture is a complex constellation of mores, values, customs, and traditions that provide a general design for living and a pattern for interpreting reality (Nobles, 1986). As such, the culture of African people is intertwined with the worldview assumption each makes about the nature of reality, who they are, where they fit into the world, and what their purpose or destiny is. Counselors and therapists alike need to explore these questions with the clients they treat.

Successfully counseling African Americans also requires a recognition that sociological variables that are used to make between group comparisons (i.e., African American vs. Caucasian) are insufficient to understand the complexity of the African American experience. This point is buttressed by a volume of research that has described the notion of psychological identity development of African-descent people (Cross, 1971; Helms, 1986; Parham, 1989; Atwell & Azibo, 1992; Kambon, 1992; Parham, 1993; Carter, 1995). In recognizing that the spirit of African-descent people in America is nurtured within a socially oppressive environment, several authors have sought to explain the identity development phenomena within this context. The models that have emerged in the psychological literature can be consolidated into themes of *psychological nigrescence,* or in some cases, as models relating to *African self-consciousness.* With respect to the nigrescence phenomena, authors such as Cross (1971, 1991), Thomas (1971), and others have developed or refined (Parham, 1989) models to explain identity development where individuals move through a series of distinct psychological stages. In these models, the stages of nigrescence represent a movement from psychological spaces of self-degradation to places of self-pride. In the African self-consciousness theme, authors such as Kambon (1992) have sought to articulate both characteristics that define an individual's identity along a continuum of high versus low African self-consciousness, as well as factors that support and sustain that identity against the force of cultural misorientation. Because the scope of this chapter limits a more thorough discussion of these identity constructs, readers are referred to the citations previously noted and in the reference list.

Although recognizing the existence of these models is important, a more salient issue revolves around understanding the importance of identity and how it functions in the context of everyday life. Parham and Parham (2002) have argued that identity serves many important functions. Identity serves as a buffer against racism and oppression, as well as white supremacy and other cultural and environmentally oppressive phenomena. They also argue that identity serves as an experience of bonding that helps each individual to form attachments with other people who share similar cultural practices and worldviews. This is synonymous with Cross's (1991) notion of reference group orientation. Identity also functions as a means of code-switching, allowing each individual to adapt to a particular environmental circumstance or situation, which may be more or less supportive of their cultural identity. Identity also serves as a bridge in helping individuals to transcend the limits of their cultural reality in breaking down barriers which prevent genuine levels of intimacy and connection across demographic boundaries. Lastly, Parham and Parham argue that identity provides a sense of individual pride and achievement in helping to create for each individual a picture of who one is and how one is connected intergenerationally to a much broader community network.

Within this context, mental health practitioners of psychotherapy will also need to understand the influence of identity development in how it relates to the dynamics of the counseling process. In fact, White and Parham (1990) have suggested that stages of identity can be used to help understand under what circumstances a clinician would have more or less difficulty in breaking down the social distance and establishing rapport with a client of African descent. In utilizing the Cross stages of Nigrescence, their analysis suggest that therapists of African or European American descent will experience varying degrees of success in dissipating the social distance based on a particular stage a client is at when he or she presents for help and assistance to a counseling agency. Their analysis is important in seeking to be more culturally sensitive with African-descent people.

The Role of the "Healer"

Traditional books on counseling and psychotherapy help to define and describe therapists and counselors. Fundamentally, therapists are thought of as individuals who are trained to assist clients in understanding and resolving life's circumstances, which have led them to experience some level of emotional distress (Ohlsen, 1983). Thus, as academicians train new generations of therapists, they are taught to create supportive, nurturing, therapeutic environments while utilizing the skills of listening, interpreting, reflecting, paraphrasing, questioning, summarizing, and goal setting, in short term treatment modalities. In addition, therapists are also trained to conceptualize client dynamics using diagnostic nosologies (i.e., DSM-IV) and theoretical orientations (i.e., client-centered, cognitive-behavioral, Gestalt), which help to provide clarity as to a client's level of psychological debilitation and a road map showing where the therapist needs to go in order to assist in restoring mental health equilibrium.

Although the skills just listed are important tools for trying to achieve positive therapeutic outcomes, the learning and demonstration of those skills sometimes fosters a belief that those techniques are sufficient to achieve the desired therapeutic progress. We contend, as Hilliard (1997) has before us, that therapists are not simply clinicians who demonstrate a broad range of counseling skills. Rather, therapists should be thought of as healers who participate with clients, rather than seeking to direct and control clients. Healers help clients confront their mental, physical, emotional, and spiritual debilitations with the use of cultural-specific attributes and techniques. Among those attributes considered the most important for healers are those less related to the context of therapy itself, and those related to the healer him- or herself. You cannot respect and nurture aspects of other people's humanness without first respecting those characteristics in yourself. In this regard, Hilliard reminds us that the task of a healer involves

- Healing thyself.
- Understanding how their sense of self has been damaged by our confrontations with oppression or privilege.
- Developing their minds, bodies, and spirits so that their consciousness can be appropriately centered on the task at hand.
- Remembering the past by promoting congruence and harmony in ways that a client's consciousness can be properly aligned with his or her passion or destiny.
- Accessing the spirit by serving as a conduit for positive energy flow that is transferred and transformed into specific mental, emotional, and behavioral strategies for helping.
- Subduing pride—becoming vulnerable to new interpretations of reality, rather than believing that their way of intervention is the best way.
- Subduing arrogance—not being deluded about an exaggerated sense of importance based on educational training and acquisition of degrees.
- Aspiring to perfection—seeking maximum congruence between what is preached and what is practiced.
- Being open to all—such that we give real value and meaning to the lessons that we learn from others' words and deeds, particularly the clients we seek to serve.

In essence, we are arguing that healers serve as a conduit through which energy flows. Healers participate with the client, not on the client, in helping to confront their expressed and unexpressed debilitations. Being a healing presence in somebody's life is a tremendous responsibility, and one that must be respected with the sacredness preserved for those who occupy the most special of positions in our communities. Indeed, "healing can be therapeutic, but not all therapy is healing" (Parham, 2002). Given the earlier discussion on spirituality, it is also important to remember that therapeutic healing must include a deliberate focus on the spiritness that permeates the emotional, behavioral, and mental aspects of the self.

Specific Techniques for Counseling and Therapy

The degree to which psychologists, counselors, and other mental health practitioners have become sensitive to the needs of African American clients says a lot about the ability to be an effective therapeutic agent. However, if sensitivity is the only criteria that one uses to measure competence, then the probability that such a skill base will be found wanting increases significantly. Rather, what is required to effectively intervene with African American populations is a level of awareness, knowledge, and skill that allows a clinician to more effectively treat that client.

One model of competency that has shown promise in this regard is that articulated by Parham, White, and Ajamu (1999). In their text entitled *The Psychology of Blacks: An African Centered Perspective,* these authors propose a list of requisite attributes that are framed in the outline of the competency model proposed by Sue, Arredondo, and McDavis (1992), including awareness, knowledge, and skills:

Awareness
- Therapist must be cognizant of his or her own personal biases and assumptions about African-descent people.
- Therapist must be aware of his or her own role as "healer."
- Therapist must be aware of how people and elements in the universe are interconnected.
- Therapist must have a sense of his or her own essence as spirit and be in touch with his or her own spirituality.
- Therapist must have a relationship with the divine force in the universe.
- Therapist must have a vision for African-descent people that embraces the transformative possibilities of the human spirit.

Knowledge
- Knowledge of African psychology and history in ancient Kemetic, historical African, and contemporary African American societies.
- Knowledge of the essential components of an African-centered worldview.
- Knowledge of the limitations of traditional Euro-American psychological perspectives when applied to African-descent people.
- Knowledge of how science has been used as a tool of oppression.
- Knowledge of the limitations of traditional approaches to therapy.
- Knowledge of the characteristics and dynamics of personality development.
  - Dimensions of the soul (Nobles, 1986; Akbar, 1991).
  - Dimensions of African character (i.e., Ma'at).
  - Models of nigrescence (i.e., Thomas, 1971; Parham, 1989; Cross, 1991).
  - Models of African self-consciousness (Kambon, 1992).
- Knowledge of assessment instruments appropriate for use with African-descent adults, youth, and children.
- Knowledge of the ethical principles germane to treating African-descent people.
- Knowledge of what racism and White supremacy are and how individual, institutional, and cultural racism impact the lives of African-descent people.
- Knowledge of the dynamics of family in the African American community.
- Knowledge of communities, institutions, and resources that provide both tangible and intangible support to the African American community.

Skills
- Ability to connect with, bond with, or otherwise establish rapport with African American clients.
- Ability to conduct and participate in rituals.

- Ability to hear both the surface structure and deep structure messages that clients communicate.
- Ability to administer and interpret culturally appropriate assessment instruments.
- Ability to advocate on behalf of clients to social agencies and institutions.
- Ability to utilize theories and constructs in forming diagnostic impressions.

Beyond the model and attributes proposed by Parham et al. (1999), it is also important that those clinicians who are serious about providing effective therapeutic treatment must recognize the need to employ or create critical elements within the therapeutic context. We would argue that these elements are important to the *development* of the relationship between the therapist and the client, the *use* of that relationship in the context of appropriate intervention strategies, and the *management* of that relationship over the course of a client's time in therapy. These elements include:

Relationships.   Therapist must have the ability to develop a relationship with African American clients that is anchored in genuine bonds of empathic connectedness. These relationships must cross lines of race, gender, class, and other variables, and be able to sustain themselves through client or therapist disappointments in each other. Wyatt (2001) reminds us all that no matter how much therapists try to avoid it, race always challenges the therapeutic alliance. Therefore, it must be managed as a component that is potentially central to the process.

Trust (Absence of Misgivings).   Therapists and other clinicians must possess the ability to establish bonds of trust with their African American clients. Given the hesitance to seek therapy and the knowledge of how some therapy has been less than helpful to African Americans historically, trust is a major issue. In this regard, care must be given to avoid externalizing the responsibility for establishing trust as therapist and clients look for the other to demonstrate attitudes and behaviors that are reciprocally acceptable. In contrast, we believe it is important to remember that real trust is not an external circumstance but an internal virtue. Therefore, the most appropriate posture to assume is not "can I trust you?" but rather "can I trust myself enough to take an intellectual, emotional, and behavioral risk with you?" (White & Parham, 1990).

Unconditional Acceptance of a Person's Humanness.   Therapists are no more immune to the evils of social ills (racism, sexism, etc.) than the majority of society. Clearly, they bring their biases and assumptions into counseling and clinical situations. Where African Americans are concerned, society is prone to view them in ways that are not only racist, but also characterize them as less intelligent, emotionally immature, poor family structures, prone to criminal activity, violent, and so on. Certainly, the media contributes heavily to these stereotypes. Therapists must recognize that each of these labels, if and when used, serve to dehumanize

African American clients. Counselors must challenge their own biases about African American people generally, and seek ways to see beyond the social or other demographic labels to a core level of humanity reflected in each individual.

A History of Giving Assistance.   Credibility is an important asset to all mental health professionals because it breeds confidence in their ability to render effective care. Because of the material orientation to reality that characterizes Western society, credibility is assumed to exist because of the attainment of degrees, licenses, and certifications by mental health professionals. Where African-descent people are concerned, credibility is often a function of service given over time. It also requires that a clinician reach out to the members of the community to establish a credible presence as a person capable of lending care and assistance, and sustaining that presence in a community over time.

Empathic Consolation.   Empathy is perhaps one of the most important components of the therapeutic process. It allows clinicians to project themselves into the story of the client while drawing on a reservoir of emotional understanding. Although the ability to empathize with a client is essential, equally important to the therapist's empathic awareness is the ability to communicate that understanding to the client. Without that communication, the empathic energy is only partially given and much more difficult for the client to receive. Consolation relates to the ability to provide support, nurturance, caring, and a voice of reassurance in understanding the client's dilemma. In working with African American clients, empathic consolation requires both the need to "feel," and the ability to communicate and express that feeling in open and honest ways the client can understand.

Ability to Bear Witness to African American Suffering, While Offering Hope for Redemption

Cornel West (1996) reminds us that within the life experiences of African-descent people, there will undoubtedly be instances of unjustified suffering, unmerited pain, and undeserved harm. While mustering the strength to deal with life's adversities is always a challenge, African Americans' frustration is often enhanced because their suffering often falls on deaf ears. African American people, like most clients who might be in pain, need to be able to tell their story. Counselors must be able to acknowledge the oppressive nature of African American life in America while simultaneously providing compassionate reassurance that things can and do change and improve.

Practical Advice

Often, therapists and counselors are taught to maintain a posture of objective distance with their clients. In that space, service providers can listen attentively, reflect, and even interpret content, but stop short of giving advice. Where African American clients are concerned, this strategy needs to be rethought.

Although some clients of African descent will appreciate a more distant, less engaged style, many more will expect and benefit from a style that is more active and engaging, as well as one where advice and practical strategies are a part of the counseling session. In this regard, therapists will need to assume a posture of a "subjective companion," rather than an objective outsider. Subjective companions do provide advice and feedback to clients as a way of assisting them with their dilemmas. Whether their problems relate to relationship difficulties, family dynamics, career or school, personal growth issues, and so on, service providers would do well to equip themselves with a collection of strategies and intervention recommendations. Assisting a client to understand their psychological pain, and to be simply all that they can in the absence of some specific advice and guidance, may violate their expectation of what the therapy process is about.

Social Engineering

Counseling interventions are often directed at intrapsychic elements of the individual personality. These strategies are dictated by theoretical constructs that see client distress as internal. Unfortunately, much of the psychological distress experienced by African American people is a reaction to sociocultural and environmentally oppressive phenomenon. Therefore, counseling effectiveness cannot be relegated to helping clients feel less anxious, depressed, or angry about their circumstances. That strategy helps them to feel better while they are then ushered out of mental health facilities still vulnerable to the social pathology that instigated their entry into the mental health system in the first place. In reality, therapists and counselors must direct some of their energies to social advocacy that addresses instances of oppression.

Those approaches must also be proactive in helping African American clients develop skills of mastery (Lee, 1991). In some cases, that advocacy and mastery training will need to be directed at social systems; in others, political and economic, or even educational systems must be the target of intervention. Certainly Sue (2001) and Neville and Mobley (2001) make this approach abundantly clear in their writings. In addition, Boyd-Franklin (1989) invites us to consider a structural family systems approach when working with African American families. We would also contend that family systems approaches have much to contribute in assisting African American families with the construct of social engineering. Structural family system approaches are useful because of their focus on problem solving. Not only is this approach a very beneficial modality to use, but it is also believed to provide a sense of empowerment and accomplishment as problems are resolved and families are restructured within the context of the therapeutic alliance. Thus, the family systems approaches proposed by Boyd-Franklin are an excellent example of the tools that therapists have at their disposal that allow them not only to think creatively about moving beyond the boundaries of intrapsychic client distress, but also to help them to help their clients navigate their way through the maze of social structures that allow them to feel more empowered and liberated.

Conclusion

With the dawning of a social climate that is perceived by many in the profession to be less hostile (at least overtly) to African-descent people, the urgency to push for more sensitivity with counseling interventions appears to have decreased somewhat. Indeed, the psychological and counseling literature is rife with models and methods that advocate for revisions in theory (Parham, 1996; D'Andrea, 2000), modifications in research methods (S. Sue, 1999), development and training for increased competence (Sue, Arredondo, & McDavis, 1992), and operationalization of therapeutic techniques (Lee, 1991; Parham, 2002). Likewise there is more emphasis on challenging the ethnocentric biases of the larger White society (Daniels & D'Andrea, 1996; Ivey, Ivey, & Simek-Morgan, 1997); intervening beyond individual competency domains to institutional, organizational, and societal levels (Sue, 2001); and creating a more socially just and humane society while challenging White people's comfortable categories of privilege (McIntosh, 1989; Daniels & D'Andrea, 2000). Without question, the explosion of counseling models, methods, and techniques creates an impressive cadre of therapeutic and intellectual resources.

The paradox of our circumstance, however, is that the new wave of multiculturalism has spawned more models of generic intervention but less understanding of specific cultural populations we seek to serve (i.e., African Americans). The literature advances and promotes more techniques, yet practitioners sometimes fail to understand the very populations they seek to serve. In reality, questions remain about whether what we have really achieved is true progress or have we merely achieved fashionable competence with little substance. In all likelihood, only time and good science, which test the efficacy of these models and methods in longitudinal ways, can provide the answers to those questions.

This chapter has attempted to support the idea that more progress in working with African Americans is still necessary. However, counselors and other service providers cannot effectively intervene with populations they do not functionally understand. Hopefully, readers will have a better understanding of African American life and culture after digesting this material. In doing so, it is important to remember that demographic profiles make for interesting comparisons but tell you very little about the cultural nuances of a person and a people. Only analysis at the cultural deep structure level (rather than the surface structure level) can broaden those insights.

Unfortunately, the lenses through which African-descent people see and relate to life are colored by a set of experiences that contextualize their psychological growth and adaptation against a backdrop of socially oppressive phenomena. As they seek psychological support for their resulting ailments, therapists and counselors must be sensitive to those realities. In addition, a counselor's ability to establish an effective therapeutic alliance will depend in part on the ability to connect with African-descent people on levels that are genuine and allow for an alignment of the spiritual energy.

DISCUSSION QUESTIONS

1. Describe and explain the rationale for culturally specific psychological models.

2. Discuss the limitations of applying traditional psychological approaches to African American clients.

3. Define culture and explain how it differs from the concept of race or other demographic variables.

4. Describe the sociocultural context in which African Americans come to therapy.

5. Identify and describe the most fundamental components of an African-centered psychological perspective.

6. In establishing a therapeutic relationship with an African American client, what are some of the more critical attributes a therapist will need to display?

REFERENCES

Akbar, N. (1991). Mental disorders among African Americans. In N. R. L. Jones (Ed.). *Black Psychology* (3rd ed., 339–352). Berkeley, CA: Cobb and Henry.

Ani, M. (1994). *Yurugu: An African centered critique of European culture, thought and behavior.* Trenton, NJ: African World Press.

Atkinson, D. R., Bui, U., & Mori, S. (2001). Multiculturally sensitive emperically supported treatments—An oxymoron? In J. G. Ponterotto, J. M. Casas, L. A. Suzuki, and C. M. Alexander (Eds.), *The handbook of multicultural counseling* (2nd ed.). Thousand Oaks, CA.: Sage.

Atkinson, D. R., Morton, G., & Sue, D. W. (1989). *Counseling American minorities.* Dubuque, IA: William C. Brown.

Atwell, I., & Azibo, D. A. (1992). Diagnosing personality disorder in Africans (Blacks) using the Azibo nosology: Two case studies. In A. K. H. Burlew, W. C. Banks, H. P. McAdoo, & D. A. Azibo (Eds.), *African American psychology: Theory, research, and practice* (pp. 300–320). Newbury Park, CA: Sage.

Boyd-Franklin, N. (1989). *Black families in therapy.* New York: Guilford Press.

Carter, R. T. (1995). *The influence of race and racial identity in psychotherapy.* New York: John Whiteley.

Cross, W. E., Jr. (1971). The Negro-to-Black conversion experience: Toward a psychology of Black liberation. *Black World, 20,* 13–27.

Cross, W. E., Jr. (1991). *Shades of black: Diversity in African American identity.* Philadelphia: Temple University Press.

D'Andrea, M. (2000). Postmodernism, constructivism, and multiculturalism: Three forces reshaping and expanding our thoughts about counseling. *Journal of Mental Health Counseling, 22,* 1–16.

Daniels, J., & D'Andrea, M. (2000). *Counseling for social justice.* Paper presented at the annual meeting of the American Counseling Association, Washington, DC.

Daniels, J. & D'Andrea, M. (1996). MCT theory and ethnocentrism in counseling. In D. W. Sue, A. E. Ivey, & P. B. Pedersen (Eds.). *A theory of multicultural counseling and therapy.* (pp. 157–174). Pacific Grove, CA.: Brooks/Cole.

Ellison, R. (1947). *Invisible man.* New York: Vintage Books.

Franklin, A. J. (1999). Invisibility syndrome and racial identity development in psychotherapy and counseling African American men. *The Counseling Psychologist, 27*(6), 761–793.

Fu-Kiau, K. K. B. (1991). *Self healing power and therapy: Old teachings from Africa.* New York: Vantage Press.

Gary, L. E., & Weaver, G. D. (1991). Mental health of African Americans: Research trends and directions. In R. L. Jones (Ed.) *Black psychology.* (3rd ed., pp. 727–746). Berkeley, CA: Cobb and Henry.

Grills, C. (2002). African centered psychology: Basic principles. In T. A. Parham (Ed.), *Counseling African descent people: Raising the bar of practitioner competence* (pp. 10–24). Thousand Oaks, CA: Sage.

Helms, J. E. (1986). Expanding racial identity theory to cover counseling process. *Journal of Counseling Psychology, 33,* 62–64.

Hilliard, A. G. (1997). *SBA: The reawakening of the African mind.* Gainsville, FL: Makare Publishing Co.

Ivey, A. E., Ivey, M. B., & Simek-Morgan, L. (1997). *Counseling and psychotherapy: A multicultural perspective* (4th ed.). Boston: Allyn & Bacon.

Jackson, G. G., and Kirshner, S. A. (1973). Racial self-designation in preferences for counselor. *Journal of Counseling Psychology, 20,* 560–564.

Jones, R. L. (1980). *Black psychology* (2nd ed.). New York: Harper & Row.

Kambon, K. (1992). *The African personality in America: An African-centered framework.* Tallahassee, FL: Nubian Nation Productions.

Lee, C. C. (1991). Counseling African Americans: From theory to practice. In R. L. Jones (Ed.), *Black psychology* (3rd ed., pp. 559–576). Berkeley, CA: Cobb & Henry.

Lindsey, K. P., & Paul, G. L. (1989). Involuntary commitment to public mental institutions: Issues involving the overrepresentation of blacks and assessment of relevant functioning. *Psychological Bulletin, 106,* 171–183.

Mbiti, J. S. (1970). *African religions and philosophy.* New York: Anchor Books.

McIntosh, P. (1989, July/August). White privilege: Unpacking the invisible knapsack. *Peace and Freedom,* 8–10.

Neighbors, H. W., Jackson, J. S., Campbell, L., & Williams, D. (1989). The influence of racial factors on psychiatric diagnosis: A review and suggestion for research. *Community Mental Health Journal, 25,* 301–311.

Neville, H. A., & Mobley, M. (2001). An ecological model of multicultural counseling and psychology processes. *The Counseling Psychologist, 29,* 471–486.

Nobles, W. (1986). *African psychology: Toward its reclamation, reascension and revitalization.* Oakland, CA: Black Family Institute.

Nobles, W. W. (1998). To be African or not to be: The question of identity and authenticity—Some preliminary thoughts. In N. R. L. Jones (Ed.), *African American identity development* (pp. 185–277). Hampton, VA: Cobb and Henry.

Ohlsen, M. (1983). *Introduction to counseling.* Itasca, IL: S. E. Peacock.

Parham, T. A. (1989). Cycles of psychological nigrescence. *The Counseling Psychologist, 17,* 187–226.

Parham, T. A. (1993). *Psychological storms: The African American struggle for identity.* Chicago: African American Images.

Parham, T. A. (1996). MCT theory and African American populations. In D. W. Sue, A. E. Ivey, & P. B. Pedersen (Eds.), *A theory of multicultural counseling and therapy* (pp. 177–191). Pacific Grove, CA: Brooks/Cole.

Parham, T. A. (2002). *Counseling African descent people: Raising the bar of practitioner competence.* Thousand Oaks, CA: Sage.

Parham, T. A., and Helms, J. E. (1981). The influence of Black students racial identity attitudes on preference for counselors race. *Journal of Counseling Psychology, 28*(3), 250–256.

Parham, T. A., & Parham, W. D. (2002). Counseling African Americans: The current state of affairs. In T. A. Parham (Ed.), *Counseling African descent people: Raising the bar of practitioner competence.* Thousand Oaks, CA: Sage.

Parham, T. A., White, J. L., & Ajamu, A. (1999). *The psychology of Blacks: An African centered perspective.* Englewood Cliffs, NJ: Prentice-Hall.

Sue, D. W. (2001). Multidimensional facets of cultural competence. *The Counseling Psychologist, 29*(6), 790–821.

Sue, D. W., Arredondo, P., & McDavis, R. (1992). Multicultural counseling competencies and standards: A call to the profession. *Journal of Multicultural Counseling and Development, 20,* 64–88.

Sue, S. (1999). Science, ethnicity, and bias: Where have we gone wrong? *American Psychologist, 54,* 1070–1077.

Thomas, C. (1971). *Boys no more.* Beverly Hills, CA: Glenco Press.

U.S. Bureau of the Census. (2001). The Black Population in the United States. March, 2000 (UPDATE) (Report No. PPL-146).

U.S. Department of Health and Human Services. (2000). *Healthy people 2010.* Rockville, MD: Author.

Utsey, S. O., Bolden, M. A., & Brown, A. L. (2001). Visions of revolution from the spirit of Frantz Fanon: A psychology of liberation for counseling African Americans confronting societal racism and oppression. In J. G. Ponterotto, J. M. Casas, L. A. Suzuki, & C. M. Alexander (Eds.), *Handbook of multicultural counseling* (2nd ed., pp. 311–336). Thousand Oaks, CA: Sage.

Vanzant, I. (1996). *The spirit of a man: A vision for transformation of Black men and women who love them.* San Francisco, CA: HarperCollins.

Vontress, C. (1971). Racial differences: Impediments to rapport. *Journal of Counseling Psychology, 18,* 7–13.

West, C. (1996, August). *Spirituality in the Black community.* Presentation given at the annual meeting of the Association of Black Psychologists, Chicago, IL.

Whaley, A. L. (2001). Cultural mistrust in mental health services for African Americans: A review and meta-analysis. *The Counseling Psychologist, 29*(4), 513–531.

White, J. L., & Parham, T. A. (1990). *The psychology of Blacks: An African American perspective.* Englewood Cliffs, NJ: Prentice-Hall.

Zhang, A., & Snowden, L. (1999). Ethnic characteristics of mental disorders. *Cultural Diversity and Ethnic Minority Psychology, 5*(2), 134–146.

7 Counseling Approaches with Asian Americans and Pacific Islander Americans

DAYA SINGH SANDHU, S. ALVIN LEUNG, AND MEI TANG

This chapter introduces Asian and Pacific Islander Americans as a distinct minority with unique characteristics, values, special needs, and concerns. After discussing their acculturative experiences, we focus on models and strategies and how to work with these populations. A summary is presented at the end of the chapter. Discussion questions are included to facilitate and challenge readers' comprehension.

There is no general consensus on the number of disparate cultural groups that are grouped under the category of Asian and Pacific Islander Americans. Chu and Sue (1984) have identified thirty-five distinct cultures as part of the Asian and Pacific Islander category. Sandhu (1997) recognized an array of more than forty such cultural groups that are called Asian and Pacific Islander Americans.

Using self-identification as a more reliable method (U.S. Bureau of the Census, 2000), Asian Indian, Chinese, Filipino, Japanese, Korean, Vietnamese, Cambodian, Hmong, Laotian, and Thai were identified as ten major Asian subgroups. In addition, fifteen other groups, such as Bangladeshi, Indo-Chinese, Pakistani, and Sri Lankan, were identified under this category. Under Pacific Islander, three major groups including Native Hawaiian, Guamanian or Chamoro, and Samoan were listed. Also, sixteen other subgroups such as Carolinian, Fijian, Tahitian, and Tongan were identified.

We agree with Kim, McLeod, and Shantzis (1992) that to organize all these diverse groups under one category of Asian American or Native Hawaiian and other Pacific Islander Americans is erratic and too simplistic. As a matter of fact, each Asian national group has its own distinctive cultural background, unique historical experiences, and reasons for immigration (Takaki, 1989).

Immigration Patterns

The Asian and Pacific Islander American population is the fastest growing minority in the United States. In 2000, there were 10,242,998 Asian Americans and 398,835 Native Hawaiian and other Pacific Islander Americans (U.S. Bureau of the Census, 2000). During the past 10 years, the Asian population increased by 48.3 percent. This increase in the Asian population is strikingly impressive when compared with the total U.S. population increase of 13.2 percent from 1990 to 2000. It may be noted during the same period, the White population increased by 5.9 percent, African American by 15.56 percent, and Native American and Alaskan Native by 26.4 percent. Within the past fifty years, the Asian and Pacific Islander American population has increased from 0.60 million to 10.24 million. It is projected that in the next 50 years, this population will increase to 34.35 million. This population is "exploding with no signs of subsiding" (Bell, 1996, p. 15).

Some Asian and Pacific Islander Americans immigrated for better economic opportunities, better lifestyles, better education, and more freedom; others sought the United States as a place for political asylum to escape untenable political conditions, starvation, and large scale massacres in their native lands.

There are clearly three main waves of immigrants from Asian countries. The first wave included immigrants as farmers or laborers during the 1800s. The U.S. Congress never seriously considered the idea of granting citizenship to these people. After the Immigration and Naturalization Act of 1965, a special provision called *preference category* attracted many highly educated people, such as medical doctors, scientists, engineers, and educators, under the second wave of immigrants. The third wave included illegal immigrants who became eligible to apply for legal residency in accordance with the revised immigration law passed by Congress in 1986. A large majority of these illegal immigrants engaged in menial work as they could not be hired legally.

Transformation of Ethnic Identities and New Challenges

When newly arrived Asian and Pacific Islanders interact with the dominant culture, their internalized cultural beliefs and behaviors are reexamined. Their sense of belonging to a native ethnic group is weakened and cultural loyalties are questioned. The uprooting experience from the homeland also casts many doubts about one's social and psychological support systems. A person may feel caught between two conflicting worlds, behaving in one way at home and in another way outside the home, thus having two totally different identities (Sandhu, 1999). The ethnic identity of the newly arrived immigrants is strongly challenged by social and cultural factors. Some of the factors include new geographic location, educational setting, interpersonal relationships, stereotypes, and experiences with racism (Yeh & Hwang, 1999).

Like most other minority groups, Asian and Pacific Islander Americans undergo a series of ethnic identity transformations. To understand this transformation process, several stage models have been proposed, such as Sue and Sue's (1999) Racial/Cultural Identity Development (R/CID) Model.

Threats to one's cultural or ethnic identity is one of the major causes of disillusionment and unfulfilled aspirations for many Asian and Pacific Islander Americans. In the process of renegotiation of identities during the acculturation process, individual identities never remain intact. These identities either become hybrid or hyphenated, leading to various psychological conflicts and afflictions (Sandhu, 1999).

Acculturative Stress for Asian and Pacific Islander Americans

Soon after the immigration process is concluded, the cultural transformation of many Asian and Pacific Islanders is initiated. In the new settings, when cultural contexts change, priorities, values, and behaviors also change. These dramatic changes cause enormous amounts of stress. Sandhu and Asrabadi (1994) identified perceived discrimination, fear, stress from culture shock, perceived hate, homesickness, and guilt as the six major contributing factors to acculturative stress of international students. We believe that these same factors contribute to the acculturative distress for the newly immigrated Asian and Pacific Islander Americans.

Posttraumatic Disorder in Asian Americans

Many refugees who sought political asylum in the United States from war-torn or repressive regimes, such as Vietnam, North Korea, China, Kampuches, and Laos, have suffered traumatic experiences because of torture, starvation, atrocities, and forced migration (Du & Lu, 1997). Consequently, these refugees silently suffer an unusually high rate of posttraumatic stress disorder (PTSD). These Asian Americans suffer from distressing and troubling recollections, nightmares, and flashbacks. Some of them may also suffer from a disorder of estrangement, irritability, hypervigilance, and sleeping disorders. Several Southeast Asian women experienced additional trauma caused by violence, torture, and multiple rapes (Chen, 1997).

A Model Minority Myth Debunked

Several writers (Butterfield, 1986; Ramirez, 1986; Hasia, 1987; Bell, 1996) described Asian Americans as a model minority. Osajima (1988) identified strong family ties, stability, and structure as the contributing factors to the success stories of Asian Americans. Bell (1996) described Asian Americans' success stories as spectacular on all fronts of life. For instance, Korean merchants run 56 percent of New York's corner grocery stores, and Vietnamese Americans, in some parts of Texas, control 85 percent of the shrimping industry. In California, 800 of the 6,000 motels in the state are owned by Asian Indian Americans.

However, the revisionists of the "Asian as a model minority" thesis (Crystal, 1989; Min, 1995; Walker-Moffat, 1995; Takaki, 1996) have recently argued that the model minority myth is detrimental to the interests of many Asian and Pacific Islander Americans. These researchers contend that the success image of a few elite, individual Asian Americans has drastic negative effects on the welfare of the Asian American group as a whole. For instance, Hurh and Kim (1989) pointed out that "Asian Americans are considered by the dominant group as successful and problem free and not in need of social programs designed to benefit disadvantaged minorities such as Black and Mexican American" (p. 528).

Asian Women's Concerns

Asian women in the United States operate under economic, social, and cultural conditions that are different from their native countries. Patriarchal traditions and strict gender-specific roles are challenged and in many cases cause marital conflicts (Homma-True, 1997; Sandhu, 1999). A significant number of Asian and Pacific Islander American women have to sustain acculturative stress because of culture shock, working in marginal occupations, and sharing the financial responsibilities for the family. When Asian American women start changing their gender roles from housewives to working outside for financial and personal reasons, marital conflicts loom. Asian men consider their new household responsibilities demeaning and an insult to their masculine identity and masculine roles (Espiritu, 1997).

Domestic violence is another major issue for Asian and Pacific Islander Americans. Because the model minority myth claims higher standards of social and moral morality, there is generally a denial of domestic violence in Asian American families (Das & Kemp, 1997). The incidence and severity of domestic violence increases when Asian American women have no friends or family members and they cannot speak English. In such cases, Asian male batterers continue to take advantage of these helpless women (Masaski & Wong, 1997). The situation worsens when women have no job skills and education, and have to depend economically on the batterer.

Challenges to Asian Values and Beliefs

Given the diversity of ethnic groups recognized as Asian and Pacific Islander Americans, it is difficult, if not impossible, to delineate values specific to each group. However, some of the core Asian and Pacific Islander American values include formality in relationships, maintaining interpersonal harmony, strong family obligations, emotional restriction, deference to authority, a passive style of interacting, utilizing guilt and shame as methods of internal control, strong group orientation, and conformity in relationships (Huang, 1994; Uba, 1994; Sandhu, 1997; Baruth & Manning, 1999).

Asian and Pacific Islander American immigrants experience a tremendous amount of stress when their family values clash with Western family values. Some of these family values are diametrically opposed. For instance, Asian families generally expect that individual family members make sacrifices for the welfare of their family; however, in the United States, the family is expected to meet the personal needs of its members. Contrary to the values of the extended family in Asia, autonomy and independence are stressed in the West (Lee, 1997).

In an interview with Morrissey (1997), Sandhu debunked Asian Americans' model minority myth and highlighted their mental health issues as follows:

> The myth of Asians as a model minority, based on the success image of a few elite individuals, has a very negative and debilitating effect on the general population of Asian Americans. Several mental health concerns and psychological afflictions, such as threats to cultural identity, powerlessness, feelings of marginality, loneliness, hostility, and perceived alienation and discrimination remain unredressed and hidden under the veneer of the model minority myth. (pp. 1, 21–22)

In summary, it is obvious that in the process of assimilation into American culture Asian and Pacific Islander Americans encounter several dramatic ecocultural changes (Sandhu, Kaur, & Tewari, 1999). These assimilation, adaptation, and acculturative experiences cause Asian Americans many psychological problems. We present the following counseling models and strategies to help Asian and Pacific Islander American clients.

Counseling Asian and Pacific Islander Americans: Multicultural Counseling Models and Process Issues

There is an array of multicultural counseling models, including models related to multicultural counseling competence (e.g., Sue, Arredondo, & McDavis, 1992), racial and ethnic identity development (e.g., Helms, 1990), and counseling ethnic minorities (e.g., Leong, 1996; Fischer, Jome, & Atkinson, 1998). However, with the exception of a few that focus on conceptual contributions (e.g., Kim, Atkinson, & Umemoto, 2001), there does not exist a comprehensive model on counseling Asian Americans.

Ponterotto, Fuertes, and Chen (2000) defined a multicultural counseling model as "conceptualizations that address the how to component of counseling, providing an explication of how therapy is conducted, the role of clients and counselors, and the mechanisms for client change and growth" (p. 640). Given that the research literature on counseling Asian Americans is still limited both in terms of quantity and scope, there might not be enough research findings and empirical data that could be used to construct a comprehensive model of counseling Asian Americans. Accordingly, our goal is not to propose a comprehensive model, but to identify a range of multicultural issues related to the process of counseling Asian Americans based on the existing multicultural counseling literature.

Consistent with the literature in multicultural counseling competencies, we take the position that effective multicultural counseling requires that the counselor develop competence in terms of attitudes, knowledge, and skills (Sue, Arredondo, & McDavis, 1992). At the same time, we agree with the use of a combined etic-emic approach in understanding the process of multicultural counseling (e.g., Ponterotto & Benesch, 1988; Fischer et al., 1998). Along this line, effective multicultural counseling is viewed as a process involving a set of global factors that are somewhat universal across cultures, as well as factors, issues, and operationalizations, that are specific to the cultural background of clients.

Based on the literature in counseling process (Hill & O'Brien, 1999), counseling is conceptualized in this chapter as an interpersonal process having exploration, insight, and action stages. We would like to examine and discuss how selective multicultural issues that are unique to Asian American individuals would affect the process of counseling Asian American clients in successive stages of counseling. We hope that the issues examined could serve as stimuli for counseling practitioners and researchers in our efforts to develop a more comprehensive framework on counseling Asian Americans.

Exploration

In the beginning stage of counseling, the counselor and the client have to engage in a process of exploration, and to examine the thoughts, feelings, and behavior of the client in relation to the presenting concerns (Hill & O'Brien, 1999). Central to this process of exploration is the development of a therapeutic alliance between the client and the counselor (Sexton & Whiston, 1994). Ponterotto and Benesch (1988) identified a number of common therapeutic factors that we feel are important in forming a strong therapeutic alliance with Asian American clients. Included in these general factors are accuracy in identifying the client's problem, the personal qualities of the counselor, consistency with the client's expectation regarding the therapeutic process, and the establishment of counselor credibility.

However, it is also important to understand how the cultural background of Asian Americans might influence their expectations, reactions, and perceptions about the therapeutic alliance. Given that relationships in Asian cultures are often governed by norms and hierarchy, the ambiguous nature of a counseling relationship might cause some Asian American clients to experience internal conflicts. For example, Yang (1995) suggested that traditional Chinese culture specified three types of relationships, which are those between family members, between familiar persons, and between strangers. It is important to note that intimate exchanges between individuals (e.g., between a client and a counselor) are unlikely to occur if a relationship is perceived as one between strangers.

Tseng, Lu, and Yin (1995) suggested that a counselor should facilitate a special personal relationship with Asian clients in the beginning stage of counseling. They suggested that counselors should work with clients in such a way that the counseling relationship would slowly evolve from one "between strangers" to one between "personal friends" or "family members." They believed that personal relationships are very important in Asian cultures and that clients are likely to give higher priority to their relationship with a personal or familial interpersonal network than a relationship with an organization or institution (e.g., Kwan, 2000). Tseng et al. (1995) believe that maintaining a professional, neutral, and distant therapeutic relationship with clients, as suggested by a number of psychotherapeutic orientations, might be detrimental to the development of these more personal relationships.

The question is how to transform a relationship between strangers to a relationship between familiar persons or family members? We believe that Rogers's concepts of empathy, respect, and congruence are applicable to Asian clients (Ivey, Ivey, & Simek-Morgan, 1993). A counselor who could competently communicate his or her understanding and respect will transform a counseling relationship between strangers to one that is more personal and familiar to the client. The balancing act between a personal counselor and an expert counselor is difficult to play. In some instances, when trust develops and the relationship starts to move, a client might develop a high degree of dependence, and expect the counselor to be someone who could solve his or her problems, as well as those experienced by other members of the family.

Insight Stage

The insight or middle stage of counseling is critical because it is when clients develop insight or self-understanding through the psychotherapeutic process (Weiner, 1998; Hill & O'Brien, 1999). Based on the insights, self-understanding, and awareness attained in this stage, the counselor and client have to develop a mutual agreement on the direction and goals of psychotherapeutic intervention. In the insight and action stages, the counselor is more likely to use intervention skills such as interpretation, challenge, confrontation, advice-giving, and immediacy to help clients tie things together. In order to benefit from the process, clients have to look into themselves and decide if the counselor's observations and viewpoints are accurate. Some Asian American clients might not be able to clearly articulate or verbalize their views, especially those that were not in agreement with what the counselor had suggested. The need for harmony and goodwill in interpersonal relationships (e.g., Yang, 1995; Kim et al., 2001), especially in formal relationships in which the other person is perceived to be an expert, might cause some clients to refrain from verbalizing their disagreement with the suggestions, interpretation, solution, or session homework offered by the counselor. In other words, Asian American clients might be reluctant to disagree because they wanted to avoid having conflicts with an authority figure (i.e., the counselor).

Two important variables to consider in setting counseling goals in the insight stage of counseling are individualism and collectivism (e.g., Duan & Wang, 2000; Kim et al., 2001). The multicultural counseling literature suggested that Asians and Asian Americans are more likely to operate under a collectivistic orientation in which group welfare (e.g., family, society) is often placed ahead of individual welfare. Counseling, more of a professional discipline in the United States, is more likely to operate under an individualistic orientation in which self-actualization is viewed as the ultimate goal. To many individuals, self-actualization and individualism are often contradictory, because individual needs and collective welfare are incompatible.

We believe that exploration and insight are necessary steps even for Asian American clients who take on a collectivistic orientation. First, it is important for the counselor to point out that the two orientations often coexist in one's reality, and to explore with the client how one could achieve or negotiate a balance between individual and collective goals in the present and future (Duan & Wang, 2000). Second, successful counseling is often accompanied by a clearer awareness of one's needs, and a sense of responsibility about decisions that one has to make. Counselors should remind Asian American clients that even if they choose to bend themselves in order to fulfill collective goals (e.g., yield to family expectations), it is a choice that they have made through a deliberate process of exploration, and they have to assume responsibility for the consequences of these decisions.

Action Stage

The implementation of some form of counseling interventions is suggested by Ponterrotto and Benesch (1988) as one of the common factors in counseling individuals from different ethnic and cultural backgrounds. The final stage of counseling often involves a process of change in which clients experiment with new ways of behaving, coping, thinking, feeling, and relating. It also involves a process of ending counseling as the concerns raised in the beginning stage of counseling are resolved. Thereafter, the client has to use the strategies they have learned in counseling to deal with real-world realities and challenges, without the assistance of formal counseling.

Many scholars in counseling and psychotherapy have suggested that Asian American clients often prefer a more directive style of counseling, and that they respond more positively to cognitive oriented and problem-solving interventions, focusing on concrete problems as well as the present and the immediate future (Waxer, 1989; S. Sue, Zane, & Young, 1994; Leung & Lee, 1996; Sue & Sue, 1999). We feel that the validity of these assertions should be further scrutinized by research (Fischer et al., 1998; Leung, 2000). On-target cognitive interventions that are practical and concrete are useful to many clients, including Asian American clients. However, we caution against the mechanical use of directive and cognitive-oriented strategies simply because the literature suggests that Asian American clients perceive a directive approach more positively. Competent multicultural counselors should have a repertoire of intervention strategies that they could use to work with diverse individuals, and the choice of specific strategies should be based on the needs and cultural background of clients.

Empirical research on counseling process and outcomes suggested that successful counseling is often accompanied by changes in the relationship between the counselor and client (Tracey, 1993). Such findings might apply to the multicultural counseling process. We propose that in order for progress to be made at the action phase of counseling and psychotherapy, the counselor has to transform the counseling relationship in such a way that his or her role as an expert or authority person is lessened. It means that the process of counseling has to become less directive as it evolves. The client has to depend less on the counselor for assurance and direction, and to become more involved in the exploration process, as well as in formulating treatment direction and action plans.

Counseling Strategies

Understanding clients (not only Asian Americans) in the cultural context is essential to interpret complexity and dynamics in a cross-cultural counseling relationship (Pedersen, 1994). Sue, Arredondo, and McDavis (1992) recommended that culturally competent counselors should be aware of their own assumptions about human behavior, values, biases, preconceived opinions, and personal limitations. They should also attempt to understand the worldviews of their clients without negative judgments and actively develop and practice appropriate, relevant, and sensitive intervention strategies and skills. These general guidelines must be incorporated into developing counselors' conceptualization and counseling strategies to effectively counsel Asian American clients.

Helping Resources and Utilization

Asian Americans have been found to have a low rate of using mental health services but have a much higher rate of premature termination of counseling sessions (Sue & Sue, 1974; Sue, 1977; Chin, 1998; Yeh & Wang, 2000). Studies found that Asian Americans preferred to seek help from familial and social relations or even from religious authorities and practices rather than from mental health professionals (Webster & Fretz, 1978; Yeh & Wang, 2000). The reasons for underutilization could be lack of bilingual therapists, stereotypes of therapists, discrimination, and therapists' inability to plan culturally appropriate forms of treatment (Sue & Zane, 1987).

What would be a culturally appropriate treatment? Knowledge about Asian American culture is only the necessary, but not the sufficient, condition for effective treatment. What is needed is the credibility that refers to the clients' perception of therapists as effective and trustworthy helpers (Sue & Zane, 1987). An accurate conceptualization of the problem, strategies for problem resolution, and goals for treatment are crucial to credibility building.

A culturally accommodating model of counseling, proposed by Leong (1996), illustrates how counselors and clients from different backgrounds can work toward effective outcomes. In essence, both counselors and clients have multidimensions of personality on a universal level (human nature across cultures), on a group level (characteristics shared by the same cultural group), and on an individual level (unique personality). Focusing on only one dimension and neglecting the other two will harm the effectiveness because Asian American clients may feel that they are either being treated as a symbolic figure of a certain cultural group (not getting their psychological problems addressed adequately) or misunderstood because counselors do not value their cultural background. For instance, an

18-year-old second-generation Asian girl who has issues of gender identity may feel misunderstood if her counselor only focuses on her group dimension of personality and ignores her unique experiences; only focusing on the group dimension minimizes this girl's struggle with gender identity because the counselor sees her as an Asian American. However, if the counselor only focuses on her gender identity issue, and does not acknowledge her as being an Asian American, neglecting her group dimension, the counselor fails to recognize the cultural contexts and values that might influence the girl in psychological being and behaviors.

Diagnosis and Assessment

Cultural variables may significantly influence symptom expression and use of clinical and personality tests (Leong, 1986). Because of stigma associated with mental illness among Asian Americans, a tendency to replace psychological symptoms with somatic ones is not a surprise. Lin and Cheung (1999) argue that overrepresentation of somatic complaints in Asian Americans occurs because of the Asian tradition of viewing body and mind as unitary rather than dualistic. Underutilization of mental health services does not mean that Asian Americans do not have emotional and mental problems. They actually have experienced great anxiety from loneliness and isolation, but they do not seek professional help because a stigma is attached to mental health problems in their culture (Sue & Kirk, 1975).

Chin (1998) argued that culturally irrelevant tests resulted in Asian Americans being more likely viewed as less verbal, having more personality problems, more neurotic, more anxious and introverted, and less dominant than Whites. Because most clinical instruments are developed and normed in Euro-American culture, counselors should not interpret the test results without considering clients' cultural contexts. Counselors also need to interpret clients' behaviors in their cultural contexts rather than viewing these behaviors as dysfunctional and symptoms of mental health problems if they are at variance from those of the dominant culture.

Factors Affecting Effectiveness

Research on counseling diverse populations identified many variables that might have influences on the treatment effects. Along with variables such as therapists' knowledge and skills, goals and strategies of treatment plan, and clients' variables (Leong, 1986; Sue & Zane, 1987; Atkinson, Thompson, & Grant, 1993), the level of acculturation of clients and experiences with majority culture are important variables to consider for effectiveness of counseling outcomes (Atkinson et al., 1993; Aponte & Barnes, 1995).

Studies about acculturation and counseling variables such as counselor preference, problem severity, helping resources, counselor effectiveness and ratings, and counseling styles have supported the effects of acculturation on counseling processes, but the results have not been consistent (Atkinson, Whiteley, & Gim, 1990; Gim, Atkinson, & Whiteley, 1990; Atkinson & Matsushita, 1991). Most studies found that with higher acculturation, minority clients tended to seek help more from professional therapists rather than families and relatives; to present more personal and emotional problems rather than academic and vocational concerns; to be more positive about the counselor of different ethnicity; and to be more accepting of nondirectional counseling styles. Related to acculturation levels, generation status also needs to be considered in counseling intervention with Asian Americans. A newly arriving immigrant and a third generation Ivy League educated professional would have very different issues to deal with because of their different levels of familiarity with culture and language.

Language is another variable frequently recognized by cross-cultural counseling that may affect counseling outcome. The underuse and early termination of counseling services might be because these services have been culturally inappropriate and linguistically incompatible (Sue, 1977; Lin & Cheung, 1999). Mutual understanding between the counselor and the client is the necessary condition in the helping process, and language is one of the major elements to build such a bridge.

Shame or losing face is another critical factor that might influence the outcome of treatment. The concept of guilt and shame among traditional Asian culture might affect how Asian Americans present their problems and which solution would save face. Shame has been identified as a major motivating force that prompts Asian Americans to do or not to do things (Sato, 1979; Berg & Miller, 1992). Therefore, counselors should use future-oriented questioning techniques and empowerment strategies to help clients restore their sense of self-worth and competence.

Family plays an important role in many aspects of Asian Americans' lives, particularly in academic aspirations and occupational choices (Leong, 1993; Peng & Wright, 1994). Family pressure on academic excellence and higher occupational status can be a motivating force or it could be just the opposite. The importance of family itself and the familial values embedded in Asian traditional culture make it viable to incorporate family dynamics into intervention strategies (Yu, 1996). Any solutions that do not consider family needs will not go too far because Asian Americans usually will not sacrifice their family benefits for individual gains.

Gender issues are another important factor for counseling with Asian Americans because women and men have traditionally defined roles and expectations. The gender-specific roles for Asian American women may conflict with these women's acculturation process and particularly when they have to become the financial supporters for the family (which often is the case at the beginning of the immigration process because women have an easier time finding service-related jobs). Counselors need to be mindful of clients' understanding and expectation of gender roles in family and at work in order to develop an effective strategy.

Differences in communication styles could also become barriers to the effectiveness of counseling with Asian Americans. Asian Americans have very complex communication styles. For instance, they generally talk in indirect ways. The communication style is elaborate, subtle, and deferential (Leong, 1993). The nature of the interpersonal relationship is hierarchical and structured, which could significantly impact the communication among the members of the group.

Preferences for Counseling Styles

For counseling styles, Asian Americans prefer a logical, rational, structured counseling approach over affective, reflective, and nondirective counseling (Atkinson, Maruyama, & Matsui, 1978). Atkinson et al. (1978) have argued that reflection and summarization of feelings might reduce counselors' effectiveness with Asian American clients. Researchers have also found counselors of the same race to be more effective than counselors of a different race. Counselors of Asian American ethnicity and counselors who were culturally sensitive were given higher ratings for effectiveness by the Asian American participants (Gim, Atkinson, & Kim, 1991).

There are pros and cons about Asian American involvement in group therapy. The advantages are that it is less threatening and that the group diversity could be a good resource for Asian Americans to learn new roles. The disadvantages are that if the group is very talkative, Asian Americans might not benefit because they are less assertive and are more emotionally withdrawn (Chu & Sue, 1984). While working with Asian American clients in a group setting, the content, size, power relationship between minority and majority members, verbal and nonverbal cues from members, and structure of the group needs to be recognized and monitored closely (Leong, 1992; Conyne, Tang, & Watson, 2001).

Conclusion

On the basis of present immigration patterns, it is safe to conclude that the number of Asian and Pacific Islander Americans will continue to increase. The acculturative experiences of this minority group are indicative of a plethora of psychological problems and pressures that this minority group endures. In this chapter, we pointed out that labeling all Asian and Pacific Islander Americans as a model minority based on the successes of a selected few elite individuals and subgroups is not only a misnomer but also a public neglect of the real and painful problems of the entire group of Asian and Pacific Islander Americans.

This chapter also discussed selective multicultural issues that are specific to Asian and Pacific Islander Americans. To meet the counseling needs of this special population effectively, three sequential stages of the counseling process, exploration, insight, and action, were described. Also, several culturally relevant counseling strategies as they apply to Asian and Pacific Islander Americans were discussed.

DISCUSSION QUESTIONS

1. Who are Asian and Pacific Islander Americans?

2. Discuss the immigration patterns of Asian Americans.

3. What is meant by acculturative stress? Discuss various factors that contribute to the acculturative stress of Asian and Pacific Islander Americans.

4. Describe in detail three stages of the counseling process as they apply to Asian Americans.

5. Discuss the counseling strategies that are culturally relevant to Asian and Pacific Islander Americans.

REFERENCES

Aponte, J. F., & Barnes, J. M. (1995). Impact of acculturation and moderator variables on the intervention and treatment of ethnic groups. In J. F. Aponte & R. Y. Rivers (Eds.), *Psychological interventions and cultural diversity* (pp. 19–39). Boston: Allyn & Bacon.

Atkinson, D. R., Maruyama, M., & Matsui, S. (1978). Effects on counselor race and counseling approach on Asian Americans' perception of counselor credibility and utility. *Journal of Counseling Psychology, 25,* 76–83.

Atkinson, D. R., & Matsushita, Y. J. (1991). Japanese-American acculturation, counseling style, counselor ethnicity, and perceived counselor credibility. *Journal of Counseling Psychiatry, 38* (4), 473–478.

Atkinson, D. R., Thompson, C. E., & Grant, S. K. (1993). A three dimensional model for counseling racial/ethnic minorities. *Counseling Psychologist, 21,* 257–277.

Atkinson, D. R., & Whiteley, S., & Gim, R. H. (1990). Asian-American acculturation and preferences for help providers. *Journal of College Student Development, 31,* 155–161.

Baruth, L. G., & Manning, M. L. (2003). *Multicultural counseling and psychotherapy: A lifespan perspective* (3rd ed). Columbus, OH: Merrill Prentice Hall.

Bell, D. A. (1996). America's greatest success story: The triumph of Asian-Americans. In R. C. Monk (Ed.), *Taking sides: Clashing views on controversial issues in race and ethnicity* (2nd ed.). Guilford, CT: Dushkin.

Berg, I. K., & Miller, S. D. (1992). Working with Asian American clients: One person at a time. *Families in Society, 73*(6), 356–363.

Butterfield, F. (1986, August 3). Why Asians are going to the head of the class. *New York Times,* Sec. 12, pp. 18, 23.

Chen, V. T. (1997). Asian and Pacific Islander Women. In K. M. Allen and J. M. Phillips (Eds.), *Women's health across the life span: A comprehensive perspective* (pp. 363–381). Philadelphia: Lippincott.

Chin, J. L. (1998). Mental health services and treatment. In L. C. Lee & N. W. S. Zane (Eds.), *Handbook of Asian American psychology* (pp. 485–504): Thousand Oaks, CA: Sage

Chu, J., & Sue, S. (1984). Asian/Pacific-Americans and group practice. *Social Work With Groups, 7,* 23–36.

Conyne, R. K., Tang, M., & Watson, A. L. (2001). Exploring diversity in therapeutic groups. In E. Welfel & R. E. Ingersoll (Eds.), *Mental health counselors' sourcebook essential for effective and responsible practice* (pp. 358–364). New York: Wiley.

Crystal, D. (1989). Asian Americans and the myth of the model minority. *Social Casework, 70,* 405–415.

Das, A. K., & Kemp, S. F. (1997). Between two worlds: Counseling South Asian Americans. *Journal of Multicultural Counseling and Development, 25,* 23–33.

Du, N., & Lu, F. G. (1997). Assessment and traumatic posttraumatic stress disorder among Asian Americans. In E. Lee (Ed.), *Working with Asian Americans: A guide for clinicians* (pp. 275–294). New York: Guilford.

Duan, C., & Wang, L. (2000). Counseling in the Chinese cultural context: Accommodating both individualistic and collectivist values. *Asian Journal of Counselling, 7,* 21.

Espiritu, Y. E. (1997). *Asian women and men.* Thousand Oaks, CA: Sage.

Fischer, A. R., Jome, L., & Atkinson, D. R. (1998). Reconceptualizing multicultural counseling: Universal healing conditions in a culturally specific context. *The Counseling Psychologist, 26,* 525–591.

Gim, R. H., Atkinson, D. R., & Kim, S. J. (1991). Asian-American acculturation, Counselor ethnicity and cultural sensitivity, and ratings of counselors. *Journal of Counseling Psychology, 38,* 57–62.

Gim, R. H., Atkinson, D. R., & Whiteley, S. (1990). Asian-American acculturation, severity of concerns, and willingness to see a counselor. *Journal of Counseling Psychology, 37,* 281–185.

Hasia, J. (1987). *Americans in higher education and at work.* Hillsdale, NJ: Erlbaum.

Helms, J. E. (Ed.). (1990). *Black and white racial identity: Theory, research, and practice.* Westport, CT: Greenwood.

Hill, C. E., & O'Brien, K. M. (1999). *Helping skills: Facilitating exploration, insight, and action.* Washington, DC: American Psychological Association.

Homma-True, R. (1997). Asian American women. In E. Lee (Ed.), *Working with Asian Americans: A guide for clinicians.* New York: Guilford.

Huang, L. N. (1994). An integrative approach to clinical assessment and intervention with Asian American adolescents. *Journal of Clinical Child Psychology, 23,* 21–31.

Hurh, W. M., & Kim, K. C. (1989). The "success" image of Asian Americans: Its validity and its practical implications. *Ethnic and Racial Studies, 12,* 512–538.

Ivey, A. E., Ivey, M. B., & Simek-Morgan, L. (1993). *Counseling and psychotherapy: A multicultural perspective* (3rd ed.). Boston: Allyn & Bacon.

Kim, B. S. K., & Atkinson, D. R., & Umemoto, D. (2001). Asian cultural values and the counseling process: Current knowledge and direction for future research. *The Counseling Psychologist, 29,* 570–603.

Kim, S., McLeod, J. H., & Shantzis. (1992). Cultural competence for evaluators working with Asian-American communities: Some practical suggestions. In M. A. Orlandi (Ed.), *Cultural competence for evaluators: A guide for alcohol and other drug abuse prevention practitioners working with ethnic/racial communities* (pp. 173–201). Rockville, MD: U.S. Department of Health and Human Services.

Kwan, K. L. K. (2000). Counseling Chinese people: Perspectives of filial piety. *Asian Journal of Counseling, 7,* 23–41.

Lee, E. (Ed.). (1997). *Working with Asian Americans: A guide for clinicians.* New York: Guilford.

Leong, F. L. (1992). Guidelines for minimizing premature termination among Asian American clients in group counseling. *The Journal of Specialists in Group Work, 17,* 218–233.

Leong, F. T. L. (1986). Counseling and psychotherapy with Asian-Americans: Review of the literature. *Journal of Counseling Psychology, 33,* 196–206.

Leong, F. T. L. (1993). The career counseling process with racial/ethnic minorities: The case of Asian Americans. *The Career Development Quarterly, 42,* 345.

Leong, F. T. L. (1996). Toward an integrative model for cross-cultural counseling and psychotherapy. *Applied and Preventive Psychology, 5,* 189–209.

Leung, S. A. (2000). *The counseling relationship: A Chinese perspective.* Paper presented at the Annual Convention of the American Psychological Association. Washington, DC.

Leung, P. W. L., & Lee, P. W. (1996). Psychotherapy with the Chinese. In M. H. Bond (Ed.), *Chinese psychology* (pp. 441–456). Hong Kong: Oxford University Press.

Lin, K.-M., & Cheung, F. (1999). Mental health issues for Asian Americans. *Psychiatric Services, 50*(6), 774–780.

Masaki, B., & Wong, L. (1997). Domestic violence in the Asian community. In E. Lee (Ed.), *Working with Asian Americans: A Guide for clinicians.* New York: Guilford Press.

Min, P. G. (Ed.). (1995). *Asian Americans: Contemporary trends and issues.* Thousand Oaks, CA: Sage.

Morrissey, M. (1997, October). The invisible minority: Counseling Asian Americans. *Counseling Today, 40* (4), 1, 21–22.

Osajima, K. (1988). Asian Americans as the model minority: An analysis of the popular press image in the 1960s and 1980s. In G. Y. Okihiro, S. Hune, & J. Liu (Eds.), *Reflections on shattered windows* (pp. 165–174). Pullman: Washington State University Press.

Pedersen, P. (1994). *A handbook for developing multicultural awareness.* Alexandria, VA: American Counseling Association.

Peng, S., & Wright, D. (1994). Explanation of academic achievement of Asian American students. *Journal of Educational Research, 87,* 346–352.

Ponterotto, J. G., & Benesch, K. F. (1988). An organizational framework for understanding the role of culture in counseling. *Journal of Counseling and Development, 66,* 237–241.

Ponterotto, J. G., Fuertes, J. N., & Chen, E. C. (2000). Models of multicultural counseling. In S. D. Brown & R. W. Lent (Eds.), *Handbook of counseling psychology* (3rd ed.), pp. 639–669. New York: Wiley.

Ramirez, A. (1986, November 24). America's super minority. *Fortune Magazine,* pp. 148–149, 152, 156, 160.

Sandhu, D. S. (1997). Pyschocultural profiles of Asian and Pacific Islander Americans: Implications for counseling and psychotherapy. *Journal of Multicultural Counseling and Development, 25*(1), 7–22.

Sandhu, D. S. (Ed.). (1999). *Asian and Pacific Islander Americans: Issues and concerns for counseling and psychotherapy.* Commack, NY: Nova Science.

Sandhu, D. S., & Asrabadi, B. R. (1994). Development of an acculturative stress scale for international students: Preliminary findings. *Psychological Reports, 75,* 435–448.

Sandhu, D. S., Kaur, K. P., & Tewari, N. (1999). Acculturative experiences of Asian and Pacific Islander Americans: Considerations for counseling and psychotherapy. In D. S. Sandhu (Ed.), *Asian and Pacific Islander Americans: Issues and concerns for counseling and psychotherapy* (pp. 3–19). Commack, NY: Nova Science.

Sato, M. (1979). The shame factor: Counseling Asian Americans. *Journal of the Asian American Psychological Association, 5*(1), 20–24.

Sexton, T. L., & Whiston, S. C. (1994). The status of the counseling relationship: An empirical review, theoretical implications, and research direction. *The Counseling Psychologist, 22,* 6–78.

Sue, D. W., Arredondo, P., & McDavis, R. J. (1992). Multicultural counseling competencies and standards: A call to the profession. *Journal of Counseling and Development, 70,* 477–486.

Sue, D. W., & Kirk, B. (1975). Asian Americans: Use of counseling and psychiatric services on a college campus. *Journal of Counseling Psychology, 22,* 84–86.

Sue, D. W., & Sue, D. (1999). *Counseling the culturally different: Theory and practice* (3rd ed.). New York: Wiley.

Sue, S. (1977). Community mental health services to minority groups: Some optimism, some pessimism. *American Psychologist, 32,* 616–624.

Sue, S., & Sue, D. W. (1974). MMPI comparisons between Asian-American and non-Asian students utilizing a student health psychiatric clinic. *Journal of Counseling Psychology, 21,* 423–427.

Sue, S., & Zane, N. (1987). The role of culture and cultural techniques in psychotherapy: A critique and reformulation. *American Psychologist, 42,* 37–45.

Sue, S., Zane, N., & Young, K. (1994). Research on psychotherapy with culturally diverse populations. In A. E. Bergin & S. L. Garfield (Eds.), *Handbook of psychotherapy and behavior change* (4th ed., pp. 783–817). New York: Wiley.

Takaki, R. (1989). *Strangers from a different shore: A history of Asian Americans.* New York: Penguin Books.

Takaki, R. (1996). The myth of the "model minority." In R. C. Monk (Ed.), *Taking sides: Clashing views on controversial issues in race and ethnicity* (2nd ed.). Guilford, CT: Dushkin.

Tracey, T. J. (1993). Interpersonal stage model of therapeutic process. *Journal of Counseling Psychology, 40,* 396–409.

Tseng, W. S., Lu, Q. Y., Yin, P. (1995). Psychotherapy for the Chinese: Cultural considerations. In T. Y. Lin, W. S. Tseng, & E. K. Yeh (Eds.), *Chinese societies and mental health* (pp. 281–294). Hong Kong: Oxford University Press.

Uba, L. (1994). *Asian Americans.* New York: Guilford.

U.S. Bureau of the Census. (2000). Facts on the Asian/ Pacific Islander Population. Retrieved July 8, 2002, from http://www.census.gov/pubinfo/www/apihot1.html

Walker-Moffat, W. (1995). *The other side of the Asian American success story.* San Francisco: Jossey-Bass.

Watts, A. (1968). *The meaning of happiness.* London: Village Press.

Waxer, P. H. (1989). Cantonese versus Canadian evaluation of directive and non-directive therapy. *Canadian Journal of Counseling, 23,* 263–272.

Webster, D. W., & Fretz, B. R. (1978). Asian American, Black, and White college students' preferences for help-giving sources. *Journal of Counseling Psychology, 25,* 124–130.

Weiner, I. B. (1998). *Principles of psychotherapy* (2nd ed). New York: Wiley.

Yang, K. S. (1995). Chinese social orientation: An integrative analysis. In T. Y. Lin, W. S. Tseng, & E. K. Yeh (Eds.), *Chinese societies and mental health* (pp. 19–39). Hong Kong: Oxford Press.

Yeh, C., & Hwang, M. Y. (1999). The sociocultural context of Asian American ethnic identity and self: Implications for counseling. In D. S. Sandhu (Ed.), *Asian and Pacific Islander Americans: Issues and concerns for counseling and psychotherapy* (pp. 59–69). Commack, NY: Nova Science.

Yeh, C., & Wang, Y. (2000). Asian American coping attitudes, sources, and practices: Implications for indigenous counseling strategies. *Journal of College Student Development, 41*(1), 94–103.

Yu, A. M. (1996). A qualitative analysis of the interaction of Asian culture and family therapy: A look through the eyes of Asian-American therapists. *Dissertation Abstracts International Section A: Humanities & Social Sciences, 56*(11-A), 4285.

8 Counseling Paradigms and Latina/o Americans: Contemporary Considerations

PATRICIA ARREDONDO AND PATRICIA PEREZ

Introduction

In a poem by Gloria Anzaldúa (1987), the Latina author writes that one must live without borders in order to survive "the Borderlands." The metaphor of the borderlands, or *la frontera,* has been used by Mexican American feminist writers to provide images of the benefits and struggles of being bicultural, bilingual, and American in a country that does not necessarily accept you. From the Latino viewpoint, there are historical perspectives of colonization, marginalization, and discrimination in the midst of countless contributions by Latinos to the development of contemporary U.S. society.

Fighting in national wars, picking the foods that are shipped across the country, and contributing to the economy through purchases and taxes are all ways in which Latinos are making a difference in the United States. Ironically, there is a new type of fascination with Latinos. Since the release of the 2000 census data, stating that the Latino population is now at 35 million (U.S. Census, 2000), a wide range of institutions are focusing on this very heterogeneous group as a potential client, customer, employee, student, or any other status that could bring Latinos into the fold. These outreach efforts occur while simultaneously Latinos are still the most underinsured cultural group in the country, have less than 5 percent representation in roles of corporate senior management, are victims of racial profiling, and continue to be labeled "illegal aliens" and considered threats to White wage earners.

At the beginning of the 1990s, there were mainstream magazine covers and other publications that forecasted the period as the decade of the Latino. By most accounts, this did not materialize in political, economic, and academic arenas. Rather, events occurred to throw up additional barriers to Latinos in general, but more so for immigrants, particularly in the educational domain. Antiaffirmative action and antibilingual education legislation, in the name of fairness and equity for all, introduced other forms of exclusion and contributed to the already excessive dropout rate of Latino school-age children.

In 1998, it was reported that for Latino youth 18 and under, 60 percent were first-generation and 24 percent were second-generation U.S. born (Estrada, 1999). This statistic alone indicates that Latinos will be in the pipeline for counseling services for the foreseeable future. Moreover, projections indicate that Latino birthrate is greater than that of other cultural groups, family size characteristically continues to be larger than that of non-Hispanics, and average household income is 12 percent less than non-Hispanics, and this gap is increasing (Arce, 1999). These data are harbingers of psychosocial stressors that will also predispose Latinos to seek some form of counseling and counseling-related resources.

Although this chapter is meant to discuss contemporary counseling considerations with Latinos, it is impossible to ignore the sociopolitical context that currently exists and demographic projections for the twenty-first century. To work with Latinas/os in counseling requires a broad base of cultural competencies because of the heterogeneity of the population. One chapter will not cover all there is to know, but it will offer both considerations and guidelines for more effective and ethical practice.

Overview of the Chapter

There is more than one counseling paradigm for working with Latinas/os in general and for the different ethnic groups who fall under this category. Therefore, this chapter is organized in three major discussions: (1) the status of Latina/o-centered counseling and psychology as portrayed through the literature; (2) general historical and sociopolitical underpinnings that have contributed to value orientations, immigration and acculturation, ethnic identity, and other developmental processes; and (3) strategies for conceptualizing counseling interventions. Some of the broad-brush comments are limitations in this discussion; however, it is anticipated that counseling professionals will continue to seek out new knowledge in the spirit of Latino-centered competency development.

Terminology

Throughout this chapter, I use the terms *Latina/o* and *Latinas/os*. The term *Hispanic* was introduced by the federal government for the census and other legislative business, thereby causing more sociopolitically-minded colleagues not to use the term. However, it should be noted that *Hispanic* is more often heard in the Southwest and California but less on the East Coast.

One of the objectives of this chapter is to raise awareness about various Spanish terms, sayings, and concepts relevant to counseling processes. In the spirit of promoting bilingualism, Spanish terms will be italicized followed by the English word.

Spanish is a romance language using both feminine and masculine terms. The collective term is typically a masculine form ending in "o." In the chapter, I will alternate between the feminine and masculine terms.

Personal Caveat

First, I am an American-born woman of Mexican heritage, a Mexican American woman and a Chicana. These are self-identifiers that I prefer to use when asked about my ethnicity. Yes, I can say that I am a Latina but that falls short of my family heritage. Second, my perspectives have been shaped by (1) independent study of Mexican and Latino history; (2) Latina feminist literature; (3) community and counseling activities with men, women, and adolescents in Latino and non-Latino agencies; and (4) review of as many studies reports, books, and book chapters as possible to learn from others. To become more culturally competent about Latinos in general and persons of Mexican heritage is my ongoing academic objective.

Finally, my worldview about Latinas and Mexican American *mujures*/women is also influenced by personal and professional experiences. There is invaluable learning I have acquired by being raised Mexican American near Cleveland, Ohio, in a predominantly White community. To this I add 30 years as a displaced Mexican American in Boston and acculturating since 1999 to Arizona. I can accurately claim both a bicultural and bilingual life experience, exposure to different worldviews as a result, and a flexibility that allows for interpersonal cross-cultural adaptation. At the same time, there is a continuous learning curve for me about the life experiences of other Latinas/os (e.g., Mexican Americans who grew up in Texas and/or on the border, and Puerto Ricans from Los Angeles versus Boston). My point in articulating these caveats is to indicate that mine is but one perspective and that the formulation of my ideas has been acquired through both personal and academic pursuits.

Status of Latina/o-Centered Counseling and Psychology

The focus on Latinos in counseling has steadily grown and evolved since the 1970s. The *Hispanic Journal of Behavioral Sciences,* first published in the 1980s, remains the singular Latino/Hispanic-oriented academic journal. Many more texts have been written, studies have been conducted, and Latino-specific models have been conceptualized primarily by Latina/o researchers and academics. All publications offer valuable perspectives on topics such as family satisfaction, sexual orientation, workplace issues, drug abuse, preferences in counseling, and ethnic-identity development.

The studies reported in this expanding literature are filling a void and enriching our understanding of the salience of the cultural context(s) and worldviews of Latinos. For example, "Factors That Predict Sexual Behaviors among Young Mexican American Adolescents: An Exploratory Study" (Liebowitz, Castellano, & Cuellar, 1999) and "An Overview of Utilization, Counselor Preference, and Assessment Issues" (Prieto, McNeill, Walls, & Gómez, 2001) invariably discuss culturally shaped value orientations and how these influence Latina/o behavior.

A second observation emerges from a review of Latina/o-focused publications. It is that Latinos bring to counseling issues that are both similar and different to those brought by clients of other cultural backgrounds. There are times a clinician may wonder about whether culture really matters and that applying a traditional research methodology or counseling intervention, regardless of the client's ethnic background, will not cause any harm or bias the outcomes of a study. My response to one who says that culture does not count is to suggest that culture-specific competency continues to be essential to effective and ethical practice, and the literature affirms this position. One only needs to look to the Surgeon General's report on the status of mental health for ethnic minorities in the United States (Center for Mental Health Services, 2001). The conclusion of this report is that "culture counts."

A third observation about the counseling and psychology literature regarding Latinos underscores the complexity of the population in general. To talk about Latino culture without consideration of within-group differences based on one's family heritage (e.g., Cuban or Puerto Rican) and other dimensions of Latino identity (Arredondo & Santiago-Rivera, 2000) is to promote cultural stereotyping (see Figure 8.1). Additionally, to report research findings about Latinos without citing generational and socioeconomic differences may also obscure the critical factors of acculturation and ethnic identity.

The purpose of these comments is not to be critical about the existing literature but to point out the strengths, limitations, and opportunities for expanding the purview of study and discourse. There are many issues to address and research to carry out because of the variability as well as the common denominators of the population. One point emerges clearly in nearly all of the existing literature on Latinos: It is essential to provide context, beginning with historical and sociopolitical references.

Historical and Sociopolitical Contexts

It has been said that the Spanish language is the thread that binds Latinos, that anchors their shared identity. With the arrival of the *conquistadores* from Spain in the fifteenth century, the Spanish language was imposed on the conquered Native American people. Although Spanish is the predominant language, some indigenous tribes have preserved their native language through today. For these groups, Spanish is their second language. There are other historical occurrences, however, that

Age/Generational Status
Culture / Euro / Mestizo / Indigenous

"A" Dimensions:	Gender / Marianísmo / Machísmo
	Language / Regional Accents
	Physical / Mental Status
	Phenotype
	Sexual Orientation
	Social Class

"B" Dimensions:	Acculturation Status
	Citizenship Status
	Educational Background
	Geographic Location
	Family Relationship Status / Familismo
	Religion / Spirituality / Folk Beliefs
	Work Experience
	Health Care Practices / Beliefs
	Identity Status (Self-referent labels)
	Economic Status

| "C" Dimensions: | Personal / Familial / Historical Eras / Events |
| | Sociopolitical Forces |

FIGURE 8.1 Latino Dimensions of Family and Personal Identity

Adapted from P. Arredondo and T. Glauner, *Personal Dimensions of Identity Model.* Boston: Empowerment Workshops. 1992.

contribute to experiences among Latinos that can be termed culturally universal and culturally variable. These constructs become important in understanding the heterogeneity among contemporary Latinos and why it is essential that counselors be familiar with the historical and sociopolitical landscape for the different groups.

Place of Origin and Residence

Latinos in the United States have a continent and a country or region of origin. Geographically, this includes North, Central, and South America (except Brazil), and the Caribbean. Thus, individuals will likely self-identify with their country of origin such as *Dominicanos* from the Dominican Republic, a Caribbean Island, and *Salvadoreños* from El Salvador in Central America. Proximity and history have influenced the presence in the United States of the three largest groups, from Mexico, Puerto Rico, and Cuba, respectively. Moreover, the historical relations of each country to the United States also varies. Whereas many countries have been conquered, invaded, or otherwise been at war with the United States, the South American countries have had the least contact and adverse experiences historically and sociopolitically.

The variability of the life experiences of Latinos from the different ethnic groups, (e.g., Costa Ricans, Colombians, and Panamanians) is further evidence of heterogeneity. Beyond these between-group differences are the within-group differences. For example, for persons of Mexican heritage, there is a range of diversity based on regional differences. Whether one or one's family is from a border town, a Southwest state, or another state such as Ohio or Michigan that became the home of many men who arrived after World War II to work in U.S. factories, there may be a shared ethnic identity, but beyond this, other differences become more salient.

Colonization

To be a Latino means to have a shared history of colonization. The Americas represented the new world to the European explorers, and the history of their invasions and conquests as well as the establishment of the African slave trade is well documented. From these conquests and slavery emerged the *mestizo* and *criollo culturas. Mestizo* refers to persons of Indian and European heritage, and *criollos* or *mulattos* refers to persons from the union of Indians, Africans and Europeans. It is these cross-cultural unions that have resulted in the wide range of phenotype and other visible physical features among contemporary Latinas/os. In the United States, color/phenotype counts; for Latinos, this bias has not gone unnoticed. Studies on phenotypes indicate that the lighter one is, the greater access one has to mainstream systems, networks, and benefits. This occurs for Latinos and individuals of African American heritage as well. The psychological consequences of colonization manifest in notions of psychic wounds, manifesting as submissiveness, learned helplessness, and identification with the oppressor (Córdova, 1999).

For Latinos, legacies of oppression and marginalization continue to occur in the United States. All Spanish-speaking countries in the Americas have had unique and similar sociopolitical relations with the United States since the late 1700s. Thus, when discussion arises about different national Latino groups' (e.g., Cubans) point of entry into this country, the answer is often "by conquest." Puerto Rico became a Commonwealth as a result of the Spanish-American War in 1898, and the Mexican-American War led to the Treaty of Guadalupe Hidalgo in 1848. Mexico's military defeat led to the secession of territory that today includes the states of California, Arizona, New Mexico, Nevada, Colorado, Texas, and Utah, home to the majority of persons of Mexican heritage today.

Sociopolitical Context and Language

Recent reports indicate that Spanish is spoken by more persons over 5 years of age than any language other than English in the United States (Estrada, 1999). It has often been said that one's primary language, learned through the age of 5, is the language of emotions, of the heart. Nevertheless, language has always been made a political issue in the United States. Antibilingual movements began in the late 1700s against German-speaking schools and continue today with antibilingual legislation successfully passing in Arizona in 2000 and in California in 1995.

There are numerous reasons why Latinos prefer to speak English versus Spanish, are monolingual English speakers, bilingual, or engage in code-switching to be culturally sensitive. Counseling professionals may consider the following: (1) Language use can be associated with generation in the United States. Recent immigrants may be monolingual Spanish speakers or speak English as a second language with a wide range of ability: (2) Many Latinos, particularly Mexican Americans, do not speak Spanish at all. These individuals were taught by their parents that in order to fit in and not be punished in school, as they had been, they could not learn to speak Spanish: (3) Being bilingual or speaking Spanish whenever possible can be viewed as an indication of comfort. However, speaking Spanish in the workplace has often been discouraged so as not to make "others" feel uncomfortable: (4) Code-switching refers to the use of Spanish and English in the same sentence. Individuals engage in code-switching to emphasize a point with a particular English or Spanish word: (5) Bilingualism is an academic, psychological, social, and economic asset, not a deficit. The need for bilingual, Spanish-speaking professionals and workers continues to increase in all work environments in both urban and rural settings. Commentaries on the importance of Spanish for safety and other public needs indicate that there are economic and sociocultural benefits that accrue to a community through the presence of Spanish speakers (Middleton, Arredondo, & D'Andrea, 2000).

The Development of Latina/o Worldviews

Counseling paradigms for application with Latinas/os draw from multiple reference points. The discussion thus far has briefly reported on some historical and sociopolitical underpinnings. It has been noted that the heterogeneity of Latinos is infinite because of intergenerational differences, country and place of origin, and other personal dimensions and national identity (Arredondo & Santiago-Rivera, 2000). However, given the shared history of colonization, the most logical place to begin the discussion of worldviews is through the tenets of *mestizo* psychology.

Mestizo Psychology

The *mestizo* experience has been given attention by feminist writers, sociologists, and psychologists. José Vasconcellos, a Mexican philosopher, is credited with describing *mestizos* as *la raza cósmica*/ the cosmic race (Vasconcellos, 1925). In Vasconcellos's writings, he constantly refers to mestizos as members of a synergistic race, a synthesis of other races, and *una raza de color*/a race of people of color. Many, including Vasconcellos, would argue that race is an artificially constructed concept; however, when used by Latinos, the term has a different quality. Ironically, there is a different meaning that race takes on based on context.

For example, October 12, known in the United States as Columbus Day, is called *día de la raza* in Spanish-speaking countries. It is a day of unity and pride, of celebrating collective personhood and pluralism. Perhaps retrospectively, it also represents the dawning of a new world in light of the historical event attributed to that date.

Mestizo-based psychology asserts principles from a strength versus a deficit perspective. In this regard, it differs from the prevailing orientations emanating from the medical model that presumes pathology, with the illness or malady typically viewed as emanating from the individual without sufficient attention to various contexts that influence psychological well-being. Forces that shaped the *mestizo* worldview were

- Survival in new environments in spite of invasions;
- Survival through cooperation, collaboration, and learning of new skills;
- Intermarriage between Native American people and European settlers;
- Synthesis of Native American and European religious practices; and
- Revolutions against European domination leading to the evolution of *la raza cósmica* ideologies, having an effect on a sense of a pluralistic identity. (Ramirez, 1998)

The combination of these perspectives serves to illustrate the interdependent thinking and behavior of people that became an infrastructure for the purpose of survival. In the midst of colonization and other forms of oppression based on spiritual beliefs, the Indians and Africans in the Caribbean (Puerto Rico, Cuba, and the Dominican Republic), Venezuela, Guatemala, and Mexico had to develop values and strategies for self-efficacy. Had they not, many of today's Latino groups would not exist.

Latina/o Value Orientations/La *Familia*

The Latina/o multicultural/multiracial worldview—beliefs, values, and practices—is strengthened by the premises of *mestizo* personality development (Ramirez, 1998). Indeed, the *mestizo* worldview is highly contextual and circumstantial. "Each set of life circumstances represents certain problems and challenges of life through which each individual finds solutions and adaptations thus developing his own personality and philosophy of life" (Ramirez, 1998, p. 68). Although the term *individual* is used, the experiences for Latinas/os have been highly relational, interdependent, and family centered. The term *allocentric* is often used to describe the Latino collectivistic orientation.

In research studies involving first- (immigrant) to third-generation individuals of different Latino background, it was reported that *la familia*/the family is still the most important focal point in their life ("Latinos in America," 2000). For clinicians and researchers, the concepts of *personalismo* and *familismo* are important for the development of a trusting relationship, one *de confianza*/trusting. Other equally relevant terms are *respeto* and *bien educado*/well-mannered—further indicative of the value placed on interpersonal amenities, particularly with those who are older, in places of authority, and with special family or group status (Falicov, 1998; Flores & Carey, 2000; Santiago-Rivera, Arredondo, & Gallardo-Cooper, 2002).

For Latinas/os, kinship systems and the extended family are also sources of strength. It is not unusual for individuals from the same town in El Salvador, Puerto

Rico, or Mexico to locate in the same community in the United States. This has always been an immigrant tradition, and Latinos are not different in this self-selection process that provides comfort and familiarity in the midst of major life events of dislocation, transition, and acclimation to a new cultural and ecological environment.

Gender Socialization

Gender roles for Latinas and Latinos are framed through the concepts of *marianismo* and *machismo.* Both have been given more attention in contemporary literature because they provide a lens for understanding principles that influence behavior and other choices individuals make. At the same time, both concepts have been misinterpreted and used as a way to blame culture.

Marianismo is rooted in the aura of the Blessed Virgin Mary. For women, the spoken and unspoken messages are to live one's life in the image of the Blessed Mother—caring, nurturing, pure, and self-sacrificing (Gil & Vazquez, 1996). Virtuous behavior is admired and reinforced, often leading to what appears to be passivity and submissiveness to one's self-detriment. Younger women have complained about watching their mothers wait on their fathers *when he clearly could pour himself a glass of water!*

A research study with Latina psychotherapy clients led to the description of the 10 commandments of marianismo (Gil & Vazquez, 1996). Sample commandments include "Do not be single, self-supporting, or independent; Do not wish for more than being a housewife; Do not ask for help; and Do not forsake tradition" (Gil & Vazquez, 1996, p. 6). The 10 commandments are useful tools in the counseling process, but they must be assessed in relationship to other mediating forces and dimensions of personal identity, including immigration, acculturation and generational status, age, religious practices, relationship status, sexual orientation, and socioeconomic status.

Machismo has often been used to portray Latinos negatively, suggesting a preference for dominating women physically, sexually, and emotionally. This interpretation of the concept is the antithesis of the true meaning of men's prescribed role as breadwinner, reliable father and spouse, and protector of the family (Santiago-Rivera et al., 2002). As recommended with the application of marianismo, there are limitations. Other mediating processes, such as education, employment, and spiritual/religious practices must be taken into account.

Religion and Spirituality

From historical perspectives, indigenous spiritual orientations and the tenets of Catholicism have shaped beliefs and practices among Latinos. Although there are other organized religions that Latinos practice, Catholicism was introduced by the friars who accompanied the *conquistadores,* and it became a tool of oppression against the Native American people.

Generation and acculturation status as well as place of origin are factors that may affect individuals' religious and spiritual orientations. Seeking help from *curanderos/espiritistas* as well as priests and ministers is not uncommon among Latinos from Puerto Rico, El Salvador, or Mexico. For counselors in predominantly Spanish-speaking environments, such as New York City, Miami, or Los Angeles, inquiring about such services is recommended. In consultation with community cultural agencies or the healers themselves it can be determined when and if such services are indicated.

In a counseling setting, exploring individual and family religious practices in the present and the past can serve to illuminate possible coping mechanisms for clients. Latinas/os may invoke the Virgin Mary, Jesus, *La Virgen de Guadalupe,* or a saint in times of duress. Common expressions by Latinas are *Ay Díos mio/*Oh my God or *Si Díos quiere/*If it's God's will (Flores & Carey, 2000). It is advisable to explore the extent of a client's religious involvement historically and in the present. If an individual or family has changed religious preferences or stopped practicing, this may be a subject to pursue. For many individuals, spiritual/religious beliefs and practices are a source of strength.

Latino/a Dimensions of Personal and Ethnic Identity

As with all other ethnic/racial minority groups in the United States, Latinas/os have a range of experiences and feelings based on self-referent identity and the perceptions of others. *Mestizo* and *criollo* roots predispose contemporary individuals to a range of phenotypical and physical characteristics, from African, Asian, and Native American to European features. Although the literature suggests a much deeper meaning with respect to ethnic identity (Helms, 1990; Ruiz, 1990; Bernal & Knight, 1993; Santiago et al., 2002), for many Latinas/os stereotype-based assumptions, low expectations, and other prejudicial judgments about language ability, work ethic, citizenship status, and educational abilities continue to occur (Niemann, 2001).

Assumptions and judgments based on phenotype continue to occur with darker-skinned members of the same family, often resulting in more discriminatory experiences. An example comes from an interview a graduate student conducted with a teenage Mexican American girl. During the discussion, the girl's brother, one year younger, sat nearby listening attentively. When asked about how she identified ethnically, the girl quickly responded, "Mexican American." She went on to comment that oftentimes her friends, primarily Anglo, do not believe her brother is really her brother. "He's much darker so they have a hard time believing we are related and that I am Mexican."

Different theories about Mexican American identity indicate that there are mediating forces that interact and affect one's sense of ethnic identity and self-efficacy. For example, the Latino Dimensions of Personal Identity Model (Arredondo & Santiago-Rivera, 2000) suggest the interdependence of different dimensions of personal identity and processes such as place of origin/geographical location and acculturation, and external forces of history and political events. Imbedded in the identity development and self-referent process are factors of education, employment, and economics.

In a counseling situation, a woman's presenting issues may be workplace stress that may nor may not have to do with her being Latina. University environments push all junior faculty to produce scholarships that makes them eligible for tenure, regardless of ethnic background. However, if the junior professor is not sufficiently mentored, has few to no Latina role models, and is overloaded with teaching and service assignments, the degree of stress is magnified. A counselor would have to be judicious about pushing an ethnic minority identity agenda if this is not a priority in the client's struggle. This is not to say that ethnic identity is unrelated, rather to not overfocus on it. Instead, looking at the B dimensions of the Latino model might be considered. In particular, attention can be given to educational and work experiences and how the client has managed stress in these situations previously. Go for her strengths.

Continuous immigration from Spanish-speaking countries introduces differences in the profile of Latinas/os primarily from South American countries who may come prepared with formal education and professional skills, and immigrants from Mexico and Central America, often from rural towns, who may be at the opposite end of the educational and employment spectrum. This is not a statement of absolutes but rather indicative of the variability of the Latino population (Arce, 1999; U.S. Bureau of the Census Report, 2001).

Implications for Counseling Practices

This chapter has been a rather cursory discussion of a paradigm for new and old considerations in counseling processes with Latinas/os, drawing on multiple concepts and models from the literature. The Latina/o-centered counseling paradigms of interacting processes (Figure 8.2) suggests that clinicians begin to conceptualize a client's presenting issues more comprehensively. The objective is to underscore the interacting processes and critical factors that contribute to the uniqueness of Latinos as individuals and as a cultural group. Presenting issues and difficult situations might be explained through acculturative stress precipitated by economic demands, workplace discrimination, and the sociopolitical climate that is unfriendly to newcomers to a previously White community. When discussions such as these begin to deconstruct a label (Latino/Hispanic) and concepts that heretofore were used to conveniently categorize a group of people, the challenges for educators, agency administrators, and clinicians expand, and new knowledge is required. A few examples and observations follow.

Challenges to Counselors

At a recent counseling workshop, a participant raised a question about the participation of migrant farm workers in therapy. She observed their failure to be "self-reflective" and introspective. She wondered how she could move clients to this process. The presenter responded with several observations: (1) Her expectation about the desirability of client reflection represented a bias in traditional

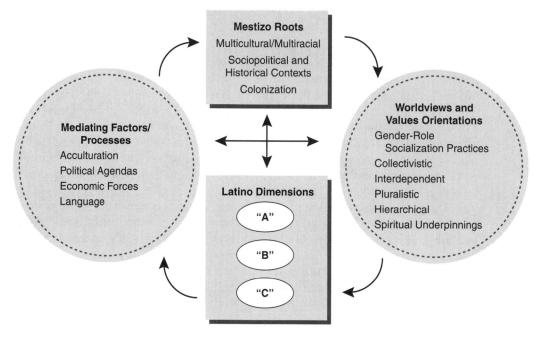

FIGURE 8.2   Latina/o Centered Counseling Paradigms: Interacting Processes

counseling. Depending on the client's need and expectations from counseling, it may or may not be a necessary process. (2) Migrant farm workers are likely capable of self-reflection; however, their context for work and living needs primary consideration. Farm worker families live in situations that introduce health, economic, and psychological stressors. Historically, their lives have been full of duress and survival against all odds. (3) Counselors need to remember that suspending judgment and meeting clients where they are allows for more effective, client-centered practice. Working with the Latino client in context, regardless of a counselor's preferred intervention processes, reflects cultural competence.

Two questions are often raised about counseling with Latinos: (1) Is there a preference for forms of help such as consultation with the clergy or family members, rather than engagement in standard counseling? and (2) Is there a particular counseling theory that works best with Latinos? Given the heterogeneity within the population as described in the Latino Dimensions of Personal Identity Model (Arredondo & Santiago-Rivera, 2000), it is reasonable to conjecture that not all Latinos will seek help from clergy or *curanderos*/indigenous healers, and that different counseling theories and modalities can be applied with Latinos.

A study of barriers to counseling among Mexicans and other Latinos, compared with Whites, pointed out the importance of within-group differences. It was reported that Mexicans do use formal counseling services, not just clergy, family, and friends (Young, 2001). Another study specifically examined the use of psychodynamic treatment with Latinos through discussions with clinicians self-described as bilingual and bicultural. Findings from these interviews were that the use of a psychodynamic approach was effective when clinicians placed an emphasis on the interpersonal relationship, the client as an individual, and external realities or context (Rosenthal, 1999). A third study, utilizing a case-study approach, found utility in applying racial identity models to assessment processes and case conceptualization (Delgado-Romero, 2001).

Community agency challenges are multidimensional. Well-intentioned practices or ones that have traditionally worked for White, monolingual-English-speaking middle-class clients may not neatly apply with low-income, immigrant, monolingual Spanish speakers. In addition to language considerations are the use of indigenous healers, multigenerational family counseling strategies, and collaboration with local cultural organizations that may provide resources not available at a community counseling agency. For example, the importance of family and the value of family support are often expected for Latinos. If it does not occur or is not in place, this line of inquiry may yield some explanations about family roles and other issues. A clinician should not immediately assume that family members do not care but learn more about the family and relationships among family members.

Latino-Centered Practices

To be culturally competent in the delivery of counseling services and for the development of institutional access for Latinos, counselors and psychologists in different roles (e.g., consultant) need to engage in relevant professional development. This is an ethical mandate. To not do so is to practice outside one's sphere of expertise.

Guiding proposed Latino-centered strategies for work with Latinos are the multicultural counseling competencies (MCC) documents (Sue, Arredondo, & McDavis, 1992; Arredondo et al., 1996). These statements address the interpersonal relationship of the client and counselor, the cultural bias and limitations of traditional assessment tools and counseling modalities, sociopolitical and historical factors, institutional racism, and the consideration of culturally different practices. These competencies or guidelines are suggested with full acknowledgment that they will still require adaptation for effectiveness with the individual Latino client and family.

Latino-Centered Strategies

Latino-centered strategies reflect the tripartite model of the MCC that address counselor self-understanding, counselor understanding about the client's worldview, and the application of this knowledge to culturally congruent interventions.

Counselor Self-Understanding
- Consider your own cultural heritage and its salience in your personal and professional development.

- Recognize feelings that arise when working with Latina clients and the meaning of these feelings.
- Review your preparation as a counselor or psychologist and how this enables and/or limits your work with Latinos.
- Examine your personal ethnic/racial identity status.
- Examine biases, both positive and negative, about Latinos in general, specific Latino ethnic groups, bilingualism, and other characteristics attributed to Latinos; know where they come from and how to address them so that they do not become barriers to effective treatment.

Counselor Understanding of the Latino Clients' Worldviews

- Be mindful of the heterogeneity of the Latino culture and ethnic groups as well as individual differences; refer to the Latino Dimensions of Personal Identity Model (Arredondo & Santiago-Rivera, 2000).
- Be knowledgeable about acculturation stressors and processes, family immigration history, ethnic and racial identity models, and sociopolitical forces such as racism that may impinge on the psychological well-being of Latinos.
- Become knowledgeable about demographic projections and the implications for counseling services for Latinos in different settings (e.g., public schools, community colleges, and community mental health centers).
- Become familiar with factors that contribute to acculturative stress, particularly for immigrants. Factors may include neighborhood, workplace stress, posttraumatic symptoms, communication limits, lack of social support/ isolation, cultural conflicts, and intergenerational conflicts.
- Become familiar with literature about "traditional" Latino worldviews based on *mestizo* psychology and other paradigms that speak about value orientations to allocentrism, *personalismo*, and *familisimo*.
- Recognize that there are varying Latino worldviews based on differences in place of origin, historical relations with the United States, education, economics, generation, citizenship, and other sociocultural and ecological factors. Consider psychohistorical frameworks (Erikson, 1975) when conceptualizing approaches to working with Latinos.
- Realize that individuals and families need to be understood in context. This suggests that there is no one best approach to work with Latinos in general. Approaches with middle-class, highly educated individuals and immigrants from rural communities will likely vary.
- Consider bilingualism an academic, psychological, social, and economic asset, not a deficit.

Application of Culturally Congruent Practices

- Be prepared to conduct culture-centered assessments that include information about gender socialization experiences, religious and spiritual orientation, language preference and use, and health care practices.
- Know when it is appropriate to use interpreters and when it is not appropriate.

- Determine the relevance of standardized psychological assessments with limited English-speaking clients.
- Know when it is appropriate to involve an indigenous healer or to refer a client to another cultural resource.
- Be prepared to use multicultural counseling competencies, the ethical guidelines, and Latino-centered knowledge.

Case Study

Manuel was a 35-year-old landscape worker referred by a physician for mental health treatment. According to the referral, recently Manuel was experiencing extensive bouts of insomnia, causing him to "fall asleep" on the job. This lack of sleep also seemed to introduce eye discomfort and headaches, to the point that reportedly his head felt like it weighed fifty pounds. His co-workers were able to cover for him for a week, until the supervisor found him napping.

Employed by the same company for the past ten years, Manuel had an excellent performance record, was well-liked by his supervisor and co-workers, and seemed to lead a model family life as well. He was married and the father of three children under the age of 12. Manuel's wife, Elsa, worked part time as a housekeeper. They were married in Mexico prior to coming to the United States fifteen years previously. Manuel and his family were regular churchgoers, and he proudly wore a medal of La Virgen de Guadalupe around his neck.

In his meeting with the therapist, Manuel shared that he had become preoccupied with the recent death of a co-worker's teenage son. They boy was killed in a neighborhood drive-by shooting by White teenagers out joy riding. His oldest child was an 11-year-old boy. In Mexico, Manuel's best friend had died in a freak traffic accident at age 15. He wondered aloud whether his son would be safe in this country. When he first arrived, Manuel had experienced discrimination because of his language limitations, "They didn't realize that I had a high school education and was preparing to be an accountant. All they saw was a dark man who couldn't speak English."

Case Conceptualization

Listening to the client's pain and providing support is the likely approach to engage initially with Manuel. He is trying to manage different stressors simultaneously in the present with precipitants from the past. Because Latino clients are known to not return to counseling after the first visit, the counselor's interpersonal behavior and cultural competence will be key. This is a man who is proud of his family and his accomplishments, yet he is also fearful and in pain. Using Figure 8.2, a clinician is reminded that Manuel may have been socialized with hierarchical relationships, thus being formal is indicated. He has been living up to the machismo principles of caring for his family, yet the work situation has created a crisis for him. Manuel's faith and reverence for La Virgen are noteworthy.

A counselor might inquire about the role of prayer and how he incorporates prayer at times when there is distress.

La familia is a central value for Latinas/os, and this is evident for Manuel. The counselor needs to inquire about his wife's awareness of the current situation. Does she know about his fears? If not, why?

Manuel is dealing with loss and the anticipation of additional loss if something happens to his son. It is also possible that losses experienced as a result of immigration and acculturation are contributing factors. Many immigrants have to postpone their sense of loss about leaving family and friends behind. A crisis can precipitate long-suppressed feelings. This may also be the case for Manuel.

All of the constructs in Figure 8.2 are relevant; it is a matter of determining if and when to operationalize them. All cases will be different, but it is the interpersonal and cultural competence of the counselor that will be the enabling force to a successful counseling experience for all parties involved.

Conclusion

In a popular song, Puerto Rican singer Ricky Martin expounds upon the challenges of living *la vida loca*/a crazy life. For contemporary Latinas/os, life introduces multiple contradictions and challenges filled with pessimism and optimism. Walking a tightrope of multiple social identities, in and out of affirming and nonaffirming environments, and with the same basic human needs of emotional and physical well-being held by other individuals are the experiences and motivators that counselors must recognize. However, recognition is insufficient.

In this chapter, I have attempted to provide an overview of the rich historical roots that have given birth to today's Latinas/os and our families, our heterogeneity, and our similarities. I encourage counselors to embark on the journey of becoming culturally competent with respect to the Latino population. Commit to learn one new fact a week, commit to become more curious, and accept the premise that this is a life-long journey. Follow the model of César Chavez who knew that in order to help the migrant farm workers who depended upon him, he needed to take heed. "When I am out with the workers, they teach me every single day. It's an amazing thing. Obviously, I don't know everything, I just know a little bit. Perhaps because I've made more mistakes than anybody else, I've had a chance to learn more than anybody else. But still, the workers teach me every single day as I teach them" (Levy, 1974, p. 521).

DISCUSSION QUESTIONS

1. What are some of the historical events between U.S. governments and the countries of Cuba, Mexico, and Puerto Rico?

2. Describe some of the contributing factors to Latino value orientations.

3. What contributes to the complexity of the Latino ethnic identity phenomenon?

4. Describe Latino-specific concepts and value orientations that may manifest in a counseling encounter.

5. Explain why the "borderlands" metaphor applies to contemporary Latinos.

REFERENCES

Anzaldúa, G. (1987). *Borderlands/La Frontera.* San Francisco, CA: Spinsters/Aunt Lute Book Company.

Arce, C. (1999). *Hispanic Association of Corporate Responsibility 1999 report.* Washington, DC: Hispanic Association of Corporate Responsibility.

Arredondo, P., & Santiago-Rivera, A. (2000). *Latino dimensions of personal identity* (adapted from Personal Dimensions of Identity Model). Unpublished document.

Arredondo, P., Toporek, R., Brown, S. P., Jones, J., Locke, D. C., Sanchez, J., & Stadler, H. (1996). Operationalization of the multicultural counseling competencies. *Journal of Multicultural Counseling and Development, 24,* 42–78.

Bernal, M. E., & Knight, G. P. (Eds.). (1993). *Ethnic identity: Formation and transmission among Hispanics and other minorities.* Albany: State University of New York Press.

Center for Mental Health Services. (2001). *Mental health: Culture, race, and ethnicity—A supplement to mental health: A report of the surgeon general.* Rockville, MD: U.S. Department of Health and Human Services, Substance Abuse and Mental Health Services Administration.

Córdova, T. (1999). Anti-colonial Chicana feminism. In R. D. Torres & G. Katsiaficas (Eds.), *Latino social movements: Historical and theoretical perspectives.* New York: Routledge.

Delgado-Romero, E. A. (2001). Counseling a Hispanic/Latino client: Mr. X. *Journal of Mental Health Counseling, 23,* 207–221.

Erikson, E. (1975). *Life history and the historical moment.* New York: Norton.

Estrada L. (1999). *Hispanic Association of Corporate Responsibility 1999 report.* Washington, DC: Hispanic Association of Corporate Responsibility.

Falicov, C. J. (1998). *Latino families in therapy: A guide to multicultural practice.* New York: Guilford Press.

Flores, M. T., & Carey, G. (2000). *Family therapy with Hispanics: Toward appreciating diversity.* Boston: Allyn & Bacon.

Gil, R. M., & Vazquez, C. N. (1996). *The Maria paradox.* New York: A Perigee Book.

Helms, J. E. (1990). *Black and White racial identity: Theory, research and practice.* Westport, CT: Greenwood.

Latinos in America: A journey in stages. (2000). *The Washington Post.* Retrieved January 15, 2000, from www.washingtonpost.com/wp-dyn/article/a51043–2000jan15.html

Levy, J. (1974). *The autobiography of César Chavez.* New York: Norton.

Liebowitz, S. W., Castellano, D. C., Cuellar, I. (1999). Factors that predict sexual behaviors among young Mexican American adolescents: An exploratory study. *Hispanic Journal of Behavioral Sciences, 21,* 470–479.

Middleton, R., Arredondo, P., & D'Andrea, M. (2000, December). The impact of Spanish-speaking newcomers in Alabama towns. *Counseling Today, 43*(6), p. 24

Niemann, Y. F. (2001). Stereotypes about Chicanas and Chicanos: Implications for counseling. *The Counseling Psychologist, 29,* 55–90.

Prieto, L. R., McNeill, B. W., Walls, R. G., & Gómez, S. P. (2001). An overview of utilization, counselor preference, and assessment issues. *The Counseling Psychologist, 29,* 18–54.

Ramirez, M. (1998). *Multicultural/multiracial psychology: Mestizo perspectives in personality and mental health.* Northvale, NJ: Jason Aronson.

Rosenthal, C. S. (1999). Toward a better understanding of the use of psychodynamically-informed treatment with Latinos: Findings from clinician experience. *Dissertation Abstracts, 59*(8-A): 3212.

Ruiz, A. S. (1990). Ethnic identity: Crisis and resolution. *Journal of Multicultural Counseling and Development, 18,* 29–40.

Santiago-Rivera, A., Arredondo, P., & Gallardo-Cooper, M. (2002). *Counseling Latinos and la familia: A practical guide.* Thousand Oaks, CA: Sage.

Sue, D. W., Arredondo, P., & McDavis, R. (1992). Multicultural competencies and standards: A call to the profession. *Journal of Counseling and Development, 70,* 477–486.

U.S. Bureau of the Census. (2001). *The Hispanic population: Census brief* (C2KBR/01–3). Washington, DC: Government Printing Office.

Vasconcellos, J. (1925). *La raza cosmica: Mision de la cultura iberoamericano (The cosmic race: Mission of the Iberoamerican race).* Mexico, D. F.: Espasa-Calpe Mexicana S. A., 1976.

Young, K. S. (2001). Barriers to counseling: Mexicans and other Hispanics compared with non-Hispanic Whites. *Dissertation-Abstracts, 61*(9-A): 3784.

9 Counseling European Americans

LEE J. RICHMOND

The New Colossus
Not like the brazen giant of Greek fame
With conquering limbs astride from land to land;
Here at our sea-washed, sunset gates shall stand
A mighty woman with a torch, whose flame
Is the imprisoned lightning, and her name
Mother of Exiles. From her beacon-hand
Glows world-wide welcome; her mild eyes command
The air-bridged harbor that twin cities frame,
"Keep, ancient lands, your storied pomp!" cries she
With silent lips. "Give me your tired, your poor,
Your huddled masses yearning to breathe free,
The wretched refuse of your teeming shore,
Send these, the homeless, tempest-tossed to me,
I lift my lamp beside the golden door!"
—Emma Lazarus, 1883

Some Early American History

The area that we call the United States has always been a land of immigration. It is commonly believed that the first inhabitants were Siberian migrants who crossed the Bering Strait and traveled southward from Alaska in search of food some 13,000 years ago. By the time the Europeans sailed to what they later called the "New World," many cities were already there, some as densely populated as the capital cities of Europe. A population of 70 million people stretched across the two American continents. By the year 1500, it is believed that the "natives" spoke 2,000 different languages. Even then, the Americas were comprised of people of diverse cultures. Some tribes hunted and gathered, whereas Aztecs and Incas, building on earlier Olmec, Mayan, and Toltec civilizations, created not only great cities but even greater empires (Gutman et al., 1989).

Who were European explorers who early encountered these natives, and why did they set sail for new lands? It is commonly held that the European explorers of the fifteenth and sixteenth centuries came as a result of the failure of the feudal system in Europe. The rulers of Europe could not obtain enough money out of the old agrarian culture to solve their commercial and military problems. Famine, disease, and seemingly endless wars had decimated the population of Europe. New rulers who sought to centralize their power needed to seek new sources of revenue. They looked beyond the European continent for these sources. They became early capitalists who sought and found gold and other riches in distant lands by financing adventurous European explorers (Gutman, et al. 1989)

Most of these European explorers came from Spain, Portugal, and the lands that now comprise Italy. Their names are all familiar to us, but none is more familiar or famous than Christopher Columbus. Son of a weaver, and thought, but not proven, to be of Spanish-Jewish descent, Columbus was born in the port city of Genoa. Regardless of whether Columbus was Jewish, it is known that six people who sailed with him were. Rodingo DeTriani, a sailor; Luis De Tores, an interpreter; Maestre Bernal, a physician; Rodrigo Sanches De Segovia, Queen Isabella's inspector; Marco, a surgeon; and Afonso DeLaCalle, a sailor, were the six men of Jewish origin. It is an interesting fact of history that his first expedition in 1492 occurred in the very year that the Inquisition was at its zenith in Spain. In fact, all Jews were expelled from Spain that year (Builders of America, The Jewish Heritage, 1991).

Early European commerce was with Central and South America. There the Spanish extracted huge sums of gold, largely from Mexico. The Portuguese, using slave labor from Africa, grew tobacco on Brazilian plantations. Subsequently, the French settled in Quebec, and the Dutch in New York, each seeking profitable trade with Europe. The English also came to North America. However, it was not until the defeat of the Spanish Armada that the English seriously set their sights on the New World. When they came, they settled mainly in Virginia and Massachusetts.

There were two groups of English settlers: those who wished to engage in the production of goods and trade, and those who sought freedom from political and religious oppression in England. So many came that the English soon represented 60 percent of the early settlers. People from Scotland, Ireland, and Wales joined the English. Thus, the American colonies were born.

The Europeans who peopled America came from several countries and had various motives. Predominantly entrepreneurial capitalists, some were simply adventurers, whereas others were seekers of political and religious asylum. Still others were prisoners and indentured servants wishing to break their shackles in an unknown and sometimes dangerous environment. There is evidence that these Europeans brought with them their old ways. The Spanish were cruel to the native people and often to their own people. The Inquisition was carried from Spain to Central America where, in 1596, in Mexico City, the sister of the governor, Doña Francesca Rodriguez Caravajal, and her three daughters and one son, Luis de Carvajal, were burned for being Jewish. In 1589, Isabel Rodriguez de Andrada, niece of

Don Luis de Caravajal, governor of the province called the New Kingdom of Leon, was tortured by the Inquisition into naming many other colonists as Judiazers. As a result many moved out of central Mexico to the land that is today New Mexico and Texas (Tobias, 1990).

It was not only the Spanish who brought old ways. In Salem the English Puritans hanged witches. The religious freedom that they sought was for themselves, not others. The religious segregation of Europe was carried to the colonies. Catholics, not welcome in New England, settled in Maryland. Not only individuals, but also nations, carried their feuds here. There was little love lost between the French and English, and between each of these countries and Spain.

Economics, however, sometimes makes strange bedfellows. For example, in 1649, a 400-year-old law forbade Jews from settling in English lands. Jews were expelled from England in 1250 A.D. However, a Dutch rabbi named Manassa Ben Israel convinced Oliver Cromwell to let Jews settle in New York. He used the messianic argument that before the final Judgment Day, Jews had to be dispersed to all nations of the earth. The idea fit Cromwell's religion but also coincidentally fit with Cromwell's desire to hasten commerce with the colonies (Builders of America, The Jewish Heritage, 1991). Hence, Jews settled in Boston in 1649 and in Newport in 1658. When the English conquered New Amsterdam in 1664, its Jewish inhabitants became English subjects living in the renamed city of New York.

Among the settlers, the ways of the Old World slowly transformed into ways of the new. Both the colonies of the industrial north and agrarian colonies of the south grew and prospered. In addition, as the colonies grew, seeds of an American democracy grew independent of European rule. When revolution cemented American independence, eyes turned to the new frontier and the opening of the American West. Here English Americans and Spanish Americans would later meet, fight, and unite, as new immigrants continued to pour in from Europe. However, the immigrants of the mid-1800s were different from those who came before. They were the poor and tempest-tossed about which the poetess Emma Lazarus wrote (Rose, 1974). They came in tens of thousands not only from Ireland, Scandinavia, Italy, and Germany but also from Eastern Europe—Poland, Czechoslovakia, and Russia. All of these, the poorest of the poor, were determined to become American citizens.

Who were these poor? They were Slavs and Poles. They were Greeks; 500,000 of them came in five waves throughout the 1800s. They were Italians: 5 million of them seeking religious freedom and seeking land because there was none available to them at home. More than 4 million Irish, poor and plagued by famine, sought a home in America. Three million people migrated from Scandinavian countries to seek a better life in America. All of these came, and along with them came Germans and Russians, Albanians, Hungarians, and Armenians. Eastern European Jews, both a cultural and a religious group, entered the United States in the late 1800s and early 1900s. They were victims of Eastern European wars, and they were also victims of poverty and homelessness (Rose, 1974).

Each new European group that came to America sought to integrate within the American culture and eventually they did, but it was not easy. Each new group was stereotyped by those who were already in the United States. The jobs that the newcomers could get were limited to the most difficult, those that required long hours of labor. Often people who came seeking streets of gold were reduced to living on streets of squalor in the poorest and dirtiest living quarters. Prejudice against each new nationality ran rampant. Gradually, as time passed, diverse European groups became less impoverished and made their way into the culture at large. For instance, by 1939, the city council of Cleveland was comprised of three African Americans, four Native Americans, and 17 people of European descent. Two of these were Jews, two Yugoslavians, two Poles, one Hungarian, six Germans, two Irish, one Bohemian, and one Italian (Wittke, 1939). Hardly a monolithic group at the outset, it is entirely possible that today, an American of European ancestry may be descended from as many as ten different immigrant groups and a multitude of religious sects. People often thought to be of Anglo origin most often are not. For example, Walt Whitman, commonly thought to be English, was actually half-Dutch, and Bret Hart, was half-Jewish. The so-called Anglo American majority has been a mystique since the colonial era. Caucasian Americans are more like a conglomerate of cultures, a cluster of minorities, who in some ways are far more different from each other than alike.

A Comparison of Groups

The Jews

An example of differences both between and within immigrant groups can be illustrated by tracing the journey of the Jews, the Irish, the Italians, and the Swedes. It has been previously demonstrated that before the founding of America, Jews were already there. Luis de Torres, who sailed with Columbus, remained in Cuba, received a grant of land from the King of Spain, married the daughters of local chiefs, and began commerce with Europe. When Oliver Cromwell lifted the ban against Jewish settlement in the English colonies, several Jews came to North America. Most of them were Spanish or Portuguese who entered the English colonies from Brazil, Central America, or the West Indies. The oldest synagogue in the United States is in Rhode Island and dates to 1658. When Roger Williams was banished from Salem, Massachusetts, in 1635 because he believed that worship should be granted to all men, he formed the colony of Rhode Island to do just that. A group of Jews then founded Congregation Jeshuat Israel. They then broke ground for their synagogue, known as the Turo Synagogue, and dedicated it in 1753.

Great Jewish families arose prior to the revolution. A second congregation was established in Charleston, South Carolina. In 1697 there were forty-four Jews living there. In New York, the Moses Levy family were merchants, as were the Jacob Franks family. A relative, David Franks, was a member of the provincial assembly in Pennsylvania in the 1700s. Another well-known family was that of Isaac Mendez Seixas. These Jewish families practiced a form of the Jewish religion called Sephardic, meaning Spanish. It was previously practiced in Spain, Portugal,

South America, and North Africa. This was the same Sephardic practice that the crypto-Jews who settled in New Spain (Mexico) brought to what is now called New Mexico. Surrounded in secrecy, because of the Inquisition, it is now known that certain Jewish practices did exist there (Tobias, 1990).

Perhaps the most famous Jew living in America at the time of the American Revolution was Hyam Soloman, who is said to have lost his fortune financing it. In any case, this much is known: at the time of the American Revolution, Jews lived throughout the colonies as loyal and sometimes powerful citizens, practicing their own form of religious Jewish Orthodoxy.

The good fortune of the Jewish people in the colonies was made clear by a 15-year-old Jewish boy named Napthali Phillips. He wrote a letter describing the 1778 ratification of the American Constitution in Philadelphia. He described long tables filled with all kinds of foods and a separate table for Jews with Kosher food because they could not, for religious reasons, eat some of the meat on other tables (Lipsett & Raab, 1995).

The next group of Jews to come to America came from Germany where, during the 1800s, anti-Semitic feeling ran high. It was not until 1848 that Jews were granted German citizenship. Nevertheless, even though German Jews had been discriminated against, many of the Jews of Germany in the 1800s benefited from the enlightenment movement in Europe. They started a branch of Judaism known as Reform Judaism. Seeking better circumstances than those that were offered to them in Europe, both Orthodox and Reform German Jews came to America. These Jews did not speak Spanish, and they were not immediately welcomed by the Sephardic Jews who arrived before them. They were also not immediately welcomed by the culture at large.

Most German Jews in America began as peddlers, traveling from place to place, selling cloth, knives, and jewelry. Though they did not make much money at first, this was the beginning of the firms that would later emerge as department stores such as Macy's, Bloomingdale's, and the Hecht Company. Moreover, Levi Strauss started out as a peddler. Guggenheim, now a name indicating power and wealth, was the name of another German Jewish immigrant. The German Jews lived in groups and adapted their enlightened Reform Judaism to the "American Way of Life." Orthodox Jewry saw this as an anathema, proclaiming Reform Judaism to be more like Christianity than like traditional Judaism.

America, by this time, was not free of anti-Semitism, but it was freer of it than the countries of Europe where trouble was never far away, particularly in Eastern Europe. Emma Lazarus, born in 1849 to a prominent fourth-generation New York Jewish family, recognized in the 1880s that her city was becoming the port of entry for Jewish immigrants from Eastern Europe, particularly those escaping the pogroms of Russia. A well-known writer and poet, Emma Lazarus was never homeless, poor, or tempest-tossed. She nevertheless used her celebrity to bring to the nation's attention the plight of Eastern European Jews and also that of other refugees from Eastern Europe (Brody, 1996). Between 1880 and 1920, Jewish immigrants, who were poor and weary victims of war and famine, flooded into America from Poland, Lithuania, Romania, Latvia, and Russia. These Jews were different from both the Orthodox Sephardic Jews and the German Jews, both in their faith and in their way of life. These 2 million Eastern European immigrants by far outnumbered the two groups who had come before, disapproved of their lifestyle, spoke a different language (Yiddish), and were just as eager to become Americans as any other group. They were called Ashkenazic Jews, came in families, and, albeit poor, were literate. They took low-paying jobs in sweatshops, took in laundry, peddled wares, resisted assimilation, and had children such as Fanny Borach, later known as Fanny Brice, the Ziegfeld girl. Jews were not often known to be soldiers, but immigrant Sergeant Benjamin Kaufman won the Congressional Medal of Honor, along with other awards from nine foreign governments for bravery in World War I (Brody, 1996). He started the Jewish-American War Veterans organization.

American patriotism was no stranger to the Jewish immigrant. Perhaps one who exemplified it in a different way was Israel Baline, better known as Irving Berlin, who wrote "This is the Army, Mr. Jones," and with it raised $10 million for army emergency relief. He is most known for writing "God Bless America." He assigned the copyright for that song to the God Bless America Fund, which has constantly raised money for the Boy Scouts and the Girl Scouts of America. Nine hundred other songs, including "Easter Parade" and "White Christmas," were also composed by the Russian Jewish immigrant who made America his home (Brody, 1996).

In summation, Jewish people are identified both as a culture and a religion. There have been three major waves of immigration, which have brought to the U.S. shores three major subgroups of Jews. Each group came by and large to escape European anti-Semitism and create a better life in America. The third group, the Eastern European Jews, were Orthodox, poor, and considered somewhat backward by the Spanish and German Jews who were already in the United States. In fact, three Jewish groups did not come together as a unit until the Nazi Holocaust attempted to do away with all Jews.

As for the Jewish religion, there are four major branches of Judaism in America today: Orthodox, Reform, Conservative, and Reconstructionist. The latter two emerged as middle of the road because Orthodoxy was considered by many to be too strict in its interpretation of the Law, and Reform was considered to be too lax. It should be noted that within Orthodoxy itself there is a wide range of practice ranging from modern Orthodoxy to Chasidim, a particular sect, made known to the public by the movie *Yentl*.

The Irish

The first Irish in America were by and large Scotch-Irish who came during the colonial period. There was an economic motive for the early emigration from Ireland—the system of mercantilism, on which the British commercial system was based (Wittke, 1939). The Scotch-Irish of the eighteenth century traveled to New England where they were immediately resented by the Puritans. After their frontier settlements in Massachusetts were destroyed by a mob during the night, the Scotch-

Irish settled in Pennsylvania where they practiced a form of Protestantism. Michael J. O'Brien (1919) wrote a history of the Irish during the American Revolution. He claimed that 38 percent of the troops were Irish. In fact, St. Patrick's Day was observed by the colonial troops by order of General George Washington (Wittke, 1939).

The Scotch-Irish who came from the North of Ireland, however, did not want to be confused with the Southern "Papist" Irish at home. The Scotch-Irish in American were mostly Presbyterians who are noted for leading the way westward and setting up academies. Princeton, the College of New Jersey, was a significant contribution of the Scotch-Irish to American higher education (Wittke, 1939).

Known for tenacity, courage, self-determination, and self-reliance, the ranks of Scotch-Irish include such political leaders as John Witherspoon, Henry Knox, James Monroe, James Madison, John Calhoun, Horace Greely, and Woodrow Wilson. Be this as it may, the great bulk of Irish immigration occurred in the mid-1800s as a result of the Great Famine. Economists agree that between 1815 and 1850 in Ireland there was a steady and progressive deterioration of farms and farmland (Wittke, 1939). England and an aristocracy of English landholders forced the native Catholic Irish into poverty. The peasants in Ireland lived in huts that were dirty, smokey, and cold; they ate only one meal a day, which consisted of potatoes and buttermilk. Then when the potato crop failed, men, women, and children ate grass. Thus, hundreds of thousands of Irish arrived in America with no money in their pockets or food in their bellies. With little education and lack of skills, they were often stranded in cities where they either roamed the streets or lived in congested shantytowns (Wittke, 1939).

From the alleys and cellars of slum areas, in the ghettos of Boston, New York, and Philadelphia, the Irish spread the diseases from which they often died. Prejudice against their Catholic religion kept them from getting many jobs, even the most menial. Nevertheless, those who survived did eventually find work building the railroads or as servants in the homes of others. With the passing of time, better jobs were eventually acquired. As difficult as life was, for most it was still better than starving to death in Ireland.

The Irish immigrants gave America not only politicians but also songwriters and storytellers and more than a few heroes. The Yankee Doodle Dandy, George M. Cohan, sang and danced America's spirit. Coincidentally, it is often said that Cohan the Irishman and Berlin the Jew were both instrumental in giving the nation Broadway.

Other European Minorities

Before 1860, there were few Italian immigrants to America, but after that year, Italians came in droves. Many never meant to stay; they were "birds of passage" and went back home. However, most stayed (Wittke, 1939). They came to earn money. Most were men, unskilled and often illiterate, who, because of heavy taxes, primitive agricultural methods, and industrial stagnation, could not earn a living at home. The Italians, largely Catholic, did the lowliest tasks for meager wages.

Living in clannish isolation, most became day laborers in the construction industry, on the railroad, in mines, and in mills. Italians stayed in their communities at first, prey to mobs that would taunt them to fight. But from these ranks came Fiorella H. LaGuardia, mayor of New York; Giovanni Martinelli of the Metropolitan Opera; Joe Di Maggio of baseball fame; and Chairman of the Board, Frank Sinatra (Wittke, 1939).

Swedish emigration occurred because of an overcrowded countryside. Many were poor and, like the Irish, had nothing but their hands with which to work. In the late 1860s, severe weather prevailed in Sweden and the crops did not. There was famine in the land, and after a succession of poor harvests in Sweden and the economic crisis of 1864–1865, there was an exodus of Swedish agricultural workers. Most often, these Swedish immigrants arrived in New York and proceeded by rail or by way of the Erie Canal to Buffalo, and then by boat or over land westward (Wittke, 1939).

Though they had come to farm, many Swedes drifted to cities. Chicago was the center of Swedish America. By 1900, Chicago had more Swedes than the second-largest city in Sweden, Gothenburg. A section of Chicago was called "Swede Town" where the immigrants lived. It has been claimed that Chicago was built by Swedes, who, rising from the lowest level of labor, learned and became skilled carpenters and bricklayers. They created Swedish newspapers and Swedish clubs, and, gradually, as they learned English, joined with other Scandinavians (e.g., Finns, Danes, and Norwegians) in building cities such as Minneapolis, Minnesota (Holmquist, 1981). Eventually, the "Vikings in America" settled throughout Minnesota, Iowa, Illinois, Michigan, Nebraska, and Kansas. One fourth of the Swedes remained farmers (Wittke, 1939). Almost universally, they were Lutherans and they formed congregations that, together, formed the Swedish Lutheran Church. Charles A. Lindbergh, Sr., and John Lind wrote their names into American history. Fiercely loyal and mainly Republican, the Swedes have had a major influence on middle American politics even to this day (Magnussen, 2001).

Jews, Irish, Italians, and Swedes were all European, but with different languages, cultures, and faiths. What they had in common was their poverty, and their willingness to work, to struggle, and to start anew. They all held hope that one day things would be better for their children. Each faced prejudice from the then "majority culture," struggled with it, and both they and America prevailed.

European Immigration Today

Today, most of the immigrants who come to the United States are not from Europe. Of those who are from Europe, very few are from the United Kingdom. The Ukraine, Russia, and Poland are the nations from where most European immigrants have come. In 1995, 720,500 people immigrated to the United States. At that time, 91 percent of the total population was native born. Of the 21,632,000 Americans who were not native born, the majority came from Mexico, the Dominican Republic, Cuba, Jamaica, Haiti, El Salvador, and Columbia. Most of the rest of the immigrants come from Pacific or Asian countries, including the Philippines, Vietnam, China, and India. There is every indication that the largest growing minority groups in the United States will continue to come from Spanish-speaking countries and from Asia. Furthermore, the fastest growing religion in America is Islam. It has come to America from Africa, the Middle East, and Asia. The shift in population growth has ramifications for European Americans who, even if banded together, would not much longer hold the hegemony. The power base in America is shifting. European Americans are a part of the minority stew. As a group, Caucasian Americans hold most, but surely not all, of the political clout in a rapidly changing economy where women and people of color are slowly but surely making strong inroads into the fist of corporate America (*Encyclopedia Britannica*, 2001).

Ramifications for Counseling

When considering Caucasian Americans as a composite of many minority groups from Europe, existing models for the counseling of American minorities pertain. Important consideration must be given to recency of immigration, number of generations in America, and values issues engendered in lifestyle. Attitudes toward self, other minorities, and the current culture of most Americans, as suggested in Atkinson, Morten, and Sue's (1989) model, is most useful. Taking a cross-generational approach to historical-cultural background, as suggested in the McFadden model, also is valuable (McFadden, 1999).

Because most counseling takes place with persons having concerns in living with self or others, or having decision-making difficulties in the educational or career area, matters relating to gender identity and social identity are significant not only for other minorities but also for European Americans. Recently, a well-known counselor, who happens to be an Orthodox Jew, spoke at a national convention about how little understood was her observance of the law pertaining to both the Sabbath and the use of Kosher food. In fact, she took to task a known professional organization for scheduling her session on Saturday. The session was changed, but she admonished the association for not being more sensitive. Counselors need to be aware of specific ethnic and cultural needs of Euro-American minorities.

Counseling Cases: A Dilemma, Some Anger, and a Bully

To illustrate further the importance of the time of immigration and the importance of culture on European Americans, consider the following cases. Samira Hashemi and Stephen Butler met and fell in love while attending a graduate school in New England that is noted for its program in business administration. On his father's side, Stephen's family had lived in America since the signing of the Constitution. The Butler family were of mixed German and English stock. Steve's German ancestry was originally Lutheran. However, Steve's paternal grandparents joined the Methodist Church, the faith in which Steve was raised. Steve's mother's family was originally Jewish, but much to the chagrin of her family of origin, Steve's mother converted to the Methodist faith when she married. Some contact was kept with the Jewish part of the family and as a youth, Steve celebrated some of the major Jewish holidays with his cousins. Steve considered himself all-American in every way—he was athletic throughout his life and engaged in sports in both high school and college.

Samira's family came to the United States in the 1970s. Her parents fled from Iran when the government changed. Her father, an employee of the deposed Shah, would have been executed had the family stayed in Iran. Although Samira was born in America, she has heard many stories about Iran from her mother, who missed her native land and found it difficult to adapt to American methods, styles of dress, and daily living. The family, however, prospered in the United States, though they did not possess the great wealth or expansive lands that they had to leave behind in Iran. Though the Hashemis continued to practice the Moslem religion, they were modern in their ways. Samira was raised as an American child. She dressed as her classmates did, and she was quite popular with both boys and girls throughout her school years. While in college she excelled in academics, developed an interest in drama, and acted in several school plays.

Steve and Samira considered themselves to be a perfect match. Both were bright and attractive, and each came from a good family. When Steve brought Samira home to meet his parents, they took to her immediately. Samira's parents also liked Steve. The couple, however, faced two problems. The first was religion. Not raised as a Christian, Samira did not see herself converting. Steve had little understanding of Islam. To him, it was a foreign faith. Steve was concerned that the Jewish part of his family might have negative feelings about Samira being Iranian and Moslem, and he did not introduce her to them. Therefore, the first problem was how the couple, who felt spiritually as one in every other way, could reconcile their religious beliefs. The second problem was that of their respective families. Although everyone who knew the couple respected them, a marriage between them would still look like that of a bird marrying a fish. Not only did religious views cause a problem, but also political views related to the situation in the Middle East could cause discomfort. A third problem loomed for the future. What about the children that Steve and Samira might have? Samira and Steve sought counseling. They knew they were in love but had no idea how they would work things out.

A different counseling case involved a young woman named Naomi Rosenstein who had applied to law school. She did not get in. A good student throughout high school and college, Naomi had always wanted to be a lawyer. In college, her interests crystallized. A social activist, Naomi wanted to be a public defender. She became close friends with an African American woman, Cheryl Smith, who had similar interests. Although bright, Cheryl did not have an academic background equal to that of Naomi and did less well in both literature and social science classes. However, both women graduated from college with honors. Both applied to their state university's law school. Only Cheryl got in; Naomi did not. At first, Naomi was glad for her friend but furious with the system. Naomi's grades were slightly better, her LSAT scores slightly higher, and although she was accepted to two lesser law schools out of town, she felt that the only reason that Cheryl got into the state university was because Cheryl was African American. Naomi began to resent Cheryl. After all, Naomi herself was from a minority group. The state had plenty of Jewish law students, she thought, but few African American ones. Her anger was blinding her. She wanted to sue. She felt that she could hardly be Cheryl's friend because of her jealousy. Naomi knew that she was not functioning well. She sought counseling.

Boris, a 10-year-old boy, was brought for counseling by his parents. Though his name was simply Boris, his classmates called him "Boris the Bully." Newly immigrated from Russia, Boris's parents could not understand his recent oppositional behavior. All of his obstinacy, they thought, occurred since he had come to America at age 7. At home in Moscow, Boris had been an obedient, even a docile, child. However, here he was a terror. What had happened?

Boris, however, faced unique problems both within himself and with his peers. He did not speak English well, and for that reason was singled out in school and thought to be slow. His clothing was different from that of his peers. Neatly dressed, but with a limited wardrobe, he did not look like the other kids. Nor did his classmates visit him at home or invite him to their houses to play.

Boris's parents wanted him to study after school. They knew how much he had to learn. They also feared letting him play outside in the neighborhood lest the other children hurt him. Gradually, Boris began to act out his frustration. He would push other kids in school. At home, he would disobey and, when punished, he would be silent or sulk. His parents did not understand. They took Boris to his school counselor and told the counselor to make him behave.

In each of these three cases, the minority person was a European American. In the first case, both Steve and Samira represented minorities, Steve with regard to a social convention. A white, Protestant Anglo-Saxon would have trouble being accepted as husband to an Iranian American citizen of the Moslem faith, as would Samira as a bride to him. Although interfaith marriages are common in the United States, they are usually between people of varying Protestant groups or between Protestants and Catholics. Marriages between Christians and Jews is considered somewhat more problematic but hardly uncommon. Marriage between Moslems and Christians, and especially those Christians with Jewish ancestry are quite uncommon, particularly among first-generation American Moslems. Yet, there is no reason to believe that Samira and Steve's is an isolated case. As more young people of the Moslem faith meet others on college campuses and in offices across the land, Steve and Samira's situation will be repeated many times.

Naomi's case is one of what Naomi believed to be reverse discrimination. Naomi could have been Lorraine, a Protestant of Norwegian descent, or Mary, a Catholic of Irish decent. The point is that she was a Caucasian. Reverse discrimination is being claimed by many Caucasians who think that they are discriminated against by colleges and corporations that may seek to bolster their numbers of African Americans, Hispanics, and Asians.

Boris is a victim. He is unaccepted by his young peers and misunderstood by parents who do not know or necessarily want to know the norms of the new culture in which their son lives. They do not understand the pressure that American children exert on their peers or the dress standards (or lack of them) to which American children adhere.

Furthermore, the importance of play in the lives of American children is frequently misunderstood by others. Newcomers to the United States frequently do not understand that American counselors do not "make" children behave. This clearly illustrates that the time of immigration and the degree of acculturation are important factors to consider when counseling European ethnic groups.

Conclusion

It is important for the counselor to have an understanding of the various ethnic groups that are comprised of European American citizens. Indeed, understanding the cultures of the various people of the world is of great importance today. In the year 2000, the International Committee for Women (ICFW) of Division 52 (International Psychology) of the American Psychological Association was tasked with writing a position paper. This paper (Rice et al., 2001), entitled "Cultural and Gender Awareness in International Psychology," was presented at the APA convention meeting in San Francisco one year later. The paper includes "principles that promote and strive toward greater cultural and gender awareness and equity." Its purpose is to guide both research and practice. The five principles are

- Understanding the experiences of individual in diverse cultures and contexts;
- Respect for pluralism based in differences;
- Awareness and analysis of power;
- Critical analysis of Western perspectives; and
- International and interdisciplinary social-cultural perspectives.

The position paper is well worth reading in its entirety. It discusses in detail the importance of valuing the history and worldviews of diverse cultures and of valuing their ways of knowing, organizing, and functioning. It stresses the importance of trying to rid ourselves of embedded cultural and gender beliefs. In a world of global coalitions against terrorism, these principles are of paramount importance.

Various European immigrant ethnic groups have succeeded in the United States because they held productivity and autonomy as virtues. They quickly learned and accepted the English language as the dominant language of the nation, thus unifying the country with a common language. Furthermore, the Judeo-Christian religions have been recognized by most to be the spiritual base of a nation that prizes separation of church and state. It should be noted that much of the economic success of the European American majority rests on a culture that was originally agrarian, especially in the South where slaves from Africa knew how to grow crops in climates familiar to them but unfamiliar to their European owners. These crops were sold for domestic and foreign use. Chinese labor helped the westward expansion of the nation. There have always been non-Europeans working for and alongside of Caucasians. The challenge of today is for European Americans who have lived in the United States in coalition with non-European Americans to interface successfully with the new American immigrants. These new groups of immigrants are different. The contrasts become less of color than of class, and less of class than ideological concepts. All of this offers a unique challenge to the field of multicultural counseling.

Equity and power issues are paramount when it comes to the concerns of these newcomers, particularly if they are female émigrés. Equity and power are very important concepts that touch all of life but they are especially significant as related to career issues. Furthermore, the newer the immigrant, the more complex these issues may become.

The face of the New York City harbor where the Statue of Liberty stands has been forever changed. So has the face of the people of the United States. Whereas before, to paraphrase President Franklin D. Roosevelt, "We have nothing to fear but fear itself," we are now convinced that we are the first line against terror, and that until the battle against it is won, we all have much to fear. At the same time, the task for European Americans and all Americans is to join with new immigrants from countries whose culture we do not understand and who look like the very people who frighten us. This is bound to have ongoing ramifications for counselors.

The statue in the harbor still holds a torch and that torch still burns brightly. That light is symbolic of hope, which still burns for America's new immigrant arrivals. Perhaps for all Americans, it never burned more brightly than now.

DISCUSSION QUESTIONS

1. When you read that European Americans are not a monolithic group but that Caucasian Americans are comprised of many very different minority ethnic groups, did you have to make adjustments in the way you think about counseling them? Does it make a difference in the way you think about minority groups?

2. Every new group that came to America experienced some sort of hardship and discrimination. In the face of such hardship, how important do you think it is to help people identify with cultural heroes? Have you thought about using the Internet as a source of information?

3. Immigrant populations often want counselors to be more directive with their children than counselors are trained to be with American youth. How should this be addressed in counseling as well as counselor education?

4. What were your feelings when you read the case of Steven and Samira? How would you help them address the issues that they face?

5. How would you address issues of perceived reverse discrimination as was claimed in Naomi's case?

REFERENCES

Atkinson, D. R., Morten, G., & Sue, D. W. (1989). *Counseling American minorities: A cross-cultural perspective* (3rd ed.). Dubuque, IA: William C. Brown.

Brody, S. (1996). *Jewish heroes and heroines of America.* Hollywood, FL: Lifetime Books. Retrieved September 14, 2001, from http://www.fau.edu/library/bro.htm

Builders of America, The Jewish Heritage. (1991). FAU Library special collections and archives. Retrieved October 30, 2001, from http://www.borisamericanjews.com

Encyclopedia Britannica (2001). [CD-ROM]. United Kingdom: Encyclopedia Britannica.

Guttman, H. G., Levine, B., Brier, S., Brundage, D., Countryman, E., Fennel, D., & Rediker, M. J. (1989). *Who built America?* New York: Pantheon.

Holmquist, J. P (1981). *They chose Minnesota.* Minnesota Historical Society Press.

Lazarus, E. (1883). The new colossus. Retrieved September 14, 2001, from http://www.libertystatepark.com/emma.htm

Lipset, S. M., & Raab, E. (1995). *Jews and the new American scene.* Cambridge: Harvard University Press.

Magnussen, L. (2001). Retrieved September 3, 2001, from http://library.thinkquest.org/26786/en/arti/cles/view.php3arKey=3&pakey=6&loKey=l&toK

McFadden, J. (Ed.). (1999). *Transcultural counseling* (2nd ed.). Alexandria, VA: American Counseling Association.

Rice et al. (2001). *Cultural and gender awareness in international psychology.* Unpublished paper. American Psychological Association.

Rose, P. I. (1974). *They and we.* New York: Random House.

Tobias, H. S. (1990). *A history of the Jews in New Mexico.* Albuquerque: University of New Mexico Press.

Wittke, C. (1939). *We who built America?* New York: Prentice-Hall.

10 The International Counseling Movement

FREDERICK D. HARPER AND NATHAN DEEN

Although it might always be questionable to determine a starting point for the development of organized, international activities in counseling, we think that there are good reasons to begin the narrative in 1951. In that year, a group of individuals from several countries came together in Paris, France, and founded the Association Internationale d'Orientation Scolaire et Professionelle (AIOSP); in English-speaking countries, better known as the International Association for Educational and Vocational Guidance (IAEVG). In 2001, the association celebrated its fiftieth anniversary, and, in terms of membership, it is still the largest international association in the guidance and counseling field (International Association for Educational and Vocational Guidance [IAEVG], 2001). Preparatory contacts and communications took place after the end of World War II, and, in 1951, the time was right for the creation of a formal organization. Founding members came from the United Kingdom (UK), Belgium, Germany, the Netherlands, France, and the United Nations Educational, Scientific, and Cultural Organization (UNESCO).

A recent publication sets forth the purpose of the IAEVG: "The objectives of the Association were designed to provide guidance professionals with the opportunity to exchange views and experiences and to benefit from mutual exchanges and experiences" (IAEVG, 2001, p. 2). Conferences, seminars, and research studies have been used to accomplish these objectives. A long list of conference venues and themes testify to the success of IAEVG's aims and objectives. Venues for past IAEVG conferences are represented by countries throughout the world, except the United States. This does not imply that Americans have not been involved in the historical movement of the IAEVG. On the contrary, American leaders in counseling had a strong influence on the development of the association. For example, past presidents of the IAEVG have included well-known Americans such as Donald E. Super and William Bingham.

While spending three years as a visiting fellow at Wolfson College in the United Kingdom, from 1976 to 1979, Super had a significant influence on the

Note: Within this chapter, the British spelling of counseling with two "l's" [counselling] is used in some cases, for example, when used in the names of counseling associations or counseling journals that spell counseling in this fashion.

counseling movement in Europe through his training, professional involvement, and consultation (Osborne, 1997). Earlier, during the 1950s, American counseling professionals such as Robert H. Mathewson and Leo Goldman fulfilled visiting professorships at the University of Amsterdam as a beginning groundwork for organized counseling in the Netherlands, although institutionalized counselor training in the Netherlands did not start before the 1970s. Moreover, through exchange programs and the support of the Fulbright-Hays Act, professors from European and non-European countries have gotten the opportunity to study counseling in American universities and to adapt their newly acquired knowledge and skills to the needs of their homeland.

Nevertheless, there remains a perception among some leaders in the counseling profession that everything that is non–United States is considered "international" (Wehrly & Deen, 1983; Stockton, Kaladow, & Garbelman, 2001). This presupposition presents a problem because one cannot discuss the international movement in counseling without addressing how the United States has had a strong impact on the establishment and development of counseling in the rest of the world. The United States has been a source of information, consultation, and inspiration for the development of counselor training, counseling services, and counseling associations in Europe. Furthermore, counseling scholars and leaders from the United States have put their stamp on counselor training and the development of counseling services in other countries (Khan, 1983; Robertson & Paterson, 1983; Artiles, 1994; Osborne, 1997; Dogan, 2000).

The counseling movement in Europe first landed in the United Kingdom in terms of its focus on career guidance (vocational counseling) for "young people" in the early 1900s (Watts & Kidd, 2000, p. 485), that is, around the same time that vocational counseling began to evolve in the United States (Gladding, 2000). It seems that the simultaneous development of career or vocational counseling in both the United States and the United Kingdom was helped by their common English language (Watts & Kidd, 2000). Career counseling became prevalent in UK universities in the 1950s, and various forms of educational guidance began to appear in the United Kingdom in the 1960s and 1970s (Avent, Sisterson, Fawcett, Watts, & Newsome, 1983; Watts & Kidd, 2000).

J. Guichard (personal communication, February 20, 2002) reports that the guidance movement in France was significantly influenced by the pioneering mental hygiene work of Edouard Toulouse and the development of intelligence testing by Alfred Binet. Guichard also notes that French legislation in 1938 made it compulsory for all school youth to receive guidance before leaving school to enter an apprenticeship; however, he reveals that the first French law that addressed guidance and counseling was enacted in France in 1922.

Germany's counseling movement received impetus during the mid-1970s from the publication of the landmark book, *Handbuch der Bildungsberatung* (*Handbook of Educational Guidance*), by Heller (1975). Also, in Germany, Lothar R. Martin, from the University of Bonn, was influential by contributing to the development of a "Fernstudienkurs" (correspondence course in counseling) and authoring several books that promoted the implementation of counseling in the German school system (Martin, 1974, 1981, 1985). Around the same time, in the European countries of

Belgium, France, Italy, and Spain, the emphasis was on career guidance. Over the past decade, developing and expanding guidance and counseling activities of a generalist nature could be observed in the southern European countries of Greece and Italy (Deen, 1987). As of 2001, the European Association for Counselling (EAC) listed seven national member associations as Britain, Greece, Ireland, Italy, the Netherlands, Russia, and Scotland (European Association for Counselling [EAC], 2001a).

As stated earlier, counseling in European countries was inspired and influenced by the counseling efforts in the United States; however, counseling in western European countries adapted to the specific needs of each country. European school systems are different from those in the United States; they are more centrally organized and have less flexibility in the curriculum. Consequently, school counselors have a different role, that is, with an accent on care for the well-being and education of students on the one hand and a focus on career guidance on the other hand. Often they spend part of their time as counselors and part as teachers. Outside the schools, European counselors will usually have roles that are more related to their U.S. counterparts (Wehrly & Deen, 1983; Palmer & Varma, 1997).

Counseling Movement in the United States and Canada

The counseling movement in Europe, which often began with a focus on career, vocational, or school guidance, was apparently influenced by the pioneering foundation work in the United States in the early 1900s and onward. Although 1908, if not earlier, is often cited as the beginning year of formalized counseling services in the United States, it was really in 1913 when the founding of the National Vocational Guidance Association (NVGA) provided momentum to an "organized," national movement of counseling in the United States. The early counseling movement in the United States, 1908 to the early 1940s, centered on vocational counseling, testing and assessment, school guidance, and college counseling. After World War II and up to the 1970s, there was a focus on group work in counseling, the development of counseling theories, and the development and consolidation of professional counseling associations. The 1970s witnessed a focus on counseling effectiveness, counseling special client groups (e.g., non-White ethnicities), and counseling in diverse counseling settings; whereas the 1980s focused on the credentialing of counselors (e.g., licensure/certification of counselors and accreditation of counselor training), professional identity of counselors, multicultural counseling, and the development of ethical standards for counselors. The 1990s witnessed continuing emphases on multicultural counseling and counselor identity, along with new and developing foci on counselor competence, counselor skills, and spirituality in counseling (Gladding, 2000; Nugent, 2000).

Robertson and Paterson (1983) note that, "The Canadian guidance and counseling movement found its origins in the United States" (p. 490) in the early twentieth century. Robertson and Paterson continue in stating that counseling in Canada began around 1921 with a vocational-guidance focus and changed to an educational-guidance focus after World War II. Starting in the 1960s, counseling took on a one-to-one focus and group approach, much influenced by the work of Carl R. Rogers. Counseling in Canada has, to a degree, paralleled the counseling movement in the United States, in terms of professional development and identity, the development of professional associations, and involvement of counseling professionals in international counseling and American Counseling Association (ACA) activities (Robertson & Paterson, 1983).

Counseling in Central and Eastern Europe

A number of counseling centers have been established at universities or in communities in central and southeastern European countries such as Hungary, Poland, Romania, Slovakia, and Turkey, but it is as yet unclear as to the national impact of counseling in some of these efforts (Harper, 2000a; Stockton, et al., 2001).

Ritoók (1998) reports that traditional counseling in Hungary, especially prior to the 1990s, was carried out primarily by psychologists, and the emphasis was on educational and career decision making; however, newly trained counselors now address personal-social problems as well as educational, career, and employment problems. Moreover, Ritoók notes that the government of Hungary passed laws for the training of school counselors in 1991 and for the training of employment counselors in 1992, that is, because of unemployment problems as a national concern.

The focus of counseling in Poland over the past decade has also been on employment concerns. Wojtasik (2000) reports that Poland went through drastic socioeconomic and sociopolitical changes in the early 1990s because of a change from a communist country to a free-market society. Vocational counseling became a priority during the 1990s because of new professions, high unemployment, and labor-market changes. Therefore, the Polish government encouraged and supported the training of counselors, beginning in 1994, and a profession of vocational counseling was legally established in 1995 (Wojtasik, 2000). Szilagyi (2001) describes similar employment and social problems caused by Romania's transition from a Communist society to a free-market one in 1989. Szilagyi, the only doctoral-trained counselor in Romania as of this writing, describes the prevalent counseling problems for the country as related to unemployment, domestic violence, poverty, and health.

In 1993, the former Czechoslovakia split into two separate countries, the Czech Republic and Slovakia. Between the two countries, Slovakia has been more actively involved in organizing and developing counseling. For example, Slovakia hosted the 1999 Conference of the International Association for Counselling. Kopcanova (2000) writes that in the former Czechoslovakia there was a focus on vocational guidance, beginning in the 1930s, and a focus on educational counseling after World War II. In the 1960s, there was the development of educational and career counseling for secondary school youth. Recently, Slovakia has focused on the improvement of its educational and psychological counseling centers, the improvement of its institutes for training and research in counseling and testing, the expansion of the role of counselors, and efforts to integrate counseling into the school system versus providing services in the community through its centers (Kopcanova, 2000).

Turkey, which overlaps parts of southeastern Europe and southwest Asia, began organized counseling in the schools in the early 1950s, based on input from American counselor educators and support from the Ministry of National Education of Turkey. The Ministry of National Education provided support for the training of counselors at the master's and doctoral degree levels (Dogan, 2000). According to Dogan, counseling in Turkey currently has a broad focus, which includes (1) educational, vocational, and personal counseling; (2) referrals to specialists; (3) counseling services in elementary and secondary schools; (4) activities of a professional counseling association and its counseling journal; and (5) training in counseling. Although theoretical orientations of practicing counselors tend to vary, Dogan suggests that early practice and training of counselors in Turkey were influenced by Rogers's (1951, 1961) client-centered therapy—sometimes referred to as person-centered therapy.

Counseling in Non-European Countries

There is very limited information in counseling journals about organized counseling efforts and associations in South America. Nevertheless, Argentina is one South American country that has recently organized counseling efforts. In 1990, Andrés Sanchez Bodas founded Holos or, by its longer name, the Argentine Center for Humanistic Psychology and Counseling. Holos was the first significant movement to train counselors in Argentina, based on a humanistic or client-centered orientation. During the following year, in 1991, students from Holos organized the Asociatión Argentina de Counselors, which became the national counseling association for Argentina. The association has approximately 400 active members, who are working with a variety of client problems and in a number of counseling settings, including private practice and employee assistance. Moreover, in 1992, the Ministry of Education of Argentina approved a plan for a profession in counseling and addressed training guidelines and concerns (Artiles, 1994).

On the continent of Africa, several countries have enacted laws to require counseling with school youth. In 1975, the Nigerian government established the Third National Development Plan to mandate counseling and guidance services in schools. In addition, the National Policy on Education was enacted in 1981, providing additional support for the development of counseling in Nigeria (Ahia & Bradley, 1984). The introduction of formalized guidance services for youth in South Africa in 1967 was mandated by the enactment of the National Education Policy Act, which focused on guidance services in the forms of vocational, educational, personal, and family guidance. Guidance services were "differentiated" for "Whites, Indians, Coloureds, and Black Africans" (Ganie, 1996, p. 198). Vontress and Naiker (1995) remind us of the role of the former racial policy of Apartheid in South Africa as a means of favoring counseling services and counselor/psychology training for Whites over Blacks and other persons of color.

Richards (2000) notes that organized counseling services in Zimbabwe, formerly Rhodesia, was originally developed for White school youth only and was based on a Eurocentric model of psychological practice. Richards indicates that under the racially oppressive government of former Rhodesia, psychology and counseling were used to suppress Black youth, that is, prior to Black freedom and independence of the country from British colonial control in 1980. Furthermore, Richards calls for counseling in Zimbabwe that is based on an Afrocentric worldview instead of the traditional orientation to a Eurocentric worldview.

Among countries in the South Pacific and nearby areas of the world, New Zealand and Australia have had organized counseling services and associations for some years. Small (1984) reports that organized guidance services began in New Zealand in the early 1920s, and, around 1925, there was widespread aptitude testing of entrants to state secondary schools as well as a child guidance clinic at a university. Nevertheless, it was not until 1960 when guidance counselor positions became available in schools and 1973 when universities began to train counselors (Webster & Hermansson, 1983). As regards Australia, Khan (1983) posits that the counseling movement in Australia has been rooted in the American model of counseling, and that the writings of Carl Rogers (e.g., 1951, 1961) had a significant influence on the early development of counseling in the country.

The International Movement: Counseling Associations

As we mentioned earlier, the International Association for Educational and Vocational Guidance was the first international counseling association. To date, the IAEVG is still a very important umbrella or parent association under which a number of national associations for careers guidance unite, and, because of these collective memberships, it must be considered quite influential in terms of the international counseling scene. Nevertheless, the growing expansion of the role of the counselor in Europe and on other continents, beginning in the 1960s, created a need for a different type of professional association, one that was directed more to professional exchange of diverse knowledge, viewpoints, skills, and experiences in counseling. As an outcome of this thinking, the International Round Table for the Advancement of Counselling (IRTAC) was founded, holding its first international conference in 1966 in Neuchâtel, Switzerland. In 1997, the IRTAC changed its name to the International Association for Counselling (IAC); nonetheless, its focus remains the same, a forum for counselors and counseling scholars worldwide with the designed purpose of exchanging knowledge and ideas about counseling (International Association for Counselling [IAC], 2001).

In our examination of the themes of IAC conferences over the years, we found a development from quite general to rather specific themes as the years advanced. During the 1960s, the IAC conferences chose general themes of counseling such as "School Counseling, Educational, and Vocational Guidance" (1966) and "Counselling in School and non-School Situations" (1967). In later years, the themes became more specific and more related to developments in the world at large, for example, "Counselling for the Integration of the Handicapped in Society" (1981), "Counselling and Ethnic Minorities" (1985), and "New Roles for Men and Women in the Family and in Work" (1986). In terms of recent IAC conferences of the past decade or so, the following are conferences by year, host country, and theme.

1990, Helsinki, Finland, "Youth in the 1990s—Challenges and Opportunities for Counselling and Education"

1991, Oporto, Portugal, "Counselling Women and Girls in Education and Employment and Counselling in Academic Life"

1992, Budapest, Hungary, "Counselling the Disabled in their Social Environment" (UN International Decade of the Disabled)

1993, Auckland, New Zealand, "Counselling Towards 2000; Reducing the Distance: Psychological, Social, and Cultural"

1994, Munich, Germany, "Counselling for the Family" (UN International Year of the Family)

1995, Valetta, Malta, "Counselling for Tolerance" (UN International Year for Tolerance)

1996, Vancouver, Canada, "Counselling in the Global Community"

1997, Cambridge, UK, "Counselling in Medical Settings"

1998, Paris, France, "Counselling as a Profession: Status, Organization and Human Rights"

1999, Bratislava, Slovakia, "Counselling Children and Youth at the Edge of the Third Millennium"

2000, Thessaloniki, Greece, "Counselling in the New Millennium: Meeting the Challenges of Diversity and Promoting Peace and Social Inclusion"

2001, Mumbai-Lonavla, India, "Families in Transition, Counselling in Transition: Meeting the Challenges Ahead"

2002, Auckland, New Zealand, "Counselling in the New Millennium: Facing Differences, Respectful Practice"

The IAC has been extremely successful in terms of bringing about a network of counselors and other helping professionals from around the world; many have become friends and colleagues for life and, thus, have created a professional association that has influenced the development of organized counseling in various parts of the world.

Internet Web sites follow for readers who would like to acquire additional information about the IAC, the IAEVG, and other international counseling associations or internationally influential professional counseling groups:

International Association for Counselling: http://www.iac-irtac.org

International Association for Educational and Vocational Guidance: http://www.iaevg.org

African Counselling Network: http://ads.x10.com/yahoo/yahgeo_elvira.htm

American Counseling Association: http://www.counseling.org

Australian Counselling Association: http://www.theaca.net.au

British Association for Counselling and Psychotherapy: http://www.bac.co.uk

Canadian Counselling Association: http://www.ccacc.ca/ccacc.htm

Counseling Journals

In close connection with the historical development of counseling associations has been the development of affiliated counseling journals. The only international journal that is truly a counseling journal, in the sense of being devoted to diverse topics of counseling, is the *International Journal for the Advancement of Counselling* (*IJAC*), now publishing in its twenty-fifth volume year. Although the *IJAC* is professionally affiliated with the IAC (formerly IRTAC), the IAEVG, and the EAC, it is owned and published by Kluwer Academic Publishers. As the title of the journal indicates, the editorial board of the *IJAC* has focused its content on international themes as consistent with its aim, "to promote the exchange of information and research about counselling throughout the world," but especially in parts of the world where organized counseling is still in a beginning or developing stage (Harper, 2001; Instructions to Authors, 2001). Published in the English language, the *IJAC* has addressed a variety of counseling topics over the years. Moreover, the *IJAC* editorial leadership has actively encouraged and assisted authors from non-English-language countries to publish articles in the journal on counseling efforts in their respective homelands (Deen, 1987; Harper, 2000b, 2001).

The IAEVG had been publishing a professional bulletin that was recently transformed into a full-fledged refereed journal, *The International Journal for Educational and Vocational Guidance*. Its first issue, a special memorial issue to Donald E. Super, was published in early 2001. A third international counseling journal is the recently developed *International Careers Journal*, which is not currently published in a printed format, but is published only on the Internet in electronic form.

Seemingly, the oldest counseling journal in the world is the *Journal of Counseling and Development*, the main journal of the ACA. It is now in its eightieth volume year of publishing. The *Journal of Counseling and Development* was originally published on a regular basis starting in 1921 under the name of the *National Vocational Guidance Bulletin*. The original *National Vocational Guidance Bulletin* kept its vocational theme in subsequent name changes until 1952, when the counseling focus of the journal was broadened and the name was changed to the *Personnel and Guidance Journal*. In 1984, the journal took on its current name, *Journal of Counseling and Development* (Gladding, 2000). Another long-running counseling journal in the United States is the *Journal of Counseling Psychology*, which is now in its forty-ninth volume year (i.e., as of 2002). Both the *Journal of Counseling and Development* and the *Journal of Counseling Psychology* occasionally publish articles with international and cross-cultural topics or implications.

Among the oldest counseling journals published outside the United States is the French journal, *L'Orientation Scolaire et Professionnelle* (*Educational and Vocational*

Guidance), edited by Jean Guichard. It has been published under its current name since 1972; however, it was previously published, beginning in 1929, as the *Bulletin de l'Institut National d'Étude du Travail et d'Orientation Professionnelle* (J. Guichard, personal communication, February 20, 2002). In addition, the *British Journal of Guidance and Counselling,* under the editorship of Anthony Watts, reached its thirty-first anniversary of publishing in 2002. As related to international subject matter, the *British Journal of Guidance and Counselling* publishes articles, at times, related to counseling in English-speaking countries other than the UK, for example, Kenya, Australia, New Zealand, and Ireland. Along the same line, the *L'Orientation Scolaire et Professionnelle* has published articles with implications for French-speaking countries other than France.

Other major counseling journals with international content or implications include the *Asian Journal of Counseling* and the *Journal of Multicultural Counseling and Development.* The *Asian Journal of Counseling* publishes articles related to China and other Asian countries and is affiliated with the Hong Kong Counselling Association. The *Journal of Multicultural Counseling and Development,* affiliated with the Association for Multicultural Counseling and Development (an ACA division), publishes articles related to national and international ethnocultural groups, for example, African Americans, Native Americans, Middle East/Arab Americans, Asian Americans and Pacific Islanders, Latinos (or Hispanics), various Caribbean ethnicities, Africans, and East Indians.

The following is a recommended list of international, continental, and national journals along with their Internet addresses. We have chosen these journals because they are international in focus or they occasionally publish articles with international or cross-cultural counseling themes:

International Journal for the Advancement of Counselling: http://www.wkap.nl/prod/j/0165-0653

International Journal for Educational and Vocational Guidance: http://www.wkap.nl/journals/ijevg

International Careers Journal: www.careers-cafe.com

Asian Journal of Counseling: http://www1.fed.cuhk.edu.hk/en/ajc

British Journal of Guidance and Counselling: http://www.tandf.co.uk/journals

Journal of Counseling and Development: http://www.counseling.org/journals/guidelines/JCD.html

Journal of Multicultural Counseling and Development: http://www.counseling.org/journals/guidelines/jmcd.html

African Counselling/Psychology Journals: http://www.geocities.com/p_moyo/links2.html

L'Orientation Scolaire et Professionnelle: http://www2.cnam.fr/inetop

People and Pioneers

However important associations and journals may be, it will always be people who bring them to life, support their development, and give them direction. This is why we think that some names have to be mentioned regarding people whose influence in the international counseling field is evident; without them counseling in many parts of the world would have a different image or no image at all. Among these people, one person in particular stands out above all others in terms of his impact on the international counseling movement: Hans Zacharias Hoxter. In a long and productive life of 90-plus years, Hoxter continues to be actively involved in the international counseling movement as honorary president for life of the IAC. He left his mark on the international movement in counseling and gave counseling a face in the work of the United Nations. He has been the ambassador of counseling, not only with UNESCO, but also with many governments of the world, in Europe, Asia, and elsewhere (Ivey, 1989).

Born in Frankfurt, Germany, Hans Hoxter migrated to France at age 18 and later settled in the United Kingdom where he has spent almost all of his adult life. After arriving in the United Kingdom, Hoxter played a significant role in providing services as a social worker and counselor, developing and directing service programs, raising funds to offer some of the first courses to train counselors in the United Kingdom, and arranging for Fulbright scholars to visit Europe in order to train counselors in the universities and create awareness about counseling across countries. Hans Hoxter was especially successful in getting support from the United Nations and the United States for the purposes of providing services for World War II refugees and children who had been handicapped by war injuries (Ivey, 1989).

Hoxter's contributions to the international counseling movement, like his physical stature and presence, have been monumental. He was one of the founders of the IAEVG in 1951, and in 1966, when the International Round Table for the Advancement of Counselling was established, it was Hoxter who initiated it and served as its president until 1998, when he was honored with the title of honorary president for life. Without question, Hans Z. Hoxter is the single most significant figure in terms of the global development of counseling and the cross-cultural exchange of counseling information and ideas.

Another name that deserves mentioning in this context is Anthony W. Watts, who, for years, edited the *British Journal of Guidance and Counselling* and made it one of the outstanding counseling journals. He also carried out important research activities in the European community, together with Peter Plant (Denmark) and others. In Denmark, Peter Plant is and was a key figure in the development of guidance and counseling. Lothar R. Martin, from the University of Bonn in Germany, is a key person in the development of counseling in that country. In France, although the emphasis in that country has been mainly on career guidance, Jean Guichard of the Institut National d'Étude du Travail et d'Orientation Professionnelle (National Institute for the Study of Work and Guidance) and Pierre Tap of the University of Toulouse promoted a broader vision of counseling. Nathan Deen established programs for the education of school counselors in the Netherlands and founded the *International Journal for the Advancement of Counselling,* of which he was managing editor for a total of fifteen years (Martin & DeVolder, 1983; Wehrly & Deen, 1983; Wehrly, 1995).

In countries other than the United States, Canada, and those of Western Europe, some of the counseling professionals who have consistently written about or helped to develop counseling in their respective countries, cultures, or geographic areas of the world include the following: Agnes Watanabe-Muraoka and Shoma Morita (Japan); O. Bojuwoye, Julius O. Akinboye, and Samuel E. Okon (Nigeria); Lionel J. Nicholas and O. Bojuwoye (South Africa); Abdul Halim Othman (Malaysia); S. Alvin Leung (China); Andrés Bodas and Manual Artiles (Argentina); Magda Ritoók (Hungary); Dagmar Kopcanova (Slovakia); Ana-Maria Andreea Szilagyi (Romania); Mika Haritos-Fatouras (Greece); Lina Kashyap and Mehroo Bengalee (India); Rachel Erhard and Moshe Israelashvili (Israel); Iffat Almas and Farah Ibrahim (Pakistan); and Gary I. Hermansson, J. Small, and Alan Webster (New Zealand).

Selected Research and Publications on International Counseling

Another source of information about the international movement in counseling is to be found in international publications. It seems appropriate in the framework of this chapter to approach this aspect by using the *International Journal for the Advancement of Counselling* as a primary source of international counseling publications. In the tenth volume of the *IJAC*, results of a content analysis of 257 articles from the first nine published volumes of the *IJAC* was published (Deen, 1987). In a content analysis, articles were summarized under fifteen distinctive headings:

1. theoretical approaches in counseling and psychotherapy
2. theoretical models of counseling
3. specific approaches of counseling
4. research with regard to specific theories, strategies, and instruments
5. vocational and career counseling
6. special populations (rehabilitation)
7. special populations (other)
8. cross-cultural counseling
9. counseling and developmental psychology
10. preparation and education of counselors
11. country studies by outside observers
12. country studies by inside observers
13. comparative studies
14. East–West or North–South relations
15. a category for "other."

Among other findings, the analysis indicated that the majority of articles were contributed by authors from the United States and Canada, closely followed by European authors. African and Asian countries were much less represented, with the exception of Nigeria, which had contributed thirteen articles in those years. Comparative studies were seldom, and most were written by well-known scholars with years of experience in counseling research and writing. Moreover, the content analysis generated a significantly greater number of within-country studies, that is, when compared to comparative studies or between-country studies.

A review of the past five volume years (1998 to 2002) of the *International Journal for the Advancement of Counselling* suggests increasing international diversity of articles by country and culture. For example, there have been an increasing number of articles on counseling-related activities in countries other than Canada, the United States, and Western Europe, including countries such as Australia, China, Hungary, India, Israel, Jamaica, Japan, Jordan, Kenya, New Zealand, Poland, Slovakia, South Africa, Swaziland, Turkey, and Zimbabwe. Moreover, in a special attempt to address international representation and continental or hemispheric balance, the December 2000 issue of *IJAC* was a special-focus issue on "Non-Western Approaches to Counseling" (Harper, 2000b).

In 1983, ACA published a special issue of its *Personnel and Guidance Journal* (now the *Journal of Counseling and Development)* on the topic of "International Perspectives on Counseling." This issue included articles on the development and practice of counseling in a number of countries, including Ethiopia, Nigeria, South Africa, Japan, Thailand, Australia, New Zealand, Ireland, Iran, and Canada (Wehrly & Deen, 1983). A similar but more recent review is a research paper that examines the development and history of international counseling (Stockton et al., 2001). In addition to reviewing the development of counseling in particular countries, the paper explores counseling practices in specific countries from the perspective of sociopolitical and cultural challenges and the phenomenon of globalization. Another publication that examines international counseling is a chapter by Wehrly (1995), titled "Multicultural Counseling on the International Scene," wherein she presents an overview of counseling in African, Asian, European, Middle Eastern, and North American countries, along with a discussion of counseling in New Zealand and Australia.

Future Developments and Cultural Implications

What will be the future of the international movement in counseling? Looking at what we have presented so far, we are led to conclude that there is a growing need for the professionalization of counseling throughout the world. The American Counseling Association in the United States may assist in this regard, as it has had a long history of experiences in the development of statements of ethics and professional identity. ACA's most recent statement can be found via its Web site address as presented earlier in this chapter. From a continental perspective, the European Association for Counselling, at its 2001 conference, presented its "Training Standards, Accreditation and Ethical Charter" (EAC, 2001b). In this way, the EAC has assumed a guiding role in setting European standards for counseling and counselor training, which will help national member counseling associations in Europe to determine their own training and ethical standards according to their cultural contexts. The standards were developed and defined by a broad-based European group of counselors, who were mandated by their respective national associations. This gives the ethical booklet its legitimization and is a clear sign toward professional maturity. Similar processes toward culturally and nationally based ethical standards for counselors are occurring in other parts of the world.

In defining the role and identity of counseling, each country or culture must consider its own cultural needs, ways, and values. Although a counseling association of a particular country may get ideas from ethical statements of other countries or associations, it should be careful to develop a culture-centered ethical statement or country-oriented professional identity that would be sensitive and relevant to its members and target clientele group.

Another perspective for the future is the increasing impact of the Internet on counseling. Most national counseling associations have Web sites of their own, and the same is true for the international associations, including the IAC and IAEVG. At the time of this writing, the EAC had begun to prepare a Web site for upload to the Internet. In addition, we have already mentioned one Web-based counseling journal that is published only in electronic form, that is, the *International Careers Journal,* edited by Michael Taylor (www.careers-cafe.com). Another Web-based counseling journal is a newly developed journal on the topic of counseling and technology, the *Journal of Technology in Counseling,* edited by Marty J. Jencius. The Web site for this journal is http://jtc.colstate.edu. In the future, counseling professionals can expect more on-line versions of counseling journals and more Web sites for professional counseling associations. Moreover, the future of counseling will more likely involve greater use of the Internet for e-mails among counseling professionals and between counselors and clients. The international counseling network can also expect additional innovations in and broader use of the Internet for web counseling and the training of counselors. As regards preventive counseling, counselors should be much more aware of the possibilities for using the Internet as a source of multicultural guidance information. (See Chapter 22 on technology and counseling for more strategies regarding the use of the Internet for international counseling and cross-cultural exchange of ideas among counseling professionals.)

In terms of the exchange of counseling knowledge on compact disk (CD), counseling professionals of the future can expect to see more counseling journal articles on CDs that will contain years of published journal volumes with hundreds of articles. This developing trend will assist tremendously in terms of easy access to international literature on counseling for the purposes of counseling research, practice, and training. Already, the ACA has developed and begun distributing all articles published in its *Journal of Counseling and Development* over a 20-year period (1979 to 1999) on a single CD (American Counseling Association [ACA], 2000). Moreover, Kluwer Academic Publishers is developing electronic access to articles from its counseling journals by way of CD-ROM and on-line retrieval.

In much of the world, the challenges to counseling professionals will continue to be influenced by the effects of globalization, global migration, ethnic and religious conflicts, terrorism and war, famine and starvation, disease (e.g., AIDS), injustice, abandonment of children, and unemployment (Harper, 1998; Harper &

Stone, 1999; Brundtland, 2000; DeLay, 2000; Vontress & Epp 2000). Delay's (2000) recent article in the *American Psychologist* delineates a number of these challenges as the raison d'être to fight for the rights and needs of children of the world. Moreover, Vontress (2000) describes the impact of immigration on Western countries. Vontress focuses particularly on the impact of immigration on France and the resulting intergroup conflicts due to ethnic differences (various Northern Africans of color versus Caucasian French nationals) as well as religious differences (Islamic versus Catholic).

Victims of globalization, war, oppression, and terrorism will continue to seek refuge or economic sufficiency in countries other than their homeland, and the survivors of violence and natural catastrophes will continue to need grief counseling or some form of psychological support. According to Deen (2002), counselors will have to develop multicultural competence and cultural empathy in order to be effective across cultures and in order to deal with these challenges. Moreover, counselors of the future, due to the urgency of client problems, will probably resort more to brief counseling or time-limited counseling (Palmer, 1997) and may have to favor specific techniques rather than theoretical models (Palmer & Varma, 1997).

In the future, it will become more self-evident that the Western approaches to counseling and counselor training, when used alone, are inadequate as a solution for the rest of the world. Various non-Western or indigenous practitioners and scholars are already demanding and developing helping approaches that address the needs and worldviews of their cultures (Richards, 2000; Bojuwoye, 2001; Szilagyi, 2001). Eastern therapies and African healing methods can offer much as complements to Western counseling approaches. Along this line, Bojuwoye (2001) recommends combining relevant Western approaches with non-Western approaches in order to bring about effective counseling and mental health services for clients, regardless of culture.

Conclusion

The international counseling movement has involved organized efforts to provide counseling, train counselors, and develop professional counseling associations in various countries in Western Europe, Central and Eastern Europe, New Zealand, North America, South America, Africa, and Asia. The chapter traces the development of international and continental professional associations in counseling, such as the International Association for Vocational and Educational Guidance, the International Association for Counselling (formerly IRTAC), and the European Association for Counselling. International and continental journals of counseling were presented, including the *International Journal for Educational and Vocational Guidance* and the *International Journal for the Advancement of Counselling* among others. Pioneers of and contributors to the international counseling movement were presented and discussed. In the concluding paragraphs, expectations and challenges for the future are presented from a global and cross-cultural perspective.

The counseling movement in most countries appears to have begun with a focus on career/vocational guidance or educational guidance. The United States, Canada, and the United Kingdom were among the first countries to pursue organized counseling efforts, and counseling in countries such as Argentina, Romania, and Greece is a newly developing phenomenon.

DISCUSSION QUESTIONS

1. What Western counseling theories and techniques seem to have global or universal value for counseling human beings, regardless of culture or country?

2. Should counseling services for youth be provided in the school setting or in community mental health centers, that is, apart from the school?

3. Can there be some universal goals for counseling individual clients, should counseling goals be couched in the needs of one's cultural or national context, or can there be a combination of both?

4. In counseling immigrant clients from non-Western countries to Western ones, should the counselor favor indigenous healing approaches, Western counseling approaches, or a combination of both? Explain and justify your viewpoint or position.

5. What should be the role of counselors and counseling associations in sociopolitical issues of justice, fairness, and human rights; for example, oppressed women, children, the poor, non-Whites, or the ethnically/religiously different?

REFERENCES

Ahia, C. E., & Bradley, R. W. (1984). Assessment of secondary school student needs in Kwara State, Nigeria. *International Journal for the Advancement of Counselling, 7,* 149–157.

American Counseling Association. (2000). *Journal of Counseling and Development, 1979–1999* [CD-ROM]. Alexandria, VA: Author.

Artiles, M. F. (1994). Historia del counseling en la Argentina (History of counseling in Argentina). *Counseling: Revista de la Asociatión Argentina de Counselors, 3,* 18–19.

Avent, C., Sisterson, D., Fawcett, B., Watts, A., & Newsome, A. (1983). Careers guidance and counselling in England. *The Personnel and Guidance Journal, 61,* 476–478.

Bojuwoye, O. (2001). Crossing-cultural boundaries in counselling. *International Journal for the Advancement of Counselling, 23,* 31–50.

Brundtland, G. H. (2000). *Outstanding issues in the international response to HIV/AIDS: The WHO (World Health Organization) perspective.* Paper presented at the XIII International AIDS Conference, Durban, South Africa.

Deen, N. (1987). Nine years in the journal, some analytic notes with regard to the development of the *International Journal for the Advancement of Counselling, 10,* 149–178.

Deen, N. (2002). (Young) newcomers in European societies: Implications for education and counselling. *International Journal for the Advancement of Counselling, 24,* 3–17.

DeLay, T. (2000). Fighting for children. *American Psychologist, 55,* 1054–1055.

Dogan, S. (2000). The historical development of counseling in Turkey. *International Journal for the Advancement of Counselling, 22,* 57–67.

European Association for Counselling. (2001a). *Counselling as a preventive process,* Eighth Annual Conference of the European Association for Counselling (EAC): Author.

European Association for Counselling. (2001b). *Training standards, accreditation and ethical character.* Drossica Attica, Greece: Author.

Ganie, L. (1996). Transformation in South Africa: The changing role of the guidance counsellor. *International Journal for the Advancement of Counselling, 19,* 197–206.

Gladding, S. T. (2000). *Counseling: A comprehensive profession* (4th ed.). Englewood Cliffs, NJ: Merrill Prentice Hall.

Harper, F. D. (1998). *Roles and challenges of counseling professionals for the new millennium.* Keynote paper presented at the Annual Conference of the International Association for Counselling, Paris, France. (Also, published: Harper, F. D. (2000). Challenges to counseling professionals for the new millennium [Editorial]. *International Journal for the Advancement of Counselling, 22,* 1–7.)

Harper, F. D. (Ed.). (2000a). European perspectives on counselling [Special focus issue]. *International Journal for the Advancement of Counselling, 22*(3).

Harper, F. D. (Ed.). (2000b). Non-western approaches to counselling [Special focus issue]. *International Journal for the Advancement of Counselling, 22*(4).

Harper, F. D. (2001). Writing for Publication in the *International Journal for the Advancement of Counselling. International Journal for the Advancement of Counselling, 23,* 1–6.

Harper, F. D., & Stone, W. O. (1999). Transcendent counseling (TC): A theoretical approach for the year 2000 and beyond. In J. McFadden (Ed.), *Transcultural counseling* (2nd ed., pp. 83–108). Alexandria, VA: American Counseling Association Press.

Heller, K. (Ed.). (1975). *Handbuch der Bildungsberatung (Handbook of Educational Guidance) I, II, and III.* Stuttgart, Germany: Klett.

Instructions to authors. (2001). *International Journal for the Advancement of Counselling, 23*(4).

International Association for Counselling (2001). *Conference program: Families in transition—Counselling in transition: Meeting the challenges ahead.* Mumbai (Bombay), India: Author.

International Association for Educational and Vocational Guidance. (2001). *The first 50 years, Maximising the world's potential through guidance.* Rivenhall, Essex, United Kingdom: Author.

Ivey, A. E. (1989). Hans Zacharias Hoxter. *Journal of Counseling and Development, 67,* 263–270.

Khan, J. A. (1983). The evolution of counseling and guidance in Australia: Or, as yet no counseling kangaroos? *The Personnel and Guidance Journal, 61,* 469–471.

Kopcanova, D. (2000). Educational and psychological counseling in Slovakia: Keeping continuity. *International Journal for the Advancement of Counselling, 22,* 209–223.

Martin, L. R. (1974). *Bildungsberatung in der Schule (Educational Guidance in Schools).* Bad Heilbrunn, Germany: Klinkhardt.

Martin, L. R. (1981). *Schulberatung—Anlässe, Aufgaben, Methodenkonzeption (School guidance: Causes, aims, conception of methods).* Stuttgart, Germany: Klett.

Martin, L. R. (1985). *Einzelfallhilfe und systembezogene Beratung (Individual counselling and systemtied guidance),* Fernstudium Ausbildung zum Beratungslehrer (Correspondence course for guidance-teachers). Tübingen, Germany: DIFF.

Martin, L. R., & DeVolder, J. (1983). Guidance and counseling services in the Federal Republic of Germany. *The Personnel and Guidance Journal, 61,* 482–486.

Nugent, F. A. (2000). *An introduction to the profession of counseling* (3rd ed.). New York: Merrill/Prentice Hall.

Osborne, W. L. (1997). Donald E. Super: Yesterday and tomorrow. Retrieved November 30, 2001, from http://icdl.uncg.edu/ft/033000-01.html

Palmer, S. (1997). Stress counselling and management: Past, present and future. In S. Palmer & V. Varma (Eds.), *The future of counselling and psychotherapy* (pp. 82–111). Thousand Oaks, CA: Sage.

Palmer, S., & Varma, V. (Eds.). (1997). *The future of counselling and psychotherapy.* Thousand Oaks, CA: Sage.

Richards, K. (2000). Counsellor supervision in Zimbabwe: A new direction. *International Journal for the Advancement of Counselling, 22,* 143–155.

Ritoók, M. (1998). Counselling in Hungary: Present and future trends. *International Journal for the Advancement of Counselling, 20,* 17–25.

Robertson, S. E., & Paterson, J. G. (1983). Characteristics of guidance and counseling services in Canada. *The Personnel and Guidance Journal, 61,* 490–493.

Rogers, C. R. (1951). *Client-centered therapy.* Boston: Houghton Mifflin.

Rogers, C. R. (1961). *On becoming a person.* Boston: Houghton Mifflin.

Small, J. J. (1984). Guidance and counselling in New Zealand. *International Journal for the Advancement of Counselling, 7,* 113–118.

Stockton, R., Kaladow, J. K., & Garbelman, J. (2001, June). *Meeting the challenges ahead: The development and history of international counseling.* Paper presented at the Annual Conference of the International Association for Counselling, Mumbai (Bombay), India.

Szilagyi, A. A. (2001, June). *Values in transition, families in transition: The need for counselling of the Romanian family of the third millennium.* Paper presented at the Annual Conference of the International Association for Counselling, Mumbai (Bombay), India.

Vontress, C. E., & Epp, L. R. (2000). Ethnopsychiatry: Counseling immigrants in France. *International Journal for the Advancement of Counselling, 22,* 273–288.

Vontress, C. E., & Naiker, K. S. (1995). Counseling in South Africa: Yesterday, today, and tomorrow. *Journal of Multicultural Counseling and Development, 23,* 149–157.

Watts, A. G., & Kidd, J. M. (2000). Guidance in the United Kingdom: Past, present and future. *British Journal of Guidance and Counselling, 28,* 485–502.

Webster, A. C., & Hermansson, G. L. (1983). Guidance and counseling in New Zealand. The *Personnel and Guidance Journal, 61,* 472–476.

Wehrly, B. (1995). *Pathways to multicultural counseling competence: A developmental journey.* Pacific Grove, CA: Brooks/Cole.

Wehrly, B., & Deen, N. (1983). International guidance and counseling [Special issue]. *The Personnel and Guidance Journal, 61*(8).

Wojtasik, B. (2000). Model of the vocational counsellor's work performance: A Polish perspective. *International Journal for the Advancement of Counselling, 22,* 197–208.

11 Understanding Immigrants: Acculturation Theory and Research

GARGI ROYSIRCAR

There are currently more than 22 million documented immigrants living in the United States, along with an even larger number of their U.S.-born offspring (U.S. Bureau of the Census, 2000). Since 1970, Asia and Latin America have provided the largest source of legal entries, with documented immigrants from Mexico accounting for more than one fourth of the total immigrant population (U.S. Bureau of the Census, 2000). Mexicans also accounted for two thirds of formerly undocumented immigrants (Rumbaut, 1997). Thus, immigrants from Mexico make up the largest population of both legal and undocumented immigrants in the United States.

The current trend in immigration appears to be diverse, indicating an increase in the proportion of political refugees and asylees, highly skilled professionals, executives, and managers, as well as undocumented laborers. Therefore, the socioeconomic statuses of current immigrants run the gamut from the very poor to the upwardly mobile. Additionally, second-generation immigrants (with at least one immigrant parent) are found excessively in the oldest (65-plus) and youngest (0–17) age categories when compared with first- (foreign-born) and third- (native-born individuals with native-born parents) generations. Jensen and Chitose (1997) attribute this generational difference in age distributions to the pause in immigration during the middle part of the 1900s, thus impacting the profiles of ethnic populations in the United States.

Demographic Trends in the U.S. Population

Latinos and Asians are the fastest growing ethnic groups in the United States (U.S. Bureau of the Census, 2000). According to the recent U.S. Census, 66 percent of the Asian and Latino population in the United States is made up of new immigrants and their children. These two groups have achieved the highest growth rate, from immigration and births in immigrant families, of all ethnic groups in the United

States (Buriel & De Ment, 1997). It is estimated that by the year 2050, Asians and Latinos will make up 33.6 percent of the total U.S. population (U.S. Bureau of the Census, 2000). African Americans and Native Americans are projected to constitute 15.5 percent (58.5 million) of the total U.S. population by the year 2050 (U.S. Bureau of the Census, 2000). Currently, the Latino population is estimated at 32.2 million (11.7 percent of the total U.S. population) and is expected to grow to 98.2 million (24.3 percent of the total population) by the year 2050 (U.S. Bureau of the Census, 2000). The Asian and Pacific Islander population is currently estimated at 11.1 million (4 percent of the total U.S. population) and by the year 2050 is expected to grow to 37.6 million or 9.3 percent of the U.S. population (U.S. Bureau of the Census, 2000).

These population estimates of immigrants to the United States point to changes in projected populations of the United States, especially for Latinos and Asian Americans. Multicultural psychology is providing an avenue to understand the relationships of acculturation, ethnic identity, and ethnic group membership (Sodowsky, Kwan, & Pannu, 1995; Roysircar-Sodowsky & Maestas, 2000; Roysircar, 2002; Roysircar, in press; Roysircar-Sodowsky & Maestas, in press). Psychologists have recognized many important questions about both the immediate and long-term impact of change in a cultural context for immigrants and their offspring (Nguyen, Messé, & Stollak, 1999; Roysircar-Sodowsky & Frey, 2003). As the area of multicultural psychology has developed, researchers have begun to identify differences, as well as similarities, within and across ethnic groups in the areas of acculturation and ethnic identity. With the various emphases of researchers, this has facilitated the evolution of both the theory and measurement of acculturation and ethnic identity.

Wide Application of the Construct of Acculturation

Currently, the shared understanding among prominent researchers in the areas of acculturation and ethnic identity (e.g., Berry, 1980; Padilla, Wagatsuma, & Lindholm, 1985; Phinney, 1991; Roysircar-Sodowsky & Maestas, 2000) is that ethnic minority individuals living in American society must address issues of their (1) relationship with the White dominant society, (2) retention of their specific ethnic or cultural heritage, and (3) the accompanying stress and other mental health concerns that arise from these processes. These three issues have been empirically and conceptually examined in the measurement domains of acculturation (including acculturative stress) and ethnic identity.

Many acculturation and ethnic identity researchers tend to work within one of the two areas, that is, acculturation or ethnic identity, and study one ethnic minority group of interest, for example, a particular Latino group, such as Mexican Americans (Padilla, 1985), or a particular Asian American group, such as Asian Indians (Sodowsky, 1991; Roysircar, 2002; Roysircar, in press; Veerasamy & Roysircar-Sodowsky, in press). A particular assumption of these researchers is that due to each group's unique culture and sociopolitical history with the dominant group, certain issues are more salient for one ethnic group than for others. For instance, Mexicans, as North Americans, have very close historical, political, trading, and farming employment ties with the United States; they have a favored immigration status with the United States; and many among them enter the United States as "economic refugees." Thus, researchers studying Mexican Americans/Chicanos investigate topics related to this preimmigration background. With regard to Asian Indians, even though also seeking economic opportunities, the majority are adult voluntary immigrants who gained U.S. entry since 1965 because of their high education and professional status (Sodowsky & Carey, 1987, 1988; Veerasamy & Roysircar-Sodowsky, in press). These two immigrant groups, Mexican Americans and Asian Indians, are quite different from each other and are of interest to different scholars.

However, despite preimmigration differences among groups, in surveying the recent multicultural literature, it appears that researchers have increasingly come to recognize that all ethnic minority individuals can, at some level, relate to issues of acculturation and retention of ethnic identity in White American society. This is evidenced by the development of several acculturation (including acculturative stress) and ethnic identity instrument measures that have been used with different ethnic minority groups in order to study specific groups empirically. It is important to note that the use of a large number of these cultural measures has preceded theory development. However, an important consequence of their use is the opportunity these cultural instruments have provided for hypotheses testing and construct building.

The acculturation instruments, in alphabetical order, and their authors are listed in Table 11.1. Psychometric properties of each instrument that met construct validation criteria set by the American Educational Research Association (1999), Anastasi and Urbina (1997), and Nunnally (1978) are reported here. These minimum criteria include acceptable degrees of internal consistency (IC) reliability, test-retest reliability (temporal stability) (T-R), criterion-related validity (CRI-R), convergent validity (CONV), and the use factor analysis, which determined the structure of some instruments. Summaries on the psychometric properties of instruments are additionally provided by the author at the Web site, www.multiculturalcenter.org, under the link Information on Multicultural Test Titles (Maestas & Roysircar-Sodowsky, 2000).

An Overview of the Constructs of Acculturation and Ethnic Identity

Acculturation issues most often affect foreign-born, first-generation, immigrant minority groups who go through the continuous process of adapting to White American society. Conversely, ethnic identity issues, related to a reverse acculturation to a minority individual's cultural group, are more relevant and meaningful to children of immigrants. The two constructs have been distinguished in the sense that "acculturation adaptation is a response to the dominant group and ethnic identity is a response to one's ethnic group" (Sodowsky & Lai, 1997, p. 213).

TABLE 11.1   A List of Acculturation, Acculturative Stress, and Ethnic Identity Measures

Instrument	Major Psychometric Properties
Acculturation Rating Scale for Mexican Americans (Cuéllar et al., 1980)	IC & T-R reliability; CONV validity; Factor analysis
Acculturation Rating Scale for Mexican Americans-II (Cuéllar et al., 1995)	IC & T-R reliability; CONV validity; Factor analysis
Acculturation Rating Scale for Mexican Americans-SF (Dawson et al., 1996)	IC reliability; CONV validity; Factor analysis
Acculturation Scale for Southeast Asians (Anderson et al., 1993)	IC reliability; Factor analysis
Acculturation Scale for Vietnamese Adolescents (Nguyen et al., 1999)	IC reliability; Factor analysis
Behavioral Acculturation Scale and Value Acculturation Scale (Szapocznik et al., 1978)	IC & T-R reliability; Factor analysis
Bicultural Acculturation Scale (Cortés et al., 1994)	IC reliability; Factor analysis
Bidimensional Acculturation Scale for Hispanics (Marín & Gamba, 1996)	IC reliability; CONV validity; Factor analysis
Brief Acculturation Scale for Hispanics (Norris et al., 1996)	IC reliability; CRI-R validity
Chicano Adolescent Acculturation Scale (Olmedo et al., 1978)	T-R reliability; Factor analysis
Children's Acculturation Scale (Franco, 1983)	IC & T-R reliability; CONV validity; Factor analysis
Cuban Behavioral Identity Questionnaire (García & Lega, 1979)	IC reliability; Factor analysis
Cultural Adjustment Difficulties Checklist (Sodowsky & Lai, 1997)	IC reliability; Factor analysis; Structural Equation Modeling
Cultural Awareness–Ethnic Loyalty Scale (Padilla, 1980)	IC reliability; Factor analysis
Cultural Life Style Inventory (Mendoza, 1989)	IC & T-R reliability; Factor analysis
Ethnocultural Identity Behavioral Index (Yamada et al., 2000)	IC & T-R reliability; Factor analysis
Hispanic Stress Inventory (Cervantes et al., 1991)	IC & T-R reliability; Factor analysis
Internal-External Ethnic Identity Measure (Kwan & Sodowsky, 1997)	IC reliability; CRI-R validity; Factor analysis
Language Acculturation Scale for Mexican Americans (Deyo et al., 1985)	Guttman coefficient of reproducibility; coefficient of scalability
Latino/Latina Adolescent Acculturation Scale (Felíx-Ortiz et al., 1994)	IC reliability; Factor analysis
LAECA Acculturation Scale (Burnam et al., 1987)	IC reliability; Factor analysis

(continued)

TABLE 11.1   Continued

Instrument	Major Psychometric Properties
Mexican American Acculturation Scale (Montgomery, 1992)	IC reliability; Factor analysis
Multigroup Ethnic Identity Measure (Phinney, 1992)	IC reliability; Factor analysis
Minority-Majority Relations Scale (Sodowsky et al. 1991); Alternate: American-International Relations	IC reliability; Factor analysis; Confirmatory factor analysis
Na Mea Hawai'i Scale (Hawaiian Ways) (Rezentes, 1993)	Empirically keyed items; CRI-R validity
Psychological Acculturation Scale (Tropp et al., 1999)	IC reliability; Factor analysis
Short Acculturation Scale for Hispanics (Marín et al., 1987)	IC reliability; Factor analysis
Short Acculturation Scale for Hispanic Youth (Barona & Miller, 1994)	IC reliability; Factor analysis
Suinn-Lew Asian Self-Identity Acculturation Scale (Suinn et al., 1987, 1992)	IC reliability; Factor analysis

Note: IC reliability = internal consistency reliability; T-R reliability = test-retest reliability; CONV validity = convergent validity; CRI-R validity = criterion-related validity

First-generation immigrants who arrive in the United States at an older age must struggle with their acculturation to White American society after having been socialized in their culture (Roysircar, 2002; Roysircar, in press). Children of immigrants and later generations must determine what aspects of their cultures are most relevant to them and, thus, to be retained (Roysircar, 2002; Roysircar-Sodowsky & Frey, 2003; Roysircar, in press). An immigrant becomes acculturated to the dominant society through exposure, experience, and both involuntary and voluntary learning. An immigrant's offspring, with the need to attach to a reference or social group, is driven to develop an ethnic identity.

The preceding conceptualization of acculturation of the first generation and ethnic identity of the second generation has found support in empirical studies. Velez (1995), who studied first- and second-generation Puerto Rican and Chinese Americans in New York City, found that second-generation subjects had higher acculturation scores than the first generation, but ethnic identity was not negatively correlated with level of acculturation. Bufka's (1998) study showed that first-generation Asian Indian adolescents were less acculturated than their second-generation peers. They also perceived more prejudice. However, the two generations did not show any differences in various components of ethnic identity. Cuéllar, Roberts, Nyberg, and Maldonado (1997) found in a sample of Mexican American first-year college students that those students who were classified as high bicultural acculturative type scored higher on a measure of ethnic identity than those students classified as low bicultural acculturative type. Thus, the empirical literature in acculturation and ethnic identity suggests that these two constructs are related but somewhat independent processes, both being experienced by ethnic minorities.

Conceptually, the relationship between acculturation and ethnic identity can be described as a push-and-pull psychological phenomenon: An ethnic individual feels both the push to acculturate to the dominant culture and the pull toward his or her ethnic group. This tension between push and pull can be described as acculturative stress and bicultural stress.

Perspectives in the Measurement of Acculturation and Ethnic Identity

Etic Versus Emic Measures

The development of the acculturation (including acculturative stress) and ethnic identity instruments has proceeded along both "etic" and "emic" approaches and has provided cross-cultural and multicultural psychology with universal and culture-specific information and theoretical conceptualizations. According to Sue (1983), the "etic approach views human phenomena across cultures and emphasizes 'universals' or core similarities in all human beings" (p. 584). Some acculturation and ethnic identity investigators have developed instruments using the etic perspective. For example, the impetus for developing the Multigroup Ethnic Identity Measure (MEIM; Phinney, 1992) stemmed from the concept that ethnic identity is a general phenomenon and that group identity is common to all humans. Phinney has included White American samples in her study of ethnic identity (Phinney, 1992). Similarly, the Minority-Majority Relations Scale (MMRS; Sodowsky, Lai, & Plake, 1991) was initially developed and validated on a sample of Latino and Asian Americans and later cross-validated with a sample of Native Americans and African Americans (Osvold & Sodowsky, 1995). Confirmatory factor analysis was performed on an international student sample from Asian, African, and South American countries (Sodowsky et al., 1991; Sodowsky & Plake, 1991, 1992). This measure has predicted varying degrees of acculturation in different Asian religious groups and their individualistic versus collectivistic coping strategies (Roysircar et al., 2001). The MMRS has also been used with White Americans in order to understand how acculturated they are to their own White American society (Frey & Roysircar-Sodowsky, 2002). In this study, White Americans' perception of normal dissociative experiences was significantly accounted for by their acculturation scores (Frey & Roysircar-Sodowsky, 2002). Instruments, such as the MEIM and the MMRS, provide information that facilitates generalizations across ethnic groups and allow researchers to make comparative analyses.

The emic perspective, however, "utilizes a culture-specific orientation whereby the influence of sociocultural variables is stressed" (Sue, 1983, p. 584).

When acculturation is quantitatively defined using such variables, that is, the degree to which an ethnic individual has adopted the sociocultural characteristics of the dominant culture, the IQ scores of Latinos have been shown to increase (Mercer, 1976). An example of a sociocultural variable would be generational status and its influence on the ethnic identity of individuals within an ethnic group. Some acculturation and ethnic identity researchers have long underscored the need to recognize the heterogeneity within Latino and Asian American ethnic groups and have developed culture specific measures (e.g., ARSMA in Cuéllar, Harris, & Jasso, 1980; SL-ASIA in Suinn, Rickard-Figueroa, Lew, & Virgil, 1987). Factors by which an ethnic group has shown wide variation among its members include sociocultural variables, such as country of ancestry, preimmigration (e.g., voluntary immigration versus political refugee status) conditions, immigration history, ethnic language, religion, and sociopolitical relationship with White American society. Latinos and Asian Americans also differ on other intraethnic variables including migration and relocation experiences in the United States, ethnic and English language proficiency, ethnic dialect, socioeconomic status, family composition and intactness, adherence to religious beliefs, and generational status. These sociocultural variables, as well as degree of acculturation and cultural ethnic identity retention, influence both interethnic (etic) and intraethnic (emic) variations (e.g., Sodowsky & Plake, 1992; Kwan & Sodowsky, 1997).

Acculturation Theories

Definition

In order to better understand the phenomenon of acculturation, the following operational definition of culture can be used.

> One of the most important scientific developments of modern times has been the recognition of culture. It has been said that the thing which a dweller in the deep sea would be least likely to discover would be water. [He/she] would become conscious of its existence only if some accident brought [him/her] to the surface and introduced [one] to air. [Humankind], throughout most of [its] history, has been vaguely conscious of the existence of culture and has owed even this consciousness to the contrasts between the customs of [its] own society and those of some other with which [it] happened to be brought into contact. (Linton, 1945, p. 125; parenthetical words added to avoid sexist language)

Sodowsky et al. (1991) further described culture as "a set of people who have common and shared values; customs, habits, and rituals; systems of labeling, explanation, and evaluation; social rules of behavior; perceptions regarding human nature, natural phenomena, interpersonal relationships, time, and activity; symbols, art, and artifacts; and historical developments" (p. 194).

The basic premise of acculturation involves the transmission of certain cultural phenomena of one cultural group to members of another distinct cultural group. One of the earliest sociological definitions of acculturation maintained that "acculturation comprehends those phenomena which result when groups of individuals having different cultures come into continuous first-hand contact, with subsequent changes in the original cultural patterns of either or both groups" (Redfield, Linton, & Herskovits, 1936, p. 149). Walter (1952) added the concept that acculturation is but one of the processes of intercultural exchange. He defined acculturation as the "interchange of cultural traits and complexes between or among alien groups" (p. 44). Walter further articulated that acculturation is a prolonged process wherein each cultural group is likely to maintain its own values and practices and resist those that compete with traditional ones. Thus, acculturation is a bidirectional process involving the acquisition of group characteristics and practices of two societies. However, one group will dominate this exchange of group characteristics (Walter, 1952). Acculturation is not to be confused with assimilation, which is unidirectional in nature and involves requiring the less powerful minority group to adopt the values, behaviors, and cultural patterns of the dominant or majority group (Cuéllar et al., 1997).

Furthermore, acculturation has been delineated to encompass the collective or group level phenomenon, as well as the psychological acculturation of the individual (Graves, 1967). Acculturation as a group-level phenomenon involves a change in the culture of the group, and psychological acculturation involves a change in the psychology of the ethnic individual (Berry, 1997). Berry (1997) further added that this distinction between levels is important "in order to examine the systematic relationships between these two sets of variables and because not all individuals participate to the same extent in the general acculturation being experienced by their group" (p. 7).

Berry (1997) has provided a conceptual framework from which to understand the individual- or psychological-level phenomenon of acculturation. According to this framework, psychological acculturation begins with an ethnic individual's subjective experience of the contact between two distinct cultures and the need to participate to varying degrees in each of the cultures. This process continues as the individual determines if this contact experience will present difficulties and the extent to which these difficulties will affect the adaptation process. At one end, the individual may view the acculturation experience as an opportunity with minimal stress, while at the other end, psychopathology may develop if the acculturation experience proves overwhelming.

Ethnic individuals engage in coping strategies to overcome the acculturation experiences that are judged to be problematic. These coping strategies are related to the four acculturation strategies outlined by Berry (1980) (i.e., integration, assimilation, separation, and marginalization) and can be active, passive, problem focused, or emotion focused. If the coping strategies are not effective, the immediate effects that follow acculturative problems give rise to physiological and emotional reactions, which are labeled acculturative stress. However, when an ethnic individual engages in effective coping strategies, the immediate effects will be positive. The end result of the psychological acculturation process is adaptation. Berry (1997) defines this adaptation as "the relatively stable changes that take place in an individual or group in response to environmental demands. [This adaptation] may or may not improve the 'fit' between individuals and their environments" (p. 20). Adaptation in this sense is not synonymous with positive adjustment or being well adapted only. "Long term adaptation to acculturation is highly variable ranging from well-adapted to poorly adapted, varying from a situation where individuals can manage their new lives very well, to one where they are unable to carry on in the new society" (p. 20).

Ultimately, acculturation, as understood by psychological researchers, is a dynamic adaptation process whereby attitudes and behaviors of individuals from one culture or minority group are modified as a direct result from contact with another cultural or dominant group (Moyerman & Forman, 1992; Sodowsky et al., 1991). The phenomenon and processes of acculturation occur at the macro- and microlevel, are multifaceted, multidirectional, and encompass bicultural and multicultural processes (Cuéllar et al., 1997).

Bidirectional Acculturation Theory

Berry and colleagues (1980, 1987, 1989, 1993) proposed a two-dimensional model of acculturation at the group level. This model provides a framework to understand the parallel process between a majority group and a minority group, both relatively autonomous with regard to their cultural ways of life, that determines the acculturation options of ethnic groups.

Ethnic minorities must confront two general issues that are in opposition and may create conflict: the maintenance and development of one's ethnic distinctiveness by retaining one's cultural identity; and the desire to seek interethnic contact by valuing and maintaining positive relations with the dominant society (Roysircar-Sodowsky & Maestas, 2000). These two general issues represent the dimensions of acculturation for the individual and can be assessed by two central questions in opposition to each other (Berry, 1990, p. 216): (1) "Is it considered to be of value to maintain cultural identity and characteristics?" and (2) "Is it considered to be of value to maintain relationships with other groups?" Both questions must be answered, and the combination of answers result in four acculturation decisions: integration (yes/yes), assimilation (no/yes), separation (yes/no), and marginalization (no/no). The integration adaptation mode is characterized by an allegiance to cultural identity and involvement in the dominant culture. Those who use the assimilation mode relinquish their cultural identity and prefer to interact only with members of the dominant society. In contrast, a separation involves the exclusive identification with and retention of one's cultural values and an avoidance of contact with the dominant society. Individuals who become marginal "lose cultural and psychological contact with both their traditional culture and the larger society" (Berry et al., 1989, p. 188). Similar to Berry's second question regarding how one relates to the dominant society, Sodowsky and her colleagues (Sodowsky et al., 1991; Sodowsky & Plake, 1992; Osvold & Sodowsky, 1995; Sodowsky et al., 1995; Sodowsky & Lai, 1997; Roysircar-Sodowsky & Maestas, 2000; Roysircar, 2002; Roysircar, in press) understand acculturation as a U.S.

minority group's conflict-reduction process of behavioral adaptation, as it attempts to reduce the majority-minority group conflict over cultural value and power differences.

Berry pointed to the individual's acculturation responses in psychological areas, such as language usage, cognitive style, personality, cultural identity, relationship attitudes toward the dominant group, and acculturative stress. These factors interact to create a multidimensional profile related to acculturation. Cuéllar et al. (1980) have argued, "One cannot assume that a minority is highly acculturated simply because he or she is fluent in English" (p. 199).

Interactional Theory of Acculturation

Padilla (1980) presented a model of acculturation that articulated the effect of psychological functioning on both the extent and rate of acculturation. This model was developed specifically for Mexican Americans, but the author contended that the critical constructs in this model are applicable to other ethnic groups. Padilla posited that there are two elements involved in acculturation: cultural awareness and ethnic loyalty. Cultural awareness is defined as the knowledge an ethnic individual possesses of cultural material regarding both his or her culture of origin and the host culture. Ethnic loyalty refers to an individual's propensity to choose one cultural orientation over the other. Padilla introduced the concept of *cultural preferences*. Preferences may vary from minor relevance, as when an individual engages in some ethnic activity for the purpose of relaxation, to critical significance, if it implies ethnic self-identification. Padilla (1980) highlighted the importance of preferences as behavioral indices of cultural awareness and ethnic loyalty because they provide information about the extent to which an individual is acculturated.

Padilla (1980) held that there were five dimensions important in the conceptualization of acculturation that could be understood using both components of acculturation (cultural awareness and ethnic loyalty). Language familiarity and usage, the first dimension, was conceptualized in terms of preferences. Previous conceptualizations of the language dimension entailed only the measurement of "use of language." Language usage has been used almost exclusively in the study of acculturation using linear models whereby an increase in the use of the dominant group's language requires a reduction in the use of the language of the culture of origin, resulting in a greater level of acculturation (e.g., ARSMA in Cuéllar et al., 1980). In Padilla's model, the *preference* for either the original culture's language or the language of the host culture is also important when studying language familiarity and usage.

Cultural heritage, the second dimension, "refers to knowledge of a wide variety of cultural artifacts and materials specific to both cultures . . . [and] refers to an individual's preference for one culture's artifacts or materials over the other" (Padilla, 1980, p. 49). Therefore, acculturative change is not exclusively dependent on the level of knowledge of either culture. It is possible, using this model, to possess a high degree of knowledge regarding the artifacts and materials of the host culture, yet *prefer* the artifacts and materials of one's culture of origin, thereby impacting acculturation level.

The final three dimensions constitute an ethnicity factor: ethnic pride and identity, interethnic interaction, and interethnic distance, the latter two being moderated by perceived prejudice. These dimensions highlight the interactional nature of acculturation and the resultant effects on acculturation level. Padilla (1980) hypothesized that cultural groups who are slow to interact with the dominant group will acculturate slower than those groups for whom interaction is facile. Therefore, acculturation is expedited by increased interethnic interaction. Interethnic distance may be maintained by such differences as skin color, speech accents, religious beliefs, and so on, and may be supported by a consensus of the ethnic group, the dominant society, or both. Sodowsky et al.'s (1991) instrument, the MMRS, has three factors that closely support Padilla's constructs of language preference, cultural heritage preference, and perceived prejudice, as these variables affect majority-minority interaction of the ethnic individual.

Linear Theory of Acculturation Within the Framework of Sociocultural Variables

Szapocznik, Scopetta, Kurtines, & Aranalde (1978) developed a linear psychosocial acculturation theory that emphasizes the type of cultural context involved in the acculturation process and the changing ethnic individual and his or her family. Specifically, "individual acculturation is a linear function of the amount of time a person has been exposed to the host culture, and the rate at which the acculturation process takes place is a function of the age and sex of the individual" (Szapocznik & Kurtines, 1980, p. 141). Therefore, the longer a person is exposed to a host culture, the more acculturated he or she will be. Additionally, there is an interaction between length of exposure to the host culture and age and gender. Ethnic individuals who are exposed to a majority culture at a younger age will acculturate more rapidly than those individuals who are exposed at an older age, with males acculturating more rapidly than females (Szapocznik et al., 1978). There is strong evidence in research on a linear relationship between time in the United States, including number of generations in the United States, and behavioral acculturation (e.g., Szopcznik et al., 1978; Padilla et al. 1985; Mena, Padilla, & Maldonado, 1987; Sodowsky, Lai, & Plake, 1991; Sodowsky & Plake, 1992; Suinn, Ahuna, & Khoo, 1992; Mehta, 1998).

This model further delineated the acculturation process into an overt behavioral dimension of functioning and an internalized value orientation. Specifically, the

> dimension of behavioral acculturation involves the gradual adoption by the individual of the more overt and observable aspects of the host culture, including the host culture's language, customs, habits, and life style. The value dimension is less overt and involves the gradual adoption by the individual of the host culture's basic value orientations. (Szapocznik et al., 1978, p. 115)

The process of behavioral acculturation was found to be positively correlated with length of exposure to the host culture, with males acculturating more rapidly than females along this dimension (Szapocznik et al., 1978). The value orientation process of acculturation was found to be more complex and related to a psycho-social stage (i.e., early adolescence, later adolescence, early adulthood, middle adulthood, and later adulthood) rather than age with no significant differences between males and females (Szapocznik et al., 1978).

Szapocznik and Kurtines (1980) also held that the "process of accommodation to a total cultural context may be either unidimensional or two dimensional depending upon the type of cultural context involved" (p. 139). When the context of acculturation is bicultural, the process is two dimensional involving the retention of culture of origin characteristics while adopting the characteristics of the host culture. The two moderating variables for this bicultural process are the amount of time the ethnic individual has been exposed to the dominant culture and the degree of support he or she receives from the culture of origin (Szapocznik & Kurtines, 1980). For example, according to the author of this writing, a divorced Asian woman may not receive much support from her traditional or conservative culture of origin. Thus, the longer she lives in White American society, the more she will adopt the attitudes and behaviors of White Americans.

Intergenerational conflict can result from acculturation differences within the family when parents and children adhere to conflicting cultural values and behaviors (Szapocznik et al., 1978). The increased rate of acculturation in children and adolescents, when compared to their parents, compounds the typical intergenerational differences with acculturation differences (Szapocznik et al., 1978). These differences further explain the phenomenon of family disruption in ethnic minority communities.

The weakness inherent in a linear conceptualization of acculturation is its inability to account for contextual factors in the acculturation process (Sodowsky et al., 1995; Roysircar, 2002; Roysircar, in press). Mendoza (1989) held that "acculturation reflects not only changes that occur as a function of passage of time, exposure to an alternate culture, and other social and psychological factors but also changes in context" (p. 374). Ethnic individuals may adopt different acculturation attitudes that are dependent on a particular context in which they function, such as, an ethnic neighborhood versus a middle-class White neighborhood versus a multicultural downtown setting; public school or state-supported higher education; and an ethnically popular occupation or trade versus an executive position in management.

Acculturative Stress and Bicultural Stress: Definitions and Empirical Findings

Acculturative Stress

Acculturative stress stems from the stressors in the context of the process of acculturation and is "mildly pathological and disruptive to the individual and the group" (Berry, 1980, p. 21). Berry, Kim, Minde, and Mok (1987) define this stress as a "Generalized physiological and psychological state . . . brought about by the experience of stressors in the environment, and which requires some reduction . . . through a process of coping until some satisfactory adaptation to the new situation is achieved" (p. 492). Dressler and Bernal (1982) state that acculturative stress occurs "when an individual's adaptive resources are insufficient to support adjustment to a new cultural environment" (p. 34). The stress is elicited by drastically new life events and cues the acculturating individual to possible dangers or opportunities. Although a certain amount of stress may be necessary or helpful in alerting the individual to respond to new situations, too much stress can threaten healthy adaptation. Thus, Berry et al. (1987) state acculturative stress could be a "reduction in health status (including psychological, somatic and social aspects) of individuals who are undergoing acculturation, and for which there is evidence that these health phenomena are related systematically to acculturation phenomena" (p. 491).

Individuals undergoing acculturation do not necessarily experience mental health problems. The level of acculturative stress may vary considerably depending on four individual and group characteristics. According to Berry and Kim (1988), there are four broad categories of mediating variables. The first mediating variable includes the nature of the dominant society, which includes factors such as its pluralistic or assimilationist ideology—as stated by Gil and Vega (1996),

> Social conditions may favor a smooth or bumpy transition. These conditions include the presence or absence of ethnic enclaves to support and advocate for new immigrants in their efforts to find housing, jobs and an accommodating cultural environment. Other environmental factors are the active resistance to new immigrants and the lack of receptivity to their culture and language. This can take the form of numerous boundary maintenance strategies, including de facto segregation, political marginalization, overt racism and cultural conflicts. (p. 437)

Acculturative stress is less predominant in multicultural societies than in unicultural societies. Multicultural societies tend to accept diversity and encourage support structures for diverse groups. Unicultural societies are more likely to expect diverse groups to assimilate to the dominant group's standards.

The second mediating variable refers to the nature of the acculturating group. Berry and Kim (1988) identified five groups that varied in degree of voluntariness, movement, and permanence of contact: immigrants, refugees, native peoples, ethnic groups, and sojourners. Individuals who voluntarily participate in the acculturation process, such as voluntary immigrants, and who are more permanently established in their communities, such as ethnic groups, experience less stress than those whose contact with the dominant group is involuntary (historically Native Americans and African Americans), who are refugees (e.g., Vietnamese), or who are sojourners (e.g., international students) making temporary contact. Osvold and Sodowsky (1993) used the first two assumptions, the assimilationist versus pluralistic ideology of the dominant society, and the nature of the acculturating group (voluntariness versus involuntariness, temporary contact of sojourners) to understand the eating attitudes of women of color and White women.

The third mediating variable is the mode of acculturation adaptation chosen: assimilation, integration, rejection, or deculturation. Berry (1980) found that among nine groups of "Amerindians" in northern Canada, those communities with the highest stress levels were those (1) with the least cultural similarity to the dominant group, (2) who had some contact, and (3) who preferred the rejection mode of adaptation. Conversely, those minorities in Canada with the least amount of stress had more initial cultural similarity to the dominant group, had experienced more contact, and preferred the integration mode of adaptation. For these minorities, acculturation was a choice and not an imposition (Berry et al., 1987).

The fourth factor includes the demographic (see Sodowsky & Carey, 1988; Sodowsky et al., 1991; Sodowsky & Plake, 1992), social (see Sodowsky & Lai, 1997), and psychological characteristics (see Kwan & Sodowsky, 1997) of the acculturating individual that can mediate the acculturation-stress relationship. Some of these characteristics also include coping strategies, education, age, gender, cognitive styles, prior intercultural experiences, and contact experiences.

Bicultural Stress

Acculturative stress is a common experience of foreign-born, first-generation immigrants as they adapt to a new society. However, U.S.-born second- and later-generation ethnic minorities experience bicultural stress owing to the conflicts that arise out of their bicultural socialization (De Anda, 1984). Biculturalism refers to the orientation of minorities in the United States who inherit two different cultural traditions. Asian Americans and Latinos undergoing a bicultural socialization process must negotiate between two disparate cultures, their ethnic culture and the White dominant culture. There is vast disparity between Asian and Western cultures. Some of the more salient cultural values and beliefs of the Asian culture include emphasis on family kinship, reciprocal duty and obligation (i.e., filial piety), hierarchical roles and social status, and respect and deference to authority figures or persons of higher social status (Sodowsky, 1991; Sodowsky et al., 1995). LaFromboise, Coleman, and Gerton (1993) concluded that "the more an individual is able to maintain active and effective relationships through alternation between both cultures, the less difficulty he/she will have in acquiring and maintaining competency in both cultures" (p. 402). The authors further suggested that the acquisition of bicultural skills is important to the physical and psychological health of ethnic minorities.

Bicultural conflict appears to involve two dimensions, the interpersonal, measured as intercultural competence concerns, and intrapersonal, measured as acculturative distress (Sodowsky & Lai, 1997). The interpersonal dimension involves having cultural conflicts with one's own ethnic group (e.g., second generation's conflicts with first generation parents) and/or with members of the dominant culture (Sodowsky & Lai, 1997). The intrapersonal dimension includes identity crisis, a personal sense of inferiority as a member of one's cultural group, lack of ethnic ego differentiation due to feeling marginalized from both cultural groups, and feelings of anger and guilt toward one or both cultural groups (Sodowsky & Lai, 1997). Golding and Burnam (1990) investigated levels of depressive symptoms of 538 U.S.-born and 806 Mexico-born Mexican Americans. They indicated that U.S.-born Mexican Americans reported significantly higher depression scores than the Mexican-born respondents, even though the U.S.-born had higher job status, income, and less financial strain than their immigrant counterparts. Also, U.S.-born subjects who had low educational achievement and low acculturation had higher levels of depression. Similarly, Dressler and Bernal (1982), upon interviewing sixty-seven Puerto Rican migrants to the northeastern United States, found that those who had lived the longest but lacked coping resources had the worst acculturative stress outcomes, such as poorer health and more behavioral problems. In addition, extreme bicultural conflict leaves the individual vulnerable to experiences of bicultural stress, which is manifested by feelings of emotional turmoil and alienation (Sue & Sue, 1990), cultural marginality (Masuda, Matsumoto, Meridith, 1970; Sodowsky et al., 1995), poor self-concept (Padilla et al., 1985), depression (Draguns, 1996), anxiety (S. Sue, 1996), disordered eating attitudes and behaviors (Osvold & Sodowsky, 1993, 1995), and career-choice indecision (Sodowsky, 1991).

Additional Information on Acculturation and Mental Health

Acculturation has been related to mental health and personality issues (see review by Roysircar-Sodowsky & Maestas, 2000), including psychiatric symptoms, alienation, and well-being or general life satisfaction for an Asian Indian immigrant sample (Mehta, 1998), cultural values conflict for Asian Indian immigrant women in relation to dating/sexuality and sex role expectations (Inman, Ladany, Constantine, & Morano, 2001), self-esteem (Phinney, Chavira, & Williamson, 1992), family conflict (Rumbaut, 1994), interpersonal and intrapersonal distress (Sodowsky & Lai, 1997), fear of loss of face and collective group self-esteem (Kwan & Sodowsky, 1997), normal dissociative states of consciousness and worldviews (Frey & Roysircar, 2002), disordered eating attitudes (Osvold & Sodowsky, 1995), perceived prejudice and racial consciousness (Sodowsky et al., 1991; Kuo & Roysircar-Sodowsky, 1999), as well as the relationship of these correlates to ethnic group memberships. The relationship between acculturation and mental health has been complex, showing that both high and low acculturation can have either positive or negative mental health effects (Roysircar-Sodowsky & Maestas, 2000).

Negative mental health effects, such as stress or depression, result from the multidirectional interaction of acculturation, pulls toward identification with one's own ethnic group, extracultural stressors in the environment (e.g., low income, unfamiliar educational system), and mediating immigrant, sociocultural, and personal variables, (Roysircar-Sodowsky & Maestas, in press). The interactions form a fully recursive model (that is, it is not unidirectional) that represents influences from two or three directions. For example, for an ethnic individual, certain mediating variables (e.g., length of residence, gender role) affect acculturation to White society. Acculturation, in turn, impacts extracultural stressors (e.g., educational experiences). Extracultural stressors also affect an individual's acculturation to White society and are themselves impacted by specific mediating variables. The recursive influence of acculturation, extracultural stressors, and mediating variables on an acculturating individual creates the experience of mental health difficulties, which vary from individual to individual (Roysircar-Sodowsky & Maestas, in press).

Acculturation has been related to gender attitudes. For instance, higher acculturation scores of Japanese American men predicted higher levels of gender role conflict as these men also became more relaxed with regard to their emotional expressions (Owen, 1996). Similarly, acculturation has been related to those who are most likely to date outside one's ethnicity or race (Mok, 1994; Murthy, 1998).

Conclusion

The phenomenon of "new immigrants" or post–World War II immigrants from Asia and Latin America and the large birthrate of U.S.-born second-generation children have begun to change U.S. society with the visibility of people of color who are different from even those who have been traditionally considered as ethnic minorities in the United States. New immigrants constitute the majority of immigrants to this country. At the individual level of acculturation, a person must confront two general issues that are in opposition and may create conflict: (1) the maintenance and development of one's ethnic distinctiveness by retaining one's cultural identity, and (2) the desire to seek interethnic contact by valuing and maintaining positive relations with the dominant society. Subsumed in these dimensions are changes in multiple domains for immigrants: physical changes, biological changes, social relationships, language change, cognitive processes, personality, identity, cultural attitudes and values, and acculturative stress. Acculturation studies to date have been involved in the measurement of length of residence in the United States, age of entry into the United States, language change, ethnic identity, social behaviors and orientation, cultural attitudes and values, family differences, and generational differences. This writing describes the constructs and empirical findings in the measurement of acculturation and ethnic identity. Acceptable measures are identified and listed, and the measurement perspectives behind the development of these measures are explored.

DISCUSSION QUESTIONS

1. You are a counselor in a middle school that is part of the public school district in a large metropolitan area. Your school is ethnically and racially diverse and, over the past 10 years, has seen a significant increase in the number of immigrant children,

particularly children of Asian and Hispanic/Latino American descent. You are in the process of planning psychoeducational support groups for these students with the goal of facilitating the adaptation of the youth within the school. In organizing a presentation for the school administration regarding such groups, you must be prepared to respond to the following questions:

(a) What are your objectives for the group that are based on your knowledge of acculturation and ethnic identity issues?

(b) How will you select participants for the group? Will participation be voluntary (explain why) or based on specific criteria developed by teachers and school counselors (explain why)? If based on specific criteria, what will they be? Will you make the group open to European immigrant students (e.g., from Bosnia, Russia) and/or to white nonimmigrant students (explain why)?

(c) What content would you cover in the group?

(d) How would you structure the group (e.g., size, age range, length and duration, in-school or after-school meetings, etc.)?

(e) What would be key acculturation knowledge, attitudes, skills, and interventions, and personal characteristics of the group leaders?

(f) How would you involve the students' families (e.g., foreign-born immigrant parents) in the planning process and in other activities related to the groups?

2. What key dimensions would you consider in assessing an individual's acculturation? Develop specific intake questions that would provide appropriate information in assessing acculturation dimensions of an individual. If you wanted to gather information regarding acculturation through observation of an individual in a community, social, school, or family environment, in what specific settings would you observe this student? What information could you gather through observation that would help you to better understand the individual's acculturation and help him or her?

3. You are a counselor in the only high school of a small, rural public school district. A female student who is the second-generation child of immigrant parents from India moves into your school district after her father is recruited to be a family physician in the community. You are interested in assisting this student in her transition into the school, which currently has no teachers or students of color. How would you approach this student and/or her family from an acculturation perspective regarding providing her with assistance? What aspects of school life would you focus your acculturation interventions on? Identify specific ways you might consider intervening with teachers and administrative personnel.

4. Review the dimensions of acculturation and acculturative stress and their interface with issues of ethnic identity. What are some of the differences among the acculturation constructs?

5. Discuss your own values about acculturation and ethnic identity. How are these cultural value orientations expressed in your approach to counseling?

6. What are some of the defining demographic characteristics of Asian and Hispanic/Latino immigrants? Suggest five different implications of the given demographics.

REFERENCES

American Educational Research Association, American Psychological Association, and National Council on Measurement in Education. (1999). *Standards for educational and psychological testing*. Washington DC, American Educational Research Association.

Anastasi, A., & Urbina, S. (1997). *Psychological testing* (7th ed.). New York: Prentice Hall.

Anderson, J., Moeschberger, M., Chen, Jr., M. S., Kunn, P., Wewers, M. E., & Guthrie, R. (1993). An acculturation scale for Southeast Asians. *Social Psychiatry and Psychiatric Epidemiology, 28*, 134–141.

Barona, A., & Miller, J. A. (1994). Short Acculturation Scale for Hispanic Youth (SASH-Y): A preliminary report. *Hispanic Journal of Behavioral Sciences, 16*(2), 155–162.

Berry, J. W. (1980). Acculturation as varieties of adaptation. In A. M. Padilla (Ed.), *Acculturation: Theory, models and some new findings* (pp. 9–25). Boulder, CO: Westview Press.

Berry, J. W. (1990). Psychology of acculturation. In J. J. Berman (Ed.), *Cross-cultural perspectives* (pp. 201–234). Lincoln: University of Nebraska Press.

Berry, J. W. (1993). Ethnic identity in pluralistic societies. In M. E. Bernal & G. P. Knight (Eds.), *Ethnic identity: Formation and transmission among Hispanics and other minorities* (pp. 271–296). Albany: State University of New York Press.

Berry, J. W. (1997). Immigration, acculturation, and adaptation. *Applied Psychology: An International Review, 46*(1), 5–68.

Berry, J. W., & Kim, U. (1988). Acculturation and mental health. In P. Dasen, J. W. Berry, & N. Sartorius (Eds.), *Health and cross-cultural psychology: Towards applications* (pp. 207–236). Newbury Park, CA: Sage.

Berry, J. W., Kim, U., Minde, T., & Mok, D. (1987). Comparative studies of acculturative stress. *International Migration Review, 21*, 491–511.

Berry, J. W., Kim. U., Power, S., Young, M., Bujaki, M. (1989). Acculturation attitudes in plural societies. *Applied Psychology: An International Review, 38*(2), 158–206.

Bufka, L. F. (1998, August). *Family factors, acculturation, and identity in second generation Asian Indians*. Paper presented at the annual convention of the American Psychological Association, San Francisco, CA.

Buriel, R., & De Ment, T. (1997). Immigration and sociocultural change in Mexican, Chinese, and Vietnamese American families. In A. Booth, A. C. Crouter, & N. Landale (Eds.), *Immigration and the family: Research and policy on U.S. immigrants* (pp. 165–200). Mahwah, NJ: Erlbaum.

Burnam, M. A., Telles, C. A., Karno, M., Hough, R. L., & Escobar, J. I. (1987). Measurement of acculturation in a community population of Mexican Americans. *Hispanic Journal of Behavioral Sciences, 9*(2), 105–130.

Cervantes, R. C., Padilla, A. M., & Salgado de Snyder, N. (1991). The Hispanic Stress Inventory: A culturally relevant approach to psychological assessment. *Psychological Assessment, 3*(3), 438–477.

Cortés, D. E., Rogler, L. H., & Malgady, R. H. (1994). Biculturality among Puerto Rican adults in the United States. *American Journal of Community Psychology, 22*(5), 707–721.

Cuéllar, I., Arnold, B., & Maldonaldo, R. (1995). Acculturation Rating Scale for Mexican Americans-II: A revision of the original ARSMA scale. *Hispanic Journal of Behavioral Sciences, 17*(3), 275–304.

Cuéllar, I., Harris, L. C., & Jasso, R. (1980). An acculturation scale for Mexican American normal and clinical populations. *Hispanic Journal of Behavioral Sciences, 2*(3), 199–217.

Cuéllar, I., Roberts, R. E., Nyberg, B., & Maldonado, R. E. (1997). Ethnic identity and acculturation in a young adult Mexican-orgin population. *Journal of Community Psychology, 25*(6), 535–549.

Dawson, E. J., Crano, W. D., & Burgoon, M. (1996). Refining the meaning and measurement of acculturation. Revisiting a novel methodological approach. *International Journal of Intercultural Relations, 29*(1), 97–114.

De Anda, D. (1984). Bicultural socialization: Factors affecting the minority experience. *Social Work, 29,* 101–107.

Deyo, R. A., Diehl, A. K., Hazuda, H., & Stern, M. P. (1985). A simple language-based acculturation scale for Mexican Americans: Validation and application to health care research. *American Journal of Public Health, 75*(1), 51–55.

Dressler, W. W., & Bernal, H. (1982). Acculturation and stress in a low-income Puerto Rican community. *Journal of Human Stress, 8*(3), 32–38.

Felíx-Ortiz, M., Newcomb, M. D., & Meyers, H. (1994). A multidimensional measure of cultural identity for Latino and Latina adolescents. *Hispanic Journal of Behavioral Sciences, 16*(2), 99–115.

Franco, J. N. (1983). An acculturation scale for Mexican-American children. *The Journal of General Psychology, 108,* 175–181.

Frey, L., & Roysircar, G. (2002). Acculturation, worldview, and normal dissociation: Self-reported differences among White Americans, South Americans, South Asians, and Southeast Asians. Submitted for publication.

García, M., & Lega, L. I. (1979). Development of a Cuban ethnic identity questionnaire. *Hispanic Journal of Behavioral Sciences, 1,* 247–261.

Gil, A. G., & Vega, W. A. (1996). Two different worlds: Acculturation stress adaptation among Cuban and Nicaraguan families. *Journal of Social and Personal Relationships, 13*(3), 435–456.

Golding, J. M., & Burnam, M. A. (1990). Immigration, stress and depressive symptoms in a Mexican American community. *Journal of Nervous and Mental Disease, 178*(3), 161–171.

Graves, T. (1967). Psychological acculturation in a tri-ethnic community. *South-Western Journal of Anthropology, 23,* 337–350.

Inman, A. G., Ladany, N., Constantine, M. G., & Morano, C. K. (2001). Development and preliminary validation of the cultural values conflict scale for South Asian women. *Journal of Counseling Psychology, 48,* 17–27.

Jensen, L., & Chitose, Y. (1997). Immigrant generations. In A. Booth, A. C. Crouter, & N. Landale (Eds.), *Immigration and the family: Research and policy on U.S. immigrants* (pp. 47–61). Mahwah, NJ: Erlbaum.

Kuo, P. Y., & Roysircar-Sodowsky, G. (1999). Cultural ethnic identity versus political ethnic identity: Theory and research on Asian Americans. In D. S. Sandhu (Ed.), *Asian and Pacific Islander Americans: Issues and concerns for counseling and psychotherapy* (pp. 71–90). New York: Nova Sciences.

Kwan, K. L. K., & Sodowsky, G. R. (1997). Internal and external ethnic identity and their correlates: A study of Chinese American immigrants. *Journal of Multicultural Counseling and Development, 25*(1), 51–67.

LaFromboise, T., Coleman, H. L. K., & Gerton, J. (1993). Psychological impact of biculturalism: Evidence and theory. *Psychological Bulletin, 114,* 395–412.

Linton, R. (1945). *The cultural background of personality.* New York: Appleton-Century-Crofts, Inc.

Maestas, M. V., & Roysircar-Sodowsky, G. (2000). *Information on Multicultural Test Titles.* Available at the Multicultural Center for Research and Practice: www.multiculturalcenter.org

Marín, G., & Gamba, R. J. (1996). A new measurement of acculturation for Hispanics: The Bidimensional Acculturation Scale for Hispanics (BAS). *Hispanic Journal of Behavioral Sciences, 18*(3), 297–316.

Marín, G., Sabogal, F., Marin, B. V., Otero-Sabogal, R., & Perez-Stable, E. J. (1987). Development of a short acculturation scale for Hispanics. *Hispanic Journal of Behavioral Sciences, 9,* 207–225.

Mehta, S. (1988). Relationships between acculturation and mental health for Asian Indian immigrants in the United Stated. *Genetic, Social, and General Psychology Monographs, 124*(1), 61–78.

Mena, F. J., Padilla, A. M., & Maldonado, M. (1987). Acculturative stress and specific coping strategies among immigrant and later generation college students. *Hispanic Journal of Behavioral Sciences, 9,* 207–225.

Mendoza, R. H. (1989). An empirical scale to measure type and degree of acculturation in Mexican-American adolescents and adults. *Journal of Cross-Cultural Psychology, 20*(4), 372–385.

Mercer, J. R. (1976). Pluralistic diagnosis in the evaluation of black and Chicano children: A procedure for taking sociocultural variables into account in clinical assessment. In C. A. Hernandez, M. J. Haug, & N. N. Wagner (Eds.), *Chicanos: Social and psychological perspectives* (2nd ed., pp. 183–195). St Louis, MO: Mosby.

Mok, T. A. (1994, August). Looking for love: Factors influencing Asian Americans' choice of dating partners. In J. Y. Fong (Ed.), *Proceedings of the Asian American Psychological Association 1994 Convention*, Los Angeles, CA.

Montgomery, G. T. (1992). Comfort with acculturation status among students from South Texas. *Hispanic Journal of Behavioral Sciences, 14*(2), 201–223.

Moyerman, D. R., & Forman, B. D. (1992). Acculturation and adjustment: A metaanalytic study. *Hispanic Journal of Behavioral Sciences, 14*(2), 163–200.

Murthy, K. (1998, August). *Implication for counseling Asian Indians: Second generation perceptions of the American milieu.* Paper presented at the 106th annual convention of the American Psychological Association, San Francisco, CA.

Nguyen, H. H., Messé, L. A., & Stollak, G. E. (1999). Toward a more complex understanding of acculturation and adjustment: Cultural involvements and psychological functioning in Vietnamese youth. *Journal of Cross-Cultural Psychology, 30*(1), 5–31.

Norris, A. E., Ford, K., & Bova, C. A. (1996). Psychometrics of a Brief Acculturation Scale for Hispanics in a probability sample of urban Hispanic adolescents and young adults. *Hispanic Journal of Behavioral Sciences, 18*(1), 29–38.

Nunnally, J. C. (1978). *Psychometric theory* (2nd ed.). New York: McGraw-Hill.

Olmeda, E. L., Martinez, Jr., J. L., & Martinez, S. R. (1978). Measure of acculturation for Chicano adolescents. *Psychological Reports, 42*, 159–170.

Osvold, L. L., & Sodowsky. G. R. (1993). Eating disorders of white American, racial and ethnic minority American, and international women. *Journal of Multicultural Counseling and Development, 25*, 149–155.

Osvold, L. L., & Sodowsky, G. R. (1995). Eating attitudes of Native American and African American women: Differences by race and acculturation. *Explorations in Ethnic Studies, 18*, 187–210.

Padilla, A. M. (1980). The role of cultural awareness and ethnic loyalty in acculturation. In A. M. Padilla (Ed.), *Acculturation: Theory, models, and some new findings* (pp. 47–84). Boulder, CO; Westview Press.

Padilla, A. M., Wagatsuma, Y., & Lindholm, K. J. (1985). Acculturation and personality as predictors of stress in Japanese and Japanese-Americans. *Journal of Social Psychology, 125*, 295–305.

Phinney, J. S. (1991). Ethnic identity and self-esteem: A review and integration. *Hispanic Journal of Behavioral Sciences, 13*(2), 193–208.

Phinney, J. S. (1992). The Multigroup Ethnic Identity Measure: A new scale for use with diverse groups. *Journal of Adolescent Research, 7*(2), 156–176.

Phinney, J. S., Chavira, V., & Williamson, L. (1992). Acculturation attitudes and self-esteem among high school and college students. *Youth and Society, 23*, 299–312.

Redfield, R., Linton, R., & Herskovits, M. (1936). Memorandum on the study of acculturation. *American Anthropologist, 37*, 149–152.

Rezentez III, W. C. (1993). Na Mea Hawai'i: A Hawaiian acculturation scale. *Psychological Reports, 73*, 383–393.

Roysircar, G. (2002). *Multicultural casebook: Conceptualization, assessment, and practice.* Manuscript in preparation.

Roysircar, G. (in press). Therapy for acculturation and ethnic identity concerns: Immigrants from South Asia and international students. In T. Smith & Richards, S. (Eds.), *Practicing multiculturalism: Affirming diversity in counseling and psychology.* Boston: Allyn & Bacon.

Roysircar, G., Gard, G., Preston, P., Utsch, H., Huynh, U., Potter, B., & Taliouridis, C. (2001 August). *Predictors of acculturation and coping for Asian International participants.* Paper presented at the Annual Meeting of the American Psychological Association, San Francisco, CA.

Roysircar, G., Webster, D. R., Germer, J., Campbell, G., Lynne, E., Palensky, J. J., Liu, J., Yang, Y., & Blodgett-McDeavitt, J. (in press). Multicultural counseling with middle school immigrant children: A practice framework. In G. Roysircar, D. S. Sandhu, & V. B. Bibbins (Eds.),

Multicultural competencies: A guidebook of practices. Alexandria, VA: American Counseling Association.

Roysircar-Sodowsky, G., & Frey, L. L. (2003). Children of immigrants: Their worldviews value conflicts. In P. Pedersen & J. C. Carey (Eds.), *Multicultural counseling in schools: A practical handbook* (pp. 61–83). Boston: Allyn & Bacon.

Roysircar-Sodowsky, G., & Maestas, M. (2000). Acculturation, ethnic identity, and acculturative stress: Evidence and measurement. In R. H. Dana (Ed.), *Handbook of cross-cultural and multicultural personality assessment* (pp. 131–172). Mahwah, NJ: Erlbaum.

Roysircar-Sodowsky, G., & Maestas, M. L. (in press). Assessment of acculturation and cultural variables. In K. S. Kurasaki, S. Okasaki, & S. Sue (Eds.), *Asian American mental health: Assessment theories and methods.* Dordrecht, The Netherlands: Kluwer Academic Publishers.

Rumbaut, R. G. (1994). The crucible within: Ethnic identity, self-esteem and segmented assimilation among children of immigrants. *International Migration Review, 28,* 748–794.

Rumbaut, R. G. (1997). Ties that bind: Immigration and immigrant families in the United States. In A. Booth, A. C. Crouter, & N. Landale (Eds.), *Immigration and the family: Research and policy on U.S. immigrants* (pp. 3–46). Mahwah, NJ: Erlbaum.

Sodowsky, G. R. (1991). Effects of culturally consistent counseling tasks on American and international student observers' perception of credibility: A preliminary investigation. *Journal of Counseling and Development, 69,* 253–256.

Sodowsky, G. R., & Carey, J. C. (1987). Asian Indian immigrants in America: Factors related to adjustment. *Journal of Multicultural Counseling and Development, 15,* 129–141.

Sodowsky, G. R., & Carey, J. C. (1988). Relationship between acculturation related demographics and cultural attitudes of Asian Indian immigrants. *Journal of Multicultural Counseling and Development, 16,* 117–136.

Sodowsky, G. R., Kwan, K. L., & Pannu, R. (1995). Ethnic identity of Asians in the United States. In J. G. Ponterotto, J. M. Cases, L. A. Suzuki, & C. M. Alexander (Eds.), *Handbook of multicultural counseling* (pp.123–154). Thousand Oaks, CA: Sage.

Sodowsky G. R., & Lai, E. W. M. (1997). Asian immigrant variables and structural models of cross-cultural distress. In A. Booth, A. C. Crouter, & N. Landale (Eds.), *Immigration and the family: Research and policy on U.S. immigrants* (pp. 211–237). Mahwah, NJ: Erlbaum.

Sodowsky, G. R., Lai, E. W. M., & Plake, B. (1991). Moderating effects of sociocultural variables on acculturation attitudes of Hispanics and Asian America. *Journal of Counseling and Development, 70,* 194–204.

Sodowsky, G. R., & Plake, B. (1991). Psychometric properties of the American-International Relations Scale. *Educational and Psychological Measurement, 51,* 207–216.

Sodowsky, G. R., & Plake, B. (1992). An investigation into acculturation options of international people and implications for sensitivity to within group differences. *Journal of Counseling and Development, 71,* 53–59.

Sue, D. W., & Sue, D. (1990). *Counseling the culturally different: Theory and practice* (2nd ed.). New York: John Wiley.

Sue, S. (1983). Ethnic minority issues in psychology: A reexamination. *American Psychologist, 38,* 583–592.

Sue, S. (1996). Measurement, testing, and ethnic bias: Can solutions be found? In G. R. Sodowsky & J. C. Impara (Eds.), *Multicultural assessment in counseling and clinical psychology* (pp. 7–36). Lincoln, NE: Buros Institute of Mental Measurements.

Suinn, R. M., Ahuna, C., & Khoo, G. (1992). The Suinn–Lew Asian Self-Identity Acculturation Scale: Concurrent and factorial validation. *Educational and Psychological Measurement, 52*(4), 1041–1046.

Suinn, R. M., Rickard-Figueroa, K., Lew, S., & Virgil, P. (1987). The Suinn–Lew Asian Self-Identity Acculturation Scale: An initial report. *Educational and Psychological Measurement, 47*(2), 401–407.

Szapocznik, J., & Kurtines, W. (1980). Acculturation, biculturalism, and adjustment among Cuban Americans. In A. M. Padilla (Ed.), *Acculturation: Theory, models and some new findings* (pp. 139–159). Boulder, CO: Westview Press.

Szapocznik, J., Scopetta, M. A., Kurtines, W., & Aranalde, M. A. (1978). Theory and measurement of acculturation. *International Journal of Psychology, 12,* 113–130.

Tropp, L. R., Erkut, S., Coll, C., Alarcon, O., & Garcia, H. A. (1999). Psychological acculturation. Development of a new measure for Puerto Ricans on the U.S. mainland. *Educational and Psychological Measurement, 59*(2), 351–367.

U.S. Bureau of the Census, Population Division. (2000). *United States population estimates by age, sex, race, and Hispanic origin and Asian origin.* Retrieved July 7, 2002, from http://www.census.gov/population/estimates/nation/intfile3

Velez, M. G. (1995). The relationship between ethnic identity and acculturation in a sample of Puerto Rican and Chinese college students. *Dissertation Abstracts International, 55*(11).

Veerasamy, S., & Roysircar-Sodowsky, G. (in press). Relationships of religious orientation and cultural identity retention: A study of South Asian Muslims and Hindus. *Cultural Diversity and Ethnic Minority Psychology.*

Walter, A. F. (1952). *Race and culture relations.* New York: McGraw-Hill.

Yamada, A., Marsella, A. J., & Yamada, S. Y. (2000). The development of the Ethnocultural Identity Behavioral Index: Psychometric properties and validation with Asian American and Pacific Islanders. *Asian American and Pacific Islander Journal of Health.*

12 Integrating Spirituality in Multicultural Counseling: "A Worldview"

MARY A. FUKUYAMA

In the October 5, 2001, *Gainesville Sun,* the Doonesbury cartoon by Gary Trudeau shows Boopsie, a young woman, speaking to Scot, who is wearing a clerical collar; she says, "It's hard to explain, Scot. So much of what I used to care about means nothing to me now. . . . Everything in my world has been profoundly shaken, not the least of which is my faith in God. I mean, what kind of God allows such terrible suffering and death?" Scot says, "Okay, so that's the #1 FAQ about God lately." She replies, ". . . Well, I thought it might be."

The cartoon appeared less than one month after the September 11 terrorist attacks on the World Trade Center in New York City and the Pentagon in Washington, D.C. These acts of violence shook Americans and troubled the world. In the words of Deepak Chopra, "Everyone is calling this an attack on America, but is it not a rift in our collective soul?" (Chopra, 2001). Making meaning in times of crisis is one demonstration of the importance and relevance of spirituality in the human condition. Worldwide, people's hearts opened to the victims and their families and friends, and many Americans returned to their churches and called upon prayer and songs like "God Bless America" for reassurance. Within this complex situation, the name of God has been invoked by extremist Islamic terrorists to fight a *Jihad,* a holy war. Backlash has erupted against Muslims in America and those who look like Muslims (e.g., Sikhs from India). Fortunately, public messages, from as high as the White House, have expressed respect for Muslims and Arab Americans and cautioned angry Americans not to act out. Even so, visible, innocent domestic "targets" of hostility have suffered, ranging from harassment to murder. Today, we live in a world that is a volatile mix of cultural and religious diversity and power clashes.

It is in this context of global relations and conflicts in the international arena, the transformation of the U.S. society into a culturally pluralistic nation, and increased individual search for meaning that this chapter is written. It is timely that this topic appear in this book, the goal of which is to include new approaches to culture in counseling. Additionally, from a holistic viewpoint, spirituality is a meaningful dimension of individual and community life.

The format of the chapter takes inspiration from the previously-mentioned Doonesbury cartoon script, that is, to examine some of the most "frequently asked questions" (FAQs) related to the integration of spirituality in multicultural counseling. I use a question-answer format to highlight key issues. I also want to generate meaningful questions for you, the reader, to explore further. In the wise words of Eli Wiesel, "There are no answers to true questions. There are only good questions, painful sometimes, exuberant at others. Whatever I have learned in my life is questions, and whatever I have tried to share with friends is questions" (Wiesel, 1974, p. 276).

FAQ 1: Why did you get involved in this topic?

In the mid-1980s, I attended a workshop titled "Spirituality and Mental Health: Professional Burn-Out." The presenter introduced a body of literature and experiences that connected personal growth, psychological insight, and spirituality (meaning, values, and consciousness). Other convergent factors included approaching midlife (age 40) and the death of my father, who was a Protestant minister and Veteran's Administration (VA) chaplain. With my father's passing, I felt more alone than ever, especially with respect to resolving the ultimate questions of life (purpose, relationship with God, and making meaning of death). Up to this time, I had devoted much of my career to the study of multiculturalism. I had unknowingly begun to integrate spirituality into my work by broadening my understanding of multicultural counseling competency to be inclusive and universal (Fukuyama, 1990). Working in the area of multicultural counseling has been a professional "growth edge" for me, and it was natural to extend this work to include spirituality, religion, and the transpersonal. These questions and the exploration of them have been a "work in progress" over the past fifteen years, culminating in the publication of a book on this topic (Fukuyama & Sevig, 1999), contribution to curriculum development (Fukuyama & Sevig, 1997), and continued inquiry about spirituality in multicultural counseling (Funderburk & Fukuyama, 2001; Fukuyama & Sevig, 2002). Why do I share this personal story with you? If you are particularly drawn to this topic, I invite you to reflect upon your personal narrative that brings you to the subject of spirituality, as self-awareness is one of the important growth tools for counselors.

FAQ 2: What is meant by *spirituality*?

Spirituality, religion, and the *transpersonal* are terms used interchangeably to refer to complex phenomena related to the "ultimate realities" in life. *Spirituality* is a concept that is ever present and yet elusive. Some of the dimensions that have been identified in the counseling literature range from esoteric mysticism to matters of everyday living. Bullis (1996) focused on spirituality as being a relationship with transcendence and as eclectic and inclusive by definition. Other authors emphasized certain spiritual values, including meaning and purpose in life, a sense of mission and goals, awareness of the sacred, helping others, and striving toward making the world better (Elkins, Hedstrom, Hughes, Leaf, & Saunders, 1988). In the simplest of terms, spirit derives from the Latin root *spiritus*, meaning breath of life. Many identify *religion* as being the ritualized expressions of a relationship with transcendence via institutions, day-to-day practices, and in community with others (Canda, 1994). Artress (1995) has suggested that religion is the container and spirituality the essences held within. However, spiritual issues that arise in counseling may or may not be associated with a religious belief system (Ingersoll, 1994). The *transpersonal* is a phrase originating in the 1960s humanistic psychology movement and refers to that which is "beyond the person," implying that there is a consciousness or self that exists beyond ego. Transpersonal psychotherapy is concerned with transcending the limitations of ego identification toward expanded states of awareness (Strohl, 1998).

FAQ 3: How are the mental health professions responding to the question of integrating spirituality, religion, and the transpersonal?

I would say that this depends on whom you ask. Historically, there have been both proponents and opponents to including spirituality as a dimension of psychology and mental health (see Kelly, 1995 for an overview). From the times of Freud and Jung, religion and spirituality have been identified as both a cause for neuroses and a place for healing and wholeness. At times, extreme religiosity has been associated with psychosis, and some contemporary psychologists view religion as irrational (Ellis, 1980). Currently, the emergence of spirituality as related to mental health has been recognized by a variety of mainstream professional groups (marriage and family therapists, social workers, mental health counselors, psychologists, and pastoral counselors) and by a wide range of alternative healing modalities (e.g., Reiki, body work, Chinese medicine, acupuncture). Spirituality can be found in helping areas such as addictions recovery, wellness, holistic health, transpersonal growth and development, and psychotherapy in general (e.g., Kelly, 1995; Bullis, 1996; Cortright, 1997; Richards & Bergin, 1997). Additionally, authors have looked at the role spirituality can play specifically in multicultural counseling (Fukuyama and Sevig, 1999; Richards & Bergin, 2000; Zinnbauer & Pargament, 2000).

The origins of the word psychology (*psyche*) refer to the study of the soul. In some professional associations, the integration of spiritual competencies has been recommended for all counselors (Miller, 1999). Current recommendations for multicultural counseling competencies ask counselors to be able to understand the concept of "worldview" of the client, and, in many instances, this worldview may include qualities of spirituality, religion, and the transpersonal. The inclusion of multiculturalism in counseling provides a "natural home" for integrating spirituality.

Finally, spirituality is imbedded in specific ethnic worldviews and related to specific populations. For example, see recent literature on the importance of spirituality in counseling African Americans (Frame, Williams, & Green, 1999; Thompson & McRae, 2001) and discussions of Native American worldviews (Dufrene & Coleman, 1994; Garrett & Garrett, 1994; Garrett & Wilbur, 1999). Spirituality is also relevant to feminist therapy and the analyses of patriarchy and traditional power structures. In considering the forces of multiculturalism, feminism, and spirituality in psychotherapy, all three of these movements emphasize consciousness, context, and connection while heightening awareness about suffering, liberation, and enlightenment (Funderburk & Fukuyama, 2001).

FAQ 4: What is the relationship between multiculturalism and spirituality?

My colleague Todd Sevig and I have discussed at length our perception that multiculturalism and spirituality are synergistic in relation to one another. On one level, cultural diversity expands the way one sees the world, and religion is no exception. In the United States, there are more than 2,000 religions and spiritual traditions. A recent trend in postmodern religion is an eclecticism in which people draw from several religious traditions to formulate their personal spirituality (see Elizabeth Lesser, 1999). In this way, culturally diverse expressions of spirituality have expanded the options for American spiritual seekers. For example, someone might attend Sunday worship in a Methodist church, attend a weekly Buddhist meditation, and participate in Sacred Earth ceremonies. On another level, cultural diversity is as challenging as it is enhancing. It does not take long for the cross-cultural sojourner to bump into differences (e.g., communication, language, and values). In addition, multicultural advocates are called to seek social justice on a variety of issues (e.g., racism, poverty, and heterosexism) and such activities frequently are challenging and overwhelming. Calling upon spiritual values (e.g., compassion, faith, and creativity) to meet multicultural challenges and using multicultural skills to negotiate spiritually challenging times demonstrate the potential synergy of these two forces. Finally, the mirror of multiculturalism provides a way to see oneself in contrast with others, and, in this way, one's identity can be strengthened and expanded as one both differentiates and connects with others who may believe differently. These principles are put into action in graduate student training through experiential learning activities, which are described in the next question.

FAQ 5: How does one get trained to deal with spiritual issues in counseling?

Ideally, this topic needs to be included as part of multicultural counseling training. In addition, it is often helpful to have a specific course devoted to new topics such as this until it can become infused into other coursework. I have taught a course based upon the theme of "spiritual issues in multicultural counseling" for a number of years with graduate students in the mental health professions (counselor education, counseling psychology, rehabilitation counseling, student personnel). I have followed the Association for Spiritual, Ethical, and Religious Values in Counseling (ASERVIC) guidelines ("Summit results," 1995) and have included the following topics: (a) understanding spiritual worldview, (b) exploring models of faith development and spiritual awakening, (c) discussing the synergy between multiculturalism and spiritual values, (d) defining both positive and negative expressions of spirituality (e.g., religious wounding), (e) exploring both content and process dimensions of spirituality in counseling, (f) working on case conceptualization (e.g., history taking), and (g) helping students to clarify what types of interventions are appropriate given where they are in their personal and professional development. This course is consistent with other descriptions of curriculum development on this topic (Ingersoll, 1997; Patterson, 2000). I do not want to make this process seem simplistic, however.

There are both content and process elements to take into consideration in planning such a course of study. I have adopted a pluralist approach in order to be as inclusive as possible (Zinnbauer & Pargament, 2000). This may be a challenge for students who follow an absolutist belief system. I also encourage experiential learning through action plans where students deepen their personal spirituality through self-selected practice. Similar to multicultural counseling training, I also recommend that students experience a religious/spiritual event that is different from their own traditions to further breakdown stereotypes and to educate themselves through experiential learning (Parker, 1998). For example, Christian students have attended Jewish synagogue services, conservative students have attended a liberal church and vice versa, and students have attended a Medicine Wheel teaching by a local Native American healer.

However, there are several areas of caution I would offer readers and suggest that if you are sincerely interested, you pursue professional training in this area through coursework, professional workshops, and supervision.

FAQ 6: What are some typical pitfalls when training in this area?

One of my observations of mental health professionals is that many have "baggage" related to spirituality and religion that requires self-awareness to prevent unconscious countertransference with clients. Often professional mental health workers are drawn to psychology and counseling out of their personal needs for healing and wholeness, and sometimes there are religious skeletons in the closet, so to speak. Personal reactions can range from negative stereotyping of various religious traditions, power struggles with authority, and fear of pressure to convert or believe or act in ways that are contradictory to self. This is one of the reasons why I encourage students to write in journals throughout the course, to develop personal self-reflection skills, and to see where prejudice or fear may be operative. Given the vast religious diversity of our nation, it is also necessary to cover a range of religious and spiritual traditions, including what may be controversial for some, for example, New Age Spirituality, Wiccan, Santeria, indigenous earth based religions, and other traditions. I also recommend that students explore spiritual traditions that are "culture-specific" to their geographical region.

It is particularly easy for counselors to "impose" their religious/spiritual values on clients without intending to do so, even with something as innocent as a question about religion. A typical concern of graduate students in training is the question of how to bring up the topic of spirituality respectfully. Work setting and professional orientation of the counselor will influence the degree to which such matters are made explicit. For example, a therapist in private practice who presents herself as doing "psychospiritual counseling" provides an open invitation to talk about spiritual issues.

There are two ways in which spiritual issues arise *explicitly* in counseling, through the client's initiative or through the counselor's inquiry. Responding to client's concerns is a respectful way to proceed. However, clients may be reluctant to bring up religious or spiritual concerns if they fear judgment or wonder if the counselor will try to change their views. Some counselors may want to routinely assess spiritual/religious histories as part of the intake process. By doing so, the subject is opened and the counselor has demonstrated willingness to discuss spiritual issues as part of counseling.

FAQ 7: How does a counselor handle a situation where the client's religious values seem to contradict mental health values?

Let us take the situation where the client is asked to take personal responsibility for his or her actions, but the client wants to defer control to God. Sometimes counselors and clients see an "either/or" dichotomy such as this one as an irreconcilable values difference. However, I find the issue of control (underlying this concept is power) to be a fundamental issue addressed by both religious doctrine and psychological principles. The twelve-step program for addiction recovery is an excellent example of where the individual needs to surrender to a higher power or something greater-than-self in order to heal. Giving up "control" in order to gain control in one's life is also a sound psychological principle. In this way, I see both spiritual and psychological principles working in harmony. If that is not the case, I find that people unnecessarily create an "either-or" dichotomy that polarizes and perpetuates unnecessary division between these two "camps." The Prophet Muhammad was said to have taught, "Pray to God and tie up your camel." The idea here is that the individual needs BOTH to take individual responsibility and to surrender one's ego. It is a paradox. In multicultural work, often problems are solved through implementing "both/and" solutions and embracing contradictions.

In another clinical case, occasionally clients will use religious/spiritual excuses to avoid life challenges. Such events have been called a "spiritual by-pass" (Battista, 1996) when spiritual or religious reasons are used to avoid a psychological or interpersonal difficulty. As an example, an overworked wife and mother may repress her anger because it wouldn't be considered virtuous, thus using a religious rationale for not engaging in necessary conflict in her marriage and family life.

In a third case example, client and counselor values may conflict regarding sexual orientation. For instance, client X says, "I pray to God and I read the Bible to try to figure out what I should do, but if I screw up, I'm going to hell. I know I don't want to be gay." Counselor Y thinks to himself, "I don't see God as punishing, but this client obviously thinks so. I don't see being gay as anti-Christian, even though some conservative Christians see it this way." Here is an obvious difference in thinking around the issue of sexual orientation and religious values. What sorts of interventions are appropriate, or what would the counselor do if the roles were reversed and the counselor had conservative religious values and the client did not? These issues deserve extensive discussion and reflection, as there is a wide range of responses and thinking regarding sexual orientation and religion (Ritter & O'Neill, 1989).

FAQ 8: Is it OK for counselors to challenge dysfunctional religious beliefs?

This touches on another difficult area for mental health professionals. How does one respond when religious doctrine seems to be supporting dysfunctional behavior, such as in the case of spouse abuse (resisting a divorce for religious reasons), or other examples of family dysfunction? In some cases, perfectionism may take on religious overtones (Heise & Steitz, 1991) and to challenge the perfectionism may entail challenging the client's religious belief system. Such confrontations naturally take place in the context of a working alliance with the client. Some counseling theories lend themselves to working with religious clients, such as taking a social constructionist approach (Frame, 1996).

The primary aim for the multicultural counselor is to elicit and understand the worldview of the client. Sometimes the worldview will challenge the reality of the counselor. For example, take the hypothetical case of Rose, a Mexican American woman, age 28, who suffers from depression. She has been hospitalized for suicidal threats. She feels that she is possessed by a great-grandmother who died a tragic, premature death. A community psychic healer has advised her to perform rituals and ceremonies to help this disembodied spirit to leave. Antidepressant medication has also been prescribed. How do you as counselor provide support for these different views of the problem? Such cases may require multiple resources and cultural experts to understand the full scope of the problem (see Fadiman, 1997).

FAQ 9: What ethical guidelines are helpful in resolving some of these issues related to integrating spirituality into multicultural counseling?

Of course, the basic premise "to do no harm" is essential to practicing competent counseling. Counselors are continually advised not to practice outside their competency areas. How does one determine competency in this area? The ASERVIC guidelines provide a place to begin, and I would suggest that these be combined with multicultural counseling competencies as well (Sue et al., 1998). Getting supervision and consulting on cases is important. Defining one's boundaries with respect to psychological work and the sacred is essential. Being able to respect the work of alternative (folk) healers and to make referrals to community resources is also important.

FAQ 10: Are there any other recommendations you would make for counselors who want to integrate spirituality into their multicultural counseling?

Generally speaking, I do not think counselors can engage in this area without having some sort of personal experiences upon which to base their interventions. If most of this chapter is being perceived as theoretical, and you want to know more, then I would recommend that you pursue personal study of spirituality so that it has an experiential reality (for example, see Walsh, 1999).

FAQ 11: Why *is* there suffering in the world?

Back to the question posed by Boopsie, the important thing for humans is to make meaning of their suffering (Frankl, 1963; Kushner, 1981). According to the teachings of the Buddha, life is suffering. But to make meaning, to find purpose, to transcend, to transform, this is what the human condition is about. Along this line, mental health workers, as well as priests, rabbis, and ministers all work toward ameliorating life's difficulties and traumas. In a best-case scenario, these helpers work in collaborative and supportive relationships, refer to each other when appropriate, and respect each other's traditions.

Conclusion

Using a personal narrative writing style, I provide an overview of the issues related to integrating spirituality in multicultural counseling. Spirituality, religion, and the transpersonal are considered to be inherent dimensions in the concept of "worldview," an essential lens through which to understand cultural differences. I explore the synergy of multiculturalism and spiritual development, highlight relevant multicultural and spiritual counseling competencies, discuss training issues, and present several case examples for your consideration.

DISCUSSION QUESTIONS

1. What meanings do the terms "spirituality, religion, and the transpersonal" have for you?

2. How have cultural-diversity experiences contributed to your understanding of spirituality, religion, and the transpersonal?

3. What would you predict to be your greatest challenge in counseling around spiritual issues? When would you refer to religious or spiritual experts?

4. Develop a course of study for deepening your understanding of this area of multicultural counseling. What sorts of "action plans" and "diversity experiences" would you pursue to enhance your educational experience?

REFERENCES

Artress, L. (1995). *Walking a sacred path: Rediscovering the labyrinth as a spiritual tool.* New York: Riverhead Books.

Battista, J. R. (1996). Offensive spirituality and spiritual defenses. In B. W. Scotton, A. B. Chinen, & J. R. Battista (Eds.), *Texbook of transpersonal psychiatry and psychology* (pp. 250–260). New York: Basic Books.

Bullis, R. K. (1996). *Spirituality in social work practice.* Washington, DC: Taylor & Francis.

Canda, E. R. (1994). Spiritually sensitive social work. In C. H. Simpkinson, D. A. Wengell, & M. J. Casavant (Eds.), *The Common Boundary graduate education guide: Holistic programs and resources integrating spirituality and psychology* (2nd ed., pp. 31–34). Bethesda, MD: Common Boundary.

Chopra, D. (2001, September 12). Message posted to Namaste mailing list, archived at http://www.chopra.com

Cortright, B. (1997). *Psychotherapy and spirit: Theory and practice in transpersonal psychotherapy.* Albany: State University of New York Press.

Dufrene, P. M., & Coleman, V. D. (1994). Art and healing for Native American Indians. *Journal of Multicultural Counseling and Development, 22,* 145–152.

Elkins, D. N., Hedstrom, L. J., Hughes, L. L., Leaf, J. A., & Saunders, C. (1988). Toward a humanistic-phenomenological spirituality: Definition, description, and measurement. *Journal of Humanistic Psychology, 28,* 5–18.

Ellis, A. (1980). Psychotherapy and atheistic values: A response to A.E. Bergin's "Psychotherapy and religious values." *Journal of Consulting and Clinical Psychology, 48,* 635–639.

Fadiman, A. (1997). *The spirit catches you and you fall down: A Hmong child, her American doctors, and the collision of two cultures.* New York: Farrar, Straus & Giroux.

Frame, M. W. (1996). A social constructionist approach to counseling religious couples. *The Family Journal, 4,* 299–307.

Frame, M. W., Williams, C. B., & Green, E. L. (1999). Balm in Gilead: Spiritual dimensions in counseling African American women. *Journal of Multicultural Counseling and Development, 27,* 182–192.

Frankl, V. E. (1963). *Man's search for meaning.* Boston: Beacon.

Fukuyama, M. A. (1990). Taking a universal approach to multicultural counseling. *Counselor Education and Supervision, 30,* 6–17.

Fukuyama, M. A., & Sevig, T. D. (1999). *Integrating spirituality into multicultural counseling.* Thousand Oaks, CA: Sage.

Fukuyama, M. A., & Sevig, T. D. (1997). Spiritual issues in counseling: A new course. *Counselor Education and Supervision, 36,* 233–244.

Fukuyama, M. A., & Sevig, T. D. (2002). Spirituality in counseling across cultures: Many rivers to the sea. In P. Pedersen, J. Draguns, W. Lonner, & J. Trimble (Eds.), *Counseling Across Culture* (5th ed., pp. 273–295). Thousand Oaks, CA: Sage.

Funderburk, J., & Fukuyama, M. (2001). Feminism, multiculturalism, and spirituality: Convergent and divergent forces in psychotherapy. *Women and Therapy, 24*(3/4), 1–18.

Garrett, J. T., & Garrett, M. W. (1994). The path of good medicine: Understanding and counseling Native American Indians. *Journal of Multicultural Counseling and Development, 27,* 134–144.

Garrett, M. T., & Wilbur, M. P. (1999). Does the worm live in the ground? Reflections on Native American spirituality. *Journal of Multicultural Counseling and Development, 27,* 193–206.

Heise, R. G., & Steitz, J. A. (1991). Religious perfectionism versus spiritual growth. *Counseling and Values, 36,* 11–18.

Ingersoll, R. E. (1994). Spirituality, religion, and counseling: Dimensions and relationships. *Counseling and Values, 38,* 98–111.

Ingersoll, R. E. (1997). Teaching a course on counseling and spirituality. *Counselor Education and Supervision, 36,* 224–232

Kelly, E. W., Jr., (1995). *Spirituality and religion in counseling and psychotherapy: Diversity in theory and practice.* Alexandria,VA: American Counseling Association.

Kushner, H. S. (1981). *When bad things happen to good people.* New York. Schocken Books.

Lesser, E. (1999) *The seeker's guide: Making your life a spiritual adventure.* New York: Villard.

Miller, G. (1999). The development of the spiritual focus in counseling and counselor education. *Journal of Counseling and Development, 77,* 498–501.

Parker, W. M. (1998). *Consciousness-raising: A primer for multicultural counseling* (2nd ed.). Springfield, IL: Charles C. Thomas.

Patterson, J. (2000). Spiritual issues in family therapy: A graduate-level course. *Journal of Marital and Family Therapy, 26,* 199–210.

Richards, P. S., & Bergin, A. E. (1997). *A spiritual strategy for counseling and psychotherapy.* Washington, DC: American Psychological Association.

Richards, P. S., & Bergin, A. E. (Eds.). (2000). *Handbook of psychotherapy and religious diversity.* Washington, DC: American Psychological Association.

Ritter, K. Y., & O'Neill, C. W. (1989). Moving through loss: The spiritual journey of gay men and lesbian women. *Journal of Counseling and Development, 68,* 9–15.

Strohl, J. E. (1998). Transpersonalism: Ego meets soul. *Journal of Counseling and Development, 76,* 397–403.

Sue, D. W., Carter, R. T., Casas, J. M., Fouad, N. A., Ivey, A. E., Jensen, M., et al. (1998). *Multicultural counseling competencies: Individual and organizational development.* Thousand Oaks, CA: Sage.

Summit results in formation of spirituality competencies. (December, 1995). *Counseling Today* (p. 30).

Thompson, D. A., & McRae, M. B. (2001). The need to belong: A theory of the therapeutic function of the black church tradition. *Counseling and Values, 45,* 40–53

Walsh, R. (1999). *Essential spirituality: The seven central practices to awaken heart and mind.* New York: Wiley.

Wiesel, E. (1974). Whatever I have learned in my life is questions. In A. Chapman (Ed.), *Jewish-American literature: An anthology* (pp. 276–278). New York: Mentor New American Library.

Zinnbauer, B. J., & Pargament, K. I. (2000). Working with the sacred: Four approaches to religious and spiritual issues in counseling. *Journal of Counseling and Development, 78,* 162–171.

13 Existential Worldview Counseling Theory: Inception to Applications

FARAH A. IBRAHIM

This chapter focuses on the development of the existential worldview counseling theory and the lens from which it was conceptualized. I have a strong belief that theories are derived from an author's cultural, social, and familial background. As a South Asian woman, I know that I bring my culture and socialization into my work. It is probably as a result of the cultural differences that I have been able to understand the universe the way I do and make some unique contributions to my field.

The Personal Dimension

My educational background when I came to the United States was a very broad liberal arts preparation in psychology, political science, and education based on a British model of higher education. I had completed my education with a master's degree in psychology, the highest degree available (at that time) in Pakistan in humanities. My goals included coming to the United States to complete my education in psychology. After coming to the states I decided that since I had a master's in psychology, maybe I should specialize in the applied domain of counseling in psychology. The missing piece in my education and training was the application of all the knowledge I had gained to clients. I am alluding to the specific theories of counseling and psychotherapy and the skills needed to be an effective therapist. Another reason for focusing on counseling was my mother's (Iffat Almas) interest in starting these services in Pakistan. My mother had been an educator for twenty years. She had also started the first Institute for Educational and Vocational Guidance (IEVG) in Pakistan. This institute was a project undertaken by the International Federation of Women (IFUW) and UNESCO. I knew that I could never go back to Pakistan based on the circumstances that had led to my departure. I still decided to first complete a master's in counseling focused on secondary school counseling and then proceed to a broader doctoral program in counseling. I was still working on the premise of institutionalizing counseling services in Pakistani schools, through my mother and the IVEG. The institute had started training school teachers in counseling skills, focused on educational and career services (Ibrahim, 1982a, 1982b; Ibrahim & Almas, 1983). Our goal was to expand this effort to formalize the education and training of school counselors and community mental health counselors.

During my work on my master's in psychology, I had undertaken an in-depth study of all major areas of psychology, including a minor in cognitive and personality assessment. The puzzles that I had not figured out were how relevant the tests were in the Pakistani context. On undertaking my studies in the states, several areas emerged as challenging questions and concerns, such as, how can the theories and techniques of counseling be relevant to all cultures and setting, including racial and ethnic minorities in the United States. Furthermore, I had similar questions regarding group counseling theories and skills, career counseling theories, and career assessment strategies. I started to ponder how all this would apply in the Pakistani context and other international settings (Das & Ibrahim, 1990).

I finished the master's and went on to the doctorate. The questions in my mind about applicability became more insistent as I progressed through each level of training. After finishing my degrees, I got permission from the Immigration and Naturalization Service (INS) to work for a year to learn to apply my knowledge and skills. The job I undertook involved the facilitation of women and international students as assistant dean of students. During my studies at Pennsylvania State University, I had run a group for abused women on a volunteer basis for two years. Throughout my doctoral education, I had also served as a volunteer peer counselor at the Student Peer Counseling Service coordinated by student affairs. Furthermore, I conducted workshops, training, and orientation workshops for international students on communication skills, adjustment issues, and so on.

I had a graduate assistantship as a counselor at the Student Assistance Center (for two years). Later, I was hired as a counselor at the Adult Therapy Clinic of the speech pathology and audiology department, counseling stroke victims and their families as well as children and adolescents with speech and hearing impairments. In all my applied work, I learned that the theories and skills I had acquired needed modification to address the needs of each person with whom I worked. There were different strategies that worked better with children, adolescents, adults, males and females, and elderly clients. Most of my training was very effective with college students from the dominant cultural group. However, I made modifications essentially instinctively as I worked with all other groups, especially racial and ethnic nondominant group members, women, gay, lesbian, and transgendered clients, children, adolescents, abused women, international students, older clients, people with disabilities, and people with different religions and spiritual beliefs.

The modifications primarily involved coming to the counseling situation from an existential-humanistic theoretical base in terms of basic questions and issues that are relevant to all humans (i.e., relationships, birth, marriage or partnership, death, success and failure, personal worth, self-respect and respect for others, and violations of human rights). These were the experiences that led to the establishment of an existential-humanistic base in my work and my personal theory of counseling (Ibrahim, 1984, 1999). I always started my work with the Rogerian principles of the necessary conditions for establishing a relationship, through warmth, genuineness, and empathy. In addition, these necessary conditions created an environment that engendered trust, and thus, the counseling relationship thrived. As Torrey (1987) notes, counselors, psychologists, psychiatrists, social workers, shamans, and medicine men or women all share these necessary conditions, whether they live in the bush in Africa, or in a Western metropolitan area. The key to establishing a trusting and respectful relationship was always being able to find common ground, or creating a shared worldview in an emotionally warm environment (Ibrahim, 1991, 1993a, 1999). During my education and the year of practical training, as the INS calls it, another critical piece started to emerge that pertained to identifying the "strengths" in the therapeutic relationship between the client and counselor. These strengths were the common ground between the client and the counselor and helped create a shared worldview (Ibrahim, 1991). This thinking led to the development of the Scale to Assess Worldview, to assess beliefs, values, and assumptions for both the client and the counselor to clarify shared values and assumptions; and to increase trust and to recognize the differences between the client and the counselor on basic values, beliefs, and assumptions, as areas where caution must be exercised about inadvertently imposing the counselor's values or worldview on the client (Ibrahim, 1984, 1985a, 1991, 1999).

I learned in my work that when I used communication skills and strategies that resonated with the client, I was more successful. Fortunately, I was exposed to the work of Minuchin (1974) in my doctoral internship. I learned that to establish a relationship, when in doubt about the appropriate verbal and nonverbal style to use, adopt the verbal and nonverbal behavioral style of the client. Minuchin calls this technique "mirroring" and considers this a very powerful technique that leads to engagement in family therapy. Because I was from another country, and in a completely different cultural context from the one I was socialized in (Takaki, 1989), I had to work hard to establish a relationship and credibility. In my work with vulnerable populations (racial-ethnic nondominant groups, gay, lesbian, transgendered, abused women and women in general, people with disabilities, and people of nondominant religions and languages), I noted a certain pathos and anxiety in some cases that resulted from being "different" or "less than others" and the residual effects of racism, sexism, homophobia, classism, and so on. This later led to the formulation of the hypothesis regarding posttraumatic stress syndrome (PTSD) as a result of being a member of a nondominant group, which involves a person being perceived (by the dominant group and by the oppressed group member) as having less power, privilege, and access to opportunity (Ibrahim, 1993b, Ibrahim & Ohnishi, 2001).

As my theoretical perspectives emerged, I realized that these were greatly dependent on my experiences from childhood to adulthood and the experience of being a woman in a third-world South Asian Islamic culture. I am quite aware that the way I am treated by individuals in the United States also has influenced my perspectives. I grew up in a particularly brutal part of Pakistan known as Sarhad (the frontier), or the North West Frontier Province (NWFP), as named by the British colonials, where a woman has less value than an indentured servant. Several groups live in this province. The largest population is of the Pakhtuns (who reside in Afghanistan and Pakistan, and lately famous as the hated and oppressive Talibans). The other groups are the Hindko-language group, the Persian-speaking group, refugees from India (Muslims forced to leave India during the partition of India and Pakistan), Afghan refugees for the past twenty-one years, and a small minority of Zoroastrians and Christians. For me, being a second-class citizen and a "minority" has been a lifelong condition. My mother was a refugee from India of Kashmiri descent and was married to my father who was from an old and respected family of Muftis (town leaders) from Peshawar. My paternal grandmother was from Afghanistan. This culture, I felt, never accepted my mother, and consequently, I believe, never accepted me.

The larger culture of Sarhad is essentially egocentric with strict hierarchies of wealth, power, and gender. Castillo (1997) accurately presents the culture of the Pakhtuns as a particularly brutal tribal culture. The Pakhtuns live in the mountains of northern Pakistan and northeastern Afghanistan. This is a highly hierarchical, very egocentric, premodern society. Dominance hierarchies in this culture are based on gender (patriarchy) and wealth. The social environment tolerates aggression and violence among individuals. This social environment is also competitive and harsh. People struggled for survival in a fairly dry and dusty, mountainous region with not many natural resources. In this system, a person who manages to aggrandize wealth is highly respected; it does not matter whether the methods to achieve this wealth were honorable or dishonorable.

My maternal grandfather, a retired businessman (Kashmiri, by ethnicity), was forced to move from Amritsar in India to the North West Frontier Province because our house was robbed every six months. I lived in terror of these robbing events because if anyone woke up during a night robbery or returned home, they were always murdered. I lived with my grandparents for several years because my father (a pilot in the Royal Indian Air Force) had come back from World War II completely devastated with what would now be diagnosed as posttraumatic stress disorder (PTSD). He subsequently began to cope by drinking and eventually abandoned us. Due to the partition of India and Pakistan, my maternal grandparents lost everything; at that point, my grandfather was already retired. My mother, who had a bachelor's degree and a teaching certificate, decided that she should not become a drain on the family and started teaching.

These were the conditions in the country where I was born and raised. My mother, for all her courage and strength of character, was twice stigmatized, as a divorced woman and a woman who had to work to support herself. I also bought into these definitions and felt stigmatized throughout my life, in spite of my mother's courage and hard work. Relating to and understanding nondominant groups, that are usually stigmatized simply for being a nondominant population, is second nature for me.

Development of the Existential Worldview Theory

In my quest to identify universal principles that are common to all human beings, I came across the works of existential thinkers and their theories. One of my unofficial mentors in this domain was Dr. Clemmont Vontress. I realized that I had stumbled onto universal principles that challenge all people at some time in their lives. These pertained to values involving the following dimensions: understanding human nature, social and familial relationships, conception of nature, understanding time, and activities people engage in over the life span (Ibrahim, 1985b, 1991, 1993a, 1999). In addition to these variables, it is critical to understand how the human life cycle is understood, such as birth, marriage or coupling, and death, because these were also universal. The rituals may differ, but these aspects are a part of every life.

The key variable that emerged as the theory started to take shape was the understanding that universal values and life cycle tasks were common to all people of the world, although within the value domains (i.e., human nature, time, etc.) there was much variation, such that, although all people ponder human nature, their values may center around human nature as good, bad, or a combination of good and bad. Coming across this information base was the catalyst that led to the development of the Scale to Assess Worldview (SAWV; Ibrahim & Kahn, 1984, 1987; Ibrahim & Owen, 1994). Worldview is the mediating variable that can help the therapist operationalize goals, process, and outcome in counseling and psychotherapy in several ways: (1) by providing an understanding of the client's cultural values, beliefs, and assumptions; (2) by helping the therapist understand how similar or dissimilar the client and the counselor are at a point in time; (3) by helping the therapist recognize that similarities between the client and the therapist represent strengths and a means of creating a shared worldview with the client that would lead to engagement in counseling and psychotherapy; (4) by recognizing that the differences in value systems represent areas where the counselor must be careful not to impose his or her values on the client; (5) by assessing the worldview of the counselor and the client, the dyad is ensured to be matched appropriately; if counselors recognize that their values are completely discordant with certain clients, especially if they are from a protected group, it would be best to refer the client; and (6) by understanding that worldview and cultural identity (Ibrahim, 1993a, 1999) can also assist in developing appropriate goals and process in counseling and psychotherapy that are consistent with the client's beliefs. To ensure that the outcome of the counseling intervention will be truly beneficial, the goals and outcome must be consistent with the client's culture and values and not pose conflicts for the client during the counseling intervention and later on in life (Ibrahim, 1984, 1985a, 1991, 1993c, 1999).

Once the existential worldview theory was explicated, and the Scale to Assess Worldview was developed, I noticed in using the scale that the information I was getting only partially clarified the client's perspectives. I realized that worldview is one aspect that is the result of socialization and is anchored within a person's racial and cultural identity. Given the racial politics of the United States and the world, it is critical to move beyond simply understanding the client's worldview to anchoring the worldview within the cultural identity of the client. Because there were no instruments to assess cultural identity, I developed the Cultural Identity Check List (CICL, Ibrahim, 1993a, 1999). This checklist allows the counselor to identify critical variables from the client's culture and socialization that have impacted his or her worldview over the life span. The CICL addresses the following variables: gender and its conceptualization by the client and the counselor's culture, sexual preference and its implications, sociopolitical history, generation in the United States and the social conditions experienced by the client's primary cultural group, history of migration of the client's group, religion, age and its meaning in the client's culture and in the dominant culture, life stage and its meaning and implications, birth order, languages spoken, and ability and disability status.

The theory and the tools that go with it (SAWV and CICL) were developed for the therapeutic context to understand the client, to arrive at an appropriate diagnosis considering the culture and its ramifications for the client, client and counselor matching, and developing an appropriate process and outcome for counseling. A review of the literature on the SAWV and the theory it is derived from show that it has been used in several contexts (Ibrahim, Roysircar-Sodowsky, & Ohnishi, 2001).

Applications

This section reviews the different contexts where the existential worldview theory, SAWV, and CICL have been used. The SAWV can be successfully used as a training tool to enhance cross-cultural counselor effectiveness in dealing with some basic existential dilemmas that people face to cope with life's challenges and questions (for training of counselors, psychologists, psychiatric nurses, and human resource personnel for diversity training purposes). The scale can also be used with different cultures to compare groups as well as to understand differences within each cultural group, and to gain important information on cross-cultural differences and similarities (Ibrahim, Frietas, & Owen, 1993). Other uses have focused on facilitation of communication and conflict resolution in schools, businesses, other institutions, and communities.

Counseling and Psychotherapy

This is the arena for which the existential worldview theory, the SAWV, and the CICL were developed. Trevino (1996) notes that several prominent theorists and researchers have made worldview the lynchpin of their theories. Sue (1978) derived worldview from attribution and social learning theories. Ibrahim (1984) derived the concept of worldview from research in anthropology on universal values and beliefs. Additionally, Helms (1986, 1990) has merged her work on racial identity with worldview, and Myers (1988) has operationalized worldview from an Afrocentric perspective. Trevino (1996) proposes a model that incorporates worldview as a unifying construct for change in cross-cultural counseling. Since the publication and adoption of the multicultural competencies by the American Counseling Association (ACA) and the American Psychological Association (APA), and the recognition that cultural issues are critical to appropriately diagnose a client using the DSM-IV, counselors and helping professionals have become aware that no therapeutic intervention is possible unless one clarifies the client's worldview and cultural identity. The chance that cultural malpractice and client violation will occur is high if these variables are not clarified (Ibrahim & Arredondo, 1986; Ibrahim & Arredondo, 1990). Clarifying these variables also helps in understanding the presenting problem and why it is such a crisis for the client that she or he is moved to seek counseling or psychotherapy. Ibrahim, Ohnishi, and Wilson (1994) and Lonner and Ibrahim (1996, 2001) give a detailed outline for an appropriate assessment in a multicultural setting to avoid issues or charges of cultural malpractice and violation of clients.

The SAWV can either be used as a paper-and-pencil assessment tool or it can be verbally administered to the client. The CICL is to be used as an initial client assessment tool for intake. This must be presented verbally and the client's responses written or tape recorded. Once these two variables are clarified, the presenting problem needs to be reframed in the context of the client's world. This contextualizing helps in determining what the presenting problem means to the client in his or her world. It also helps in determining what the options are for the client given the specific cultural and ethnic identity, gender, sexual orientation, age, life stage, social class, and religion. In addition, these assessments will help the counselor to determine what communication mode to use (i.e., directive, nondirective, or as mutual collaborators that work together to find a solution and to bring the client's issues to resolution). Beyond individual and group counseling, worldview has also been applied to counseling cross-cultural couples (Ibrahim & Schroeder, 1990) and in family therapy (Thomas, 1998).

Training of Helping Professionals

Training counselors in the use of the SAWV results in the client's perception that the counselor truly understands him or her and the problem that is under consideration, and leads to a perception of the therapist as effective, and therefore credible and trustworthy (Sadlak & Ibrahim, 1986; Cunningham-Warburton, 1988).

Using the SAWV and the CICL in training helps professionals to focus on their own cultural and gender identity and worldview. It reduces the possibility of the counselor imposing his or her value systems or culturally dominant beliefs on the client, such as paternalism or condescension, or labeling the client as "sick" (Cayleff, 1986; Ibrahim & Arredondo, 1986; Hickson, Christie, & Shmukler, 1990).

The existential worldview theory, the SAWV, and the CICL fit into the awareness, knowledge, and skills paradigm suggested for training in working with clients across cultures or in a diverse society such as the United States. These three variables, whether they are applied to oneself or to a client, force one to become aware of cultural relativity and all the different ways people, communities, and societies live. They increase the helping professional's capacity for understanding and engender respect of all cultural systems available in our communities, in our nation, and the world. This theoretical orientation increases awareness and knowledge. The awareness creates a desire to seek out knowledge to gain effectiveness with a diverse clientele. Understanding and knowing various systems of being increase the helping professional's knowledge base and also clarify for professionals the limits of their knowledge and expertise. Finally, learning to do a cultural assessment using the SAWV and the CICL gives helping professionals the knowledge to conduct educational and therapeutic interventions with culturally different clients.

Existential worldview theory is a cognitive-humanistic perspective that empowers helpers and clients to learn about their own systems of thinking and make changes where the behavior or cognitions are self-defeating (Ibrahim, 1999). This perspective gives the clients the power to make changes in their thinking patterns, to separate problems that have an external cause (such as racism, sexism, heterosexism, and abuse), and to identify problems and issues that are internal to the client (chemical imbalance, irrational thinking, etc.). This perspective is also very empowering because once cultural identity and worldview are clarified, it helps clients to recognize and act powerfully within the framework of their values and their world, clarifying values, assumptions, cultural and political history of their group, and the strength of their cultural or racial group in surviving and finding their rightful place within their social, political, and cultural world.

Several studies have addressed worldview and preferred counseling style, directive or nondirective. Links were made to worldview and the style of counseling, and commitment of the client to counseling (D'Rozario, 1996). In general, the research shows that traditional values and a hierarchical view of social relationships lends itself to directive or more active counseling strategies. Additionally, Odenweller (1997) demonstrates that counseling process style is related to a specific worldview and perception of the counselor. She also shows that African American, Latino/a American, and Caucasian students did not differ in their preferences for specific counseling styles. Mahalik, Worthington, and Crump (1999) investigated the relationship between racial ethnic membership of therapists and their worldview. They found that all the therapists had a similar worldview regardless of race or ethnicity. This implies that there is a therapist worldview that may supercede racial or ethnic beliefs and values and may respond to values and beliefs of the profession. This is a critically important finding because therapists' values do have a powerful impact on the course and quality of a therapeutic intervention.

Mapping Cultural Differences in Worldview

Several researchers have studied cultural assumptions of different groups using the SAWV and existential worldview theory. Barrett (1998) examined whether racial or ethnic classification can be used to identify dominant cultural descriptions of most members of a group. Although racial or ethnic classifications did not predict dominant value systems, other variables did. These included home configuration, highest educational level, and religious participation. This study lends support to Ibrahim's (1984) hypothesis that educational level, religion, and several other demographic variables influence worldview.

Furn (1986) investigated worldview of women and men to determine if they were different, as posited by several theorists. Worldview of men and women could be differentiated. Women tended to regard human nature as either good or bad, relationships as hierarchal, and they favored an activity orientation of being (spontaneous) and being-in-becoming (material and spiritual development). Men were more likely to endorse subjugation and control of nature, or the power of nature, and present-time orientation. This research supported the contention that men and women have different realities. The results also indicated that contrary to expectations, women experience relationships as positional with a superior-inferior component, as opposed to mutual relationships.

Gordon (1997) investigated the worldview of deaf male and female adolescents. Her results showed that cultural identity influences the sense of self, the time orientation, and the activity orientation. Adolescents with a bicultural identity had higher self-esteem and valued activities that enhanced all aspects of the self as an integrated being (being-in-becoming). In addition, it was found that gender influenced the way the participants evaluated themselves. Thompson (1997) investigated whether traditional worldview, interpersonal flexibility, and degree of similarity on these variables predicted marital satisfaction among thirty-five interethnic couples. The results suggested that degree of similarity did predict marital satisfaction among interethnic couples.

Ngumba (1996) studied the relationship between worldview, African self-consciousness, and adjustment among African, African American, and Caucasian American students. Significant differences were found among the three groups. A larger number of African American students, when compared to Africans and Caucasians, perceived human nature as essentially bad, social relationships as collateral-mutual, and had a time focus on the past and the future. African students, when compared to African American and Caucasian students, perceived human nature as essentially good or bad and social relations as hierarchical.

Gender differences were also reported in terms of women favoring social relationships as collateral-mutual and believing in activities that would allow the whole self to develop (external and internal value systems). The men favored hierarchical social relationships. Academic adjustment was related to worldview. The worldview orientations that predicted better adjustment were human nature as bad, individualistic social relations, and a lower future-time orientation. Lockney (1999) investigated worldview and accuracy of interpersonal perceptions. The participants were Latino and Caucasian American students at a southwestern university. The two groups were different and the Latino group had not acculturated to mainstream culture. In addition, each group saw the other group in an extremely stereotypic manner.

Gerber (1998) studied the impact of worldview and social class on psychosocial development in Chile. Results showed that worldview varied by social class. Lo (1996) studied the role of culture on worldview and the impact of Western influence on professionals in Taiwan. She found that Taiwanese professionals had the beliefs, values, and assumptions that would be considered typical for Taiwan and showed a similarity to Western values only on the construct of worldview. Ibrahim, Frietas, and Owen (1993) compared the worldview of Brazilians and Americans and found that Brazilians favored a traditional worldview whereas American participants favored a modern worldview that was progressive and sought equality in relationships.

Educational and Business Settings

Several researchers have investigated congruence of worldview and job satisfaction, similarity of worldview and survival in an institution, and perception of organizational culture. The higher the discrepancy between the employees and the institutional or business setting, the higher the dissatisfaction, regardless of race or ethnicity (Boatswain, 1997). Moreover, in educational settings people who have a harder time surviving do not have a congruent worldview to the faculty (Chu-Richardson, 1988). Hansman, Grant, Dale, and Jackson (1999), considering the changes in demographics, investigated the worldview of graduate students in professional preparation programs. In investigating worldview and perception of organizational culture, Toczyska (1996) found that there were significant worldview differences between managers and nonmanagers. This could lead to problems in an organization because discrepancy in worldview can lead to conflict and dissatisfaction.

Conclusion

This chapter detailed the origin and contribution of the existential worldview theory and the assessment tools that were developed to apply it to therapeutic, educational, work, and international settings. The original focus of the theory was on therapeutic interventions. Research shows that these constructs can be utilized to facilitate human growth and development in educational, institutional, and business settings. In addition, this theoretical perspective, along with the SAWV and the CICL, can assist in mapping cultural differences within our communities, nation, and the world, and can lead to better communication and conflict resolution.

DISCUSSION QUESTIONS

1. Considering the construct of worldview, as conceptualized by Ibrahim (1984), discuss how this can be used effectively in counseling and psychotherapy, both within and between cultures.

2. Discuss what mechanisms were available to therapists before Ibrahim operationalized the construct of worldview. What were the limits and strengths of these approaches? How were they used within and between cultures?

3. Ibrahim (1991) states that worldview must be anchored within a cultural identity that primarily must address race/culture, gender, sexual orientation, age, religion, social class, educational level, family composition, and ability and disability concerns. Do you agree or disagree with this statement? Provide a rationale for your position.

4. How can information about worldview and cultural identity assist you in developing goals and process for a specific counseling intervention? Could these two variables assist in both within- and between-culture interventions?

5. Discuss what research has shown about the validity of the existential worldview perspective. What areas exist that still must be explored in counseling and psychotherapy and cross-cultural research? How would this theory, with its tools, be effective into uncharted domains?

REFERENCES

Barrett, A. (1998). Race ethnicity and pattern of values. *Dissertation Abstracts International, 59-4A*, 1075.

Boatswain, B. P. (1997). The relationship between cultural values and job satisfaction among African-American managers and higher-level professionals. *Dissertation Abstracts International, 58-11B*, 6264.

Castillo, R. J. (1977). *Culture and mental illness: A client-centered approach.* Pacific Grove, CA: Brooks/Cole.

Cayleff, S. E. (1986). Ethical issues in counseling gender, race and culturally distinct groups. *Journal of Counseling and Development, 64*, 345–347.

Chu-Richardson, P. B. (1988). Worldview, learning style, and locus of control as factors of institutional culture differentiating academically unsuccessful students, academically successful students, and faculty. *Dissertation Abstracts International, 49*, 2152.

Cunningham-Warburton, P. (1988). *A study of the relationship between cross-cultural training, the Scale to Assess Worldview, and the quality of care given by nurses in a psychiatric setting.* Unpublished doctoral dissertation. University of Connecticut.

Das, A. & Ibrahim, F. A. (1990). International consultation: Case study. In B. Herlihy and L. Golden (Eds.), *American Association for Counseling and Development Ethics Handbook* (4th ed., 91–100). Alexandria, VA: American Counseling Association.

D'Rozario, V. A. (1996). Singaporean and United States college students' worldviews, expectations of counseling, and perceptions of counselor effectiveness based on directive and nondirective counseling style. *Dissertation Abstracts International, 56,* 2564.

Furn, B. G. (1986). The psychology of women as a cross-cultural issue: Perceived dimensions of worldviews. *Dissertation Abstracts International, 48-01A,* 0234.

Gerber, M. H. (1998). Worldview, social class, and psychosocial development. *Dissertation Abstracts International, 60,* 2983.

Gordon, R. D. (1997). Worldview, self-concept, and cultural identity patterns of deaf adolescents: Implications for counseling. *Dissertation Abstracts International, 58,* 4448.

Hickson, J., Christie, G., & Shmukler, D. (1990). A pilot study of black and white South African adolescent pupils: Implications for cross-cultural counseling. *South African Journal of Psychology, 20,* 170–177.

Ibrahim, F. A. (1982a). A systems approach to guidance: A model for Pakistan. *Counsellor, 1,* 2–26.

Ibrahim, F. A. (1982b). Creating and elevating awareness in teachers who plan to do counseling in Pakistani schools. *Counsellor, 1,* 46–60.

Ibrahim, F. A. (1984). Cross-cultural counseling and psychotherapy: An existential-psychological perspective. *The International Journal for the Advancement of Counseling, 7,* 159–169.

Ibrahim, F. A. (1985a). Effective cross-cultural counseling and psychotherapy: A framework. *The Counseling Psychologist, 13,* 625–638.

Ibrahim, F. A. (1985b). Effectiveness in cross-cultural counseling and psychotherapy: A framework. *Psychotherapy, 22,* 321–323.

Ibrahim, F. A. (1991). Contribution of cultural worldview to generic counseling and development. *Journal of Counseling and Development, 70,* 13–19.

Ibrahim, F. A. (1993a). Existential worldview theory: Transcultural counseling. In J. McFadden (Ed.), *Transcultural counseling: Bilateral and international perspectives* (pp. 23–58). Alexandria, VA: American Counseling Association.

Ibrahim, F. A. (1993b). Why cultural diversity for everyone in the counseling profession. *Dialog, 21,* 13–16.

Ibrahim, F. A. (1993c, August). *Paradigm shift in organizational development theories.* Paper presented at the annual meeting of the American Psychological Association. Toronto, Canada.

Ibrahim, F. A. (1999). Transcultural counseling: Existential worldview theory and cultural identity. In J. McFadden (Ed.), *Transcultural counseling* (2nd ed., pp. 23–58). Alexandria, VA: American Counseling Association.

Ibrahim, F. A., & Almas, I. (1983). Guidance and counseling in Pakistan. *The International Journal for the Advancement of Counseling, 6,* 93–98.

Ibrahim, F. A., & Arredondo, P. M. (1986). Ethical standards for cross-cultural counseling: Preparation, practice, assessment and research. *Journal of Counseling and Development, 64,* 349–351.

Ibrahim, F. A., & Arredondo, P. M. (1990). Essay on law and ethics: Multicultural counseling. In B. Herlihy & L. Golden (Eds.), *American Association for Counseling and Development: Ethics Casebook* (4th ed.). Alexandria, VA: AACD Press.

Ibrahim, F. A., Frietas, K., & Owen, S. V. (1993, August). *Comparison of Brazilian and American worldviews.* Paper presented at the annual meeting of the American Psychological Association, New York.

Ibrahim, F. A., & Kahn, H. (1984). *Scale to Assess Worldview* (SAWV). Storrs, CT: Unpublished document.

Ibrahim, F. A., & Kahn, H. (1987). Assessment of worldviews. *Psychological Reports, 60,* 163–176.

Ibrahim, F. A., & Ohnishi, H. (2001). Post traumatic stress disorder and the minority experience. In D. Pope-Davis & H. Coleman (Eds.), *The intersection of race, class, and gender: Implications for multicultural counseling.* Thousand Oaks, CA: Sage.

Ibrahim, F. A., Ohnishi, H., & Wilson, R. (1994). Career counseling in a pluralistic society. *Journal of Career Assessment, 2,* 276–288.

Ibrahim, F. A., & Owen, S. V. (1994). Factor analytic structure of the Scale to Assess Worldview. *Current Psychology, 13,* 201–209.

Ibrahim, F. A., Roysircar-Sodowsky, G. R., & Ohnishi, H. (2001). World view: Recent developments and future trends. In J. G. Ponterrotto, M. Casas, L. Suzuki, & C. Alexander (Eds.), *Handbook of Multicultural Counseling* (2nd ed.), pp. 425–456. Thousand Oaks, CA: Sage.

Ibrahim, F. A., & Schroeder, D. (1990). Cross-cultural couple counseling. *Journal of Comparative Family Studies, 21,* 193–205.

Lockney, J. P. (1999). Worldview: Accuracy of interpersonal perceptions on diversity. *Dissertation Abstracts International, 60-06B,* 3018.

Lo, Y.-H. (1996). The role of culture and subculture in worldviews: The impact of western influence and profession in Taiwan. *Dissertation Abstracts International, 57-04B,* 2948.

Lonner, W. J., & Ibrahim, F. A. (1996). Appraisal and assessment in cross-cultural counseling. In P. B. Pedersen, W. J. Lonner, J. Trimble, & J. Draguns (Eds.), *Counseling across cultures* (4th ed.). Thousand Oaks, CA: Sage.

Lonner, W. J., & Ibrahim, F. A. (2001) Assessment in cross-cultural counseling. In P. B. Pedersen, W. J. Lonner, J. Draguns, & J. Trimble (Eds.), *Counseling across cultures* (5th ed.). Thousand Oaks, CA: Sage.

Mahalik, J. R., Worthington, R. L., & Crump, S. (1999). Influence of racial/ethnic membership and therapist culture on therapists' worldview. *Journal of Multicultural Counseling and Development, 27,* 2–18.

Minuchin, S. (1974). *Families in family therapy.* Cambridge, MA: Harvard University Press.

Ngumba, E. W. (1996). The relationship between worldview, African self-consciousness, and adjustment of African and African-American students: A comparative study. *Dissertation Abstracts International, 57,* 2877.

Odenweller, T. (1997). *Worldview and ethnicity: Factors in preferred counseling styles and perceptions of counselors.* Doctoral Dissertation University of Florida (DAI, 58-07B, p. 3931).

Sadlak, M. J., & Ibrahim, F. A. (1986, August). *Cross-cultural counselor training: Impact on counselor effectiveness and sensitivity.* Paper presented at the annual meeting of the American Psychological Association, Washington, DC.

Sue, D. W. (1978). Eliminating cultural oppression in counseling: Toward a general theory. *Journal of Counseling Psychology, 25,* 419–428.

Takai, R. (1989). *Strangers from different shores: A history of Asian Americans.* Boston: Little Brown and Co.

Thomas, A. J. (1998). Understanding culture and worldview in family systems: Use of the multicultural genogram. *Family Journal, 6,* 24–33.

Thompson, M. L. (1997). Traditional worldview, interpersonal flexibility, and marital satisfaction among interethnic couples. *Dissertation Abstracts International, 58-07A,* 2864.

Toczyska, M. A. (1996). Worldview and perception of organizational culture: Factors distinguishing dominant cultures from subcultures and managers from non-managers in northeastern United States workplaces. *Dissertation Abstracts International, 57(A-4),* 1737.

Torrey, E. F. (1986). *Witchdoctors and psychiatrists.* New York: Harper & Row.

Trevino, J. G. (1996). Worldview and change in cross-cultural counseling. *The Counseling Psychologist, 24,* 198–215.

14 Stylistic Model for Counseling Across Cultures

JOHN MCFADDEN

Counseling across cultures has historically presented numerous challenges for helping professionals because of limited emphasis on intercultural competency in counselor education programs. Although this trend is changing, it is imperative that nontraditional models, theories, and approaches for counselor training be incorporated into counselor education curricula throughout colleges and universities. New approaches should be blended with traditional ones as counselor trainees seek to be interculturally effective and efficient. Stylistic counseling constitutes one of these relatively new approaches, and this chapter is designed to introduce to some and expand for others an array of information on the evolution of this model and its historical context.

The Stylistic Model for counseling across cultures is a framework from which helping professionals might establish a basis to promote growth of their clients. It purports to establish a graphic reference point on which counselors can identify as they work with clients.

The hierarchical nature of this model manifests itself in a sequential manner that challenges its users to understand the need to progress in an ascending direction during the counseling relationship. At the same time, counselors are able to maintain their own mode or style when applying this model.

Stylistic counseling advocates basic principles that are essential in promoting transculturalism. The author recognized the importance of incorporating a worldview in designing the Stylistic Model, one that features a global framework for individuals, their culture, and society. Knowledge, competencies, and skills are built on this foundation and allow counselors to excel in their practice. Evidence of successful application of these competencies and skills rests with effective interventions through transcultural counseling, which assumes a stance that counseling and other helping ventures can occur across cultures, nations, and continents (Ibrahim, 1999). The linkage between stylistic counseling and the International Association for Counselling and the American Counseling Association is clear, as the model is known to have been presented at numerous institutes, workshops, and conferences.

Emerging originally from a cry to provide counseling services for African Americans through assistance, training, programming, consultation, coordination, and outreach, a model for stylistic counseling found a niche in counselor preparation. Current application of the model suggests its applicability for individuals and groups without specific regard to race, ethnicity, disability, tribe, nationality, gender, or sexual orientation, to name a few. Just as there is a longing for diversity training in management, so should there be a call for counselor training with emphasis on transculturalism. The Stylistic Model for counseling across cultures is merely one alternative to achieving this training.

The emergence of stylistic counseling began in the 1960s when people in the generation now referred to as baby boomers were aggressively exploring their identities and seeking something to which to cling. They had a style—a way through which they could express themselves. The term *stylistic counseling* began to form in the early 1970s and represented an opportunity for counselors to assemble their cultural insights and skills pertinent to promoting growth with their clients. Stylistic counseling, therefore, is known to embrace a quality of imagination and individuality by persons in the counseling profession. Although it is multidimensional in design and interdisciplinary in scope, it allows for each individual who chooses to use this model to apply his or her own primary professional orientation and formulate his or her own style of counseling.

Anatomy of Stylistic Counseling

Stylistic counseling is a model based on the belief that the implications of culture are multilayered and that effective transcultural counseling requires successfully uncovering those layers on behalf of both the client and the counselor. Although it is represented by twenty-seven cubes, it is composed of three basic dimensions (see Figure 14.1). At the foundation of this model is the cultural-historical (CH) dimension, predicated on the assumption that our broad cultural backgrounds provide the core for who we are. The second dimension, psychosocial (PS), assumes that our social interactions and psychological responses are interrelated and relevant to our cultural base. Then, the third dimension, scientific-ideological (S-I), is action oriented and allows us to express our concreteness.

Cubical descriptors have been grouped on the three tiers of cultural-historical, psychosocial, and scientific-ideological. Whereas some of the descriptors might be uniquely placed elsewhere, the author (McFadden, 1999) grouped the nine cubes on each dimension based on historical, psychological, or scientific relevance. Even though it may appear that the various cubical descriptors are fixed, the model is intended to allow for horizontal, vertical, or diagonal movement through the respective lines with fluidity. In fact, it could be said that the lines surrounding each cube are transparent.

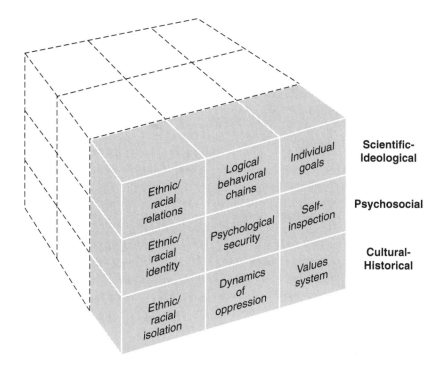

FIGURE 14.1   Scientific-Ideological, Psychosocial, Cultural-Historical Model of Stylistic Counseling

Source: Reprinted from *Transcultural Counseling* (2nd ed.) by J. McFadden (Ed.), 1999. Copyright © ACA. Reprinted with permission. No further reproduction authorized without written permission of the American Counseling Association.

Several significant qualities of the model exist, one being its hierarchical nature. Each subsequent dimension builds on those previous to it. As such, counselors can progress vertically or diagonally through the cubical columns, always in an ascending manner. The basic rationale is that our cultural identities are deeply ingrained and the result of historical influences and social interactions cannot be separated from our actions. To effect positive changes, counselors must likewise have a strong sense of cultural awareness.

The twenty-seven cubical descriptors (see Figure 14.2) of the Stylistic Counseling Model are structured by dimensions, (i.e., nine cubes for each layer: cultural-historical, psychosocial, scientific-ideological). Building upon each other is a key to understanding the structure and flow of stylistic counseling, which permits counselors to interface their theoretical orientation within the framework of this model. In other words, the counselor's individual style for promoting client growth is defined and supported.

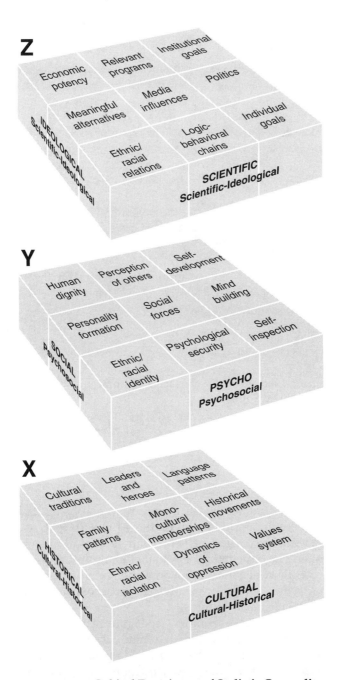

FIGURE 14.2   Cubical Descriptors of Stylistic Counseling

Source: Reprinted from *Transcultural Counseling* (2nd ed.) by J. McFadden (Ed.), 1999. Copyright © ACA. Reprinted with permission. No further reproduction authorized without written permission of the American Counseling Association.

Cubical Descriptors*

Each of the three dimensions (cultural-historical, psychosocial, and scientific-ideological) encompasses nine cubical descriptors that are graphically depicted in Figure 14.2 and concisely described in the following section.

1. Ethnic/racial discrimination: An emphasis on historical and cultural effects of discrimination on ethnic/racial groups. This component is important because one cannot counsel another person transculturally unless one is extremely knowledgeable and sensitive to discrimination the client may have experienced.
2. Ethnic/racial identity: A study of the psychological and social aspects of ethnic/racial identity of underrepresented persons. This component includes factors that involve the sociological and psychological impact of discrimination affecting the self-concept and identity of ethnic/racial groups. This component is designed to address ingredients essential in the formation of individual identity.
3. Ethnic/racial relations: An analysis of the science of race relations and ethnic interactions and the ideology of these relations as they influence a particular nationality. This is a cubical descriptor for an action-oriented dimension of the model.
4. Dynamics of oppression: A history of the major aspects of oppression as they affect the formation of various ethnic/racial cultures.
5. Psychological security: A study of the psychology of the oppressed as it pertains to internal and external sense of security. The psychosocial dimension of counseling individuals allows them to build their sense of psychological security in relation to coping skills required in managing the dynamics of oppression.
6. Logic-behavioral chains: An investigation of the scientific logic that undergirds one's thoughts and behaviors. This component allows a client to be directed or helped behaviorally, based on a logical pattern that emerges from a sense of psychological security reflected in the form of survival skills.
7. Value system: An exploration of the history of values embraced by a given culture and how these values influence the lives of an ethnic or racial group. The evolution of the value structure and the value orientation of a group of people from infancy to adulthood become crucial in this component.
8. Self-inspection: A psychological and social study of an individual's self-concept formation. This entails the definition of self-concept and its development toward a mentality of how one feels or perceives oneself.
9. Individual goals: A scientific exploration of the identification of goals of historically underrepresented ethnic/racial groups and their aspirations toward the development of a clear ideology for goal attainment.

10. Family patterns: An examination of the various family patterns to which particular ethnic/racial persons belong. The family patterns are based on the history of the oppressed groups.

11. Personality formation: Identification of the ways personalities are formed among ethnic groups and races—how they develop varying personalities to build a system of survival.

12. Meaningful alternatives: Selection of a variety of situations and alternatives that govern efficient and productive lives; scientific examination of choices for effective decision making and successful career development.

13. Monocultural membership: A description of the advantages and limitations of monocultural membership. The advantages of belonging to a particular cultural group and ways to optimize this fundamental membership are assessed.

14. Social forces: A discussion of social forces that affect the lives of persons outside the mainstream of society, such as unemployment, underemployment, alcoholism, substance abuse, and homelessness.

15. Media influences: An examination of the positive and negative ways by which the media influence ethnic/racial perceptions in society, as well as the controlling force of print and audio-visual media.

16. Historical movements: An indication of the impact of certain historical and legislative movements and the alteration of government and community programs as related to ethnic/racial groups.

17. Mind building: Conditioning of one's mental capacity to become productive and useful to oneself and others through transcultural methods.

18. Politics: An indication of the influences of ethnic/racial groups in politics; the variation in ways that politics embrace and establish parameters within which the public is expected to function.

19. Cultural traditions: A reflection of the culture that, by virtue of its beginning and tradition, manages to be transferred from one generation to another; how cultural traditions develop to affect others through continuity.

20. Human dignity: Maintenance of identity so that individuals can have feelings of self-satisfaction, self-enhancement, empowerment, dignity, and ethnic or cultural pride.

21. Economic potency: Ability of ethnic/racial groups to unify and solidify their power (i.e., influence, ability, and impact on the economics of a particular system).

22. Leaders and heroes: Individuals who, by virtue of their function in society, have attained a level of respect as leaders or heroes. They serve as mentors and role models for ethnic/racial groups.

23. Perception of others: Ideas and visions of people based on certain experiences that may have emerged as a result of interaction with a societal context toward a level of transcendency.

24. Relevant programs: Formation of a programmatic thrust within a particular group. Such programs are perceived to have true meaning and significance as they bond with values that ethnicities and races may hold to be special.

25. Language patterns: The development of languages and linguistic orientation that prove themselves to be optimally communicative between or among individuals, allowing for and respecting dialects and language differences.
26. Self-development: The enhancement or improvement of oneself so that one can provide for oneself and others within an ethnic/racial context. It is self-improvement aimed at reaching a level of productivity or orientation for accomplishment.
27. Institutional goals: Aspirations of an institution, organization, community, or society that may have some utility to an ethnic/racial group. These goals are geared to serve a large group of people and can be linked to a cultural or sociological context that could have significance.

Principles of Stylistic Counseling

Following are the principles of stylistic counseling.

1. Stylistic counseling proposes a model for formulating an individual counseling program compatible with the counselor's orientation and conducive to effectively meeting the needs of clients.
2. Stylistic counseling suggests that cubical descriptors of a person's behavior are hierarchical in nature.
3. Stylistic counseling is an approach to helping others that integrates the cultural-historical, psychosocial, and scientific-ideological dimensions of human behavior.
4. Stylistic counseling advocates the establishment of a cultural-historical base as the foundation for effective helping relationships.
5. Stylistic counseling states that one's psychosocial experiences are inherent factors that affect one's perception of self and others.
6. Stylistic counseling encourages implementation of an active dimension to the helping professions through clear articulation at the scientific-ideological level.
7. Stylistic counseling requires that the counselor develop a genuine concern and commitment to the client's best interest regardless of cultural differences.
8. Stylistic counseling requires that the counselor develop an ability to open and maintain effective cross-cultural channels of communication.
9. Stylistic counseling requires that the counselor develop the attitude that each client in a counseling situation has a cultural experience unique to the client.
10. Stylistic counseling requires that the counselor develop an active awareness of his or her own attitudes and feelings toward minority individuals and groups.
11. Stylistic counseling requires that the counselor's role become that of an agent and helper within the scope of the client's frame of reference.
12. Stylistic counseling requires that the problem be redefined with emphasis placed on societal responsibility for human dignity and enhancement.

The Stylistic Counseling Model is structured in a manner to accommodate a variety of counseling theoretical orientations. At the same time, it is intended to promote credibility of culture and history as some base of our existence and the foundation for our being. Thus, the three dimensions of cultural-historical (CH), psychosocial (PS), and scientific-ideological (SI) emerge. The model is structured with its twenty-seven cubical descriptors, nine per dimension, in a manner to allow its users to progress through the design in an ascending manner from one descriptor to the other.

Recognizing that clients present dilemmas across the spectrum, it is possible for counselors to begin working with their clients on any of the three dimensions. The author of stylistic counseling recommends that in order to optimize application of this model, counselors demonstrate a master knowledge of the cubes on each dimension prior to the presenting one by their clients. So, situations presented to the counselor should be clearly identified and associated with a particular cubical descriptor in order to promote a starting point to solve problems.

Stylistic counseling is applicable across a variety of settings, such as school, mental health, family, criminal justice, community, higher education, rehabilitation, social services, and career development. Although these settings represent a cross-section of venue where the stylistic counseling may be applied, other sources appropriate for applicability of this model also exist. Stimuli for use of stylistic counseling are known to emerge from academic, social, economic, developmental, political, financial, physical, marital, and family sources, to name a few.

Using the Stylistic Model to Counsel Native Americans at Colleges or Universities With Native American Mascots

The code of ethics of the American Psychological Association (1992) states that "helping professionals must be aware of cultural, individual, and role differences, including those due to age, gender, race, ethnicity, national origin, religion . . . language, and socioeconomic status" (Herring, 1999, p. xi). As a result, many researchers and helping professionals have begun to develop methods designed to better serve diverse populations. Heinrich, Corbine, and Thomas (1990) state that "although Native Americans are a small minority of the U.S. population, they are burdened with a disproportionate share of social and economic problems" (pp. 132–133). Consequently, it is crucial that counselors who serve Native American clients have an understanding of their clients' cultural experiences and foundations.

To promote this understanding, the Stylistic Model "allows persons who already have initial training in counseling or those who are receiving training to develop their own mode or style so that they can be effective in helping others who have experienced oppression" (McFadden, 1999, p. 62). This model, comprised of three dimensions of cubical descriptors that move hierarchically in a vertical, horizontal, or diagonal motion, can help counselors "master a knowledge of and feeling for the culture and history of the client whose life has been marked by separation, disregard, and oppression" (p. 61). Many Native Americans view Native American mascots as a sign of this separation, disregard, and oppression. Consequently, the Stylistic Model can be used to counsel Native Americans on the issue of mascots.

Cultural-Historical Dimension

The first dimension of the Stylistic Model, cultural-historical, is "the basic and fundamental dimension . . . relating specifically to the culture of a people and how their history evolved over time" (McFadden, 1999, p. 64). This dimension operates under the premise that an effective counselor-client relationship cannot be established without the counselor's fundamental understanding of the client's view of his or her heritage or role in the greater social context and how his or her cultural norms and values function within the surrounding social forces. Some cubical descriptors in the cultural-historical dimension include ethnic/racial discrimination, value systems, and leaders and heroes. Exploring these cubicals can help the counselor to "identify with the culture of the particular race or ethnicity he or she is counseling" (p. 64).

The exploration of the ethnic/racial discrimination cubical descriptor can help to establish a foundation based on the experiences of clients resulting from their race or ethnicity. As a counselor, this component is important because one cannot counsel another person transculturally unless one is extremely knowledgeable and sensitive to the discrimination that clients may have experienced. In relation to Native American mascots, it will be important to determine what oppressive or discriminatory experiences the clients have had in college as a result of the mascot. "Historically, White institutions such as government bureaus, schools, and churches have deliberately tried to destroy Native American cultural institutions" (Heinrich, Corbine, & Thomas, 1990, p. 129). Thus, it will also be important for counselors to learn the oppressive or discriminatory history experienced by their clients, if any. This history could help both counselors and clients to understand reactions to the mascot.

Another cubical descriptor in the cultural-historical dimension is "value systems." Discussing value systems includes an "exploration of the history of values embraced by a given culture and how these values influence the lives of an ethnic or racial group" (McFadden, 1999, p. 66). "While keeping in mind the enormous diversity among Native Americans it is possible to identify similarities in values that exist across tribes and regions" (Heinrich, Corbine, & Thomas, 1990, p. 129). When counseling students concerning mascots, the exploration of these values will help to determine the impression and feelings of clients on the mascots. In addition, it will help counselors understand whether the practices of mascots and fans accurately portray the values of the culture of their clients. This will be beneficial in establishing whether the identity development of their clients clashes with how their identity is defined by the majority culture.

Leaders and heroes, still another cubical descriptor in the cultural-historical dimension, focuses on the idea that there are "individuals, who by virtue of their function in society, have attained a level of respect as leaders or heroes" (McFadden, 1999, p. 68). First and foremost of the historical leaders and heroes for Native Americans are tribal chiefs. It can be humiliating for Native Americans to see the image of their chiefs reduced to caricatures and halftime shows, says Charlene Teeter in an article by Rodriguez (1998). Leaders and heroes serve as mentors and role models for ethnic and racial groups and, as a result, the inaccurate portrayal of these leaders and heroes can lead to confusion or negative identity development. Exploring perceptions by clients of their leaders and heroes will help counselors to better understand how to approach the issue of mascots. A current trend that is proving to be useful in leadership modeling for young people is mentoring programs in many communities. An example of counselors collaborating with such a program since 1988 is the Benjamin E. Mays Academy for Leadership Development at the University of South Carolina (McFadden et al., 2001).

Psychosocial Dimension

The second dimension of the stylistic model, psychosocial, "relates specifically to the psychological framework, the formation of a mindset of how a person's psychic influence affects his or her scope and development, such as in the case of a person's interaction based on how the person sees his or her own cultural heritage" (McFadden, 1999, p. 64). The psychosocial dimension is important because it helps counselors determine how a person's cultural-historical foundation affects his or her social motivations and interactions. Some of the psychosocial cubical descriptors include social forces, human dignity, and perception of others.

The social forces cubical is logistically, and perhaps figuratively, the core of the stylistic model. An exploration of this cubical includes "a discussion of social forces that affect the lives of persons outside the mainstream of society" (McFadden, 1999, p. 68). This cubical is recognized as serving as a centrifugal force for the remaining twenty-six cubes. Social influences in our lives govern much of what we think and do and thereby, chart our psychological equilibrium. Thomason (1991), author of "Counseling Native Americans: An Introduction for Non-Native American Counselors," asserts that, given the diversity of the Native American population, one must be careful to avoid stereotyping Native Americans based on general assumptions. However, Thomason (1991) also argues that "although most of the psychological information available on Native Americans focuses on deviant patterns of adjustment such as suicide, alcoholism, and unemployment," these generalizations are important social forces pressing on the Native American community (p. 324). Mascots and other stereotypical symbols perpetuated by the media can also be considered serious social forces.

Human dignity, another cubical descriptor in the psychosocial dimension, focuses on the "maintenance of identity so that individuals can have feelings of self-satisfaction, self-enhancement, empowerment, dignity, and ethnic or cultural pride" (McFadden, 1999, p. 86). Ancis, Choney, and Sedlacek (1996) postulate the following:

> It is thus likely that students, having been exposed to negative and stereotypical imagery of American Indians throughout the educational process, hold prejudicial attitudes toward them. Because prejudicial attitudes are implicated in the degree to which academic environments foster the emotional, academic, and vocational achievement of American Indians, it seems necessary to assess the exact nature of student's attitude. (p. 27)

Consequently, Native American mascots, an example of negative and stereotypical imagery, may have profound effects on college students' perceptions of Native Americans. Because the human dignity cubical is linked so closely to identity development, it is important for counselors to explore this cubical when focusing on the psychosocial dimension.

The perception of others cubical is defined as "ideas and visions of people based on certain experiences that may have emerged as a result of interaction within a societal context toward a level of transcendency" (McFadden, 1999, p. 68). Charlene Teeter's experience with trying to change the University of Illinois's mascot (Chief Illiniwek), cited in the article by Rodriguez (1998), is a prime example of perception of others. Not only was Teeter's perception of those around her changed after she viewed their behavior, but the following week when she returned to the stadium to protest, she was met with hostility and rejection from many students and spectators. According to Teeter, these experiences had a profound impact on her perception of her fellow students. In order to help Teeter and students with concerns like hers, an exploration of her perception of others is a vital step toward a higher level of transcendency.

Scientific-Ideological Dimension

The third dimension in the Stylistic Model, scientific-ideological, "refers specifically to an action-oriented aspect of counseling" (McFadden, 1999, p. 64). Not only does this dimension deal with how people of different ethnicities and races function, communicate, and relate to people of their ethnic or racial groups as well as those outside of it, but it also deals with how the cultural-historical and psychosocial dimensions motivate people to take action. The scientific-ideological dimension involves a "developmental process of empowering an individual to function given that there is a support system whereby the client becomes optimally productive" (p. 65). Some cubical descriptors in the scientific-ideological dimension are individual goals, economic potency, and media influences.

The individual goals cubical descriptor includes a "scientific exploration of the identification of goals of historically underrepresented ethnic/racial groups and their aspirations toward the development of a clear ideology for goal attainment" (McFadden, 1999, p. 66). When exploring this descriptor it is important to help clients set goals based upon their cultural-historical and psychosocial explorations.

The cubical is marked by a client's understanding of what he or she wants to accomplish in order to achieve a greater sense of transculturalism. In regard to mascots, this may include actions such as the exploration of social forces, action based on the goal of abolishing the mascots, and involvement of other cultures to work toward multicultural and transcultural education.

Economic potency, another cubical descriptor in the scientific-ideological dimension, deals with "the ability of ethnic/racial groups to unify and solidify their power (i.e., influence, ability, and impact on the economics of a particular system)" (McFadden, 1999, p. 68). Although Native Americans are a small minority of the U.S. population, "defining precisely the perimeters of the American Indian population would be a less important matter if it did not determine the apportionment of economic resources and opportunities" (Snipp, 1997, p. 680). In order to receive federal assistance, many Native American individuals and groups must provide proof of blood quantum or tribal membership. However, many agencies do not have the means and equipment to assess these qualities. "Consequently, self-identification is the most widely used method for determining ethnic background" (p. 680). Exploring this descriptor of the scientific-ideological dimension as it concerns mascots would involve the client's empowerment to transcend these barriers in influencing the higher education system.

Media influences, still another descriptor in the scientific-ideological dimension, involves "an examination of the positive and negative ways by which the media influence ethnic/racial perceptions in society, and community programs as related to ethnic/racial groups" (McFadden, 1999, p. 68). When examining this descriptor a counselor and client should explore not only how Native Americans are portrayed by the media but also the effects the portrayals have on the Native American culture. Media influences have a tremendous impact on the use of Native American mascots. The media decide how it chooses to cover athletic events that use racist mascots. In addition, supporters and opposers of Native American mascots use various forms of media to convey their views toward them. Because the scientific-ideological dimension is action oriented, it is appropriate for counselors to explore with their clients ways by which the clients choose to use the media to encourage transculturalism.

Subsets of Cubical Descriptors

Each of the twenty-seven cubical descriptors has nine subsets (cubes) in order to acknowledge the multiple components that exist even within any cultural group. Another way of expressing variability even within cultures is offered here. To illustrate the meaning of this discussion, the cubical descriptors of language patterns may be subdivided as shown in Figure 14.2 (p. 212).

As counselors work with their clients, linguistics becomes a crucial consideration in optimizing the client-counselor relationship. In further understanding clients as regards the cultural-historical dimension of stylistic counseling, articulation through pertinent subsets of the "language patterns" cubical is essential. It is general knowledge among multicultural/ transcultural educators that language lies at the core of a person's identity. To acknowledge and understand the client's language base and to promote the client's ownership and alignment with that base is to ensure the foundation for securing positive cross-cultural communication between the counselor and client.

Although this discussion pertains to subsets of the cubical descriptor identified as language patterns, a similar illustration can be extended to each of the cubes of the stylistic counseling model. The further subdivision of the primary 27 cubical descriptors, as seen in Figure 14.2, means that this model can potentially yield 9 × 27 or 243 subcubical descriptors as counselors seek to comprehend their clients.

A Stylistic Counseling Self-Assessment has been developed in order to assist counselors in further understanding the model. The Stylistic Counseling Self-Assessment provides counselors with an opportunity to rate themselves in relation to a particular client. Twenty-seven of the questions pertain to a particular cubical in the Stylistic Counseling Model. Using this as a guide, counselors can discern where they tend to spend the bulk of their time when working with their clients. The instrument is a practical tool that counselors can use in learning more about stylistic counseling. A copy of the instrument can be found at the end of this chapter.

Cross-Cultural Counseling Critical Incident 1: A New Insight on Caucasian Culture

Biodata

This incident involves an African American female of 23 who comes from a socioeconomic background of middle income. The setting is at a singing/dancing bar filled with middle- to lower-income Caucasians. The singing/dancing pub is located in a rural county in the southern United States. The people call themselves "down to earth Rednecks" and seem to form their own isolated society of "regulars" and friends.

Background

The African American female was invited to this singing/dancing experience by a co-worker. At first she was hesitant to go but when she learned that other African Americans would be there she agreed to participate. She rode with a group of fellow African American friends and when they opened the door to the small, smoke filled, country-music playing, Caucasian-dominated pub, the cultural dilemma began.

The African American female has many preconceived ideas about lower-socioeconomic Caucasians that stem from racist experiences she has encountered through her adolescent years at a predominately Caucasian high school. She feels that most lower-income Whites are racist and feels as if she does not belong in their environment. This philosophy is also reinforced by her parents' opinion that all Whites should be approached with caution.

Dilemma

The dilemma begins as she opens the door to the pub only to find hundreds of these lower-income Whites staring at her. She immediately feels uncomfortable and wonders if she should go inside or forget the whole thing and return home. Some of her Caucasian friends beckon her to come in, but she feels torn as to what she should do. Although she loves to have new experiences and meet new people, because of her preconceived ideas of how these individuals will react to her, she feels insecure that this will be a positive experience. She decides to go inside the bar but stays close to her group of African American friends. She wants to interact with individuals within the bar but is very fearful of their reaction.

Intervention

As a counselor, I would use my stylistic approach with the young woman and explore her cultural background. I would first take a cultural-historical look at her ethnic/racial experiences of isolation and discrimination with this particular population. The fact that she has had some traumatic experiences with this type of group is very relevant to this case. I would then dive into a more psychological-social realm and allow her to discuss her ethnic/racial identity and what this identity means to her. I would try to develop a Venn diagram with my client on how she views herself and this target population. By moving to the scientific-ideological dimension, I am trying to determine my client's ethnic/racial relations with this particular group. I would ask her to draw a Venn diagram of how she would like her relations with this new group to grow, develop, and change. In this way I would obtain my client's individual goals, giving both of us something to work toward in our counseling sessions.

Also, taking into account that my client is an African American female, I would make sure to examine not only her ethnic/racial issues but also her gender issues. Does she feel more comfortable around women or men in this population, and if so why? I would take a look at Harper and Stone's (1999) transcendent counseling approach and determine what phase my client was experiencing multiethnically with this population group (i.e., whether she were at the ethnoentrophy stage and felt isolated and tended to avoid this cultural population when possible, the ethnocentrism phase and felt superior to this other ethnic group, the ethnosycretism stage and felt accepting of the other culture, the transethnicity state where she wanted to experience this other culture more fully, or maybe at the panethnicity stage and had a view of herself as a member of all ethnic groups of the world). What stage in development my client was at would determine how she would react in this situation and also determine what individual goals would be realistic to her developmental case of cultural identity.

Questions

1. As a counselor, is there any other way of viewing or dealing with this situation aside from the ethnic/cultural issue?
2. As an African American in the panethnicity phase of development, how would you react in this particular situation?
3. If encountering a client at the bottom of the totem pole, the ethnoentrophy phase, and knowing that progress within this stage is minimal, how can you as a counselor aid in transcending the client?
4. If a client develops goals that you do not feel will promote personal growth, should you as a counselor accept and reinforce the client's decision?
5. How might you as a counselor have handled this situation differently?

Cross-Cultural Counseling Critical Incident 2: Chow in America

Biodata

Ming Chow is a 16-year-old Asian American male sophomore at Baker High School in Sandy Hills. Coach Jack Jacobs is a 42-year-old Caucasian male who has been coaching the Baker High basketball team for the past six years.

Background

Ming Chow was born in North America and reared by his Asian-born parents in a middle-income community in Sandy Hills. Ming has a younger brother. His parents own a local Chinese restaurant. Coach Jacobs and his wife, who is a homemaker, have three children and live in a middle-income community.

Dilemma

Coach Jacobs notices Ming's great athletic abilities in basketball during several physical education classes. Basketball tryouts are in two weeks. Coach Jacobs knows that Ming could be a valuable asset to the team, so he asks Ming if he's going to try out for the team. Even though he has grown to love basketball (he only plays at school), Ming knows his parents won't allow him to join the team. Later that day after school, Coach Jacobs and I talk to each other as the students wait for their parents to pick them up. As soon as Coach Jacobs tells me about Ming, he notices Ming's parents driving up. He decides that he's going to talk to them at once about Ming's athletic ability. As counselor, I stop Coach Jacobs and ask him to come into my office for a talk.

Intervention

Once Coach Jacobs and I get to my office, we begin to discuss his plan of speaking with the Chows to persuade them to allow Ming to play basketball. I challenged Coach Jacobs to think of the Chinese culture and the things which the culture values. McFadden's Stylistic Model is a useful way to explain the Chinese culture's values and beliefs to Coach Jacobs. Beginning in the cultural-historical dimension, we examine the value systems of the Chinese culture. A culture's value systems are critical in understanding the background of an individual. Asians have a profound respect for their elders. They believe that older persons possess a great deal of knowledge and maturity. Asians also place a great deal of importance on education and expect scholarly excellence from their children. Thus, if Coach Jacobs had approached the Chows with hopes of recruiting another player, it is possible that Mr. Chow could have felt insulted by the Coach because he questioned his authority in the presence of his wife and children. Also, Coach Jacobs could have appeared as if he were undermining the importance of education to the Asian culture. As we move to the psychosocial dimension of the model, we explore the self-inspection cubical. I ask Coach Jacobs to think of the possible implications Mr. Chow could have felt if Coach Jacobs had spoken to him. Coach Jacobs states that Mr. Chow could have questioned his culture and whether he should try to acculturate to some of America's practices. Mr. Chow could have also questioned his competency as a parent. For example, he may wonder if he's depriving his child of the American high school experience or, if he allows Ming to play basketball, whether he's letting go of his cultural beliefs. Another way that Mr. Chow may examine himself is by wondering, if he allows American beliefs and values to affect his family, what will his parents and family who are still in China think about him. Will they think Mr. Chow is abandoning his culture? Will that, in turn, affect Mr. Chow's feelings about himself? All of these things are to be taken into consideration when considering the possible ways Mr. Chow's self-worth could have been affected if Coach Jacobs had spoken with him. Finally, the scientific-ideological dimension of the Stylistic Model addresses the individual goals cubical. A goal for the Asian culture is to do well in higher education in order to attain wealth and prestige. Mr. Chow might have felt that, if Ming played basketball, it might detract from his education, therefore, lessening his chances of achieving wealth. Another general goal of the Asian community is to produce good grades. In Mr. Chow's mind he may feel that basketball practice and games will take too much time away from Ming's studies and, as a result, limit Ming's successes.

By exploring the different dimensions of McFadden's Stylistic Counseling Model, Coach Jacobs was able to see the effects his talk with the Chows could have had. He didn't realize that dealing with another culture required so much knowledge, sensitivity, and understanding. Coach Jacobs now realizes that he should consider the cultural background of those of a different culture and respect their heritage.

Questions

1. Should Coach Jacobs consider the possible ramifications when dealing with those individuals of different cultures?
2. Have you as the counselor done a proficient job in explaining the cultural differences among Asians to Coach Jacobs?

Cross-Cultural Counseling Critical Incident 3: The Challenges Surrounding a Heterosexual Father's Conversion to a Homosexual Lifestyle

Biodata

This cross-cultural incident involves a divorced gay male who is 26 years of age. At the age of 19 the identified client was married to a heterosexual partner and remained in the relationship for seven years. During the marriage the couple had two children. They are an 8-year-old son and a 6-year-old daughter.

The client in this study is a Caucasian and was reared in a Protestant, middle-income family with a subsystem of three children. When he was 9 years of age, his mother died of breast cancer. Subsequently, his father remarried and the children were reared by their father and a Hispanic stepmother. After remarriage, the father spent limited time at home and traveled extensively for his job. The stepmother worked full time and placed few restrictions on the children's activities.

The identified client's family of origin is labeled as dysfunctional for the following reasons. Succeeding the mother's death, the father became withdrawn and refused to discuss his wife or her death with his children. The problems associated with the denial of the mother's death manifested in the father's abuse of alcohol.

Background

After being married for seven years, the client is now in the process of a divorce. He admittedly struggled with his sexuality prior to the marriage, and although he dated women throughout high school, he remained confused about his physical attraction to persons of the same sex. While married, he thought that the birth of a child would eliminate the conflicting feelings but the denial of these feelings only heightened his physical attraction to other men.

After the birth of their second child, the identified client became sexually involved with another male while still married to his wife. After admitting this to his wife, the couple unsuccessfully tried resolving their marital discord through counseling but it resulted in their filing for a divorce.

Dilemma

The mother now wants full custody of the children and has stated to her attorney that a gay father is not capable of rearing children. The father has a solid relationship with both of his children and the older child has expressed an interest in living with his father after the divorce. The father wants his son to live with him but he is having difficulty managing his multiple identities: father of two children, divorced parent, and homosexual partner. He has been involved in a serious relationship with another male for the past year, and as a result, the couple has decided to commit to each other long term. This scenario requires the client to integrate numerous roles while balancing his identity shifts and changing his sense of self.

In trying to decide what living environment is best for his son, the father has sought the guidance of a family counselor. The child's mother does not approve of her ex-husband's homosexual relationship and is adamantly opposed to her son's living with him. This situation has caused the father to question his ability to serve in the role of a father and it has forced him to evaluate his partner's parenting capacity.

Intervention

If assigned this case as a counselor, I would apply a stylistic counseling framework as a tool for examining the client's background. The initial assessment would begin with an exploration of the cultural-historical dimension of the client's life. Building on this base, the client and I could examine his family patterns and value system. The hierarchical nature of stylistic counseling requires the counselor to integrate a person's psychosocial descriptors, and in this case, I would review his perception of others, psychological security, and self-development. The framework culminates in the scientific-ideological dimension where the counselor empowers the client to set goals and review meaningful lifestyle alternatives.

The SAWV (Scale to Assess Worldview) instrument is a valuable tool for helping the client understand his or her worldview (Baldwin & Hopkins, 1990), and in this particular case its application would also provide the counselor with a starting point for understanding the client's culturally diverse world.

In an attempt to help the client understand his multiple roles and his shifting sense of self, I would recommend an affirmative counseling approach. This particular approach emphasizes the adoption of a positive gay identity as a means to assist the client in examining each portion of his identity.

The client in this case would benefit by rising above the negativity that is surrounding both his lifestyle change and the divorce proceedings. In a transcendent counseling model the counselor helps the client accept the transition to a gay lifestyle by providing him with the techniques and skills for achieving a positive, successful lifestyle change. Further client-therapist discussions could include the consequences of change if the son does live in the same household as the father and his gay partner.

Questions

1. As a counselor, how would you proceed to help the client learn his children's feelings toward his new partner?
2. Discuss approaches you would apply in helping the client recall obstacles, if any, he may have experienced during adolescence in expressing his sexuality.
3. To what extent would you have the client explore insights about sexual experiences and beliefs and values together with his partner?
4. What specific steps would you take in helping the client make projections of his relationship in two years?
5. Identify how in your counseling role you plan to promote your client's examination of his fatherly functions and how these complement or conflict with his having taken a new partner.

Another Dimension

As the Stylistic Model for counseling continues to be used in a variety of settings, it has become more evident that another dimension to this model potentially exists. Students inquire about the counseling stage beyond the scientific-ideological dimension. Researchers seek more insight into transcultural dynamics of transcendental components of counseling across cultures that might occur between counselor and client at a transspiritual level. I maintain an ongoing interest in this aspect of the model and am exploring the meaning of another dimension to the Stylistic Model for transcultural counseling. It is advocated that this particular dimension, although not identified by label, does contain features of spirituality and existentialism. Furthermore, it is believed that it may be advisable for the counselor and client to value the presence of another dimension and celebrate it but, at the same time, not affix a label thereto. This exploratory dimension to stylistic counseling could serve as a basis upon which transcultural counselors can venture into areas of unknown creativity and development.

Conclusion

Societal issues imposed on clients can be understood when the Stylistic Counseling Model is used as a point of reference. The three dimensions of this model, cultural-historical (CH), psychosocial (PS), and scientific-ideological (SI), represent developmental patterns through which counselors emerge as they provide counsel on societal issues that impose immediacy. Toward accomplishment of this function, stylistic counseling is based on the premise that the CH dimension provides "reflection" by and for clients. In other words, their worldview can be understood historically. The PS dimension offers "insight" into essential dynamics encompassing problematic areas of clients' lives. Ultimately, counselors should aspire to achieve "action" on the part of their clients. The SI dimension is the plane where this occurs in the Stylistic Counseling Model.

It is appropriate to acknowledge that, while this model is layered by three key dimensions, in a futuristic sense a fourth dimension or level is implied, yet not currently identified in title. This considers that fact that it is existentially and spiritually reasonable for there to be an additional dimension that represents a client-counselor relationship. I therefore wish to encourage this dimension or level to evolve between client and counselor and, at the same time, not label it. The hierarchial nature—that is, twenty-seven cubical descriptors—of stylistic counseling offers counselors the opportunity to participate actively and chronologically with their clients. Moreover, they journey with their clients and experience reciprocal learning that is culturally enriching.

Stylistic counseling, through each dimension permeated by mind-body-spirit, offers a framework within which counselors can apply their particular theoretical orientation in the counseling relationship, and thereby assist clients in accomplishing their goals.

DISCUSSION QUESTIONS

1. Given your cultural/ethnic heritage, process and discuss one of the cubical columns in the anatomy of stylistic counseling.

2. What is the significance of the cubical descriptor "social forces" being at the core of the stylistic counseling model?

3. Identify what you perceive as another dimension, beyond "scientific-ideological," for stylistic counseling.

4. Compare and contrast your preferred counseling theory/technique with the basic framework of the stylistic counseling model.

REFERENCES

Ancis, J. R., Choney, S. K., & Sedlacek, W. E. (1996). University student attitudes toward American Indians. *Journal of Multicultural Counseling and Development, 24,* 26–36.

Baldwin, J. A., & Hopkins, R. (1990). African-American and European-American cultural differences as assessed by the worldviews paradigm: An empirical analysis. *Western Journal of Black Studies, 14*(1), 38–52.

Harper, F. D., & Stone, W. O. (1999). Transcendent counseling (TC): A theoretical approach for the year 2000 and beyond. In J. McFadden (Ed.), *Transcultural counseling* (2nd ed., pp. 83–108). Alexandria, VA: American Counseling Association.

Heinrich, R. K., Corbine, J. L., & Thomas, K. R. (1990). Counseling Native Americans. *Journal of Counseling and Development, 69,* 128–133.

Herring, R. D. (1999). *Counseling with Native Americans and Alaska Natives.* Thousand Oaks, CA: Sage.

Ibrahim, F. A. (1999). Transcultural counseling: Existential worldview theory and cultural identity. In J. McFadden (Ed.), *Transcultural counseling* (2nd ed., pp. 23–58). Alexandria, VA: American Counseling Association.

McFadden, J. (Ed.). (1999). *Transcultural counseling* (2nd ed.). Alexandria, VA: American Counseling Association.

McFadden J., Johnson, R., Dogan, T., et al. (2001). *The Benjamin E. Mays Academy for Leadership Development Participant Survey Report.* Unpublished manuscript. University of South Carolina at Columbia.

Rodriguez, R. (1998, June 11). Plotting the assassination of little red sambo: Psychologists join war against racist campus mascots. *Black Issues in Higher Education, 15*(8), 20–24.

Snipp, C. M. (1997). Some observations about racial boundaries and the experiences of *American Indians. Ethnic and Racial Studies, 20*(4), 667–690.

Thomason, T. C. (1991). Counseling Native Americans: An introduction for non-native American counselors. *Journal of Counseling and Development, 69*(4), 321–327.

Appendix 14.1
Stylistic Counseling
Self-Assessment

JOHN McFADDEN AND MARTY JENCIUS

Directions: **In your role as counselor, respond to the following questions in relationship to a particular client.**

Question	Never	Occasionally	Frequently	Always
1. Are you knowledgeable and sensitive to client's history of oppression?				
2. Are you aware of ways in which discrimination has impacted the psychological self-concept of your client?				
3. Are you aware of how race relations influence your client's racial identity and behavior?				
4. Do you have an understanding of the major aspects of oppression and how it impacted your client's formation of personal culture?				

(continued)

Question	Never	Occasionally	Frequently	Always
5. Do you understand how oppression of your client's ethnic origins has led to issues of internal and external security?				
6. Do you understand the logic of your client's thoughts and behaviors?				
7. Do you understand the history of values embraced by your client's culture?				
8. Do you understand the psychology and sociology of your client's self-concept formation?				
9. Do you understand the goals and goal attainment of your client's self-concept?				
10. Do you understand the historic family patterns of the client with whom you work?				
11. Do you understand the personality formation of your client?				
12. Do you understand the examination of choices for effective decision making made by your client?				
13. Do you understand your client's affiliation with a particular ethnic group and the ways in which he/she has optimized his/her membership to that group?				
14. Do you understand the nature of social forces that impact your client's life and behavior?				
15. Do you understand the positive and negative ways in which the media impacts society's view of your client's culture?				

Question	Never	Occasionally	Frequently	Always
16. Do you understand the impact of historic movements and the alteration of community and government programs and their impact on your client?				
17. Do you understand how your client conditions his or her own mental capacity to become productive and useful?				
18. Do you understand the ways in which political groups influence your client's ethnic group?				
19. Do you understand how your client's cultural traditions have developed and created continuity across generations?				
20. Do you understand how your client maintains his or her unique identity within the cultural context?				
21. Do you understand the potential ability of your client's ethnic group to unify and solidify his or her power?				
22. Are you aware of the culture-specific mentors and role models in your client's life?				
23. Do you understand the ideas and visions of people your client has that emerged as a result of interfacing with others?				
24. Are you aware of programs for your client that help him or her bond with values that your client's ethnicity holds special?				
25. Do you understand the development of language within your client's culture?				

(continued)

Question	Never	Occasionally	Frequently	Always
26. Do you understand the ways in which your client can enhance or improve him or herself within a cultural/ethnic context?				
27. Do you understand how institutions, organizations, community, or society has an impact on your client's cultural group?				
28. Do you understand the culture of your client and how it evolved historically across time?				
29. Do you understand your client's psychological framework and mindset, and how it has influenced his or her scope of development?				
30. Do you focus on the action-oriented aspect of the counseling process with your client?				

Never = 1; Occasionally = 2; Frequently = 3; Always = 4

Cultural-historical dimension: 1, 4, 7, 10, 13, 16, 19, 22, 25, 28
Psychosocial dimension: 2, 5, 8, 11, 14, 17, 20, 23, 26, 29
Scientific-ideological dimension: 3, 6, 9, 12, 15, 18, 21, 24, 27, 30

15 Transcendent Counseling: An Existential, Cognitive-Behavioral Theory

FREDERICK D. HARPER AND WINIFRED O. STONE

We originated transcendent counseling as a theory for counseling African Americans (Harper & Stone, 1973; Harper & Stone, 1974). As the first two African American, male, Ph.D. graduates in counselor education from Florida State University, we concluded that traditional counseling theories were not relevant for effective counseling with African Americans. In 1985, after twelve years of writing, speaking, and training on the topic of transcendent counseling with African Americans, we refocused and expanded our theory to be applicable across cultures or to be a multicultural theory of counseling (Stone & Harper 1985; Harper & Stone, 1986). Over the years, we have been asked on a number of occasions during conference presentations, how would we classify our counseling theory in terms of the traditional schools of thought. We hesitated to address this issue; however, in a previous publication on transcendent counseling, we reluctantly classified the theory as a cognitive-behavioral model (Harper & Stone, 1999). Just recently, Exum, Moore, and Watt (1999) categorized transcendent counseling as a behavioral model of counseling, perceiving it as having a central focus on learning principles.

In preparation for writing this chapter, we carried out a content analysis of concepts and counseling strategies from theoretical statements of the theory (Harper & Stone, 1986, 1993, 1999) and concluded that transcendent counseling can be categorized as an existential, cognitive-behavioral theory of counseling. Therefore, we will call it, for the purposes of this chapter and possibly hereafter, an existential, cognitive-behavioral theory of counseling that has broad applications for counseling diverse clientele groups. For example, (1) existential themes of our theory include the concepts of "choice," "transcendence," and "meaningful activity;" and (2) cognitive-behavioral counseling strategies and concepts include "lifestyle modification," "cognitive reorientation," "behavioral rehearsal," and "approval." Based on our content analysis, Table 15.1 presents qualitative data and results of a simple analysis indicating how concepts and strategies of transcendent counseling are classified under existential, cognitive, and behavioral counseling categories.

TABLE 15.1 **Existential, Cognitive, and Behavioral Themes of Transcendent Counseling**

Existential	Cognitive	Behavioral
Action to change lifestyle	Attitudes about living	Approval
Choice to change lifestyle	Beliefs (about a way of life)	Behavioral rehearsal
Meaning in life and work	Cognitive reorientation	Biofeedback
Transcendence	Memories in life	Fieldwork or homework
Will power to change	Perceptions	Learned lifestyle
	Persuading client to rethink	Lifestyle modification
	Teaching a new way of life	Relaxation techniques
	Thoughts drive lifestyle	Role modeling

Note: Lifestyle modification and lifestyle change are used interchangeably.

An Overview of the Theory

Before discussing specific aspects of transcendent counseling, it may be feasible here to present a brief overview of the theory. As regards culture and diversity, transcendent counseling can be viewed as a multicultural, cross-cultural, transcultural, intracultural, transethnic, transnational, transgender, and metacultural theory of counseling (Harper & Stone, 1999). In other words, our theoretical approach can be used across cultures, within cultures, across ethnic groups, across nations, across gender lines, and even beyond cultures (e.g., various age groups). Transcendent counseling goes beyond cultures in that it is designed to be employed with special or diverse populations, including persons with disabilities, children, and persons of diverse identities (e.g., sexual identity or orientation). Transcendent counseling focuses on the goals of positive lifestyle change, need-fulfillment, holistic health, meaningful work or activity, and self-understanding/improved relations with others. Nevertheless, the central goal of transcendent counseling is positive lifestyle change. The five steps of counseling, as represented by the acronym APART, are assessment of lifestyle, prescription for a new lifestyle, action toward change, review of the client's progress and change, and transcendence of one's old lifestyle or one's negative environment. Transcendent counseling focuses on any of six modules or areas of living and uses both training modalities and fieldwork/homework, along with counseling, in order to achieve positive lifestyle change and other transcendent counseling goals. The modules of living include (1) survival, (2) holistic health, (3) human/ethnic relations, (4) knowledge about self and living, (5) meaningful and productive work or activity, and (6) self-regulation of body energy. One-to-one counseling skills of transcendent counseling include supportive skills (reassurance and approval), teaching skills (information giving, modeling, and advice giving), and action-provoking/action-sustaining skills (motivating, confronting, and encouraging).

Goals of Counseling

The primary goal of transcendent counseling is positive lifestyle change. Lifestyle is defined as a person's way of life or one's daily or weekly habits, activities, and behavior patterns. A person's lifestyle reflects his or her values in life and attitudes about living. Moreover, as appropriate to the client's concerns or problems, secondary goals of counseling are need-fulfillment, holistic health, meaningful work or activity, self-understanding, and improved relations with others.

Need-Fulfillment

Need-fulfillment involves satisfying the basic needs that are common to all human beings, regardless of cultural background, ethnic origin, or gender. As delineated by Maslow (1970), basic human needs include physiological maintenance, safety, belongingness and love, esteem, and self-actualization. The ability of a client to satisfy his or her basic needs is often influenced by the client's ethnic, social, political, religious, or economic status within a given culture or country as well as the drive or motivation of that client toward the self-fulfillment of needs. Need-fulfillment also depends on the ability of a culture or country to meet the needs of its people at a given time in history (Maslow, 1968, 1970; Harper & Stone, 1999).

Holistic Health

The goal of holistic health is defined as an interdependent state of physical, psychological, and spiritual health. Holistic health is a welding together of a healthy mind, body, and spirit into one synergistic, fully functioning, whole person.

Meaningful Work or Activity

Meaningful work or activity includes a meaningful job or career that yields financial compensation as well as personal self-fulfillment, based on a useful service or product for other human beings. This goal also includes nonpaid, meaningful activity such as (1) volunteer service to one's community or the world ecology; (2) meaningful leisure activity; and (3) training, formal education, travel, or other learning experiences.

Self-Understanding and Improved Relations With Others

This goal involves one's improved understanding of self in terms of perceived identities (e.g., human identity, ethnic identity, physical self, family identity, sexual identity, and work identity) and perceived worth as a human being (self-esteem). This counseling goal also includes effective relationships with other human beings regardless of their background, identity, or way of living.

Theoretical Assumptions

A theory can be defined as a set of interrelated assumptions or propositions (Harper & Bruce-Sanford, 1989) that can be used as a model or guide for practice, as in the case of counseling (Gladding, 2000). We developed a set of assumptions for transcendent counseling from its beginning (Harper & Stone, 1973, 1974). These were expanded in 1986 (Harper & Stone, 1986) and then parsimoniously reduced to ten assumptions in our last published theoretical statement (Harper & Stone, 1999). The assumptions that follow are essentially the same ten statements from 1999, except for minor changes in language.

1. Counseling is a dynamic growth experience wherein people learn to change the way they live, the way they perceive themselves, and the way they perceive their world.
2. Lasting change in one's behavior comes with a change in lifestyle. The lifestyle of a person tends to be influenced by that person's genetic predisposition, life experiences, and self-perceptions of experiences. One's cultural background is reflected by that person's way of life as it evolves over time, place, experiences, and social class. A person's basic cultural orientation is developed during the formative years of childhood; however, it continues to evolve with cross-cultural and cross-social-class experiences over the life span.
3. Cultural differences are often represented by lifestyle differences in terms of a person's daily activities, behavioral patterns, customs, habits, language, and ritualistic ways. These lifestyle activities are influenced by learned thoughts that are demonstrated by one's attitudes, beliefs, values, and perceptions.
4. Although people differ across cultures with regard to lifestyle and worldview, they have the same basic needs, drives, emotions, and capacity for thought (Maslow, 1970).
5. As biological and social organisms, human beings are limited by inherent human frailty and vulnerability; nevertheless, they are capable of self-improvement and transcendence.
6. Human beings are relatively fixed in a daily lifestyle; however, they are capable of changing that lifestyle toward a direction of self-improvement and ultimate transcendence of a socialized and often ineffective way of living. This assumption is further explained by seven "we" subassumptions:
   - We tend to do today what we did yesterday, and we likely will do tomorrow what we do today.
   - We do what we do until we perceive the need to do differently, a need that is often precipitated by a crisis and/or awareness that lead to cognitive reorientation.
   - We do what we do until we acquire the will power to do what we must do.
   - We and only we can change our life; nobody can do it for us because we and only we are the masters of our energy—our own vessel of life.
   - We must change; otherwise, we will be destined to live our miseries over and over in our memories and in our experiences. If we change, we will

discover the fulfillment, happiness, and peace that come with existential choice and action.

- We cannot know what true happiness is until we experience it. We experience happiness by seeking it, and we experience pain by letting it capture us.
- We are nobody until we feel like somebody. Our life remains an empty shell until we fill it with meaningful experiences that are worthy of our memories and our living.

7. Regardless of one's cultural background or ethnic identity, the "good life" can be universally defined as a lifestyle characterized by (1) holistic health; (2) meaningful activity or work; (3) positive self-management of one's energy; (4) a healthy, respectful, and homeostatic relationship with life and life's spiritual source; and (5) effective interpersonal relations.

8. Presenting behaviors that come to counseling are often interrelated in a mosaic pattern that has developed over time. The route to changing patterns of behavior is through a sustainable change in one's lifestyle. This road to positive change of lifestyle takes time, patience, and consistency; and it is a road that is not free from temporary setbacks, human frustration, and personal resignation.

9. Behaviors, to a great degree, are need driven, mood driven, and even programmed over time as automatic responses. Nevertheless, the human being is capable of self-initiation (starting and maintaining behavior) and self-control (pacing and stopping behavior). This possibility for change comes with new ways of perceiving and relating to one's world from day to day and, thus, new ways of acting and living.

10. Awareness, cognitive reorientation, will power, and action make up the orderly sequence toward lifestyle change and transcendence (Figure 15.1). The most powerful resource of a human being is the capacity to change, that is, to transcend social conditions and human imperfections to a high level of holistic health, self-fulfillment, and human functioning.

Steps of Transcendent Counseling

Represented by the acronym APART, the five steps of transcendent counseling are (1) assessment, (2) prescription, (3) action, (4) review, and (5) transcendence. Symbolically, the APART acronym connotes the term *apart*, as in apart from the old self or old lifestyle and toward a new self and a new way of living.

Assessment (Step 1)

As the initial step of the counseling relationship, the transcendent counselor establishes rapport with the client and assesses the client's problem or concern. The counselor focuses on the needs and lifestyle of the client in terms of need deficiencies, daily habits, recurring activities, and behavioral patterns. Moreover, the counselor solicits the client's input about things that he or she would like to change and

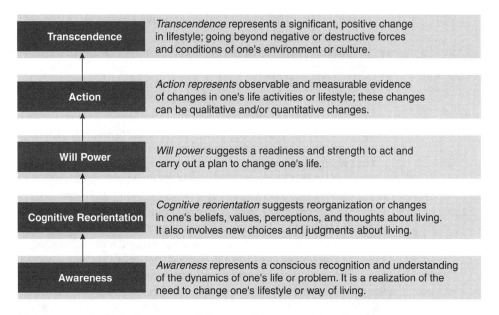

Figure 15.1   Orderly Sequence of Human Change or Lifestyle Change

evaluates this input along with other interview information, historical information, and assessment data about the client.

Along with a focused or structured interview, the counselor might use an
assessment technique that employs a dual listing and sorting of lifestyle activities
that cover the span of a week or longer. This technique would involve the priori-
tizing or ranking of daily activities and habits that the client would like to stop or
minimize (on the left side of a sheet) as compared to a listing of things the client
would like to start or maximize in life (on the opposite side or right side of the
sheet). The counselor may choose to assign a negative (–1), neutral (0), or positive
(+1) value to noteworthy daily habits or recurring lifestyle activities. The counselor
should always note that when a neutral or positive activity in life becomes excessive, it can become a negative habit or lifestyle activity and, therefore, be assigned
a negative value (–1). For example, eating is a positive and essential life activity for
survival; however, excessive eating can lead to obesity and health problems. By the
same token, moderate alcohol consumption is not a negative life practice; however,
excessive, frequent use of alcohol can lead to alcohol addiction, illness, social problems, and economic losses, among other lifestyle consequences. In addition, a
deficit or lack of an essential activity in one's lifestyle can yield a negative value,
for example, sedentary living or an absence of exercise, a dire lack of food for survival, or absence of a job or meaningful activity in life.

In assessing lifestyle, the counselor should be cognizant of criteria of assessment such as the nature, frequency, absence, and/or intensity of a lifestyle activity

as well as the lifestyle activity as related to the cultural context and developmental stage of the client. Subsequent to the collection of information about the client's lifestyle, the transcendent counselor categorizes significant negative or deficit lifestyle activities into one or more modules or areas of living as preparation for developing goals and intervention strategies for counseling. The assessment stage can take one counseling session or several sessions as necessary in order to accurately assess the client's human needs and lifestyle.

Prescription (Step 2)

After the counselor's assessment of the client's lifestyle and needs, goals of counseling and a prescription of intervention modalities are derived for lifestyle modification. Moreover, the prescription results in additional counseling sessions for the primary purpose of information giving as well as facilitating, motivating, and monitoring the prescribed actions for the client. The prescription may also provide for activities such as self-practice modalities, group training modalities (e.g., relaxation training, meditation, and biofeedback), and/or group counseling activities (e.g., role playing, behavioral rehearsal, nonverbal exercises, and psychodrama). In prescribing activities for lifestyle modification, the counselor involves the client in the development of the action program and its activities and solicits a sense of client commitment to action and follow through.

Action (Step 3)

The counseling process and subsequent client change normally involve the orderly stages of exploration, understanding, and action (Egan, 2002; Okun, 2002). However, wherein traditional counseling theories tend to focus on change of behavior, transcendent counseling emphasizes the client's change in lifestyle through action. The client's action is based on the prescribed program or activities of Step 2 and involves motivation, support, and necessary information giving from the counselor in order to enhance the client's progress. If appropriate, the counselor serves as a role model or exposes the client to positive models of successful lifestyle change.

In counseling cases with minors (children and youth), issues of survival (e.g., starvation or suicide risk), or clients who have physical or psychological limitations (e.g., clients with disabilities, rape survivors, or spousal abuse survivors), the counselor may have to take the necessary action to access social justice, social services, or appropriate resources on behalf of the client. Nevertheless, the counselor must be careful not to enable inaction but to assist initiation of action until a client is capable of assisting in the lifestyle change or sustaining a lifestyle change. Moreover, the counselor (1) anticipates barriers, pitfalls, and problems of lifestyle change; (2) follows the client's actions or lifestyle change closely; and (3) encourages a record of daily and weekly successes and changes in lifestyle activities. Both the client and the counselor keep complete records of lifestyle activities and successes.

Review (Step 4)

Step 4 involves a review or evaluation of the client's progress based on the preestablished goals of Step 2. The review is based primarily on formative evaluation or ongoing feedback during the counseling relationship (Weiss, 1998). If there is a lack of sufficient success as related to preestablished criteria of progress, the counselor and client may have to repeat a previous stage. This recycling process is for the purpose of accountability, and, when appropriate, it may suggest a need to revise the assessment of lifestyle, statement of goals, and use of modalities and counseling strategies.

Transcendence (Step 5)

Transcendence is evidenced by a significant change in a major area or module of the client's life to a point where it is suggested that the change will be maintained or sustained over time. Evidence of sustained lifestyle change is indicated by significant, observable, and measurable changes in life activities. For example, an alcoholic who no longer drinks alcohol, has been involved in inpatient treatment, and has been attending Alcoholics Anonymous (AA) meetings regularly would be a candidate for transcendence of a previous lifestyle of alcoholism or a lifestyle that was characterized by frequent, heavy drinking and all its accompanying life problems and interpersonal conflicts. As a part of Step 5, upon termination of counseling, follow up is required in order to minimize the client's relapse to the previous, ineffective lifestyle.

Modules and Modalities of Change

As stated previously, transcendent counseling identifies six major modules or areas of human living that are related to Steps 1 and 2 of transcendent counseling. The six modules are related to the goals of counseling (Step 2) and represent the lifestyle areas of the client's problem or concerns based on the counselor's assessment (Step 1). The modules are (1) survival, (2) holistic health, (3) human/ethnic relations, (4) knowledge about self and living, (5) meaningful and productive work or activity, and (6) self-regulation. These modules are not mutually exclusive but may overlap in terms of areas of living. The modules of living are described as follows:

1. Survival represents client problems related to striving to satisfy basic needs for physical survival in circumstances or conditions such as starvation, life-threatening disease (e.g., cancer and AIDS), inadequate shelter, natural or climactic catastrophes (e.g., earthquakes, tornadoes, cyclones, and hurricanes), accidental catastrophes (e.g., airplane crashes, vehicular accidents, and structural failures), and violence or violent threat (e.g., violent crime, terrorism, and warfare). Furthermore, the module of "survival" involves client issues related to psychological survival in cases such as

(a) sexual rape, (b) grief because of the death of a loved one or other significant losses, (c) suicidal ideation of clients, (d) child sexual or physical abuse, (e) psychological or physical abandonment as a child, or (f) spousal abuse.

2. Holistic health addresses lifestyle concerns or problems that impede physical, psychological, and spiritual well being. Some of the counseling problems within this module include (a) physical disease, (b) eating disorders and other lifestyle-related mental disorders (American Psychiatric Association, 1994), (c) improper nutrition, (d) sedentary living versus exercise, (e) stressful living (rushing and overloading activities), (f) lack of spiritual meaning or awareness in life, (g) lack of meaningful work in life, and (h) drug addiction. Transcendent counseling values communing with outdoors and nature. It also values regular physical exercise that contributes to cardiovascular and respiratory benefits, disease prevention, physical health enhancement, and psychological benefits of relaxation and stress reduction. Persons with physical disabilities are encouraged to participate in physical exercise or physical activities based on their abilities and with the aid of prosthetics, instrumentation, or assistance from others. For example, a person with an ambulatory, physical disability may be assisted in climbing a mountain with the aid of prosthetics and a team, or a person who is visually impaired may be assisted in jogging or track and field competition.

3. Human/ethnic relations focus on areas of ongoing tension or conflict in interpersonal relations, human relations, and ethnic or race relations. Examples of problems of counseling that are represented within this module are within-family conflict (e.g., marital, parent–child, or sibling conflict), job-related interpersonal conflict, romantic conflict, friendship conflict, intergroup conflict (racial, ethnic, religious, age, etc.), and teacher–student conflict. These conflicts in relationships are lifestyle problems because they recur as a theme of life and, thus, interfere with effective and harmonious living.

4. Knowledge about self and living represents problems in life that are centered on a lack of accurate and relevant information for self-understanding and effective living. This knowledge includes appropriate information, attitudes, values, and skills transmitted to the client by way of counseling, training, printed materials, media, personal and vicarious experiences, and other methods. Knowledge about self and effective living includes information about health, family, child care, emotional management, financial management, human sexuality, human behavior, job opportunities, training opportunities, career and educational planning, and information about available social services and resources for survival and self-improvement. The "knowledge" modules overlap other modules of transcendent counseling to some degree because information given in counseling cuts across diverse counseling concerns such as education, job placement, career planning, personal-social problems, and health.

5. Meaningful and productive work or activity implies that the holistically healthy person must have some meaningful and/or productive work or activity in life. Lack of such activity creates a void in one's life that can result in feelings of depression, lowered self-esteem, emptiness, and a sense of unworthiness. Meaningful and productive work or activity, whether for pay or not, should result in self-fulfillment; a useful or aesthetic product for society; a service to society; and/or preparation for a future career, job, or endeavor. Examples of meaningful and productive work/activity include higher-education study, career or vocational training, career work, volunteer service, and a chosen hobby.

6. Self-regulation involves an area of living that affects all human beings, regardless of culture or ethnicity. It relates to the person's ongoing effort to regulate or manage his or her human energy in terms of (a) achieving or maintaining organismic balance, peace, or equilibrium; (b) energizing the self for work or activity; and (c) relaxing or slowing down body energy because of stress, extreme anxiety, or physical exertion. This module also focuses on client awareness of environment and how the person's energy may interact with environmental conditions and forces.

Phases of Multiethnic Identity Development

Within the modules of human/ethnic relations and knowledge about self and living, transcendent counseling accounts for lifestyle problems and concerns of ethnic identity, multiethnic identity development, and ethnic relations. The two modules accommodate ethnocultural development and maturity through individual counseling, skills training, group work, and information giving. We view ethnic identity in terms of how the client perceives his or her ethnicity and relationship to other ethnic groups. We view multiethnic identity development as growth on a developmental continuum from ethnoentropy (alienation from one's ethnicity of origin) to panethnicity (the highest level of ethnic maturity as identification with the entire human race). Figure 15.2 presents a schema of phases of multiethnic identity development that demonstrate the various levels of ethnic maturity from the least matured to the most matured ethnic phase (Stone, 1975, 1984; Harper & Stone, 1993, 1999). As with our model of multiethnic identity development, most ethnic identity models suggest that the client or counselor grows from accepting his or her own ethnicity of origin to accepting all races, ethnicities, and cultures of the world or toward cultural or ethnic maturity at the highest level (e.g., Cross, 1980; Carter & Helms, 1992).

We conceptualize ethnic identity as having two dimensions, state and trait, in the same manner as state-trait anxiety and state-trait anger (Spielberger & Sydeman, 1994). Therefore, ethnic identity can be assessed in terms of how the client feels about his or her ethnic identity and relationship to other ethnic groups from "moment to moment" (state ethnic identity) and how the client "generally feels" about his or her ethnic identity and relationship to other ethnic groups (trait ethnic identity). As compared to state ethnic identity, trait ethnic identity is more stable and less affected by racial or ethnic incidents or experiences. The state-trait principle of multiethnic identity development is represented by the reversed pairs of arrows between each level of the five phases of development in Figure 15.2. These pairs of arrows (pointed up or down) in the

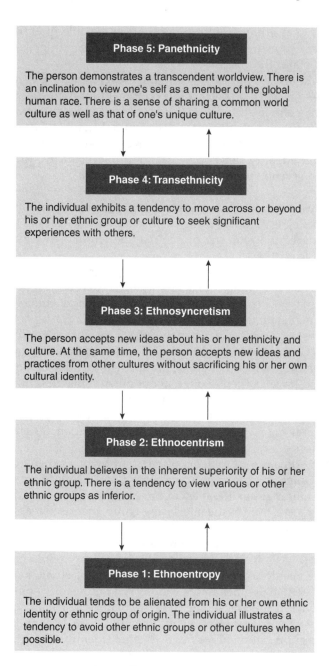

Phase 5: Panethnicity

The person demonstrates a transcendent worldview. There is an inclination to view one's self as a member of the global human race. There is a sense of sharing a common world culture as well as that of one's unique culture.

Phase 4: Transethnicity

The individual exhibits a tendency to move across or beyond his or her ethnic group or culture to seek significant experiences with others.

Phase 3: Ethnosyncretism

The person accepts new ideas about his or her ethnicity and culture. At the same time, the person accepts new ideas and practices from other cultures without sacrificing his or her own cultural identity.

Phase 2: Ethnocentrism

The individual believes in the inherent superiority of his or her ethnic group. There is a tendency to view various or other ethnic groups as inferior.

Phase 1: Ethnoentropy

The individual tends to be alienated from his or her own ethnic identity or ethnic group of origin. The individual illustrates a tendency to avoid other ethnic groups or other cultures when possible.

FIGURE 15.2   A Paradigm of Phases of Multiethnic Identity Development

paradigm indicate that ethnic identity has fluid or flexible qualities that can change, in either direction, depending on environmental conditions and circumstances, especially state ethnic identity.

Using our paradigm of multiethnic identity development, the transcendent counselor identifies the stage or phase of development for each client by way of matching the client's ethnic attitudes, self-perceptions, and experiences with the criteria of an appropriately matching phase (see Figure 15.2 for criteria appropriate to each phase). Thereafter, the counselor intevenes with strategies that will enhance multiethnic identity development and ethnic maturity. The following implications and interventions for each phase are provided:

1. Ethnoentropy (Phase 1). Within this phase, the prognosis for progress of individual counseling is minimal. If the client is terminated early in the individual counseling relationship, he or she may be referred to a group on the theme of ethnic relations.

2. Ethnocentrism (Phase 2). The prognosis for progress is improved in this phase. Individual and group counseling strategies may be effective in achieving desired goals. Also, information groups (about race, ethnicity, and culture) and ethnic-relations training may be considered.

3. Ethnosyncretism (Phase 3). Clients in this phase are often interested in feeling more comfortable with their own ethnic identity and ethnic group versus seeking experiences with other ethnic groups. They tend to assume that they are liberal and have learned enough about other ethnicities for the present time. In this case, the counselor encourages ongoing cross-cultural learning or lifestyle changes by way of bibliocounseling (multicultural books), ethnic or multicultural courses, cross-cultural group experiences, cross-cultural travel, and cross-ethnic relationships.

4. Transethnicity (Phase 4). Problems of rejection by one's own ethnic group may be encountered when significant contact and interface are maintained with another ethnic group. Resistance or rejection may be received from one's own ethnic group as well as the interfacing group. Increased reassurance and encouragement by the counselor and the development of awareness by the client are realistic areas of focus for counseling.

5. Panethnicity (Phase 5). This phase of ethnic identity represents transcendence for the client, or attaining the highest level of ethnic maturity. Evidence of self-actualizing behaviors is observed and readily apparent in the client's lifestyle. At this phase, the client (a) realizes a state of comfort with human beings regardless of ethnicity or culture; (b) is comfortable with knowing and appreciating his or her own ethnic identity of origin; and (c) is not affected by the negative, ethnic reactions, rejections, or comments from persons of other ethnic groups or his or her own ethnic group. The client who is in this phase has reached the highest level of ethnic identity maturity and multiethnic identity development; therefore, the panethnic is not likely to need counseling for concerns related to ethnic or cultural identity, development, or relations.

Modalities of Counseling

In addition to one-to-one counseling, transcendent counseling employs modalities in the forms of structured training and fieldwork/homework practice. Modalities serve as adjuncts to counseling for the purpose of facilitating positive lifestyle changes. The examples of modalities discussed within this section are those recommended for specific modules of counseling. Nonetheless, the counselor should not limit his or her creativity to our recommendations but should explore additional therapeutic modalities that could be effective in changing the client's lifestyle.

The modalities are designed to bring about lifestyle changes for the purposes of therapy and prevention as related to specific lifestyle modules. For example, a client's tendency to rush through life, make excessive errors, and react to insignificant events or distractions in daily living would fall under the module of "self-regulation," and would incorporate modalities of stress reduction such as relaxation training, meditation, time-management training, or biofeedback. Any one of these modalities can be incorporated into the client's lifestyle through a formal group (e.g., meditation or relaxation group) or via individualized homework or fieldwork that allows for self-practice between counseling sessions. Fieldwork is differentiated from homework, wherein it occurs outside the home setting or in any natural setting. The counselor may also suggest daily practice or learning strategies for time management, for example, techniques related to focusing, organizing, listening, and starting on time to avoid rushing. Following are listed the six modules of transcendent counseling with suggested modalities in parentheses for each module.

1. Survival (counselor's acquisition of social services and resources to fulfill the daily needs of the client, self-help groups, bibliocounseling, grief group counseling, consultation, and survival information groups).
2. Holistic health (health-information groups, AIDS/HIV prevention groups, human sexuality guidance, encounter groups [other growth groups], anger management, stress-reduction exercises, nutritional guidance, meditation training, spirituality activities, bibliocounseling, therapeutic poetry, walking, jogging, dancing, swimming, aerobic exercises, mountain climbing, and biking).
3. Human/ethnic relations (psychodrama, sociodrama, role playing, behavioral rehearsal, bibliocounseling, interpersonal-effectiveness training, encounter group, group counseling, ethnic relations training, cross-cultural travel, and academic courses in multiculturalism and/or ethnic studies).
4. Knowledge about self and living (psychological assessment, bibliocounseling, information groups, growth groups, values orientation groups, attitudinal exploration groups, career workshops, effective relationship workshops, seminars about race and racism, various seminars and growth groups related to living).
5. Meaningful and productive work/activity (career information groups, college courses, career practicum experiences, volunteer work experiences, occupational/vocational training, and career planning).

6. Self-regulation (biofeedback, meditation, relaxation therapy, therapeutic touch, hypnosis or self-hypnosis, yoga, anger management, and energy management exercises). Note: Therapeutic touch, as a healing adjunct, is being taught in nursing and medical schools. This modality facilitates relaxation and, thus, client self-disclosure during the therapeutic process (Krieger, 1993). The counselor may also recommend therapeutic massage as a relaxation or stress-reducing modality.

The Transcendent Being of the Counselor

The overall goal of the transcendent counselor is to help the client to make a positive lifestyle change, a change that is relatively permanent and not transient or subject to recidivism. The transcendent counselor comes to counseling with a holistically healthy attitude about self, the client, and life, and, thus, possesses the same ideals for himself or herself that are held for the client, that is, ideals of holistic health and continual striving for self-improvement and growth. By doing so or by being and becoming, the transcendent counselor is more qualified to present himself or herself as a positive role model for the client's imitation and inspiration.

The transcendent counselor believes that all clients, regardless of culture, ethnicity, social class, gender, sexual identity, or state of ability, are equally worthy of help, growth, and holistic health to the highest degree possible. Therefore, the counselor attempts to understand and help while avoiding bias against and prejudicial judgment about the client as a member of any socially defined group. The transcendent counselor attempts to understand the client as a unique person and not as a stereotypical social image—although cultural and social knowledge about the client's background may or may not play a part in assisting the counselor to understand and address the client's problems and needs.

The transcendent counselor perceives the counseling relationship as an opportunity for professional and personal self-growth. As a mutual growth experience, the counseling relationship becomes an experience from which both the client and the counselor grow. The transcendent counselor views healthy ethnic identity as approximating or attaining a panethnic view of the world or an acceptance of oneself as a member of the human race or world culture of humankind. The counselor values the positive ways, customs, habits, and achievements of all cultures of origin and rejects or transcends cultural ways that are nonproductive or unnaturally destructive to human beings or the global ecology. In addition, the transcendent counselor encourages clients to make the same type of cultural evaluation and analysis for themselves and their overall need-fulfillment and growth. Lastly, the transcendent counselor continually strives to seek and acquire cross-cultural education and experiences that promote personal and professional growth as well as greater understanding of self and clients.

The Counseling Process

Transcendent counseling takes the viewpoint that thoughts drive not only behavior but also lifestyle. Therefore, the counseling process aims to assist and persuade the client to change ways of thinking and thus change undesirable ways of living; in other words, to modify his or her lifestyle. The transcendent counselor serves in the role of an information giver, facilitator, motivator, role model, group trainer, and, at times, a teacher of living. The counselor goes about facilitating change in the client's ways of thinking and living by (1) teaching the client to say "I won't" and not "I can't"; (2) initially persuading the client to make an expressed promise, resolution, or commitment to change at least one significant thing in his or her daily living and intermittently soliciting an expression of recommitment if necessary (the counselor emphasizes incremental changes); (3) motivating the client to take action based on his or her expression of commitment or taking action on behalf of the client; and (4) guiding the client to focus on the two "W's," "what" and "when," that is, "*What* are you going to do about your life and *when* are you going to do it?"

Frequently, clients state "I can't" when they really should be saying, "I won't." That is, the client is often allowed, in therapy and counseling, to use and think "I can't change my life" as an excuse for inaction or resistance to action. This dichotomy of terminology, "won't" versus "can't," suggests further that people often know what they need to do, but they have not acquired the will power to act and to do what has to be done.

The transcendent counselor persuades the client to think about initiating something new and constructive in his or her daily living and eliminating something that is old and destructive. Constructive habits in life are based on activities that are valued for health, interpersonal effectiveness, existential meaning, personal growth and fulfillment, achievement based on one's talent and ability, and harmonious living with others and with Earth's ecology. While holding important these universal values of the human race and the global community, the counselor also takes into consideration the client's cultural perspective about what is the good and constructive life. The counselor's rapport and effective helping relationship are facilitated by his or her orientation to continually (1) grow as a person; (2) maintain a state of peace and balance as much as possible; (3) strive toward a healthy self in mind, body, and spirit; and (4) maintain a constant orientation of helping and giving.

In working with the client, the counselor maintains a respect for the client as a human being and not a physical image or stereotypical identity that represents preconceived and predefined attributes of personality, gender, culture, social class, physical ability, or educational level. Moreover, the counselor believes in the client as a person who is capable of changing his or her way of living, and, therefore, holds high expectations for the client's possibilities while maintaining patience and the realization that relatively permanent change takes time.

The transcendent counselor primarily employs verbal counseling skills that can be taxonomized into three categories: supportive skills, teaching skills, and action-provoking/action-sustaining skills. Examples and descriptions of these skills are as follows:

Supportive Skills

Approval: verbal reward or positive reinforcement that is dispensed intermittently after the client's positive expression of commitment or completion of a positive act in daily lifestyle practice or activities.

Reassurance: a verbal expression of comfort or support toward the client during a difficult or painful step in changing one's life or during a difficult period of transition in life.

Teaching Skills

Information giving: basic verbal, media, or printed information about effective living that the transcendent counselor shares with the client; the information should be related to the client's problem, concern, or lifestyle goals.

Modeling: the use of social modeling or role modeling as learning examples for the client (e.g., live role models, vicarious models in books and media, personal illustration, and impersonal illustration). The purpose is to use positive or successful role models in order to inspire the client to imitate the positive lifestyle of the model, whether the model is real or vicarious. Although not always feasible or appropriate, the counselor considers the use of models that reflect a client's ethnic or cultural image or a client's gender or identity.

Advice giving: the counselor shares a number of options, courses of action, or solutions for the client's consideration. Moreover, the counselor solicits the client's feedback and opinions, especially as related to the client's worldview and based on his or her cultural worldview and experiential perspective. This exchange becomes a learning experience for the client's decision making rather than a telling experience by the counselor.

Action-Provoking/Action-Sustaining Skills

Motivating: verbal motivation, encouragement, and inspiration as a means of persuading the client to start or stop an activity or habit in life as well as to maintain a positive activity or habit once it is started.

Confrontation: in a case where the client is consistently resistant or in denial, the counselor confronts the client in a nonthreatening manner in order to facilitate awareness and remove emotional blocks to choice and action. The client can often provide illogical or nonsignificant reasons for procrastination or avoiding action that is necessary for growth and lifestyle change.

Encouragement: a verbal expression of motivation and support for the client during an ongoing pursuit of a difficult goal or challenge in life.

Conclusion

Transcendent counseling is a theoretical approach to counseling that has a central focus on positive lifestyle change. It has applications across diverse clientele groups and with a variety of human problems and concerns. Transcendent counseling is an existential, cognitive-behavioral approach; therefore, it focuses on client choice and meaning in life and it employs cognitive and behavioral intervention strategies in ways that yield observable and measurable outcomes in terms of lifestyle changes. Unlike traditional counseling theories, transcendent counseling is a holistic approach that addresses body, mind, and spirit as integrated, related, and interdependent aspects of overall health. The process of counseling is viewed not only as a helping process for clients but also as a learning process for both the counselor and the client. Along this line, Axelson (1999) classifies transcendent counseling under "synergetic cultural/environmental models," or models that involve the counselor and client working together toward a common goal that is important for the client from his or her cultural context.

To a degree, transcendent counseling is also a psychoeducational experience wherein the counselor teaches the client effective ways of living. Transcendent counseling involves one-to-one counseling as well as treatment-training modalities, fieldwork or homework, and self-practice—all for the purpose of developing new knowledge, attitudes, skills, habits, and values that contribute to lifestyle change, effective living, and transcendence. An effective lifestyle or the "good life" is defined universally, without regard to culture or social group, as a life of (1) holistic health, (2) meaningful activity or work, (3) positive self-management of one's energy, and (4) effective interpersonal relations.

Transcendent counseling is both a therapeutic (remediative) and preventive theoretical approach. That is, by positively changing one's lifestyle, the client transcends negative conditions of environment, transcends destructive and ineffective ways of living, minimizes or even eliminates human problems that already exist, and prevents the possibility of the occurrence of new human problems. Transcendent counseling is also consultative in that the counselor can service the the role of a consultant in terms of training and educating persons to change their lifestyle.

For examples of counseling cases that demonstrate the process of transcendent counseling, see the earlier publication by Harper and Stone (1993). Moreover, for additional applications of transcendent counseling, beyond what has been discussed in this chapter, see Harper and Stone (1999).

D I S C U S S I O N   Q U E S T I O N S

1. What is the role of assessment and testing within the theory of transcendent counseling? Moreover, what are the implications of assessment (Step 1 of counseling) with regard to the cultural diversity of clientele and other steps of the transcendent counseling process?

2. What counseling problems have no relationship to lifestyle or human need in terms of their etiology, dynamics, or consequences?

3. What diagnostic group or mental disorders of the DSM-IV or International Classification of Diseases (ICD-10) have diagnostic criteria that are related to lifestyle patterns or implications?

4. What are areas, lifestyle habits, or behavioral patterns in your life that you would like to change? Moreover, how could you go about making such changes with the use of transcendent counseling strategies?

5. What is the significance of the ethnicity, cultural background, gender, or sexual orientation of the counselor in achieving the primary goals of transcendent counseling for the client?

6. Why is lifestyle change viewed as more substantial progress for the client as compared to specific behavioral changes?

7. How important or nonsignificant are the phases of multiethnic identity development in the counseling of diverse clientele?

8. Based on the theory of transcendent counseling, what are some of the important personal and professional attributes that a transcendent counselor should communicate and manifest?

REFERENCES

American Psychiatric Association. (1994). *Diagnostic and statistical manual of mental disorders (DSM-IV)* (4th ed.). Washington, DC: Author.

Axelson, J. A. (1999). *Counseling and development in a multicultural society* (3rd ed.). Pacific Grove, CA: Brooks/Cole.

Carter, R. T., & Helms, J. E. (1992). The counseling process as defined by relationship types: A test of Helms' Interactional Model. *Journal of Multicultural Counseling and Development, 20,* 181–201.

Cross, W. E., Jr. (1980). Models of psychological nigrescence: A literature review. In R. L. Jones (Ed.), *Black Psychology* (pp. 81–98). New York: Harper & Row.

Egan, G. (2002). *The skilled helper: A problem-management approach to helping* (7th ed.). Pacific Grove, CA: Brooks/Cole.

Exum, H. A., Moore, Q. L., & Watt, S. K. (1999). Transcultural counseling for African Americans revisited. In J. McFadden (Ed.), *Transcultural counseling* (2nd ed.). Alexandria, VA: American Counseling Association.

Gladding, S. T. (2000). *Counseling: A comprehensive profession* (4th ed.). Englewood Cliffs, NJ: Merrill/Prentice Hall.

Harper, F. D., & Bruce-Sanford, G. C. (1989). *Counseling techniques: An outline and overview.* Alexandria, VA: Douglass.

Harper, F. D., & Stone, W. O. (1973). *Toward a theory of counseling Blacks.* A paper presented at the annual convention of the American Counseling Association, Atlanta.

Harper, F. D., & Stone, W. O. (1974). Toward a theory of transcendent counseling with Blacks. *Journal of Multicultural Counseling and Development, 2,* 191–196.

Harper, F. D., & Stone, W. O. (1986). Transcendent counseling: Toward a multicultural approach. *International Journal for the Advancement of Counselling, 9,* 251–263.

Harper, F. D., & Stone, W. O. (1993). Transcendent counseling: A transcultural theory. In J. McFadden (Ed.), *Transcultural counseling: Bilateral and international perspectives* (pp. 83–107). Alexandria, VA: American Counseling Association.

Harper, F. D., & Stone, W. O. (1999). Transcendent counseling (TC): A theoretical approach for the year 2000 and beyond. In J. McFadden (Ed.), *Transcultural counseling* (2nd ed., pp. 83–108). Alexandria, VA: American Counseling Association.

Krieger, D. (1993). *Accepting your power to heal: The personal practice of therapeutic touch.* Sante Fe, NM: Bvear.

Maslow, A. H. (1968). *Toward a psychology of being* (2nd ed.). New York: Van Nostrand Reinhold.

Maslow, A. H. (1970). *Motivation and personality* (2nd ed.). New York: Harper and Row.

Okun, B. F. (2002). *Effective helping: Interviewing and counseling techniques* (6th ed.). Pacific Grove, CA: Brooks/Cole.

Spielberger, C. D., & Sydeman, S. J. (1994). The State-Trait Anxiety Inventory and the State-Trait Anger Expression Inventory. In M. Maruish (Ed.), *The use of psychological testing for treatment planning and outcome assessment* (pp. 292–321). Hillsdale, NJ: Erlbaum.

Stone, W. O. (1975). Career development for ethnic minorities. In R. C. Reardon & H. D. Burck (Eds.), *Facilitating career development: Strategies for counselors.* (pp. 248–267). Springfield, IL: Charles C. Thomas.

Stone, W. O. (1984). Serving ethnic minorities. In H. D. Burck & R. C. Reardon (Eds.), *Career development interventions* (pp. 267–291). Springfield, IL: Charles C. Thomas.

Stone, W. O., & Harper, F. D. (1985). *Multicultural and multimodal concepts of transcendent counseling: Supportive research.* A paper presented at the International Round Table for the Advancement of Counselling, Utrecht, the Netherlands.

Weiss, C. H. (1998). *Evaluation* (2nd ed.). Upper Saddle River, NJ: Prentice Hall.

CHAPTER

16 Culture-Specific Counseling Cases

The following nine counseling cases include counseling problems or concerns in which culture, race, or ethnicity was a significant factor in the dynamics of the presenting problems or the dynamics of the counselor–client relationship. Case 1 involves a Chinese working mother who believed that dissatisfaction of her ancestors about her taking a job, versus staying home full time to care for her children, contributed to an industrial accident on her job. Case 2 is a problem of ethnic-identity confusion involving a southern African woman of color who had been passing for White, but, as an adult, was trying to get in touch with her African ethnic heritage and reestablish a relationship with her estranged African family. Case 3 is a case of an Islamic family of young, adult siblings who migrated to the United States to study and attend college; however, family conflict became a problem because of cultural differences related to gender roles and religious practice. Case 4 is a counseling case of an AIDS patient who resisted Western drugs and medical treatment in favor of his own preference for African-centered therapy, healing, and herbal use.

Case 5 involves a White, lesbian psychotherapist who counsels a middle-aged, African American lesbian couple. The couple lived together and presented intracultural issues (e.g., skin color) that interacted with sexual identity, family reactions, personality differences, and their conflicting viewpoints about "outness" or "coming out" with their lesbianism. In addition, one of the clients was diagnosed with posttraumatic stress disorder related to severe physical, sexual, and emotional abuse during her childhood. Case 6 is a case of drug abuse and depression in a Latina client and involves a team-counseling approach of an African American case manager, a Latina secondary counselor, and a group-counseling leader. Case 7 is a counseling dilemma of a biracial teenage female with multiple problems, including academic problems in school, inappropriate sexual behaviors, substance abuse, racial-identity problems, and family conflict. Case 8 involves a biracial student who is Native American/African American in a predominantly African American elementary school and is dealing with grief issues as well as struggling with spirituality challenges. Case 9 presents dilemmas for an African American male who has been confronted consistently with criminality and youthful indiscretions.

These cases do not only address cultural dynamics but they also examine culture and ethnicity as these factors intersect with counseling problems related to areas of living such as family relations, child rearing, romantic unions, clinical behaviors (e.g., posttraumatic stress and depression), human development, religious beliefs and practice, legal problems, and psychosocial problems (e.g., physical abuse, drug use, grief, inappropriate sexual behavior, and educational learning).

Case 1: Incorporating Confucian Chinese Spiritual Beliefs into Cognitive-Behavioral Therapy for Posttraumatic Stress Disorder

Case Background/History

Judy Cheng was a 40-year-old, married, Confucian Chinese immigrant with two sons, ages 9 and 15. She had been working full time on an assembly line in a meat packaging plant since she arrived in Canada from Mainland China in 1995. When residing in her country of origin, she stayed at home to raise her children. Mrs. Cheng was forced to seek employment outside of the home after relocating in order to assist her underemployed husband with paying the bills. Because she had only completed two years of university in China before giving birth to her first son and was experiencing difficulty acquiring the English language, her employment prospects were limited. Mrs. Cheng was referred for counseling by her caseworker at the local Workers' Compensation Board after experiencing a severely traumatic work-related accident.

Presenting Problem and Diagnosis

Mrs. Cheng reported having a near-death experience when the sleeve of her shirt was caught in the conveyer belt of the machine on which she was working. Her shirt was devoured by the machine, leaving her physically exposed in front of her co-workers. The physical contact between Mrs. Cheng's body and the steel edges of the conveyer belt resulted in multiple injuries, including the "slicing" of her left breast and bruising on her arm and shoulder, as well as on the left side of her neck and face. A co-worker immediately switched off the machine in response to Mrs. Cheng's screams.

Mrs. Cheng reported that she thought she was going to die when the accident occurred. She stated that the most frightening aspect of the event was an image that she saw of herself as a skeleton. She attributed the image to the disappointment of the spirits of her ancestors. When asked why her ancestors may be displeased with her, she identified her perceived neglect of her children since she entered the workforce as evidence of poor parenting. Because of the perceived disapproval of her role-shift by her ancestors, Mrs. Cheng noted that her fears were generalizing to events outside of the work setting: She found herself being preoccupied with anxiety about terrible things happening to her children and was constantly attempting to restrict their activities outside of the home. Her fears were accompanied by several symptoms of posttraumatic stress disorder, including recurrent nightmares and daytime flashbacks of the event, an exaggerated startle response, sleep difficulties, feelings of detachment from others, and an avoidance of all reminders of the event, including her co-workers.

Mrs. Cheng's self-reports of her symptoms were consistent with the counselor's observations. Her pupils were dilated and she visually scanned the room for any danger. She spoke in a shrill voice, her breathing was very shallow, and she could not sit still or control her fidgeting. This attests to her heightened anxiety response. There were two main issues that Mrs. Cheng wanted to address in the counseling relationship: (1) her fears about returning to work given her family's need for the second income, and (2) her changing relationships with her husband and children, who had also become the targets of her fears. Mrs. Cheng was already receiving treatment for her physical injuries through her participation in a rehabilitation and pain management program.

Counseling Intervention and Follow-Up

Because of the potency of Mrs. Cheng's spiritual beliefs in perpetuating her experience of posttraumatic stress and the generalization of her fears to other family members, a focus on these beliefs was incorporated into the counseling process. Mrs. Cheng's belief that her ancestors would be displeased with her for neglecting her children was examined using cognitive techniques derived from the schema-focused approach. We collaboratively searched for evidence of inadequate versus good parenting. The only factor supporting a change in Mrs. Cheng's involvement in her children's lives was the reduced amount of time that she spent with them after entering the workforce. In response to my Socratic questions, she generated multiple examples of very responsive parenting during the time that she spent with her children. Because she saw her time at work as detracting from her contributions to her family, we explored the reasons why she had entered the workforce in the first place. This led Mrs. Cheng to reconceptualize her entry into the workforce as representing an even greater contribution to her family than her previous role of a homemaker; she was now contributing to her family both financially and in terms of her role as a mother.

As a result of the cognitive interventions, Mrs. Cheng seemed to feel that her ancestors would be more likely to be pleased with her than displeased. Thus, she felt comfortable invoking and communicating with the spirits of her ancestors in the subsequent counseling session. Mrs. Cheng brought food offerings to the next session to invoke the spirits. She communicated with them covertly in silence, as the counselor also engaged in the process of taking a moment of silence in the session. Mrs. Cheng reported that the results of her communication with the spirits were positive.

Because Mrs. Cheng was no longer afraid of additional negative events befalling herself and her family through the displeasure of her ancestors, she had become receptive to the use of imaginal exposure techniques. The specific technique used involved having her recall the accident in detail, with a back-up self-generated relaxation scene as a stabilizer for instances when the exposure became too stressful. It was also important to encourage Mrs. Cheng to start talking about the event with her husband and to reinitiate interactions with her co-workers after the imaginal exposure was over. In addition to discussing her symptoms with family members, she was encouraged to slowly lift off all of the restrictions she had placed on her children's behavior since the time of the accident. Mrs. Cheng successfully followed through with each of the counselor's recommendations. She was also effectively able to implement a graduated return to work program after her physical injuries were addressed in the rehabilitation program. A follow-up telephone call six months after the termination of the counseling relationship indicated that Mrs. Cheng had returned to her previous level of functioning.

Cultural Implications

Although a counselor who was uninformed about Mrs. Cheng's cultural heritage could have erroneously interpreted her spiritual beliefs as delusional, a consideration of the central tenets of the Confucian Chinese tradition elucidates that a strong duty to maintain the regard of one's ancestors is an integral part of the culturally defined reality. Incorporating a focus on these spiritual beliefs in the counseling process achieved two aims: (1) validation of the client's worldview and the establishment of a solid therapeutic alliance and (2) removal of barriers to the implementation of imaginal and in vivo exposure methods of intervention. The use of the exposure techniques served to ameliorate the client's posttraumatic stress symptoms, enabling her to return to work and improving her family functioning. Because the cognitive interventions and invocation of the ancestral spirits alleviated some of Mrs. Cheng's self-blame regarding the accident, the stigma that she attached to her experience decreased. This in turn, decreased her need to "save face" and conceal her symptoms from other people; it enabled her to reinitiate interactions with her co-workers in order to access their support in the return-to-work process.

Counselor's Reflection and Self-Evaluation

The counselor's postponement of the standard exposure-based protocol for posttraumatic stress was necessitated by the potent nature of the client's belief that her accident and symptoms were caused by the displeasure of the spirits of her ancestors. In hindsight, it seems that soliciting the involvement of Mrs. Cheng's husband in the counseling process in order to have him provide feedback regarding his perception of Mrs. Cheng's contributions to her family could have enhanced the effectiveness of the cognitive-reframing intervention and promoted the access of family support. Mrs. Cheng's case elucidates the fact that acknowledgment of the culturally derived meaning of a client's experience and incorporation of cultural factors in intervention help to ensure a positive counseling process and outcome.

Noorfarah Merali, Ph.D.
Chartered Psychologist and Assistant Professor of Counseling Psychology
University of Alberta, Edmonton, Alberta, Canada

Case 2: Black or White: Ethnic-Identity Confusion

Case Background/History

A high school graduate, Mary, was an intelligent and well-groomed 25-year-old single female, who worked as a secretary and lived with her mother. Mary's father left Rhodesia (what became Zimbabwe in 1980) when she was 12 years old. He rarely communicated with the family after his departure. When Mary was 23, she visited her father in Greece. She stated he behaved as if he was ashamed of her and would not introduce her to her relatives in the area because of her mixed racial heritage. Mary stated that her mother was British, Dutch, and Asian Indian, and her maternal great, great grandmother was a Shona (an indigenous ethnic group in Zimbabwe). The client did not describe her mother as a Shona, although she would have been part Shona. I thought Mary was a White female until she revealed her racial identity. The client was a devout Jehovah's Witness although she was not brought up in that faith.

Presenting Problem and Diagnosis

Although the client mentioned that she had been sexually abused at the age of 14, she stated the focus of her problem was her racial and ethnic identity. Mary also said she felt overwhelming guilt because she had been brought up as a White person and had a degree of White privilege, although she was not White. During the separatist period in Rhodesia, she went to Whites-only schools, lived in a Whites-only neighborhood, and never protested the Rhodesian government's racist colonial policies. Though she knew some of her cousins, aunts, and uncles on her mother's side, her family did not associate with them for fear of losing their privilege and safety. She stated that her relatives had Asian Indian identities, but that she did not. Mary also noted that her mother's relatives did not greet her with open arms. The client said even though she could associate with her relatives freely now under the new government in Zimbabwe, she still avoided them and this bothered her. Mary felt that she did not really belong anywhere and that her life as a White person was a lie. The client wanted to go out and meet people of various racial and cultural backgrounds, but she was scared of the potential social and financial consequences of doing that, and was afraid of not being able to "say the right things" and of being rejected or possibly hated by non-Whites.

The client was not sure what to do with her non-White African identity. She believed that she did not deserve to have an African identity because she thought she betrayed Africans during Rhodesia. The client said she was scared to be who she really was, yet she desired to know all aspects of herself. The client believed the only way of solving this dilemma was to "just die," because she perceived that there was no way out of the dilemma. Although Mary stated that she "thought about killing herself," she had no specific plan for attempting suicide. Mary said she was so distraught about her identity that every night when she went to bed she wished she would not wake up the next morning. Although a diagnostic category was not assigned to this African client, her concerns centered on a conflict of ethnic identity and some degree of depression with guilt and intermittent suicide ideation.

Counseling Intervention and Follow-Up

Mary came to counseling once a week for eight months and rarely missed a session. She was willing to talk about her life and her ethnic identity issues, but was resistant at first to actually taking action to resolve her identity crisis. As she became less resistant, her eagerness to explore who she was grew. To engage this client, a friendly "girl talk" atmosphere seemed to be essential, so sometimes the counseling session would wander and be rather casual. However, the counseling would eventually find its way back to the central issue of the client's identity development and her resulting depression. As the client started to explore her racial and cultural identity, I designed homework around this exploration. Because the client feared exploring her identity because of possible repercussions, initial homework was to explore in private some aspects of the cultures she wanted to understand. Eventually the client was willing to take on more public exploration of racial/cultural themes in Zimbabwe, such as attending an indigenous art festival. This gave her the opportunity to view various facets of the cultures she wanted to explore and to see who attended such affairs. Since we met in the city center, we attended some of these activities together and I modeled multicultural social skills for her. Some assertiveness training and role playing was done with the client to help develop her multicultural social skills. Eventually, Mary believed she could try to strike up conversations with people of various racial/cultural groups. Though it was initially difficult and uncomfortable for the client to do, she was able to take some action. At times, she felt that she made mistakes in how she communicated, but she kept trying. Eventually the client went from visiting the African Village on display at Victoria Falls, to actually visiting her ancestral village, where she was welcomed. Prior to visiting her village, she had begun taking Shona language lessons. The client also explored being sexually abused and how that affected her identity development.

The client subsequently lost her job and believed it was the result of her claiming her ethnic identity. Mary was angry about losing her job and the injustice of it. However, the job loss was reframed as an opportunity to explore further herself and her heritage without as many social hindrances. Mary soon joined a company that had a multiracial staff. This provided her with greater opportunity to enjoy the company of people of varying racial and cultural backgrounds, gain multicultural communications skills, and broaden her support system. Losing her job was even more beneficial to her because it inspired her to examine issues of equity, justice, and her own prejudices. She did have to deal with some White community backlash, but she now had garnered support from people of the various racial communities in Zimbabwe, even from some individuals from the White community.

Mary tried to develop a better relationship with her mother's family members, and, in turn, this brought her mother back into the family circle as well. Mary was able to integrate some new social and cultural aspects into her life and continued to explore her racial and cultural identity. She stated that she had become friends with a few females who were also of mixed racial/cultural heritage and who had been "passing for White." She seemed to be satisfied with the new friendships. After eight months, Mary stopped coming to counseling because she felt she was managing her identity development and her life in a better way.

Cultural Implications

The counseling process and the client's related activities were done from a multi-cultural framework. The client did at times express cultural conflict in her observations and communications with Zimbabweans outside of the White community. She knew how to behave and socialize in the White community, but not in any other racial/cultural community in Zimbabwe. She was at first resistant in taking the steps to learn how to communicate with non-White Zimbabweans. This resistance lessened to discomfort and eventually she looked forward to trying out multicultural social situations.

As the counselor, on the one hand, having experienced both violence and the loss of privilege because of my social and political activities, at times I felt annoyed by the client's resistance to giving up some of her privilege. On the other hand, I understood in part what she was experiencing, and I knew how some individuals in the White community in Zimbabwe might behave toward those they believed "betrayed" them.

Counselor's Reflection and Self-Evaluation

Three months prior to the client being referred to me, I returned to Zimbabwe after getting a master's degree in counseling in the United States. I was an inexperienced counselor, but was experienced in multicultural communication in Zimbabwe. Although I had studied racial identity development models on my own, I had no counseling training or experience in working with clients with racial and cultural identity issues or working with clients from multicultural backgrounds.

I had problems identifying a counseling theory that I felt was appropriate for my setting and me. I found the Euro-American theories I had been taught all had something to offer, but none of them were completely relevant to me and my counseling situation. I was then floundering because I had no specific model to follow and at the same time I only had these Euro-American counseling perspectives. There seemed to be no one I could turn to for supervision. I was the only professional counselor in Zimbabwe at the time.

I felt very lost at times, and this must have hindered the counseling process. I was trying to develop my own ideas about counseling in the Zimbabwe context. My client experienced both my failures and successes in that regard, and my own insecurities of being a new counselor. One of the good things that came out of this was that I started thinking about how to do counseling in Zimbabwe. I am now developing a counseling model (Liberation Therapy) and a model of counselor supervision (Release Counselor Supervision). The counseling model is in the early developmental stage and the supervision model was presented at the 2000 American Counseling Association conference. A lot of the ideas for these models came from this particular case.

In hindsight, I wish I had believed in myself more. If I had, I may have been able to more rapidly adapt what I learned in the United States to my counseling work in Zimbabwe. Instead, I felt I was not a good counselor because I did not have a theory that seemed to work for me. Later I found that many people from outside of the United States who were trained in the United States have those same feelings when trying to use Euro-American models back home. Nevertheless, having those doubts is what led me to explore theories of counseling I had not been taught, and eventually to develop my own counseling and supervision models.

Kimberly Richards, NCC, SACC
Lecturer, Department of Human Services
California State University, Fullerton

Case 3: Counseling With an Islamic Immigrant Family

Case Background/History

Mr. A. was a 24-year-old, single, Muslim male from West Africa. He came to the United States in the 1990s to study business at a private college. Mr. A. had two mothers, his biological mother, who was deceased, and his other mother who came into the family as his father's second wife. Mr. A. is the oldest sibling in his combined family. Mr. A. has six siblings, two female and four male. His biological mother had five children altogether, and his second mother had two children from his father. Among offspring born to his biological mother, Mr. A., the oldest, is a year older than the second born (a sister), two years older than the third born sibling, five years older than the fourth born sibling, and five years older than the youngest sibling born to his biological mother. He is eight years older than the first child and twelve years older than the second child of his second mother.

All six siblings from both of his mothers were sent to the United States at different times to live with him and to attend college or public U.S. schools. The second oldest child on his biological mother's side was sent to the United States in the early 1990s. After that, three children were sent one after another, all within the next three years. Around the mid-1990s, the two children from his second mother were sent to the United States together.

Mr. A. was not employed while attending college. He was sent here to study, and all his financial needs were taken care of with money that was being sent from back home. Mr. A.'s economic status was well above that of a typical U.S. college student from a middle-class family background. He occasionally and proudly alluded to his father's tribal status and wealth back home.

During our initial interview, Mr. A. presented himself as very cordial, polite, and reserved. His demeanor reflected that of a person who is important and confident but respectful. Mr. A. was sure to indicate to me that he is a proud Muslim and a "true believer" that Islam should play a major role in the family. His identity, as he communicated to me, is very much connected to his culture and not the U.S. culture. He made it clear that, as the oldest male sibling, it was his role to play the father figure and be the overseer of his younger siblings while they were living here with him in the United States. According to him, this role is expected of Muslim males. Mr. A.'s culture and religion was also very evident in how he expressed his feelings and formulated his beliefs and thoughts about Muslim families in general. He stated that his beliefs were centered on strict values and traditions that were instilled in him as a child. For example, he shared with me that in his culture, the man should provide discipline for the family. Other beliefs he shared were that a Muslim man should live his life according to the teachings of Islam. Mr. A. strongly believed that problems should be resolved within the family. He indicated that he prays five times a day and attends prayer meetings at the local mosque. Mr. A. spoke of having a good relationship with his male siblings but not his female siblings. He stated that he was having a difficult time, particularly with his oldest female sibling from his biological mother's side.

It was apparent that he was a bit disturbed about being in this situation. He stated a couple of times, "I can't believe I have to be here." Mr. A. was in constant conflict with his female sibling. The conflicts had to do with his older sister's increasingly antagonistic attitude and opposition toward him as the family's overseer. In addition, he was disturbed by what he saw as her negative influences on the younger female sibling's attitude toward Islam. He stated that the older female sibling constantly disobeyed him and the rules that he had established for their home. According to Mr. A., she did not agree with the discipline he had established for them. He indicated that when he confronted her about things that he felt were against the teachings of Islam, "she lied" and ignored him. When I asked him to describe her behaviors and actions that were disagreeable to him, he only commented that she was not being a "true Muslim."

As the counseling relationship progressed and client trust developed, Mr. A. volunteered an example of his older sister not being a "true Muslim." He indicated that one morning he asked her to get out of the bed to pray. She refused. After a short while, he noted that she got out of the bed and instead of praying, she turned on the television. Mr. A. revealed that he became angry and turned off the television. His sister then pushed him and they began to fight. After the fight, Mr. A.'s sister reportedly called the police who arrested him and gave him a citation for domestic violence. Mr. A.'s citation mandated that he be assigned to a probation officer and that he participate in a set number of counseling sessions for anger management. Shortly after the incident and immediately before beginning counseling, Mr. A. moved out of the family home and to another residence that he shared with his male siblings.

Presenting Problem and Diagnosis

Mr. A. came to the multicultural counseling center to learn effective, nonviolent ways to communicate with his female sibling and to learn strategies for controlling his anger as ordered by the court. He was in denial of the inappropriateness of his actions and explained that his actions were in line with his cultural and religious beliefs. Mr. A. felt that his ability to carry out his culturally prescribed family responsibilities had been challenged by U.S. culture and laws. Moreover, Mr. A. expressed resentment about his sister going against his deceased mother's wish never to bring shame on the family. He expressed frustration about not being able to control his female siblings and not being able to exercise his responsibilities as his father would have if he were here with them. He shared that the older sister had negatively influenced the attitudes of their younger female sibling to also act in a rebellious manner. Mr. A. expressed feelings of unhappiness about his female siblings not following their Islamic religion. He was distressed over the thoughts of them ignoring or even forgetting their cultural and religious beliefs and ways. While Mr. A. was going through stress here in the United States with his sisters, he was also under stress related to problems of his father, who was facing serious tribal conflict and issues back home.

Mr. A. appeared uneasy about explaining his problem and the reasons for having to attend counseling. When he was asked to explain what happened regarding the conflict with his older sister, he continually shifted the blame on his sister. Mr. A. was not clear about what he needed to do to meet the goals of the court, although the court had stipulated that he attend a fixed number of counseling sessions, specifically for anger management. Mr. A.'s. diagnosis was intermittent explosive disorder as established by the *DSM-IV*. It was also apparent that Mr. A. was experiencing adjustment problems as an immigrant to the United States from a non-Western culture; therefore, he could have been diagnosed with a *DSM-IV* adjustment disorder.

Counseling Intervention and Follow-Up

The primary treatment goal for Mr. A. was to reduce his situational anger. Secondary goals included assisting Mr. A. to take responsibility for his actions, understand the impact of his actions, improve his relationship with his sibling, adjust to cross-cultural stress, and acquire education about domestic violence. The counseling approach was cognitive-behavioral in terms of allowing him to examine his thought processes as related to his belief system. Questions were directed to assist him in understanding the impact of his actions and what he needed to do to get himself out of this situation. He received information on domestic violence and physical violence regarding state laws and related federal laws. Mr. A. learned anger management strategies such as cognitive reframing, self-talk, and relaxation therapy.

Cultural Implications

Mr. A. was very immersed in his culture and religion. As he built trust in the counseling relationship, he shared with me many aspects of his religion and culture that influence how he thinks and acts. In addition, he shared with me how anger is handled in his country. He stated that in his country, conflict is seen as normal. This is due in part to tribal conflicts that often occur in his country. He says when someone in the family does something wrong, the individual is physically punished by people inside the home and outside the home. Mr. A. says when he hit his sister, his intent was not to hurt her, but to bring shame on her for bringing shame on the family. He indicated that he was also concerned about how she was becoming acculturated or "Americanized," and, thus, losing her ethnic and Islamic way of life.

Counselor's Reflection and Self-Evaluation

Mr. A. and I established a therapeutic relationship in which he was willing to let down his guard and accept responsibility for his actions and behavior. Toward the end of our sessions, Mr. A. began to bring the Koran to sessions to share with me verses that explained his beliefs and values. I used the information that he was sharing with me in the Koran to assist him in therapy.

> *Jacqueline A. Harper*
> School Guidance Counselor, Prince William County Public Schools
> Former Counselor, Center for Multicultural Human Services
> Falls Church, Virginia

Case 4: An AIDS Patient: Traditional Therapy Versus African-Centered Therapy

Case Background/History

Mr. T., a 45-year-old African American male, came to the clinic for supportive therapy related to an HIV+ diagnosis, which he had been aware of for ten years. Mr. T. appeared younger than his stated age and was stately in appearance. He was tall and slender, well groomed, and conservatively dressed. He wore crisp white shirts, bow ties, and suits for his weekly appointments. His visual presentation was consistent throughout the two and a half years of therapy except toward the end of our sessions when his HIV status advanced to AIDS with subsequent wasting and low energy. Although he spoke in an articulate manner, at times his speech pattern became loquacious, which required the therapist to ask him to clarify his responses. He maintained eye contact and engaged himself fully during the therapy sessions.

Mr. T. was single and had never been married, but had had two long-term relationships with cohabitation. He denied a current relationship with a significant other, but verbalized a desire to have such a relationship. Mr. T. reported he did not like to use "labeling" terms to describe his sexual orientation. He also did not want to be described or categorized based on "what he did in the privacy of his intimate moments." He preferred to consider himself as both a lover of men and of women but did not wish to describe himself as "bisexual." He was the younger of two male siblings. His older brother was gay.

Family Background.   Mr. T.'s residence was in the eastern region of the United States; however, he was born in a small southern community where the neighbors were well acquainted with one another. His developmental years through adolescence were spent in the northeastern region of the United States, as he was reared by his maternal grandparents. He reported a very good relationship with his now-deceased grandmother, nearly to the point of idealizing her characteristics. Mr. T. reported having an estranged relationship with his biological mother, which presented a challenge as he considered the need to divulge his HIV status and accept the possibility of her providing end-of-life care for him.

Presenting Problem and Diagnosis

Mr. T. entered the therapeutic relationship to work through grief issues related to his HIV diagnosis, which was now becoming symptomatic. He had significant experience with therapy and was "impatient" with therapists who were not his "intellectual equal" or did not honor his health care decisions, which were considered nonconventional. A primary concern for the therapeutic relationship was that his spiritual and intellectual capacity would be respected, particularly surrounding treatment issues and his choices for alternative methods of treatment.

Mr. T. entered therapy expressing concern that his history with other therapists had been challenging for two reasons. The primary reason, from the client's perspective, was that his belief system and preferred methods of problem solving were often "disrespected" in therapy and within the medical system. Mr. T. further reported that his spiritual beliefs, which were African based, were difficult for some therapists to support. He was seriously involved in an African religion and he was training to become a priest within this spiritual community. Mr. T. considered this community to be a primary emotional, physical, and spiritual support for him. The spiritual community was aware of his HIV status and sexual orientation, both of which were not stigmatized by his sisters and brothers in this community. He sought Western medical service to monitor his CD4 and viral-load levels while he received primary care for his HIV-related symptoms from an herbal doctor. He also utilized Eastern methods of health care such as acupuncture, and he practiced yoga. Spirituality and the meaning of events in his life were predominant themes throughout the therapeutic relationship. During the two years of weekly and sometimes more frequent visits, Mr. T.'s physician, who primarily monitored his CD4 and viral-load levels, would seek the support of the therapist to "convince" Mr. T. to begin antiviral treatments, particularly when his health began to deteriorate and he was hospitalized for pneumonia and generalized wasting.

Psychological assessment and diagnosis of this client revealed DSM-IV adjustment disorder, with mixed anxiety and depressed mood. Symptoms of anxiety appeared during a period of time when he had considerable conflict on the job. The depressed mood predominated when he explored the desire for a stable relationship with a significant other. Although he had periods of situational depression, he never met the full criteria of major depressive disorder. He denied a history of mania or psychosis, and had no evidence of personality disorders. He was a recovering alcoholic, having been sober for 15 years. He denied current drug or alcohol use and had no history of legal difficulties.

The client's primary method of defense was intellectual. He used increased verbiage, ambiguous speech patterns, and complex sentence structure early in the therapeutic relationship. Initially, the client "tested" the therapist's competence, intelligence, and willingness to accept his right to choose his method of care. After the initial period of "testing," the client engaged and was able to join the therapeutic process. During the working phase of the relationship, much of the client's sharing was framed in a spiritual context as he sought to gain meaning for the events that challenged him from day to day. He discussed his future, and later, as his symptoms became more difficult to manage, the reality of death in terms of his "transition." He was psychologically ready for therapy and demonstrated a capacity to explore deep-level core issues.

Counseling Intervention and Follow-Up

To facilitate the client joining the therapeutic process, the therapist provided unconditional positive regard as she assisted the client's input in understanding his spiritual belief system. Spiritual terms and concepts that were shared with the therapist were integrated with a cognitive-behavioral approach as the therapist assisted the client in his search for the meaning of events in his life. A phenomenological approach allowed the therapist to experience the client's presenting problems and primary defenses, mainly intellectualization, within the context of the experience of an African American male in the United States. Within this contextual framework, the therapist provided space for the client to work through his defenses and beliefs that his intelligence, ability to make logical decisions, and ability to articulate himself in a meaningful way would be minimized by a Western trained therapist. He was able to identify cognitive distortions, evaluate his use of intellectualization as a primary defense against anxiety, and integrate his spiritual understanding of life into the challenges of family origin issues, social isolation, and end-of-life decisions. As his health deteriorated, spiritual themes became more dominant and his reliance on the therapist to "defend" his decision against pharmacotherapy with the primary care physician helped to solidify the therapeutic relationship and assist him through a meaningful transition into death.

Cultural Implications

Faith in spiritual belief systems is an integral part of life for many African Americans and Africans of the Diaspora. For these clients, spiritual connectedness takes precedence over linear patterns of belief. These belief patterns sometimes come in direct conflict with health care systems whose goal and focus is to "master disease and illness" through "research-based" interventions. When the client's belief system consists of traditional healing practices and a general modus of trust in divine powers, conflict with Western views of illness is often inevitable. The ensuing power struggles between these two systems have the potential for undermining the counselor–client therapeutic relationship.

Similar conflicts were observed in southern Africa where the role of spiritual beliefs and use of traditional methods of treatment were inextricably linked. In these instances, the clients would give verbal support and acknowledgment of Western-based views of illness and disease transmission; however, when they returned to their homesteads and places of familiarity, the traditional belief systems were followed. This was particularly challenging when the counseling interventions were related to the transmission of HIV in a country where the HIV prevalence was the second highest in the world and traditional beliefs included polygamy and limited rights of women to negotiate their sexual encounters within the marital relationship. In addition to these challenges, some traditional methods of treatment in African countries involve rituals such as cutting the skin, which put the client at greater risk for exposure to HIV transmission. Within international as well as domestic settings, the counselor is challenged to understand and support the fact that the ultimate decision for self-direction lies with the client.

Counselor's Reflection and Self-Evaluation

The counselor practices within the framework of "do no harm" when providing counseling for clients. When supporting the client comes in direct conflict with common medical practice, particularly within the framework of life-and-death decisions, the culturally sensitive therapist is challenged from within and from without.

As a direct effect of a good therapeutic relationship, the counselor will invest some degree of emotional energy into the well-being of the client. In this case, when the client's views of health, their right to self-determination, coupled with the need for emotional support of those decisions conflicted with the counselors commitment to do no harm, the therapist questioned her ethical position and felt emotionally drained. She learned that the training she received in cultural diversity and cross-cultural counseling provided information that assisted her in providing culturally sensitive care; however, the conflicting feelings she had as she supported her client's right to choose the way he would live and the way he would die were not expected. At times, the therapist felt like an advocate and other times like a coconspirator to client behavior and choices that could lead to a premature death. In spite of a lifetime commitment to support clients' rights to make decisions that were best for them, this therapist learned valuable lessons about the meaning of life from the perspective of this client and African American client groups. Quality of life can only be determined and ultimately directed by the individual whose responsibility it is to live it.

Barbara Q. Tobias, Ph.D., MSN, RN, Assistant Professor
College of Pharmacy, Nursing, and Allied Health Sciences
Howard University
(Dr. Tobias has a Ph.D. in counseling psychology.)

Case 5: Discussing Heterosexism
With a Lesbian Couple

Case Background/History and Diagnosis

The effect of "isms," such as racism and sexism, and how they affect identity development and psychological adjustment are increasingly being discussed as important components of multicultural counseling. Although many lesbian, gay, and bisexual clients mention *coming out* issues, rarely do they come to therapy seeking to reduce their internalized heterosexism; yet heterosexism pervades social customs and institutions (such as legal systems and religion) as well as individual attitudes and behaviors (Herek, 1990), creating a major impact on these clients' lives.

Lesbian clients already face discrimination based on gender and sexual identity. These issues are further complicated when lesbian women also have to contend with discrimination and stigmatization based on ethnicity, age, physical appearance, disability, socioeconomic status, and other factors. Weaving the interactions among multiple sources of oppression becomes an important part of the discussion. Clients can see that I am a White female, and I encourage any discussion we may need to have about the implications of those aspects of my identity to their therapy. My sexual identity is not automatically visible, so some clients may know that I am a lesbian and some may not. Regardless of what clients know of my identity, I believe it is vital that I not remain noncommittal in response to any form of oppression but serve as an ally, an advocate, and an activist (Mallon, 2000; Reynolds & Hanjorgiris, 2000) in empowering the client and dismantling the "ism."

Drawing clinical data from three lesbian clients with similar experiences and concerns, this composite case will offer a couple of situations to show how I bring an exploration of the impact of heterosexism and other forms of oppression into the therapeutic exploration.

Charlayne, a 48-year-old African American lesbian woman came to treatment because of ongoing problems from severe posttraumatic stress and dissociative disorders. Her history included many years of severe physical, sexual, and emotional abuse from her alcoholic and dissociative mother and a father with a severe bipolar disorder who committed suicide when Charlayne was 11 years old. Charlayne was currently in a nine-year relationship with Denita, a 50-year-old African American woman. Although Denita knew that Charlayne was an abuse survivor, both women were adamant that Charlayne not disclose the particulars or even the severity of her abuse. Charlayne reported that generally their relationship was good. Charlayne had worked as a nurse, prior to the increase in trauma symptoms that led to getting on long-term mental disability, and her partner worked for a small publishing company.

Charlayne's sexual history included sexual abuse perpetrated by both women and men. She reported that she had boyfriends in high school, had supported herself in her late teens as a sex-worker servicing primarily male clients, was briefly married to a man in her early twenties, and had a couple of short and abusive relationships with two women prior to becoming involved with her current partner, Denita. Charlayne was open about her lesbian identity in most situations. Her partner was not as comfortable identifying as a lesbian to herself or with others, and this sometimes created friction within the relationship.

Counseling Intervention and Follow-Up

Although much of the therapy focused on a stage-oriented treatment of posttraumatic and dissociative disorders (Courtois, 1991), there were some times when sexual identity concerns and discussing the effects of oppression, particularly from heterosexism and racism, became key. As part of her therapy, Charlayne participated in a local mental health agency's psychotherapy group for abuse survivors. She found much about this group helpful, and it provided a good adjunct for the individual therapy treatment. However, Charlayne felt that the therapists, both heterosexual women, although fairly competent in dealing with issues of race and ethnicity, frequently did not understand the ways in which they failed to recognize their own heterosexism.

As Charlayne strengthened her ability to stay emotionally present in the group, she began to point out when she perceived the therapists and some group members acting in heterosexist ways, such as their devaluing her relationship as less "real" because she was not legally married, telling her they accepted her "even though" she was gay, referring to her partner as her "friend," and questioning whether in fact she might be heterosexual or bisexual because of her sexual history. She recounted times when she had overheard comments referring to someone being "too dykey" and "such a fag." As someone who had done activist work, Charlayne referred to herself as *queer.* When confronted that she was using derogatory language, she explained that queer is a term being reclaimed within the lesbian, gay, bisexual, and transgender (LGBT) communities, much as African Americans reclaimed the word *Black* in the late 1960s, then a term of insult. Charlayne was most upset that one of the group therapists, Mathilda, had suggested that her lesbian identity was her choice, given that she had been sexually active with males in her youth, and that her refusal to have sex with her partner stemmed from her desire to be sexual with men. Charlayne felt very disempowered because her attempts to confront these views were met with disregard by the therapists and group members. Charlayne reported that Mathilda said, "This group is not heterocentric. Your issues with your homosexuality are creating your problem. You are using this to alienate yourself from the group."

Charlayne came back to individual therapy asking, "Am I crazy? I know she is wrong, but I have thought I have been right and found out that I was wrong before. Do I have issues with my sexual identity? I am afraid I am going to find out she's right." It was important for me not only to listen in a noncommittal way but to respond clearly, "No. You are not crazy. What you are describing is heterosexism. Heterosexism is wrong." Further, I acknowledged to her that she was not a lesbian *because* she had been sexually abused by either women or men, nor was she not a lesbian because she had been sexually active with men in her youth, much of which had been in the context of the abuse. We discussed how prostitution was about financially supporting herself as she attempted to get out of an abusive home, not about sexual preferences. Charlayne frequently lamented that she loved Denita deeply and wanted to make love to her in the way she deserved, but abuse memories and flashbacks would intrude, making it difficult for Charlayne to distinguish present from past. I reminded her of her lament as a way of countering her fear that her sexual difficulties with Denita stemmed from some confusion about her sexual identity. We even discussed the ways in which she did alienate herself from others to discern that her sexual identity was not one.

Charlayne relaxed the most when I added, "It is not your responsibility as a client to educate your therapists about sexual identity concerns or heterosexism. Therapists should take primary responsibility to learn about these issues."

We discussed possible interventions, and I told Charlayne that I was willing to speak to the therapists but wanted us first to explore any ramifications she might experience if I did so. We explored various interventions and how they might affect Charlayne's relationships with the therapists and group members and the relationships among treatment team members as we related to her. Charlayne and I decided that I would first speak to the supervisor of the therapists, whom I knew to be an ally on sexual identity concerns, to alert her to the need for additional training for the staff and to shield my client as much as possible from what can be a politically sensitive issue. When Mathilda left a message for me indicating concerns that our client was using derogatory language by "throwing around the term 'queer,'" I was provided with my entrée to begin a discussion with her about the evolving process of language and LGBT concerns in psychotherapy and offer some recent articles and any support I could give as an educator in this field.

Cultural Implications

Often, differing approaches to managing one's sexual identity produce conflicts for same-sex partners, and a discussion of heterosexism can increase empathy for the complexity involved in each one's choices. Denita's family lived only a couple of hours away, and so Charlayne and Denita frequently visited them. When the family came to visit, Denita would give up "her" bedroom and stay in "Charlayne's" room, and when the two women visited Denita's family, they would sleep in separate places. Although Denita's family loved Charlayne, they never acknowledged the two women as partners.

Charlayne had become an activist, working for sex workers' rights with COYOTE ("Call Off Your Old Tired Ethics"), an organization to assist sex workers in their rights as well as their choice to change occupations, and with the local Black Lesbian and Gay Coalition. Denita, however, was much more reserved. She was not out at work, and said she was uncomfortable labeling herself, although she knew she loved Charlayne and wanted to be with her forever. Denita often was uncomfortable with how "butch" she thought Charlayne looked, wanting her to look a little more "femme," at least around the family.

Denita was willing to acknowledge that her family had often treated her with disrespect; however, she was very loyal to them. Charlayne often felt hurt and betrayed that Denita would render their relationship invisible to maintain the family's acceptance. At one point when this conflict was causing considerable distress for the couple, the two of them came together to a session with me.

Denita was often included in therapy, as a way of supporting the couple as they dealt with the daily effects of Charlayne's abuse. This had allowed Denita to build her own therapeutic alliance with me. As we began to address the conflicts caused by the differences in their outness, I asked Denita about what she feared she would lose if she confronted their status as a couple more directly with her family. She depended on her family for many things, including a sense of belonging. She had grown up in a working-class family, in a small city still rife with racial discrimination. Being seen as "like" the others gave her a much-needed sense of belonging and a refuge from racism, and her early feelings for women were an unsettling reminder of how "different" she was. Denita had grown up in a family without racial or class privilege, leaving heterosexual privilege as the one available to her. Having been forced to manage without a familial safety net at such an early age, Charlayne was angry that Denita was still trying to "pass" as straight and deny the reality of their relationship to preserve her place in her family.

To help the couple find an area of common understanding of the costs and benefits of passing, I asked Denita and Charlayne what their experiences were regarding privilege associated with skin color. They agreed that both families had experienced tension around this issue. A lively discussion of those family members who more closely met Eurocentric standards of beauty or were able to pass as White, and ways in which those with darker skin had been given less regard helped the women identify feelings of jealousy, pressure to perform and produce, freedom, resentment, anger, and internalized shame. As we explored how many of those feelings might be experienced regardless of skin color and the losses and gains experienced either way, I wondered aloud how it might be similar to issues of loss and privilege resulting from passing as heterosexual versus being out as a lesbian. In this context, Charlayne and Denita were more able to appreciate how, as African American lesbian women, they had been affected by racism, sexism, and heterosexism, and the difficult choices they each faced. They could explore the choices they had made regarding expression of gender identity (in this case, choices to appear or act more butch or femme), sexual identity, and as women of color. We discussed the ways these forces had affected them as individuals and in their relationship, and what losses each one might have sustained had she made different choices.

Although this discussion certainly did not solve all of the problems created by their different levels of outness, it increased empathy and understanding between them. Charlayne reported at her next individual session that she and Denita had noted new insights that were resulting in positive changes in their discussions about dealing with Denita's family and increased acceptance of each partner's hopes, fears, and inconsistencies.

Counselor's Reflection and Self-Evaluation

With clients who identify as lesbian, gay, bisexual, or transgender, as well as with those who are questioning their sexual or gender identities, there are times when it is not therapeutic to take a value-free approach to the exploration of their concerns.

Multicultural counseling is certainly enhanced when the therapist communicates that multiple sexual and gender expressions of identity can be explored, and that no one expression of identity carries a de facto superiority over another. However, as shown in the preceding example with Charlayne and her partner Denita, there are times when it is imperative that the multicultural counselor more actively teach clients to recognize and name the "ism" for what it is, and, when need be, takes on a more activist role to create societal change.

Becky Carroll, Ph.D.
Licensed psychologist in private practice
3000 Connecticut Avenue NW, Suite 400A
Washington, DC 20008–2527

Case 6: Depression and Drug Abuse With a Latina Client

Case Background/History

Maria, a 38-year-old Hispanic female, was born in Cuba. She has been living in the United States for seventeen years, moving to the United States with her mother at the age of 20. Her mother currently resides in Florida. She is very close to her mother. Her father is deceased. She indicates that she has close relationships with her siblings despite not speaking to them in many years. Her siblings are still in Cuba, but Maria does have one sister who lives in Canada. She has never been officially married, but has three children from a previous relationship with someone she refers to as her "ex-husband." Her children were taken away from her when they were young, and they have since been adopted by a family in Pennsylvania. She has not seen nor had any contact with them since they were taken from her care. She has no knowledge of the families that adopted her children, because, at the time, her drug problem was very severe.

Maria is currently living with a man she refers to as her "husband"; however, they are not legally married. She has been in her current relationship for almost a year. Maria's male mate speaks no English. Maria speaks and understands English on a limited basis, although she prefers to communicate in Spanish. She completed the ninth grade while in Cuba and, thereafter, stopped attending school in order to work. She did not pursue any additional education upon coming to the United States. Maria has a very limited work history and states she had been supporting herself through prostitution in order to survive and support her drug habit. She began using cocaine at the age of 24.

Presenting Problem and Diagnosis

Maria was brought to my attention by a judge who had been assigned to her case. She had been arrested for prostitution and possession of cocaine. A forensic evaluation was ordered by the judge, and it was determined that Maria was dually diagnosed with major depression and cocaine abuse. She was ordered to spend 45 days at a forensics hospital for further evaluation and treatment. After Maria completed her evaluation period, she reappeared before the judge. The report completed on Maria stated that she was competent, had responded well to medication, but would need additional outpatient treatment and resources (mental health and substance abuse counseling) in order to remain stable in the community. The judge asked that I intervene and become Maria's primary counselor to provide Maria with mental health and substance abuse counseling and other services to ensure not only that she would return to court but also to assist Maria in successfully changing her life.

Immediately upon being discharged from the forensics hospital, Maria reported to my office for a biopsychosocial assessment. In this assessment, I focused on the following areas: what she felt were her problems, daily routine, lifestyle and activities, and behaviors. It was important for me to do this in order to assess what Maria felt were her problems and areas in her life that she felt needed change. After reading the forensics report and interviewing Maria, I knew she needed services and counseling in almost every area of her life.

Counseling Intervention and Follow-Up

As an African American female, my primary caseload and work experience had been with the African American population. Working with Maria would be my first Hispanic client. Although I have friendships with numerous Hispanic individuals, a therapeutic relationship is not quite the same. The first thing I did was to enlist the assistance of an agency that provided substance abuse and mental health services with the Hispanic community. Maria and I went to the agency and met with a counselor who would be assigned to Maria. We all agreed that it would be a team effort with Lena (a Latina) being the secondary counselor and myself as primary because I was responsible for her through the court. The first thing we did was sign a release of information for both agencies to communicate with each other with respect to Maria and her treatment. Second, we developed a treatment plan to which we all agreed. Lastly, we incorporated an action plan as to reasonable time frames to have Maria's most immediate needs and services addressed and who would be responsible for assisting her in those areas. We all knew the counseling aspect with respect to Maria's life would be an ongoing process because the agency we connected her with provided long-term treatment. Maria also agreed to once-per-week sessions with me.

Following are the areas in Maria's life that needed services and treatment and the interventions implemented by the counselors assigned to her case:

1. Medical: Maria had not had a physical in several years and did not have medical insurance. She reported feeling tired a great deal of time and was concerned about whether she was HIV positive because of her drug use and sexual behaviors. Maria was immediately referred to a local clinic for medical attention; a physician was on staff who spoke Spanish. Additionally, Maria was taken to the local social services agency, where she completed the necessary paperwork for state medical insurance.

2. Substance abuse: Maria had not used drugs in six weeks when we began working with her. At our treatment meeting, we discussed whether she should be placed in residential treatment for a period of four to six months; however, she stated that she wanted to try an outpatient program. The assigned counselor and I were skeptical about her decision but decided that we would try Maria in an intensive outpatient program with the stipulation that if she was experiencing any problems we would immediately transition her to an inpatient program. Maria's "husband" did not feel she needed a drug program because he did not want her leaving the house. After several counseling sessions with him involved, he finally agreed that she could participate. The substance abuse program that the counselor and I thought would be most appropriate for Maria was a program that had counseling groups for Spanish-speaking clientele. Maria went to one session and immediately asked to be placed in another program. Although the program we had selected for her was for Spanish-speaking substance abusers, many of the individuals in the program were people she used drugs with in the past. She felt being in the same environment with them would be a trigger. Lena and I immediately found another program; however, the substance abuse treatment was in English. We found there were limited Spanish-speaking substance abuse services in the metropolitan area.

3. Individual counseling: My counseling approach is an existential, cognitive-behavioral approach. Maria had numerous areas in her life that we were going to focus on in individual counseling. We decided that we would work on whatever came up, and the sessions would be for her to address issues in her life that had caused her to lose her children, become addicted to drugs, and engage in a lifestyle that was counterproductive. Maria needed to make immediate lifestyle changes for a number of reasons. She was on a path of self-destruction, and, if she did not take responsibility immediately, she was possibly going to jail or could even end up dead.

Sessions were once per week with homework assignments. One of her homework assignments was to list the negative and positive aspects of her life. Because Maria was of a different cultural background from myself, I did not want to impose any of my values on her, but we both agreed that she needed to make changes in her life in order to stay alive and be a productive member of society. Her goals were to be drug free, secure a job, get her own apartment, maintain her mental health by continuing to take medication, and continue counseling to address the problems that had caused her to fail in some of these areas. Maria's final goal was to eventually see and have some type of relationship with her children.

4. Action plan: After we had developed counseling goals, we negotiated an action plan. I involved the secondary counselor in this area because I wanted to make sure that culturally I was not expecting something to happen when it could have been my value system and not Maria's. Overall, we all agreed on an action plan that was culturally sensitive and appropriate for Maria. I encouraged Maria to keep a journal in either English or Spanish, which she brought to each session. The journal was for her to discuss daily activities, thoughts, feelings, and behaviors. As our time for individual counseling was ending because of the disposition of her case, we reviewed her progress biweekly. Maria had made a great deal of progress. She was drug-free for more than six months, was actively participating in substance abuse and mental health treatment, and the treatment agency was seeking employment opportunities for her. It has been more than a year and reports indicate that Maria is doing quite well. She continues to be drug free and to participate actively in Narcotics Anonymous and AA meetings. Also, she successfully graduated from the outpatient treatment program and obtained a job. As of this writing, Maria has not been rearrested and has not engaged in sexual solicitation since her last arrest and court referral to treatment. She was placed on probation and remains drug-free. She is still working with Lena and her agency and is compliant with her treatment plan at the agency. She is working full-time and is happy with her new job. She often thinks about her children and, at this writing, is attempting to find them in order to have some sort of relationship with them.

Cultural Implications

As an African American female, whose clientele are predominantly Black, this was my first time working with a Hispanic client. Several times in our sessions, Maria would state that she had to ask her "husband" for permission in order to complete certain tasks and homework assignments, especially as it related to her doing some things on her own. A part of me was not comfortable or even understood this, especially because some of the treatment and services required that she be outside of the home. There were times when her "husband" objected to her treatment and services. I started to think that he was controlling and did not want to see her become self-sufficient. I had to take a step back and examine my own feelings and myself. I had to think about my own cultural background and upbringing (African American) and Maria's (Hispanic). I learned from Lena, the Hispanic counselor, that in some Hispanic cultures, men play a very strong role in the family. What I saw as dominance and overbearing was possibly a way of culture.

Counselor's Reflection and Self-Evaluation

I began to understand, as a counselor who had never worked with a Hispanic client, how important it was for me to enlist the assistance of another agency to help me ensure the success of this client. Never once did I feel I was so culturally knowledgeable and aware and could totally relate to all of Maria's issues as a Hispanic female. As I reflect on my six months of working with Maria, I think one of the best things I could have ever done as a counselor was to enlist the help of another agency that specialized in Hispanic services and which complemented my work with the client. At this point, I would not do anything differently.

Teresa M. Grant, LPC, LCADC
Treatment Specialist
Pretrial Services, Superior Court
Washington, DC

Case 7: A Biracial Teenage Female
With Multiple Problems

Case Background/History

Doris is a 15-year-old biracial female with a long history of behavior problems in the home as well as the school environment. She has had an extensive history of psychiatric treatment. She reported that she received counseling at age 8 after her foster father died. Subsequently, she was hospitalized at least on five occasions for sexual promiscuity, stealing, breaking and entering, as well as defiance at school, leading to suspensions and expulsion for sexual misconduct and hitting a girl.

Presenting Problem and Diagnosis

Doris has been diagnosed with attention deficit disorder, oppositional defiant disorder, depression, and alcohol and marijuana abuse. Records indicated she has difficulty complying with family rules and is vulnerable to attention of males in an indiscriminate way. She had been treated with numerous medications including Wellbutrin, Paxil, Adderall, Ritalin, Depakote, Risperdal, and Prozac.

Doris indicated that she is perceived to be depressed by others. She reported a history of mood swings and being very impulsive and easily distracted. Doris admitted to having temper problems and throwing things in the past. She reported miscarrying after she became pregnant, stating, further, that she had been hanging out with boys who "get in trouble with the law."

Doris indicated that she was placed in a foster home at 2½ years of age because her parents were in jail for robbery and selling drugs. She has had only one contact with her natural parents, which occurred at age 7. Doris and her biological brother and sister lived with foster parents until Doris was 6 years old at which time their foster father died. Doris and her sister were then placed with her current adoptive parents, who are both Caucasian. Another family adopted her brother, but Doris and her sister keep in contact with him. Her adoptive parents have other biological children in the home. She reported having a strained relationship with her adoptive mother, and indicated that they do not get along well. She denied a history of physical or sexual abuse.

Doris confided that she started using marijuana when she was 13 years old about three times a week. However, she indicated that she quit about a year prior to this counseling. She reported significant problems from marijuana including failing seventh grade as well as engaging in unsafe sexual conduct and problems in school. Doris reported that she has an inability to follow rules when she is in the community. She also reported that she has been "looking for love," has had sixteen sexual partners, and believes she is at risk for HIV.

Counseling Intervention and Follow-Up

Doris was receptive to treatment intervention. This was demonstrated through verbal expression during several individual counseling sessions. The primary focus was to engage Doris to develop a healthier lifestyle and address her poor impulse control. Doris attended intensive outpatient treatment because of her high-risk behaviors in the community, and her extensive alcohol and drug history. She attended treatment sessions three times weekly for approximately three months. Each session was a minimum of three hours. Doris did well; however, she often needed to be redirected because of her distraction around male peers. The following are some of the barriers to Doris's treatment as observed:

> She participated in individual sessions on a regular basis because of the inability to encourage her adopted parents to support her treatment need by attending family sessions. This lack of family support ultimately caused Doris to be unstable in the home and wreck havoc in the community.

> Doris's adopted mother never made time for Doris's scheduled family session, and she often would not be home when Doris returned from evening treatment groups. On many occasions, Doris would find herself locked out of the house.

> Doris's adopted father would assume some responsibility; however, his work out of town would cause him to be absent from the home on a regular basis.

> Doris's medication would often leave her tired or fogged.

> Doris's promiscuous behaviors led to barriers as well.

Cultural Implications

Being biracial (Doris's biological father is African American and her biological mother is Caucasian), she was initially placed in foster care with an African American family; however, after the death of her foster father, she was placed with a Caucasian family who subsequently adopted her. Doris only had one contact with her biological parents. Her major conflicts developed with her adopted parents. While in treatment, Doris interacted well with both African American and Caucasian peers. At school, she mostly hung out with African American males; however, she would often find comfort with whoever accepted her often delinquent behavior. Doris never brought her African American friends home because of her fear that her parents would embarrass them.

Counselor's Reflection and Self-Evaluation

Doris was able to refrain from any alcohol or drugs during her twelve months in the treatment program, with the exception of one positive alcohol screen. Although Doris's home life continued to be in turmoil, she was able to progress enough to complete the program successfully. Unfortunately, however, Doris is back in the system because of a substance abuse relapse.

To understand Doris's socialization and to best serve Doris's developmental and educational needs, the counselor needs to begin the counseling process by working with Doris on developing her identity formation. A counselor needs to understand that ethnicity plays an important role in child development. Doris has never been able to establish an identity because she has been a member of both an oppressed and a privileged group, and because neither one of these sets of parents have ever discussed her sense of ethnic or cultural identity with her. Therefore, the counselor needs to understand that Doris's need for acceptance is part of her lack of not only a sense of self and belonging but also a sense of racial identity confusion or conflict. Compounding Doris's lack of identity formation is her experience with abandonment by all of her caregivers. She has had no contact with her natural parents because they are incarcerated; her foster father died; and adoptive parents have had little communication or interaction with her.

Moreover, the counselor needs to gather information on parenting styles of the foster parents and the adoptive parents. It is possible that these two sets of parents had two distinct parenting styles and beliefs. Thus, Doris would clearly not be able to integrate fully these differences.

As mentioned earlier, Doris was on a multitude of medications. One of her medications, Risperdal, is given to patients who suffer from psychotic disorders. Usually, psychotic disorders appear when a person is in their late teens, 20s, or 30s. Yet, Doris had been taking Risperdal, an antipsychotic, since she was about 11 years old. A personal psychiatric history of Doris and either her natural, foster, or adopted family was not available in any of her documentation, nor were any references to her suffering the symptoms of psychotic episodes such as delusions or hallucinations. Doris had also been taking Depakote, which is a medication given to people who suffer from bipolar disorder. Again, no mention of any manic or depressive episodes was present in her clinical records. Additionally, because she was also diagnosed with attention deficit disorder, and prescribed Ritalin and at one point Adderall, a nutritional history should also have been taken with careful attention to the amount of caffeine likely to be circulating in her system. Small amounts of caffeine in some at-risk individuals can precipitate loss of concentration or anxiety. Doris also was taking Wellbutrin for depression. Moreover, Doris's substance-abusing patterns complicated or perhaps also precipitated any onset of depression or anxiety.

Because of the varied medications prescribed to Doris, a complete examination by a physician, with a six-week follow-up, should have been conducted to learn not only about her medications, their indications, and major contraindications but also to accurately assess whether she was bipolar or suffered from a psychotic disorder and attention deficit disorder.

Sue Sadik, Ph.D., Consultant
South Carolina Department of Alcohol and Other Drug Abuse Services
Columbia, South Carolina

Case 8: A Challenge of Spirituality in Elementary School

Case Study Background/History

Brook Heights Elementary School is nested in an evolving neighborhood inhabited primarily by blue-collar workers as recently as twenty years ago. Since then, the neighborhood has retained a portion of its long-time inhabitants who are now retired; passed through a time when most of the families would be described as residing in low-income housing; and is now emerging as a strong community of solid, mostly African American yet diverse middle-class households.

Darien arrived as a new second-grade student to the school. His nonobtrusive demeanor, pleasant smile, and physical features of an African American would have made it easy for many to overlook him. Those adults who didn't overlook him seemed to be caught up in the struggle of deciding whether Darien was a boy or a girl, a difficult task mostly because of his hair being braided into thick cornrows.

Presenting Problem and Diagnosis

Darien began to visit with the school counselor after his mother told the teacher that he was "expressing grief." During his first visit with the counselor, Darien drew clouds and rain with a light blue crayon on a sheet of drawing paper. He drew family members and a house in pencil. Darien lives alone with his mother. His drawing, however, included his mother, father, stepsister, stepbrother, himself, and his deceased sister, Sonya. Sonya was 11 years old when she died.

"When I had dreams, I could go to her room and sleep with her. She been good too. And she asked if she could go to the bathroom and the teacher said 'no.' She said could she go home and the teacher said 'no.' She got to the fence and she collapsed. The kids took her back to school. She said everything went black. My mom picked her and me up. We took her to a doctor. Doctor said she could go home. The next morning, she started throwing up green. We took her to Charleston. I stayed with my Auntie. I couldn't see my sister. We go down to her grave and put flowers on her grave and talk to her. My dad didn't know my sister. She babysat me. She kept the doors locked. I didn't cry. I went past my sister." It was during this first session with Darien that the counselor began to learn of Darien's Native American heritage.

Counseling Intervention and Follow-Up

Subsequent counseling sessions with Darien continued to incorporate play in addition to client–counselor dialogue but were less directive in that Darien was able to choose the play medium. Darien's preference for creating fighting scenes in the sand tray was second only to him sharing his dreams. "My mom makes me sleep with a cross on every night. I used to have a dream catcher. Sometimes, when you have dreams, it catches all the bad dreams and gives you the good dreams."

Most of Darien's sand tray scenes could be described as well choreographed (as opposed to violent) battles with action warriors in which teams were balanced. Battles with no clear winners and losers were customary. Let me reiterate that while the sand tray was his medium of choice, Darien frequently shared his dreams. Once he dreamt that he and his father were getting in a car with the police. Darien shared with much animation and enthusiasm. "Me and him ran together, got up in the car and drove off. We turned around pointing the car downhill, drove through the woods and couldn't get back up because it was a hill." Darien had a unique way of honoring his dreams. He was able to give them a value comparable to real-life events without dimming the brightness of the line that separates them from reality. His dreams often reflected aspects of his life. "I had a dream about Grandma's husband. He's whipping me. My momma said, 'he aint gonna whip ya.'" As Darien continues, he frames this dream within the context of his life. "He was beating up my grandma but now he's in jail. Now she [grandmother] is trying to get him out. If he gets out I won't be able to visit."

Generally, Darien's play served a number of purposes. His play was a way for the counselor to gather information. Through his play, Darien was able to explore aspects of his world more thoroughly by making his world concrete. His play also afforded him a greater sense of control over his world as he made decisions on how to use symbols to represent events, concepts, and feelings.

Darien was invited to participate in a grief group with his peers. One member of the group lost both parents. Two other members' parents died. One member's teenage brother committed suicide. The group experience provided a different kind of therapeutic power where members could move through the grief process together. Characteristics such as trust and openness surfaced as group norms that became infused in their collective struggle to preserve their resiliency. Among the comments by members of the grief group, Brittany said, "I know how my dad died, but sometimes I wonder why." Darien spoke of his sister's spirit being around him and his mom. Darien talked about times when he attributed credit to his sister's spirit for protecting him from bullies and even helping him catch balls on the playground that he would have normally considered impossible to catch, "but somehow the ball ends up in my hands." Willie spoke of being afraid at his mom's stone. Paul asked Willie, "How did you feel when your mother died?" Willie responded by saying, "I felt like it was my fault." Paul said he felt the same way. "I said some mean things to my brother two days before he died," Paul added. As the group prepared for the holidays the counselor mentioned that he would be visiting the grave of his mother. Darien said, "That is your gift to her."

Sometimes, group meetings were supplemented with individual sessions with Darien. My counselor notes follow: "Discussed getting sick and seeing colors. Darien went to the doctor yesterday. The doctor said that if he continues to see colors they would do 'an x-ray on his brain.' That made him feel sad. He 'made a face' to his dad at the doctor's office and his dad smiled. When I inquired about what made him sad, Darien said that if they do the x-ray, they will be able to see what I am thinking when I gets home."

Cultural Implications

Darien continues to struggle with (1) grieving the loss of his sister and (2) his own personal safety and health. He is aware of threats from bullies, an abusive grandfather, strangers and drunken friends of his father who have tried to harm him or his family, and his own mortality. In contrast, a safety/protection theme is equally present in the therapeutic content associated with his close family members.

His counselor must be able to deal with a variety of cultural issues. One overarching challenge for the counselor involves sorting through the filtering effects of his own cultural identity. For example, would an abusive grandparent and drunken associates of Darien's father serve to perpetuate previously held stereotypes adversely affecting the counselor's level of commitment?

A second issue involves being able to understand how Darien's developmental level impacts his ability to negotiate the challenges he faces. The counselor must determine how to handle Darien's fear of his parents being able to see what he is thinking when they get the results of the "x-ray of his brain." Similarly, his counselor needs to have the skill level to determine whether Darien's wish for a new baby sister as a Christmas present is an inappropriate means of coping or developmentally normal.

Other considerations take a systemic perspective. The counselor may struggle with determining the relevance of the teacher and physician's role in the grieving process and the family's legal options. Neither seemed to have given adequate attention to Sonya's (Darien's deceased sister's) critical medical condition. How might this view conflict with the cultural beliefs held by the family? Might attributing blame contradict the spiritual beliefs of the family? How might the counselor control for his own subjectivity?

Finally, is there an inherent contradiction between the typical task of saying goodbye to a loved one who has died with Darien's firm belief that his sister is ever-present and in fact an active agent in his life? How might the counselor strike a balance between his theoretical orientation and the cultural framework of his client?

Counselor's Reflection and Self-Evaluation

Gathering data for assessment from multiple sources across time, using multiple counseling modalities (individual and group counseling), utilizing a variety of skills and techniques (e.g., bibliotherapy, play, drawings, dreams, sand tray, and dialogue), maintaining a developmental perspective and a reverence for the cultural heritage of the client, and incorporating evaluative components all helped shore up the counselor's effectiveness. Evidence of effectiveness can be seen through client disclosures. Both the client and the counselor appear to have bridged many cultural barriers that enabled open, honest, and comprehensive communication. A later drawing of blue clouds and rain showed progression in therapy as Darien decided to include a heart with wings with smaller hearts enclosed centered in the sky above two green trees full of fruit and supported with strong trunks. Darien's ability to summarize counseling sessions and describe aspects of sessions that he considered helpful was an indication of efficacy. Effectiveness may have been bolstered through the inclusion of specific activities that accentuated and celebrated certain cultural practices. The counselor could have provided a dream journal and a replacement dream catcher for the one lost. These seemingly small gestures coupled with additional readings from appropriate Native American authors may have strengthened Darien's power of endurance.

As Darien approaches adolescence and his thinking becomes more sophisticated, he will be confronted with the challenge of reevaluating his beliefs and values as he works through the amorphous stage of identity development. Currently, he is ready to adopt the beliefs shared by his closest family members who incorporate customs and traditions from various origins. It seems difficult to predict whether his exposure to differing cultural practices will make this process more facile or problematic.

Robert A. Horak, Jr., M. Ed., Ed.S.
Intermediate/Middle School Counselor
Heathwood Hall Episcopal School
Doctoral Student in Counselor Education
Columbia, South Carolina

Case Study 9: An African American Male Confronts Issues of Criminality

Presenting Problem and Diagnosis

Robert is a 23-year-old, single, African American male who presented for treatment in an urban county detention center "because I know I need some insight into my anger because I don't want to be a repeat offender." Robert believes counseling will help to "better myself, get out of my dorm, and to show the court I'm doing positive things." Currently, Robert has served 10 months in the county detention center and is awaiting trial. Robert was prescreened in order to assess for his motivation and appropriateness for individual counseling.

Robert is a man of slightly above average height and average build. His hair is kept in cornrows and his dentistry is remarkable for gold dental work on lower teeth. Robert also has a tattoo image of barbed wire on his left upper arm. Robert's mood and affect during our sessions was congruent to the topics of conversation. No significant medical history was reported. His speech was notable for terms indicative of the street and the prison system. Robert had no prior history of counseling or substance abuse treatment.

Robert grew up in a family that consisted of his mother, grandmother, and two uncles. Although Robert's mother lived in the home, he considers her neglectful and views his grandmother as the one "who raised me." He has never known his birth father but believes he is a successful military man based on stories his mother told him as a youth. His uncles are slightly older and serve as his male role models, but he acknowledges their behavior is not always "the best."

At age 4, his mother married his stepfather and they moved in with him. This period of Robert's life was marked by verbal, physical, and emotional abuse at the hands of his stepfather. Often, his stepfather would "kick me out." He continues to feel a great deal of anger and resentment toward his mother, whom he feels chose an abusive relationship over him.

At age 13, his grandmother died and a close cousin was shot and killed by police. Robert believes his "hatred of authority" started here and he began to view the police as the "enemy." Already reeling from the abuse at home, fighting and truancy increased at school. Seeking comfort from his pain, Robert began drinking alcohol, which marked his fall into a cycle of substance abuse and crime.

He reports quickly progressing "from wine to hard liquor." By age 15, he reported daily use of alcohol and marijuana. When asked how he supported his habits, he replied "selling drugs and robbery." Because of his incarceration, Robert has been clean for more than ten months. This is the longest period of sobriety since he began using drugs and alcohol as a 13-year-old.

Fighting and truancy marked Robert's behavior in school, and by his junior year he had dropped out to "be on the streets with my friends." This period of his life involved escalating drug and alcohol use and criminal activities. He was arrested and given the option of juvenile detention or placement in a Job Corps program. Robert chose the Job Corps and was sent to a training facility out of state. Here, he completed his GED and stayed clean and sober for more than a year. Upon completion of the Job Corps, he moved to South Carolina to be near his family and enrolled in a junior college. He reported liking his classes but dropped out after one semester to "be on the streets having fun and making the kind of money I was used to." He relapsed into a cycle of escalating criminal activity geared toward supporting his drug and alcohol habits. This ended with Robert's arrest and current incarceration. When asked about his employment history, Robert replied, "installing cable, construction on the side, and robbery." Employment usually ended because of substance use or because he felt undercompensated and returned to selling drugs.

Although Robert minimizes his criminal history, he reports seven arrests and many criminal actions where he was "not caught." His charges include control of a dangerous substance (cocaine), resisting arrest, assault on a police officer, aggravated assault with intent to kill, and his current charge of accessory to murder. He spoke of his criminal activities in a detached manner.

Counseling Intervention and Follow-Up

Robert was seen for individual counseling once a week for a period of ten weeks. Each session took place in the correctional facility in a room where Robert was monitored by staff from outside the room. Robert was not taking any medication. Therapy was based on a cognitive-behavior model and the basic philosophy of this therapy was explained to him during the initial session.

The first three sessions involved establishing rapport and further assessing his history and current level of functioning. Robert verbalized an understanding between right and wrong, but minimized the need to adhere to the rules of society. During the initial sessions, Robert showed himself to be bright and insightful as we worked together to identify realistic goals and to clarify his expectations. Termination was also discussed.

During the next few sessions, the focus shifted to his thinking patterns. Soon thereafter, behavior interventions were introduced. The therapist explained cognitive restructuring and worked to reconstruct his thinking. As a result, Robert began reporting increased insight into the negative views he held and began to work to change them. More specifically, he cited improvements in his views that "all cops were bad," "you can't trust women because they will hurt you," and his tendency to minimize his past negative behaviors. Another positive aspect was the clarification of his cycle of violence. With guidance from the therapist, Robert explored his triggers and underlying feelings about anger. He reported insight into his thought processes surrounding anger, and worked to improve his coping strategies and develop a more realistic thinking style. Confrontation was used successfully to keep Robert from placing blame and to take responsibility for his behavior. The final session involved summarizing treatment and dealing with any unresolved questions Robert had regarding his therapy. Robert's release from prison was not imminent at the time termination occurred.

During the course of the ten weeks, Robert made significant progress in treatment. He reported a boost in self-esteem from his ability to identify, monitor, and manage/reframe his faulty thinking. He met the goals we had set at the beginning. Robert was referred to community mental health and substance abuse centers and strongly urged to seek out these services when possible.

Although I would like to be more positive, I regard Robert's prognosis as guarded at best. His history of substance abuse, violence, and ambivalence to his past criminal (often violent) activities indicates a high likelihood for relapse outside of a controlled environment. Additionally, his intention to return to his social circles shows he is not yet ready to make the wholesale changes required to improve his chances of remaining sober and clear of criminal activity. There were many positive results of treatment, but the fact remains he has little support once released.

Cultural Implications

There are numerous racial, social, and cultural implications in this case. The therapist was a European American raised in a middle-class, suburban environment. I attempted to monitor myself so as to remain sensitive of the social and cultural differences with Robert.

One of the reasons for choosing cognitive-behavioral therapy was because of the collaborative nature of the therapeutic relationship. Counseling literature shows that African Americans often view the counseling relationship as unequal. I believe, in this case, that Robert greatly benefited from the collaborative nature of the relationship. This was indicated by the initiative he took during the course of treatment to improve himself. The correctional facility was also a big factor in this case. Often during the sessions, we dealt with issues specifically related to his relationships with other inmates as well as his emotional adjustments while incarcerated. As a therapist, I had limited experience working with incarcerated clients.

Counselor's Reflection and Self-Evaluation

I believe using cognitive-behavioral therapy was the right choice in this case. It allowed for a collaborative relationship, which allowed Robert to become involved in all aspects of his treatment. The cognitive strategies were effective, but the behavior interventions (specifically behavioral rehearsal, diversion techniques, and graded task assignments) allowed Robert to engage in activities outside of the session.

In hindsight, I would refocus attention more on his substance abuse patterns. Our sessions often touched on his cycle of substance abuse, but in-depth substance counseling was not provided because I was not trained in substance abuse treatment. Although Robert denies it, I believe he remains highly susceptible to relapse and I confronted him on critical issues that pointed toward a relapse. I felt his answers to my questions regarding substance use were often meant to appease me and deflect attention to other areas where he felt less vulnerable.

In future cases such as this one, I would consider utilizing systemic or group work. Although I feel positive about Robert's improvements, I often felt we were missing core issues related to his family history. I would have liked to help him further develop his relationship with his family and understand the influence it had on him. In addition, Robert's insight would be beneficial to other inmates in a group setting.

Daniel B. Kissinger, M.Ed., LPC
Doctoral Student in Counselor Education
University of South Carolina
Columbia, South Carolina

Conclusion

This chapter includes nine counseling cases that have multicultural implications. Most of these cases reveal how cultural worldview can influence a client's perception of his or her lifestyle and problem or can affect how an individual functions in the real world, especially across cultures. These cases also demonstrate how culture and ethnicity can intersect with religious beliefs; sexual identity or orientation; gender; ethnic or racial identity, heritage and style; age group or developmental stage in life; and other diverse affiliations or status situations. Even more, these counseling cases demonstrate how the client's worldview can be miles apart from the counselor's perception of the client's problem or diagnosis, thus causing the counselor, at times, to adjust diagnoses and intervention approaches in order to be effective in helping the client in real and practical ways.

REFERENCES

Courtois, C. (1991). Theory, sequencing, and strategy in treating adult survivors. In J. Briere (Ed.), *Treating victims of child sexual abuse* (pp. 47–60). San Francisco: Jossey-Bass.

Herek, G. M. (1990). The context of anti-gay violence: Notes on cultural and psychological heterosexism. *Journal of Interpersonal Violence, 5*(3), 316–333.

Mallon, G. (2000). Always watch your back: Advice on radical practice. *In the Family, 6*(1), 6–13.

Reynolds, A. L., & Hanjorgiris, W. F. (2000). Coming out: Lesbian, gay, and bisexual identity development. In R. M. Perez, K. A. DeBord, & K. J. Bieschke (Eds.), *Handbook of counseling and psychotherapy with lesbian, gay, and bisexual clients* (pp. 35–55). Washington, DC: American Psychological Association.

17 Using Bibliotherapy in Transcultural Counseling

JOHN McFADDEN AND MARYANNE BANICH

Integrating art and science is the work of counselors. There are myriad theories and techniques from which to draw. However, unless the professional can weave the science with the art of language, culture, empathy, communication, human experience, and holistic awareness, counseling will become stagnant. From a scientific viewpoint, counselors must be intentional with clients. From the artistic viewpoint, counselors must be creative with clients.

Bibliotherapy Defined

Bibliotherapy is the intentional use of art for healing and growth. There are several definitions of bibliotherapy discussed in the literature. Hynes and Hynes-Berry (1986) define three methods as reading, interactive, and developmental. Cohen (1989) defines bibliotherapy as "that which occurs with the guidance and skill of a professional and that which occurs through self-help books" (p. 41). For the purposes of this chapter, Cohen's former definition is applied.

How to Use Bibliotherapy

As simplistic as it may seem, there is more to the method than merely suggesting a short story, novel, poem, or movie to a client. The process of bibliotherapy does not happen each time a client reads a book or sees a movie. Through the intentionality of selecting the reading material and processing it with the client, bibliotherapy becomes an agent for a change in affect or behavior. Professionals in the field of bibliotherapy have defined four stages required for the process to be successful: "(1) identification, (2) selection, (3) presentation, and (4) follow-up " (Pardeck & Pardeck, 1993, p. 109). Each stage should be guided by the counselor and each stage is equally important. The first stage involves the counselor's identifying the client's issue(s). The second and third stages include the counselor's knowledge of the client's reading level, the counselor's skill in selecting appropriate reading material, and the timing and method of introducing the concept to the client. Without the final stage of processing the accomplishment with the client, this activity becomes common reading or watching a movie instead of some form of therapeutic relevance.

Follow-up activities can include discussing the reading, viewing a film, drawing or painting, or role playing and journaling.

The Use of Bibliotherapy Through Different Counseling Approaches

Because of the increasing diversity of clients and the issues with which they present, the counselor must learn to integrate cultural factors into the assessment and treatment of the client. "Harm can come to clients who are expected to fit all the specifications of a given theory, whether or not the values espoused by the theory are consistent with their own cultural values" (Corey, 2001, p. 460). Rather than attempting to merge the client into the counselor's theory, professionals must make their theory complement the unique needs of each client. "This requirement calls for counselors to possess knowledge of various cultures, be aware of their own cultural heritage, and have skills to assist diverse clients in meeting their needs within the realities of their culture" (Corey, 2001, p. 460). In this, the twenty-first century, a challenge has been issued by Corey that "merely assisting clients in gaining insight, expressing suppressed emotions or making specific behavioral changes is not enough" (p. 460). According to Corey, the counselor has responsibility to find strategies and techniques to help clients question the impact of their culture and the impact that their culture continues to have on their lives and to make decisions about what they want to celebrate or change.

There are several theories mentioned in the counseling literature that suggest bibliotherapy as a supplement to other techniques. The first of these is multimodal therapy developed by Arnold Lazarus (1990). The counselor who uses this approach believes individuals have a variety of issues and that it is appropriate to use multiple modes of treatment strategies to ensure change. Multimodal therapists such as Martin-Causey and Hinkle (1995) and Curtis and Davis (1999) typically use techniques such as biofeedback, thought stopping, the empty chair, and meditation. Each of these lends itself to blending with bibliotherapy.

Rational emotive behavior therapists (REBTs), including Ellis (1996), believe in confronting clients with full acceptance but without empathy or too much understanding of pointless behaviors. REBTs also believe in using bibliotherapy to foster independence in their clients. The emphasis in these two therapies is on a variety of cognitive and behavioral techniques tailored to the individual client. Reading or watching a film would be considered homework for their clients. "Bibliotherapy has been used to increase academic and emotional development with children, to enhance self-esteem in children, and to help clients cope with stress and change. It can also be used as a way of helping clients through grief, and to increase socialization and self-actualization" (Capuzzi & Gross, 1997, p. 273).

The goals and objectives of bibliotherapy become the same as those for other counseling sessions, that is, to foster understanding or insight, to inspire growth and health, and to promote satisfying relationships. According to Pardeck and Pardeck (1993), bibliotherapy provides the counselor and the client with an opportunity for discussion of an issue with which others have dealt, while sharing the experience of reading or watching a film, which aids in building trust between the counselor and client. As is presented throughout this textbook, both counselors and clients are cultural beings in every likeness. Bibliotherapy can be a method of discussing cultural issues for both counselor and client, while helping the counselor with unfamiliar issues and at the same time helping the client identify with familiar issues.

Bibliotherapy should be used as an adjunct to other more traditional counseling techniques such as art, music, and play therapy. The counselor who decides to use this approach should have prior knowledge of the written materials or films being used, which means that the counselor should have read the material previously or should have seen the film (the counselor also may read or watch the material, or parts of it, again along with the client). The counselor should have assessed formerly the mental status of the client and have a trusting counseling relationship. Bibliotherapy is not something to be taken lightly or too quickly with a client. At the same time, it is not a method to be used with severely emotionally unstable individuals or in a time of crisis. The client with a deep-rooted psychological or psychosocial issue probably is served most effectively with intensive traditional therapy. "The counselor also must be adept at 'reading' the reader's response to discussions of third persons" (Byrne, 2001). "For example, a client who is considered to be empathic may be unmoved by the portrayal of death in a novel or movie, while another client considered to be less empathic may be profoundly moved even in a non-verbal way" (Byrne, 2001). Clients may be able to use more easily transference or countertransference of feelings, emotions, and beliefs to literary characters. Therefore, counselors must be astute at listening and helping the client define the relationship that develops between the client and the literary character(s). A counselor who is highly adept at reading both verbal and nonverbal communication will find it easier to use bibliotherapy. For example, many clients will find it less threatening to deal with their own issues through the third person—the literary character—but the discerning counselor will be able to apply imaginative issues to real-life situations.

It is important that the counselor do the work during the introduction stage of counseling in order to gain insight into the client's previous experience with reading and watching films and how that may affect the use of bibliotherapy. During the selecting and presenting stages, the counselor should introduce the concept as well as the chosen literature or film—perhaps through characters—to the client (the counselor may also ask the client to help choose the literature or film). The client must have time for reading or viewing the film and reflecting between sessions or during a session with the counselor. In the follow-up stage, the counselor should be able to provide discussion that will lead the client from merely recalling the information to interpreting, applying, analyzing, synthesizing, and evaluating the reading in relation to the client's own life. Finally, there must be a session for closure of that particular reading or film. Bibliotherapy is especially effective for clients who process things visually as opposed to auditorily (Capuzzi & Gross, 1997).

The manner in which bibliotherapy is used is as varied as the clients whom counselors encounter. Bibliotherapy is not limited to novels, short stories, poetry, or films; it is not limited to fiction, nonfiction, science fiction, children's stories, or fairy tales. There is a plethora of material waiting to be selected from the shelves of public libraries, bookstores, video rental stores, and even the Internet. The story or novel may even be one that was told to the client by a mother, grandmother, grandfather, and so on, which was written for posterity. The possibilities are limitless, as is the potential for clients to gain healing and understanding that will enhance their knowledge for today and their future problem-solving abilities. Chosen literature should have some literary merit or poignancy for the client. Some of the published literature on bibliotherapy suggests that "a poorly written novel with stereotyped characters and simplistic answers to complex questions is worse than not reading anything at all and can even lead to a negative view of literature by the client" (White, 1989, p. 10). We believe that novels with stereotyped characters might be primarily the manifestation with which a client who has experienced such judgments can connect in a therapeutic setting through guidance of a professional. Such material offers the counselor an opportunity to discuss with the client what it is like to experience discrimination. This is the time for self-evaluation by the counselor as well as the client. Depending on the developmental and reading skills of the client, the counselor may recommend literature in which the characters are different from the client or similar to the client. This offers an opportunity to introduce relevant issues pertaining to race, gender, ethnicity, spirituality, disability, sexual orientation, and so on. Because of the personal nature of reading and film preference as well as the client's predisposition to reading, this becomes an area that the counselor can only determine with each individual client.

The underlying assumption is that reading is a dynamic process (Schlichter & Burke, 1994). When people read or view films, the characters and experiences, the setting, and the tone of the literature or movie are translated into something personal by the reader or viewer. Bibliotherapy can be used to work with many different clients with a variety of issues. Counselors who find themselves counseling those of different cultural backgrounds or those with culture-based issues should use culturally relevant bibliotherapy to bring that perspective into the sessions as appropriate. Cohen's (1994, p. 41) study, for example, suggests that "readers recognized themselves, significant others, and their situations in what they read. This aspect of therapeutic reading appeared to be crucial to the evolution of the entire experience. Those participants who strongly and personally recognized themselves in literary characters obtained greater benefit from their reading." We believe the ability of the client to recognize the self in literary characters through the use of bibliotherapy is especially important for the client and counselor who are from different cultural backgrounds, or at the very least, for those with different cultural experiences. According to McFadden (1999), this can promote manifestation of transcultural encounters in the interest of human potential. Transcultural differences can offer positive qualities to the counseling experiences.

Research

Johnson, Wan, Templeton, Graham, and Sattler (2000) provide guidelines for teachers of students with disabilities in the use and benefits of bibliotherapy relative to application for traditional classroom teaching. The authors delineate effective practices for providing a supportive, safe, and positive discussion with students with disabilities. They also provide an extensive list of children's literature for bibliotherapy.

Most of the research on bibliotherapy concentrates on children and adolescents with developmental issues (Sauerman, 1980; Walter, 1993; Gillespie, 1994), divorce issues (Sheridan, 1982; Bunting, 1984; Forrer, 1985; Brennan, 1989; Nuccio, 1997; Freitag, Ottens, & Gross, 1999), grief (Adams, 1994; Lelah, 1994; Barbis, 1997; Davis, 2000; Doka, 2000), and a plethora of other topics. Two such studies were conducted with children in hospital settings. The first used bibliotherapy to encourage the hospitalized child's self-esteem and self-concept. In this study, by Mathews and Lonsdale (1992), the research used eleven British hospitals in which play therapy staff were surveyed and interviewed about the efficacy of the bibliotherapy. The staff was asked if it used bibliotherapy with the children for communication, education, treatment, and coping with feelings. The responses were grouped into three categories: growth, education, and play. Most of the interviewees had positive responses. They indicated that the research suggested that there should be greater awareness of bibliotherapy among all professions concerned with caring for children in medical centers and similar settings. Mathews and Lonsdale concluded their study by reporting that further research with bibliotherapy with hospitalized children is needed.

The second study used bibliotherapy to reduce the anxiety level of the hospitalized child. Bibliotherapy in this investigation was used along with other therapeutic approaches for the treatment of children who had been burned. Because other treatments were applied, the researchers could not assess the positive effects of bibliotherapy alone, although positive outcomes were measured when including other approaches used for this study.

Sipsas-Herrman et al. (1996) used a pretest and posttest experimental design on a group of sixth graders to examine the effects of fiction and nonfiction on the increasing acceptance of children with disabilities. The researchers concluded that nonfiction was found to be the only effective approach. Other research on the effects of bibliotherapy with children with disabilities has either proven to be inconclusive or shown that children with disabilities do not like to read about other children with disabilities—they would rather read and compare themselves to children without disabilities.

A group of second graders was the focus in a study to measure the results of bibliotherapy on personal and social development and it was found that there is evidence to suggest that definite improvement can be achieved by using bibliotherapeutic intervention. A similar study by Blake (1988) used the Culture Free Self-Esteem Inventories for Children and Adults as a pretest and posttest comparison measure. The hypothesis was that the self-esteem of 11 and 12 year olds would be increased through the use of bibliotherapy. Although the scores were not statistically significant, the research did reflect a positive correlation between using the bibliotherapeutic intervention.

Another area that has used bibliotherapy as an adjunct to counseling techniques is the use of fiction with gifted children and adolescents. "For too long the social and emotional needs of gifted youngsters have been underestimated—one could even say ignored" (Byrne, 2001). She proceeds to indicate that the lack of interest can be attributed to the thinking that gifted children face few problems in the realm of their development. This is based on the belief that, because the children are gifted, they will not have social or emotional maturation problems. "Quite simply, gifted youngsters must face the same problems as other children as well as a unique set of problems that arise from being gifted" (Byrne, 2001). For example, gifted adolescents are more often referred for counseling because of their depression. This happens when the capacity to assimilate information about disturbing events is greater than their capacity to either process or understand this information. Counselors should choose literature for these children and adolescents not based solely on their reading level but also on their emotional developmental level. This provides a safe place for the child or adolescent with guidance to be his or her introspective self.

Doll and Doll (1997) provide annotated bibliographic resources that contain tips and ideas for bibliotherapy activities with young people and reflective of culturally diverse interests. The counselor must also decide whether to use bibliotherapy in group settings. The parameters for individual, family, and group therapy would, of course, apply first; then bibliotherapy could be considered. For example, Barrett-Kruse (2000) describes bibliotherapy and storytelling as methods for facilitating positive mother–daughter relationships within the variety of family constellations that exist today.

The four aforementioned stages of identification, selection, presentation, and follow-up would apply with group counseling as well. Group counseling with bibliotherapy may be an avenue for those who do not gravitate to being singled out or those who may be able to discuss the literary characters more easily than focusing on themselves. Reinforcing the point: joining a book club is not bibliotherapy—the process must be intentionally guided by a professional counselor. In addition, if it is to reflect cultural enrichment, the process must include diversity across cultures.

In addition to literature, movies can be used as a bibliotherapy tool, although some would refer to this as cinematherapy. This approach could be particularly effective with adolescents who spend much time watching television and movies but who do not enjoy reading. The counselor should choose movies that depict events or emotions that can facilitate insight, change, or offer coping skills for the client. Recognizing the potential that movies can have on influencing the viewing audience and careful identification of video material that is culturally appropriate and broad in content is another step toward transculturalism.

Bibliotherapy also may be used in the classroom by counselor educators. It is a well-known fact that counselor education programs struggle nationally with providing students with real-life situations while in training. Bibliotherapy is one avenue that should be explored partially to alleviate this dilemma. Introducing students to "clients" and their "issues" through literature and cinema is an excellent option. For example, using *As Good As It Gets,* in which Jack Nicholson plays an obsessive-compulsive character, gives educators a chance to show portions of the film in the classroom; then have students write and discuss case studies from different theoretical viewpoints. "Some therapists, such as Harvey Roy Greenberg, Clinical Director of Psychiatry at the Einstein School of Medicine, write movie reviews to help students analyze characters" (Melanson, 2001).

Organizations such as the World Organization for Research Into the Therapeutic Use of Motion Pictures are dedicated to the study of films for patients but also films as patients (Melanson, 2001). Melanson also makes the point that research studies have shown that literature and movies play a significant role in the desensitization of violence among young people. Those media also can play a significant role in developing positive coping skills.

Examples of Literature and Films to Use in Bibliotherapy

The following examples represent a partial list of books and movies that might serve as bibliotherapy sources for professionals to use in transcultural counseling:

LITERATURE

Children/Adolescents
The Little Chairs
Kate Salley Palmer

Mean Soup
Betsy Everitt

The Cat Ate My Jumpsuit
P. Danziger

Harriet the Spy
L. Fizhugh

The Stone Book
A. Garner

The Planet of Junior Brown
V. Hamilton

Father's Arcane Daughter
E. L. Konigsburg

George
E. L. Konigsburg

A Wrinkle in Time
M. L'Engle

Very Far Away From Anything Else
U. Le Guin

The Bridge to Terabithia
K. Paterson

Freaky Friday
M. Rodgers

Dancing in the Wings
Debbie Allen

Brownwen, the Traw and the Shape-Shifter
James Dickey

Charlotte's Web
E. B. White

The Giving Tree
Shel Silverstein

Oh the Places You'll Go
Dr. Suess

The House at Pooh Corner
A. A. Milne

Go Ask Alice
Anonymous

Catcher in the Rye
J. D. Salinger

Zen and the Art of Motorcycle Maintenance
Robert Pirsig

Sitting Pretty
Dinah Johnson

Little Women
Louisa May Alcott

Soul Looks Back in Wonder
Tom Feelings

Moja Means One: Swahili Counting Book
Muriel Feelings

The Soul of Christmas
Helen King

Free as a Frog
Elizabeth Jamison Hodges

Adults
Problems
John Updike

Nine Stories
J. D. Salinger

The Collected Stories of Eudora Welty
Eudora Welty

Selected Poems
Robert Frost

Poems on Love and Life
Frederick Douglas Harper

Clover
Dori Sanders

The Bodacious Book of Succulence
Sark

The Fisherman's Tale
Emily Whittle and Jeri Burdick

Divine Secrets of the Ya-Ya Sisterhood
Rebecca Wells

Healing Stories: Narrative in Psychiatry and Psychotherapy
G. Roberts and J. Holmes

Post Office
Charles Bukowski

Roots
Alex Haley

The Ladder of Years
Anne Tyler

And So I Rise
Maya Angelou

Medicine and Poetry
S. Rojcewicz

A Shining Thread of Hope
Darlene Clark Hine and Kathleen Thompson

Bridget Jones's Diary
Helen Feilding

MOVIES

Children/Adolescents
Heathers
The Parent Trap
Now and Then
National Velvet
Paper Moon

The Secret Garden
The Wizard of Oz
Ever After
Table for Five

Adults
The Joy Luck Club
Postcards From the Edge
Coal Miner's Daughter
Muriel's Wedding
Driving Miss Daisy
Soul Food

Fried Green Tomatoes
Steel Magnolias
The Turning Point
A Room With A View
On Golden Pond

Conclusion

Bibliotherapy is an adjunctive tool that counselors can use transculturally with children, adolescents, and adults through individual, couples, and family counseling. It has many uses such as bridging a cultural gap between counselor and client, changing affect, and building mechanisms for coping skills. This chapter defines bibliotherapy, demonstrates how to use it, and presents research examples. It also offers both print and media examples to use with clients of all ages who present many different issues. Likewise, it provides some background information for individuals to consider through a bibliotherapeutic approach in achieving goals of counseling across cultures.

DISCUSSION QUESTIONS

1. Describe a counseling case or case study in which you would use bibliotherapy.

2. What are some of the aspects to consider when recommending literature or film to a client for use in therapy?

3. What role can bibliotherapy play in bridging a cultural gap between the client and the counselor?

4. What role can bibliotherapy play in helping clients with transcultural issues?

5. What is the difference between clients reading a book or watching a film with and without the guidance of a counselor?

6. How is bibliotherapy integrated with other theoretical techniques? Discuss which counseling theories the counselor might consider using along with bibliotherapy.

REFERENCES

Adams, K. N. (1994). Bereavement counseling groups with elementary school students (Doctoral dissertation, University of Florida, 1994). *Dissertation Abstracts International, 56,* 4277.

Barbis, H. E. (1997). The impact of a loss and separation support group on school children: An evaluation of the footsteps program (Master's thesis, California State University, 1997). *Masters Abstracts International, 36,* 0318.

Barrett-Kruse, C. (2000). Strengthening the mother-daughter relationship through bibliotherapy and story telling. *TCA Journal, 28*(2), 111–114.

Blake, S. M. (1988). *The effect of bibliotherapy on the self-esteem of sixth graders* (Report No. CS009105, ERIC Document Reproduction Service, ED 293 101).

Brennan, D. J. (1989). Effects of group counseling and interactive bibliotherapy on children's adjustment to separation and divorce (Doctoral dissertation, Hofstra University, 1989). *Dissertation Abstracts International, 51,* 0413.

Bunting, K. P. (1984). The use and effect of puppetry and bibliotherapy in group counseling with children of divorced parents (Doctoral dissertation, The College of William and Mary, 1984). *Dissertation Abstracts International, 45,* 3094.

Byrne, G. R. (2001). An introduction to bibliotherapy. AAEGT Conference, June 1998.

Capuzzi, D., & Gross, D. R. (1997). *Introduction to the counseling profession.* Boston: Allyn & Bacon.

Cohen, L. J. (1989). Reading as a group process phenomenon: A theoretical framework for bibliotherapy. *Journal of Poetry Therapy, 3*(2), 73–83.

Cohen, L. J. (1994). Bibliotherapy: A valid treatment modality. *Journal of Psychosocial Nursing, 32,* 40–44.

Corey, G. (2001). *Theory and practice of counseling and psychotherapy.* Belmont, CA: Brooks/Cole.

Curtis, R. C., & Davis, K. M. (1999). Spirituality and multimodal therapy: A practical approach to incorporating spirituality in counseling. *Counseling and Values, 43*(3), 199–210.

Davis, J. (2000). When a pet dies: Books can help children learn to grieve. *Texas Child Care, 24*(3), 28–33.

Doka, K. J. (Ed.). (2000). *Living with grief: Children, adolescents, and loss.* Washington, DC: Hospice Foundation of America.

Doll, B., & Doll, C. (1997). *Bibliotherapy with young people: Librarians and mental health professionals working together.* Englewood, CO: Libraries Unlimited.

Ellis, A. (1996). The humanism of rational emotive behavior therapy and other cognitive behavior therapies. *Journal of Humanistic Education and Development, 35*(2), 69–88.

Forrer, S. L. (1985). Divorce discussion groups for elementary-age children: A curriculum plan (Doctoral dissertation, The University of Akron, 1985). *Dissertation Abstracts International, 46,* 3252.

Freitag, R., Ottens, A., & Gross, C. (1999). Deriving multicultural themes from bibliotherapeutic literature: A neglected resource. *Counselor Education and Supervision, 39*(2), 120–133.

Gillespie, C. M. (1994). A case study utilizing developmental bibliotherapy methodology in the secondary remedial reading classroom to enhance reading proficiency and self-esteem (Doctoral dissertation, Temple University, 1994). *Dissertation Abstracts International, 55,* 0916.

Hynes, A., & Hynes-Berry, M. (1986). *Bibliotherapy. The interactive process: A handbook.* Boulder, CO: Westview Press.

Johnson, C. E., Wan, G., Templeton, R. A., Graham, L. P., & Sattler, J. L. (2000). *Booking it to peace: Bibliotherapy guidelines for teachers* (Report No. EC308303, ERIC Document Reproduction Service ED 451 622).

Lazarus, A. A. (1990). Multimodal applications and research: A brief overview and update. *Elementary School Guidance and Counseling, 24*(4), 243–247.

Lelah, R. (1994). Children and adolescents during maternal terminal illness: Phenomenology and bibliotherapy (Doctoral dissertation, Rutgers the State University of New Jersey, 1994). *Dissertation Abstracts International, 55,* 2643.

Martin-Causey, T., & Hinkle, S. J. (1995). Multimodal therapy with an aggressive preadolescent: A demonstration of effectiveness and accountability. *Journal of Counseling and Development, 73*(3), 305–316.

Mathews, D. A., & Lonsdale, R. (1992). Children in hospital: Reading therapy and children in hospital. *Health Libraries Review, 9,* 14–26. Cited in E. DeVault, *Using words that heal. Bibliotherapy in child life settings.* Retrieved April 10, 2002, from http://home.earthlink.net/~esmejake/litrev.htm

McFadden, J. (1999). *Transcultural Counseling* (2nd ed.). Alexandria, VA: American Counseling Association.

Melanson, R. (2001, January). Movies as therapy: Not just vacations of the mind. *New Brunswick Telegraph Journal.*

Nuccio, L. M. (1997). The effects of bibliotherapy on the self-esteem and teacher-rated classroom behavior on third-grade children of divorce (Doctoral dissertation, The University of Southern Mississippi, 1997). *Dissertation Abstracts International, 59,* 0409.

Pardeck, J. T., & Pardeck, J. A. (1993). Bibliotherapy: A tool for helping preschool children deal with developmental change related to family relationships. *Early Child Development Care, 47,* 107–129.

Sauerman, T. H. (1980). A guide for dealing with five major life issues of young children (ages 2–7): Death, hospitalization and illness, separation and divorce, new baby, and moving (Doctoral dissertation, Temple University, 1980). *Dissertation Abstracts International, 41,* 1939.

Schlichter, C. L., & Burke M. (1994). Using books to nurture the social and emotional development of gifted students. *Roeper Review, 16,* 280–283.

Sheridan, J. T. (1982). Structured group counseling or explicit bibliotherapy as an in-school strategy for preventing problems in children from changing families (Doctoral dissertation, The Pennsylvania State University, 1982). *Dissertation Abstracts International, 43,* 0677.

Sipsas-Herrman, A. et al. (1996, March). The differential effects of fiction and nonfiction literature: Increasing acceptance of children with disabilities. Paper presented at the annual meeting of the National Association of School Psychologists, Atlanta, GA. (Report No. EC304715, ERIC Document Reproduction Service, No. ED 394 219).

Walter, V. A. (1993). *War and peace literature for children and young adults: A resource guide to significant issues.* Phoenix, AZ: Oryx Press.

White, R. (1989). *Bibliotherapy and the reluctant student* (Report No. CS009734, ERIC Document Reproduction Service, No. ED 309 390).

18 Preventive Counseling in a Multicultural Society

CHARLES E. DURANT AND JOHN McFADDEN

Prevention has become a prevalent term in contemporary society. This term is found extensively in popular magazines and books, newspapers, professional and trade journals, dissertations and monographs, and governmental studies. Prevention models found in medical journals differ, however, from those in counseling journals and monographs. For most counselors and other helping professionals, prevention emphasizes development of client empowerment skills.

Prevention is a fundamental tenet of the counseling profession. *Prevention* and *counseling,* as terms and techniques, are fundamentally misunderstood by the public. And to add to the conundrum, as a term and as a concept, *primary prevention* has not been static, even within and among the counseling disciplines. Each term (primary prevention and counseling) is contextual. Some ascribe a mental health or developmental perspective, whereas others perceive a medical model with a pathological or illness orientation.

For the most part, *primary prevention* as used herein refers to a comprehensive set of proactive and collaborative activities directed toward forestalling the antecedent (probable or suspected affective or behavioral) incidences from ever occurring by seeking fundamental changes in a population or high-risk group. Emphasis is on proactive measures (e.g., instruction) and is targeted toward groups of people who may be at-risk as opposed to remediation and individualized services.

Prevention models abound in the literature. Guetzloe (2000) identified causal factors known to be associated with violence and aggression and delineated practical strategies for addressing violence in the school and in the classroom. O'Neal (1997) presented a group work model for special education students that provided an alternative approach for addressing academic and social skills development. Forness et al. (2000) described a prevention model that utilized a self-determination curriculum to address both emotional and behavioral disorders. Albee and Ryan-Finn (1998) cited two monographs, the *American Journal of Community Psychology* and *14 Ounces of Prevention* by Price, as excellent resources. These models and those cited in a monograph by Dusenbury et al., (1997) provide practitioners with a framework for identifying high-risk populations, assessing variables to address, and formulating preventive interventions. For example, Albee (1982) developed an incidence formula in which the occurrence of mental illness is attributed to seven components: organic factors or behaviors that contribute to disease or illness (smoking, drug abuse, poor nutrition), stress, feelings of powerlessness, exploitation, coping skills, self-esteem, and support group. In a later publication by Albee and Gullotta (1998), the incidence formula is operationalized. Also, an expanded version of Albee's design may be found in the ten-step model developed by Dickel and Boytim (1991). Population identification, goals, objectives, and strategies are the supplemental items found in the latter model.

Preventive Counseling: A Hierarchical Framework

Caplan (1964) is attributed with having classified prevention into three categories: primary (preventing an occurrence), secondary (diagnosis of an occurrence), and tertiary (slowing the onset or preventing long-term consequences). This triadic classification system has many detractors (Albee, 1982; Cowen, 1983, 1997; Baker & Shaw, 1987; Lorion, Price, & Eaton, 1989; Conyne, 2000) because of the debates as to whether a difference exists between primary and secondary prevention (Romano & Hage, 2000) and whether secondary and tertiary preventions are not preventions but remediation (Baker & Shaw, 1987; Bower, 1987). Tertiary prevention has also been conceptualized as treatment (Cowen, 1983) or rehabilitation (Albee, 1995). Situations do exist where secondary and tertiary, but not primary, prevention can be provided (Shaffer et al., 1990). Shaffer et al. suggested that primary interventions are not applicable to the prevention of specific adolescent disorders: conduct disorders, learning disorders, drug and alcohol abuse, and suicide.

Primary prevention focuses on the development of educational programs for individuals or communities that have the potential to be affected by an issue (Conyne, 1987, 1997, 2000; Shore, 1998; Kiselica, 2001). For girls, prenatal care has been a prime beneficiary of primary intervention programming. Warning labels on several consumer items (e.g., cigarettes, alcohol, drugs) inform pregnant women of potential risks to their unborn children. Educational programs describe the effects of alcohol and poor nutritional habits. Posters on buses, trains, and subways depict characteristics of fetal alcohol syndrome at birth. With these and other media, there has been increased attention to the relationship between child development issues and adolescent and inexperienced mothers.

Secondary prevention is based on the premise that an identified dysfunction already exists (Simeonsson, 1991) and that early detection and intervention lead to successful outcomes. Early remediation is paramount in alleviating the problem from becoming worse. Whereas the goal of primary prevention is to prevent the occurrence of an incidence or to reduce additional occurrences, the goal of secondary prevention is reducing the prevalence or severity of existing stresses or disorders through counseling interventions. Beneficiary secondary interventions are able to mediate attendant stressors with an effective support system.

Tertiary prevention counseling occurs when an established affective or behavioral disorder is exacerbated in an individual. This level of counseling seeks to minimize the negative impact of the occurrence and to prevent related complications through direct interventions.

The efficacy of prevention approaches has been and continues to be debated (Lewis et al., 1990; Durlak & Wells, 1997; Franklin, Grant, Corcoran, Miller, & Bultman, 1997; Sagrestano & Paikoff, 1997; Trickett, 1997; Weissberg, Kuster, & Gullotta, 1997; Dowell, 2001). As an example, two community-based strategies for preventing youth violence, redirecting youth behavior, and shifting peer group norms, have shown a lack of effect in reducing youth violence. In fact, because both approaches tend to group high-risk youths together, they can actually increase the cohesiveness of delinquent peer groups and facilitate deviancy training (Dishion, Andrews, & Crosby, 1995; Elliott & Menard, 1996; Patterson & Yoerger, 1997).

Measurable evaluative standards for prevention programs remain elusive. In some cases, the misuse of scientific methodologies used to perform a review of prevention programs has served to discredit some evaluative efforts. Of those prevention programs that utilize assessment strategies, most investigate short-term quantitative measures of effectiveness, such as participant competence, as well as employ qualitative evaluations. Several attempts to develop empirical measures with a theoretical approach, however, do appear in the literature (Robinson, 1980; Caulkins, Rydell, Sohler-Everingham, & Bushway, 1999; Nitsch, 1999; Riley, 2000; Sapia, 2000; Silverman, 2000).

Durlak and Wells (1998) provided evidence that many primary prevention methods bring significant, positive outcomes despite glaring deficiencies in intervention conceptualization, documentation, and implementation. Most troubling to Durlak and Wells (1997) was that their meta-analytic review found that participant race and ethnicity was not found in 48 percent of the studies, "an especially problematic finding in a field where the sociocultural appropriateness of interventions is critical" (p. 150). On the other end of the spectrum, compelling evidence shows that drug abuse education programs, such as DARE (Drug Abuse Resistance Education), CARE (Chemical Assistance Reaching Everyone), and SADD (Students Against Driving Drunk), popular with police departments, school systems, community agencies, and parent groups do not deter drug use among adolescents and teens. As a result, the U.S. Department of Education has rescinded funding support. Staunch supporters contend that, despite dubious outcomes, these programs are tremendous public relations tools for law enforcement, particularly with students.

Preventive Intervention Formats

Prevention activities and programs can be applied in three targeted forums: (1) individual, (2) groups, and (3) environmental.

Individual

Individualized preventions generally focus on secondary and tertiary interventions. Friedmann (1998) described a flexible eating disorder prevention program.

The gender-based model operationalizes contemporary theories of female develop-ment, validates feelings, reframes experiences, and provides understanding of soci-etal pressures. Beginning with preadolescents, it teaches girls to recognize when they feel fat and to tell the stories that lie underneath (Friedmann, 1998). Dibrino (1998) created a checklist to help identify adolescents at risk for self-mutilation and the behavioral symptoms that predispose such behaviors. In addition, primary and secondary strategies for adolescent clients were delineated in the checklist.

Groups

Groups tend to be effective mechanisms for expanding knowledge (secondary and tertiary prevention strategies) among those who share similar concerns and cul-tural perspectives. Thematic groups, which use expressive interventions (drama, dance, music, sand tray, bibliotherapy, phototherapy, poetry, etc.), help clients feel less isolated and more free to unlock feelings. For example, play therapy has proven to be an effective intervention component (Shen, 1998). In addition, stimu-lus drawings (SDs) and techniques were developed in the 1960s for use with deaf children at a time when manual communication was forbidden in their schools (Silver, 1991). During the next decade, the drawings were expanded for use with learning disabled children, adult stroke patients, and others with communication disorders (Silver, 1991).

Weinstein (2000) purported that group context is the most constructive ther-apy for girls with eating disorders because of its high-relational characteristics. Support from the group is an integral aspect of helping clients to identify behaviors and attitudes that may or may not be detrimental, as well as to formulate alterna-tive options. Groups that focus on the many emotional and physical abuse mani-festations (e.g., intimidation, coercion, domestic violence, rape) of alcohol abuse empower clients to confront denials, unravel cultural perceptions and identity per-spectives, increase disclosure of maladaptive behaviors, and set realistic attitudi-nal and behavioral goals.

Life span issues transcend both individualized and group contexts. Using a life span approach that focuses on the four developmental ages (i.e., adolescents, young adults, middle adults, older adults), comprehensive prevention programs target each age group in terms of their particular needs or the distinctive factors that influ-ence their well-being. With increased numbers of people living past 70, Westerhof et al. (2001) contend helping professionals should be cognizant not to make use of the deficit model of aging that predominates both gerontology and the medical sciences. The authors suggest further research with respect to cultural differences in the mean-ing of health in old age as well culture-specific gerontological interventions.

Many communities have established educational forums to discuss issues faced by older adults such as transition from one level of independence to another (Burger, Fraser, Hunt, & Frank, 1996), grief and loss, family interactions, social services and caregiving (Agee & Blanton, 2000), life-threatening behaviors (McIn-tosh, 1995), and health education (Caserta, Lund, & Rice, 1999). For example, the Cooperative Extension Service has increasingly targeted educational programs to older people and families. The service provides preventive educational materials (i.e., support groups, newsletters, radio, television, correspondence courses, and newspaper articles) that help individuals make informed decisions and develop living skills while they are undergoing life transitions. Notwithstanding, education, health promotion, counseling intervention, and public policy should form the interlocking basis when considering the different disorders and conditions that affect this population.

Environmental

Churches.   Churches play a pivotal role in many ethnic communities. For example, the African American church is a vanguard institution; serves as a spiritual, psychological, social foundation (Frame, Williams, & Green, 1999); and provides an alternative point of access to certain hard-to-reach elements in the African American community (Rashid, Brock, Key, Amulera-Marshall, & Meehan, 1987). It also plays critical advocacy roles in primary and secondary prevention strategies.

Schools.   With education in the United States being mandated for those less than 16, the school facility is a primary learning and interaction context for children and adolescents. It also serves a critical community laboratory for educational interventions and can address a range of community and national issues. For these reasons, massive government funds are given to school districts to promote social and affective (mental, emotional, and health) activities that complement academic learning. These funds support activities for the identification of endangered or at-risk student populations, as well as prevention and remediation programs.

A plethora of primary and secondary prevention strategies exists that targets high-risk populations (women, adolescents, children of alcoholics, college students). For example, children of alcoholics (COAs) are at higher risk of alcohol abuse simply by virtue of their family history of alcoholism. High-risk populations among youth include children of parents with affective disorders, youth involved with the family court system, youth in poverty, and Native American youth (Wodarski & Smyth, 1994).

School-based mental health programs have been established in many public school systems. Most of these systems utilize a three-tiered approach to identify and eliminate risk factors and increase protective factors in students. Rowney and Quinn (2000) suggest that schools that use this approach believe that students must be taught not only appropriate behaviors but how to use these skills effectively in multiple environments. School-based interventions include the following:

- Elementary schools for students with serious emotional disturbances (Eber, Rolf, & Sullivan, 1998; Hussy, Guo, & Schlegelmilch, 1999), overt behavioral problems (Oliver, Oaks, & Hoover, 1994; Eber et al., 1998; Hussey & Bennice, 1998; Pietrucha, 1998), alcohol use (Mackay, 1995), and those in crisis settings (Schonfeld & Newgass, 2000);
- Middle schools for students with mental disorders (Reeves, 1998; Greenberg, Domitrovich, & Bumbarger, 2001) and students with emotional and behavior

disorders (EBDs) (Minnesota State Department of Human Services, 1997; Pelton, 1998) and those at risk (Hoover & Achilles, 1994; Graham, 1999); and

- High schools to prevent or delay the onset of substance abuse among target populations, such as female adolescents with a history of childhood abuse (Davis, 1994; Mitchell, Gabriel, Hahn, & Laws, 1996; Kist-Kline & Quantz, 1998), those at risk for dropping out (Walsh, 1999) or at risk for suicide (Degroot, 1995; Ceperich, 1997; McArt, Shulman, & Gajary, 1999; King, 2001), and gang involvement (Esbensen, 2000; Vera, 2000).

Examinations of the efficacy of these interventions as well as tertiary (treatment) strategies abound in the literature. For example, school-based alcohol and drug abuse prevention and intervention programs employ strategies with primary and secondary aspects (Hadge, 1992). In primary prevention, districts develop a climate conducive to the understanding of alcohol and drug abuse prevention and intervention through staff training (Hadge, 1992). In the next phase, secondary prevention, intervention concentrates on the effects of alcohol or drug abuse on students via the formulation of a school drug policy, student counseling groups, and a broad-based employee assistance program (Hadge, 1992). Because of liability issues, school systems do not provide treatment. Tertiary responses generally include guidelines that stipulate conditions upon which adults and students can return to the school.

As a fundamental tenet of transcultural counseling, prevention and intervention programs occur in a cultural context and often target disparate individuals and populations rather than the systemic issues that situate them at the margins. Moreover, clients from marginalized populations and groups with collective identities share the injurious effects of systemic methodologies. These clients face culturally determined barriers (Diaz, Prigerson, Desai, & Rosenheck, 2001) and find it difficult to differentiate between internal and external sources of distress. A critical understanding of systemic barriers as well as how they operate are critical aspects in designing effective prevention and intervention programs of a transcultural nature.

The effect of historical oppression through governmental policies and actions has exerted a profound influence on Native American and Alaskan Native communities. Herring (1999) articulates that the negative impact of historical and contemporary discriminatory policies and practices on Native American and Alaskan Native peoples has devastated their standard of living and created major cultural conflicts. Herring adamantly stresses the need for counselors to develop advocacy strategies to assist their clients and all Native American and Alaskan Native peoples. Priority areas for counselor understanding and appreciation of these communities should include the complex nature of being subjected to systemic oppression both as an internal phenomenon and in its interrelationships with adaptive and functional aspects of institutionalized poverty.

With increasing cognizance that the fundamental counseling theories and prevention interventions are embedded with a Westernized cultural bias, counselor training programs must develop systemic strategies throughout the curriculum that incorporate an awareness of culturally learned assumptions and biases.

Acquisition of effective counseling skills to engage clients from marginally racial and marginally ethnic populations and others (e.g., persons with disabilities, women, gays, lesbians, bisexuals, the aged) as well as measures of competencies has become a pivotal issue for the profession.

Preventive Counseling in a Multicultural Society

In order to eradicate culturally myopic prevention counseling models, it is imperative that a transculturally integrative approach be devised. Many transcultural counselor educators (d'Ardenne & Mahtani, 1989; Ibrahim, 1999; McFadden, 1999) have emphasized competencies that transcend cultural contexts, worldviews, and nations. Primary to the development of these competencies is an understanding of the sociohistorical milieu (separation, disregard, and oppression) that shape backgrounds and perspectives of clients from racial, cultural, and ethnic communities. Transcultural counseling models have implications for use across gender, sexuality, disability, age, and economic categories (McFadden, 1999).

Transcultural prevention counseling integrates prevention models with the three hierarchical dimensions (cultural-historical, psychosocial, and scientific-ideological) advocated by McFadden. A successful transcultural prevention counseling intervention is predicated on two perspectives. First, the counselor must acquire sensitivity to forces of oppression and discrimination incurred by disparate communities, respond to the belief system and worldview affecting the client, become aware of and refrain from utilizing monocultural or Westernized counseling paradigms, and transcend preconceived philosophies. Second, the challenge for the counselor is to not proscribe a singular set of interventions but culturally appropriate paradigms that effectively respond to a client's needs (McFadden, 2000). The client should be empowered to incorporate developmental, identity, religious, ethical, spiritual, and family perspectives into the design of the intervention.

Disparate Populations and Cultures

Although marginalized racial and ethnic populations and groups with collective identities (persons with disabilities, women, gays, lesbians, bisexuals, the aged) have been subjected to various forms of discrimination, oppression, and stereotyping, the counselor should recognize that each client embodies unique cultural characteristics. Many communities possess cultural orientations different from those of majority populations, and within-community differences also exist (Kohatsu, 2000; Coon & Kemmelmeir, 2001; Phelps, Taylor, & Gerard, 2001).

Religion and spirituality are the cornerstones of many racial and ethnic cultural communities. For example, religion and spirituality were predominate issues in the recovery of the Japanese fishing vessel sunk by a U.S. Navy submarine in 2001. Japanese families were anxious to reclaim the remains because of their belief that if a body is not returned or located, its soul is considered lost. For those families, closure would be difficult because spirit and body are continuous or considered one; they are not distinct from each other. Separation of the body from one of its many souls might create havoc and even haunt family members (Frye, 1995).

At the other end of the spectrum, religious fanaticism brought about the September 11, 2001, tragic events at the World Trade Center in New York City, in Shanksville (near Pittsburgh, Pennsylvania), and at the Pentagon (near Washington, D.C.) by a zealous segment of the Muslim community, fearing cultural encroachment by Western society, and thereby seeking to destroy its cultural icons. Contrary to the tenets of religion, spiritual and religious convictions of the Taliban—a radical and fundamentalist faction of the Muslim community—allow for eradication of those with a divergent worldview (Marsden, 1999; Norval, 1999; Khalilzad & Byman, 2000; Lloyd, 2000; Islamic countries should rein in the Taliban, 2001).

Increasingly, counselors are having to acknowledge client issues of religion (Richardson & June, 1997; Aalsma & Lapsley, 1999; Oakes, 2000) as well as other constructs of religion and spirituality (Evans, 2000; Faiver, O' Brien, & Ingersoll, 2000) in the design of prevention strategies. Such interventions should incorporate empirical constructs of religion and spirituality that may be dissimilar to the perspectives of the counselor. These constructs convey the client's way of viewing the events in his or her world; they provide a way of explaining or interpreting that world. Client constructs are critical aspects of decision making and communication.

Ntu is an emergent prevention model that incorporates spiritual constructs. Ntu utilizes a pluralistic approach to the dissemination of mental health to address systems needs of the client (Gregory & Harper, 2001). It is framed in an Afrocentric construct of the world and accommodates the client's perspectives, processes, and learning styles (Gregory & Harper, 2001). Gregory and Harper have indicated that the Ntu model is framed by six characteristics (spiritually oriented, family focused, culturally competent, competency based, holistic/ systemic, and values driven) and by three principles (harmony, balance, and interconnectedness and authenticity).

Women present unique issues, also. For example, does the prevailing perspective of women's worldview apply to disparate cultures? This operant perspective purports that women view reality from five different perspectives (silence, received knowledge, subjective knowledge, procedural knowledge, and constructed knowledge), and that their self-concepts and ways of knowing are intertwined (Austin, 1999). Without extensive research within disparate racial and ethnic populations, it is ill advised to formulate prevention interventions based on the premise that all women view reality from a shared perspective. Notwithstanding, prevention interventions for women clients from marginalized populations should address collusion and its role in oppression.

Case Studies

Case studies provide practitioners an opportunity to apply paradigms, methodologies, and techniques to a set of conditions. Principles learned from such case study activities help practitioners integrate theories, formulate practices, and articulate perspectives. The following case studies illustrate conceptual perspectives of prevention interventions at three foci (primary, secondary, and tertiary) and can foster the design of additional learning activities.

Transcultural Adoption

A church with a large congregation has collaborated with an international adoption agency to bring refugee adolescents to a small southern community. Twenty-six families were approved for adoption. Eleven families have received their Sudanese adoptees, and the remaining families anticipate custody within 6 weeks.

A counselor has agreed to provide family counseling services twice a week in the basement of the church. Design of any potential strategies with these families must also address the likelihood that both the couple and the adoptee fear misunderstandings brought about by perceptual and emotional issues. For example, person-centered strategies are culturally appropriate, values-based approaches that focus on a person's choices, vision, and support circle. These strategies and trust-building activities provide both parties a forum for creating trust and rapport, recognize barriers to healthy relationships, and strengthen ongoing collaboration with their circle of support.

During the primary phase the counselor seeks to strengthen and enhance family dynamics by (1) getting a better understanding of the family environment or climate—socioenvironmental characteristics, interpersonal relationships shared and valued, disciplinary practices, spiritual beliefs, parenting styles, and rites of passage (McEachern & Kenny, 2002; Sanders & Bradley, 2002); (2) helping the families identify cultural bridges that can facilitate a reduction of dysfunctional communication patterns (McFadden, 1993); and (3) identifying within-community differences (Khaleefa et al., 1996; Kohatsu, 2000; Coon & Kemmelmeir, 2001) that may exist among the Black and Arab Sudanese adoptees. Secondary phase measures by the counselor may include exploring issues that promote self-concept, racial identity, social adjustment, and adoptive family life. Several sessions may explore the history of the Sudanese adoptee experiences and living conditions, familial relationship development, and feelings of alienation. The goal is to decrease the severity of those misunderstandings brought about by perceptual and emotional issues. The focus of the tertiary phase is to empower all parties to stipulate specific step-by-step goals within the framework of relationship enhancement. The counselor seeks to facilitate healing and prevent familial crisis.

Violence

Aggression and force are inseparable aspects of violence, and violence, in its many manifestations, is of concern to every cultural group. In this case study, a state-funded social services agency has hired a counselor to establish and administer a violence prevention program for high school students in a predominantly Latino community. To abate male violence against females, the counselor conducted a presentation with the social services board to gain its support for adoption of a board-approved violence prevention policy, inservice programs for all staff, and parental awareness programming. Subsequent to gaining board acceptance of these primary prevention strategies, the counselor elected to make use of a prevention program that integrated Caplan's (1964) prevention model with an approach developed by Hage (2000).

> At the initial client contact stage, the primary focus included establishment of a communicative climate to engage and empower the Latino teens (Low & Organista, 2000). Again, activities were designed to encourage both self-actualization and emotional adjustments to cement robust, culturally effective relationships, which tend to be the most effective (Altarriba & Bauer, 1998). Having observed language switching in the initial sessions and knowing that it can be an effective form of treatment to objectify difficult issues (Pizarro, 1995), repress painful memories (Altarriba & Santiago-Rivera, 1994), or remain emotionally distant from important issues under consideration (Yamamoto, Whittaker, & Davis, 1998), the counselor utilized Paniagua's (1994) acculturation scales (*respeto, personalismo-formalismo, machismo-marianismo, familismo,* etc.) to gain a perspective on the possibility of premature termination. Another component of this initial stage included having both male and female participants identify those factors that increase the onset of abusive behaviors within their community.
>
> Reducing the impact of men's violence was a critical aspect of the secondary and tertiary prevention strategies. This was accomplished through group-developed activities designed to strengthen knowledge, attitudes, and behavior, thus promoting healthy relationships between the two genders (Hage, 2000). Drama was found to be effective to stimulate cooperative learning because of its heuristic value in dealing with violence, sexual abuse, and male aggression.

Suicide and Life-Threatening Behaviors

Native Americans and Alaska Natives are subject to exceptionally high rates of suicide for males and life-threatening behaviors for both males and females. Despite the expansive need for mental health and counseling services, the Native American and Alaska Native communities remain underserved by the mental health profession. Any comprehensive prevention should include primary, secondary, and tertiary components. Primary activities should focus on raising individual, family, and tribal awareness of warning signs, risk factors, and referral agencies. Secondary activities may include steps that friends, family members, and tribal leaders should take upon the presentation of suicide ideation or life-threatening behavior. At this stage it is incumbent to assess the risk level for suicide or life-threatening behavior as well as the appropriate mental health services needed. The counselor should collaborate with traditional healers to focus on the client's subtle verbal and nonverbal components of communication. A suicide or homicide is a traumatic event in any community. Counselor knowledge of community tribal structure, acculturation stress and social integration of the tribe, intratribal group heterogeneity, and tribal wordview will increase the likelihood of well-designed tribe-specific tertiary activities.

Eye Disease

Glaucoma poses a very serious and challenging health problem in many communities of the marginalized population. Glaucoma is a group of eye diseases and is the leading cause of irreversible blindness. It is most prevalent with individuals having two or more of the following factors: (1) age greater than 60; (2) a family history of glaucoma, diabetes or vascular block, or myopia; (3) the prior use of steroid preparations; and (4) belonging to a dark-skinned race, especially of African descent.

> The counselor elected to utilize both environment-centered and person-centered interventions as described by Durlak and Wells (1997). During the primary phase, prevention strategies occurred in community education programs with population-specific (African Americans, Latinos, Asians) media (posters, illustrated booklets, brochures, 10-question true-false quizzes, reproducible art, factsheets, elementary school lesson plans, etc.) and slogans ("Get the first checkup for glaucoma when you need reading glasses") to increase awareness among those at risk about the importance of early detection and treatment of glaucoma.
>
> Secondary phase activities, interventions designed by an agency counselor, sought to reduce client distress brought on by the onset of glaucoma. Several exercises were designed to develop affiliations among the attendees as well as elicit pertinent family support information on each. Here, the agency counselor sought to have each client verbalize perceptions of past, present, and future behaviors that could address their respective glaucoma stage.
>
> Notwithstanding, tertiary preventions strategies, developed by the agency counselor, minimize the impact of the disease and prevent additional complications because of client neglect. Paramount during this final stage is the empowerment of the client to formulate additional activities that will ensure their acquisition of self-determined goals.

Conclusion

This chapter examined issues surrounding prevention within the counseling profession. It explored models of prevention and focused on a triadic classification scheme (primary prevention, secondary intervention, tertiary postintervention) The principles of each stage were elaborated and applied to several cultural communities in the form of case studies.

Clients' cultural and social contexts are of primacy in prevention counseling. In accordance with prevention counseling principles, accurate information must be obtained with regard to the causal factors, prevalence, severity, and outcome of the issue within both the marginal and major cultural populations. An important aspect of obtaining accurate information is a risk-factor assessment. Such an assessment includes identification of those items (predisposing factors, early predictors, precipitating events, opportunity factors, family factors, cultural factors, etc.) contributing to the discomfiture of the clients. Regardless of whether the issue presented or perceived by the client is complex, it may manifest itself within a myriad of attendant cultural factors.

Practical information, materials, and initiatives to design culturally appropriate interventions as well as to adapt prevention paradigms for disparate communities were provided. It is incumbent upon counselor-education training programs to play a pivotal role in increasing the number of clinicians competent to employ culturally sensitive and appropriate prevention strategies. Without such a transcultural commitment, counseling will continue to be perceived as an ineffective mental health option for disparate communities. Counseling can choose, by its professional standards and credentialing criteria, to be inclusive or exclusive.

DISCUSSION QUESTIONS

1. Describe the three stages of prevention counseling and compare them with multicultural counseling.

2. Describe the circumstances under which it is appropriate to terminate a primary, secondary, or tertiary intervention.

3. What are the universal elements that appear to be common to transcultural and multicultural prevention counseling?

4. What role can primary prevention play in the elimination of racism, oppression, poverty, and stressful social conditions to which disparate populations are subjected?

5. What are some of the ethical responsibilities of a counselor in designing prevention interventions for adolescents and senior citizens? How are these responsibilities similar and dissimilar?

6. Life span challenges, according to Austin (1999), are a result of the extent to which change or transition occurs in various developmental spheres. Life span challenges tend to be classified within three life junctures: the period from birth to the adolescent or teen years, adulthood, and the senior years. For each of these life junctures, describe a counseling intervention that incorporates the concepts of primary, secondary, and tertiary prevention with a developmental sphere.

REFERENCES

Aalsma, M. C., & Lapsley, D. K. (1999). Religiosity and adolescent narcissism: Implications for values counseling. *Counseling and Values, 44*(1), 17–29.

Agee, A., & Blanton, P. W. (2000). Service providers' modes of interacting with frail elders and their families: Understanding the context for caregiving decisions. *Journal of Aging Studies, 14*(3), 313–333.

Albee, G. W. (1982). Preventing psychopathology and promoting human potential. *American Psychologist, 37,* 1043–1050.

Albee, G. W. (1995). Counseling and primary prevention. *Counseling Psychology Quarterly, 8*(3), 205–211.

Albee, G. W., & Gullotta, T. P. (Eds.). (1998). *Primary prevention works.* Thousand Oaks, CA: Sage.

Albee, G. W., & Ryan-Finn, K. Y. (1998). An overview of primary prevention. *Journal of Mental Health, 7*(5), 441–449.

Altarriba, J., & Bauer, L. M. (1998). Counseling the Hispanic client: Cuban Americans, Mexican Americans, and Puerto Ricans. *Journal of Counseling and Development, 76*(4), 389–396.

Altarriba, J., & Santiago-Rivera, A. L. (1994). Current perspectives on using linguistic and cultural factors in counseling the Hispanic client. *Professional Psychology: Research and Practice, 25*(4), 388–397.

Austin, L. (1999). *The counseling primer.* Levittown, PA: Accelerated Development, Taylor & Francis Group.

Baker, S. B., & Shaw, M. C. (1987). *Improving counseling through primary prevention.* Columbus, OH: Merrill.

Bower, E. M. (1987). Prevention: A word whose time has come. *American Journal of Orthopsychiatry, 57*(1), 4–5.

Burger, S. G., Fraser, V., Hunt, S., & Frank, B. (1996). *Nursing homes: Getting good care there.* San Luis Obispo, CA: American Source Books.

Caplan, G. (1964). *Principles of preventive psychiatry.* New York: Basic Books.

Caserta, M. S., Lund, D. A., & Rice, S. J. (1999). Pathfinders: A self-care and health education program for older widows and widowers. *Gerontologist, 39*(5), 615–620.

Caulkins, J. P., Rydell, C. P., Sohler-Everingham, S. M., Chiesa, J. R., & Bushway, S. (1999). *An ounce of prevention, a pound of uncertainty: The cost-effectiveness of school-based drug prevention programs.* Santa Monica, CA: Rand.

Ceperich, S. R. D. (1997). Coping interventions for high school-based suicide prevention (Doctoral dissertation, Arizona State University, 1997). *Dissertation Abstracts International, 58,* 1599.

Conyne, R. K. (1987). *Primary preventive counseling: Empowering people and systems.* Muncie, IN: Accelerated Development Inc.

Conyne, R. K. (1997). Educating students in preventive counseling. *Counselor Education and Supervision, 36*(4), 259–269.

Conyne, R. K. (2000). Prevention in counseling psychology: At long last, has the time now come? *The Counseling Psychologist, 28*(6), 838–844.

Coon, H. M., & Kemmelmeir, M. (2001). Cultural orientations in the United States. *Journal of Cross-Cultural Psychology, 32*(3), 348–364.

Cowen, E. L. (Ed.). (1982). Research in primary prevention in mental health [Special issue]. *American Journal of Community Psychology, 10*(3).

Cowen, E. L. (1983). Primary prevention in mental health: Past, present, and future. In R. D. Felner, L. A. Jason, J. N. Moritsugu, & S. S. Farber (Eds.), *Preventive psychology: Theory, research, and practice* (pp. 11–25). Elmsford, NY: Pergamon.

Cowen, E. L. (1997). On the semantics and operations of primary prevention and wellness enhancement (or will the real primary prevention pleas stand up?) *American Journal of Community Psychology, 25*(3), 245–255.

d'Ardenne, P., & Mahtani, A. (1989). *Transcultural counseling in action.* Newbury Park, CA: Sage.

Davis, E. J. (1994). Suicide prevention program effectiveness for junior and senior students (Doctoral dissertation, Temple University, 1994). *Dissertation Abstracts International, 55,* 2278.

Degroot, C. D. (1995). The roles of high school professional personnel in school-based suicide prevention programs (Doctoral dissertation, University of Southern California, 1995). *Dissertation Abstracts International, 57,* 1097.

Diaz, E., Prigerson, H., Desai, R., & Rosenheck, R. (2001). Perceived needs and service use of Spanish speaking monolingual patients followed at a Hispanic clinic. *Community Mental Health Journal, 37*(4), 335–346.

Dibrino, C. I. (1998). Self-mutilation in adolescence (Doctoral dissertation, Adler School of Professional Psychology, 1998). *Dissertation Abstracts International, 59,* 5077.

Dickel, C. T., & Boytim, J. A. (1991). *A ten-step model for team planning for primary prevention* (ERIC Document Reproduction Service No. ED 340 955).

Dishion, T. J., Andrews, D. W., & Crosby, L. (1995). Adolescent boys and their friends in adolescence: Relationship characteristics, quality and interactional process. *Child Development, 66,* 139–151.

Dowell, K. A. (2001). Impact of exposure to school-based and parental sexuality education on adolescent sexuality and pregnancy (Doctoral dissertation, University of Maryland Baltimore County, 2001). *Dissertation Abstracts International, 62,* 1241.

Durlak, J. A., & Wells, A. M. (1997). Primary prevention mental health programs for children and adolescents: A meta-analytic review. *American Journal of Community Psychology, 25,* 115–152.

Durlak, J. A., & Wells, A. M. (1998). Evaluation of indicated preventive intervention mental health programs for children and adolescents. *American Journal of Community Psychology, 26*(5), 775–802.

Dusenbury, L., Falco, M., Lake, A., Brannigan, R., & Bosworth, K. (1997). Nine critical elements of promising violence prevention programs. *Journal of School Health, 67*(10), 409–414.

Eber, L., Rolf, K., & Sullivan, M. P. (1998). *School-based systems of care: Early intervention and day treatment examples from Illinois* (ERIC Document Reproduction Service No. ED 433 637).

Elliott, D. S., & Menard, S. (1996). Delinquent friends and delinquent behavior: Temporal and developmental patterns. In J. D. Hawkins (Ed.), *Current theories of crime and deviance* (pp. 28–67). Newbury, CA: Sage.

Esbensen, F. A. (2000). *Preventing adolescent gang involvement. Youth gang series. Juvenile Justice Bulletin* (ERIC Document Reproduction Service No. ED 445 160).

Evans, L. (2000). Ethics, philosophy, and culture: Exploring the issues involved in the spirituality-religion-counseling debate. *The Journal of the Pennsylvania Counseling Association, Volume 2, 2*(2), 9–20.

Faiver, C. M., O' Brien, E. M., & Ingersoll, R. E. (2000). Religion, guilt and mental health. *Journal of Counseling and Development, 78*(2), 155–161.

Forness, S. R., Serna, L. A., Nielsen, E., Lambros, K., Hale, Mary J., & Kavale, K. A. (2000). A model for early detection and primary prevention of emotional or behavioral disorders. *Education and Treatment of Children, 23*(3), 325–345.

Frame, M. W., Williams, C. B., & Green, E. (1999). Balm in Gilead: Spiritual dimensions in counseling African American women. *Journal of Multicultural Counseling and Development, 27,* 182–192.

Franklin, C., Grant, D., Corcoran, J., Miller, P., & Bultman, L. (1997). Effectiveness of prevention programs for adolescent pregnancy: A meta-analysis. *Journal of Marriage and the Family, 59*(3), 551–567.

Friedmann, S. S. (1998, March). Girls in the 90s: A gender-based model for eating disorder prevention. *Patient Education and Counseling, 33*(3), 217–224.

Frye, B. A. (1995). Use of cultural themes in promoting health among southeast Asian refugees. *American Journal of Health Promotion, 9*(4), 269–280.

Graham, J. E. (1999). The effects of school-based services on at-risk behaviors in youth (Doctoral dissertation, The University of Texas at Arlington, 1999). *Dissertation Abstracts International, 60,* 3792.

Greenberg, M. T., Domitrovich, C., & Bumbarger, B. (2001). The prevention of mental disorders in school-aged children: Current state of the field. *Prevention and Treatment, 4,* Article 1. Retrieved March 30, 2002 from http://journals.apa.org/prevention/volume4/pre0040001a. html

Gregory, W. H., & Harper, K. W. (2001). The Ntu approach to health and healing. *Journal of Black Psychology, 27*(3), 304–320.

Guetzloe, E. (2000). Teacher preparation in the age of violence: What do educators need to know? *Teacher Educator, 35*(3), 19–27.

Hadge, C. (1992). *School-based prevention and intervention programs. Clearinghouse fact sheet* (ERIC Document Reproduction Service No. ED 372 329).

Hage, S. M. (2000). The role of counseling psychology in preventing male violence against female intimates. *The Counseling Psychologist, 28*(6), 797–828.

Herring, R. (1999). *Advocacy for Native American Indian and Alaska Native clients and counselees* (ERIC Document Reproduction Service No. ED 435 908).

Hoover, S., & Achilles, C. M. (1994). *What does one look like? A school and community approach* (ERIC Document Reproduction Service No. ED 366 065).

Hussey, D. L., & Bennice, J. A. (1998). *Forging partnerships with high-risk families through school-based mental health services* (ERIC Document Reproduction Service No. ED 433 638).

Hussey, D. L., Guo, S., & Schlegelmilch, A. (1999). *School-based mental health services in urban elementary education: Child, family, and teacher perspectives* (ERIC Document Reproduction Service No. ED 445 462).

Ibrahim, F. A. (1999). Transcultural counseling: Existential worldview theory and cultural identity. In J. McFadden (Ed.), *Transcultural counseling* (2nd ed., pp. 23–57). Alexandria, VA: American Counseling Association.

Islamic countries should rein in the Taliban. (2001, May 26). *The Economist, 359,* p. 88.

Khaleefa, O. H. et al. (1996). Creativity in an indigenous Afro-Arab Islamic culture: The case of Sudan. *Journal of Creative Behavior, 30*(4), 268–282.

Khalilzad, Z., & Byman, D. (2000). Afghanistan: The consolidation of a rogue state. *Washington Quarterly, 23*(1), 65–78.

King, K. A. (2001). Developing a comprehensive school suicide prevention program. *The Journal of School Health, 71*(4), 132–137.

Kiselica, M. S. (2001, March 30). Overcoming barriers to the practice of primary prevention: An agenda for the mental health professions. *Prevention and Treatment, 4,* Article 8. Retrieved March 30, 2001 from http://www.journals.apa.org/prevention/volume4/pre0040008c.html

Kist-Kline, G. E., & Quantz, R. A. (1998). Understanding a school-based mental health program: Creating a caring environment. *Journal for a Just and Caring Education, 4*(3), 307–322.

Kohatsu, E. L. (2000). Using racial identity theory to explore racial mistrust and interracial contact among Asian Americans. *Journal of Counseling and Development, 78*(3), 334–343.

LeVine, E. S., & Sallee, A. L (1987). *Critical phases among adoptees and their families: Implication for therapy.* (ERIC Document Reproduction Service No. ED 291 479).

Levinger, B. (1996). *Critical transitions: Human capacity development across the lifespan.* Newton, MA: Education Development Center, Inc.

Lewis, C., et al. (1990). School-based primary prevention: What is an effective program? *New Directions for Child Development, 50,* 35–59.

Lloyd, J. (2000, October 2). A faraway struggle that began in the West. *New Statesman, 129,* 31–32.

Lorion, R. P., Price, R. H., & Eaton, W. W. (1989). Basing preventive interventions on theory: Stimulating a field's momentum. In R. P. Lorion (Ed.), *Protecting the children: Strategies for optimizing emotional and behavioral development: Prevention in human services* (pp. 7–31). New York: Haworth.

Low, G., & Organista, K. C. (2000). Latinas and sexual assault: Towards culturally sensitive assessment and intervention. *Journal of Multicultural Social Work, 8*(1–2), 131–157.

Mackay, M. A. (1995). An evaluation of a school-based drug prevention program at the elementary level. (Doctoral dissertation, Loyola University of Chicago, 1995). *Dissertation Abstracts International, 56,* 0112.

Marsden, P. (1999) *The Taliban: War, religion and the new order in Afghanistan.* New York: Zed Books.

McArt, E. W., Shulman, D. A, &. Gajary, E. (1999). Developing an educational workshop on teen depression and suicide: A proactive community intervention. *Child Welfare, 78*(6), 793–806.

McEachern, A. G., &. Kenny, M. C. (2002). A comparison of family environment characteristics among white (NonHispanic), Hispanic, and African Caribbean Groups. *Journal of Multicultural Counseling and Development, 30,* 40–58.

McFadden, J. (Ed.). (1993). *Transcultural counseling: Bilateral and international perspectives.* Alexandria, VA: American Counseling Association.

McFadden, J. (1999). Stylistic model for transcultural counseling. In J. McFadden (Ed.), *Transcultural counseling* (2nd ed., pp. 59–81). Alexandria, VA: American Counseling Association.

McFadden, J. (2000). *Transcultural vignettes for helping and management professionals.* Louisville, TN: Dura-Nuance Associates.

McIntosh, J. L. (1995). Suicide prevention in the elderly (age 65–99). *Suicide and Life-Threatening Behavior, 25*(1), 180–192.

Minnesota State Department of Human Services, Mental Health Division. (1997). *Children and youth at risk of emotional disturbance: Risk factors and symptoms* (ERIC Document Reproduction Service No. ED 427 456).

Mitchell, S. J., Gabriel, R. M., Hahn, K. J., Laws, K. E. (1996). *Portland public schools project chrysalis: Year 2 evaluation report* (ERIC Document Reproduction Service No. ED 412 487).

Nitsch, R. E. (1999). An evaluation of selected characteristics of project D.A.R.E. (Doctoral dissertation, Arizona State University, 1999). *Dissertation Abstracts International, 60,* 0609.

Norval, M. (1999). *Triumph of disorder: Islamic fundamentalism, the new face of war.* Indian Wells, CA: Sligo Press.

Oakes, K. E. (2000). Reflection on religiousness and mental health. *Counseling and Values, 44*(2), 113–117.

Oliver, R., Oaks, I. N., & Hoover, J. H. (1994). Family issues and interventions in bully and victim relationships. *The School Counselor, 41,* 199–202.

O'Neal, G. S. (1997). Focusing on strengths in a special education class: A primary prevention approach. *Social Work in Education, 19*(4), 279–284.

Paniagua, F. A. (1994). *Assessing and treating culturally diverse clients: A practical guide.* Thousand Oaks, CA: Sage.

Patterson, G. R., & Yoerger, K. (1997). A developmental model for late-onset delinquency. In D. W. Osgood (Ed.), *Motivation and delinquency* (Vol. 44, pp. 119–177). Lincoln: University of Nebraska Press.

Pelton, R. P. (1998). *Improving the consistency of interventions in a public middle school therapeutic program for students with severe emotional/behavioral disorders* (ERIC Document Reproduction Service No. ED 430 353).

Pietrucha, C. A. (1998). Social-cognitive intervention program: Toward the reduction of children's aggressive behavior through modification of social goals (peer acceptance). (Doctoral dissertation, University of Maine, 1998). *Doctoral Dissertation Abstracts International, 59,* 1865.

Phelps, R. E., Taylor, J. D., & Gerard, P. A. (2001). Cultural mistrust, ethnic identity, racial identity, and self-esteem among ethnically diverse Black university students. *Journal of Counseling and Development, 79*(2), 209–216.

Pizarro, C. J. (1995). Emotional intensity in a second language: A study on fluent Spanish-English bilingual individuals when discussing emotional topics (Doctoral dissertation, The University of Iowa, 1995). *Dissertation Abstracts International, 55,* 0096.

Price, R. H., Cowen, E. L., Lorion, R. P., & Ramos-McKay, J. (Eds.). (1988). *14 Ounces of Prevention: A casebook for practitioners.* Washington, DC: American Psychological Association.

Rashid, H., Brock, R., Key, A., Amulera-Marshall, O., & Meehan, S. (1987). Prevention models for Black youth at high risk: Family and religion. Panel Summaries. In Ura J. Oyemade & Deloris Brandon-Moyne (Eds.). *Ecology of alcohol and other drug use: Helping Black high-risk youth.* Proceedings of the Howard University School of Human Ecology Forum. OSAP Prevention Monograph-7 (ERIC Document Reproduction Service No. ED 336 456).

Reeves, M. A. L. (1998). A program evaluation of a school-based mental health program. (Doctoral dissertation, University of Denver, 1998). *Dissertation Abstracts International, 59,* 1580

Richardson, B. L., & June, L. N. (1997). Utilizing and maximizing the resources of the African American church: Strategies and tools for counseling professionals. In L. C. Courtland (Ed.), *Multicultural issues in counseling: New approaches to diversity* (pp. 155–170). Alexandria, VA: American Counseling Association.

Riley, M. A. (2000). Program evaluation of a home-based, diversion/family preservation program: Lessons learned (Doctoral dissertation, University of Hartford, 2000). *Dissertation Abstracts International, 61,* 3858.

Robinson, A. L. (1980). The development of standards and an evaluation procedure for primary prevention programs in mental health centers (Doctoral dissertation, United States International University, 1980). *Dissertation Abstracts International, 41,* 1523.

Romano, J. L., & Hage, S. M. (2000). Prevention in counseling psychology: Revitalizing commitments for the twenty-first century. *The Counseling Psychologist, 28*(6), 733–763.

Rowney, G. C., & Quinn, M. M. (2000). Prevention of behavior problems in schools. *Reclaiming Children and Youth, 9*(2), 107–110.

Sanders, J. L., & Bradley, C. (Eds.). (2002). *Counseling African American families.* Alexandria, VA: American Counseling Association.

Sapia, J. L. (2000). Determining the efficacy of an eating disorder prevention program among college women (Doctoral dissertation, State University of New York at Buffalo, 2000). *Dissertation Abstracts International, 61,* 2780.

Schonfeld, D. J., & Newgass, S. (2000). *School crisis preparedness and response* (ERIC Document Reproduction Service No. ED 450 486).

Shaffer, D. E., et. al. (1990). *Prevention in child and adolescent psychiatry: The reduction of risk for mental disorders.* (ERIC Document Reproduction Service No. ED 321 468).

Shen, Y-J. J. (1998). Phenomenological approach to counselor educators and school counselors use of play therapy in elementary schools of Taiwan (China) (Doctoral dissertation, The Pennsylvania State University, 1998). *Dissertation Abstracts International, 59,* 2872.

Shore, M. F. (1998). The making, unmaking and remaking of primary prevention *Journal of Mental Health, 7*(5), 471–477.

Silver, R. A. (1991). *Stimulus drawings and techniques in therapy, development, and assessment* (4th ed. rev.). Sarasota, FL: Ablin Press Distributors.

Silverman, A. B. (2000). Evaluating the efficacy of the Rhode Island teen dating violence prevention program (TDVPP): A process and outcome approach to determining the success of both primary and secondary prevention projects (Doctoral dissertation, University of Rhode Island, 2000). *Dissertation Abstracts International, 61,* 5581.

Simeonsson, R. J. (1991). Primary, secondary, and tertiary prevention in early intervention. *Journal of Early Intervention, 15*(2), 124–134.

Trickett, E. J. (1997, April). Ecology and primary prevention: Reflections on a meta-analysis. *American Journal of Community Psychology, 25*(2), 197–205.

Vera, E. M. (2000). Aspirations, barriers, and community strengths: A qualitative survey of urban Chicano youth and families. *Occasional Paper No. 38. Latino Studies Series* (ERIC Documentation Reproduction Service No. ED 455 084).

Walsh, E. M. (1999). Suicide-risk behaviors and drug involvement among potential high school dropouts (Doctoral dissertation, University of Washington, 1999). *Dissertation Abstracts International, 60,* 0250.

Weinstein, E. S. (2000). *School-based eating disorder prevention programs for pre-adolescents and adolescents: A review of recent literature* (ERIC Documentation Reproduction Service No. ED 440 332).

Weissberg, R. P., Kuster, C. B., & Gullotta, T. P. (1997). Introduction and overview: prevention services—From optimistic promise to widespread, effective practice. *Issues in Children's and Families' Lives, 9,* 33–51.

Westerhof, G. J., Katzko, M. W., Dittmann-Kohli, F., & Hayslip, B. (2001). Life contexts and health-related selves in old age: Perspectives from the United States, India, and Congo/Zaire. *Journal of Aging Studies, 15,* 105–126.

Wodarski, J. S., & Smyth, N. J. (1994). Adolescent substance abuse: A comprehensive approach to prevention intervention. *Journal of Child and Adolescent Substance Abuse, 3*(3), 33–58.

Yamamoto, K., Whittaker, J., & Davis, O. L. (1998). Stressful events in the lives of UK children: A glimpse. *Educational Studies, 24*(3), 305–314.

CHAPTER

19

Breaking Barriers for Multiracial Individuals and Families

BEA WEHRLY

One of the most rapidly growing populations in the United States of America is the interracial/multiracial population. The *Loving v. Virginia* 1967 U.S. Supreme Court decision overthrew a major barrier to interracial marriage through repeal of the last fourteen state antimiscegenation laws. By 1992, Maria Root stated, "The emergence of a racially mixed population is transforming the face of the United States" (p. 3).

The number of mixed marriages grew from 150,000 in the 1960s to more than 1 million in 1990 (Eddings, 1997). Recent U.S. Census data show the dramatic increase in the number of children living in mixed-race families: in 1970: 460,000; in 1980: 996,070; and in 1990: 1,937,496 (U.S. Bureau of the Census News, 2001). The U.S. Census 2000 Profile of Demographic Characteristics lists 6,826,228 people of two or more races in this country. This is 2.4 percent of the total U.S. population of 281,421,906.

In this brief chapter, I hope to achieve two goals: (1) to introduce readers to issues, challenges, and barriers faced by multiracial individuals and interracial families in the United States and (2) to suggest counseling strategies for helping people in the mixed-race population to overcome these barriers. Readers interested in more details are encouraged to pursue the readings cited in the chapter and listed in the References at the end of this chapter.

The history of race mixing in the United States is addressed in Wehrly (1996) and Wehrly, Kenney, and Kenney (1999) and will not be repeated here. After a section on definitions of terms pertinent to the interracial population, this chapter will concentrate on societal and professional issues related to work with the mixed-race population and on counseling strategies to assist mixed-race individuals and families in breaking barriers that may be inhibiting the attainment of their full human potential.

Defining Terms

Miscegenation, or racial mixing by sexual union, is a term that was often associated with children born to African American slave women who were fathered by the

White slave owners, but the term applies to any mixing of races. Laws against miscegenation were common in many states until the Supreme Court repealed these laws in the 1967 Supreme Court case referred to in the opening paragraph of this chapter.

An **interracial family** is a family grouping that includes members of more than one racial heritage. Family is defined very broadly as any grouping that lives together. Some families become interracial by marriage; some families become interracial through partnering or living together; some families become interracial through transracial adoption. The Kaeser and Gillespie (1997) book, *Of Many Colors—Portraits of Multiracial Families,* includes photographs and brief narrative descriptions of thirty-nine multiracial or interracial families.

It should be noted that the terms *interracial* and *multiracial* are often used interchangeably in the popular press as well as in the professional literature. Readers will note the interchangeable use of these terms in this chapter.

A **multiracial person** is an individual whose parents are of different racial heritages. The book *Black, White, and Jewish: Autobiography of a Shifting Self,* by Rebecca Walker (2001), tells the life story of Ms. Walker, whose mother was the well-known African American author Alice Walker, and whose father was a White, Jewish lawyer, Mel Leventhal.

The term **transracial adoption** is used in adoption across cultures. Transracial adoption may occur through adoption within a country and through adoption of a child from a different country. J. Douglas Bates (1993) addresses the challenges of transracial adoption within the United States in *Gift Children: A Story of Race, Family, and Adoption in a Divided America.* Some of the authors who have addressed intercountry transracial adoption are Alstein et al. (1994), Borders (1995), Kim (1995), and Register (1991).

During the nineteenth and early twentieth centuries, the term **mulatto** was often used to indicate the individual with more than one racial heritage. Chiong (1998) addresses the pre-Civil War history of the mulatto population as it related to slavery. Today, the term, *mulatto* is viewed as pejorative and is rarely used.

With the broadening of the definition of the term **culture** to include any diverse population, the terms **bicultural** and **multicultural** do not accurately describe people with more than one racial heritage. The terms *multicultural* and *multiracial* are not synonymous.

Societal and Professional Issues of the Mixed-Race Population

Societal barriers faced by people of mixed-race heritage are numerous. Among these barriers are the myths and stereotypes that continue to plague interracial families and multiracial individuals (Wehrly, 1996; Chiong, 1998). Some of the long-standing myths are those of White superiority and the dangers of miscegenation, the negative motives of one or both partners participating in an interracial relationship, the automatic labeling of mixed-race children by the parental race with lesser social status, and the continuing application of the "one drop" rule that labels all mixed-race people with some White heritage as non-White. Many of these myths persist because they have become stereotypes that are learned in the process of socialization.

Watts and Henricksen (1998) developed "The Interracial Couple Questionnaire" (ICQ) as a tool for facilitating discussion of sensitive issues in an interracial relationship in a nonthreatening manner. From the use of the ICQ with five White females married to African American males, Watts and Henricksen (1999) presented a composite case study of Paula, a White female married to Larry, an African American male. Messages received by Paula from both her White culture and Larry's African American culture appeared to be heavily influenced by the negative overtones of the myths and stereotypes listed in the previous paragraph.

A major issue that begins at an early age for the multiracial child and that may continue throughout the individual's lifetime is the development of a positive racial identity. Because of a phenotype that does not fit common racial descriptors, the mixed-race child will hear the question "What are you?" at an early age. At first, the child may be flattered by this attention. When the questions continue as the child gets older, the individual may wonder what is wrong with him- or herself. By the time the individual reaches adolescence, the mixed-race young person may be asking not only "Who am I?" but "Where do I fit?" (Gibbs, 1987). Questions about physical appearance may plague mixed-race persons throughout their lifetimes. Sometimes mixed-race children and adolescents are ostracized based on their appearance; this nonacceptance by others can lead to loneliness and a blaming of self for being different.

Another barrier faced by adolescents with more than one racial heritage emerged from early research that concentrated on work with multiracial adolescents in therapy (Gibbs, 1987). Some people generalized the results of this research to indicate that all multiracial adolescents had an excess of psychological problems. The results of the Gibbs and Hines's (1992) two-year study of the psychosocial adjustment of biracial adolescents not in therapy and the information from the Phinney and Alipuria (1996) research that compared large samples of multiethnic and monoethnic high school and college students have helped to dispel the early stereotype that all mixed-race young people have serious emotional problems.

Mixed-race individuals may feel ongoing pressures to identify with only part of their racial heritages. Pressures may come from within the family as well as from outside the family and can lead to denial of part of the self. These external pressures are sometimes so strong that the person is automatically labeled and given no choice in self-identification.

Lillian Comas-Diaz (1994) addresses the multiple challenges faced by the LatiNegra. As the daughter of Latino and Western Hemisphere African American parents, the LatiNegra is seen as Black by both maternal and paternal families. Comas-Diaz (1994) described the situation as "a classic example of racial exclusion, marginality, and disconnection" (p. 36). The combination of race, ethnicity, and gender results in the LatiNegra being a minority within a minority. LatiNegra lesbians face the "additional stress of coping with the gay and lesbian community's racism, plus the heterosexism, sexism, and internalized racism of their own ethnic community" (Comas-Diaz, 1994, p. 43).

Individuals who engage in interracial relationships are sometimes rejected and even disowned by their families. Minerbrook's (1996) *Divided to the Vein: A Journey Into Race and Family* is the story of the author's endeavors to connect with his mother's White family, who had denied his existence. Other recent autobiographies that tell similar stories of denial by part of the family are McBride's (1996) *The Color of Water: A Black Man's Tribute to His White Mother* and Williams's (1995) *Life on the Color Line: The True Story of a White Boy Who Discovered He Was Black.*

The challenge of checking one's racial categorization looms large for mixed-race individuals who are faced with checking just one of their racial heritages or checking "other" on many registration blanks. Chiong (1998) gives a detailed description of challenges for school registration in her book, *Racial Categorization of Multiracial Children in Schools.* In Wehrly (1996), I discuss the need to legitimize an identity for interracial people. The U.S. Census 2000 did make a major change by permitting people to check more than one racial heritage.

Killian (2001) discusses results of his dissertation research of ten interracial Black-White couples. Semistructured, in-depth interviews were conducted with spouses and with the couples (30 total interviews) to obtain information on racial histories and identities. Mixed support for the couples from the families of origin was reported. Some family members refused to attend the couple's wedding ceremony. Some interracial couples opted for brief civil ceremonies to circumvent the problem of nonattendance at weddings by family members. The general public also sent messages to the interracial couples such as avoiding the couples, excluding them in conversations, and outright staring. Sixteen of the twenty participants reported negative public reactions that brought pain and frustration to them.

One important aspect evident in Killian's (2001) interviews was a deemphasis on history and ethnic heritage and an avoidance of discussion of incidents of prejudice. Killian noted many "silent histories" and "silent partners." It appeared that silence served as a survival mechanism for some interracial couples when issues were too painful to discuss.

A professional barrier that has impeded culturally sensitive service to mixed-race people is that most racial identity development theories are monoracial theories. Recently, biracial and multiracial theories have been proposed for work with multiracial individuals (Poston, 1990; Root, 1990, 1998; Reynolds & Pope, 1991; Jacobs, 1992; Phinney, 1993). Application of concepts from some of these theories is discussed in the next section.

The professional counseling literature has been slow to address the needs and strengths of the burgeoning mixed-race population (Wehrly, 1996; Wehrly, Kenney, & Kenney, 1999), whereas the popular press has highlighted the interracial population since the early 1990s (Mathabane & Mathabane, 1992; Bates, 1993; Funderberg, 1994; Haislip, 1994; Perkins, 1994; Pressley, 1994; Cose, 1995; Courtney, 1995; von Sternberg, 1995).

Related to the dearth of professional literature on counseling the mixed-race population is the fact that the majority of multicultural counseling textbooks give little or no attention to work with the interracial population. My 1999 unpublished research of the Council for Accreditation of Counseling and Related Education Program's (CACREP) accredited institutions revealed confusion among counselor educators as to the inclusion of training counseling students to work with mixed-race clients and families. It appeared that some counselor educators thought that training for multicultural counseling was synonymous with training for multiracial counseling (Wehrly, 2000).

Counseling Strategies to Assist Mixed-Race Individuals and Families in Breaking Barriers

In Wehrly (1996), I propose counselor self-study of ethnic-racial heritage as an initial step in working with multiracial individuals and interracial families. Included in this study is self-examination of the origins of stereotypes and myths that come to mind regarding the mixed-race population and in-depth examination of how these myths and stereotypes influence current behavior. The results of Goodwin's (1999) dissertation research of Texas licensed professional counselors support my position that a major first step toward competency in counseling people of more than one racial heritage is "a thorough self-examination of personal values, biases, beliefs, feelings, and attitudes toward topics such as interracial dating, interracial couples, interracial unions, and children of interracial unions" (Wehrly, 1996, p. 27).

A counseling technique that can be of great value in work with multiracial individuals and interracial families is culturally sensitive active listening and speaking. Counselor awareness of the cultural impact on nonverbal behavior is of special importance. Eye contact, touching behavior, the use and meaning of silence, the distance kept between the people when speaking, and bodily gestures are all culturally conditioned and will be unique to each situation. Role playing, including role reversal, and sculpting can be used in culturally sensitive ways.

Awareness of the dangers of stereotyping is another priceless counselor trait. Knowing clients on an individual basis enables the counselor to learn what clients consider important in their lives. Cultural characteristics should never be ascribed based on physical appearance.

Bibliotherapy, the use of stories and books for therapeutic purposes, is a counseling technique that can be used with clients of all ages, including people of mixed-race heritage. The process of bibliotherapy involves the client in reading, hearing, or seeing a story acted out on the stage or in a video or movie. Cornett and Cornett (1980) suggest three assumptions or guidelines that support the use of this technique:

1. A current or future problem exists for the client;
2. The client identifies with the character or situation in the story; and
3. The client becomes personally involved with the character or situation in the story and is able to gain insight for solving present or future problematic situations.

Bibliotherapy must be used in an age-appropriate manner for the client to experience the three stages of the process: identification, catharsis, and insight. Benefits that the client reader or listener may receive are several. First, because the experience is vicarious, happening to someone else, the process is safe with very little threat to the participant. Second, clients begin to realize that other people, also, have similar problems and that they are not alone. Third, through following ways in which the lead character in the story solves a problem, clients realize that most problems have several alternatives for solution. Fourth, participants learn initial steps in problem solving by engaging in the process of bibliotherapy.

Bibliotherapy involves advance planning in order to select age-appropriate and situation-specific books for use with clients. If clients are to read the books by themselves, it usually helps to have more than one book from which clients choose. Appendix B of Wehrly (1996) includes an introduction to the bibliotherapeutic process and a list of books that are appropriate for use in bibliotherapy with interracial individuals. Additional books not included on this 1996 list are Kandel (1997), McBride (1996), Minerbrook (1996), Walker (2001), and Williams (1995).

A Case Study Using Bibliotherapy

A case study applying the use of bibliotherapy follows.

> I am a tenth-grade counselor in a suburban New York City school. School has been in session about six weeks when my secretary tells me that a new student named Sarah has made an appointment to see me. Before my appointment with Sarah, I look at the school records from her previous school in California. It appears that Sarah has attended schools in several cities since entering kindergarten. She has maintained a strong B grade point average in spite of the many moves that she has made. On her registration form, Sarah is listed as a person of mixed-race heritage.
>
> Early in the first session, Sarah tells me how lonely she feels from the annual moves from the home of one parent to the other parent. Sarah says she just begins to get to know her peers when it is time to move again. Since the breakup of her parents' marriage five years ago, Sarah has alternated living with her father and mother. The previous year, Sarah lived with her African American mother in San Francisco. Now she is living in New York with her father and new stepmother who are both White and Jewish.
>
> I compliment Sarah on maintaining such a good academic record in spite of her constant moves and school changes. She smiles when I say this and begins to talk about how exciting it is to learn so many new things. Sarah talks at length about the topics being addressed in her classes and how she has learned to go "on-line" to look up additional information related to these topics. She tells me that getting involved in her schoolwork helps her to forget that she is lonely. Sarah asks if she can come to see me again next week.

Our second session opens with Sarah excitedly telling me how well she has done on two recent tests. I respond that I can see how excited she is about these achievements. Sarah's facial expression changes as she confides that her peers say she is African American and can't be White, and they sometimes make fun of her appearance. She also says that the African American students say she is snobbish because she acts like a "White girl." So far, she doesn't feel a part of any school social group.

Sarah tells me that some of her father's family never speak to her at family gatherings; "They look away or act as if they just don't see me when they are looking my way." Sarah feels as if they don't want to include her as part of their White, Jewish family. When I comment that it must be hard to feel excluded at school and by part of her family, Sarah heaves a big sigh, nods her head, and looks down.

Sarah returns for a third session and tells me again how great her classes are. When I ask Sarah to tell me what she likes to do when she isn't studying, she says that she loves to read and spends a lot of time reading—even late at night when she hides under the covers and reads, using a flashlight.

I ask Sarah if she would like to read a book about a young woman who has faced challenges similar to the ones she faces. Her face lights up as she answers with an excited "Yes!" I show Sarah a copy of Rebecca Walker's 2001 book, *Black, White, and Jewish.* Sarah takes the book and thumbs through several pages, saying, "May I borrow this book?" I tell Sarah that we can use this book as a guideline for discussion for several sessions. I ask her to read at least the first fifty pages and do the following two things by the time we meet again:

1. Select passages to which you can relate. During our next session, be prepared to discuss what it is that makes these book passages significant for you.
2. Keep notes on your own feelings as you read how Rebecca Walker reveals her deep feelings, questions, and concerns. Be prepared to share these feelings with me.

At the next session, Sarah tells me that she can really relate to how Rebecca felt more comfortable in airports than in the several houses in which her parents lived. Sarah says, "I know exactly what to do in airports. I can feel relaxed in airports; but I don't feel relaxed when I go to the houses where my family gets together with my father's relatives." Then Sarah adds information to illustrate how stressful some of the family reunions have been.

Sarah then turns to page 41 of Walker's book and tells how she really relates to the last paragraph on the page that began with the incident of Rebecca's being told that she "acted like a White girl." Sarah wonders if the darker-skinned girls in her school feel that she is taking something away from them when she, Sarah, answers questions in class and speaks to some of the popular boys in the hallway.

Sarah tells me she never thought about how the other students may interpret her behavior. This leads to Sarah's saying, "But I have to be me!" Sarah's thoughtful insights as to how her behavior influences others and how she can remain true to being herself are the basis of much discussion during this and subsequent counseling sessions.

As Sarah continues to relate to incidents in *Black, White, and Jewish,* more "a-ha" reactions surface during our counseling sessions. Sarah begins to wonder if she uses her negative reactions as an excuse not to reach out to others. This self-understanding leads to a form of catharsis for Sarah and the recognition that she is not alone in facing rejection by peers. Together, we discuss alternatives for dealing with rejection. Sarah begins to feel empowered when she realizes she can choose other alternatives for dealing with rejection.

Killian's (2001) research of interracial couples resulted in suggestions for helping professionals. Members of the interracial couples hoped that helping professionals would advocate for them rather than emphasize their differences as a reason to end the relationships, or rather "focus on synthesis, not on division" (Killian, 2001, p. 34). Interracial couples also hoped to have a helping professional who would serve as a mediator when impasses occur during therapy. Killian suggested the value of cultural genograms, discussion of hypothetical scenarios (which have advantages similar to bibliotherapy in that the cases discussed are external to self), letter writing, and the need for the counselor to maintain an ongoing atmosphere of support and sensitive interest as the couples disclose painful memories. A caution issued was the danger of the therapist allying with one partner against the other.

Families that have become interracial through cross-racial adoption usually rejoice that they have been able to add a much-wanted member to the family. Beneath the joyous atmosphere of this family addition, the adoptive parents may have buried feelings of sadness because they have been unable to give birth to the child themselves. For adoptive children, concerns about why their birth mother gave them away may eventually surface.

In cross-racial placement of an older child, both the adoptive parents and the child can benefit from counselor-facilitated, cross-cultural sensitivity training that includes discussion of parental and child expectations in the new environment. Ideally, the counselor will have time to work with the family and the child on a regular basis to help with the cross-cultural adjustment of all family members. The counselor can encourage regular family meetings to talk about daily challenges and triumphs. Parents can be encouraged to raise the adoptive children in a manner that will help these children to understand and take pride in their birth cultures.

A powerful intervention with multiracial individuals and interracial families is to focus on strengths. When asked about strengths, many clients will respond immediately and say things about the benefits they get from living in two cultures and how it helps them to get along better with others who are different. With a little encouragement, other multiracial clients will get involved in thinking about and exploring their own strengths.

When asked about the strengths of growing up multiracial, a biracial college student emphasized the importance of the "lived" experience of growing up in a multiracial and multicultural home: "Culture is key here because it, as opposed to race, provides the real benefit of multiracial families. Multiracial families provide us with a tremendously powerful experience of diversity right at home, where I believe it's the most beneficial" (Shaka Smart, personal communication, March 31, 1999).

Suggestions from the research and models of multiracial identity development are worth noting. Concepts from the work of Jacobs (1992), Root (1990, 1992, 1998), and Phinney (1989, 1993) will be noted.

After fifteen years of research on the identity development of biracial Black-White children, Jacobs (1992) proposed a three-stage model. During the second stage of their identity development, Jacobs found that biracial Black-White children often need help in acquiring a biracial or interracial label. At this point, parents can work with their children to decide on an accurate label for their family so that children can reply forthrightly when asked questions such as, "What are you?" Without a specific label for their family of origin, biracial children seem to have difficulty in moving on to the third and last of Jacobs's stages. Counselors can help members of the interracial family to understand the importance of working together to decide on a label for their family. (For further discussion of Jacobs's model, see Jacobs, 1992.)

Root (1990, 1992, 1998) has given many years to researching the ethnic identity development of multiracial Americans. Root (1990) presented a "Schematic Meta-model" for the resolution of biracial identity in which she proposed four possibilities for biracial identity resolution. The four resolutions are not mutually exclusive, and the individual can move back and forth among the resolutions. Root was one of the first theorists to propose situational racial reference group identification. Root's (1998) Ecological Identity Model incorporates a host of factors that influence identity development, any or all of which could be topics of discussion during therapy.

Phinney and colleagues (1989, 1993, 1996) devoted years to the study of minority/ethnic identity development. Phinney's model of adolescent ethnic identity development includes three stages: (1) unexamined ethnic identity, (2) ethnic identity search (moratorium), and (3) achieved ethnic identity. In discussions of this model with diverse groups, I have found that many counselors see this as a model that can be used with people of mixed-race heritage at both the adolescent and adult stages. Readers may want to pursue the details of Phinney's three-stage model and use it in work with multiracial individuals.

Conclusion

After an introductory section and definitions of terms related to helping professionals' work with multiracial individuals and interracial families, this chapter gave a cursory overview of some of the issues, challenges, and barriers facing this population. In addition, the chapter introduces counseling strategies that can be used by helping professionals to aid multiracial individuals and interracial families to reach their full human potential.

DISCUSSION QUESTIONS

1. What is the difference between the terms *multicultural* and *multiracial*?

2. Name and discuss some of the myths and stereotypes about people of mixed-race heritage.

3. What aspects of counselor self-study are important as a major first step toward competency in counseling the mixed-race population?

4. How can bibliotherapy be used in counseling with a multiracial person?

5. Discuss contributions of Maria Root to the formulation of appropriate multiracial ethnic identity development models.

REFERENCES

Alstein, H., Coster, M., First-Hartling, L., Ford, C., Glasoe, B., Hairston, S., Kasoff, J., & Grier, A. W. (1994). Clinical observations of adult intercountry adoptees and their adoptive parents. *Child Welfare, 73*, 261–269.

Bates, J. D. (1993). *Gift children: A story of race, family, and adoption in a divided America.* New York: Ticknor & Fields.

Borders, L. D. (1995, July/August). The passing of innocence. *Adoptive Families, 28*(4), 26–28.

Chiong, J. A. (1998). *Racial categorization of multiracial children in schools.* Westport, CT: Bergin & Garvey.

Comas-Diaz, L. (1994). LatiNegra: Mental health issues of African Latinas. *Journal of Feminist Family Therapy, 5*(3/4), 35–74.

Cornett, C. E., & Cornett, C. F. (1980). *Bibliotherapy: The right book at the right time.* Bloomington, IN: Phi Delta Kappa.

Cose, E. (1995, February 13). One drop of bloody history. *Newsweek,* p. 70, 72.

Courtney, B. A. (1995, February 13). Freedom from choice: Being biracial has meant denying half of my identity. *Newsweek,* p. 16.

Eddings, J. (1997, July 14). Counting a "new" type of American. *U.S. News & World Report, 123,* 22–23.

Funderburg, L. (1994). *Black, White, other: Biracial Americans talk about race and identity.* New York: William Morrow.

Gibbs, J. T. (1987). Identity and marginality: Issues in the treatment of biracial adolescents. *American Journal of Orthopsychiatry, 57,* 265–278.

Gibbs, J. T., & Hines, A. M. (1992). Negotiating ethnic identity: Issues for Black-White biracial adolescents. In M. P. P. Root (Ed.), *Racially mixed people in America* (pp. 223–238). Thousand Oaks, CA: Sage.

Goodwin, R. B. (1999). The efficacy of a self-examination study of racial/ethnic heritage concerning Black/White romantic unions in improving multicultural counseling competency (Doctoral dissertation, Southwestern Baptist Theological Seminary). *Dissertation Abstracts International, 60–11,* B5752.

Haislip, S. T. (1994). *The sweeter the juice.* New York: Simon & Schuster.

Jacobs, J. H. (1992). Identity development in biracial children. In M. P. P. Root (Ed.), *Racially mixed people in America* (pp. 190–206). Thousand Oaks, CA: Sage.

Kaeser, G., & Gillespie, P. (1997). *Of many colors—Portraits of multiracial families.* Amherst: University of Massachusetts Press.

Kandel, B. (1997). *Growing up biracial: Trevor's story.* Minneapolis, MN: Lerner Publications.

Killian, K. D. (2001). Reconstituting racial histories and identities: The narratives of interracial couples. *Journal of Marital and Family Therapy, 27,* 27–42.

Kim, W. J. (1995). International adoption: A case review of Korean children. *Child Psychiatry and Human Development, 25,* 141–154.

Mathabane, M., & Mathabane, G. (1992). *Love in black and white: The triumph of love over prejudice and taboo.* New York: HarperCollins.

McBride, J. (1996). *The color of water: A Black man's tribute to his White mother.* New York: Riverhead Books.

Minerbrook, S. (1996). *Divided to the vein: A Journey into race and family.* New York: Harcourt Brace & Co.

Perkins, M. (1994, March 7). Guess who's coming to church? *Christianity Today,* pp. 30–33.

Phinney, J. S. (1989). Stages of ethnic identity development in minority group adolescents. *Journal of Early Adolescence, 9,* 34–49.

Phinney, J. S. (1993). A three-stage model of identity in adolescence. In M. E. Bernal & G. P. Knight (Eds.), *Ethnic identity: Formation and transmission among Hispanics and other minorities* (pp. 61–79). Albany: State University of New York Press.

Phinney, J. S., & Alipuria, L. L. (1996). At the interface of cultures: Multiethnic/multiracial high school and college students. *The Journal of Social Psychology, 136,* 139–158.

Poston, W. S. C. (1990). The biracial identity development model: A needed addition. *Journal of Counseling and Development, 69,* 152–155.

Pressley, S. A. (1994, August 22). The color of love. In a country transfixed by race, black-white couples turn to each other for support. *The Washington Post,* pp. B1, B4.

Register, C. (1991). *"Are those kids yours?" American families with children adopted from other countries.* New York: Free Press.

Reynolds, A. L., & Pope, R. L. (1991). The complexities of diversity: Exploring multiple oppressions. *Journal of Counseling and Development, 70,* 174–180.

Root, M. P. P. (1990). Resolving "other" status: Identity development of biracial individuals. In L. S. Brown & M. P. P. Root (Eds.), *Diversity and complexity in feminist therapy* (pp. 185–205). New York: Haworth Press.

Root, M. P. P. (1992). Within, between, and beyond race. In M. P. P. Root (Ed.), *Racially mixed people in America* (pp. 3–11). Thousand Oaks, CA: Sage.

Root, M. P. P. (1998). Multiracial Americans: Changing the face of Asian America. In L. C. Lee & N. W. Zane (Eds.), *Handbook of Asian American psychology* (pp. 261–287). Thousand Oaks, CA: Sage.

U.S. Bureau of the Census. (2000). *Profile of general demographic characteristics.* Washington, DC: U.S. Department of Commerce.

U.S. Bureau of the Census News. (2001, March 14). Questions and answers from Census 2000 data on race. Washington, DC: U.S. Department of Commerce.

von Sternberg, B. (1995, April 12). "Biracial" doesn't mean one or the other. *Star Tribune,* pp. A1, A10.

Walker, R. (2001). *Black, White, and Jewish: Autobiography of a shifting self.* New York: Riverhead Books.

Watts, R. E., & Henriksen, R. C. (1998). The interracial couple questionnaire. *The Journal of Individual Psychology, 54,* 368–372.

Watts, R. E., & Henriksen, R. C. (1999). Perceptions of a White female in an interracial marriage. *The Family Journal: Counseling and Therapy for Couples and Families, 7,* 68–70.

Wehrly, B. (1996). *Counseling interracial individuals and families.* Alexandria, VA: American Counseling Association.

Wehrly, B. (2000). *Diversity research of CACREP counselor education programs.* Unpublished manuscript. Western Illinois University, Macomb.

Wehrly, B., Kenney, K. R., & Kenney, M. E. (1999). *Counseling multiracial families.* Thousand Oaks, CA: Sage.

Williams, G. H. (1995). *Life on the color line: The true story of a White boy who discovered he was Black.* New York: Dutton.

20 Cultural Considerations in Counselor Training and Supervision

DON C. LOCKE AND MARIE FAUBERT

Multicultural counseling theory and practice has come unto its own. It has been called the fourth force in counseling (Ivey, Ivey, & Simek-Morgan, 1997) placing it on a par with psychoanalytic, cognitive-behavioral, and existential-humanistic traditions. It has developed a body of knowledge, skills, and competencies (Arredondo et al., 1996a) that have been accepted cognitively by most counselor educators and counselor education programs. The time has come to suggest how counselor educators can operationalize counselor training and supervision in such a way that students graduate culturally competent and confident.

In this chapter, we begin with a brief reflection on the history of the conversation about multicultural counseling. We continue with a consideration of how multiculturalism is defined generally and for the purposes of this chapter. Then we consider the lack of research and dialogue on how to successfully graduate competent and confident counselors who are knowledgeable and skilled in working with diverse populations. In addition, we offer some concrete suggestions and reflections regarding training using social constructionism and postmodernism. Finally, we complete our discussion by reflecting on the characteristics of a sound program in counselor education and supervision using a cognitive-behavioral theoretical framework.

Brief Consideration of the History of Multicultural Counseling

Multiculturalism in the field of counseling can be traced back to the 1960s. That counseling has failed to fulfill its promises to the culturally different has been a frequent theme in counselor education and supervision literature since then. Wrenn's (1962) description of "the culturally encapsulated counselor" was among the earliest reports. The term refers specifically to (1) the substitution of model stereotypes for the real world, (2) the disregard of cultural variations and a dogmatic adherence to some universal notions of truth, and (3) the use of a technique-oriented definition of the counseling process. The results of cultural encapsulation are that counselor roles are rigidly defined, implanting an implicit belief in universal values and universal concepts of "health" and "normalcy."

We know that cultural values and traditions offer special strengths that should help guide counselor education and supervision. We believe that counselor education and supervision is more effective when provided within the most relevant and meaningful cultural, gender-sensitive, and age-appropriate context for students and the clients they serve. It is important that standards for counselor education and supervision mirror practices that are appropriate for the clients whom students and counselors will serve.

As early as 1977, Derald W. Sue and David Sue (Sue & Sue, 1977) indicated that most graduate programs in counselor education gave inadequate treatment to mental health issues of culturally different ethnic group members. Cultural influences affecting personality formation, career choice, educational development, and the manifestation of behavior disorders were infrequently part of mental health training programs. As a result, professionals who dealt with mental health problems of the culturally different were lacking in understanding and knowledge about ethnic values and their consequent interaction with a racist society.

To avoid this narrowness, it is necessary for counselors to challenge their beliefs and reorganize old knowledge when it no longer fits. Through increasing one's personal awareness and through training, it is possible to avoid being culturally encapsulated. A multicultural perspective recognizes a client's culturally based beliefs, values, and behaviors and emphasizes sensitivity to the client's cultural environment (Pedersen, 1994).

Definition of Multicultural Counseling

There are two perspectives concerning multicultural counseling. One has been developed by people such as Fukuyama (1994) and is called the universal view, and the other by people such as Locke (1998) and is named the focused view (Faubert, 1998). The former includes issues of race, gender, religion, spirituality, sexual orientation, socioeconomic issues, and other variables of difference under one umbrella. The latter separates issues of culture from issues of diversity. This perspective is the one used in this chapter because the authors believe that issues of diversity are subsets of issues of culture (Faubert, 1998). For example, gender issues and issues of physical and mental challenge are different from culture to culture and need to be examined and practiced within the cultural context.

For purposes of this chapter, multicultural counselor education and supervision will be defined as those relationships in which there is a counselor educator–student or supervisor–supervisee relationship where there are cultural differences based on race or ethnicity. We recognize that other differences are salient and deserving of consideration in counselor education and supervision. Some might argue that the material related to race and ethnicity is directly applicable to other cultural differences. Our professional focus has been on race and ethnicity and we will continue that focus in this chapter.

Approaches to Cultural Sensitivity

In general, the study of counselor education and supervision includes a variety of approaches to cultural sensitivity. Some of the approaches include topics such as applying a cognitive-behavioral approach to counselor education (Faubert, Locke, & Lanier, 1996), teaching about racism (Locke & Kiselica, 1999), critical incidents in supervision (Fukuyama, 1994), and multicultural case conceptualization (Constantine, 2001).

We do know a number of things about including a diversity perspective in counselor education and supervision. For example, we know that a major objective of American education is to teach people the academic and social skills necessary to live successfully in a democratic society. In counselor education, we operationalize this concept by teaching our students those skills that will prepare them to participate fully in our society. We also teach them how to help others live fully.

Diversity is a fact of life in the United States and will be even more so as the twenty-first century continues. The population of the United States is growing and changing dramatically. Present and projected changes in the ethnic composition of the United States present a challenge for how we do counselor education and supervision.

The process of becoming educated is made easier for students when the full range of their life experiences is used (Freire, 1973, 1993). As the demographics of counselor educators and supervisors change and as the ethnic composition of counselor education students changes, the opportunity for the use of this diverse ethnic composition as a source of rich classroom material becomes evident.

Finally, we believe that diversity can be integrated into the curriculum only by deliberate and intentional efforts on the part of counselor education faculty. We continue to debate whether courses specific to the diverse populations counselors serve are necessary while simultaneously claiming that content, which will produce confident and competent counselors, has been infused into the curriculum or that the similarities among people outweigh the need for "separate" courses. Regardless of which side of this issue we find ourselves, we must be deliberate and intentional in providing content and experiences that prepare our graduates for service in a world that is diverse and continues to change. We believe that cultural competence requires attaining the knowledge, skills, and attitudes to enable counselors to provide effective service to diverse populations.

Dinsmore and England (1996), after examining how counselor educators are wrestling with how to provide multicultural counseling training, concluded that there are few studies describing what counselor education programs are doing in the area of multicultural counseling program development. There is no general consensus regarding what set of program characteristics constitutes a standard for multicultural program competence. They concluded that "multicultural training of counselors follows no universally agreed on set of standards for program content and design, and it is difficult to determine where the progression stands in relationship to program development in multicultural counseling" (p. 2). Nonetheless, Bernard and Goodyear (1998) suggested that the supervisor is responsible for ensuring that multicultural issues receive attention in supervision.

Multicultural Counseling Training

Kiselica (1999) identified several converging themes regarding the current status of the practice of multicultural counseling training. These themes included the following:

- Multicultural counseling training requires organizational support;
- Multicultural counseling training focuses on providing knowledge about the culturally different, examining cultural biases, and developing culturally appropriate skills in order to reduce ethnocentrism and prejudice;
- Discomfort is a necessary but manageable aspect of multicultural counseling training;
- Multicultural counseling training and educational strategies and processes must be adjusted according to the differing developmental levels of students;
- The cultural and racial identity of the instructor influences the dynamics and outcomes of multicultural counseling training;
- Experiential and clinical learning activities are central to comprehensive multicultural education.

Kiselica and Ramsey (2001), describing the future of the profession, posited that multicultural training will become infused throughout counselor education curricula. The question becomes, "What is it that multicultural counselor education will look like?"

The first multicultural counseling competencies were presented to the profession by Sue, Arredondo, and McDavis (1992). These standards were "operationalized" by the Professional Standards and Certification Committee of the Association for Multicultural Counseling and Development in 1996 (Arredondo et al., 1996). This process identified a number of training standards for the profession, including the following:

- Culturally skilled counselors seek out educational, consultative, and training experiences to improve their understanding and effectiveness in working with culturally different populations. Being able to recognize the limits of their competencies, they seek consultation, seek further training or education, refer to more qualified individuals or resources, or engage in a combination of these.
- Culturally skilled counselors possess specific knowledge and information about the particular group with which they are working. They are aware of

the life experiences, cultural heritage, and historical background of their culturally different clients. This particular competency is strongly linked to the minority identity development models available in the literature.

- Culturally skilled counselors should familiarize themselves with relevant research and the latest findings regarding mental health and mental disorders that affect various ethnic and racial groups. They should actively seek out educational experiences that enrich their knowledge, understanding, and cross-cultural skills for more effective counseling behavior.

- Culturally skilled counselors have a clear and explicit knowledge and understanding of the generic characteristics of counseling and therapy (culture bound, class bound, and monolingual) and how they may clash with the cultural values of various cultural groups.

- Culturally skilled counselors are able to engage in a variety of verbal and nonverbal helping responses. They are able to send and receive both verbal and nonverbal messages accurately and appropriately. They are not bound to only one method or approach to helping, but recognize that helping styles and approaches may be culture bound. When they sense that their helping style is limited and potentially inappropriate, they can anticipate and modify it.

We believe that the assumptions of social constructionism serve as a basic foundation for all counselor education and supervision. Simply, social constructionism recognizes the multiple understandings of reality that persons have when making meaning of their experiences. For example, in any family, each member has a different telling of the same event. In a similar manner, clients come to counseling with multiple meanings and voices, some very different from counselors (Anderson, 1997; Gergen, 1999; Holzman & Morss, 2000; Shotter, 2000). These may involve such things as whether they believe they have opportunities (as is taught by the dominant culture), how they experience grief, or what explanation they give for illness.

In a similar manner, counselor education students have multiple experiences and varying understandings and explanations for their experiences. Skilled counselor educators can use the lived experiences and multiple understandings of students to enhance their ability to have conversations with clients (Anderson, 1997) in such a way that clients feel the understanding of counselors. Counselor education classes and counseling are most effective when they engage collaborative language and dialogical conversation (Anderson, 1997).

Postmodernism is a fundamental paradigm shift from the traditional modernistic points of view presented in the psychoanalytic, cognitive-behavioral, and existential-humanistic views of the first three forces in counseling. It is less dependent on the natural sciences and more dependent on the phenomenological experiences of the conversants. Postmodern thought offers an opportunity for structuring counselor education and supervision for maximum effect in graduating culturally competent and confident counselors. Postmodern experiences in the classroom prepare students to meet the needs of a diverse clientele (Rigazio-DiGilio, Ivey, & Locke, 1997). The foundational elements of social constructionism and postmodernism include

- Individuals exist and function within a context;
- Context shapes perceptions of self and others;
- Perceptions become realities;
- Contexts can change and people can change;
- Multiple realities exist for every person;
- Marginalized views, multiplicity, and diversity are valued;
- Expertise is a shared endeavor.

Characteristics of Sound Programs

A sound multicultural counselor education and supervision program must provide a number of traits and characteristics to make it effective and relevant to the needs of a diverse clientele. We have identified a dozen components of an effective multicultural counselor and education program.

1. Effective multicultural counselor education and supervision includes a rationale and philosophy to clarify its nature, premises, and aims. An introductory course explores the multiple interpretations and definitions of multiculturalism and diversity so that counselor trainees discern the underlying beliefs, assumptions, and goals inherent in each perspective.

2. Effective multicultural counselor education and supervision includes opportunities for reflection on how culture and gender shape our behavior, beliefs, expectations, values, identity, and personal biases. An understanding of one's own cultural heritage and worldview invites understanding and acceptance of other cultural groups. Cultural self-understanding evolves through repeated intercultural experiences, reflection on personal feelings and expectations, exploration of one's own values and beliefs, and exposure to a variety of ideas, beliefs, and cultural perspectives.

3. Effective multicultural counselor education and supervision includes direct and meaningful experiences with people from diverse backgrounds. Students are exposed to a multicultural clientele throughout their program. To understand others, people must understand themselves; to understand themselves, people must interact with others. Personal experiences with a diverse mix of people can lead to better understanding of our own cultural identity through comparison and contrast with other cultural groups. Additionally, intercultural experiences help reduce the anxiety experienced in unfamiliar cross-cultural encounters. The reduced anxiety boosts self-confidence, increases cultural competency, and improves cross-cultural communication.

4. Effective multicultural counselor education and supervision includes an exploration of issues related to gender, age, ethnicity, family, and language within multicultural settings. An overview of the cultural underpinnings in people's attitudes toward females, males, ethnic groups, and language differences develops greater sensitivity and understanding of cross-cultural behaviors and attitudes. It encourages counselors to examine their own feelings, attitudes, and beliefs about these important issues.

5. Effective multicultural counselor education and supervision includes a cross-cultural examination of family roles and family values. The family, the oldest human institution, is the basic unit of culture. As such, it is responsible for the socialization of children. The manner in which the culture organizes itself in kinship patterns provides useful information on its structure.

6. Effective multicultural counselor education and supervision includes verbal and nonverbal communication strategies attuned to ethnic, racial, linguistic, and cultural differences. Attention is given to language, including languages other than English, dialect, and slang. The acquisition of cross-cultural communication strategies increases cultural competency. Through knowledge of key areas of cultural miscommunication and awareness of cross-cultural communicative strategies, counselors can approach cross-cultural communication with greater confidence, sensitivity, and awareness.

7. Effective multicultural counselor education and supervision includes instruction in knowledge of cultural and individual differences in responses to psychological stresses and how to accommodate these differences in counseling. To be culturally different does not equate to deviancy, pathology, or inferiority. Each culture has strengths and limitations and their differences are inevitable. Counselors must evaluate behaviors from the perspective of the group's values system, as well as other standards used in determining normality and abnormality. When functioning as health care providers in multicultural environments, counselors, in assessing and diagnosing mental disorders, need to be aware of three possible inaccurate consequences: overdiagnosis, underdiagnosis, and misdiagnosis. An important source for this issue is Castillo (1997).

8. Effective multicultural counselor education and supervision includes identification of cultural bias towards age, gender, ethnic groups, language, and physical and mental handicaps. Lack of awareness and sensitivity to bias in counseling strategies and techniques will lead to the perpetuation of stereotypes. Through effective multicultural counselor education and supervision, counselors discern the covert messages, misrepresentations, omissions, and misinformation that are sometimes present in counseling theory and practice.

9. Effective multicultural counselor education and supervision includes a presentation of counseling methods and strategies that meet the needs of diverse populations. As counselor education student demographics change, counselor educators and supervisors must be sensitive to the appropriateness of methods, strategies, and techniques to this changed student population. Effective counselor educators and supervisors will adapt their methods and strategies to the students they teach or supervise.

10. Effective multicultural counselor education and supervision includes the identification and use of assessment strategies and techniques that are appropriate to the cultures of the clients. Counselor trainees learn about test selection, test bias, appropriate test administration procedures, and how to interpret test results in a cultural context.

11. Effective multicultural counselor education and supervision programs demonstrate an appreciation of diverse research methodologies. Both qualitative and quantitative research methods are apparent in faculty and student research. There is clear faculty research productivity in multicultural issues, which is evidenced by journal publications and conference presentations. Students are mentored in multicultural research.

12. Effective multicultural counselor education and supervision recognizes that all efforts may not be provided within the counselor education department or the student field placement. Some issues require that counselor educators and supervisors become active in the communities in which they live and from which their clients come. This is particularly true for social justice issues where counselor educators and supervisors have an opportunity to model community involvement for their students.

A Proposed Theoretical Framework for Infusing Cultural Issues in Counselor Education and Supervision

Cognitive-behavioral therapies provide a possible theoretical framework for infusing cultural issues in counselor education and supervision (Faubert, Locke, & Lanier, 1996). They interact well with constructivism and postmodernism because they both deal with cognition and meaning making, which can lead to feelings and behavior more acceptable to clients. Cognitive restructuring helps clients decide how they want to change their internal conversations concerning the meaning that they give to their lived experiences in order to feel better and function effectively.

Cognitive therapy has interacted with behavior therapy with its emphasis on empirical factors with favorable results, especially in areas of irrational thinking and dysfunctional beliefs (Beck, 1993). Cognitive therapy has been said to be integrative and eclectic, so distinctions among cognitive, behavioral, and cognitive-behavioral therapies are becoming obfuscated (Beck, 1991) and can be applied effectively in a constructivist, postmodern framework.

Cognitive-behavioral therapy can be defined as a series of therapeutic procedures that result in modifying a client's worldview. Clients come to counseling wanting to change their way of thinking, feeling, and behaving. Dialogical conversations between counselors and clients facilitate this transformation. A constructivist, postmodern way of being and doing helps counselors avoid telling clients rather than carrying on a transforming conversation with clients, who want to take on a more satisfying, successful way of seeing the world and being in the world. Clients come to counseling wanting to change, and the dialogical posture between counselors and clients proposed by postmodernism provides a setting in which cognitive-behavioral therapy can become culturally appropriate.

Applying cognitive-behavioral theories in counselor education programs that integrate multicultural issues provides unique mixes of rigorous academic discipline, profound investigation of feelings, and effective counseling behaviors with the purpose of producing culturally competent and confident professionals. What follows is a description of how cognitive-behavioral perspectives and approaches in a supportive postmodern setting can help all students in a program that centers on multicultural counseling issues feel included and become culturally competent mental health professionals.

In programs that have multicultural counseling as a core, one of the primary goals is to help students reflect on their thinking and how that thinking influences their feelings toward clients and their behaviors with clients. The theories that provide frameworks for implementing such an intent are the cognitive-behavioral theories, which have as one of their primary concepts the theory that thinking has a profound influence on feeling and behaving (Beck, 1992; Thase & Beck, 1993). Using cognitive-behavioral theory in a postmodern setting ensures that the cognitive behavioral theories remain respectful of student and client conversations.

Students of counselor education and supervision come to counselor education programs with perspectives learned from years of family, cultural, and societal influence. Meichenbaum (1993) found that cognitions can act as conditioners of behavior, and that cognition influences behavior change. Students can be helped to restructure their cognitions, which will result in behavior change toward people for whom they may feel initial fear, apprehension, anxiety, anger, animosity, resentment, or any other of the plethora of feelings that counselors can have as a result of interfacing with clients different from them.

Using student voices when developing cognitive restructuring for the purpose of enhancing cultural competence and confidence integrates postmodernism with more traditional modernist cognitive-behavioral activities. This wedding of the two perspectives mitigates against the danger of indoctrination, which can result from erroneously understanding and applying cognitive-behavior theory and methods.

Cognitive Restructuring

Beck (1976, p. 217) summarized the stages of intervention of cognitive therapy; these same stages can be used in counselor education for the purpose of changing the cognitions of students in order that they can think more sensitively, feel more positively, and behave more effectively toward clients. The stages can be paraphrased as follows:

1. Students become aware of what they are thinking.
2. Students become conscious that what they are thinking is not helpful to understanding clients.

3. Students substitute helpful cognitions for insensitive ones.
4. Students receive feedback that supports the fact that their new cognitions are better constructs for their dialogical conversations with clients.

Suppositions and Perspectives That Underlie Cognitions

When there are socially determined power differences between counselors and clients, activities adapted from Pinderhughes (1989) are helpful. These activities can take the form of dialogue between two students, among three to five students in a group, or as an outside-of-class assignment. During the class discussion, which follows the students' sharing with one another or after the writing of a short reaction paper, assumptions and viewpoints that underlie cognitions will surface.

In the process, students become conscious of social power differences. Students give up denial of social power differences and substitute more genuinely accurate power perspectives. Students receive feedback from the counselor educator and from one another, which supports them in their new cognitions.

Another effective way to challenge the thinking of students is to assign them to dialogue with people of other cultures than their own. As a consequence of an intercultural dyad, one European American student said that she was surprised to find out that her African American friend did not want to be European American. She said that she had assumed that her friend would want to be European American because "it was easier to be European American in the United States than it was to be African American."

When the student body is diverse, another effective way to challenge the thinking of students is to share their reflections concerning what has transpired among them during the class. During one of these sessions, a Native American student said that in all of her more than 40 years, she had never talked about race in a racially mixed group until she had participated in the multicultural counseling class. She said that she had worked with African Americans and European Americans all her life, but she had never talked about race with them.

Some African American and European American students concurred with her and shared that they too had never spoken of race in a mixed group. Some African American and Native American students said that they had spoken of race often at home; others said that they had not. A number of European American students said that race was never a subject of conversation at home.

The dialogue ensued around the reasons for the differences in whether race was a subject of conversation in the home. Students became aware of whether they talked about race frequently. Students became conscious of the inaccuracy of their belief that talking about race is not common. Students substituted the cognition that if race were a survival issue, it was often a subject of conversation; likewise, if the dominant culture displayed the culture of the individual or family, it often was not a subject of discussion. Feedback from the counselor educator and other students provided support and encouragement in the new cognitions of the students.

Behavioral Consequences Resulting From Dysfunctional Thinking and Feeling

It is helpful to share concrete examples of avoiding contact with individuals different from self or reflecting on specific feelings in the presence of individuals different from self. In addition, use of imagery is appropriate as long as it is used with sensitive mastery. The discussion of the possible consequences of communicating negative feelings unconsciously to clients is penetrating and generates healing.

Students become conscious of their feelings and consequent avoidant behavior. Students face their behavior as others see it and practice changing it by interacting honestly in class with the counselor educator and other students. Students receive feedback from the professor and one another, which supports them in their new awareness.

Previously, we said that we believed that constructivist and postmodern perspectives helped in developing culturally competent and confident counselors. In addition, we said that the logical-linear-modernist perspective can result in insensitivity to clients' truths. We have not thrown the baby out with the bath water. This discussion has illustrated how modernist theories and practices can interact with postmodernism to make students more sensitive to the stories of their clients.

Finally, we have been using the phrase "confident and competent." To be confident without competence will do harm to clients. To be competent without confidence will result in not being able to function. Both are equally important to develop in students in an effective counselor education program. They will come with challenge and support. We have shared our conversations with you, and in the spirit of postmodernism, we welcome your reflections on our thoughts and methods that we have found fruitful.

Conclusion

The counselor education and supervision curriculum of today is very different from what it was as recently as a decade ago. Multiculturalism and cultural competence have taken their rightful place in the education of counselors. Education for cultural competence is a challenge that requires significant deliberate activity on the part of both the faculty and students. Knowledge of scholarship on cultural diversity provides a foundation for exploration of personal beliefs, values, and attitudes about culturally different individuals and groups. This knowledge not only makes for good counseling but also changes the personal lives of clients, students, counselor educators and supervisors, and the profession of counseling.

DISCUSSION QUESTIONS

We believe that each of us brings a personal history to the process of becoming culturally competent and confident, and that personal history serves as the basis of how we approach counselor education and supervision. To determine how your culture influences you in counselor education and supervision, ask yourself the following questions:

For Students

1. What knowledge do I possess concerning my own racial/ethnic group?

2. Who am I racially/ethnically?

3. What is the history of my racial/ethnic group?

4. How does my racial/ethnic identity influence how I relate to other racial/ethnic groups?

5. At what stage of development am I in terms of my own racial identity?

6. What would I like to change about how I relate to others in my racial/ethnic group?

7. What is my relationship with individuals in different racial/ethnic groups? How do my relationships with individuals influence my beliefs, attitudes, or opinions of racial/ethnic groups?

8. What knowledge do I have of culturally different individuals' experiences of living in a predominantly White society? How did I come by this information?

9. Have I discussed racial issues with individuals from different racial/ethnic groups?

10. How did discussions about racial issues commence and how did they end? How did I feel about having those discussions?

11. What is my comfort level with the differences that exist between me and racially/ethnically different people in my environment? How does this level of comfort/discomfort manifest itself?

12. Am I aware of any stereotypical views I adhere to concerning racial/ethnic groups with whom I interact? How do these stereotypes impact how I relate to these individuals or groups?

13. What inhibitions do I have about working with racially/ethnically different clients?

For Counselor Educators and Supervisors

1. How do I create an open, comfortable, and challenging multicultural classroom or supervision environment? What do I do to encourage students to discuss openly their fears about dealing with differences? How do I help students feel comfortable with sharing views and experiences that may offend other students in the class? What kind of ground rules do I establish in the class or in supervision?

2. How do I help students integrate theoretical material with their personal experience? What kind of assignments do I give? What kind of activities do I plan for the classroom?

3. How do I help students learn from dynamics that directly result from the class composition or the counseling composition?

4. How can an instructor encourage students to say what they think without supporting "racist" views?

5. How do I use my own race, ethnicity, gender, or other relevant social characteristics to personalize issues or to represent another point of view or experience in the discussion? How do I use the counselor education department demographics and the diversity represented therein in conversations about race, ethnicity, gender, or other relevant social characteristics?

6. What do I do to empower "underrepresented voices" in the classroom?

7. How do I assess student learning and evaluate my teaching throughout the semester?

8. What do I do when a student in class discussion makes an explicit racist or sexist remark? In supervision?

9. What do I do when a student asks a question with apparent racist implications?

10. What do I do when there is a racial conflict in the classroom between students of different racial/ethnic backgrounds?

11. What do I do when a student challenges what I said as being biased?

12. What do I do when there is only one member (or a very small number) of an identified ethnic group in the class? How do I use the student's ethnic group membership while also protecting that student from becoming the spokesperson for his or her group?

13. What do I do when one group in the class dominates discussion, using a "debate" format where the only apparent goal is to "win" the discussion?

For Supervisees

1. What sort of supervisor do I need? How does the race/ethnicity of the supervisor affect supervision?

2. What inhibitions do I have about working with a supervisor who is racially/ethnically different? How may these inhibitions impede supervision?

3. What qualities do I expect my supervisor to have? How will I determine if they have those qualities? Does my supervisor have specific training in cross-cultural supervision?

4. How will I go about discovering whether my supervisor has an understanding of my worldview and the worldview of my client?

5. How will I share my own views about race and its place in supervision?

6. How will I bring my personal racial identity to supervision and how will it influence my own approach to supervision?

7. How will my supervisor evaluate my competence in working with racially/ethnically different clients?

8. Will my supervisor be capable of providing relevant guidance to me on culture-specific issues? Will my supervisor be able to help me assess the impact of various cultural factors on clients' presenting issues and develop an appropriate treatment plan based on that information?

REFERENCES

Anderson, H. (1997). *Conversation, language, and possibilities: A postmodern approach to therapy.* New York: Basic Books.

Arredondo, P., Toporek, R., Brown, S. P., Jones, J., Locke, D. C., Sanchez, J. & Stadler, H. (1996). Operationalization of the multicultural counseling competencies. *Journal of Multicultural Counseling and Development, 24,* 42–78.

Beck, A. T. (1976). *Cognitive therapy and the emotional disorders.* Madison, CT: International Universities.

Beck, A. T. (1991). Cognitive therapy as the integrative therapy. *Journal of Psychotherapy Integration, 1,* 191–198.

Beck, A. T. (1992). Cognitive therapy: A 30 year retrospective. In J. Cottraux, P. Legeron, E. Mollard (Eds.). *Which psychotherapies in year 2000?* (pp. 13–28). Amsterdam, Netherlands: Swets & Zeitlinger.

Beck, A. T. (1993). Cognitive therapy: Past, present, and future [Special section]. *Journal of Consulting and Clinical Psychology, 61,* 194–198.

Bernard, J. M., & Goodyear, R. K. (1998). *Fundamentals of clinical supervision.* Boston: Allyn & Bacon.

Castillo, R. J. (1997). *Culture and mental illness: A client-centered approach.* Pacific Grove, CA: Brooks/Cole.

Constantine, M. G. (2001). Independent and interdependent self-construals as predictors of multicultural case conceptualization ability in counsellor trainees. *Counselling Psychology Quarterly, 14*(1), 33–43.

Dinsmore, J. A., & England, J. T. (1996). A study of multicultural counseling training at CACREP-accredited counselor education programs. *Counselor Education and Supervision, 36,* 58–77.

Faubert, M. (1998, September). Cultural competence/building awareness. *The Examiner.* Austin, TX: Texas State Board of Examiners of Professional Counselors.

Faubert, M., Locke, D. C., & Lanier, S. (1996). Applying a cognitive-behavioral approach to the training of culturally competent mental health counselors. *Journal of Mental Health Counseling, 18,* 200–215.

Freire, P. (1973). *Education for critical consciousness* (M. Bergman Ramos, Trans.). New York: Continuum (Original work published 1969).

Freire, P. (1993). *Pedagogy of the oppressed: New revised twentieth-anniversary edition* (M. Bergman Ramos, Trans.). New York: Continuum.

Fukuyama, M. A. (1994). Critical incidents in multicultural counseling supervision: A phenomenological approach to supervision research. *Counselor Education and Supervision, 34,* 142–152.

Gergen, K. J. (1999). *An invitation to social construction.* Thousand Oaks, CA: Sage.

Holzman, L., & Morss, J. (Eds.). (2000). *Postmodern psychologies, societal practice, and political life.* New York: Routledge.

Ivey, A. E., Ivey, M. B., & Simek-Morgan, L. (1997). *Counseling and psychotherapy: A multicultural perspective* (4th ed.). Boston: Allyn & Bacon.

Kiselica, M. A. (1999). Reducing prejudice: The role of the empathic-confrontive instructor. In M. S. Kiselica (Ed.), *Confronting prejudice and racism during multicultural training* (pp. 137–154). Alexandria, VA: American Counseling Association.

Kiselica, M. S. & Ramsey, M. L. (2001) Multicultural counselor education: Historical perspectives and future directions. In D. C. Locke, J. E. Meyers, & E. L. Herr (Eds.), *The handbook of counseling* (pp. 433–451). Thousands Oaks, CA: Sage.

Locke, D. C. (1998). *Increasing multicultural understanding: A comprehensive model* (2nd ed.). Thousand Oaks, CA: Sage.

Locke, D. C., & Kiselica, M. S. (1999). Pedagogy of possibilities: Teaching about racism in multicultural counseling courses. *Journal of Counseling and Development, 77,* 80–86.

Meichenbaum, D. (1993). Changing conceptions of cognitive behavior modification: Retrospective and prospect *Journal of Consulting and Clinical Psychology, 61,* 202–204.

Pedersen, P. (1994). *A handbook for developing multicultural awareness* (2nd ed.). Alexandria, VA: American Counseling Association.

Pinderhughes, E. (1989). *Understanding race, ethnicity, and power: The key to efficacy in clinical practice.* New York: Free Press.

Rigazio-DiGilio, S. A., Ivey, A. E., & Locke, D. C. (1997). Continuing the postmodern dialogue: Enhancing and contextualizing multiple voices. *Journal of Mental Health Counseling, 19,* 233–255.

Shotter, J. (2000, October). *Constructing "resourceful or mutually enabling" communities: Putting a new (dialogical) practice into our practices.* Paper presented at the meeting of the Meaning of Learning Project Learning Development Institute Presidential Session at AECD Denver, CO.

Sue, D. W., Arredondo, P., & McDavis, R. J. (1992). Multicultural counseling competencies and standards: A call to the profession. *Journal of Counseling and Development, 70,* 477–483.

Sue, D. W., & Sue, D. (1977). Ethnic minorities: Failures and responsibilities of the social sciences. *Journal of Non-White Concerns in Personnel and Guidance, 5,* 99–106.

Thase, M. E., & Beck, A. T. (1993). An overview of cognitive therapy. In J. H. Wright, M. E. Thase, A. T. Beck, J. W. Ludgate (Eds.), *Cognitive therapy with inpatients: Developing a cognitive milieu* (pp. 3–34). New York: Guilford Press.

Wrenn, C. G. (1962). The culturally encapsulated counselor. *Harvard Educational Review, 32,* 444–449.

21 Traditional Counseling Theories and Cross-Cultural Implications

MARTY JENCIUS AND JOHN WEST

Traditional counseling theory (e.g., theory written from a psychodynamic, cognitive-behavioral, or humanistic focus) may have limitations in terms of applicability in a multicultural society. The evolution of counseling theory may be viewed as following historic changes occurring in society, and counseling theories may also be viewed as associated with the idiosyncratic personalities of their originators (Monte, 2002). Only recently have traditional counseling theories been considered in light of the cultural context of the client; in most cases, the cultural context is considered as an afterthought from the original theory. Organizing one chapter as an overview of all of the counseling theories and their relationships to cross-cultural principles becomes a challenge when one considers the number of possible theories. Central to the idea that multicultural counseling is becoming a new movement in the counseling profession, Paul Pedersen (1990) described multicultural counseling as the "fourth force" in counseling. Multicultural counseling follows historic progression from the "first force" psychoanalysis and ego systems theories, to the "second force" behavioral theories, which are directly followed by Carl Rogers and the "third force" of humanistic theories.

A major criticism of multiculturalism as a new force in counseling theory tends to focus on the imposition of the multicultural framework as yet another paradigm that devalues the individual by its group-based generalizations. Weinrach and Thomas (1998) stated

> We believe that the diversity-sensitive counseling movement currently tends to lack moderations in its attempts to superimpose its agenda on the counseling relationship. As important as diversity-sensitive counseling is, there is no compelling evidence that it should transcend, supercede, or eclipse every aspect of the counseling process. (p. 116)

They continued, "Placed in this proper perspective, diversity-sensitive counseling is not, as Pedersen would have us to believe, a 'Fourth Force' " (p. 116). Weinrach and

Thomas went on to discuss the futility in a postmodern society of using diversity-sensitive counseling as a way to advance traditional counseling theories to meet the needs of all clients. This argument parallels Patterson's (1996) argument that diversity theory and training are really movements toward universality in counseling. McFadden (1996), in his critique of Patterson's premise regarding a movement toward universality in counseling theory, countered that:

> Multicultural counseling does not presuppose the abandonment of traditional counseling, nor does it dilute the process. On the contrary, it is an attempt to blend cultural views and create a broad social base toward understanding problems in a pluralistic society, ultimately providing the most effective service for clients. (p. 232)

McFadden continued with a counterargument that, when counseling is considered to be generic, it minimizes the client's uniqueness.

> To suggest that all counseling is generic in nature, as opposed to incorporating insights and knowledge of cultural diversity when working with special populations, contributes to the retardation of the developmental process of those populations. (p. 232)

For the purposes of organizing this discussion in a concise fashion, we adopt Pedersen's (1990) typology of "forces" as major shifts in the lenses by which counselors see clients. Inclusive but distinguished from the typology of "forces" will be a discussion of social construction and narrative approaches and their convergence with multiculturalism. For a comparison of the "forces" and "waves" of counseling, see Table 21.1.

First Force—Psychoanalytic and Ego Psychology

The first counseling force alluded to in Pedersen's (1990) typology is psychoanalytic and ego psychology. Therapy associated with personality changes is done by helping the client become more aware of unfinished business from their childhood. Psychoanalysts focus on uncovering these unconscious drives and addressing the client's defense mechanisms in order to help the client with a corrective emotional experience (Alexander & French, 1946). A major portion of the therapy is the client's reaction to the counselor because the client's reaction is seen to constitute their internal unresolved conflicts with significant life figures (objects). These displaced reactions are considered reflective of the client's initial object relations that the counselor experiences as the client's transference. Psychoanalytic and ego psychology emphasize a developmental process that contains developmental stages that the client must navigate successfully in order to be free of symptoms. Failure to transverse a developmental stage or trauma associated with that stage will fixate the client within that stage. Theorists who would fit clearly under this first force

TABLE 21.1   Forces/Waves in Counseling

From Pedersen (1990)	From O'Hanlon (1997)
First Force	*First Wave*

Psychoanalytic and Ego-Psychology-Oriented Theories
  Pathology focused and dominated by
  biological determinism
  • Freud, Erikson
  • Initially Adler, Jung, and Perls
  Object Relations
  • Klein, Kohut, Mahler
	Psychoanalytic and Ego-Psychology-Oriented Theories

Second Force	*Second Wave*

Behavior and Cognitive-Behavioral-Oriented Theories
  Personality is influenced by multiple
  external factors and internal cognitions
  • Wolpe, Dollard and Miller, Bandura,
    Meichenbaum, Beck, Ellis
  • Glasser—Reality Therapy
	Problem Centered–Oriented Theories

Third Force	

Humanistic-Oriented Theories
  Clients have an innate ability to grow given
  the proper therapeutic conditions
  • Rogers
  Existential Theories
  • Frankl, May	

Fourth Force	
Multiculturalism-Oriented Theories	
	Third Wave

	Social-Construction and Narrative-Oriented Theories
	    • Gergen, Berger and Luckmann,
	      Freedman and Combs, Epston and
	      White, Monk
	    • West, Bitter and Bubenzer—Family
	      Therapy approaches

category include Sigmund Freud, Erik Erikson, and modern day derivatives of psychodynamic approaches such as object relations (Klein, 1932; Kohut, 1977; Mahler, Pine, & Bergman, 2000). Disputably under this category would be Freud's contemporaries, Alfred Adler and Carl Jung, because early in their careers they broke from some of Freud's theoretical tenants.

There are many considerations when reflecting on how first force theories fail to adequately address a multicultural context. Helms and Cook (1999) suggested that the client's recall of unconscious material could be interpreted differently depending on the client's racial or cultural origin. Psychoanalytic approaches consider heavily the role of the parents (particularly the mother) in the sound psychological development of the child. Locke (1991) pointed out that traditional counseling theory, as in the case with first force theories, overemphasizes the development of individuals without considering their larger social context. In a collectivist culture, clients develop an understanding of themselves in relationship to their social community and how that fits within a larger society. Psychoanalytic and ego psychology approaches rely heavily on an understanding of parent-child relationships and intrapsychic conflicts. Inherent in first force theories is the goal of developing an autonomous and well-integrated individual identity. This goal conflicts with collectivist cultures that emphasize the importance of familial and communal relationships; thus, a well-integrated individual identity may not be the primary goal of the client (Helms & Cook, 1999).

Other considerations of first force theories and their multicultural applications include their emphasis on defense mechanisms (compensatory reactions), developmental sequences, parental influence, and the counselor's stance. Without considering the cultural-historical context of the client (McFadden, 1999), a counselor using first force approaches may erroneously attribute a client's defense mechanism to an internal unresolved fixation rather than historic and oppressive experiences. First force developmental sequences are contradicted by evidence that many cultures do not follow the same developmental stages and time frames as the dominant White culture in America (Triandis, 1994). Family structure and childrearing, which is a critical aspect of psychoanalysis, does not occur with similar dynamics across cultures (Lau, 1984). The counselor's stance in the psychoanalytic approach is to remain noninvasive in the client's process. Clients from collectivist cultures may find that this a violation of cultural norms of cooperation, hierarchy in relationships, and the culture's belief that the healer should take on an active role (Helms & Cook, 1999).

Second Force—Cognitive Behavioral Approaches

The second force theories rely on addressing a range of client behaviors and cognitions that are creating problems for the client. These theories emerged in the 1950s and were an attempt to remedy some of the focus on pathology in the past from the first force theories. These theories generally focus on the here and now versus highlighting a client's historical development. With these theories, clients are involved in the assessment process and collaboration occurs within the confines of the therapeutic relationship. The counselor will often use psychoeducation as part of a process that involves the client in his or her own assessment and treatment. Homework assignments are also created to help generate client involvement in the treatment. Included under second force theories are cognitive and cognitive-behavioral theorists such as Aaron Beck, Donald Meichenbaum, and Albert Ellis, with more traditional behavior theorists such as John Dollard and Neal Miller, Joseph Wolpe, and Albert Bandura, and theorists such as William Glasser who adopt pragmatic behavioral interventions based on client goals.

Second force theories can fail to address multicultural contexts by the lack of a holistic appreciation of the client, by counselors' failings to recognize the client's personal history, and by the language-bound nature of cognitions. Second force theories often initiate an innate dualistic problem, focusing mind against body, in lieu of the holistic nature of mental health seen in many cultures. Similar to what is seen in first force theories, problems in second force theories can be oversimplified into a few areas (e.g., self-defeating cognitions) and the historic-cultural aspects of the client's oppression can be forgotten in context. Counselors who do not take the time to explore the cultural contexts of their client may not be able to accurately understand the client's view of reality. Language barriers influence these interventions when a client's self-perceptions are retained and coded by the client using language that is specific to a particular context. Casas (1988) critiques cognitive-behavioral approaches and their failure to look at race, ethnicity, and culture as a part of their major paradigm.

Because many of the second force theories are counselor driven but create a collaborative relationship where clients are treated as partners toward wellness, second force theories do hold promise for clients coming from more collectivist cultures. The counselor can become an ally for the client in dealing with an oppressive world. Clients who have consistently been challenged by institutional racism can benefit by having a counselor who will encourage them to develop an empowered way of thinking (Helms & Cook, 1999). Counselors become more active participants in the process of the second force theories, which support cultural worldviews that seek active-oriented counselors.

Third Force—Humanistic Approaches

The primary goal of humanistic theories is to create a working environment where the client can achieve self-actualization. Self-actualization is the client's innate capacity to become all that she or he can bring forth (Maslow, 1968). Third force theories emphasize the creation of a therapeutic environment that can hold the client's problems in an accepting manner in order to allow the client to move toward self-actualization. There are no formal assessment practices in third force theories but there is a focus on what the client says while also looking for incongruencies that may signal areas in the client that are yet to be fully developed. The counselor is nondirective and makes an effort to create conditions in therapy displaying genuineness, unconditional positive regard, and exhibiting empathic understanding of the client's world. Once the therapeutic environment is created and held by the counselor, the client is permitted to explore his or her feelings and attitudes with greater depth in a safe environment. In the presence of such a therapeutic environment, the client can experience growth. Carl Rogers was a major theorist associated with third force humanistic approaches, and also associated with the third force theories would be the works of existential theorists such as Victor Frankl and Rollo May, who addressed core issues of existence for clients with aspects of what Rogers would call transcendence.

Concerns regarding the third force humanistic approaches are their reliance on the mutual counselor-client understanding of the spoken word, forgoing of societal barriers (assuming that self-actualization is not externally impeded), and the nondirective nature of the intervention. This overdependence on clearly understanding nuances in language would come into play when dealing with clients whose first language is not the same as that spoken by the counselor (Helms & Cook, 1999). In an attempt to create a sense of hope for the client, third force counselors who ignore the reality of institutional racism may forget to address this barrier when creating a therapeutic holding place for client efforts at self-actualization. The overemphasis on clients doing their own growth, with the assumption that they are only holding themselves back, may inadvertently reinforce messages of oppression that the client is receiving from society. Finally, the nondirective nature of the intervention comes at the loss of opportunities for counselors to act as client advocates and help them navigate an oppressive culture.

Moving Beyond the First Three Theoretical Forces

Pedersen (1990) proposed the fourth force of counseling to be multiculturalism. Bill O'Hanlon (1994) developed a typology in which the second wave would be inclusive of Pederson's second and third forces; O'Hanlon's third wave was inclusive of the social construction approach (see Table 21.1, p. 341). The social constructionist approaches allow solutions to rest in clients and their social networks. These third wave approaches allow for the inclusion of racism and sexism to be understood within the client's contextual space. Key concepts for the social constructionist include collaborative-based counseling with the client being honored as understanding her or his own experiences. The counselor acts as a person with whom the client enters a dialogue to explore idiosyncratic experiences along with resources and with whom the client creates additional meaning. Questions from the counselor are meant to empower clients and allow for their own diverse experiences to be recognized and appreciated. Interpretations of these questions create narratives for clients' lives and these narratives or stories make meaning out of life events. Kenneth Gergen is a major theorist who has influenced the direction of social construction theory.

Gergen and Kaye (1992) noted that "Therapeutic theories (whether behavioral, systemic, psychodynamic, or experiential/humanist) contain explicit assumptions regarding (1) the underlying cause or basis of pathology, (2) the location of this cause within clients or their relationships, (3) the means by which such problems can be diagnosed, and (4) the means by which the pathology may be eliminated" (p. 169). Speaking of modernist approaches to therapy that begin with a priori stories about pathology and therapy, Gergen and Kaye went on to write that "Of all possible modes of acting in the world, one is set on a course emphasizing, for example, ego autonomy, self-actualization, rational appraisal, or emotional expressiveness, depending on the brand of therapy inadvertently selected" (p. 172). These theories can be likened to narratives that help clinicians and researchers to understand certain aspects of life and, as a possible further clarification to our understandings, Berger and Luckmann (1967) have discussed how our views of life can be socially constructed.

Gergen (1999) has also mentioned that well-formed narratives about life contain, in part, a valued ending point and an arranging of the events that are relevant to the ending point. For example, depending on the particular theory of therapy—as suggested previously—the desired ending point might highlight an increased degree of client independence, a heightened level of self-disclosure, or a more rational consideration. The events that lead to the desired ending point might include the assessment of the client's life history, the establishment of a diagnosis and agreement on therapeutic goals, and the establishment of counselor-developed interventions in line with the valued outcome. As an illustration, the interventions might emphasize empathic understanding while highlighting one's emotions and internal locus of evaluation; they might stress examining the consequences of one's beliefs or assumptions with the intent to challenge and reconstruct self-defeating thoughts; or they might highlight a system of reinforcement for sequential approximation to a goal. The problem identified by Gergen and Kaye (1992) is that theories may contain a certain a priori picture, perhaps describing health, pathology, or the process of therapy, and that picture may have become "decontextualized" or "cut away from particular cultural and historical circumstances" (p. 172). More recently, Gergen (2001) added, "what one takes to be real, what one believes to be transparently true about human functioning, is a by-product of communal construction" (p. 806). He went on to write, "At the same time, to propose that human beings live in a socially constructed world does not make it a world of any less significance" (p. 807). White and Epston (1990) have suggested that narratives that are socially constructed can help people "organize and give meaning to their experience" and they can help in "shaping lives and relationships" (p. 12) so these narratives (which include theories of counseling) impact how life is lived. So, for example, narratives can highlight individuation and differentiation, supportive and communal living, rational thought, emotional expression, equity in relationships, respect for hierarchy in relationships, primacy of the nuclear family, or preservation of the extended family. Gergen (2001) also proposed that as one considers traditions of understanding (which, we believe, includes theories of counseling), one needs to ask, "What do they accomplish in cultural life, what institutions do they champion, what do they silence?" (p. 807).

Referring to a postmodern and social construction view, Freedman and Combs (1996) noted, "While no self is 'truer' than any other, it *is* true that particular presentations of self are preferred by particular people within particular cultures. But a 'preferred self' is different from an essential or 'true' self" (p. 35). Similarly, Gergen (1994) pointed out that the way "we account for the world" is "not dictated by the stipulated objects of such accounts" but our "understanding of the world and ourselves are social artifacts, products of historically and culturally situated interchanges among people" that are "sustained across time" by "social processes" (pp. 49, 51). These perspectives, on how we account for ourselves and our understandings of the world and human behavior, would seem to have meaning for theories of counseling. That is, they would suggest that theories are grounded in local conversations that reflect the contexts within which people live; for example, a certain time in history, a particular region in the country or the world, or a particular grouping within a defined region. The understanding of counseling theory, therefore, needs to have a local or cultural appreciation rather than simply a monolithic and universal perspective.

With regard to research and theories of counseling, Gergen (1999) suggested that "Data can never prove a theory true or false; whatever counts as data, and how it is credited, requires an interpretive forestructure" (p. 93). The act of interpreting life as well as the interpretations of data from previous research forms the foundation for the questions that are subsequently studied. Jerome Bruner's (1987) comment on our perceptual process, and its alignment with what we expect, appears to have meaning for interpretive efforts:

> Leo Postman and I conducted an amusing demonstration experiment many years ago, involving the recognition of tachistoscopically presented playing cards—giving the subject only milliseconds of exposure to our displays and increasing exposure successively. The displays consisted of both normal playing cards and ones in which color and suit were reversed—a red six of clubs, for example. The reversed cards, as one would expect, took much longer to recognize. However, more interestingly, our subjects went to extraordinary lengths to "regularize" the reversed cards to make them conform to their canonical pattern. (p. 47)

Bruner then went on to mention that "In fact, what human perceivers do is to take whatever scraps they can extract from the stimulus input, and if these conform to expectancy, to read the rest from the model in their head" (p. 47). Gergen (1999) also noted "there is no privileged relationship between world and word. For any situation multiple descriptions are usually possible, and in principle there is no upper limit on our forms of description" (p. 34). Comments by Bruner and Gergen appear to be calling into question our ability to find universally validated theories of counseling. Because this would seem to be the case, one might begin to consider the place of the local culture when reflecting on theories of counseling. Of course, local culture certainly refers to issues of race, ethnicity, and gender, and it also considers issues of age and income, educational levels, and geographical locale, all within the context of a particular period in time. Like Gergen (2001, p. 811), counselors may find themselves wondering how to "more directly enrich forms of practice that might better serve society," and Roberto Cortez Gonzalez, Joan L. Biever, and Glen T. Gardner (1994) have offered the social constructionist perspective as a vehicle for helping understand multicultural counseling.

Blending Social Constructionist and Multicultural Counseling

In looking at a social constructionist's perspective for understanding multicultural counseling, Gonzalez et al. (1994) pointed out that the social constructionist's ideas have not been incorporated into a multicultural perspective. Suggestions for converging social constructionist's precepts into the multicultural counseling process include the following, as mentioned by Gonzalez et al. (1994):

1. The social constructionist approach sees the counselor as maintaining a learning position with regard to the client. With each person in a culture having a unique perspective (emic), social constructionism interprets the counselor's role as needing to explore how the client sees oneself as unique in attitudes, beliefs, and resources.
2. The counselor is open to all ideas that the client brings in about oneself. This approach allows for diverse clients to feel respected in their presentation of self to the counselor.
3. The counselor maintains a role of interest in the client's narrative or story. Careful, patient listening and maintaining inquisitive questions from a curious stance derails any prior assumptions that the counselor has about the client.
4. The focus is on a collaborative relationship between counselor and client instead of a relationship that has the counselor in a dominant and authority position.
5. Social constructionists keep the focus of the session on what the client presents and do not try to interpret below the surface of the presenting problem. This therapeutic position—that the client's presenting problem "is" the problem—respects the diverse views that clients bring to therapy without trying to add the counselor's personal constructs to them.
6. In the social constructionist's approach, the counselor's understandings of the client's story are considered to be tentative, not "factual" interpretations of the client's worldview. These understandings add to the client's ability to create a new, alternative narrative for the future.
7. Because narratives from underrepresented cultures can be impacted greatly by the dominant culture's interpretations, the counselor attempts to remain open to the client's story. Clients need to feel that they have an open space to describe their reality in their terms, not to be revised by the dominant culture.

8. The social constructionist attempts to look for client opportunities instead of framing barriers to progress. This does not mean to minimize the oppressive experiences of clients but to characterize clients in terms of what works for them.

Gonzalez et al. (1994) pointed out that there are challenges to incorporating these two converging paradigms (i.e., the multicultural and social constructionist paradigms). For example, this framework requires that counselors see reality as somewhat fluid and as somewhat different for each client. The personal, individualized approach of the social constructionist blends well with the emic perspective of multicultural counseling. The emic perspective recognizes that the historic experience of a client may be applicable to only one culture at best and, most likely, is applicable to the individual client at hand. Social constructionists recognize that reducing the individual to a generic theoretical orientation and to a uniform set of techniques imposes an external worldview on a client who may have already experienced cultural oppression. This imposition of external constructs could create a client-counselor system that mimics what the client has been experiencing throughout life. In that way counseling remains a threatening and challenging environment instead of a place where clients can feel free to emerge.

Conclusion

Counseling theories have developed in association with the course of events within the dominant culture and have been impacted by the personal nature of the major theorists. Looking at the types of counseling theories, one can identify four major forces in counseling (Pedersen, 1990). The fourth force is considered to be multiculturalism. There is simultaneously a growing acceptance of social constructionist's theory, which has many principles similar to the precepts of multiculturalism. Principle convergence of both social constructionism and multiculturalism create opportunities for diverse clients. Challenges to adopting the two converging paradigms include issues of assessment, viewing problems as fluid, and adopting a therapeutic stance that makes room for a collaborative client relationship.

DISCUSSION QUESTIONS

1. Name and describe the elements of the first three forces in counseling. What elements enhance multicultural counseling and what elements detract from effective multicultural counseling?

2. Consider the three forces and identify the progression of (a) how the client is viewed by the counselor, and (b) how the counselor views emotional disturbance.

3. Describe some of the major concepts associated with social constructionist approaches.

4. Given what is described in the chapter, what might be the next steps in advancing counseling theories toward a better convergence with the multicultural perspective?

5. Consider a particular diverse population. Describe a scenario that uses social constructionist approaches with that particular client.

REFERENCES

Alexander, F., & French, T. M. (1946). *Psychoanalytic therapy.* New York: Roland Press.

Berger, P., & Luckmann, T. (1967). *The social construction of reality: A treatise in the sociology of knowledge.* New York: Anchor.

Bruner, J. (1987). *Actual minds, possible worlds.* Cambridge, MA: Harvard University Press.

Casas, J. M. (1988). Cognitive behavioral approaches: A minority perspective. *Counseling Psychologist, 16*(1), 106–110.

Freedman, J., & Combs, G. (1996). *Narrative Therapy: The social construction of preferred realities.* New York: Norton.

Gergen, K. J. (1994). *Realities and relationships: Soundings in social construction.* Cambridge, MA: Harvard University Press.

Gergen, K. J. (1999). *An invitation to social construction.* Thousand Oaks, CA: Sage.

Gergen, K. J. (2001). *Social construction in context.* Thousand Oaks, CA: Sage.

Gergen, K. J., & Kaye, J. (1992). Beyond narrative in the negotiation of therapeutic meaning. In S. McNamee & K. J. Gergen (Eds.), *Therapy as social construction.* Thousand Oaks, CA: Sage.

Gonzalez, R., Biever, J. L., & Gardner, G. T. (1994). The multicultural perspective in therapy: A social constructivist approach. *Psychotherapy, 31,* 515–524.

Helms, J. E., & Cook, D. A. (1999). *Using race and culture in counseling and psychotherapy: Theory and practice.* Boston: Allyn & Bacon.

Ivey, A. E., & Ivey, M. B. (1998). Reframing DSM-IV: Positive strategies from development counseling and therapy. *Journal of Counseling and Development, 76*(3), 334–350.

Klein, M. (1932). *The psycho-analysis of children.* London: Hogarth.

Kohut, H. (1977). *The restoration of the self.* New York: International University Press.

Lau, A. (1984). Transcultural issues in family therapy. *Journal of Family Therapy, 6,* 91–112.

Locke, D. C. (1991, March). The Locke paradigm of cross-cultural counseling. *International Journal for the Advancement of Counseling, 14,* 24.

Mahler, M. S., Pine, F. & Bergman, A. (2000.) *The psychological birth of the human infant: Symbiosis and individuation.* New York: Basic Books.

Maslow, A. H. (1968). *Toward a psychology of being* (2nd ed.). New York: Van Nostrand Reinhold.

McFadden, J. (1996). A transcultural perspective: Reaction to C. H. Patterson's "Multicultural counseling: From diversity to universality." *Journal of Counseling and Development, 74*(1), 232–235.

McFadden, J. (1999). *Transcultural counseling* (2nd ed.). Alexandria, VA: American Counseling Association.

Monte, C. (2002). *Beneath the mask* (6th ed.). New York: Wadsworth Press.

O'Hanlon, B. (1994). The third wave: The promise of narrative. *The Family Therapy Networker.*

Patterson, C. H. (1996). Multicultural counseling: From diversity to universality. *Journal of Counseling and Development, 74*(1), 227–231.

Pedersen, P. (1990). The multicultural perspective as a fourth force in counseling. *Journal of Mental Health Counseling, 12,* 93–95.

Triandis, H. S. (1994). *Culture and social behavior.* New York: McGraw-Hill.

Weinrach, S. G., & Thomas, K. R. (1998). Diversity sensitive counseling today: A Postmodern clash of values. *Journal of Counseling and Development, 76*(2), 115–122.

White, M. & Epston, D. (1990) *Narrative means to therapeutic ends.* New York: W. W. Norton.

22 Applications of Technological Advances for Multicultural Counseling Professionals

MARTY JENCIUS

Technology challenges the modern multicultural counselor in ways never anticipated only twenty years ago. The developing multicultural counselor needs to address how new technology, even though not evenly distributed among cultures, can become a supportive tool for their efforts to become more personally aware of their own cultural heritage, knowledgeable of different cultures, and develop skills associated with becoming an effective multicultural counselor. The convergence of two contemporary disciplines, multiculturalism and technology, evolves from the clearer development of both disciplines during the past twenty years. The Cross-Cultural Counseling Competencies (American Counseling Association [ACA], 2001) are training guidelines from which multicultural counselors can assess their professional development as concerns diversity. Significant to the development of the technologically competent counselor is the creation of Technology Competencies (ACES Technology Interest Network, 1999; Jencius, 2000a) from which counselors can address technology skill development.

The professional literature during the past few years has described technology use in counseling and counselor training (Wilson, Jencius, & Duncan, 1997), including multicultural counselor training (McFadden, 2000; McFadden & Jencius, 2000), web counseling (Bloom, 2000), and marriage and family counseling (Jencius & Sager, 2001). With the expansion of such on-line publishing outlets as the *Journal of Technology in Counseling* (jtc.colstate.edu) that use technology in describing its application to counseling (Jencius & Baltimore, 2000), counselors are beginning to recognize that technology is more than a passing fad. Technology is becoming a major force in how we connect with people and how we do our work as counselors.

Writing about technology for this chapter in a paperbound book adds its own particular challenges to describing the digital medium. The Internet is a rich collection of text, audio, graphics, movies, slide presentations, databases, interactive

Web sites, computer simulations, and live broadcasts. It is difficult to describe a fluid environment such as the Internet using only text on a page. This problem is similar in nature to a social anthropologist trying to describe the richness of a culture in an ethnographic description. The social anthropologist might be able to have sample artifacts from the culture but the only way to describe the artifact is by using words outside of the culture it came from. Lacking the ability to put the actual artifact on the printed page, the social anthropologist must rely on his or her own richness of description in order to convey meaning. The best way for the reader to understand the culture would be to become immersed in it because the description, although rich and thorough, still lacks the full experience of the culture. Similarly, the best way to understand the Internet is to become immersed in it and experience the variety of content and diversity of presentation found there.

Technology Within a Cultural Context

The gap of available technology resources among various cultures is now referred to as the "digital divide." The term, as applied, refers to those differences in communities of people that can effectively use the resources of new technology, for this discussion the Internet, and those that have limited access and resources (The Digital Divide Network, 2001). Data supports the fact that technology is not evenly available or distributed among various classes, cultures, and global regions. The United States has more computers than any other country worldwide. Forty-one percent of the global on-line population is in the United States and Canada; 27 percent in Europe, the Middle East, and Africa (25 percent of European homes are on-line); 20 percent of the on-line population logs on from Asia/Pacific (33 percent of all Asian homes are on-line); and only 4 percent of the world's on-line population is in South America. Even more startling is the cultural gap as it relates to the United States. In fall of 2000, the U.S. Department of Commerce (2000) found that 51 percent of all U.S. homes had a computer and 41.5 percent of all U.S. homes had Internet access. White (46.1 percent) and Asian American and Pacific Islander (56.8 percent) households continued to have Internet access at levels more than double those of African American (23.5 percent) and Hispanic (23.6 percent) households. Looking at earned income and Internet usage, 86.3 percent of households earning $75,000 and above per year had Internet access compared to 12.7 percent of households earning less than $15,000 per year. U.S. rural areas (38.9 percent) though still lagging behind urban areas (42.3 percent), had surpassed inner cities (37.7 percent) in Internet availability and use. Despite being outdated numbers (in relation to the rapid growth of the Internet), this data shows the alarming reality that there are large differences in the ways in which cultures and people from various socioeconomic groups have access to technology.

What does one do with data that indicates that there is a vast difference in how a culture has access to contemporary technology? Finding easier ways to begin to provide access to the technology seems like the simplest solution to this gap. However, simply providing hardware access to the culture does not seem to address more subtle aspects of technology adoption. Ebo (1998) suggests that simply providing the hardware makes the false assumption that evolving from that will be equal access or a cybertopia. Supporters of equal access to technology see the Internet as becoming the great equalizer. Internet communities create the possibility of equal contributions from every member of society. Ebo suggests the other perspective that is referred to as "cyberghetto." In this perspective, the argument is that the Internet is simply another dimension of traditional communal relationships, with all its built-in bias regarding culture, race, class, and gender. Critics claim that the Internet is male centered and as a result gender issues will always be evident by the nature of its male dominated development (Ebo, 1998).

The historic cultural differences in adoption of technology have been a reality long before the invention of the Internet. The Internet, with its open forum of content where anyone with the technology can contribute to the electronic community, offers challenges to worldviews that extend beyond access to equipment. The Internet provides ready access to a great deal of information, some of which may challenge a culture's adopted norms. One has to take into consideration the culture's context and their access to information. The degree to which a culture accepts differences in power (Hofstede, 1983) may be a limiting factor in the equal adoption of the Internet across that culture. The question of access, in this case, may be more about a culture's acceptance of the potential for everyone to have open information from the Internet that could challenge and shape the culture. A culture that is more accepting of power differences among members of the culture may see the Internet as another challenge to power differences within the culture.

Gender differences in the adoption and use of technology is a well-documented phenomena. Research looking at gender differences in computer attitudes and behavior provides a clearer understanding of where the greatest differences exist. Whitely (1997) did a meta-analysis of studies that showed that men and boys exhibited greater sex-role stereotyping of computers. Men and boys also have a higher computer self-efficacy than women and girls. The greatest effect sizes found in computer attitudes occurred in the age group of high school boys. There were negligible differences in gender beliefs and behaviors around computing. Adding the cultural factor to computer attitudes and anxieties, an interesting study by Bronsan and Lee (1998) suggests differences between United Kingdom nationals and Hong Kong nationals. The United Kingdom sample reported more computer experience, less anxiety, and more positive attitudes. There were no gender differences between male and female computer anxiety, but males held better attitudes than the females in the sample from the United Kingdom. For the Hong Kong sample, there were no gender differences in computer attitudes, but males reported greater computer anxiety than females. This is one of the first samples where males have been found to have more computer anxiety than females. An item-by-item analysis identifies Hong Kong males as being more anxious when *anticipating* computer use rather than when *actually using* computers. Differences in Eastern and Western European attitudes toward computing were shown in a study by Durndell, Cameron, Knox, Stocks, and Haag (1997). Romanians reported less experience with computers than Scottish students but

Romanians were far more positive about the experiences. This applied to both male and female Romanian students.

Resources

Finding available multicultural resources on the Internet can be challenging for the multicultural counselor. As this author has done, one can go to the Internet and look for available resources on multicultural counseling, return six months later and find that the resources are gone and have been replaced at different locations by new (but not necessarily better) choices. The fluid nature of the information available is a challenge for scholars looking to extend what they can find in journals, books, and at professional conferences. Of greater value to the multicultural counselor is not the location of particular sites (which constantly change) but the knowledge of how to find Internet resources and the ability to discern good information from what may be suspect.

The Internet cultural researcher's first tool remains the Internet search engine. To be effective in finding information, it is suggested that one learns to use a variety of good search engines. Search engines include *standard* search engines, which draw from a variety of sources for their data (personal submission to the engine, automated Internet scans, paid-for submission of data) and *meta* search engines, which are search engines that will draw data taken simultaneously from multiple standard search engines. At first glance, one may think that meta search engines would be the most comprehensive sources of data. Often, the data returned from meta search engines can be overwhelming to wade through and one may find using a series of standard Internet search engines more containable. Examples of standard search engines include Google (www.google.com), AltaVista (www.altavista.com), and Excite (search.excite.com). Examples of meta search engines include Dogpile (www.dogpile.com), MetaCrawler (www.metacrawler.com), and Highway 61 (www.highway61.com). Most search engines conform to Boolean search strategies that involve the use of search modifiers (AND, OR, etc.) included in the search string that focuses the requested information.

Once information is retrieved from the Internet, the multicultural counselor is faced with trying to assess whether the information is valid. Alexander and Tate (1999) suggest when evaluating information Web pages that the Internet researcher use the following areas of criteria: authority, accuracy, objectivity, currency, and coverage. *Authority* refers to the Web site author having professional status in the content area. If there is a sponsoring organization for the Web site, does the organization hold particular notoriety for providing accurate information? Researchers should note if the information is copyrighted and who owns the copyright of the information. *Accuracy* refers to the factual information provided and whether this information can be verified through other sources presented by the Web site author. *Objectivity* relates to the way the information is provided and whether advertising is associated with it. Information provided as a public service without advertising is considered to be of greater objectivity. *Currency* is the quality of the timeliness of the information and whether there is evidence on the Web site that indicates when the information was created, posted to the Web, and updated. Finally, *coverage* addresses issues of extensiveness of the material on the site and whether the material seems complete or is still being modified. Multicultural counselors should consider these five areas as templates for judging the quality of Internet information.

Technology Parallels to Human Interactions

Given that our direct, immediate exposure to various cultures is one way to develop in our multicultural nature (Lee, 1999), how does this experience translate to the Internet environment? A typology suggested by Jencius (2000b) for creating technology-enhanced teaching environments can be adapted for use in developing multicultural technology based interactions (McFadden & Jencius, 2000). The typology asks the counselor to culturally consider two major distinctions related to the immediacy of the interaction, asynchronous and synchronous Internet interactions. Asynchronous interaction involves an interaction that is delayed in nature, where one person communicates through text, audio, or video and the person receiving the communication, at a later time, gets the data to respond to it. Synchronous interaction involves immediate, real-time interaction with another person or persons. Multicultural resources on the Internet can be thought of as falling into these two broad asynchronous and synchronous resources. Although these resources are always subject to change, the following provides the reader with some ideas on how Internet-based asynchronous and synchronous technologies can be used to increase multicultural awareness and understanding.

Asynchronous

Asynchronous technologies primarily involve text-based platforms: e-mail, listserv or discussion groups, and Web sites. There are asynchronous methods applying to audio and video platforms in which the multicultural counselor can download audio samples of a language, watch short films, and even watch live video stream from other countries. Asynchronous opportunities allow for passive exploration of cultures and measured responses to questions about cultures.

Listservs.   The multicultural counselor using asynchronous methods can read posts published to listservs (also, the e-mail archives). Most listservs are open for public access, free of charge, and require multicultural counselors to subscribe from their e-mail addresses. The multicultural counselor will then receive periodic e-mails from the list with other member's posts. The best source for locating listservs is a listserv engine, such as CatList (www.lsoft.com/lists/listref.html), which catalogs all lists that use the listserv software (at the time of this writing more than 57,000 public discussion lists existed in CatList). As an example, a search of public lists using the word "culture" found 237 entries from which to select. Multicultural counselors looking to gather an understanding of a particular culture could search the site for appropriate discussion lists to join. Many lists have searchable archives so the subscribed members can search the history of posts on a particular topic. This is useful as a way to gather information from past discussions regarding a particular culture. Specific to diversity and multicultural counseling is Diversegrad-L, a forum for discussing diversity issues in the counseling profession. In order to subscribe to Diversegrad-L@listserv.american.edu, send the message

SUBSCRIBE DIVERSEGRAD-L <full name>

to Listserv@listserv.AMERICAN.EDU. In addition, professional organizations related to multicultural counseling are developing message boards. The Association for Multicultural Counseling and Development has an on-line message board found at their home site, www.amcd-aca.org. The Southern Regional division of the Association for Counselor Education and Supervision maintains a listserv for its Multicultural Counseling Interest Network called SACESMCIN@listserv.kent.edu. Interested counselors can join the discussion by sending the message

SUBSCRIBE SACESMCIN <full name>

to listserv@listserv.kent.edu. Some lists also have a Web browser-based interface so members can review posts and even contribute to the discussion through a friendlier Web browser interface.

Web Sites.   Web sites are another source of cultural information and are primarily noninteractive in nature. Web sites allow the multicultural counselor to explore a variety of information on various cultures. The skill of exploration starts with the ability to find current, well-researched Web sites on culture. The rules of searching for resources described previously apply. Use multiple standard search engines, as well as meta search engines, and apply the rules of assessment of Internet information of authority, accuracy, objectivity, currency, and coverage. Table 22.1 presents a sampling of active Web sites at the time this book went to press.

The preceding examples of listservs or discussion groups and Web site resources provide asynchronous methods of gathering information from the Internet about other cultures. These interactions are limited in that they do not involve real, immediate interactions with people of other cultures. Multicultural counselors accessing the Internet for asynchronous material can do so without being challenged to change their frame of reference or worldview. It is through the more challenging synchronous interactions that the counselor is being immediately placed in the position of having to exercise his or her multicultural abilities.

Synchronous

Synchronous interactions on the Internet across cultures are not readily available. Considerable preemptory work needs to be done by the multicultural counselor to help establish these kinds of interactions. The following examples are technically possible, but the establishment of such experiences still depends on the efforts of people to extend themselves across cultures. The technology simply becomes the vehicle to do so, with human effort to create these experiences still the initiating force.

TABLE 22.1   Web Sites Related to Culture and Ethnicity

The Association for Multicultural Counseling and Development: http://www.amcd-aca.org

Diversity resources (from Wright State University): http://www.ed.wright.edu/diversity

Diversity information: http://home.earthlink.net/~dboals1/diversit.html

Comprehensive site for eldercare issues: http://www.elderweb.com

Social class in contemporary society: http://www.spc.uchicago.edu/SocialClass/about.html

Women of Color Resource Center: http://www.coloredgirls.org

Bilingual education: http://www.ncela.gwu.edu/links/biesl

African American Resources: http://www.aawc.com/aar.html

Asian Studies Virtual Library: http://coombs.anu.edu.au/WWWVL-AsianStudies.html

The Library of Congress, Hispanic reading room: http://lcweb.loc.gov/rr/hispanic

Native Web: http://www.nativeweb.org

Native culture Web: http://www.nativeculture.com

The Gay, Lesbian, and Straight Education Network (GLSEN): http://www.glsen.org

---

Text.   Text-based live chat rooms are one of the earliest methods of synchronous interaction on the Internet. This allows for real-time meetings of people of different cultures. Because of the nature of the chat technology, the discussion can be disjointed and broken, members choosing not to respond to remarks or delayed responding because of various typing speeds. The platform does not screen members for the on-line group and this can result in members having diverse reasons for being in the chat room. An example of a culture-specific, public chat room is Native American On-line Chat at www.naolchat.net. Another example is the About Network that has available chat rooms on various cultures and cultural topics. The Chinese Culture Chat can be found at chineseculture.about.com/gi/chat/cs.htm.

Audio Chat.   Live chat programs that allow for real-time audio conversations are possible on the Internet. One such program that has been used in group supervision discussions (Page et al., 2001) and as a guest speaker mechanism for instruction (Jencius, Baltimore, Crutchfield, Albrecht, & Jones, 2000) is PalTalk (www.paltalk.com). PalTalk allows for simultaneous audio discussion by multiple logged on members. The potential exists for multicultural counselors to exchange regular interactive communications with diverse cultures at a distance using audio-based technology. At this time there is no service that provides structured opportunities for such exchanges, and counselors seeking this experience need to be creative in making the human connection before they attempt the technology-assisted connection. Some providers, such as PalTalk, have group rooms that one can join for audio discussion, but none are currently organized specifically around cultural exchanges. PalTalk's group function does have unmonitored group rooms available that appear to be dedicated to particular languages, but discussions can be idiosyncratic like text-based discussion groups.

Videoconferencing. Videoconferencing currently faces the same challenges of synchronous interactions that text-based and audio-based chat rooms do. There appears to be no central clearing house for such experiences and the cultural videoconference experience relies heavily on the individual efforts of the counselor. Videoconferencing combines live audio and video in a connection that is real time and can be extended worldwide through the Internet. Desktop (personal computer systems) videoconferencing allows for anyone with an Internet connection to connect worldwide without extensive hardware. As suggested by McFadden and Jencius (2000), videoconferencing is a powerful way to extend diversity into geographical regions where diversity is not available. Rotter, McFadden, Lee, and Jencius (1999) and Woodford, Rokutani, Gressard, and Berg (2001) describe the use of videoconferencing in distance classroom instruction. Videoconferencing was extended to include supervision (Baltimore, Jencius, & Iris, 1999; Crutchfield, 2001) and for multicultural counselor training (Jencius et al., 2000). As we continue to pursue videoconferencing as the closest parallel technology has to direct human interaction, opportunities for incorporating this platform into multicultural training and practice will occur.

Two advanced multicultural counseling classes (one by the chapter author originating at Kent State University and one by the second book editor originating from the University of South Carolina) connected using a Polycom videoconference system to share ideas regarding transculturalism. Later in the conference, they were joined by members from the University of Georgia and a University of Georgia professor on a Fulbright Scholarship currently at the University of Tokyo. The connection spanned four universities on two continents providing synchronous audio and video at all four sites. This process can provide for global research collaboration in the field of counseling.

Technology and Cultural Communication

A question arises as to how well technology can adapt to the transcultural experience. In particular how do communication styles from cultures transform themselves into the technology medium? If the technology availability was unlimited in a culture would their communication patterns adapt to the new medium? These types of questions become critical research questions when addressing the adoption of technology by other cultures.

I had a cross-cultural experience related to teaching a counseling course in the Bahamas and using Internet chat rooms for virtual office hours. My coinstructor and I would meet with students one evening a week in the chat room to discuss class projects and answer questions on the course content. Internet chat rooms can provide their own communication chaos but we were aware of some students sitting next to each other in the college computer labs having conversation and at the same time posing questions to us simultaneously. They did not seem to self monitor their postings to the group even though they were sitting next to classmates in the lab raising similar questions. For my coinstructor and I both monitoring the room together it was hard to follow the communication patterns.

This kind of communication pattern did not make sense to me until a few weeks later when I was teaching the class in the Bahamas. After class the students encouraged me to join them for dinner at a "truly Bahamian restaurant" far from the tourist choices. While at dinner with six of the students, I witnessed six different conversations simultaneously occurring across the table. At one point one of the students stopped a conversation to turn to me and say, "Dr. Jencius, I am sorry, are you able to follow this? We all talk at the same time." The chat room experience, with the instructors' perception of chaos, was simply a different cultural communication pattern that the class was comfortable with.

Entering the Multicultural Technology Paradigm

So how does the emerging multicultural counselor engage the Internet if it is a fluid ever-changing entity? First, accept one's limitations in trying to keep current with all that the Internet can provide in terms of information and contact with other cultures. By the time you finish reading the chapter, the Internet has changed. From January 1998 to January 2001, the Internet grew from 29 million named host sites to 109 million named host sites. Those numbers only represent the equivalent of named domains, each of which could have the potential of limitless amounts of information at each host site. With the continual expansion of the Internet and all the information available, the best method for training multicultural counselors is not to train them about specific sites but to teach them how to effectively use Internet search engines to seek information. The multicultural counselor also has to move away from a reductionism approach to the Internet and instead accept a more constructivist view that there is always something out there that they will not know about the Internet.

Second, consider learning how to access and find resources as your greatest Internet skill. This chapter introduced you to some basic suggestions in using search engines to look for information on multicultural counseling on the Internet. The more one learns about using Internet search engines and selecting good material from the search results, the greater the benefits reaped from the Internet.

Third, learn from those around you who are a step ahead of you. Learn the Internet developmentally (Jencius, 2000b) following the way in which Internet tools were introduced historically. That way you will learn a process of knowing the Internet similar to its own natural growth and progression. This translates roughly to learning technology in this order: e-mail, listserv or discussion groups, search engines, graphics, presentation software, Web site design, text chat, audio chat, and videoconferencing.

Fourth, follow one type of technology (e-mail, Web sites, text chat, audio chat, videoconferencing). Instead of trying to learn across all technology types, adopt one technology method at a time until your repertoire extends across all types (Jencius, 2000b). The multicultural educators would do best to pick up one technology piece and apply it to coursework each time they teach the multicultural counseling course. Multicultural counselors can expand their awareness and skills with other cultures by focusing their learning on one type of Internet technology at a time.

Technology in Multicultural Training

There has been considerable writing about technology entering the realm of multicultural education. Roblyer, Dozier-Henry, and Burnette (1996) discuss ways in which technology and multicultural education coexist. They see current practices of technology in multicultural education involving telecommunications with people of differing cultures, using technology to address English as a second language learning, and use of multimedia devices to enhance visual learning and to increase exposure to diversity. Roblyer et al. describe the educational limits of technology and culture as the built-in cultural bias in technology as a platform, problems of equal access and equity, and biases in selection and application of technology. A goal that is considered legitimate by Roblyer is creating interest in communicating with people who are different. The second-level change goal of appreciating people of different beliefs and value systems through the use of technology has yet to be adequately demonstrated.

Recently there has been increasing scholarship around technology in multicultural counseling training. Early work in this area by D'Andrea (1995) introduced ways in which the school counselor can create a multicultural learning environment in the school with technology. D'Andrea suggests (similar to Roblyer, Dozier-Henry, & Burnette, 1996) that telecommunications systems can promote the connection of schoolchildren to cultures other than their own. D'Andrea suggests using computers to explore a culture's art, music, and dialect. Moving from applied technology approaches to more pedagogical issues, McFadden and Jencius (2000) suggest ways in which technology can be included in multicultural counseling training class by using the stylistic model by McFadden (1999). Using CD-ROM technology Thompson, Keller, and Maiorella (2001) have created a CD-ROM that contains various student-developed scenarios used in training counselors about race, culture, and oppression. Jencius (2001) has created a CD-ROM supplement for a multicultural counseling course. The CD-ROM contains all of the content and lecture material usually provided in the class and typically delivered live by the instructor. The students use the CD-ROM to time shift the content portion of the class outside of the regular class meeting times. Class time focuses on reviewing concepts from the CD-ROM and practicing multicultural counseling skills. Anecdotal reports from students indicate that once they overcome anxiety about the technology, they appreciate the ability to review lecture content and time shift their work. They also recognize that considerably greater effort has to be put into the class because of the increased training hours now available through the use of the CD-ROM.

Future Trends

The future of technology for the multicultural counseling professionals will likely occur on multiple fronts. First, advances in access and equity will continue to be addressed. The optimistic ideal would be to eliminate barriers to technology that prevent equal access. As a function of equity, the profession will also need to look at how technology addresses the difference in genders, cultures, and learning styles inherit in technology. Some advancement is being made in making sure that special needs populations have the fullest available use of technology by building "accessibility features" into software. Microsoft has established a growing effort to address accessibility needs for special populations (www.microsoft.com/enable). Efforts should also be directed toward addressing salient gender and cultural differences in technology. Second, the use of technology in a variety of platforms (Web sites, CD-ROMs, live video streaming) to assist counselors to become familiar with different cultures will continue to increase in the coming years. There is little in the form of technology product on the market to meet the growing rate of interest in multiculturalism. Third, research on the pedagogy of instruction related to the training of multiculturally competent counselors will expand. As a profession, we will want to know valid and effective ways to use the technology tools based on outcome research. Finally and foremost, core questions about how human beings communicate using technology need to be addressed. The cultural lens needs to be included in looking at using technology for human interactions.

Conclusion

The twenty-first century holds the convergence of two major paradigms, technology and multiculturalism. The counseling profession has begun to make advances in both paradigms: the Cross-Cultural Counseling Competencies (ACA, 2001) and technology competencies for counselors (ACES TIN, 1999; Jencius, 2000a). Issues of equal access to technology across cultures are evident with professional books and government publications addressing the differences (Ebo, 1998; The Digital Divide Network, 2001). Counselors need assistance in finding multicultural resources using available search engines and judging the credibility of such information using authority, accuracy, objectivity, currency, and coverage. There are technology platforms that can create asynchronous and synchronous learning environments. Those tools include listservs, Web sites, text chat, audio chat, and live videoconferencing. Technology adoption in the training of the multicultural counselor is in its youth but future trends include equal access to technology, using a variety of computer platforms, addressing the pedagogy of teaching culture through technology, and understanding the cultural lens that is placed on computer mediated communications.

DISCUSSION QUESTIONS

1. What are ways in which "the digital divide" can be spanned? What are the barriers to success in complete equity in access?

2. How can you develop creative efforts to use technology in the multicultural classroom?

3. What are a few of the major research questions associated with the convergence of technology and culture?

4. Create a research project that explores the use of technology in multicultural exchange, teaching, or practice. What resources would you need to be able to do this project?

5. Review the Cross-Cultural Competencies (ACA, 2001) and discuss experiences using technology that these competencies could address. Do not limit yourself to what you know about technology but extend the possibilities.

6. Describe criteria that you would use to determine accurate information versus suspect information about cultures found on the Internet.

REFERENCES

ACES Technology Interest Network. (1999). Technical Competencies for counselor education students: Recommended guidelines for program development. Retrieved November 1, 2001, from http://filebox.vt.edu/users/thohen/competencies.htm

Alexander, J., & Tate, M. A. (1999). *Web wisdom: How to evaluate and create information quality on the Web.* Mahwah, NJ: Erlbaum.

American Counseling Association (ACA). (2001). Cross-Cultural Counseling Competencies and Objectives. Retrieved on November 1, 2001 from http://www.counseling.org/multi_diversity

Baltimore, M., Jencius, M., & Iris, K. (1999). Supervision and technology: Efficacy and uses for Internet video conferencing. Paper presented at the American Counseling Association 1999 World Conference, San Diego, CA.

Bloom, J. K. (2000). Technology and web counseling. In H. Hackney (Ed.), *Practice issues of the beginning counselor.* Boston: Allyn & Bacon.

Brosnan, M., & Lee, W. (1998). A cross-cultural comparison of gender differences in computer attitudes and anxieties: The United Kingdom and Hong Kong. *Computers in Human Behavior, 14*(4), 559–577.

Crutchfield, L. (2001). *Long Distance Video Supervision: A Case Study.* Presentation at the Southern Association of Counselor Education and Supervision, October 26, 2001, Athens, GA.

D'Andrea, M. (1995). Using computer technology to promote multicultural awareness among elementary school-age students. *Elementary School Guidance and Counseling, 30*(1), 45–54.

Durndell, A., Cameron, C., Knox, A., Stocks, R., & Haag, Z. (1997). Gender and computing: West and East Europe. *Computers in Human Behavior, 13*(2), 269–280.

Ebo, B. (1998). *Cyberghetto or cybertopia? Race, class and gender on the Internet.* Westport, CT: Praeger.

Hofstede, G. (1983). National cultures revisited. *Behavior Science Research, 18*(4), 285–305.

Jencius, M. (2000a). The Technology Competencies Matrix. In J. Bloom & G. Waltz (Eds.), *Cybercounseling and cyberlearning: Strategies and resources for the millennium.* Alexandria, VA: American Counseling Association.

Jencius, M. (2000b). Technology-enhanced instruction: Developing your digital vision. ERIC/ACA Cybercounseling and Cyberlearning online document. Retrieved November 1, 2001 from http://cybercounsel.uncg.edu/learn.htm

Jencius, M. (2001). Facilitating students' skill development in multicultural counseling. Presentation at the Southern Association of Counselor Education and Supervision, October 26, 2001, Athens, GA.

Jencius, M., & Baltimore, M. L. (2000). Professional publication in cyberspace: Guidelines and resources for counselors entering a new paradigm. In J. Bloom & G. Waltz (Eds.), *Cybercounseling and cyberlearning: Strategies and resources for the millennium.* Alexandria, VA: American Counseling Association.

Jencius, M., Baltimore, M., Crutchfield, L., Albrecht, A., & Jones, D. (2000). *Distance supervision and distance learning in counselor education.* Paper presented at the preconference learning institute at the Southern Association of Counselor Education and Supervision Annual Conference, October 26, 2000, Greensboro, NC.

Jencius, M. & Sager, D. L. (2001). The practice of marriage and family counseling in cyberspace. *The Family Journal, 9*(3), 295–301.

Lee, W. L. (1999). *An introduction to multicultural counseling.* Philadelphia: Accelerated Development.

McFadden, J. (1999). *Transcultural counseling* (2nd ed.). Alexandria, VA: American Counseling Association.

McFadden, J. (2000). Computer-mediate technology and transcultural counselor education. *The Journal of Technology in Counseling.* Retrieved November 1, 2001 from http://jtc.colstate.edu/vol1_2/transcult.html

McFadden, J., & Jencius, M. (2000). Using cyberspace to enhance counselor's cultural transcendence. In J. Bloom & G. Waltz (Eds.), *Cybercounseling and cyberlearning: Strategies and resources for the millennium.* Alexandria, VA: American Counseling Association.

Page, B., Jencius, M., Rehfuss, M., Dean, E., Foss, L., Olson, S., Petruzzi, M., & Sager, D. (2001). Computer based audio discussion groups: How can they be set up and how can they benefit students. Presentation at North Central Association for Counselor Education and Supervision. Chicago, IL, October 13, 2001.

Roblyer, M. D., Dozier-Henry, O., & Burnette, A. P. (1996). Technology and multicultural education: The "uneasy alliance." *Educational Technology, 13*(3), 5–12.

Rotter, J., McFadden, J., Lee, R., & Jencius, M. (1999). *The infusion of technology in counselor education programs.* American Counseling Association 1999 World Conference.

The Digital Divide Network. (2001). Retrieved November 1, 2001 from http://www.digitaldividenetwork.org/content/sections/index.cfm

Thompson, D., Keller, H., & Maiorella, R. (2001). Enhancing multicultural training through technology. Presentation at the American Counseling Association Annual Conference. March 18, 2001, San Antonio, TX.

U.S. Department of Commerce. (2000). Falling through the net. Retrieved November 1, 2001 from http://www.ntia.doc.gov/ntiahome/fttn00/contents00.htm

Whitley, B. E. (1997). Gender differences in computer-related attitudes and behavior: A meta-analysis. *Computers in Human Behavior, 13*(1), 1–22.

Wilson, R. F., Jencius, M., & Duncan, D. (1997). Introduction to the Internet: Opportunities and dilemmas. *Counseling and Human Development Monograph, 29*(6), 1–16.

Woodford, M. S., Rokutani, L., Gressard, C., & Berg, L. B. (2001). Sharing the course: An experience with collaborative distance learning in counseling education. *The Journal of Technology in Counseling.* Retrieved November 1, 2001 from http://jtc.colstate.edu/vol2_1/Sharing.htm

23 Ethical Issues and Multicultural Competence in Counseling

BARBARA HERLIHY AND ZARUS E. WATSON

Although issues of cultural diversity were virtually ignored by the counseling profession during its early years of development, multicultural counseling has moved from the periphery of our attention to a position of prominence. In parallel fashion, the profession has paid increasing attention to ethics and has recognized that multicultural counseling competence is essential to ethical practice. Even with these trends, the profession has struggled to create codes of ethical behavior that can encompass the increasingly diverse nature of its clientele. The literature continues to reveal disappointing therapeutic outcomes, the probable result of counselor–client cultural incongruence. Client perceptions of counselor shortcomings include a lack of sensitivity to issues of sociorace, class, and gender. These major dimensions of diversity-based incongruence apparently have led to premature termination of services because of perceived counselor incompetence. Unfortunately, many practitioners fail to realize the destructive effects of their well-meaning but value-laden interpretations of client behavior and cognitions (Ridley, Mendoza, Kanitz, Angermeier, & Zenk, 1994; Helms & Cook, 1999).

Such disturbing trends should not be surprising because social and behavioral theorists have stressed that a person's perception of self, others, and the environment is experientially shaped (Sue, 1977; Cross, 1990). These theorists maintain that each person's perceptions are shaped not only by their own experiences during their lifetime but also by the current and past experiences of their self-identified sociogroup. In addition, they contend that most conditioned thoughts are unconscious in operation and, therefore, are enacted assumptively.

These social forces act transgenerationally and regularly with effectiveness on the population at large, and counselors, as members of the population, are not exempt from their effects. The counseling profession is unavoidably situated within U.S. history that is built on and steeped in oppression through racial and gender superiority, class separation, and intolerance of differences. Attention to such macrosystemic conditioning must underlie any attempts to improve the multicultural sensitivity of ethical standards and practices of counselors.

The American Counseling Association's (ACA) first version of its code of ethics, published in 1961, paid scant attention to multicultural concerns. By contrast, the current code (1995) shows unprecedented concern for cultural diversity and calls for input into future revisions to continue to address that concern. Although these are encouraging developments, sustained progress is essential if the ideal of ethical multicultural practice is to be met. Among the ethical issues that continue to present problems in this regard are developing and maintaining multicultural counseling competence, defining the boundaries of the counseling relationship, and using diversity-sensitive procedures in assessment and diagnosis. Most importantly, counselors need to apply culturally aware ethical reasoning and decision-making skills to the ethical dilemmas they encounter in their day-to-day practice.

Competence

It is unethical for counselors to provide services to culturally diverse clients when the counselors are not competent in working with such clients. The development and maintenance of multicultural counseling competence may be the most pressing ethical issue the profession faces in today's increasingly pluralistic society. Concern about mental health professionals' lack of preparedness to effectively counsel culturally diverse clients is not a new phenomenon. Early impetus came from the American Psychological Association's (APA) Vail Conference in 1973, when its Follow-Up Commission published a declaration that forged the link between competence to serve culturally diverse clients and ethical practice (Korman, 1974). The APA's continued attention to this issue has resulted in the publication of several guidelines, such as the competencies for culturally competent counseling promulgated by the Education and Training Committee of Division 17, Counseling Psychology (1980), and the *Guidelines for Providers of Psychological Services to Ethnic, Linguistic and Culturally Diverse Populations* (APA, 1993).

The ACA and its divisions have also been responsive to the mandate that counseling services must be responsive to the needs of a diverse client population. In the 1970s, the standards for the preparation of counselors developed by the Association for Counselor Education and Supervision (ACES, 1977) contained specific recommendations for counselors practicing in a multicultural society. A joint effort by ACES and the Association for Multicultural Counseling and Development (AMCD) produced the *Multicultural Counseling Competencies and Standards* (Arredondo et al., 1996) that define the components of competency. More recently, the Association for Specialists in Group Work (ASGW) published a set of *Principles for Diversity-Competent Group Workers* (ASGW, 1998).

As multicultural counseling competencies have been defined and refined, writers have continued to point out the inextricable link between these competencies and ethical practice (Paradis, 1981; Pedersen & Marsalla, 1982; Casas, Ponterotto, & Gutierrez, 1986; Pedersen & Ivey, 1987; Lee & Kurilla, 1997; Remley & Herlihy, 2001; Welfel, 2002). Professional codes of ethics have underscored practitioners' ethical responsibility to be multiculturally competent. The ACA code of ethics (1995) states in its preamble that association members recognize diversity in our society and embrace a cross-cultural approach in support of the worth, dignity, potential, and uniqueness of each individual. This statement represents a step in rectifying inadequacies of previous codes (Sue, 1995); however, its emphasis on individuality reflects an assumptive stance that reveals the continued and powerful influence of traditional values. By endorsing the goal of directing counseling competencies toward the development of the individual, the statement ignores values such as family, community, and group identity that are given equal or greater importance in some minority cultures.

Dimensions of Competence

Developing multicultural counseling competence is an ongoing and complex task. Sue and Sue (1990) identified three primary areas of multicultural competence: awareness, understanding, and skills. Other writers have included the dimensions of nonbiased beliefs and attitudes, knowledge of diverse cultures, sensitivity, respect and tolerance for differences, appreciation of the ongoing problems of oppression and discrimination, expertise in using assessment tools appropriately, and psychological maturity (Arredondo et al., 1996; Lonner & Ibrahim, 1996; Ivey, D'Andrea, Ivey, & Simek-Morgan, 2002).

However one labels the competencies, the first step is to gain awareness of one's own biases, values, and assumptions about human behavior. The ethical responsibility to gain self-awareness is emphasized in the ACA code of ethics, which states that counselors are aware of their own values, attitudes, beliefs, and behaviors and how these apply in a diverse society, and avoid imposing their values on clients (Standard A.5.b.). An integral part of this process is for counselors to learn how their cultural/ethnic/racial identity impacts their values and beliefs about the counseling process (Standard A.2.b.). Counselors, regardless of their cultural background or racial or ethnic identity, must examine how their personal histories both inform and bias their work (LaFromboise, Foster, & James, 1996). Developing an awareness of issues around countertransference and identification is essential. Ethical counselors work from a foundation of self-awareness and continual scrutiny of their inherent worldviews and personal biases (Burn, 1992).

The second area of multicultural competence identified by Sue and Sue (1990) is to gain knowledge and understanding of the worldviews of culturally diverse clients. This competency is reflected in the standard that requires counselors to actively attempt to understand the diverse cultural backgrounds of the clients with whom they work (ACA Code of Ethics, Standard A.2.b.). The third step is to translate the acquired self-awareness and knowledge into skills for multicultural practice. Counselors have an ethical obligation to demonstrate a commitment to gain knowledge, personal awareness, sensitivity, and skills pertinent to working with a diverse client population (Standard C.2.a.). The initial responsibility for helping practitioners acquire multicultural awareness and knowledge, and begin to practice their skills under supervision, lies with our counselor training programs.

Training Issues

Earlier debates regarding the most effective way to help prospective counselors gain multicultural awareness and knowledge centered around separate-course or area-of-concentration approaches versus infusion models of counselor training. Over time, it has become clear that relegating the development of multicultural counseling competence to a single, discrete course is inadequate. The infusion model has been identified as the preferred model (D'Andrea, Daniels, & Heck, 1992), and counselor education programs generally share a commitment to integrating multicultural training into the entire curriculum. The training standards of the Council for Accreditation of Counseling and Related Educational Programs (CACREP, 1994) require the infusion of multicultural training into the core curriculum, and practicum and internship experiences.

Counselor training programs need to be composed of socioculturally diverse faculty who are representative of the composition of society as a whole, the program's student body, and the clientele who eventually will be served by those students. CACREP standards (1994) require that counselor education programs have diverse faculty representation, and the ACA Code of Ethics (1995) exhorts counselor educators to be responsive to the needs of their institutions and programs in the recruitment and retention of faculty with diverse backgrounds (Standard F.2.i.). Nonetheless, the counselor education professoriate counts very few minority faculty members among its ranks: racial or ethnic minorities comprise only about 15 percent of counselor educators nationwide (Glosoff, Herlihy, & Watson, 2000). The underrepresentation of minority faculty in counselor preparation programs remains an intransigent problem.

If students are to become multiculturally competent counselors, they must be trained by multiculturally competent counselor educators. Although counselor education programs are attempting to infuse diversity issues throughout the curriculum, the infusion model is difficult to implement because it requires the active involvement of all individuals who deliver the programs (Holcomb-McCoy & Myers, 1999). Although some nonminority faculty possess the requisite multicultural sensitivity and knowledge to effectively train multiculturally competent counselors (LaFromboise, Foster, & James, 1996), the question remains as to whether all faculty who teach across the curriculum possess the competencies to accomplish this infusion. The continuing commitment of counselor educators to increase both their own multicultural competence and their representation of diverse faculty is vital if the profession is to realize its training goal of producing culturally responsive and skilled counselors.

Maintaining Competence

The development of multicultural counseling competence is an unending endeavor. Practitioners are obligated to take steps to maintain competence in the skills they use and keep current with the diverse and/or special populations with whom they work (ACA Code of Ethics, Standard C.2.f.).

Counselors have an ethical responsibility to practice only within the boundaries of their competence (ACA Code of Ethics, Standard C.2.a.). One difficulty for practitioners, in attempting to apply this standard, is determining just where their boundaries of competence lie. Competence in counseling is hard to define. Counseling is an exceptionally broad profession and counselors could never be competent to offer therapeutic services in all areas of practice, to every client who seeks their services (Remley & Herlihy, 2001). It would be impossible for a counselor to be fully knowledgeable about the cultural values, beliefs, and behaviors of every potential client in our richly diverse society. However, counselors have a dual obligation—to remain within the boundaries of competence in providing services, yet strive to be available to and effective with a wide variety of clients in need. This can place conscientious practitioners in a quandary. If they routinely refer clients who are culturally different from themselves, they avoid causing any harm that might result from their lack of preparedness but they stagnate as professionals. Counselors have a responsibility to stretch their boundaries of competence by gaining knowledge and skills for working with diverse client populations (ACA Code of Ethics, Standard C.2.g.), but must be careful to protect clients while they are doing so.

Clients themselves are the most expert source of knowledge about their own cultural beliefs, values, and customs, and they are often willing to teach their counselors. Counselors can increase their repertoires of culturally appropriate helping skills by reading on the topic, attending continuing education workshops, and seeking specialized training. Most importantly, counselors should work under supervision when they are gaining experience with client populations that are new for them.

When clients seek counseling, they invest a great deal of trust in their counselors to be capable of assisting them in resolving their problems. They make themselves vulnerable and rely on having a safe environment in which to confront their fears and concerns. They have the fundamental right to expect that their counselors will be competent.

Boundary Issues

Defining the boundaries of the counseling relationship has been a controversial issue among mental health professionals. Widely varying opinions exist around questions of dual or multiple relationships, in large measure because of differences between Eurocentric and other cultural views of the counseling relationship and therapeutic process. Professional codes of ethics exhort counselors to make every effort to avoid dual relationships with clients (APA, 1992; ACA, 1995). The underlying rationale, that such relationships could impair professional objectivity or judgment and thus increase the risk of harm to clients, is grounded in a traditional, Western worldview. Sue (1997) has pointed out that some cultural groups value multiple relationships with helping professionals. Parham (1997), noting that the concern over dual relationships is not widely shared in the African American community, has challenged the need for objectivity rather than emotion and for dichotomous relationships rather than multiple roles.

The counselor role and the therapeutic process, as they typically have been defined, may be inconsistent with the needs and values of minority clients. The conventional role of psychotherapist often has been misapplied in working with ethnic and racial minority clients (Atkinson, Thompson, & Grant, 1993). Alternative counselor roles that have been suggested as more appropriate include advocate or social change agent, consultant, and liaison with indigenous support systems.

The traditional one-on-one, in-the-office approach may have limited value with clients whose problems originate in societal discrimination and oppression. Counselors operating as advocates, social change agents, and consultants can help minority clients learn skills they can use to interact successfully with various forces within their community. The client and counselor, working together collegially, can address unhealthy forces within the system and design prevention programs to reduce the negative impact of discrimination and oppression (Herlihy & Corey, 1997). Many minority clients are reluctant to seek help in the form of counseling and often are more willing to turn to social support systems within their own community. Counselors, acting as facilitators of indigenous support systems, can encourage clients to make full use of community resources, such as extended families, neighborhood social networks, churches, community centers, and advocacy groups. Counselors can then structure their activities to complement or augment these resources (Herlihy & Corey, 1997).

A nondirective facilitation style is typically taught in counselor training programs, yet a more directive counseling process may be required to address environmental problems that are contributing to clients' concerns. This process includes assisting clients to recognize oppressive forces in the community as a source of their problems and teaching them strategies for dealing with these environmental barriers. For example, recent immigrants may need advice on coping with problems that they are facing in the job market or that their children are encountering at school. Clients who confront discrimination and poverty in their daily lives may need to receive assistance in dealing with the complexities of their legal and financial rights.

A number of writers have argued that some dual relationships are unavoidable (Hedges, 1993; Herlihy & Corey, 1997; Sue, 1997). Counselors who work in rural communities are likely to be acquainted in some capacity with most if not all of their clients. A counselor's cultural or racial/ethnic identity, sexual orientation, membership in a religious community, or substance dependence recovery status can create small worlds even in urban areas. Clients often seek out counselors who hold values similar to their own, counselors they may have met at social, political, or faith-based events. This increases the potential for dual relationships to occur (Herlihy, 2001). Some specific counselor practices that have been addressed in the literature on dual relationships include counseling friends or acquaintances, self-disclosure, accepting gifts from clients, and bartering for goods or services. Codes of ethics caution against counseling friends or close acquaintances. However, for counselors of color, this prohibition may be difficult to honor. For example, the only Latino, Spanish-speaking counselor at a university counseling center may know the Latino students very well. In fact, these students may come to the center specifically because of that connection. The restriction against treating family members may be extremely problematic for a Native American counselor whose reservation community is made up of extended family members. In certain Asian cultures, self-disclosing to a stranger is considered a violation of familial and cultural values. Therefore, these cultures may encourage dual relationships in which the helper is also a relative or close personal friend.

Gift giving is a common practice in many Asian communities as a means to show respect, gratitude, and the sealing of a friendship. Refusing a gift is considered an insult (Sue, 1997). Counselors may have a general policy against accepting gifts from clients, but they should be willing to make exceptions based on an awareness of the cultural meaning of gifts for the client (Herlihy, 2001).

Codes of ethics discourage bartering but do not prohibit the practice. For ACA members, bartering with a client for counseling services may be acceptable if clients request it and if it is a commonly accepted practice among professionals in the community (Standard A.10.c.). This flexibility in the code allows counselors to practice with multicultural sensitivity. They can respond to the needs of clients who live in rural communities where bartering is not unusual, or clients who lack financial resources whose pride does not allow them to accept free services.

The ethical guidelines that caution against dual relationships should not be applied rigidly to working with culturally diverse clients. Although avoiding harm to clients must remain a paramount goal, different worldviews, multicultural definitions of counseling roles and the therapeutic relationship, and cultural perceptions of helping practices must all be taken into consideration (Sue, 1997). A thoughtful interpretation of these guidelines is essential to multiculturally sensitive practice.

Assessment and Diagnosis

Assessment

In the area of client/issue assessment and testing, uncertainty regarding the nature and impact of sociorace and culture on the reliability and validity of the largely pretherapeutic process is profound. A central issue is the use of traditional assessment and testing models that have been developed, designed, constructed, and validated on mostly homogeneric populations by theorists and practitioners who are themselves lacking in both diversity and multicultural training (Helms, 1993; Helms & Cook, 1999).

Most norming populations employed in the development of traditional approaches to assessment and testing within counseling tend to have been of European extraction and middle class. Again, this directly reflects the homogeneity of both assessment developers and practitioners. Yet, the populations affected by testing and assessment practices are increasingly heterogeneric, especially along the lines of sociorace and culture, class, and gender. The counseling field has begun to address these issues of assessment/testing and population incongruence.

Assessment models and tests have been developed that can psychosocially address transgenerational sociogroup collective identity issues and that lend themselves to both between- and within-group perceptual differences (Helms, 1992; Ridley et al., 1994).

Theorists and practitioners who would engage in a pluralistic or inclusive multicultural approach to client assessment and sociobehavioral testing would expand their knowledge base and thereby increase appropriateness of service type and delivery to the client population. Such an approach would reverse course on what has been a dual trend of multiculturalism as a noneffect and the limited adherence to selective cultural diversity as culture relegated to certain population groups (Helms, 1994; Ridley et al., 1994).

The literature is replete with examples of the misuse of assessment with ethnic and racial minorities, women, clients with limited English proficiency, the physically challenged, and other special client populations. Ethical practice requires that counselors understand how clients' cultures and worldviews can affect their performance on traditional achievement, aptitude, and ability tests (Whiston, 2000). Counselors need to be able to evaluate assessment instruments to identify any bias against client groups and when such biases are found, to choose other methods of assessment. The ACA Code of Ethics (1995) underscores this responsibility by cautioning counselors to avoid culturally inappropriate practices in test selection, use, and interpretation. Counselors recognize the effects of age, color, culture, disability, ethnic group, gender, race, religion, sexual orientation, and socioeconomic status on test administration and interpretation (Standard E.8).

Competence in using assessment with clients from diverse cultures requires that counselors understand differences in worldviews and influences of language and culture on test performance. Test results must always be placed in perspective with other factors in evaluating clients. A helpful guide to responsible and competent assessment with multicultural populations is the *Handbook of Multicultural Assessment* (Suzuki, Meller, & Ponterotto, 1996).

Diagnosis

One form of assessment that poses particular problems for multicultural counseling practice, given current trends, is the diagnosis of mental disorders. Counselors, as a professional group, are struggling to establish themselves as legitimate providers of mental health services in our society (Remley & Herlihy, 2001). Although many counselors are ambivalent about diagnosing mental disorders (Hohenshil, 1996), this push for parity as providers encourages their use of the prevailing system, the *Diagnostic and Statistical Manual of Mental Disorders* (DSM). From a macrosystemic perspective, use of the DSM with diverse clients presents at least three ethical problems. First, because the DSM is based on the medical model of mental illness that defines the problem as residing within the individual, it tends to overlook contextual factors. Second, the system pathologizes the problems of minority and women clients. Third, the DSM system perpetuates a paternalistic approach to mental health care that reinforces the societal oppression of these clients.

The DSM, by defining mental disorders in intrapsychic terms, fails to consider the impact of social-political-cultural factors in clients' lives. This individualistic stance is not appropriate to working with clients whose cultures give primacy to the well-being of the family, tribe, group, or community. The majority of cultures and societies in the world have a more collectivist notion of identity and do not define the psychosocial unit as the individual (Sue & Sue, 1990). Thus, counselors who view culturally diverse clients through an individualistic diagnostic lens do these clients a serious disservice.

The DSM diagnostic system pathologizes any difference from the standards of mental health established by the dominant group in society. Studies have demonstrated that members of ethnic minorities receive more severe diagnoses than their majority counterparts for the same symptoms. For example, African Americans and Latinos are more likely to be diagnosed as suffering from schizophrenia than are Euro-Americans (Pavkov, Lewis, & Lyons, 1989; Manderscheid & Barrett, 1991). Also, depression is a component that is common to numerous diagnoses of major mental disorders. In a systemic view, ethnic minority clients and women have many more reasons to experience depression. Their subordinate status in society—along with their experiences of poverty, marginalization, oppression, and discrimination—results in a sense of powerlessness that can present as symptoms of depression. Diagnostic categories contribute to bias against other groups who have been stigmatized in our society. For instance, although homosexuality has not been diagnosed as a mental disorder for more than twenty years, 14 percent of counselors surveyed by Gibson and Pope (1993) still believed it was unquestionably ethical to treat homosexuality per se as pathological.

Reliance on the traditional medical model has implications for both the perpetuation of an economic system that oppresses women and minorities and for the counselor-client relationship. As long as social problems such as racism and sexism are medicalized, the solution to these problems remains in the hands of the medical and mental health establishments (Rave & Larsen, 1995). The medical, psychopharmaceutical, and psychotherapy industries profit tremendously from the treatment of mental disorders. Women receive more prescriptions than men in all classes of drugs and particularly psychotropic medications (Cooperstock, 1981). This example illustrates how the prevailing medical system fosters client dependency. The medical model is hierarchical and assumes that the physician or other professional provider is the member of the dyad who can best make treatment decisions; thus, the authority of the provider is an integral part of the healing process. This power relationship mirrors the dominant/subordinate relationships between the powerful establishment and minorities and women that are found in the larger culture because most providers come from the majority culture and most clients are members of minority cultures (Pedersen, 2002).

Counselors who are ethically committed to diversity-sensitive diagnosis will find only limited guidance in the ACA Code of Ethics (1995) to assist them in addressing these problems. Use of the DSM system is well entrenched in other mental health professions such as psychiatry and clinical psychology. The ACA code advises counselors to be respectful of approaches to professional counseling that differ from their own and to take into account the traditions and practice of other professional groups with which they work (Standard C.6.a.). This standard that addresses relationships with other professionals could be interpreted as lending support to the status quo.

At the same time, the ACA Code of Ethics (1995) does acknowledge that mental health and mental illness are defined in a cultural context, stating that counselors recognize that culture affects the manner in which clients' problems are defined. Clients' socioeconomic and cultural experience is considered when diagnosing mental disorders (Standard E.5.b.). This standard sets forth a multiculturally sensitive principle, but counseling practitioners still must grapple with the question of *how* to take cultural factors into account while working within a mental health system that fails to adequately address the needs of minority and women clients.

Applying ethical reasoning skills within a multicultural framework, counselors will need to consider the client's problems within the larger sociocultural context of the client and the meaning of that context for the client, rather than assessing only symptoms and behaviors. Within this broader view, many symptoms can be understood as coping mechanisms and evidence of survival skills in an oppressive culture rather than as evidence of pathology. When symptoms are reframed as coping skills and pathology is renamed as distress, the inapplicability of many DSM diagnostic categories becomes apparent. Multiculturally sensitive counselors, viewing the client as the expert member of the therapeutic dyad who is knowledgeable about his or her own distress and its social meaning (Herlihy & McCollum, 2003), take care to avoid replicating in the counseling relationship the inequities experienced by culturally diverse clients in their larger social worlds.

The goal of counseling from a multicultural orientation is to avoid fostering client dependency and to empower the client to effect change at multiple levels—personal, relational, and sociopolitical. Multicultural/feminist approaches stress that oppressive aspects of the client's reality—such as racism, sexism, homophobia, and age discrimination—need to be addressed directly (Ivey et al., 2002). Counselors, recognizing that they are only one potential source of assistance for the client, help clients access other resources within their communities.

The interface between the values of diversity-sensitive counselors and medical model practitioners will continue to present ethical dilemmas for some time to come. Beyond reconceptualizing client concerns to include cultural variables and utilizing client empowerment strategies, counselors have an ethical responsibility to influence the mental health system when its assumptions and procedures are harmful to minority clients. Concerns voiced by multiculturalists have led to some positive steps: The fourth edition of the DSM offers guidelines for therapists in viewing clients in their cultural context (Dana, 1998), and case analyses of minority clients have been made available through the journal, *Culture, Medicine, and Psychiatry* (Mezzich, Kleinman, Febrega, & Parron, 1996). Nonetheless, work remains to be done. Ethical multicultural practice involves continuing to actively advocate for change in the way mental health services are delivered in our society.

Legal Issues

Counselors need to be knowledgeable about laws that relate to multicultural counseling practice. At the same time, it is important to be aware of differences between laws and ethics. Laws dictate the minimum standards of behavior that society will tolerate, whereas ethics represent the aspirations or ideals of the profession. Laws tend to inform counselors about what they *must* do, whereas ethics are a guide to what they *should* do to practice at the optimal level of client care (Remley & Herlihy, 2001). Although counselors have become increasingly concerned in recent years about legal liability issues, few lawsuits have been filed against counselors. Because legal standards set a minimal or threshold level of behavior whereas ethics cover a wider range of behaviors devoted to client welfare, the best protection from legal entanglements is to practice ethically (Welfel, 2002).

Each of the ethical issues in multicultural counseling discussed in this chapter has some legal implications. At the opposite end of the spectrum from a high level of *competence* is gross incompetence, which could form the basis for a malpractice lawsuit. With respect to *boundary issues,* most legal actions have involved sexual dual relationships with clients. However, lawsuits could be filed based on other types of boundary violations if clients believed they had suffered injury or harm. Court cases such as the seminal *Larry P. v. Riles* (1979) have established that *testing* cannot be misused to discriminate against individuals.

Most legal challenges in the area of multicultural counseling relate to the issue of discrimination. The legal system has recognized the rights of culturally diverse groups through federal statutes such as the Civil Rights Act of 1964 and the Americans with Disabilities Act of 1990. Nondiscrimination is an ethical as well as a legal mandate. The ACA Code of Ethics (1995), for instance, contains several standards (A.2.a., C.5.a., D.1.i.) that prohibit counselors from engaging in or condoning discrimination based on color, culture, race, ethnic group, gender, age, sexual orientation, disability, socioeconomic status, religion, or marital status. Knowledge of ethical standards, self-awareness and willingness to examine one's own cultural biases and assumptions, and a commitment to continuing to develop competency in counseling diverse client populations are the best strategies for avoiding legal problems.

Ethical Reasoning and Decision Making

Multiculturally competent counseling in the complex world of actual practice requires that counselors be skilled at ethical reasoning and decision making. The context in which these skills are developed is often overlooked in the area of professional behavior and ethics. The ethical reasoning of every counselor is embedded within the counselor's worldview, which is shaped by a larger social conditioning mechanism that directly but often unconsciously influences the counselor's identity, cognitions, and behaviors (Helms & Cook, 1999). Holding this perspective, we conclude the chapter with a critical examination of the assumptions that underlie ethical standards and guide ethical decision making and suggest how they might be reinterpreted to foster diversity-sensitive practice.

Certain moral principles, or shared beliefs and agreed-on assumptions that guide the behavior of mental health professionals, are generally presented as the foundation for ethical reasoning. These principles are (1) autonomy (respect client choice, reduce client dependency), (2) nonmaleficence (do no harm), (3) beneficence (do good, or promote mental health), and (4) justice (be fair). Scholars in the field of multicultural counseling have noted that these moral principles are not universally endorsed by all cultures. To form a useful basis for ethical reasoning, they must be thoughtfully interpreted through a multicultural lens.

The principle of autonomy is often misapplied when Euro-American counselors work with clients whose cultural identity differs from their own. For many clients, choices and decisions are made in the context of family, group, or community. Burn (1992) has suggested that the guiding principle for counselors should be *cultural* autonomy. Counselors who adopt this principle will allow the client's cultural self-definition and belief system to direct the course of the therapeutic endeavor. They will be better able to meet their obligation to provide services that facilitate self-determination and the ability to make culturally appropriate life decisions.

All counselors hope to practice nonmaleficence, to do no harm to those they serve. Nonetheless, harm can occur, however unintentionally, when counselors who work with culturally diverse clients are not multiculturally competent. Harm can be inflicted on clients when a counselor's cultural biases go unexplored or are disregarded (Tsiu & Schultz, 1988). Without cross-cultural awareness, sensitivity, knowledge, and skills, counselors are not capable of protecting the welfare of their culturally diverse clients. Thus, developing and continually working to increase one's multicultural counseling competence is essential to upholding the principle of do no harm.

When counselors fail to practice with an appreciation for a client's belief systems and a respect for the client's cultural identity, the principle of beneficence is violated (Cayleff, 1986). Counselors who are sensitive to their dominant power position in the counseling relationship will be able to avoid the assumption that they should decide what is good for the client. When counselors consider their clients as cultural equals, they make ethical decisions *with* the client rather than *for* the client.

In applying the principle of justice with clients whose problems arise from discrimination and oppression, counselors are alert to personal biases and skill deficits that could interfere with the delivery of empowering multicultural interventions. The ethical duty of counselors to promote the welfare and interests of their clients may entail challenging the predominant social institutions in order to further the rights of culturally different individuals and groups.

If these ethical principles are to have any practical value, counseling professionals must be able to apply them in their everyday work with clients. Numerous ethical decision-making models have been offered to assist counselors in translating principles and standards into actual practice. Although a few of these models have addressed counselor self-awareness, the importance of context, and a collaborative client–counselor relationship (e.g., see Meara, Schmidt, & Day, 1996; Tarvydas, 1998; Remley & Herlihy, 2001), very little is actually known about the process of ethical decision making. Research on ethical decision-making is surprisingly scant (Cottone & Claus, 2000). The impact of multicultural competency on ethical reasoning has not been investigated. Acknowledging the centrality of multicultural competence to ethical practice is only a starting point. Much work remains to be done if the counseling profession is to meet the challenge of ethically and effectively serving *all* clients in a culturally diverse society.

Conclusion

Multicultural counseling competence is essential to ethical practice. Disappointing therapeutic outcomes can result when counselors work with culturally diverse clients and are unaware of the effects of the macrosystemic cultural conditioning that shapes their respective worldviews.

It is unethical for counselors to provide services to culturally diverse clients when the counselors are not competent in working with these clients. Although a number of guidelines exist to assist counselors in developing multicultural competence, developing and maintaining such competence is an ongoing and complex task that requires awareness, understanding, and skills. Gaining multicultural counseling competence begins with training in the academic setting and continues throughout a counselor's career.

Issues of dual or multiple relationships in counseling take on new dimensions when viewed through a multicultural lens. The boundaries of the counseling relationship and therapeutic process, as traditionally defined, may need to be redrawn in working with socioculturally diverse client groups. When working with these clients, ethically conscientious counselors will need to thoughtfully interpret the ethical codes' cautions against practices such as counseling friends or acquaintances, accepting gifts, and bartering.

Traditional approaches to assessment may be inappropriate when applied with a diverse clientele. Ethical practice requires that counselors develop new competencies and knowledge in testing. Diagnosis using the prevalent DSM system presents major ethical problems that need to be addressed by the counseling profession.

Multiculturally competent counseling in the complex world of actual practice requires counselors to have sound ethical reasoning and decision-making skills. Ethical standards and decision-making models require thoughtful interpretation and application when working with culturally diverse clients.

DISCUSSION QUESTIONS

1. What ethical issues do you think you might need to consider in working with clients who are culturally different from you?

2. To what extent do you believe that you are competent to counsel culturally diverse clients? What are some ways you can increase your multicultural counseling competence during your graduate training?

3. Do you believe it is ever ethical to counsel a close acquaintance? To accept a gift from a client? To barter with a client for counseling services? What is your rationale for your beliefs about these issues? Is your rationale compatible to working with socioculturally diverse client groups?

4. Why should counselors consider multicultural issues when assessing a client?

5. What factors do you think you need to consider in diagnosing mental disorders with culturally diverse clients?

REFERENCES

American Counseling Association. (1995). *Code of ethics and standards of practice.* Alexandria, VA: Author.

American Psychological Association. (1992). *Ethical principles of psychologists and code of conduct.* Washington, DC: Author.

American Psychological Association. (1993). *Guidelines for providers of psychological services to ethnic, linguistic and culturally diverse populations.* Washington, DC: Author.

American Psychological Association Education and Training Committee of Division 17. (1980, September). *Cross-cultural counseling competencies, a position-paper.* Paper presented at the meeting of the American Psychological Association, Montreal, Canada.

Arredondo, P., Toporek, R., Brown, S. P., Jones, J., Locke, D., Sanchez, J., & Stadler, H. (1996). Operationalization of the multicultural counseling competencies. *Journal of Multicultural Counseling and Development, 24,* 42–78.

Association for Counselor Education and Supervision, Commission on Standards and Accreditation. (1977). Standards for the preparation of counselors and other personnel service specialists.*Personnel and Guidance Journal, 55,* 596–601.

Association for Specialists in Group Work. (1998). *Principles for diversity-competent group workers.* Alexandria, VA: Author.

Atkinson, D. R., Thompson, C. E., & Grant, S. K. (1993). A three-dimensional model for counseling racial-ethnic minorities. *Counseling Psychologist, 21,* 257–277.

Burn, D. (1992). Ethical implications in cross-cultural counseling and training. *Journal of Counseling and Development, 70,* 578–583.

Casas, J. M., Ponterotto, J. G., & Gutierrez, J. M. (1986). An ethical indictment of counseling research and training: The cross-cultural perspective. *Journal of Counseling and Development, 64,* 347–349.

Cayleff, S. E. (1986). Ethical issues in counseling gender, race, and culturally distinct groups. *Journal of Counseling and Development, 64,* 345–347.

Cooperstock, R. (1981). A review of women's psychotropic drug use. In E. Howell & M. Bayes (Eds.), *Women and mental health* (pp. 131–140). New York: Basic Books.

Cottone, R. R., & Claus, R. E. (2000). Ethical decision-making models: A review of the literature. *Journal of Counseling and Development, 78,* 275–283.

Council for Accreditation of Counseling and Related Educational Programs. (1994, January). *CACREP accreditation standards and procedures manual* (2nd ed.). Alexandria, VA: Author.

Cross, W. E., Jr. (1990). *Shades of black.* Philadelphia: Temple University Press.

Dana, R. H. (1998). *Understanding cultural identity in intervention and assessment.* Thousand Oaks, CA: Sage.

D'Andrea, M., Daniels, J., & Heck, R. (1992). Evaluating the impact of multicultural counseling training. *Journal of Counseling and Development, 70,* 143–150.

Gibson, W. T., Pope, K. S. (1993). The ethics of counseling: A national survey of certified counselors. *Journal of Counseling and Development, 71,* 330–336.

Glosoff, H. L., Herlihy, B., & Watson, Z. (2000, March). *Cultural differences among counselor educators: Issues related to rank and tenure.* Paper presented at American Counseling Association Conference, Washington, D.C.

Hedges, L. E. (1993, July/August). In praise of dual relationships. Part II: Essential dual relatedness in developmental psychotherapy. *The California Therapist,* pp. 42–46.

Helms, J. E. (1992). Why is there no study of cultural equivalence in cognitive ability testing? *American Psychologist, 47,* 1083–1091.

Helms, J. E. (1993). I also said, A White racial identity influences White researchers. *Counseling Psychologist, 21,* 240–243.

Helms, J. E. (1994). How multiculturalism obscures racial factors in the therapy process. *Journal of Counseling Psychology, 41,* 378–385.

Helms, J. E., & Cook, D. A. (1999). *Using race and culture in counseling and psychotherapy: Theory and practice.* Boston: Allyn & Bacon.

Herlihy, B. (2001). Managing boundaries. In E. R. Welfel & R. E. Ingersoll (Eds.), *The mental health desk reference* (pp. 465–471). New York: Wiley.

Herlihy, B., & Corey, G. (1997). *Boundary issues in counseling.* Alexandria, VA: American Counseling Association.

Herlihy, B., & McCollum, V. (2003). Feminist theory. In D. Capuzzi & D. R. Gross (Eds.), *Counseling and psychotherapy: Theories and interventions* (3rd ed., pp. 332–350). Upper Saddle River, NJ: Merrill/Prentice Hall.

Hohenshil, T. H. (1996). Editorial: The role of assessment and diagnosis in counseling. *Journal of Counseling and Development, 75,* 469–477.

Holcomb-McCoy, C. C., & Myers, J. E. (1999). Multicultural competence and counselor training: A national survey. *Journal of Counseling and Development, 77,* 294–302.

Ivey, A. E., D'Andrea, M., Ivey, M. B., & Simek-Morgan, L. (2002). *Theories of counseling and psychotherapy: A multicultural perspective* (5th ed.). Boston: Allyn & Bacon.

Korman, M. (1974). National conference on levels and patterns of professional training in psychology: Major themes. *American Psychologist, 13,* 615–624.

LaFromboise, T. D., Foster, S., & James, A. (1996). Ethics in multicultural counseling. In P. B. Pedersen, J. G. Draguns, W. J. Lonner, & J. E. Trimble (Eds.), *Counseling across cultures* (4th ed., pp. 47–72). Thousand Oaks, CA: Sage.

Larry P. v. Riles, (1979). 495 F. Supp. At 971.

Lee, C. C., & Kurilla, V. (1997). Ethics and multiculturalism: The challenge of diversity. In *The Hatherleigh guide to ethics in therapy* (pp. 235–248). New York: Hatherleigh Press.

Lonner, W. J., & Ibrahim, F. A. (1996). Appraisal and assessment in cross-cultural counseling. In P. B. Pedersen, J. G. Draguns, W. J. Lonner, & J. E. Trimble (Eds.), *Counseling across cultures* (4th ed., pp. 293–322). Thousand Oaks, CA: Sage.

Manderscheid, R., & Barrett, S. (Eds.). (1991). *Mental health in the United States, 1987* (National Institute of Mental Health, DHHS Publication No. ADM-87-1518). Washington, DC: U.S. Government Printing Office.

Meara, N. M., Schmidt, L. D., & Day, J. D. (1996). Principles and virtues: A foundation for ethical decisions, policies, and character. *Counseling Psychologist, 24,* 4–77.

Mezzich, J. E., Kleinman, A., Fabrega, H., & Parron, D. L. (1996). *Culture and psychiatric diagnosis: A DSM-IV perspective.* Washington, DC: American Psychiatric Press.

Paradis, F. E. (1981). Themes in the training of culturally effective psychotherapists. *Counselor Education and Supervision, 21,* 136–151.

Parham, T. A. (1997). An African-centered view of dual relationships. In B. Herlihy & G. Corey, (Eds.) *Boundary issues in counseling* (pp. 109–111). Alexandria, VA: American Counseling Association.

Pavkov, T. W., Lewis, D. A., & Lyons, J. S. (1989). Psychiatric diagnosis and racial bias: An empirical investigation. *Professional Psychology: Research and Practice, 20,* 364–368.

Pedersen, P. B. (2002). Ethics, competence, and other professional issues in culture-centered counseling. In P. B. Pedersen, J. G. Draguns, W. J. Lonner, & J. E. Trimble (Eds.), *Counseling across cultures* (5th ed., pp. 3–27). Thousand Oaks, CA: Sage.

Pedersen, P. B., & Ivey, A. (1987). The ethical crisis for cross-cultural counseling and therapy. *Professional Psychology, 13,* 492–500.

Rave, E. J., & Larsen, C. C. (1995). *Ethical decision making in therapy: Feminist perspectives.* New York: Guilford Press.

Remley, T. P., & Herlihy, B. (2001). *Ethical, legal, and professional issues in counseling.* Upper Saddle River, NJ: Merrill/Prentice Hall.

Ridley, C. R., Mendoza, D. W., Kanitz, B. E., Angermeier, L., & Zenk, R. (1994). Cultural sensitivity in multicultural counseling: A perceptual schema model. *Journal of Counseling Psychology, 41,* 125–136.

Sue, D. W. (1977). Barriers to effective cross-cultural counseling. *Journal of Counseling Psychology, 24,* 420–429.

Sue, D. W. (1995). Ethical issues in multicultural counseling. In B. Herlihy & G. Corey, *ACA ethical standards casebook* (5th ed., pp. 193–197). Alexandria, VA: American Counseling Association.

Sue, D. W. (1997). Multicultural perspectives on multiple relationships. In B. Herlihy & G. Corey (Eds.), *Boundary issues in counseling* (pp. 106–109). Alexandria, VA: American Counseling Association.

Sue, D. W., & Sue, D. (1990). *Counseling the culturally different: Theory and practice.* New York: Wiley.

Suzuki, L. A., Meller, P. J., & Ponterotto, J. C. (1996). *Handbook of multicultural assessment.* San Francisco: Jossey-Bass.

Tarvydas, V. M. (1998). Ethical decision making processes. In R. R. Cottone & V. M. Tarvydas (Eds.), *Ethical and professional issues in counseling* (pp. 144–155). Upper Saddle River, NJ: Prentice-Hall.

Tsiu, P., & Schultz, G. L. (1988). Ethnic factors in group process: Cultural dynamics in multiethnic therapy groups. *American Journal of Orthopsychiatry, 58,* 136–142.

Welfel, E. R. (2002). *Ethics in counseling and psychotherapy: Standards, research, and emerging issues* (2nd ed.). Pacific Grove, CA: Brooks/Cole.

Whiston, S. C. (2000). *Principles and applications of assessment in counseling.* Pacific Grove, CA: Brooks/Cole.

24 Conclusions, Trends, Issues, and Recommendations

FREDERICK D. HARPER AND JOHN McFADDEN

This closing chapter (1) summarizes background information on concepts and history, (2) presents conclusions and implications about concepts and historical phenomena, (3) delineates trends as to where the field of culture and counseling appears to be headed, (4) discusses some of the prevailing issues in the field, and (5) provides recommendations for consideration and action.

Background and Conclusions

In the breadth of 23 chapters, *Culture and Counseling: New Approaches* includes discussions on a broad range of topics written by notable counseling authorities. Among the numerous topics of the book are ethnocultural concepts, ethnocultural history, counseling specific non-White and White ethnic groups, multicultural and cross-cultural counseling models, multicultural counselor training and supervision, the international counseling movement, counseling immigrants, spirituality and multicultural counseling, counseling cases, bibliotherapy, preventive counseling, multiracial and biracial clientele, cross-cultural implications of traditional counseling theories, multicultural counseling and ethical/legal concerns, and technology and multicultural counseling.

As an orientation and foundation, the first chapter provides background explanations of concepts and historical developments of the culture and counseling movement or the broader ethnocultural counseling movement. The ethnocultural movement in counseling began with counseling the culturally deprived and disadvantaged during the late 1960s and was transformed into a movement of counseling non-Whites or American minorities in the 1970s. The currently popular cultural movement in counseling did not take root and flourish as a historical movement until the late 1970s and early 1980s, although several authors had used cultural terms in the titles of several counseling publications during the late 1960s and the early 1970s (e.g., Vontress, 1969; Smith, 1973). The beginning of the current culture and counseling movement was characterized by an increase in course offerings (Copeland, 1983; Hollis & Dodson, 1999) and a significant and persistent increase in the publication of textbooks, special issues of journals, and articles with titles that included culturally related terms such as "counseling across cultures" (Pedersen, Lonner, & Draguns, 1976; Pedersen, 1978), "cross-cultural counseling" (Copeland, 1983), and "counseling the culturally different" (Sue, 1981).

The multicultural counseling movement was launched in the mid-1980s. It was influenced by a popular campaign for inclusion of special groups that had been excluded from the culture, racial, and ethnic circles of discussion, for example, groups affiliated with gender issues, sexual identity/orientation, and persons with disabilities. Moreover, the trend toward a focus on multicultural counseling was enhanced by the Association for Non-White Concerns in Personnel and Guidance's decision and action, in 1985, to change its name to the Association for Multicultural Counseling and Development.

In order to put the overall ethnocultural counseling movement in perspective, a summary of the various phases and foci of the movement, including the cultural movement, are provided for the past 40-plus years.

1960s	Counseling the culturally deprived or counseling the disadvantaged
1970s	Counseling non-Whites, ethnic groups, and American minorities
1976 to 1985	Cross-cultural counseling, counseling across cultures, counseling the culturally different, and intercultural counseling
1985 to present	Multicultural counseling and cross-cultural counseling (also, limited use of counseling across cultures, counseling the culturally different, and transcultural counseling)

Within the literature of topics on culture and counseling and counseling ethnic minorities, the concepts of multicultural counseling, cross-cultural counseling, culture, ethnicity, and race are frequently discussed; however, they lack consensus in terms of their definitions. Therefore, there was an effort to clarify some of these concepts in Chapter 1 and in the glossary. As co-editors, we also encouraged contributors to define or clarify terms in discussing concepts of and related to culture within their respective chapters. Among all the culture and counseling terms, the most popular and often used concepts in the field at this time appear to be "cross-cultural counseling" and "multicultural counseling."

As stated previously, we chose the term "culture and counseling" as the title for this book because we believe it serves as an umbrella concept that covers all culture-related counseling terms, for example, cross-cultural counseling, multicultural counseling, counseling the culturally different, transcultural counseling, counseling across cultures, intercultural counseling, cultural-diversity counseling, culture-centered counseling, and culture-specific counseling. The use of so many terms to discuss culture as related to counseling has confused counseling professionals and counseling students and has raised the question as to which terms are interchangeable and which ones are mutually exclusive or overlapping constructs. We have found that there is no consensus in the counseling literature regarding this issue. Nevertheless, there does appear to be interchangeable use of some of these terms (e.g., cross-cultural counseling, intercultural counseling, and counseling across cultures). Moreover, writings seem to suggest multicultural counseling as the most inclusive culture-related counseling concept in terms of diversity of clientele groups (Pedersen, 1991). On the one hand, Pedersen chooses to define multicultural counseling or multiculturalism in the broadest sense of going beyond culture and ethnicity to include various status, identity, and affiliation groups; however, on the other hand, Locke and Faubert (Chapter 20) and Weinrach and Thomas (1998) view multicultural counseling much less broadly as addressing cultural concerns and issues only.

In the current midst of scholarly confusion and lack of consensus in defining cultural terms related to counseling, it is our thinking that a comprehensive term that best encompasses cultural and ethnic concerns in counseling is "ethnocultural counseling," and a concept that is inclusive of multicultural counseling, cross-cultural counseling, and other culturally related counseling terms is "culture and counseling." Nonetheless, we agree with those authors who posit that no culture and counseling term is as comprehensive as "diversity" counseling and that diversity goes beyond multiculturalism to address nonethnic special populations (Weinrach & Thomas, 1998; see also Chapter 20). Therefore, diversity, as compared to ethnoculturalism and multiculturalism, is a broader concept with regard to context and inclusiveness. Diverse groups can not only be found within a culture but also across various cultures. We agree with Weinrach and Thomas's position that diversity counseling can be defined to include cultural groups as well as ethnicity, gender, race, disability, educational level, language, physique, religion, residential location (i.e., urban, suburban, and rural), sexual identity/orientation, socioeconomic status, and state of trauma.

As a related matter, we believe that culture should not be brought into counseling as a concern with a client of a diverse status, identity, affiliation, or gender group unless there are implications for cultural dynamics, context, and/or cultural worldview. Nonetheless, there are numerous instances when culture can interact with noncultural concerns of counseling. One example of how culture can interact with gender role is described in Case 1, in Chapter 16. In this case, culture and gender (role as a mother) were mediating factors in a working Chinese woman's reactions to a traumatic industrial accident. Although the client was diagnosed with posttraumatic syndrome after a near-death accident on the job, she was more concerned initially, from her cultural worldview, that the accident occurred because her ancestors were displeased with her for taking a job and not being at home to care for her children full time. The culture-based thought of the possibility of disfavor by her ancestors created anxiety and shock that rivaled the posttraumatic reaction to her near-death experience.

Current Status and Developing Trends

Over the past decade or more, the field of culture and counseling has witnessed a significant increase in the publication of textbooks and the offerings of counseling courses in multiculturalism and diversity throughout the United States (Ancis, 1998; Hollis & Dodson, 1999). This growing need for information and training in multiculturalism and diversity has been driven apparently by professional requirements for such courses in counseling by accreditation boards (e.g., Council for Accreditation of Counseling and Related Educational Programs [CACREP], 1994), counselor certification boards (e.g., the National Board of Certified Counselors, 1997), and standards for cultural competence as set forth by the Association for Multicultural Counseling and Development (e.g., see Appendix C). There has been diversity and multiculturalism counseling training requirements by various accrediting bodies such as the CACREP (1994) and the American Psychological Association (accreditation of doctoral counseling psychology training). Moreover, ethical statements by the American Counseling Association (1995), the American Psychological Association (1992, 2001), and the National Board of Certified Counselors have spoken to cultural competence as related to various roles and ethical responsibilities of counseling professionals or providers of psychological services. Because of the increasing professional requirements and the trend toward greater diversity of groups and cultures within the United States and the global community, it seems that the need for culturally competent counseling professionals is here to stay. Therefore, a trend toward the publication of textbooks and the offering of courses on culture and counseling will continue and possibly increase in the future. Specific trends that we project as continuing or beginning follow.

The Development of Cultural Assessment Instruments

The proliferation of inventories and instruments for measuring various aspects of multicultural and cross-cultural counseling phenomena and behaviors are likely to increase. An increasing number of cultural assessment instruments have been developed, researched, and written about in the past couple of decades, that is, instruments to measure multicultural counselor competencies, multicultural competence training, acculturation, cross-cultural counseling effectiveness, cultural lifestyle, cultural stress, and cultural adjustment (Ponterotto, Rieger, Barrett, & Sparks, 1994).

Identity Development Theory and Assessment

Since the early 1970s, there has been a rapidly developing trend to construct theories on identity and identity development in a number of areas including African American identity development (Cross, 1971); White and Black racial identity development (Helms, 1990); ethnic identity development; gay, lesbian, and bisexual identity development; cultural identity development; and biracial identity development among others. As with the proliferation of theoretical schemes on identity development and identity, there also has been a proliferation of psychometric instruments for the assessment of these concepts and developmental stages (Ponterotto & Casas, 1991; Lee, 2002). This trend will probably continue in the form of expanded counseling literature in terms of books, book chapters, and articles and with the anticipation of new assessment instruments on various themes of identity and identity development.

Challenge to Multicultural Counseling

There will be both a rising challenge to what some perceive to be an overemphasis on multicultural counseling as well as a challenge to the current multicultural terminology and the proliferation of so many ethnocultural counseling terms. There is a movement afoot to deemphasize cultural-sensitive or diversity-sensitive counseling in practice, research, and theory and to return to a focus on the individuality of the client, the one-to-one counseling relationship, and simply a helping focus that would minimize if not ignore cultural cues, context, and worldviews (ACA, 2000). Moreover, Helms (1994) posits that the sociopolitical issue of race and racism in counseling has been obscured by the overemphasis on multiculturalism, whereas others see the need to focus on other elements or conditions of effective counseling in the one-to-one relationship (ACA, 2000). It seems there is a need to search for balance while maintaining cultural awareness, knowledge, skill, and commitment in the debate on essentials of the effective counseling relationships.

Focus on International Counseling and U.S. Diversity

The increased diversity of the U.S. population and its recent immigrants have forced counseling professionals to look beyond the traditional U.S. ethnicities (African Americans, Asian Americans and Pacific Islanders, Latino/as, and Native Americans) to address the needs and problems of immigrant clients who represent diverse countries, global cultures, and diverse religions. Some of these nontraditional immigrant groups include persons from Africa, India, Eastern Europe, various Middle Eastern countries, Central America, and South America. The movement to gain greater awareness and knowledge about nontraditional U.S. ethnicities will probably be magnified in the future. Furthermore, increasing collaboration between U.S. counseling professionals and counseling professionals from other countries, through international professional associations, will become more prevalent in the future. In addition, the growing development of new counseling associations and services in countries throughout the world will lead to greater involvement and leadership of U.S. counseling professionals in the international counseling movement (see Chapter 10).

Issues and Future Perspectives

Much of the ethnocultural counseling literature, especially textbooks, is generic or abstract. That is, theories, models, literature reviews, and research seem to address mainstream concepts and populations and tend to lack a focus on cultural sub-groups (e.g., gender groups, children, middle class, and homeless) and special problems or concerns of culture and counseling (e.g., health/disease, violence, relationship problems, family issues, cross-cultural employment and career issues, and human injustice). There is a need to focus more on problems and concerns within cultures and between cultures (Ponterotto, Casas, Suzuki, & Alexander, 1995; Harper & Ibrahim, 1999; DeLay, 2000; Mays, 2000; Lee, 2002).

Another issue is whether U.S. multicultural and cross-cultural counseling professionals should continue to isolate and encapsulate themselves and their cross-cultural concerns to the United States, or should U.S. counseling professionals and the U.S. cultural movement in counseling give greater attention to linking issues at home with common issues abroad and vice versa, for example, AIDS, homelessness, violence and terrorism, women and children's issues, justice and opportunity, incarceration and criminal rehabilitation, hunger and starvation, and universal suffering from natural and human-created disasters. As the world shrinks and becomes one global community of interdependent cultures, cross-cultural issues in one part of the world will increasingly affect the lives of our clients here in the United States. Moreover, a number of immigrants to the United States will continue to bring problems and worldviews from their native homelands with them, attempting to find adjustment and balance in a new land and culture while practicing the ways of their native culture here in the United States.

The most detrimental and devastating violent attack ever on U.S. soil—September 11, 2001—demonstrates how a single event in the United States can affect the entire country as well as the global community in terms of psychological state, unemployment, national economies, spiritual reawakening, and cultural transformation. A question is, "What should be the role of the counseling profession in the prevention of violent destructive acts and the remediation of pain and loss caused by violence, disruption, and human displacement?" The following are specific pro and con issues and related examples of counseling dilemmas that we perceive to be worthy of presenting:

Issue 1

- In cases where the client is impacted by racism, oppression, or racial prejudice, the counselor should give more effort to counseling the client to overcome the psychosocial consequences of such injustices.

    versus

- The counselor should serve primarily as a consultant or advocate in situations of oppression or prejudice to address changing a racist or oppressive system and its prejudicial implementers.

Example of a Counseling Dilemma. A "credible" African American college student, who is on the dean's list, reports that a White English instructor refused to read and evaluate her essay paper because the instructor stated to the student that she did not believe that an African American undergraduate student could write that well. The counselor evaluates with the client the possible solutions for resolution of the problem, including weighing whether to address the college system and consult with the instructor or whether to assist the student in working this out with the instructor if possible.

Issue 2

- The DSM-IV (American Psychiatric Association, 1994) is oriented to Western disorders and symptoms and has limited value for non-Western client problems.

    versus

- The DSM-IV has made adjustments to accommodate cultural symptoms and, even more, psychological disorders are universal reactions, although their symptoms may be identified and manifested in different ways.

Example of a Counseling Dilemma. A high school student from Africa has come to the United States with his father, on the father's divorce from his mother and assumption of a job in the United States at his country's embassy. The student is referred to counseling by one of his teachers who overheard him confide to a peer that he had, more than once, received spiritual messages from his deceased maternal grandmother that he must return to his homeland of West Africa or face doom in the near future. The question is whether this is a serious psychiatric concern, a genuinely perceived cultural experience based on acceptable spiritual phenomena of his culture, or whether the phenomenon represents a problem caused by anxiety, loneliness, and cross-cultural adjustment.

Issue 3

- Most APA and ACA's ethical criteria or standards are not relevant to non-Western cultures because of their different cultural expectations, religious beliefs, customs, and lifestyle practices.

    versus

- Most ethical standards can be interpreted within the context of non-Western cultures and thus have universal value for what is professionally appropriate and ethically acceptable.

Example of a Counseling Dilemma. Is it acceptable for a client to live in the home of an indigenous healer for several weeks during treatment? Is this practice comparable to a client in the United States who is in inpatient care at a treatment center under the supervision of a therapist or therapists? Is it the context of treatment or is it the relationship of trust between the healer and the client that constitutes ethical behavior? Moreover, how would one address the fact that the poverty of some villages in poor and developing countries does not allow for the construction and privilege of an inpatient facility for healing or counseling?

Issue 4

- As a goal of counseling, should non-Western immigrants be encouraged to make visible adjustments (acculturate or assimilate to some degree) to U.S. culture and, thus, compromise some values and ways of their culture of origin?

    versus

- Should immigrants be counseled to maintain essential remnants and practices of their culture of origin regardless of the discomfort to native-born U.S. citizens or the risk of not getting a job because of a "failure to fit in," for example, with regard to their national dress and cultural practices?

Example of a Counseling Dilemma. A first-year college student from India who is a believer of Sikhism comes to counseling in ambivalence. He is debating whether to cut off his beard, shed his turban, and stop wearing his cultural or national dress because of stares and social harassment by people in a small-town community as well as some students at his college. Residents and college students have called him names such as "Muslim terrorist," "cult follower," and "psychic con man." He is very depressed and discouraged because people in what he thought was a country of freedom do not understand or accept his culture or religion.

Underemphasized and Overlooked Factors Regarding Culture

Culture and counseling literature often discusses multicultural and cross-cultural counseling as if there are no within-cultural differences for clients who present themselves to counseling. There has been a tendency to look at the client as one stereotypical cultural or ethnic image while overlooking gender, age, social class, and geographic origin. Even more, there has been a tendency to overlook or underemphasize certain problems and issues that exist within cultures or across cultures such as health, unemployment, homelessness, spousal abuse, alcoholism and drug addiction, violence, and family conflict, among others.

The lack of emphasis and outright omissions in discussing subgroups and specific problems within and between cultures are much more prevalent in multicultural and cross-cultural textbooks vis-à-vis multicultural and cross-cultural counseling journals, such as the *Journal of Multicultural Counseling and Development* and the *International Journal for the Advancement of Counselling*. These two journals and others often address a number of culture and counseling issues with regard to gender, age group, ethnicity, nationality, religion, health, counseling problem, counseling setting, and counseling modality. (See Chapters 1 and 10.)

Becoming a Culture-Sensitive and Culture-Competent Counselor

Culture-sensitive counseling is defined here as being sensitive to cultural ways and preferences of diverse clientele, but, at the same time, not being overly sensitive to the point of stereotyping or prejudicially making inaccurate assumptions about the client. The following are dicta, adages, or do's and don'ts for counseling across cultures and within cultures.

- Do not make prejudicial judgments about a client because of the client's image or identity. For example, do not stereotype all Arab-speaking persons as being Islamic, or all persons of Latina/o heritage as being able to speak Spanish, or all Chinese as being born in China or preferring a certain type of Chinese food.
- Learn about the client's ethnicity and culture not only through printed literature, film media, and travel but also through the eyes or worldview of the client.
- Be aware of cross-cultural similarities, cross-cultural differences, and within-cultural differences. In regard to cultural similarities, be aware of universal themes of human nature that transcend culture or permeate all cultures, for example, love, family, human sexuality, anxiety, anger, shame, guilt, jealousy, loneliness, psychological resistance, and the drive to satisfy basic human needs.
- Allow your focus to be on helping the client based on the presenting problem and needs of the client as well as the client's perceptions of possible solutions. Do not intellectualize a simple problem or try to overly empathize or identify with the culture or identity of the client. Do accept the client unconditionally as a human being while avoiding premature judgments about the client based on culture, identity, status, image, or affiliation.
- Use skills and approaches that are appropriate both for the cultural background of the client and the client's problem or concern. Do not allow your own worldview or cultural beliefs to make you adverse to the client's viewpoints of a counseling solution.
- As appropriate, be aware of and address within-cultural factors such as ethnicity, gender issues, sexual identity/orientation, age, religion, family issues, lifestyle, relationships, and social class.
- As a multicultural or diversity-sensitive counselor, learn about traditional and nontraditional ethnic and religious groups, for example, Arabic-speaking persons, Middle Eastern persons (including non-Arabs such as Iranians), persons who practice Islam, Asian Indians, and persons from various African countries. Although seeking knowledge and awareness of various diverse groups and cultures of the country and world, try first to learn more about the cultural and ethnic groups with whom you work and the cultural background or heritage of a particular client with whom you work.
- Do travel cross-culturally or attend international or continental conferences or any professional meeting that include persons from a number of diverse

countries and cultures. Moreover, travel to different areas of the United States to learn about within-cultural differences based on diverse geographic regions, ethnic groups, and religions of the United States.

- Seek feedback from persons of other cultures or ethnic groups regarding your own prejudices or cultural insensitivity. This type of personal growth in cultural awareness and sensitivity can occur by becoming a member or coleader in a counseling group of diverse membership; enrolling in multicultural, ethnic, or diversity courses; supervising, consulting, or serving as an administrator in a counseling-related setting with culturally diverse constituencies; hosting a student or students from other countries; and, in general, learning from personal and professional relationships with persons of various cultures and ethnicities.

Recommendations

As persons with college degrees, counselor educators and other counseling professionals tend to think convergently versus divergently. Kuhn (1970) posits that new ideas, paradigms, and concepts are difficult for people to adopt, but once adopted they are difficult to change. Along this line, it has been forty years since Wrenn (1962) wrote about the encapsulated counselor, an article that basically warned counselors about the importance of change and adapting to changing times. Although Wrenn's article is cited frequently in the multicultural literature, it did not provide any insight or lay a foundation for the field of multicultural counseling or ethnocultural counseling as we know it today. The main value of Wrenn's article was to warn the White counseling profession, in the main, about the need to prepare for and adjust to cultural changes of the time. Wrenn stated, "the counselor is drawing upon his [or her] yesterday to help the student with his [or her] today and tomorrow" (p. 448). In addition, it is interesting to note that Wrenn "suggested" the need for traditional U.S. counselors to change because of advents in technology, world politics (e.g., communism), and new occupations of the early 1960s; however, he had practically no discussion about the impact of controversial, sociopolitical, national issues of the time such as African American racial protests for civil rights and the impact of the Vietnam War, both of which became catalysts to change our country, culture, and the counseling scene forever.

The point of this backdrop to recommendations is that counseling professionals must stop to think about culture and counseling in a divergent, creative, practical, real-life, real-time, and futuristic way. To a great degree, this means addressing the controversial issues that face the United States and the world today, for example, terrorism, racism, religious conflicts, racial and ethnic violence, school violence, violence and abuse within families, human sexuality, physical and psychological abandonment of children, parental murder of children, human injustice, AIDS and other diseases, the human impact of globalization and natural disasters, and alcohol and other drug addiction (Shelby & Tredinnick, 1995; Harper & Ibrahim, 1999; Delay, 2000). These are all real problems and conditions of the human race that cut across and impact cultures and ethnic groups; nevertheless, the inclination of human nature is to ignore or repress uncomfortable issues until a crisis forces reactions and subsequent action. It is worthy to note that Wrenn warned counseling professionals of impending cultural change, but it is also evident how the counseling profession avoided addressing the uncomfortable issues undergirding the social and cultural changes of the time, that is, changes from racial segregation to racial desegregation, civil protest to civil rights laws, and war abroad to violence at home on the university campuses and in the streets. It is also interesting that the American Counseling Association had a Human Rights Committee in the late 1960s, but, at the same time, it was not willing to deal voluntarily with the real issues of racial insensitivity to its own membership, that is, until forced to do so by a Black Caucus of the 1969 APGA convention that pushed for an Office of Non-White Concerns and eventually an APGA Division, the Association for Non-White Concerns in Personnel and Guidance (McFadden & Lipscomb, 1985).

Nowadays, the counseling profession is being affected more than ever by interrelated global events and traumatic disasters and by rapid changes within cultures, across cultures, within ethnic groups, and within families. These events and changes have implications for counseling practice, counselor preparation, supervision of counselors, counselor consultation, counseling research, and the administration of counseling services and training programs. In regard to these professional counseling roles and contexts, the following are recommendations from an ethnocultural and culture and counseling perspective. Keep in mind that there are recommendations within individual chapters, and some of the ones following may even overlap with suggestions that are made by chapter authors. Nonetheless, we have chosen the following recommendations based on what we perceive to be their importance for the counseling profession of today and tomorrow.

Preventive Counseling

Counselors in schools need to counsel children and youth on the acceptance or tolerance of diverse cultural, ethnic, identity, and status groups. There should be counseling to facilitate student knowledge, awareness, and understanding about group differences for the purpose of preventing hatred and avoiding intergroup harassment and violence (Harper & Ibrahim, 1999). Multicultural counseling prevention should be carried out at all levels of school (preschool through 12), but should especially start with preschools and elementary schools. Moreover, college and university orientation courses and groups should focus on ethnic, cultural, and group diversity and the need for college students to understand and appreciate cultural and group differences.

Counselor Preparation

Because of the rapidly increasing number of Spanish-speaking Latino/a immigrants, residents, and citizens in the United States and the projected population growth of Latinos/Hispanics for the next several years, training programs in counselor education and counseling psychology need to consider requiring courses and experiences that will lead to minimal language proficiency in Spanish. Alternative languages may be considered as a requirement based on the clientele group with whom student counselors plan to work.

Regarding religion and spirituality, counselor training programs need to provide accurate and balanced knowledge and awareness about the major religions of the world in order to help counselors in training to understand clients who may come to counseling with different religious and spiritual worldviews. The present trends suggest that the United States will continue to become a country of diverse religions and spiritual beliefs. Moreover, counselor preparation programs should train students to deal with personal issues of universal spirituality such as meaning in life, peace, unselfish giving, love, forgiveness, and how to deal with human suffering and loss.

Counseling professionals and counselors in training should be required to gain cross-cultural experiences such as (1) working with ethnocultural groups that are different from their own, (2) attending multicultural conferences within the United States or attending international counseling conferences—preferably in other countries, (3) spending a summer in a non–English-speaking country to get exposure to a different language and culture, (4) attending a house of worship that is different from one's own faith or religious heritage, and (5) volunteering to help or counsel clients of special populations (e.g., homeless, HIV/AIDS patients, LGBT, low-income urban or Appalachian youth, and immigrants). Cross-cultural exposure and experiences involve risk, but the reward of cognitively restructuring one's worldview is worth the challenge of the initial dissonance and discomfort.

The goals of multicultural counseling training should be the acquisition of multicultural counseling knowledge, awareness, skills, and commitment to helping. Lastly, counselor preparation programs must be sensitive to the goals of acquiring and maintaining ethnic and gender diversity in their program faculty and student enrollment.

Consultation in Counseling

The culturally competent counselor should consult with appropriate persons toward eliminating discrimination and unfairness based on race, ethnicity, cultural background, nationality, gender, status of ability or disability, religion, LBGT identity, and other distinguishing features of identity, affiliation, status, or heritage. As mental health and professional consultants, counseling professionals must be cognizant of their responsibility and role in bringing about human equity and justice. Mays (2000) states that "No one should have their future, their health, or their well-being compromised for reasons of class, gender, national origin, physical and psychological abilities, religion, sexual orientation, or as a result of unfair distribution of resources" (p. 326).

Counseling Research

A question that can be raised is whether multicultural and cross-cultural counseling textbooks are sufficiently reporting meaningful empirical research and translating the implications of research for practice in the scientist-practitioner mode. Another question is whether enough meaningful and creative research is being carried out on important questions and populations of the cross-cultural and within-cultural spheres. Ponterotto and associates have been among the leaders who have consistently examined the nature of ethnocultural and multicultural research and publications as well as provided guidelines for cross-cultural research (Ponterotto, 1986; Ponterotto & Casas, 1991; Ponterotto et al., 1994; Ponterotto, Casas, Suzuki, & Alexander, 2001).

Advances have been made in the development of self-report instruments for the purposes of multicultural assessment and measures of various themes of identity development. Nevertheless, multicultural and cross-cultural counseling studies would benefit from a number other data-collecting techniques in addition to these self-report measures, which often have their limitations in terms of validity, reliability, available norm groups, and types of data that can be generated (e.g., thoughts, attitudes, perceptions, and opinions versus actual overt behavioral responses within a defined cultural context).

In order to study the dynamics of culture-related behaviors, worldviews, and interactions within defined cultural contexts, there is a need for more studies that employ direct observation (versus self-report) of multicultural events or actual cross-cultural counseling (group counseling and individual counseling). Culturally competent judges or observers can be used to code behavioral events in naturally occurring counseling contexts or noncounseling cultural contexts. One-way mirror or videotape recorded situations can be used in order to make the data collection unobtrusive for the participants who are being observed. Direct observation studies versus self-report studies are highly beneficial in generating data for analysis that will help counseling professionals to better understand the content and process of what happens between individuals of two or more different cultures.

Cross-cultural and multicultural counseling research needs to give more attention to a number of different counseling concerns, problems, and settings in areas of career counseling, group work, gender issues, help-seeking orientations, health and culture, addictive behaviors, culture and family functioning/therapy, nontraditional healing, and the impact of prejudice and injustice on client behaviors and the counseling relationship. Regarding research methods and statistical procedures, counseling researchers need to consider a variety of often-overlooked methods and procedures for carrying out creative research studies that will yield meaningful outcomes for professional practice. Some of these overlooked research and statistical methods include (1) nonparametric statistics for small samples; (2) multiple regression for predicting culture-related phenomena; (3) discriminant analysis for identifying variables that distinguish specific cultural groups; (4) factor analysis for developing cultural assessment instruments and for defining cultural and psychosocial dimensions; (5) nontraditional cross-cultural variables in qualitative and quantitative analyses; (6) historical studies in assessing the development and usefulness of traditional and indigenous helping methods in various countries and cultures; and (7) excellent case studies that will yield in-depth knowledge on diverse groups, multicultural situations or contexts, ethnic communities, and student cultures in educational settings.

REFERENCES

American Counseling Association. (1995, June). American Counseling Association code of ethics and standards of practice. *Counseling Today, 37,* 33–40.

American Counseling Association. (2000). "Alternative views to multicultural counseling" (Program Chair, Morris Jackson, A Multicultural Counseling Summit). Annual conference of the American Counseling Association, Washington, DC.

American Psychiatric Association. (1994). *Diagnostic and statistical manual of mental disorders (DSM-IV)* (4th ed.). Washington, DC: Author.

American Psychological Association. (1992). Ethical principles of psychologists and code of conduct. *American Psychologist, 47,* 1597–1611.

American Psychological Association. (2001). Ethical principles of psychologists and code of conduct [Draft Six of Revised Copy]. Retrieved March 24, 2002 from http://anastasi.apa.org/draftethicscode/draftcode.cfm#toc

Ancis, J. R. (1998). Cultural competency training at a distance: Challenges and strategies. *Journal of Counseling and Development, 76,* 134–143.

Copeland, E. J. (1983). Cross-cultural counseling and psychotherapy: A historical perspective, implications for research and training. *The Personnel and Guidance Journal, 62,* 10–15.

Council for Accreditation of Counseling and Related Educational Programs. (1994). *CACREP accreditation standards and procedures manual* (2nd ed.). Alexandria, VA: Author.

Cross, W. E., Jr. (1971). The Negro-to-Black conversion experience: Toward a psychology of Black liberation. *Black World, 20,* 13–27.

DeLay, T. (2000). Fighting for children. *American Psychologist, 55,* 1054–1055.

Harper, F. D., & Ibrahim, F. (1999). Violence and schools in the USA: Implications for counseling. *International Journal for the Advancement of Counselling, 21,* 349–366.

Helms, J. E. (Ed.). (1990). *Black and White racial identity: Theory, research and practice.* Westport, CT: Greenwood Press.

Helms, J. E. (1994). How multiculturalism obscures racial factors in the therapy process. *Journal of Counseling Psychology, 41,* 162–165.

Hollis, J. W., & Dodson, T. A. (1999). *Counselor Preparation 1999–2001* (10th ed.). Muncie, IN: Accelerated Development.

Kuhn, T. S. (1970). *The structure of scientific revolutions* (2nd ed.). Chicago: The University of Chicago Press.

Lee, C. C. (Ed.). (2002). *Multicultural issues in counseling: New approaches to diversity* (3rd ed.). Alexandria, VA: American Counseling Association.

Mays, V. M. (2000). A social justice agenda. *American Psychologist, 55,* 326–327.

McFadden, J., & Lipscomb, W. D. (1985). History of the Association for Non-White Concerns in Personnel and Guidance. *Journal of Counseling and Development, 63,* 444–447.

National Board of Certified Counselors (1997). NBCC Code of Ethics. Retrieved March 24, 2002 from http://www.nbcc.org/ethics/NBCCethics.htm

Pedersen, P. B. (Ed.). (1978). Counseling across cultures [Special issue]. *Personnel and Guidance Journal, 56*(8).

Pedersen, P. B. (1991). Multiculturalism as a generic approach to counseling. *Journal of Counseling and Development, 70,* 6–12.

Pedersen, P. B., Lonner, W. J., & Draguns, J. G. (Eds.). (1976). *Counseling across cultures* (pp. 17–44). Honolulu: East-West Center Press.

Ponterotto, J. G. (1986). A content analysis of the *Journal of Multicultural Counseling and Development. Journal of Multicultural Counseling and Development, 14,* 98–107.

Ponterotto, J. G., & Casas, J. M. (1991). *Handbook of racial/ethnic minority counseling research.* Springfield, IL: Charles C. Thomas.

Ponterotto, J. G., Casas, J. M., Suzuki, L. A., & Alexander, C. M. (Eds.). (1995). *Handbook of multicultural counseling.* Thousand Oaks, CA: Sage.

Ponterotto, J. G., Casas, J. M., Suzuki, L. A., & Alexander, C. M. (Eds.). (2001). *Handbook of multicultural counseling* (2nd ed.). Thousand Oaks, CA: Sage.

Ponterotto, J. G., Rieger, B. P., Barrett, A., & Sparks, R. (1994). Assessing multicultural counseling competence: A review of instrumentation. *Journal of Counseling and Development, 72,* 316–322.

Shelby, J. S., & Tredinnick, M. G. (1995). Crisis intervention with survivors of natural disaster: Lessons from Hurricane Andrew. *Journal of Counseling and Development, 73,* 491–497.

Smith, E. J. (1973). *Counseling the culturally different.* Columbus, OH: Merrill.

Sue, D. W. (1981). *Counseling the culturally different: Theory and practice.* New York: Wiley.

Vontress, C. E. (1969). Counseling the culturally different in our society. *Journal of Employment Counseling, 6,* 9–16.

Weinrach, S. G., & Thomas, K. R. (1998). Diversity-sensitive counseling today: A postmodern clash of values. *Journal of Counseling and Development, 76,* 115–122.

Wrenn, C. G. (1962). The culturally encapsulated counselor. *Harvard Educational Review, 32,* 444–449.

GLOSSARY

Aborigines—Australian aborigines; indigenous people of Australia who are believed to have migrated to Australia from Asia approximately 40,000 years ago; in general, the indigenous or earliest known population of a country or identifiable land or territory.

Acculturation—the process of an individual taking on the ways and behaviors of a particular culture; refers to a person taking on values and behaviors of the dominant culture, while also retaining some attributes and practices of one's own culture of origin.

Affirmative Action—policies or a program that is designed to ensure equal opportunity in education, employment, and economic opportunity as a means of rectifying or redressing past discrimination.

African American—a person of African descent who is a citizen of the United States; sometimes used interchangeably with Black American or the less popular Afro-American.

Afrinesian—a concept of ethnic identity that classifies persons of African descent who reside in the hemisphere of the Americas. Also, persons of African descent who reside in North America, South America, Central America, or the Caribbean Islands who have Black African heritage plus Indian or White European heritage or ancestry (Harper, 1994).

Afrocentric—reference to an African-centered process, such as African-centered education or counseling; derived from the concept of Afrocentricity or the belief that thought and practice of African people should reflect the cultural images, history, and traditions of Africa and the African Diaspora.

Aggressive counseling—a term developed and used by Clemmont Vontress (1971), with reference to active and directive counseling with African American students. The strategies involve directive counseling techniques, outreach counseling, encouragement, personal assistance, and active follow-up.

Allocentrism—also, collectivism; refers to a culture or society that focuses more on the needs and goals of the group versus those of the individual.

Amae—in traditional Japanese culture, values for interdependence (versus individualism), a sense of hierarchy or order of position as important in relationships, and defined obligations according to a person's position in his or her family and in society. *See also* Enryo.

Amerasian—a person of American and Asian descent or genetic background, for example, American and Vietnamese.

American—a term of national identification used to describe a citizen of the United States; also used in compound terms to identify ethnic Americans such as African Americans, Mexican Americans, and Native Americans. Also, a term used to identify any person from the hemisphere of the Americas, including North America and South America.

American Indian—*see* Native American.

Amerindian—*see* Native American.

Amish—a cultural and religious group, primarily of southeastern Pennsylvania, that refuses to be acculturated to modern American cultural ways and practices.

Anglo-American (or Anglo)—a term used to refer to an individual of White, English descent; sometimes used with reference to White Americans in general, except for White Hispanics.

Appalachian—referring to inhabitants or cultural ways of a geographic region of the eastern United States, including North Carolina, West Virginia, Pennsylvania, Tennessee, and Kentucky; a mainly impoverished region of the country that includes coal mining.

Apple—in colloquial usage, a Native American who is "red on the outside and white on the inside"; a Native American who tries to act White in order to succeed and adjust in the White world.

Arab Americans—Americans from Arabic-speaking countries who tend to be Islamic in religious preference or background; people from Arabic-speaking countries or cultures of origin, including Saudi Arabia, Syria, Sudan, Tunisia, Morocco, Egypt, and Jordan. Note that not all Arabs are Islamic, although a sizable group is.

Asian Americans—Americans of Asian descent, mainly of South and East Asian ancestry or origin, including East Indians, Southeast Asians, Chinese, Koreans, Japanese, Filipinos, and Indonesians.

Assimilation—the process by which an ethnic or cultural group adopts the ways of another culture or adopts a majority culture's traditions, values, beliefs, attitudes, and customs.

Association for Multicultural Counseling and Development (AMCD)—a division of the American Counseling Association that addresses multicultural concerns and issues in counseling; formerly named the Association for Non-White Concerns in Personnel and Guidance (ANWC).

Biculturalism—biculturalism or bicultural refer to U.S. minorities or U.S. immigrants who inherit two different cultural worldviews, a phenomenon that often creates conflict or dissonance.

Bilingual—refers to a person who is able to use two different languages, or one who is fluent in two languages.

Biracial—persons who are first-generation offspring of parents of two different races (e.g., White and Black, or Asian and White).

Black American—*see* African American.

Black identity development—refers to stages of ethnicity identity development for African Americans (*see* Cross's stages of Black identity development).

Boufée delirante—a mental disorder or syndrome that is observed in Haitian and West African culture; it is characterized by sudden outburst, marked confusion, psychomotor excitement, and, sometimes, hallucinations and paranoid ideation.

Buddhism—the doctrine or religious way that is attributable to Buddha; beliefs include suffering is a way of life or suffering is inseparable from human existence; also, Buddhism focuses on spiritual enlightenment by deemphasizing the self and worldly desire.

Caucasian—this term is no longer popular in usage; a racial category that describes individuals who are White. Originally, the term referred to persons who lived in Caucasus or a geographic area that is now part of southeast Europe and Russia.

Chicano—has reference to persons of Mexican American descent, usually residing in California or the far western United States; a term that is used with ethnic pride by some Mexican Americans, but sometimes viewed as derogatory by others.

Counseling—a helping process between a helping professional (a counselor) and a client for the purpose of helping the client to resolve a problem, make a decision, or develop as a human being.

Creole—a French dialect spoken by people of Haiti or Haitian background; also, spoken by persons of African American and European mix (French, Spanish, or Portuguese) who primarily reside in Louisiana; a spicy food that is prevalent in Louisiana.

Cross-cultural counseling—a counseling relationship or situation in which the client and the counselor are from different cultural backgrounds.

Cross's stages of Black identity development—William E. Cross (1971) pioneered Black identity development or Nigrescence, beginning in the early 1970s; his five stages of Black identity development are (1) pre-encounter, (2) encounter, (3) immersion-emersion, (4) internalization, and (5) internalization-commitment.

Cultural competence—one's awareness, knowledge, and skills as related to communication or counseling with a person or persons of another culture.

Cultural inventory—a self-report instrument that can be used by the counselor to obtain information about the client's perceptions of his or her culture as related to topics such as family, religion, friends, education or school, community, and language.

Cultural literacy—possessing knowledge about a particular culture.

Culturally different—a concept that became popular in the 1970s as an alternative to negative and deficit-oriented ethnic terms such as disadvantaged and culturally deprived.

Cultural relativism—the viewpoint that people should have as much right to their cultural beliefs as those of other cultures, and that the concept of cultural viewpoint is a relative term versus an absolute term; also, the general idea that cultural truths and values are not absolute, or the idea that there is no cultural way that is right or superior to that of another culture.

Culture—a way of living and behaving by an identifiable group of human beings, that is, a way that is characterized by a group's habits, perceptions, customs, values, language, communication style, traditions, rituals, artistic expressions, personal preferences, social rules, and worldview.

Culture-bound syndrome—refers to culture-specific or locality-specific patterns of behavior that may not be covered by a particular DSM-IV diagnostic category but are considered by indigenous persons of a given culture to be a mental illness or affliction (American Psychiatric Association, 1994).

Culture shock—anxiety, stress, and confusion caused by sudden immersion into a new and different culture; also refers to a rapidly changing American culture where very few things are stable and constant.

Dominant culture—the major or most powerful culture within a society or country that represents the norm or mainstream way of living and behaving. The dominant culture often represents the standard or yardstick for comparing other cultures or ethnic groups in terms of being culturally different.

Dominant group—in the United States, the European American ethnic group that comprises the majority, most powerful, or mainstream sociocultural group; the ethnic or religious group in any country that is the mainstream or dominant sociocultural group.

Ebonics—a language system or vernacular English that is used by a number of African Americans, which is different from that used by mainstream White America; a dialect of English that is learned and transmitted across generations, and one that has roots in West Africa, English-speaking Europe, and Native American culture.

Emic (emic vs. etic)—culture-specific attributes; a viewpoint from a particular culture rather than the dominant culture.

Enryo—in traditional Japanese culture, values for a sense of respectfulness and modesty along with doing one's best and controlling one's emotions.

Ethnic identity—one's ethnic identification of self with a defined ethnic group; also, one's perceptions of one's own ethnic group in relationship to other ethnic groups.

Ethnicity (ethnic group)—a group of human beings who share in common specific physical traits, behavioral style, religious orientation, language, cultural heritage, or a common national or regional origin.

Ethnocentrism—a belief by an ethnic group or culture that its ways are right or superior to the cultural beliefs, styles, images, symbols, and practices of another cultural or ethnic group; an exaggerated preference for one's own ethnic group while disfavoring or diminishing the value of other ethnic groups.

Ethnography—a branch of anthropology that observes specific group behaviors and practices over time and within the context of human environment or culture; also, the study of scientific descriptions of specific human cultures.

Ethnopsychiatry—a term used by Tobie Nathan of France, as well as Clemmont Vontress and Lawrence Epp (2000) of the United States. It has reference to cross-cultural counseling with African immigrants to France, and it combines indigenous healing practices with Western psychotherapeutic methods.

Ethnorelativity—a sense of realizing that one's own cultural ways and rules are not the only way; culture viewed as relative and variable based on the values and principles of specific cultures and the reality that there are no cultural rights and wrongs.

Etic (etic vs. emic)—cultural ways or perspectives that are reflective of the dominant culture or the mainstream culture of a country or society.

Eurocentric—refers to White American culture or White, Western, European cultural ways, behaviors, and people; that which is oriented to White Western culture.

External ethnic identity—observable ethnocultural behaviors such as language, involvement in ethnic activities and traditions, and proportion of friendships from one's own ethnicity. *See also* Internal ethnic identity.

Farsi—The national language of Iran, spoken by persons of Iran.

Feminism—a belief in the economic, political, and social equality between females and males or between the sexes.

Filipinos—inhabitants or citizens of the Philippine Islands in the South Pacific, southeast of China.

First Nation—refers to North American Indians of Canada.

Folktales—ethnic stories that reflect the values, problems, and symbolism of a particular culture or people.

Gullah—refers to a people of African ancestry who live on coastal islands east of South Carolina, Georgia, and northern Florida. The Gullah culture has retained much of its African ways, and its people speak a dialect that is a combination of English and West African languages.

Hanukkah—also Hanukah and Chanukah; an 8-day religious festival of Judaism—a rededication of the Temple at Jerusalem.

Hijab—a head scarf for women, usually has reference to Islamic women.

Hindi—an official language of much of India, especially northern India.

Hinduism—predominantly in India; a religion that is characterized by a belief in reincarnation and the belief that a Supreme Being can be of many forms.

Hispanics—the ethnic term used by the U.S. government to denote American citizens or residents of Spanish descent or heritage, including persons of Spanish descent or heritage from Central America, Cuba, Dominica, Mexico, Puerto Rico, and South America; alternative terms for Hispanic include Latino, Latin American, and Spanish-speaking American.

Homophobia—usually refers to an aversion to or disdain for gay and lesbian persons; also, negative action toward gay, lesbian, or bisexual persons based on prejudice and contempt.

Indigenous healer—a person of the indigenous or traditional culture of a country who may involve rituals, herbs, and a variety of other non-Western approaches to holistic healing of the mind, body, and soul or spirit.

Internal ethnic identity—cognitive, moral, and affective dimensions of ethnic-related-identity behaviors, including a knowledge of the history and values of one's ethnic group (the cognitive dimension), feelings about one's obligations to his or her ethnic group (moral dimension), and feelings of attachment to and identification with one's ethnic group (affective dimension). *See also* External ethnic identity.

International Association for Counselling—an international counseling association that meets once a year and addresses international and cross-cultural concerns of counselors from various countries of the world (http://www.iac-irtac.org).

International Journal for the Advancement of Counselling (IJAC)—a cross-cultural counseling journal that also addresses international issues and concerns of counseling. The *IJAC* is primarily affiliated with the International Association for Counselling.

Interracial family—a family that includes members from two or more racial groups.

Islam—a monotheistic religion that is characterized by a belief in submission to Allah or God and following the ways and practices of Mohammed (or Muhammad), the chief prophet of Allah. The scriptures of Islam advocate peace, acceptance of the prophets of Christianity and Judaism, and prayer five times a day.

Jihad—an Arabic term that refers to a holy Islamic war or crusade; a holy struggle against infidels and nontrue Moslems.

Journal of Multicultural Counseling and Development (JMCD)—the counseling journal that is affiliated with the Association for Multicultural Counseling and Development; it publishes articles related to ethnicity and multicultural counseling. The *Journal of Multicultural Counseling and Development* was formerly named the *Journal of Non-White Concerns in Personnel and Guidance.*

Journal of Psychology in Africa—a continental journal that addresses topics and issues related to psychology in Africa; some articles are related to counseling and therapy.

Koran—*see* Qu'ran.

Kwanzaa (also, Kwanza)—A seasonal celebration between December 26 and January 1 in order to give thanks for the gifts of the year; the term is derived from the Swahili word "Kwanzaa," which means "first fruits." This holiday season is celebrated in the United States mainly by African Americans.

La familia—Spanish for the family.

Latinos—Hispanics or persons of Spanish descent or Latin American descent; a term of ethnic identification that includes persons of Latin background from Mexico,

South America, Central America, Puerto Rico, Cuba, and other Spanish-speaking regions of the Americas.

LGBT—an acronym that refers to the lesbian, gay, bisexual, and transgender community.

Machismo—has reference to an exaggerated sense of masculinity, macho attitude, or chauvinistic behaviors in Latino culture. Some Latinos see machismo in a positive cultural sense regarding the male's accepted roles as breadwinner, reliable father, responsible spouse, and protector of his family.

Maori (or Maoris)—native or indigenous people of New Zealand of Polynesian and Melanesian descent; an ethnic group in New Zealand with its own language, cultural ways, and traditions.

Marianismo—in Latino or Hispanic culture, a focus on femininity or an exaggerated, cultural emphasis on traditional attributes of femininity. Also, in a positive sense, a woman's responsible focus on her duties and role as a mother or a female.

Minorities—in Western or American cultures, has reference to ethnic or racial minorities of color; a term that is not favored by persons of color in the United States, that is, because persons of color make up a majority of the world's population, although a minority in the United States.

Monocultural—to view the world through the lens of one cultural perspective, without considering other cultural views; in general, a reference to an emphasis or orientation to one's cultural way.

Morita therapy—a therapy based on the work of a Japanese psychiatrist Shoma Morita. The therapy focuses on existential and transpersonal levels of human functioning, and its attempts to get the client to accept life, be obedient to nature, resolve conflicts, and become free of fixations. Morita therapy sometimes uses letter writing between the therapist and the client or can use a client diary and the counselor's feedback on the commentary within the diary.

Multicultural competency (or multicultural competencies)—refers to sufficient awareness, knowledge, and skills related to effective multicultural counseling.

Multicultural counseling and therapy (MCT)—associated with the work of Allen E. Ivey (1995); a conceptual framework for counseling research, theory, and practice that focuses on the human condition in social or cultural context and the need to change systems versus blaming the person or victim; a liberating psychotherapy that allows the client to view self in relationship to cultural influencers.

Multicultural counseling assessment—the use of self-report instruments or other measures in order to assess multicultural competence; often measured in terms of multicultural awareness, knowledge, and skills. Some of the popular multicultural counseling assessment instruments are the Multicultural Awareness-Knowledge-Skills Survey, the Multicultural Counseling Awareness Scale, and the Multicultural Counseling Inventory.

Multicultural Counseling Inventory (MCI)—an instrument developed by Gargi Roysircar (formerly Roysircar-Sodowsky) that measures multicultural counseling competencies: multicultural counseling skills, multicultural awareness, multicultural counseling relationship, and multicultural counseling knowledge. (See Chapter 11 of this book.)

Multicultural counseling training—training counselors in multiculturalism as part of counselor education or counseling psychology training; also refers to goals, objectives, and instructional methods for including multicultural counseling as part of the counseling training curriculum.

Multiethnic—a variety of ethnic groups; sometimes, the term is perceived as an alternative to multicultural or used in conjunction with multicultural.

Multiracial person—an individual whose biological parents are of different racial groups; a person whose racial heritage or identity consists of two or more racial groups.

Native American—reference to native or indigenous citizens of the United States; sometimes called American Indians, First Americans, Native American Indians, Amerindians, or simply Indians.

Nigrescence—associated with the racial-identity work of Cross (1971); the process of becoming Black in terms of racial consciousness and identity.

Oppression—the suppression or subversion of a sociocultural group by a dominant or more powerful societal group, that is, in terms of limiting the oppressed sociocultural group's economic, educational, political, and social opportunities and privileges.

Oreo cookie—in colloquial usage, an African American who is "black on the outside and white on the inside"; one who tries to act White in order to succeed, adjust, and be accepted in a White world.

Pakeha—from the language of the indigenous Maori people of New Zealand, Whites who settled in New Zealand in the nineteenth century; in general, refers to White Europeans.

Patois—a regional dialect that is spoken by some people of Jamaica and other Caribbean Islands.

Pluralistic society—a society that has a number of distinct ethnic, religious, or cultural groups within the same society or country.

Prejudice—incorrect or faulty conclusions about a cultural group or a person from a particular cultural or ethnic group; hostile misconceptions that are based on false and stereotypical assumptions and not facts; also hostility toward another person or sociocultural group based on illogical generalizations.

Pseudospeciation—a false sense of cultural specialness; a sense of feeling that one's cultural group is the best as compared to other cultural groups.

Qu'ran (also, Koran or Qur-an)—the sacred writings of the Islamic religion; the revelations of God as communicated to and through the prophet Mohammed (or Muhammad).

Race—a classification of human beings based on attributes that may include hair texture and color, skin color, and other physical features; a distinct human population that is often distinguished by genetic characteristics or genotypic traits, geographic origin or distribution, and a common history.

Racial identity—one's conception of self as a racial being; also one's beliefs, attitudes, and values of self as related to other racial groups (Helms, 1994).

Racism—the belief and behavioral expressions that one's race is superior to that of another or other races; three types of racism include individual racism, institutional racism, and cultural racism.

Roots (or rootwork)—used by some persons of the Caribbean Islands, mainly Haiti, and the southeastern United States to refer to casting a hex or evil spell on another to cause illness, death, or some form of misfortune. In cultures that practice or believe in roots, it is thought that the ill consequences of roots or rootwork can be removed by ceremonies or work of a root doctor or indigenous healer. Also, the term has reference to a person's family lineage.

Sexism—a belief that one's sex (e.g., the male sex) is superior to another; and, thus, the presupposition that one's sex should be entitled to certain privileges and power roles in society. A sexist is one who holds such beliefs about dominance and privilege of one sex over the other.

Shenjing shuairuo—in Chinese culture, an anxiety-related condition or syndrome characterized by physical and mental fatigue, dizziness, headaches, gastrointestinal problems, sexual dysfunction, irritability, excitability, and difficulty in concentrating.

Sikhism—a religion of India that combines elements of Hinduism and Islam; the followers are referred to as Sikhs.

South Pacific Islanders—persons who originate from any of the South Pacific Islands, including Guam and Somoa.

Stereotype—preconceived generalizations by an individual about a person from a particular sociocultural group; also, a preconceived image or opinion about a sociocultural group.

Stylistic counseling—a model thematically constructed around three dimensions that focus on the development of a framework for counselors to apply to their knowledge and skills across cultures; a counseling theory founded by Gunnings and Simpkins (1972).

Systemic counseling—a multicultural theory of counseling that focuses on changing the system in order to accommodate the needs and cultural style of the client (i.e., versus changing the client to adjust to the system).

Transcendent counseling—an existential, cognitive-behavioral theory that focuses on lifestyle change, fulfillment of basic needs, holistic health, and transcendence of negative environmental influencers; a metacultural counseling theory founded by Harper and Stone (1999).

Transcultural counseling—working across, through, or beyond one's cultural differences instead of simply counseling across culture as in cross-cultural counseling; transcultural counseling is a reciprocal process of client and counselor (see d'Ardenne & Mahtani, 1989).

Transracial adoption—adopting an infant or child from a race or ethnic group that is different from that of the adopting parents.

Worldview (also, world view)—one's view of the world based on his or her cultural perspective and life experiences; one's cultural viewpoint or one's Weltanschauung (German for worldview); the way a person perceives and experiences his or her relationship to the world.

Xenophobia—an unrealistic fear and disdain for immigrants or internationals from countries other than one's own; a fear of strangers who are culturally different.

REFERENCES

American Psychiatric Association. (1994). *Diagnostic and statistical manual of mental disorders (DSM-IV)* (4th ed.). Washington, DC: Author.

Cross, W. E., Jr. (1971). The Negro-to-Black conversion experience: Toward a psychology of Black liberation. *Black World, 20,* 13–27.

d'Ardenne, P., & Mahtani, A. (1989). *Transcultural counseling in action.* London: Sage.

Gunnings, T. S., & Simpkins, G. (1972). A systemic approach to counseling disadvantaged youth. *Journal of Non-White Concerns in Personnel and Guidance, 1,* 4–8.

Harper, F. D. (1994). Afrinesians of the Americas: A new concept of ethnic identity (Editorial). *Journal of Multicultural Counseling and Development, 22,* 3–6.

Harper, F. D., & Stone, W. O. (1999). Transcendent counseling (TC): A theoretical approach for the year 2000 and beyond. In J. McFadden (Ed.), *Transcultural counseling* (2nd ed., pp. 83–108). Alexandria, VA: American Counseling Association.

Helms, J. E. (1994). Racial identity in the school environment. In P. Pedersen & J. C. Carey (Eds.), *Multicultural counseling in schools: A practical handbook* (pp. 19–37). Boston: Allyn & Bacon.

Ivey, A. E. (1995). Psychotherapy as liberation: Toward specific skills and strategies in multicultural counseling therapy. In J. G. Ponterotto, J. M. Casas, L. A. Suzuki, & C. M. Alexander (Eds.), *Handbook of multicultural counseling.* Thousand Oaks, CA: Sage.

McFadden, J. (Ed.). (1993). *Transcultural counseling.* Alexandria, VA: American Counseling Association.

Vontress, C. E. (1971). *Counseling Negroes.* Boston: Houghton Mifflin.

Vontress, C. E., & Epp, L. R. (2000). Ethnopsychiatry: Counseling immigrants in France. *International Journal for the Advancement of Counseling, 22,* 272–288.

APPENDIX A

Annotated Bibliography on Culture and Counseling

Baruth, L. G., & Manning, M. L. (2003). *Multicultural counseling and psychotherapy: A lifespan perspective* (3rd ed.). Upper Saddle River, NJ: Prentice Hall. 464 pages

Multicultural Counseling and Psychotherapy: A Lifespan Perspective looks at five of the most prevalent subgroups in the United States: African Americans, Asian Americans, Hispanic Americans, Native Americans, and European Americans. The text looks at each of these groups to provide majority-culture counselors and minority-culture counselors with tools for counseling outside of their specific group identity. The authors explain that it is likely that majority-culture counselors will deal with minority-culture clients and minority-culture counselors will deal with majority-culture clients. Client issues are examined from a life span perspective; that is, the authors consider age when discussing what counselors should be aware of when counseling across cultures.

Bucher, R. D. (2000). *Diversity consciousness: Opening our minds to people, cultures, and opportunities.* Upper Saddle River, NJ: Prentice Hall. 223 pages

Diversity Consciousness: Opening Our Minds to People, Cultures, and Opportunities focuses on informing those in educational and business settings about the current state of diversity issues in the United States. The author writes with twenty-five years of professional and personal experience as an educator at Baltimore City Community College. He uses a two-dimensional approach to explore diversity issues. One dimension examines the relationship between success and diversity awareness. The other dimension views how individuals can enhance their diversity understanding.

Fu, V. R., & Stremmel, A. J. (Eds.). (1999). *Affirming diversity through democratic conversations.* Upper Saddle River, NJ: Prentice Hall. 205 pages

Affirming Diversity Through Democratic Conversations presents scholarly narratives on issues of difference in a pluralistic America. Editors of the text contend that these narratives are a response to a particular multicultural conference, which silenced democratic conversations that do not fit stereotypical views about diversity issues. Educators and counseling practitioners are encouraged to use this text as a reader to stimulate reflections and discussions about their own diversities as unique individuals; use of this work as a sole textbook is not encouraged. All chapters are written by individuals in higher education who have been affected by multiculturalism in a profound way. The text is divided into three sections: Conversations in Diversity, Practices in Diversity, and Journeys in Diversity. The book contains thirteen chapters.

Garcia, J. G., & Zea, M. C. (Eds.). (1997). *Psychological interventions and research with Latino populations*. Boston: Allyn & Bacon. 284 pages

Psychological Interventions and Research With Latino Populations focuses on the behaviors of Mexican Americans, Cuban Americans, Central Americans, Puerto Ricans, and other Latino groups. The editors comment that within the past twenty years much has taken place with the Latino populations in America and the societal experiences of recent Latino immigrants; thus, this text attempts to respond to the evolution of conceptualizations of Latino psychology within that time span. The book is divided into three sections: The first section describes current theories about Latino populations in America; the second section covers mental health treatment research and intervention; and the third section covers descriptions of health and rehabilitation research and interventions. There are fourteen chapters of material that are primarily directed to educators. It can be used as a textbook or reference tool in multicultural psychology, counseling, social work, and related disciplines.

Herring, R. D. (1997). *Counseling diverse ethnic youth: Synergetic strategies and interventions for school counselors*. Fort Worth: Harcourt Brace. 545 pages

Counseling Diverse Ethnic Youth includes eleven chapters on topics related to counseling diverse groups of youth in the schools. The diverse youth groups of focus are (1) Native Americans and other indigenous youth (including Alaskan Natives), (2) Asian Americans, (3) African Americans, (4) Hispanic Americans, (5) European Americans, (6) Arab Americans, (7) biethnic/multiethnic youth, (8) international youth, (9) at-risk youth, and (10) youth with disabilities. The book also addresses sexuality and gender issues as well as roles and responsibilities of the school counselor. A variety of information and resources is included in eleven appendices.

Ivey, A. E., D'Andrea, M., Ivey, M. B., & Simek-Morgan, L. (2002). *Counseling and psychotherapy: A multicultural perspective* (5th ed.). Boston: Allyn & Bacon. 456 pages

Counseling and Psychotherapy: A Multicultural Perspective presents the traditional or foundational theories of counseling from a culture-centered perspective, while also presenting multicultural theories and viewpoints of counseling as a fourth force of the counseling and psychotherapy movement. The book contains fourteen chapters that include topics on the three traditional forces or schools of thought in counseling (psychodynamic, cognitive-behavioral counseling, and existential-humantic), a chapter on family counseling and therapy, and chapters that focus on multicultural competence and practice.

Kiselica, M. S. (1999). *Confronting prejudice and racism during multicultural training*. Alexandria, VA: American Counseling Association. 204 pages

Confronting Prejudice and Racism During Multicultural Training discusses issues of how those undergoing diversity training need to deal with their unfair biases and prejudices. Sexism, homophobism, classism, and racism are addressed by fifteen educational professionals in counselor education. The text proposes to answer the following questions and others: What specific conditions facilitate the examination of ethnocentrism and racism? What training techniques and group processes foster the reduction of prejudice while promoting multicultural sensitivity and appreciation for cultural diversity? What are the potential classroom dynamics when the student and the instructor are from different racial backgrounds? The text targets a broad audience that includes counselors, psychologists, social workers, physicians, nurses, teachers, ministers, and those who conduct multicultural workshops. There are twelve chapters in this text; the last chapter addresses the cross-sections that emerge from thoughts expressed by the contributing authors.

Lee, C. C. (Ed.). (2002). *Multicultural issues in counseling: New approaches to diversity* (3rd ed.). Alexandria, VA: American Counseling Association. 500 pages

Multicultural Issues in Counseling: New Approaches to Diversity examines culturally relevant intervention strategies and methods for those in the mental health field that work with multicultural clients. Scholars in the field of mental health provide theoretically sound and practical direction for optimal mental health intervention with groups and individuals. The text contains twenty-two different client groups that are examined in detail and a number of case studies that discuss and illustrate the foundations of culturally responsive counseling. This third edition offers new chapters on multicultural counseling in the twenty-first century that focus on counseling in the cross-cultural zone, multiracial individuals and families, sexuality, disabilities, socioeconomic disadvantaged clients, and other multicultural issues.

Lee, W. M. L. (1999). *An introduction to multicultural counseling.* Philadelphia, PA: Accelerated Development. 259 pages

An Introduction to Multicultural Counseling is a text that grew out of the author's eighteen years of experience as a multicultural educator. According to the author, most multicultural education texts exclude issues related to gender, sexual orientation, physical disability, and aging, which provided her with the impetus to write her own. The author addresses the aforementioned topics as well as multicultural issues related to Native Americans, African Americans, Latino Americans, Asian and Pacific Islander Americans, and European Americans. According to the author, her text is intended to be used as a primer and as a general introduction to counseling issues by classroom educators. There are sixteen chapters, and most include recommended readings for further study.

Locke, D. C., Myers, J. E., & Herr, E. L. (Eds.). (2001). *The handbook of counseling.* Thousand Oaks, CA: Sage. 757 pages

The Handbook of Counseling targets students and educators who are new to the field and experienced professionals who need a comprehensive text. It examines the development of counseling from a historical perspective of educational trends and from the perspective of a field that has been established through scholarly research. There are seven in-depth parts to this text: Part I examines the historical foundation of counseling. Part II presents theoretical concepts used in the counseling field. Part III discusses sites, such as schools and medical offices, where counseling professionals are employed. Part IV examines methods of training used in the field. Part V focuses on methodological and epistemological research in counseling. Part VI deals with critical issues and emerging topics. Part VII attempts to summarize the text by examining themes for the future of the profession based on the emerging ideas from the eighty-five contributing authors. The handbook comprises forty-four chapters.

McFadden, J. (Ed.). (1999). *Transcultural counseling* (2nd ed.). Alexandria, VA: American Counseling Association. 416 pages

Transcultural Counseling, second edition, focuses on theories, models, and approaches to counseling with an emphasis on various racial, cultural, and ethnic groups served by helping professionals. Special attention is also devoted to transcultural assessment and curriculum trends to be considered for the twenty-first century. Paradigms and assumptions are discussed toward articulating the meaning and practice of transcultural counseling. This publication is designed to support curriculum changes in counselor education programs in order to maximize advantages across all academic lines. The text contains fourteen chapters.

Okun, B. F., Fried, J., & Okun, M. L. (1999). *Understanding diversity: A learning-as-practice primer.* Pacific Grove, CA: Brook/Cole. 288 pages

Understanding Diversity: A Learning-as-Practice Primer focuses on how individuals and groups interact. The text examines cultural differences that affect how people communicate with each other. Practical exercises presented in each chapter provide an opportunity for self-reflection of covered material and an opportunity to gauge one's level of cultural sensitivity. The purpose of the text is to provide educators with a method of teaching others how to facilitate communication across cultures. One of the major goals of the text, according to its authors, is to assist readers in gauging personal comfort and discomfort zones that will enable them to establish cross-cultural relationships. This text comprises seven chapters.

Pedersen, P. (1999). *Multiculturalism as a fourth force.* Philadelphia, PA: Brunner/Mazel. 213 pages

Multiculturalism as a Fourth Force attempts to answer the question of whether multiculturalism qualifies as a "fourth force" or a dimension of psychology. The author invites readers—educators and students in counseling fields—to contemplate how multiculturalism can be used to strengthen or supplement three earlier theoretical forces of humanism, behaviorism, and psychodynamism. *Multiculturalism as a Fourth Force* attempts to achieve a balance between universalism and relativism viewpoints about multicultural groups. Identified in this text are distinctive perspectives of specific cultural groups and some of the more general perspectives different groups share with one another in an extensive view about the field of multiculturalism. The text is divided into two parts (general issues and particular issues) with ten chapters.

Pedersen, P. (2000). *A handbook for developing multicultural awareness* (3rd ed.). Alexandria, VA: American Counseling Association. 230 pages

A Handbook for Developing Multicultural Awareness addresses multicultural assessment issues for those in the counseling field. The following underlying assumptions held by the author are revealed to allow readers ample information to agree or disagree with his positions: Culture is defined based on *The Interpretations of Cultures* by Clifford Geertz; all counseling takes place in multicultural settings; culture includes obvious and unobvious symbols; cultural differences and commonalities are equally important; and the most important elements of multiculturalism can only be learned, not taught. This text contains ten chapters that cover a broad range of issues pertinent to becoming more aware of the effect of multiculturalism on the counseling field. Each chapter presents readers with major objectives and secondary objectives to make reading productive. The text contains references for further and more in-depth reading.

Pedersen, P. B., Draguns, J. G., Lonner, W. J., & Trimble, J. E. (2002). *Counseling across cultures* (5th ed.). Thousand Oaks, CA: Sage. 472 pages

This fifth edition of *Counseling Across Cultures* includes six sections and a total of eighteen chapters. There are chapters on the traditional U.S. ethnic groups under the section heading of "ethnocultural populations" as well as chapters on "broadly defined cultural groups" that address gender, international students/sojourners, refugees, the aged, and "marginalized and underserved groups." Applications for counseling and assessment are included along with perspectives on cross-cultural counseling research. In addition, *Counseling Across Cultures* presents cross-cultural counseling issues such as those related to spirituality, health, cultural empathy, and competence.

Ponterotto, J. G., Casas, J. M., Suzuki, L. A., & Alexander, C. M. (2001). *Handbook of multicultural counseling* (2nd ed.). Thousand Oaks, CA: Sage. 926 pages.

Handbook of Multicultural Counseling (second edition) contains perspectives from eighty-five scholars in the field of counseling. The purpose of the text is to provide comprehensive coverage for counseling professionals and educators about issues of cultural diversity that affect our society. Contributing authors use an array of methods to contribute to the comprehensiveness of this text; methods range from qualitative to quantitative research to in-depth oral histories. There are eight parts in this text: Part I focuses on historical perspectives; Part II discusses ethical and professional issues; Part III examines the counselor's role in understanding and fighting oppression; Part IV presents research on psychological measurement of multicultural constructs; Part V presents the latest developments about theories and designs in multicultural counseling; Part VI examines multicultural issues from a family-oriented perspective; Part VII discusses the commonalties of multicultural identities; and Part VIII focuses on supervision of multicultural issues at colleges and universities. Each of the eight parts of the text begins with an introduction and an overview; the text contains forty chapters.

Purnell, L. D., & Paulanka, B. J. (1998). *Transcultural health care: A culturally competent approach.* Philadelphia: F. A. Davis Company.

Transcultural Health Care: A Culturally Competent Approach was written in response to the growing diversity of North America's population and the paucity of health care literature on minority groups. The text is written primarily for educators, and it is designed to introduce students to new and evolving conceptual models about culture, to present a macroapproach and microapproach on cultural studies, and to describe specific characteristics of selected ethnocultural groups. Most chapters in the book are written by authors who have personal experience as minorities as well as academic and professional expertise in the area in which they write and research. This text challenges readers to consider not only the differences that make up the various cultural groups in North America but also similarities that permeate across cultures. Readers are provided with eighteen chapters; also, the text comes with an electronic disk that has an additional eleven chapters.

Ramirez III, M. (1999). *Multicultural psychotherapy: An approach to individual and cultural differences* (2nd ed.). Boston: Allyn & Bacon. 236 pages

Multicultural Psychotherapy: An Approach to Individual and Cultural Differences uses multiple approaches of psychotherapy to offer theoretical methods for counseling diverse populations; the author includes discussions on ethnic groups, sexual orientation, age-related issues, and disabilities. Humanistic, ethnopsychological, cognitive, and behavioristic are among the different approaches that the author makes use of in his theoretical formulation of psychotherapy for multicultural populations. The text also offers ten case studies of multicultural families and individuals; these case studies are introduced in the first chapter of the text and referenced throughout the remainder of the text as the author offers analyses of previous psychotherapy research and contextualizes his own theory. The author writes for an audience of practitioners and educators in mental health fields. There are fourteen chapters and fourteen appendices.

Sandhu, D. S. (Ed.). (1999). *Asian and Pacific Islander Americans: Issues and concerns for counseling and psychotherapy.* Commack, NY: Nova Science Publishers. 335 pages

Asian and Pacific Islander Americans [APAs]: Issues and Concerns for Counseling and Psychotherapy offers those in the field of counselor education and other mental health fields a contemporary view of research on APAs. The editor argues that the collection of essays here differs from other works in the field in three ways: The essays (1) offer new research about APAs that is more inclusive, moving beyond research that traditionally focused on Japanese and Chinese Americans; (2) address the scarcity of research related to racial identity and acculturation among APAs; and (3) provide practical implications for persons in mental health disciplines. All chapters are written by professionals in the field of counseling and mental health; the text is divided into twenty chapters.

Sciarra, D. T. (1999). *Multiculturalism in counseling.* Itasca, IL: F. E. Peacock Publishers. 203 pages

Multiculturalism in Counseling encourages counselors to look at the similarities and cross-sections of different cultures and advocates that they look at how universal counseling principles affect multicultural groups. It is written for an audience that includes professors, students, and practitioners of counseling. According to the author, the uniqueness of this text lies in its "integration and reworking of traditional counseling concepts and principles within the framework of multiculturalism." It is divided into two parts: Part I examines fundamentals in multicultural counseling, and Part II is arranged around counseling modalities. There are six chapters of information; all chapters contain overviews of pertinent counseling modalities and summaries of discussed materials, and Chapters 4 through 7 contain detailed case study examples.

Sue, D. W., Ivey, A. E., & Pedersen, P. B. (Eds.). (1996). *A theory of multicultural counseling and therapy.* Pacific Grove, CA: Brooks/Cole. 265 pages

A Theory of Multicultural Counseling and Therapy attempts to address the need for theoretical models for counseling African Americans, Asian Americans, Native Americans, Latino Americans, and women. The text can be used as a major or supplementary graduate-level text for courses in psychology, counselor education, and social work. The editors explain that their reason for producing it is to transcend their own biased assumptions and to address educational scholarship that has presented minorities as negative stereotypes. Chapters 1, 2, and 3 present multicultural counseling therapy (MCT); Chapters 4 to 15 are responses to their MCT from counselors who are members of multicultural populations; Chapter 16 is an editorial response to the contributor's reaction to MCT.

Tucker, C. M. (1999). *African American children: A self-empowerment approach to modifying behavior problems and preventing academic failure.* Boston: Allyn & Bacon. 372 pages

African American Children: A Self-Empowerment Approach to Modifying Behavior Problems and Preventing Academic Failure examines issues that concern African American students and argues that their success and failure impact all students in academic settings. Using the most current research, the text defines problems associated with

African American students, and it offers strategies to educators and counselors on how to deal with these problems. Also, attention is given to explaining how to provide African American students with skills for success in an academic culture that differs from their home culture. Central themes of self-empowerment, self-motivation, self-praise, engagement in success behaviors, and development of adaptive skills for success within and without the academic setting permeate this text. Each chapter begins with a brief abstract and ends with a conclusion that presents suggestions for future research; the text contains fifteen chapters.

Vacc, N. A., De Vaney, S. B., & Wittmer, J. (Eds.). (1995). *Experiencing and counseling multicultural and diverse populations.* Bristol, PA: Accelerated Development. 376 pages

Experiencing and Counseling Multicultural and Diverse Populations analyzes America's subgroups, such as Blacks, Native Americans, and Asians, as unique populations that want to maintain their culture. Providing educators and mental health professionals with tools for working with America's subgroups is the purpose of this work. The editors of the text suggest that it is helpful as a teaching tool for college professors and helpful as a reference tool for educators in K–12 and professionals in the mental health field. Historically, this text answers questions raised by proponents of the civil rights era; that is, it provides a hindsight view of why this era took shape. A representative of a multicultural population wrote each chapter; the chapters highlight perspectives that mainstream America may not understand or appreciate. The text comprises fifteen chapters.

Vontress, C. E., Johnson, J. A., & Epp, L. R. (1999). *Cross-cultural counseling: A casebook.* Alexandria, VA: American Counseling Association, 242 pages

Cross-Cultural Counseling: A Casebook is an excellent collection of multicultural counseling cases. It starts out in Chapters 1 and 2 with background knowledge and theory on cross-cultural counseling with an orientation toward existential concepts. The balance of the book includes ten cases (a case per chapter) and a final chapter that presents the authors' reflections. The counseling cases cut across culture, nationality, and client concern—concerns such as disability, sexual identity, abuse, meaning in life, and anger among others. Each case provides in-depth discussion of client history, cultural background, presenting problem, diagnosis, behavioral/family dynamics, intervention strategy, existential or theoretical perspective, and case analysis. Discussion questions are presented after each chapter except the last.

Wehrly, B. (1995). *Pathways to multicultural counseling competence: A developmental journey.* Pacific Grove, CA: Brooks/Cole. 280 pages

Pathways to Multicultural Counseling Competence provides twelve chapters that are divided into two parts: (1) Multicultural Counselor Preparation: Pathways to the Present and (2) Multicultural Counselor Preparation: Pathways from the Present to the Future. The content of Part I includes the influence of cultures on counseling, the "history and rationale for multicultural counselor preparation," models for counselor education, ethnic identity development, and international perspectives of multicultural counseling. Part II presents an overview of a stage model of multicultural counselor preparation and follows with chapters on each of the five stages of the developmental model. The last chapter wraps up the book with a discussion of future needs and directions. Eight appendices provide valuable information on cross-cultural competencies, objectives, suggested resource materials (e.g., books), and evaluation instruments for counselor preparation (practicum and internship).

Past Presidents of the Association for Multicultural Counseling and Development (AMCD)

1970s
Samuel H. Johnson (1972–1974)
Gloria S. Smith (1974–1975)
Robert L. Clayton (1975–1976)
Willie S. Williams (1976–1977)
Joyce H. Clark (1977–1978)
William E. Gardner (1978–1979)
Queen D. Fowler (1979–1980)

1980s
Thomas S. Gunnings/Thelma C.
    Lennon (1980–1981)
Thomas S. Gunnings (1981–1982)
Horace Mitchell (1982–1983)
John McFadden (1983–1984)
Aaron B. Stills (1984–1985)
Wanda D. Lipscomb (1985–1986)
Marilyn Jefferson-Payne
    (1986–1987)
Janice M. Jordan (1987–1988)
Courtland C. Lee (1988–1989)
Linda Torrence (1989–1990)

1990s
Thomas Parham (1990–1991)
Clemmie Solomon (1991–1992)
Quincy L. Moore (1992–1993)
Dottye J. Seales (1993–1994)
Marlene R. Rhodes (1994–1995)
Sherlon P. Brown (1995–1996)
Patricia Arredondo (1996–1997)
Marcelett C. Henry (1997–1998)
Joyce Washington (1998–1999)
Bernal C. Baca (1999–2000)

2000s
Victor E. Bibbins, Sr. (2000–2001)
Gargi Roysircar (2001–2002)
Roger Herring (2002–2003)

Note: This information was derived from the official Web site of the Association for Multicultural Counseling and Development (http://www.amcd-aca.org/pastpres.html).

Thirty-One Multicultural Counseling Competencies of the Association for Multicultural Counseling and Development (AMCD)

In April 1991, the Association for Multicultural Counseling and Development (AMCD) approved a document outlining the need and rationale for a multicultural perspective in counseling. The work of the professional standards committee went much further in proposing thirty-one multicultural counseling competencies and strongly encouraged the American Counseling Association (then known as the American Association for Counseling and Development [AACD]) and the counseling profession to adopt these competencies in accreditation criteria. The hope was to have the competencies eventually become a standard for curriculum reform and training of helping professionals.

I. Counselor Awareness of Own Cultural Values and Biases

A. Attitudes and Beliefs

1. Culturally skilled counselors have moved from being culturally unaware to being aware and sensitive to their own cultural heritage and to valuing and respecting differences.
2. Culturally skilled counselors are aware of how their own cultural backgrounds and experiences and attitudes, values, and biases influence psychological processes.
3. Culturally skilled counselors are able to recognize the limits of their competencies and expertise.
4. Culturally skilled counselors are comfortable with differences that exist between themselves and clients in terms of race, ethnicity, culture, and beliefs.

(See the AMCD's Web site at www.amcd-aca.org for updates.)

B. Knowledge

1. Culturally skilled counselors have specific knowledge about their own racial and cultural heritage and how it personally and professionally affects their definitions of normality-abnormality and the process of counseling.

2. Culturally skilled counselors possess knowledge and understanding about how oppression, racism, discrimination, and stereotyping affect them personally and in their work. This allows them to acknowledge their own racist attitudes, beliefs, and feelings. Although this standard applies to all groups, for White counselors it may mean that they understand how they may have directly or indirectly benefited from individual, institutional, and cultural racism (White identity development models).

3. Culturally skilled counselors possess knowledge about their social impact on others. They are knowledgeable about communication style differences, how their style may clash or foster the counseling process with minority clients, and how to anticipate the impact it may have on others.

C. Skills

1. Culturally skilled counselors seek out educational, consultative, and training experience to improve their understanding and effectiveness in working with culturally different populations. Being able to recognize the limits of their competencies, they (a) seek consultation, (b) seek further training or education, (c) refer out to more qualified individuals or resources, or (d) engage in a combination of these.

2. Culturally skilled counselors are constantly seeking to understand themselves as racial and cultural beings and are actively seeking a nonracist identity.

II. Counselor Awareness of Client's Worldview

A. Attitudes and Beliefs

1. Culturally skilled counselors are aware of their negative emotional reactions toward other racial and ethnic groups that may prove detrimental to their clients in counseling. They are willing to contrast their own beliefs and attitudes with those of their culturally different clients in a nonjudgmental fashion.

2. Culturally skilled counselors are aware of their stereotypes and preconceived notions that they may hold toward other racial and ethnic minority groups.

B. Knowledge

1. Culturally skilled counselors possess specific knowledge and information about the particular group they are working with. They are aware of the life experiences, cultural heritage, and historical background of their culturally different clients. This particular competency is strongly linked to the "minority identity development models" available in the literature.

2. Culturally skilled counselors understand how race, culture, ethnicity, and so forth may affect personality formation, vocational choices, manifesta-

tion of psychological disorders, help-seeking behavior, and the appropriateness or inappropriateness of counseling approaches.

3. Culturally skilled counselors understand and have knowledge about sociopolitical influences that impinge upon the life of racial and ethnic minorities. Immigration issues, poverty, racism, stereotyping, and powerlessness all leave major scars that may influence the counseling process.

C. *Skills*

1. Culturally skilled counselors should familiarize themselves with relevant research and the latest findings regarding mental health and mental disorders of various ethnic and racial groups. They should actively seek out educational experiences that foster their knowledge, understanding, and cross-cultural skills.

2. Culturally skilled counselors become actively involved with minority individuals outside of the counseling setting (community events, social and political functions, celebrations, friendships, neighborhood groups, and so forth) so that their perspective of minorities is more than an academic or helping exercise.

III. Culturally Appropriate Intervention Strategies

A. *Attitudes and Beliefs*

1. Culturally skilled counselors respect clients' religious and/or spiritual beliefs and values, including attributions and taboos, because they affect worldview, psychosocial functioning, and expressions of distress.

2. Culturally skilled counselors respect indigenous helping practices and respect minority community intrinsic help-giving networks.

3. Culturally skilled counselors value bilingualism and do not view another language as an impediment to counseling (monolingualism may be the culprit).

B. *Knowledge*

1. Culturally skilled counselors have a clear and explicit knowledge and understanding of the generic characteristics of counseling and therapy (culture bound, class bound, and monolingual) and how they may clash with the cultural values of various minority groups.

2. Culturally skilled counselors are aware of institutional barriers that prevent minorities from using mental health services.

3. Culturally skilled counselors have knowledge of the potential bias in assessment instruments and use procedures and interpret findings keeping in mind the cultural and linguistic characteristics of the clients.

4. Culturally skilled counselors have knowledge of minority family structures, hierarchies, values, and beliefs. They are knowledgeable about the community characteristics and the resources in the community as well as the family.

5. Culturally skilled counselors should be aware of relevant discriminatory practices at the social and community level that may be affecting the psychological welfare of the population being served.

C. Skills

1. Culturally skilled counselors are able to engage in a variety of verbal and nonverbal helping responses. They are able to *send* and *receive* both *verbal* and *nonverbal* messages *accurately* and *appropriately.* They are not tied down to only one method or approach to helping but recognize that helping styles and approaches may be culture bound. When they sense that their helping style is limited and potentially inappropriate, they can anticipate and ameliorate its negative impact.

2. Culturally skilled counselors are able to exercise institutional intervention skills on behalf of their clients. They can help clients determine whether a "problem" stems from racism or bias in others (the concept of health paranoia) so that clients do not inappropriately personalize problems.

3. Culturally skilled counselors are not averse to seeking consultation with traditional healers and religious and spiritual leaders and practitioners in the treatment of culturally different clients when appropriate.

4. Culturally skilled counselors take responsibility for interacting in the language requested by the client and, if not feasible, make appropriate referral. A serious problem arises when the linguistic skills of a counselor do not match the language of the client. This being the case, counselors should (a) seek a translator with cultural knowledge and appropriate professional background and (b) refer to a knowledgeable and competent bilingual counselor.

5. Culturally skilled counselors have training and expertise in the use of traditional assessment and testing instruments. They not only understand the technical aspects of the instruments but are also aware of the cultural limitations. This allows them to use test instruments for the welfare of the diverse clients.

6. Culturally skilled counselors should attend to as well as work to eliminate biases, prejudices, and discriminatory practices. They should be cognizant of sociopolitical contexts in conducting evaluation and providing interventions and should develop sensitivity to issues of oppression, sexism, elitism, and racism.

7. Culturally skilled counselors take responsibility in educating their clients to the processes of psychological intervention, such as goals, expectations, legal rights, and the counselor's orientation.

Source: Reprinted by permission of the Association for Multicultural Counseling and Development (AMCD).

NAME INDEX

Aalsma, M. C., 303
Aburdene, P., 62
Achenback, G. B., 50
Achilles, C. M., 300–301
Adams, D. W., 67, 69, 72
Adams, K. N., 289
Adler, A., 342
Agee, A., 299
Ahia, C. E., 151
Ahuna, C., 168, 174
Ajamu, A., 82, 83, 91, 92
Akbar, N., 86, 91
Akinboye, J. O., 157
Alarcon, O., 168
Albee, G. W., 296–297
Albrecht, A., 356
Alexander, C. M., xv,
    xvii, 3–5, 9, 384, 391,
    407
Alexander, F., 340
Alexander, J., 353
Alipuria, L. L., 315
Almas, I., 157, 197
Alstein, H., 314
Altarriba, J., 305
Amos, W. E., 6
Amulera-Marshall, O.,
    300
Anastasi, A., 166
Ancis, J. R., 218–219, 382
Anderson, H., 328
Anderson, J., 167
Andrews, D. W., 298
Angermeier, L., 363,
    370
Ani, M., 82–83
Anzaldúa, G., 115
Aponte, J. F., 108
Aranalde, M. A., 167,
    174, 175
Arce, C., 116, 125
Arnold, B., 167
Arredondo, P. M., xv,
    xviii, 9, 12, 14, 53, 54,
    77, 91, 95, 103–104,
    107, 115–132, 118,
    121–124, 126–128, 202,
    203, 324, 327, 365
Artiles, M. F., 148, 151,
    157
Artress, L., 188
Asrabadi, B. R., 101

Atkinson, D. R., 3, 5, 7, 9,
    81, 82, 103–106,
    108–110, 141, 368
Atwell, I., 86, 88
Austin, L., 303
Avent, C., 148
Axelson, J. A., 5, 77,
    249
Azibo, D. A., 86, 88

Baker, S. B., 297
Baldwin, J. A., 226
Baltimore, M. L., 350,
    356, 357
Bandura, A., 343
Banich, M., xix, 285–295
Bank, W., 6
Barbis, H. E., 289
Barlow, A., 74
Barnes, J. M., 108
Barona, A., 168
Barrett, A., 9, 204, 382,
    391
Barrett, S., 371
Barrett-Kruse, C., 290
Barrois, C., 25
Baruth, L. G., 102, 403
Bates, J. D., 314, 316
Battista, J. R., 191
Bauer, L. M., 305
Beauvais, F., 32
Becarra, J. E., 73–74
Beck, A. T., 331–333,
    343
Beck, J. D., 7
Bell, D. A., 100, 101
Benesch, K. F., 104, 106
Bengalee, M., 157
Ben Israel, M., 135
Bennice, J. A., 300
Berg, I. K., 109
Berg, L. B., 357
Berger, P., 345
Bergin, A. E., 188
Bergman, A., 342
Berkman, C. S., 74
Berkman, L. F., 74
Berlin, I., 138, 139
Bernal, H., 176, 178
Bernal, M. E., 124, 134
Bernard, J. M., 327
Bernstein, P., 59

Berry, J. W., 165, 171, 172,
    175–177
Berryhill-Paapke, E., 75
Biever, J. L., 347–348
Binet, A., 148
Bingham, W., 147
Blake, S. M., 289
Blanton, P. W., 299
Blocker, H. G., 56–57
Bloom, J. D., 74
Bloom, J. K., 350
Boatswain, 205
Bodas, A., 157
Bojuwoye, O., 157, 160
Bolden, M. A., 83
Borach, F., 138
Borders, L. D., 314
Bosworth, K., 296
Bova, C. A., 167
Bower, E. M., 297
Boyd-Franklin, N., 94
Boytim, J. A., 297
Bradley, C., 304
Bradley, R. W., 151
Brannigan, R., 296
Braun, M., 66–69
Breggin, G. R., 27
Breggin, P. R., 26–27
Brennan, D. J., 289
Brice, F., 138
Brier, S., 133, 134
Brock, R., 300
Brody, J. A., 74
Brody, S., 137–138
Brooks, G. C., Jr., 7
Brosnan, M., 352
Brown, A. L., 83
Brown, S. P., xviii, 81–98,
    127, 324, 327, 365
Bruce-Sanford, G. C., 236
Brundage, D., 133, 134
Brundtland, G. H.,
    159–160
Bruner, J., 346–347
Bryde, J. F., 7
Buber, M., 50
Bucher, R. D., 403
Bufka, L. F., 168
Bui, U., 82
Bullis, R. K., 187–188
Bultman, L., 298
Bumbarger, B., 300

Bunting, K. P., 289
Burger, S. G., 299
Burgoon, M., 167
Buriel, R., 164–165
Burke, M., 288
Burn, D., 365, 374
Burnam, M. A., 167, 178
Burnette, A. P., 359
Bushway, S., 298
Butler, S., 141–142
Butterfield, F., 101
Byman, D., 303
Byrne, G. R., 287,
    289–290

Cadier, J. B., 27
Calhoun, J., 139
Cameron, C., 352–353
Cameron, S. C., xviii,
    66–80
Campbell, L., 82
Canby, Jr., W. C., 68–71
Cancian, F., 53
Canda, E. R., 188
Caplan, G., 297, 305
Capuzzi, D., 47, 286, 287
Carey, G., 122, 124
Carey, J. C., 166, 177
Carroll, B., 266–270
Carter, R. T., 9, 44, 82, 88,
    192–193, 242
Carvajal, L. de, 134–135
Casas, J. M., xv, xvii, 3–6,
    9, 12, 192–193, 343,
    364, 382–384, 391,
    407
Caserta, M. S., 299
Castellano, D. C., 118
Castillo, R. J., 199, 330
Cattani-Thompson, K., 2
Caulkins, J. P., 298
Cayleff, S. E., 203, 374
Ceperich, S. R. D., 301
Cervantes, R. C., 167
Chanda, J., 56, 57
Chavez, C., 130
Chavez, G. F., 73–74
Chavira, V., 178
Cheatham, H., 53
Chen, E. C., 103
Chen, M. S., Jr., 167
Chen, V. T., 101

415

Cheung, F., 108, 109
Chin, J. L., 107, 108
Chiong, J. A., 314, 316
Chitose, Y., 164
Choney, S. K., 75, 218–219
Chopra, D., 186
Christie, G., 203
Chu, J., 99, 110
Chu-Richardson, P. B., 205
Clark, J., 11
Claus, R. E., 375
Cohan, G. M., 139
Cohen, L. J., 285, 288
Cole, K., 13
Coleman, H. L. K., 177
Coleman, V. D., 188–189
Coll, C., 168
Collins, P., 10–11, 13
Columbus, C., 134, 136
Comas-Dias, L., 14, 315–316
Combs, G., 346
Constantine, M. G., 14, 178, 326
Conyne, R. K., 110, 297
Cook, D. A., 342–344, 363, 369, 373
Coon, H. M., 302, 304
Cooper, M. L., 69
Cooperstock, R., 371
Copeland, E. J., 1, 2, 4–6, 379–380
Corbine, J. L., 216, 217
Corcoran, J., 298
Cordero, J. F., 73–74
Córdova, T., 120
Corey, G., 286, 368
Cornett, C., 26
Cornett, C. E., 317
Cornett, C. F., 317
Cornoni-Huntley, J., 74
Cortés, D. E., 167
Cortez Gonzalez, R., 347
Cortright, B., 188
Cose, E., 316
Coster, M., 314
Cottone, R. R., 375
Countryman, E., 133, 134
Courtney, B. A., 316
Covey, S. R., 52
Cowen, E. L., 297
Cox, C. I., 3
Craig, B. H. R., 69
Crano, W. D., 167
Cromwell, O., 135, 136
Crosby, L., 298
Cross, W. E., Jr., 6, 11, 88, 91, 242, 363, 382, 395, 396, 400

Crump, S., 203
Crutchfield, L., 356, 357
Crystal, D., 102
Cuéllar, I., 118, 167, 168–169, 171, 172, 173
Cunningham-Warburton, P., 202
Curtis, R. C., 286

Daley, T. T., 11
Dana, R. H., 372
D'Andrea, M., 76, 77, 95, 121, 359, 365, 366, 372, 404
Daniels, J., 77, 95, 366
d'Ardenne, P., xv, xvii, 3, 302, 401
Das, A. K., 1–3, 102, 197
Davis, E. J., 301
Davis, J., 289
Davis, K. M., 286
Davis, O. L., 305
Dawson, E. J., 167
Day, J. D., 374–375
Dean, E., 356
De Anda, D., 177
DeBlassie, R. R., 7
Deen, N., xviii, 147–163, 148, 149, 154, 156–158, 160
Degroot, C. D., 301
DeLaCalle, A., 134
DeLay, T., 159–160, 384, 388–389
Delgado-Romero, E. A., 127
De Ment, T., 164–165
Desai, R., 301
De Tores, L., 134
DeTriani, R., 134
De Vaney, S. B., 409
DeVolder, J., 156
Deyo, R. A., 167
Diallo, Y., 24, 25
Diaz, E., 301
Dickel, C. T., 297
Dickinson, G., 26
Diehl, A. K., 167
Diener, E., 52
Di Maggio, J., 140
Dimotrovich, C., 300
Dinsmore, J. A., 326–327
Dishion, T. J., 298
Dittmann-Kohli, F., 299
Dodson, T. A., 379–380, 382
Dogan, S., 148, 151
Dogan, T., 218
Doka, K. J., 289

Doll, B., 290
Doll, C., 290
Dowell, K. A., 298
Dozier-Henry, O., 359
Draguns, J. G., xv, xvii, 2, 5, 7–9, 11, 380, 406–407
Dreamer, O., 59
Dressler, W. W., 176, 178
D'Rozario, V. A., 203
Du, N., 101
Duan, C., 105, 106
Dufrene, P. M., 12, 188–189
Duncan, D., 350
Durant, C. E., xix, 296–312
Durlak, J. A., 298, 306
Durndell, A., 352–353
Dusenbury, L., 296

Eaton, W. W., 297
Eber, L., 300
Ebo, B., 351–352, 360
Eddings, J., 313
Egan, G., 239
Elkins, D. N., 188
Elliott, D. S., 298
Ellis, A., 188, 286, 343
Ellison, R., 82–83
England, J. T., 326–327
Epicurus, 50
Epp, L. R., xvii, 3, 9, 21–24, 48, 159–160, 397, 409
Epston, D., 345
Erhard, R., 157
Erikson, E., 128, 340–342
Erkut, S., 168
Esbensen, F. A., 301
Eschbach, K., 71–72
Escobar, J. I., 167
Espiritu, Y. E., 102
Estrada, L., 116, 120
Evans, L., 303
Exum, H. A., 233

Fabrega, H., 372
Fadiman, A., 192
Faiver, C. M., 303
Falco, M., 296
Falicov, C. J., 122
Fanon, F., 83
Faubert, M., xix, 50–51, 324–338, 325, 326, 331, 381
Fawcett, B., 148
Felíx-Ortiz, M., 167
Fennel, D., 133, 134
First-Hartling, L., 314
Fischer, A. R., 103, 104, 106

Fleming, C. M., 66
Flores, M. T., 122, 124
Ford, C., 314
Ford, K., 167
Forman, B. D., 172
Forness, S. R., 296
Forrer, S. L., 289
Foss, L., 356
Foster, S., 365, 366
Fouad, N. A., 192–193
Frame, M. W., 188–189, 192, 300
Franco, J. N., 167
Frank, B., 299
Frank, J. D., 25
Frankl, V. E., 51–52, 193, 344
Franklin, A. J., 82–83
Franklin, C., 298
Franks, D., 136
Fraser, V., 299
Frattaroli, E., 26, 27
Freedman, J., 346
Freeman, D. H., Jr., 74
Freire, P., 50–51, 326
Freitag, R., 289
French, T. M., 340
Fretz, B. R., 3, 107
Freud, S., 340–342
Frey, L. L., 168, 169, 178
Fried, J., 406
Friedman, M., 50
Friedmann, S. S., 298–299
Frietas, K., 201, 205
Frye, B. A., 303
Fu, V. R., 403
Fuertes, J. N., 103
Fu-Kiau, K. K. B., 86
Fukuyama, M. A., xviii, 14, 186–195, 187, 188, 325, 326
Funderburg, L., 316
Funderburk, J., 187
Furn, B. G., 204

Gabriel, R. M., 301
Gajary, E., 301
Gallardo-Cooper, M., 122–124
Gamba, R. J., 167
Ganie, L., 151
Garbelman, J., 148, 150, 158
Garcia, H. A., 168
Garcia, J. G., 404
García, M., 167
Gardner, G. T., 347–348
Garrett, J. T., 189
Garrett, M. W., 189
Gary, L. E., 85

Geilen, U. P., 36
Gelso, C. J., 3
Gerard, P. A., 302
Gerber, M. H., 205
Gere, D., 58
Gergen, K. J., 328, 344–347
Gerton, J., 177
Gibbs, J. T., 315
Gibson, W. T., 371
Gil, A. G., 176
Gil, R. M., 123
Gillespie, C. M., 289
Gillespie, P., 314
Gim, R. H., 101, 108–110
Giordiano, J., 69
Gladdings, S. T., 57–58, 148, 149, 154, 236
Glasoe, B., 314
Glasser, W., 343
Glosoff, H. L., 366
Golding, J. M., 178
Goldman, L., 148
Gómez, S. P., 118
Gonzalez, R., 347–348
Goodwin, R. B., 317
Goodyear, R. K., 327
Gordon, C. E., 11
Gordon, R. D., 204
Graham, J. E., 300–301
Graham, L. P., 288–289
Grambs, J. D., 6
Grant, D., 298
Grant, S. K., 108, 368
Grant, T. M., 270–273
Graves, T., 171
Greely, H., 139
Green, E. L., 188–189, 300
Greenberg, M. T., 300
Gregory, W. H., 303
Gressard, C., 357
Grier, A. W., 314
Grills, C., 84, 86
Gross, C., 289
Gross, D. R., 47, 286, 287
Guetzloe, E., 296
Guichard, J., 148, 154–155, 156
Gullotta, T. P., 297, 298
Gunnings, T. S., 7, 401
Guo, S., 300
Guthrie, R., 167
Gutierrez, J. M., 364
Gutkin, T. B., 9
Guttman, H. G., 133, 134

Haag, Z., 352–353
Hadge, C., 301
Hage, S. M., 297, 305
Hahn, K. J., 301

Hairston, S., 314
Haislip, S. T., 316
Hale, M. J., 296
Halifax, J., 24
Hall, M., 24, 25
Hanjorgiris, W. F., 266
Hansen, L. S., 51–52
Haritos-Fatouras, M., 157
Harper, F. D., xvii, xviii, xix, 1–19, 7, 9, 12, 147–163, 150, 154, 158, 159–160, 233–251, 234, 235, 236, 242, 249, 379–393, 384, 388–389, 394, 401
Harper, J. A., 259–262
Harper, K. W., 303
Harre, R., 36
Harris, L. C., 167, 170, 173
Hart, B., 136
Hashemi, S., 141–142
Hasia, J., 101
Hayslip, B., 299
Hazuda, H., 167
Heath, A. E., 3
Heck, R., 77, 366
Hedges, L. E., 368
Hedstrom, L. J., 188
Heinrich, R. K., 216, 217
Heise, R. G., 192
Heller, K., 148
Helms, J. E., 1, 9, 12, 14, 81–82, 88, 103, 124, 242, 342–344, 363, 369, 370, 373, 382, 383, 400
Hendersen, D., 57–58
Henderson, G., 3, 7
Henriksen, R. C., 315
Herek, G. M., 266
Herlihy, B., xix, 363–378, 364, 366, 367, 368, 369, 370, 372, 373, 374–375
Hermansson, G. I., 152, 157
Herr, E. L., 3, 47–48, 51–52, 62, 405
Herring, R. D., 2, 3, 5, 9, 12, 216, 301, 404
Herskovits, M., 171
Hewson, M. G., 24
Hickson, J., 203
Highlen, P. S., 3
Hill, C. E., 104, 105
Hilliard, A. G., 89–90
Hines, A. M., 315
Hinkle, S. J., 286
Hofstede, G., 352
Hohenshil, T. H., 370

Holcomb-McCoy, C. C., 3, 366
Hollis, J. W., 379–380, 382
Holmquist, J. P., 140
Holzman, L., 328
Homma-True, R., 102
Hoover, J. H., 300
Hoover, S., 300–301
Hopkins, R., 226
Horak, R. A., Jr., 277–280
Horejsi, C., 69
Hough, R. L., 167
Hoxter, H. Z., 156
Huang, L. N., 102
Hughes, L. L., 188
Hunt, S., 299
Hurh, W. M., 102
Hussey, D. L., 300
Hynes, A., 285
Hynes-Berry, M., 285

Ibrahim, F. A., xviii–xix, 2, 8, 9, 14, 157, 196–208, 197, 198, 200, 201, 202, 203, 204, 205, 209, 302, 365, 384, 388–389
Ingersoll, R. E., 188, 190, 303
Inman, A. G., 178
Iris, K., 357
Israelashvili, M., 157
Ivey, A. E., 3, 23, 35–36, 42, 76, 95, 105, 156, 192–193, 324, 328, 364, 365, 372, 399, 404, 408
Ivey, M. B., 23, 42, 76, 95, 105, 324, 365, 372, 404

Jackson, A., 68
Jackson, G. G., 81
Jackson, J. S., 82
Jackson, M. L., 4, 5, 9–10, 12–13, 22, 23
Jacobs, J. H., 316, 321
James, A., 365, 366
Jasso, R., 167, 170, 173
Jencius, M. J., xix, 59, 60, 159, 229–232, 339–349, 350–362, 354, 356–360
Jensen, L., 164
Jensen, M., 192–193
Johnson, C. E., 288–289
Johnson, J. A., 48, 409
Johnson, J. S., xvii, 9, 21–24
Johnson, R., 218
Johnson, R. S., 62
Johnson, S. H., 6–7, 11
Jome, L., 103, 104, 106

Jonas, G., 58
Jones, D., 356, 357
Jones, J., 127, 324, 327, 365
Jones, R. L., 82
June, L. N., 303
Jung, C., 51–52, 342

Kaeser, G., 314
Kahn, H., 200
Kaladow, J. K., 148, 150, 158
Kambon, K., 88, 91
Kandel, B., 318
Kanitz, B. E., 363, 370
Karno, M., 167
Kashyap, L., 157
Kasl, S., 74
Kasoff, J., 314
Katz, R., 24
Katzko, M. W., 299
Kaur, K. P., 103
Kavale, K. A., 296
Kaye, J., 345
Keller, H., 359
Kelly, Jr., E. W., 188
Kelsey, R., 10
Kemmelmeir, M., 302, 304
Kemp, S. F., 102
Kenney, K. R., 54, 313, 316
Kenney, M. E., 313, 316
Kenny, M. C., 54, 304
Key, A., 300
Khaleefa, O. H., 304
Khalilzad, Z., 303
Khan, J. A., 148, 152
Khoo, G., 168, 174
Kidd, J. M., 148
Killian, K. D., 316, 320
Kim, B. S. K., 103, 105
Kim, K. C., 102
Kim, S. J., 100, 110
Kim, U., 172, 175–177
Kim, W. J., 314
King, K. A., 301
King, M. L., 6
Kirby, K., 68
Kirk, B., 108
Kirshner, S. A., 81
Kiselica, M. S., 9, 31, 297, 326, 327, 404
Kissinger, D. B., 280–283
Kist-Kline, G. E., 301
Klein, M., 342
Kleinman, A., 372
Knight, G. P., 124
Knox, A., 352–353
Knox, H., 139
Knox, J., 50

417

Koelsch, P., 58
Kohatsu, E. L., 302, 304
Kohut, H., 342
Kopcanova, D., 150–151, 157
Korman, M., 364
Krieger, D., 246
Krippner, S., 24
Krishnamurti, J., 51
Kuhn, T. S., 388
Kunn, P., 167
Kuo, P. Y., 178
Kurilla, V., 364
Kurtines, W., 167, 174, 175
Kushner, H. S., 193
Kuster, C. B., 298
Kwan, K. L. K., 104–105, 165, 167, 170, 175, 177, 178

Ladany, N., 178
LaFromboise, T. D., 14, 177, 365, 366
LaGuardia, F., 140
Lai, E. W. M., 166–169, 172, 174, 177, 178
Lake, A., 296
Lambert, M. J., 2
Lambros, K., 296
Lanier, S., 326, 331
LaPlantine, F., 26
Lapsley, D. K., 303
Larsen, C. C., 371
Larson, P. C., 3
Lau, A., 342
Laws, K. E., 301
Layne, P., 11
Lazarus, A. A., 286
Lazarus, E., 133, 135, 137
Leaf, J. A., 188
Lee, C. C., xv, 5, 8, 9, 12, 13, 94, 95, 364, 382–384, 405
Lee, E., 103
Lee, P. W., 106
Lee, R., 357
Lee, W. M. L., xv, 3, 352, 354, 405
Lega, L. I., 167
Lelah, R., 289
Leo, L., 74
Leong, F. T. L., 107, 108–110
Lesser, E., 189
Leung, P. W. L., 106
Leung, S. A., xviii, 99–114, 106, 157
Leventhal, M., 314
Levine, B., 133, 134
Levine, D. N., 36
Levy, J., 130

Levy, M., 136
Lew, S., 168, 170
Lewis, C., 298
Lewis, D. A., 371
Lewis, J. A., 7, 11
Li, P. S., 56
Liebowitz, S. W., 118
Lin, K.-M., 108, 109
Lind, J., 140
Lindbergh, C. A., Sr., 140
Lindholm, K. J., 165, 174, 178
Lindsey, K. P., 82
Linton, R., 170, 171
Lipscomb, W. D., 4, 6, 10, 11, 389
Lipset, S. M., 137
Lloyd, J., 303
Lo, Yen-Hung, 205
Locke, D. C., xix, 9, 31, 50–51, 127, 324–328, 324–338, 331, 342, 365, 381, 405
Lockney, J. P., 205
Lonner, W. J., xv, xvii, 2, 5, 7, 8, 9, 11, 202, 365, 380, 406–407
Lonsdale, 289
Lorion, R. P., 297
Low, G., 305
Lu, F. G., 101
Lu, Q. Y., 104–105
Luckmann, T., 345
Lund, D. A., 299
Lyons, J. S., 371

Maben, P., 31
McArt, E. W., 301
McBride, J., 316, 318
McCollum, V., 372
McCullough, D., 69
McDavis, R. J., xv, 9, 12, 53, 54, 77, 91, 95, 103–104, 107, 127, 327
McEachern, A. G., 304
McFadden, J., xv, xvii, xix, xviii, 3–6, 9–11, 47–65, 49, 50, 57, 59, 60, 141, 209–232, 210–213, 216–220, 285–295, 288, 296–312, 302, 304, 340, 342, 350, 354, 357, 359, 379–393, 389, 405–406
McGoldrick, M., 69
McIntosh, J. L., 299
McIntosh, P., 95
Mackay, M. A., 300
McLeod, J. H., 100
McNeill, B. W., 118
McRae, M. B., 188–189

Madison, J., 139
Maestas, M. V., 165, 166, 172, 178, 179
Magnussen, L., 140
Mahalik, J. R., 203
Mahler, M. S., 342
Mahtani, A., xv, xvii, 3, 302, 401
Maiorella, R., 359
Maldonado, M., 174
Maldonado, R. E., 167–169, 171, 172
Malgady, R. H., 167
Mallon, G., 266
Manderscheid, R., 371
Manning, M. L., 102, 403
Manson, S. M., 74
Marin, B. V., 168
Marín, G., 167, 168
Marsden, P., 303
Marsella, A. J., 167
Martin, L. R., 148, 156
Martin, R., 130
Martin-Causey, T., 286
Martinelli, G., 140
Martinez, Jr., J. L., 167
Martinez, S. R., 167
Maruyama, M., 110
Masaki, B., 102
Maslow, A. H., 51–52, 235, 236, 343
Mathews, 289
Mathewson, R. H., 148
Matsui, S., 110
Matsushita, Y. J., 108–109
May, R., 51–52, 344
May, T., 53
Mays, V. M., 384, 390
Mazrui, A. A., 55
Mbiti, J. S., 84
Meara, N. M., 374–375
Meehan, S., 300
Mehl-Madrona, L., 72, 77
Mehta, S., 174, 178
Meichenbaum, D., 332
Melanson, R., 291
Meller, P. J., 370
Mena, F. J., 174
Menacker, J., 7
Menard, S., 298
Mendez Seixas, I., 136
Mendoza, D. W., 363, 370
Mendoza, R. H., 167, 175
Merali, N., 253–255
Mercer, J. R., 170
Mess, L. A., 165, 167
Methabane, G., 316
Methabane, M., 316
Meyers, H., 167
Mezzich, J. E., 372
Middleton, R., 121

Miechenbaum, D., 343
Miller, G., 188
Miller, J. A., 168
Miller, P., 298
Miller, S. D., 109
Min, P. G., 102
Minde, T., 172, 175–177
Mindus, L. A., 7
Minerbrook, S., 316, 318
Minuchin, S., 198
Mitchell, S. J., 301
Mobley, M., 53, 82, 94
Moeschberger, M., 167
Mok, D., 172, 175–177
Mok, T. A., 179
Monroe, J., 139
Monte, C., 339
Montgomery, G. T., 168
Moore, Q. L., 233
Morano, C. K., 178
Mori, S., 82
Morita, S., 157, 400
Morrissey, M., 103
Morss, J., 328
Morten, G., 3, 5, 7, 9, 141
Morton, G., 81
Moyerman, D. R., 172
Murthy, K., 179
Myers, D. G., 52
Myers, J. E., 3, 5, 366, 405
Myers, L. J., 3

Naiker, K. S., 151
Naisbitt, J., 62
Nathan, T., 25–26
Neighbors, H. W., 82
Neimeyer, G. J., 3
Neville, H. A., 82, 94
Newcomb, M. D., 167
Newgass, S., 300
Newsome, A., 148
Ngumba, E. W., 204
Nguyen, H. H., 165, 167
Nicholas, L. J., 157
Nielsen, E., 296
Niemann, Y. F., 124
Nitsch, R. E., 298
Nobles, W. W., 83, 84, 86, 88, 91
Norris, A. E., 167
Norval, M., 303
Nuccio, L. M., 289
Nugent, F. A., 149
Nunnally, J. C., 166
Nwachuku, U. T., 3
Nyberg, B., 167–169, 171, 172

Oakes, K. E., 303
Oaks, I. N., 300

418

O'Brien, E. M., 303
O'Brien, K. M., 104, 105
O'Brien, M. J., 138–139
Odenweller, T., 203
Oetting, E. R., 32
O'Hanlon, B., 341, 344
Ohlsen, M., 89
Ohnishi, H., 198, 201, 202
Okon, S. E., 157
Okun, B. F., 239, 406
Okun, M. L., 406
Oliver, R., 300
Olmeda, E. L., 167
Olson, S., 356
O'Neal, G. S., 296
O'Neill, C. W., 192
Organista, K. C., 305
Osajima, K., 101
Osborne, W. L., 147–148
Ostfeld, A. M., 74
Osvold, L. L., 169, 172, 176–178
Otero-Sabogal, R., 168
Othman, A. H., 157
Ottens, A., 289
Owen, S. V., 9, 200, 201, 205

Pablo, J., 69
Padilla, A. M., 7, 165, 167, 173–174, 178
Page, B., 356
Palmer, S., 149, 160
Palomares, U. H., 11
Paniagua, F. A., 305
Pannu, R., 165, 175, 177, 178
Paradis, F. E., 364
Pardeck, J. A., 285, 286–287
Pardeck, J. T., 285, 286–287
Pargament, K. I., 188, 190
Parham, T. A., xviii, 9, 81–98, 82–85, 88–89, 89–92, 95, 367
Parham, W. D., 88–89
Parker, W. M., 5, 190
Parron, D. L., 372
Paterson, J. G., 148, 149–150
Patterson, C. H., 5, 340
Patterson, G. R., 298
Patterson, J., 190
Paul, G. L., 82
Paulanka, B. J., 407
Pavkov, T. W., 371
Pearce, J., 69

Pedersen, P., xviii, 2, 5, 8, 9, 41, 42
Pedersen, P. B., xv, xvii, 2, 3, 5, 7, 11, 12, 31–46, 48–49, 107, 325, 339, 340, 341, 344, 348, 364, 371, 380, 381, 406, 406–407, 408
Pelton, R., 300–301
Peng, S., 109
Perez, P., xi–xii, xviii, 115–132
Perez-Stable, E. J., 168
Perkins, M., 316
Petruzzi, M., 356
Pevar, S. L., 67, 68, 70, 71
Phelps, R. E., 302
Phillips, N., 137
Phinney, J. S., 165, 168, 169, 178, 315, 316, 321
Pietrucha, C. A., 300
Pinderhughes, E., 333
Pine, F., 342
Pizarro, C., 305
Plake, B., 168–170, 172, 174, 177, 178
Plant, P., 156
Pollack, E., 7
Ponterotto, J. G., xv, xvii, 3–6, 8, 9, 12, 44, 103, 104, 106, 364, 370, 382–384, 391, 407
Pope, K. S., 371
Pope, R. L., 316
Poston, W. S. C., 316
Pratt, R., 69
Pressley, S. A., 316
Price, L., 11
Price, R. H., 297
Prieto, L. R., 118
Prigerson, H., 301
Purnell, L. D., 407

Quantz, R. A., 301
Quinn, M. M., 300

Raab, E., 137
Raabe, P. B., 50
Ramirez, A., 101
Ramirez, M., 122
Ramirez, M., III, 407–408
Ramsey, M. L., 327
Rashid, H., 300
Rave, E. J., 371
Reader, J., 21
Redfield, R., 171
Rediker, M. J., 133, 134
Reeves, M. A. L., 300
Register, C., 314

Rehfuss, M., 356
Remley, T. P., 364, 367, 370, 373, 374–375
Reynolds, A. L., 266, 316
Rezentez, W. C., III, 168
Rice, 144
Rice, S. J., 299
Richards, K., 152, 160, 256–259
Richards, P. S., 188
Richardson, B. L., 303
Richardson, E. H., 70
Richmond, L. J., xviii, 133–146
Rickard-Figueroa, K., 168, 170
Ridley, C. R., 9, 363, 370
Rieger, B. P., 9, 382, 391
Riessman, F., 6
Rigazio-DiGilio, S. A., 328
Riley, M. A., 298
Ritoók, M., 150, 157
Ritter, K. Y., 192
Robbins, R. R., 75
Roberts, R. E., 167–169, 171, 172
Robertson, S. E., 148, 149–150
Robinson, A. L., 298
Roblyer, M. D., 359
Rodriguez, R., 218, 219
Rodriguez Caravajal, F., 134–135
Rogers, C. R., 2, 23, 51–52, 105, 150–152, 339, 344
Rogler, L. H., 167
Rokutani, L., 357
Rolf, K., 300
Romano, J. L., 297
Roosevelt, F. D., 145
Root, M. P. P., 313, 316, 321
Rose, P. I., 135
Rosenheck, P., 301
Rosenstein, N., 142–144
Rosenthal, C. S., 127
Rotter, J., 357
Rowney, G. C., 300
Roysircar, G., xviii, 14, 164–185, 168, 169, 175, 178, 399
Roysircar-Sodowsky, G. R., 165–166, 168, 172, 178, 179, 201
Ruiz, A. S., 124
Ruiz, R., 7
Rumbaut, R. G., 164, 178
Ryan-Finn, K. Y., 296
Rydell, C. P., 298

Sabogal, F., 168
Sadik, Sue, 274–276
Sadlak, M. J., 202
Sager, D. L., 350, 356
Salgado de Snyder, N., 167
Sanches De Segovia, R., 134
Sanchez, J., 127, 324, 327, 365
Sanchez Bodas, A., 151
Sanders, J. L., 304
Sandhu, D. S., xviii, 12, 99–114, 100–103, 408
Santiago-Rivera, A. L., 118, 121–124, 126–128, 305
Sapia, J. L., 298
Sato, M., 109
Sattler, J. L., 288–289
Sauerman, T. H., 289
Saunders, C., 188
Schlegelmilch, A., 300
Schlichter, C. L., 288
Schmidt, L. D., 374–375
Schonfeld, D. J., 300
Schroeder, D., 202
Schultz, G. L., 374
Schuster, S. C., 50
Sciarra, D. T., 408
Scopetta, M. A., 167, 174, 175
Sedlacek, W. E., 5–6, 7, 218–219
Segal, L., 58
Seligman, L., 7
Serna, L. A., 296
Sevig, T. D., 187, 188, 189
Sexton, T. L., 104
Shaffer, D. E., 297
Shantzis, 100
Shaw, M. C., 297
Shelby, J. S., 388–389
Shen, Y-J. J., 299
Sheridan, J. T., 289
Shmukler, D., 203
Shore, J. H., 74
Shore, M. F., 297
Shotter, J., 328
Shulman, D. A., 301
Silver, R. A., 299
Silverman, A. B., 298
Simek-Morgan, L., 23, 76, 95, 105, 324, 365, 372, 404
Simeonsson, R. J., 297
Simpkins, G., 7, 401
Sinatra, F., 140
Sipsas-Herrman, A., 289
Sisterson, D., 148

Small, J. J., 152, 157
Smart, D. W., 1, 3
Smart, J. F., 1, 3
Smart, S., 321
Smith, C., 142
Smith, E. J., xv, xvii, 3, 6, 7, 8, 9, 12, 14, 379
Smith, G., 6–7, 11
Smith, J. A., 36
Smith, P. M., 7, 11
Smyth, N. J., 300
Snipp, C. M., 220
Sodowsky, G. R., 9, 165–170, 172, 174–178
Sohler-Everingham, S. M. J. R., 298
Soloman, H., 137
Sparks, R., 9, 382, 391
Speight, S. L., 3
Stadler, H., 127, 324, 327, 365
Steitz, J. A., 192
Stern, M. P., 167
Stills, A. B., 8
Stocks, R., 352–353
Stockton, R., 148, 150, 158
Stollak, G. E., 165, 167
Stone, W. O., xix, 7, 159–160, 233–251, 234, 235, 236, 242, 249, 401
Storr, A., 25
Strauss, L., 137
Stremmel, A. J., 403
Strohl, J. E., 188
Sue, D. W., xv, xvii, 3, 5, 7, 9, 11, 12, 35–36, 53, 54, 77, 81, 82, 91, 94, 95, 101, 103–104, 106–108, 127, 141, 178, 192–193, 202, 325, 327, 363, 365, 367, 368, 369, 371, 380, 408
Sue, S., 3, 7, 95, 99, 107–109, 110, 169, 178
Suinn, R. M., 168, 170
Sullivan, M. P., 300
Sunn, R. M., 174
Super, D. E., 147, 154
Suzuki, L. A., xv, xvii, 3–5, 9, 370, 384, 391, 407
Szapocznik, J., 167, 174, 175
Szilagyi, A. A., 150, 157, 160

Taffe, R. C., 9
Takaki, R., 100, 102, 198
Talleyrand, R., 9

Tang, M., xviii, 99–114, 110
Tap, P., 156
Tarvydas, V. M., 374–375
Tate, M. A., 353
Taylor, J. D., 302
Taylor, M., 159
Tchetche, G. D., 26
Teeter, C., 218, 219
Telles, C. A., 167
Templeton, R. A., 288–289
Tewari, N., 103
Thase, M. E., 332
Thio, A., 53
Thomas, A. J., 202
Thomas, C., 88, 91
Thomas, K. R., xv, 1, 3, 216, 217, 339–340, 381
Thomason, T. C., 218
Thompson, C. E., 108, 368
Thompson, D. A., 188–189, 359
Thompson, M. L., 204
Thornton, R., 67, 68
Tillmanns, M., 50
Tobias, B. Q., 262–265
Tobias, H. S., 135, 137
Toczyska, M. A., 205
Toporek, R., 127, 324, 327, 365
Torres, L. de, 136
Torrey, E. F., 24, 26, 198
Toulouse, E., 148
Tracey, T. J., 106
Tredinnick, M. G., 388–389
Trevino, J. G., 202
Triandis, H. S., 342
Trickett, E. J., 298
Trimble, J. E., xv, xvii, 2, 5, 8, 9, 406–407
Tropp, L. R., 168
Trudeau, G., 186
Tseng, W. S., 104–105
Tsiu, P., 374
Tucker, C. M., 408–409
turtle-song, i., 66–80

Uba, L., 102
Umemoto, D., 103, 105
Uno, R., 58
Urbina, S., 166
Utsey, S. O., 83

Vacc, N. A., 409
van den Berghe, P. L., 21
van Langenhove, L., 36
Vanzant, I., 87
Varma, V., 149, 160

Vasconcellos, J., 121
Vasquez, M. J. T., 8, 12
Vazquez, C. N., 123
Veerasamy, S., 165–166
Vega, W. A., 176
Velasquez, R. J., 12
Velez, M. G., 168
Vera, E. M., 301
Virgil, P., 168, 170
Voelke, A-J., 24
von Sternberg, B., 316
Vontress, C. E., xv, xvii–xviii, 2, 3, 5, 6, 7, 9, 10, 20–30, 21–26, 48, 81, 151, 159–160, 200, 379, 394, 397, 409

Wagatsuma, Y., 165, 174, 178
Waldman, C., 66–69
Waldrop, M. M., 36–37
Walker, A., 314
Walker, R., 314, 318, 319
Walker-Moffat, W., 102
Walkup, J. T., 74
Walls, R. G., 118
Walsh, E. M., 301
Walsh, R., 193
Walter, A. F., 171
Walter, V. A., 289
Wan, G., 288–289
Wang, L., 105, 106
Wang, Y., 100, 107
Washington, G., 139
Watanabe-Muraoka, A., 157
Watson, A. L., 110
Watson, Z. E., xix, 363–378, 366
Watt, S. K., 233
Watts, A. G., 148
Watts, A. W., 155, 156
Watts, R. E., 315
Waxer, P. H., 106
Weaver, G. D., 85
Webster, A. C., 152, 157
Webster, D. W., 7, 107
Wehrly, B., xix, 4, 5, 9, 14, 54, 148, 149, 156, 158, 313–323, 314, 316, 317, 318, 409
Weiner, I. B., 105
Weinrach, S. G., xv, 1, 3, 339–340, 381
Weinstein, E. S., 299
Weiss, C. H., 240
Weissberg, R. P., 298
Welch, P., 24
Welfel, E. R., 364, 373

Wells, A. M., 298, 306
Wengrower, H., 58
West, C., 93
West, J., xix, 339–349
Westbrook, F. D., 5–6, 7
Westerhof, G. J., 299
Wewers, M. E., 167
Whaley, A. L., 82
Whiston, S. C., 104, 370
White, J. L., 82, 83, 89, 91, 92
White, M., 345
White, R., 288
Whiteley, S., 108–109
Whitley, B. E., 352
Whitman, W., 136
Whittaker, J., 305
Wiesel, E., 187
Wilbur, M. P., 188–189
Williams, C. B., 188–189, 300
Williams, D., 82
Williams, G. H., 318
Williams, R., 136
Williamson, L., 178
Wilson, R. F., 202, 350
Wilson, W., 139
Wise, S., 9
Witherspoon, J., 139
Wittke, C., 136, 138–140
Wittmer, J., 409
Wodarski, J. S., 300
Wojtasik, B., 150
Wolpe, J., 343
Wong, L., 102
Woodford, M. S., 357
Worthington, R. L., 203
Wrenn, C. G., 5, 10, 32, 324, 388
Wright, D., 109

Yamada, A., 167
Yamada, S. Y., 167
Yamamoto, K., 305
Yang, K. S., 104, 105
Yeh, C., 100, 107
Yin, P., 104–105
Yoerger, K., 298
Young, K. S., 106, 126
Yu, A. M., 109

Zaharna, R. S., 55
Zane, N., 106–108
Zaretti, J. L., 56
Zea, M. C., 404
Zenk, R., 363, 370
Zimmer, E., 58
Zinnbauer, B. J., 188, 190

SUBJECT INDEX

Acculturation
  Asian American/Pacific
    Islander, 101–103, 108–109
  dimensions of, 173–174
  measurement issues, 169–170
Acculturation theory and research,
    164–180
  acculturation, defined, 170–171
  acculturative stress, 101, 102,
    167–168, 175–177, 178
  application of construct of
    acculturation, 165–169
  bicultural stress, 177–178
  bidirectional acculturation
    theory, 172–173
  demographic trends, 164–165
  interactional theory of
    acculturation, 173–174
  linear theory of acculturation,
    174–175
  measurement issues, 167–168,
    169–170
  mental health and, 178–179
  strategies of acculturation,
    171–172
Acculturative stress, 101, 102,
    167–168, 175–177, 178
Action stage, of multicultural
    counseling, 106–107
Adoption
  transcultural, 304
  transracial, 314
African Americans, xv, 81–96
  African traditional healing,
    24–26, 89–90, 262–265
  Black Identity Development
    model, 6–7, 11
  case studies, 256–259, 262–265,
    280–283
  criminality (case study),
    280–283
  as culturally deprived, 5–6, 22
  culture and, 87–90
  demographic trends, 165
  mental health and, 85–87
  suffering of, 93–95
  technology and, 351
  treatment approaches, 82–85,
    90–95
  White–Black counseling, 5
  worldview, 83–85, 86–87, 88, 204

African self-consciousness, 88
Afrocentrism, 202, 303
Alcohol use, Native American/
    Alaskan Native, 73, 74–75
Allocentrism, 122
AltaVista, 353
American Counseling
    Association (ACA), 6, 9–10,
    12, 13, 150, 158, 159, 202,
    209–210, 350, 364–367,
    371–372, 382, 385–386,
    389
American Educational Research
    Association (AERA), 166
American Personnel and Guidance
    Association (APGA), 6–7, 10,
    11, 13, 14
American Psychological
    Association (APA), 202, 216,
    364, 382, 385–386
American Psychologist, 160
American Revolution, 137
Americans with Disabilities Act
    (1990), 373
Annihilation policy, Native
    Americans/Alaskan Natives,
    68
Antibilingual movements, 120
APART, 234, 237–240
Art, 55–57
Artifacts, as works of art, 56
Asian Americans/Pacific
    Islanders, xv, 99–110
  case studies, 253–255
  demographic trends,
    164–165
  ethnic identity transformations,
    100–103
  immigration patterns, 99–100
  model minority myth, 101–102,
    103
  multicultural counseling
    models, 103–110
  as "neglected" minority, 7, 11
  spirituality, 253–255, 302–303
  Stylistic Model with, 223–225
  technology and, 351
Asian Journal of Counseling,
    155
Assessment, ethical issues in,
    369–370

Assimilation process
  Asian American/Pacific
    Islander, 101–103
  Native Americans/Alaskan
    Natives, 69
Association for Counselor Education
    and Supervision (ACES), 364
Association for Multicultural
    Counseling and Development
    (AMCD), 4–5, 8, 9, 10, 12, 13,
    15, 327–328, 364, 380, 382, 410,
    411–414
Association for Non-White
    Concerns in Personnel and
    Guidance (ANWC), 4–5, 6–7,
    11, 15, 380, 389
Association for Spiritual, Ethical,
    and Religious Values in
    Counseling (ASERVIC),
    189–190, 192–193
Association for Vocational and
    Educational Guidance, 160
Association Internationale
    d'Orientation Scolaire et
    Professionelle (AIOSP), 147
Asynchronous technology, 354–355
Audio chat, 356–357

Behavioral acculturation, 174–175
Behaviorism, 24, 35
Bibliotherapy, 285–293
  case study, 318–320
  defined, 285
  goals and objectives of, 286–287
  guidelines to support, 317–318
  materials for, 291–293
  for multiracial individuals,
    317–321
  research on, 288–291
  using, 285–288
Bicultural stress, 177–178
Bidirectional acculturation theory,
    172–173
Bilingualism, 120–121
Biopsychiatry, 26–28
Black Identity Development, 6–7, 11
Boundary issues, 367–369, 373
*British Journal of Guidance and
    Counselling*, 155, 156
Bureau of Indian Affairs (BIA), 69,
    70, 71

CARE (Chemical Assistance Reaching Everyone), 298
Career/vocational counseling, 148–149. *See also* International counseling movement
Case studies, 252–283
   African Americans, 256–259, 262–265, 280–283
   bibliotherapy, 318–320
   biracial, 274–276
   Confucian Chinese, 253–255
   European Americans, 141–144
   Latinos/as, 129–130, 270–273
   Muslim family, 259–262
   in preventive counseling, 303–306
   sexual identity, 266–270
   spirituality in elementary school, 277–280
CatList, 354
Caucasians. *See* European Americans
CD-ROM technology, 359–360
Churches, role in ethnic communities, 300
Civil Rights Act (1964), 373
Civil rights movement, 6
Client-centered therapy, 151
Code-switching, 121
Cognitive-behavioral psychology, 341, 342–343
Cognitive-behavioral theory of counseling, 233–234, 331–334
   behavioral consequences of dysfunctional thinking, 334
   cognitive restructuring, 332–333
   stages of intervention, 332–333
   suppositions and perspectives of, 333
Cognitive restructuring, 332–333
Collaborative approach, 53
Collectivity
   African American, 84
   Asian American/Pacific Islander, 105–106
Colonial period, 120, 135, 137
Communication styles, Asian American/Pacific Islander, 109
Competence, 364–367, 373
   dimensions of, 365
   maintaining, 366–367
   training issues, 366
Competency model, 91–92
   awareness, 91
   knowledge, 91
   skills, 91–92
Complexity theory, 36–37
Consubstantiation, African American, 84

Consultation, 390
Council for Accreditation of Counseling and Related Educational Programs (CACREP), 317, 366, 382
Counseling across cultures. *See* Cross-cultural counseling
Counseling minorities, 3
Counseling Psychologist, 11–12
Counseling special populations, 3
Counseling the culturally different, xv, xvii, 2, 3, 6, 7, 22
Counseling theory. *See also* Acculturation theory and research
Counselor preparation
   characteristics of sound programs, 329–331
   competence in, 366
   dealing with spiritual issues, 189–191
   existential worldview and, 202–204
   multicultural counseling, 43–44, 327–334
   recommendations, 389–390
   technology in, 354–360
   transcendent counseling, 246
   transcultural counseling, 59–62
Countertransference, 365
Cross-cultural counseling, xv, xvii, 2, 7, 8, 380
   language in, 109
   nature of, 22–23
   research on, 391–392
Cross-Cultural Counseling Competencies, 350
Cross-cultural sensitivity training, 320
Cultural accommodation model, 107–108
Cultural congruence, 128–129
Cultural encapsulation, 324–325
Cultural Grid, 37–41, 44
   Interpersonal, 39–41
   Intrapersonal, 38–39
Cultural heritage, 173–174
Cultural-historical dimension of Stylistic Model, 213–215, 217–218
Cultural Identity Check List (CICL), 201, 202, 203
Cultural intentionality, 76
Cultural preferences, 173
Cultural sensitivity, 320, 326–327, 387–388
Culture
   defined, 1–2, 32, 314
   elements of, 32–34

   ethnic identity and, 1
   extending concept of, 87–90
   influence on worldviews, 2
   nature of, 21–22
   technology and, 351–354, 357–358
Culture-centered counseling, 3, 31–44
   case studies, 252–283
   developing multicultural knowledge, 34–37
   developing multicultural skill, 37–43
   increasing multicultural awareness, 32–34, 48–49
   multicultural counselor education, 43–44
Culture-fair tests, 43
Culture-Free Self-Esteem Inventories for Children and Adults, 289
Culture-free tests, 43
Cyberghetto, 352

Dance, 57–59
DARE (Drug Abuse Resistance Education), 298
Dawes Act (1887), 69
Decision making, ethics in, 373–375
Decontextualization, 345
Diagnostic and Statistical Manual of Mental Disorders, 23, 26, 202, 370–372, 385
Direct observation studies, 391
Diversegrad-L, 355
Diversity-sensitive counseling, 1, 326
Dogpile, 353
Domestic violence, Asian American/Pacific Islander, 102
Drug abuse educational programs, 298
Drug-based approach, 27
Dysfunctional thinking, 334

Eclectic approach, 48
Ecological culture, 21
Ecological Identity Model, 321
Education
   African American, 81
   of counselors. *See* Counselor preparation
   Native American/Alaskan Native, 69, 74
   role of schools in ethnic community, 300–302

Elementary schools
    school-based intervention, 300
    spirituality in (case study),
      277–280
Empathy, 93
Environmental prevention
    programs, 300–302
Ethics, 363–375
    in assessment and diagnosis,
      369–372
    boundary issues, 367–369, 373
    competence, 364–367, 373
    legal issues, 373
    in reasoning and decision
      making, 373–375
    spirituality and, 192–193
Ethnic identity, 1
    African American, 256–259
    Asian American/Pacific
      Islander transformation
      patterns, 100–103
    case study, 256–259
    confusion in, 256–259
    construct of, 166–169
    Latino/a, 124–125
    measurement issues, 167–168,
      169–170
    transformation patterns,
      100–103
Ethnocentrism, 244
Ethnocultural movement, 4–15,
    381
    1960s, 5–6
    1970s, 6–8
    1980s, 8
    1990s, 9–10
    chronology, 10–13
    gender and, 13–14
Ethnoentropy, 242, 244
Ethnopsychiatry, 3, 25–26
Ethnosyncretism, 244
Etic-emic approaches, 104, 169–170
European Americans, 133–145
    case studies, 141–144
    counseling, 141–144
    "encapsulated" institutions, 5
    historical context, 133–136
    immigration today, 140–141
    Irish, 138–139
    Italians, 139–140
    Jews, 134–135, 136–138, 141
    other groups, 135, 139–140
    Scotch-Irish, 138–139
    Stylistic Model with, 221–223
    Swedes, 140
    technology and, 351
    worldview, 204
European Association for
    Counselling (EAC), 154,
    158–160

Excite, 353
Existential counseling, 23–24,
    233–234
Existential worldview
    applications of, 201–205
    development of, 200–201
Extracultural stressors, 179
Eye disease, 306

Forced removal policy, Native
    Americans/Alaskan Natives,
    68
Freedom of Religion Act (1978),
    70
Future perspectives, 62, 83–85,
    158–160, 383–386

Gender
    acculturation and, 179
    Asian American/Pacific
      Islanders and, 102, 109
    and ethnocultural history,
      13–14
    European Americans and,
      144–145
    existential worldview and,
      204–205
    Latinos/as and, 123
    in preventive counseling, 303
    technology and, 352–353
Gift giving, 369
Glaucoma, 306
Google, 353
Great Famine, 139
Group prevention programs,
    299–300

Haitians, as "neglected" minority,
    7
"Healer" role, 89–90
Health
    African American, 81, 306
    Native American/Alaskan
      Native, 72–75, 305–306
Heterosexism, 266–270
High-context cultures, 35
High schools, school-based
    intervention, 301
*Hispanic Journal of Behavioral
    Sciences,* 117
Hispanics/Latinos. *See* Latinos/as
Holistic health
    goal of, 235
    in transcendent counseling, 241,
      245
Holistic treatment approaches,
    76–77
Homosexuality
    heterosexism, 266–270
    Stylistic Model with, 225–227

Human/ethnic relations, in
    transcendent counseling, 241,
    245
Humanistic approaches, 35, 341,
    343–344

Identity development
    African American, 6–7, 11
    phases of multiethnic, 242–244
    theory and assessment, 382–383
Immigrant populations, xvi–xvi,
    140–141. *See also*
    Acculturation theory and
    research; *specific groups*
Immigration and Naturalization
    Act (1965), 100
Indian Child Welfare Act, 70
Indian Civil Rights Act (1968), 70
Individualistic perspective, 35,
    105–106
Individual prevention programs,
    298–299
Inner connectedness, African
    American, 84
Inquisition, 134–135, 137
Insight stage, of multicultural
    counseling, 105–106
Intentional Group Microskills,
    42–43
Interactional theory of
    acculturation, 173–174
Intercultural counseling. *See* Cross-
    cultural counseling
Intergenerational conflict, 175
International Association for
    Counselling (IAC), 10,
    152–153, 154, 156, 159, 160,
    209–210
International Association for
    Educational and Vocational
    Guidance (IAEVG), 147, 152,
    153, 154, 156, 159
International Careers Journal, 154,
    159
International Committee for
    Women (ICFW), 144
International counseling
    movement, xvi, 54–55,
    147–161
    in central and eastern Europe,
      147–149, 150–151, 154–155,
      156, 160
    counseling associations, 147,
      149, 150, 152–158
    future developments, 158–160
    in non-European countries,
      151–152, 155, 158
    in the United States and
      Canada, 149–150, 154,
      157–158

International Journal for Educational and Vocational Guidance, 154, 160

International Journal for the Advancement of Counselling (IJAC), 10, 11, 12, 154, 158, 160, 386

International Round Table for the Advancement of Counselling (IRTAC), 152, 156, 157, 158, 160

International studies, 54–55

Internet, 159, 351–352, 353–354, 358

Interracial Couple Questionnaire (ICQ), 315

Interracial family, 314

Invisibility Syndrome, The (Franklin), 82–83

Irish, 138–139

Islam, 141, 186, 259–262, 303

Italians, 139–140

Jews, 134–135, 136–138, 141

Journal of Counseling and Development, 12, 154, 158, 159

Journal of Counseling Psychology, 154

Journal of Multicultural Counseling and Development, 8, 9, 12, 15, 155, 386

Journal of Non-White Concerns in Personnel and Guidance, 7–8, 11, 15

Journal of Technology in Counseling, xix, 159, 350

Kitty Cole Human Rights Award, 13

Knowledge about self, in transcendent counseling, 241, 245

Language
in acculturation process, 173
Asian American/Pacific Islander, 109
Latino/a, 120–121

Larry P. v. Riles, 373

LatiNegra, 315–316

Latino Dimensions of Personal Identity Model, 124, 126

Latinos/as, xv, 115–131
case studies, 129–130, 270–273
counseling and psychology literature, 117–118
counseling practices and strategies, 125–129
demographic trends, 141, 164–165
historical context, 118–120

sociopolitical context, 120–125
technology and, 351
within-group differences, 118, 119–120
worldview, 117, 121–124, 128, 205

Legal issues, 373

Liberal arts, 49–59
art and music, 55–57
international studies, 54–55
moving beyond, 61
philosophy, 49–51
religion, 51–52
sociology, 52–54
theater and dance, 57–59

Life span counseling, 299

Linear theory of acculturation, 174–175

Listservs, 354–355

Loving v. Virginia, 313

Machismo, 123

Marianismo, 123

Meaningful work/activity
nature of, 235
in transcendent counseling, 241–242, 245

Mental health and disorders
acculturation and, 102, 167–168, 175–177, 178–179
African American, 85–87
Asian American/Pacific Islander, 101–103
Native American/Alaskan Native, 74–75
spirituality and, 191–192

Mestizo psychology, 121–122

MetaCrawler, 353

Middle schools, school-based intervention, 300–301

Minority-Majority Relations Scale (MMRS), 169

Miscegenation, 313–314

Mulatto, 314

Multicultural counseling, xv, xvii, 2, 3, 165, 324–334, 341, 344–347
action stage, 106–107
Asian American/Pacific Islander, 103–110
challenge to, 383
competencies in, 103–104
counselor development model, 43–44, 327–334
Cultural Grid, 37–41, 44
cultural sensitivity and, 320, 326–327, 387–388
defined, 103, 325–326
developing, 37–43

developing multicultural knowledge, 34–37
exploration stage, 104–105
history of, 324–325
increasing awareness, 32–34, 48–49
insight stage, 105–106
Intentional Group Microskills, 42–43
research on, 391–392
spiritualism and, 189, 193
strategies in, 107–110, 127–129
transcultural counseling versus, 48–49
Triad Training Model, 3, 41–42

Multicultural counseling competencies (MCC), 127–129

Multicultural counseling theory (MCT), 35–36

Multiculturalism
social construction and, 347–348
technology and, 358–359

Multiethnic identity development, phases of, 242–244

Multigroup Ethnic Identity Measure (MEIM), 169

Multimodal therapy, 286

Multiracial individuals and families, 313–322
counseling strategies, 317–321
defined, 314
professional barriers and, 316–317
societal barriers and, 314–316
terminology, 313–314

Music, 55–57

National Association of Student Affairs Professionals (NASAP), 10

National culture, 21

National Vocational Guidance Association (NVGA), 149

Native Americans/Alaskan Natives, xv, 66–78
defining, 71–72
demographic trends, 165
early European Americans and, 133–134
health issues, 72–75
policies toward, 67–70, 301
in postcontact period, 67–70
in precontact period, 66–67
preventive counseling, 301, 305–306
Stylistic Model for, 216–220
treatment approaches, 75–77, 216–220, 301, 305–306

Need-fulfillment, nature of, 235

New Age movement, 50

Nigrescence, 88, 89
Normal, as term, 34–35
Nouvelle Revue d'Ethnopsychiatrie
(*The New Journal of
Ethnopsychiatry*), 26

*L'Orientation Scolaire et
Professionnelle* (*Educational and
Vocational Guidance*), 154–155

Panethnicity, 242, 244
Pedagogy of the Oppressed (Freire),
50–51
Pentagon terrorist attack (2001),
186, 303, 384
Personnel and Guidance Journal, 7,
11, 158
Phenomenology, 24
Philosophy, 49–51
Postmodernism, 328–329, 346
Posttraumatic stress disorder
(PTSD), 101, 198, 199,
253–255
Poverty, Native American/
Alaskan Native, 74
Preference categories, 100
Preventive counseling, 296–307
case studies, 303–306
intervention formats, 298–302
in multicultural society, 302–303
primary prevention, 296, 297,
300
recommendations, 389
secondary prevention, 297, 300
tertiary prevention, 297, 298, 301
Primary prevention, 296, 297, 300
Psychoanalysis, 24
Psychoanalytic and ego
psychology, 340–342
Psychodynamics, 35
Psychological nigrescence, 88
Psychosocial dimension of Stylistic
Model, 213–215, 218–219
Puritans, 135

Racial/Cultural Identity
Development (R/CID)
Model, 101
Racio-ethnic culture, 22
Rational emotive behavior therapy
(REBT), 286
Rationalism, 24
Reductionism approach, 358
Regional culture, 21–22
Relationship development, 92
Religion, 141. *See also* Spirituality
counselor preparation and, 390
European American, 135
integrating with spirituality and
transpersonal, 188–189

Latino/a, 123–124
in liberal studies, 51–52
Native American/Alaskan
Native, 67, 70, 72–73
nature of, 188
Relocation policy, Native
Americans/Alaskan Natives,
70
Research. *See also* Acculturation
theory and research
bibliotherapy, 288–291
recommendations, 391–392
Reverse acculturation, 166–167

SADD (Students Against Driving
Drunk), 298
Scale to Assess Worldview
(SAWV), 198, 200–204, 226
Schematic Meta-Model, 321
Schools, role in ethnic
communities, 300–302
Scientific-ideological dimension of
Stylistic Model, 213–215,
219–220
Scotch-Irish, 138–139
Search engines, 353
Secondary prevention, 297, 300
Self-actualization, 343–344
Self-awareness, 53
Self-Determination and Education
Act (1975), 70
Self-determination policy, Native
Americans/Alaskan Natives,
70
Self-healing power, 86–87
Self-knowledge, African American,
84–85, 86, 88–89
Self-reflection, Latino/a, 125–126
Self-regulation, in transcendent
counseling, 242, 245, 246
Self-understanding, nature of, 235
September 11, 2001 terrorist
attacks, 186, 303, 384
Shame, outcome of treatment and,
109
Social constructionism, 328, 346–348
Social engineering, 94–95
Social power differences, 333
Sociology, 52–54
Spiritness, African American,
83–84, 86
Spirituality, 186–193
African American, 83–84, 86
Asian American, 253–255,
302–303
case studies, 253–255, 277–280
contradiction of mental health
values, 191–192
counselor preparation and, 390
ethical guidelines, 192–193

integrating, 188–189, 193
Latino/a, 123–124
multiculturalism and, 189, 193
Native American/Alaskan
Native, 72–73
nature of, 187–188
in preventive counseling,
302–303
training to deal with, 189–191
Stress
acculturative, 101, 102, 167–168,
175–177, 178
bicultural, 177–178
extracultural, 179
Structural family system, 94
Stylistic Counseling Self-
Assessment, 221, 229–232
Stylistic Model, 209–228
anatomy of stylistic counseling,
210–212
another dimension, 227
for Asian Americans/Pacific
Islanders, 223–225
for conversion to
homosexuality, 225–227
Cubic Descriptors, 211–215,
220–221
for European Americans,
221–223
for Native Americans/Alaskan
Natives, 216–220
principles of, 215
Suicide
Native American/Alaskan
Native, 73, 74–75, 305–306
preventive counseling, 305–306
Survival, in transcendent
counseling, 240–241, 245
Swedes, 140
Synchronous technology, 354,
355–357

Technology, 350–361
cultural communication and,
357–358
within cultural context, 351–354
multiculturalism and, 358–360
parallels to human interaction,
354–357
Termination policy, Native
Americans/Alaskan Natives,
70
Terrorist attacks (September 11,
2001), 186, 303, 384
Tertiary prevention, 297, 298, 301
Text-based chat rooms, 356
Theater, 57–59
Traditional healing, 24–26
African, 24–26, 89–90, 262–265
ethnopsychiatry, 25–26

Traditional healing *(continued)*
  Native American/Alaskan
    Native, 72–73
  spiritual, 72–73
Transcendent counseling, 233–249
  assumptions of theory, 236–237
  behavioral theme, 233–234
  cognitive theme, 233–234
  counseling process in, 234,
    237–240, 247–248
  counselor in, 246
  existential theme, 233–234
  goals of counseling, 235
  modalities of, 245–246
  modules of, 240–242
  overview of theory, 234
  phases of multiethnic identity
    development, 242–244
  skills of counselor, 247–248
  steps of, 234, 237–240
Transcultural adoption, 304
Transcultural counseling, xv, xvii,
  2, 3, 47–63
  bibliotherapy in, 285–293
  counselor development model,
    59–62
  future and, 62
  liberal arts in theory
    development, 49–59
  multicultural counseling versus,
    48–49
  preventive, 302, 304
  Stylistic Model, 209–210, 220

Transcultural counseling theory, 61
Transethnicity, 244
Transpersonal
  integrating with spirituality and
    religion, 188–189
  nature of, 188
Transracial adoption, 314
Treatment approaches. *See also*
    Case studies; Counselor
    preparation
  African American, 82–85,
    90–95
  Asian Americans/Pacific
    Islanders, 103–110
  bibliotherapy, 285–293,
    318–320
  European Americans, 141–144
  Latinos/as, 125–129
  multiracial counseling, 317–321
  Native American/Alaskan
    Native, 75–77, 216–220, 301,
    305–306
  in transcendent counseling, 234,
    237–240, 247–248
Triad Training Model, 3, 41–42
Trust, 92

Unconditional acceptance, 92–93
United Nations Educational,
    Scientific, and Cultural
    Organization (UNESCO), 147,
    156
Universal culture, 21

Values. *See also* Worldview
  challenges to Asian, 102–103
  Latino/a, 122–125
  shared, 32–33
Videoconferencing, 357
Violence, preventive counseling,
    304–305

Web sites, 353–354, 355, 356
White–Black counseling, 5
Whites. *See* European Americans
World Health Organization
    (WHO), 26
World Trade Center terrorist
    attacks (2001), 186, 303, 384
Worldview. *See also* Existential
    worldview; Religion;
    Spirituality
  African American, 83–85, 86–87,
    88, 204
  Asian American/Pacific
    Islander, 107
  European American, 204
  explaining concept of, 188
  influence of culture, 2
  Latino/a, 117, 121–124, 128, 205
  mapping cultural differences in,
    204–205
  measuring, 198, 200–204, 226
  Native American/Alaskan
    Native, 72–73
  personal dimension, 117,
    196–200